# Agenda for Improving Governance

**The Editor**

BIBEK DEBROY is Director, Rajiv Gandhi Institute for Contemporary Studies, New Delhi. He is the author and editor of several books, papers and popular articles. Bibek Debroy's special interests are international trade (in particular the WTO), law reform and the political economy of liberalization in India.

**About RGICS**

The Rajiv Gandhi Institute for Contemporary Studies (RGICS), New Delhi is part of the Rajiv Gandhi Foundation and functions as a think tank. The target audience of the RGICS includes parliamentarians, legislators and representatives of political parties, public policy makers and their advisers, the intelligentsia, the media and various interest groups. To interface with these groups, RGICS uses different modes of communication like books, monographs, working papers, symposia, discussions, talks and lectures. The RGICS research work is focused on international economic relations, law reforms, IT and economic reforms in India.

# Agenda for Improving Governance

Edited by

Bibek Debroy

PUBLISHED BY ACADEMIC FOUNDATION IN ASSOCIATION WITH

RAJIV GANDHI INSTITUTE FOR CONTEMPORARY STUDIES, NEW DELHI

Academic Foundation

NEW DELHI

First Published in 2004 by

ACADEMIC FOUNDATION

4772-73 / 23 Bharat Ram Road, (23 Ansari Road),
Darya Ganj, New Delhi - 110 002.
INDIA.

Phones : 23245001, 02, 03, 04.
Fax : +91-11-23245005.
e-mail : academic@vsnl.com
www : academicfoundation.com

*Published in association with*
Rajiv Gandhi Institute for Contemporary Studies, New Delhi.



*Agenda for Improving Governance*
edited by Bibek Debroy
**ISBN 81-7188-358-3**

Designed and typeset by Italics India, New Delhi
and printed at Print Perfect, New Delhi.

# Contents

## Authors / Contributors


Bibek Debroy ............ Director, Rajiv Gandhi Institute for Contemporary Studies, New Delhi.

Debashis Chakraborty ..... Research Associate, Rajiv Gandhi Institute for Contemporary Studies, New Delhi.

Rahul Mukherji ........... Assistant Professor, Centre for Political Studies, JNU, New Delhi.

Amir Ullah Khan .......... Research Fellow, India Development Foundation, Gurgaon.

Jayaprakash Narayan ....... Campaign Coordinator, Lok Satta, Hyderabad.

P.S.A. Sundaram .......... Ex-civil Servant and consultant to various International organizations on Governance Reforms.

P.D. Kaushik ............. Fellow, Rajiv Gandhi Institute for Contemporary Studies, New Delhi.

Mohammed Saqib ......... Fellow, Rajiv Gandhi Institute for Contemporary Studies, New Delhi.

C.H. Hanumantha Rao ..... Chairman, Centre for Economic and Social Studies, Hyderabad.

**D. Shyam Babu** ............ Fellow, Rajiv Gandhi Institute for Contemporary Studies, New Delhi.

**Paromita Shastri** ........... Assistant Editor, *Outlook*, New Delhi.

**P.V. Indiresan** .............. Former Director, IIT, Chennai and Columnist.

**Laveesh Bhandari** ........... Chief Economist, Indicus Analytics, New Delhi.

**Aarti Khare** ............... Research Associate, Indicus Analytics, New Delhi.

**Arnab Kumar Hazra** ........ Economic Advisor, Embassy of the Republic of Korea, New Delhi.

**Shubhashis Gangopadhyay** ... Founder-Director, India Development Foundation, Gurgaon.

# Introduction

## *The Reform Agenda in Governance*

BIBEK DEBROY

### Introduction

The 1990s represent the reform decade for the Indian economy. While no one can dispute this proposition, a caveat is in order. This was not the first attempt to reform the Indian economy. There was an earlier reform attempt in the 1980s, or even the second half of the 1970s. While that was more limited and certainly not as ambitious, it wasn't non-existent. One shouldn't lose sight of this continuity.

Why bother to reform the economy? There is a short-term answer, as well as a long-term one. The short-term answer concerns the balance of payments (BoP) crisis in 1990-91. If we hadn't reformed, we would have defaulted on external debt repayments. Triggered by this BoP crisis, there have been five strands to reforming the external sector – phasing out quantitative restrictions (QRs) on imports, rationalizing export subsidies, reducing tariffs, revamping the exchange control regime and a more open policy towards foreign direct investments (FDI) and portfolio investments. Not even the harshest critic of liberalization can deny success in the external sector, regardless of the yardstick used and different criteria are possible – rate of growth in exports, percentage of imports financed by exports, size of current account deficit (converted sometimes, even to a surplus), size of foreign exchange reserves, FDI inflows, debt service ratio and share of short-term debt in total external debt.

Fair enough. But what about the long-term reason? This can be stated in complicated fashion. However, the simple proposition is the following. Poverty eradication and unemployment reduction require growth, although the composition of growth is also important. Growth is a necessary condition, though it may not be sufficient. Without growth, the size of the cake doesn't increase and redistributive policies amount to redistributing poverty, not redistributing wealth. Growth requires efficiency and efficiency requires competition. The reform agenda can be unbundled in different ways. But all of it represents greater competition. Here is what the core reform agenda looks like. Even if one adds other items, these five points constitute the core. These reforms concern the domestic economy rather than the external sector. These reforms are also still on the agenda. They still haven't been implemented, except in a very marginal kind of way.

- Reform agriculture and the rural sector. With two-thirds of the population employed in the rural sector, agricultural reforms are critical in eliminating poverty and reducing unemployment. The resultant income and consumption growth is also necessary to dispel the myth that reforms are anti-poor and pro-rich.
- Rehabilitate Central and State government finances. This requires scrutiny of expenditure (privatization of PSUs that don't generate sufficient returns, downsizing expenditure on surplus government employees, re-targeting subsidies and charging appropriate user charges from those who can afford them) and revenue (PSU reform, as well as removing exemptions for both direct and indirect taxes). It also requires accountability, transparency and decentralization in government expenditure.
- Improve social sector outcomes, especially in education and health. Where possible, alternatives to public sector provisioning can be offered, thereby injecting competition. Where outright private provisioning is impossible, public provisioning must be judged in terms of tangible improvements in outcomes, not through expenditure alone. This is also linked to the point about re-targeting subsidies and increasing accountability and transparency. Similar points can also be made about existing anti-poverty programmes. For these, leakage and unnecessarily high administrative costs have been documented in several studies.
- Improve physical infrastructure, and this doesn't mean telecom or airlines alone. Despite the National Highway Development

Programme (NHDP) and the Pradhan Mantri Gram Sadak Yojana, the road sector is in a mess and despite talk about power sector reforms, so is electricity. Drinking water, irrigation water, sewage treatment, sanitation, railways and ports are all part of infrastructure. What improvements have we witnessed here? Instead, both in social and physical infrastructure, thanks to fiscal compulsions, there has been an abdication of the State's responsibility. This reinforces the belief that reforms are anti-poor. There has also been an increasing trend of inter-State and inter-regional disparities and inadequate social and physical infrastructure accentuate these regional differences.

- Improve governance. The word governance means all kinds of different things to different people. At one level, it concerns political and electoral reform. At another level, it concerns interface between administration and citizens. At a narrower level, it means the law and order and justice system. In none of these, have there been discernible improvements. The inspector raj, working through the administrative law (rules, orders, regulations) system, continues to hurt as much as it used to. Despite the new Civil Procedure Code, the backlog of court cases is just as heavy, with the exception of the Supreme Court.

The expression "second generation" reforms is often used. What this expression means is extremely unclear. Some reforms were talked about in 1992. Logically, that ought to be the first generation of reforms and the five points mentioned above figured in that agenda. But these reforms haven't been implemented. If the agenda of first generation reforms hasn't yet been implemented, what is the point of talking about the second generation? Having said this, two possible interpretations of "second generation" can be given. First, first generation reforms concern the external sector. Since the trigger for reforms was an external sector BoP crisis and since the external sector doesn't impinge on most of the Indian economy, those reforms were implemented. The political economy of resistance, lobbying and vested interests wasn't that important. Thus, second generation connotes domestic economic reforms and those will always confront the political economy problem, with vested interests represented by organized labour, inefficient trade and industry, bureaucracy, large farmers and the urban middle class (beneficiaries of subsidies). *Ipso facto,* in the absence of reforms, unorganized labour, efficient trade and industry, small farmers, consumers and the genuinely poor will continue to suffer. Second, one must remember that India is a federal country. Some areas are in the Union List, still others in the State List and some more in the Concurrent List. In general, first generation concerns items that the Centre alone could reform. The second generation set concerns areas reserved for States.

Has the objective of stepping up growth been accomplished? Yes and no. Till the Fifth Plan (1974-79), the Indian economy chugged along at real annual rates of growth of no more than 3.5 per cent, the so-called Hindu rate of growth. Beginning with the Fifth Plan and throughout the 1980s, growth rates increased to between 5.5 per cent and 5.8 per cent and remember, there were some reforms in the 1980s. The Eighth Plan (1992-97) brought 6.8 per cent. More importantly, in three of those years (1994-95 to 1996-97) the economy grew at 7 per cent plus and in 1996-97, even crossed 8 per cent. Other countries have grown at 8 per cent and more for decades. The Eighth Plan's record suggested that we could also dream of 8 per cent plus. The Ninth Plan (1997-2002) brought us down to earth with an average of 5.35 per cent. Although the Tenth Plan (2002-07) still talks of 8 per cent, no one believes that to be possible. It is easy to blame the growth retardation on external (global slowdown, 9/11, Iraq War) or internal (Gujarat, earthquake, cyclone, tension with Pakistan) bogeys. For any large country, like India and China, sources of growth are primarily endogenous. Thus, despite these unfavourable factors also affecting the Chinese economy, China continues to grow at more than 7 per cent. To get that 8 per cent and more, we need the core reform agenda to be implemented, especially in the rural sector.

Has this higher growth trickled down and made the life of the poor better? In a poor country like India, with 34.7 per cent of the population below the international poverty line of 1 US dollar per day, that's indeed the right question to ask. But it's also a meaningless question to ask, because most of the reforms (the five-point agenda) that would have improved the lot of the poor haven't been implemented. So the favourable impact on the poor has only been through the growth effect. There are some question marks about the quality of NSS (National Sample Survey) data and about whether

1993-94 figures are comparable with 1999-2000. Subject to that, the percentage of population below the poverty line has dropped from 36 per cent in 1993-94 to 26 per cent in 1999-2000. At an all-India level that's a fairly sharp drop, though that all-India figure masks significant inter-State differences. Trickle down works in States where there is growth to trickle down. Not in States that are stagnating. One should also mention that the literacy rate has improved from 52 per cent in 1991 to 65 per cent in 2001 and the rate of population growth has also slowed to something like 1.8 per cent.

2020 has a nice vision kind of ring to it. Therefore, several people have speculated about what the Indian economy will be like in 2020. Will India become a developed economy? That's an impossible question to answer, because the phrase "developed economy" doesn't have a precise definition. Per capita income is only one yardstick in judging development. Even if India doesn't grow at 8 per cent, but grows at 6.5 per cent instead, the per capita income in 2020 will be around 1200 US dollars, in today's dollars. The percentage of population below the poverty line will drop to around 10 per cent or less. The literacy rate will increase to around 85 per cent, if not more. On a slightly different note, the infant mortality rate will drop to around 35 per thousand. These are big changes, the implications of which we understand only imperfectly today. However, that doesn't catapult India into the high human development category. It takes India to where China is now, more or less. If developed economy means a per capita income of 10,000 US dollars and a high human development categorization, that's a long way off.

But these changes can be speeded up, without waiting for 2020. To ensure that, we need 8 per cent rates of growth and we need reforms. Despite a decade of reforms, we have still not sorted out what we want the government or the State to do and what we don't want it to do. Any debate about liberalization can invariably be traced to confusion about the State's role. Reforms are not about the government abdicating its responsibility. Otherwise, no government need exist. Governments exist because they offer governance. While the expression governance is often used, it lacks a precise definition. Clearly social infrastructure, physical infrastructure and law and order form the core elements of governance. Add to that the government's role in protecting the disadvantaged and the deprived, those who are likely to be bypassed by the market. This is a minimal set of what citizens should demand from the State, especially poor citizens, who can't exercise the privatization option in these areas. Interpreted differently, the five-point agenda listed above is precisely about this and about ensuring how the State obtains the revenue to perform these core functions. It is this that needs sorting out. The opportunity costs of lost growth are considerable.

This collection of papers is about governance, variously defined and interpreted. In July 2002, the Rajiv Gandhi Institute for Contemporary Studies (RGICS) organized a series of seminars on governance. These seminars focused on five areas important for improving public governance in India - agriculture, rural development, education, infrastructure and administrative reforms. Each seminar was designed to throw up the issues in that particular sector, in addition to suggesting a roadmap for reform. Following this seminar, RGICS brought out a series of working papers on the agenda for improving governance. Barring two, all 16 papers included in this volume are from that published series. There is an obvious utility in collating separately published papers into a consolidated volume.

The first paper is collated, and not authored, by Bibek Debroy and represents the gist of that first series of seminars. It throws up issues confronting the State in those five areas of agriculture, rural development, education, infrastructure and administrative reforms. The second paper, by Debashis Chakraborty tracks the performance of the State across the $8^{th}$ and $9^{th}$ Plan periods and makes the point that all is not well.

Improved governance is often equated with administrative reform and the two terms are sometimes used synonymously, depending on what one means by administrative reform. Administrative reform is also sometimes equated with civil service reform, since public delivery of goods and services does require civil service reform, including greater accountability and transparency. Sometimes, administrative reform is interpreted in a broader sense, as Jayaprakash Narayan's paper does. The third, fourth, fifth and sixth papers, by Rahul Mukherji, Amir Ullah Khan, Jayaprakash Narayan and P. S. A. Sundaram, are all about administrative reform. Collectively, one obtains a sense of recommendations made in various committee reports, attempts by the Centre and various State governments and what remains to be done. Accountability and transparency become easier with e-governance. Accordingly, the seventh paper by P. D. Kaushik documents e-governance initiatives by different States.

Despite possibilities of unbundling and possibilities of private sector participation, most people will agree, in some areas of infrastructure, the State has a role to play, not just in financing, but sometimes in provisioning as well. The eighth paper by Debashis Chakraborty catalogues reform recommendations in the infrastructure sector. To state the obvious, most of these reforms haven't yet been implemented. The ninth paper by Mohammed Saqib focuses on water management issues alone. The tenth paper by C. H. Hanumantha Rao outlines the reform agenda for agriculture and agriculture is a sector where the State will continue to have a major role to play.

From the eleventh paper, we move on to the State's role in social sectors. There is no dearth of government-run social sector schemes. Many of them have doubtful success rates. The eleventh paper by D. Shyam Babu documents the success of central social sector schemes. The twelfth paper by Paromita Shastri documents the state of India's education, meaning primarily the school education system, while the thirteenth paper by P. V. Indiresan sets out an action plan for reforming education. Health forms another plank of social infrastructure. This explains the inclusion of the fourteenth paper by Laveesh Bhandari and Aarti Khare on the health status of Indians, although this paper was not originally part of the RGICS governance series. Together with the social sectors, law and order (and defence) are core State functions. Law and order includes the criminal justice system as a sub-set. Therefore, the fifteenth paper by Arnab Kumar Hazra is on the criminal justice system.

The sixteenth paper by Bibek Debroy, Shubhashis Gangopadhyay and Laveesh Bhandari was also not part of the RGICS governance paper series. This is an attempt to rate India's States on the basis of economic freedoms that citizens in these States enjoy. The proposition is the following. Having performed the core governance function, the role of the State is to provide an enabling environment so that individual entrepreneurship can bloom. However, States also differ in the extent to which citizens in these States enjoy economic freedom. This paper is an exercise to map economic freedom across States.

Taken collectively, these sixteen papers set out the reform agenda for governance, or alternatively, for the role of the State. This is a critical subset of second or third generation reforms. If this agenda is implemented, the 2020 dream will materialize sooner rather than later.

# 1

# Agenda for Improving Governance

BIBEK DEBROY

The Rajiv Gandhi Institute for Contemporary Studies (RGICS) organized a series of seminars in July 2002. These seminars focused on five areas important for improving public governance in India - agriculture, rural development, education, infrastructure and administrative reforms. Each seminar was designed to throw up the issues in that particular sector, in addition to suggesting a roadmap for reform. This paper summarizes the gist of the discussions.

Prior to the seminar, RGICS circulated brief notes on what might be the main issues in those sectors. These were indicative and were not meant to be exhaustive. Nor were they meant to influence the discussions in any way. These notes are also included in this paper. The discussions that are summarized in this paper are not verbatim transcripts. What is reproduced is also a broad consensus, since there were instances where participants disagreed with one another. These proceedings are being published to stimulate a further debate on these issues, so that a consensus on the reform agenda can emerge.

## 1. Agriculture

### *1.1 Initial Note*

The most visible aspect of failure in agriculture is the food mountain. So obviously, the distribution problem needs to be discussed. What can be done to the PDS and the food subsidy? There is the short-term problem of eliminating the food mountain through schemes like Food for Work, but there is also the longer-term problem. Should there be a subsidy for people above the poverty line? How does one identify people below the poverty line (BPL)? Can food stamps work? Do all States have the administrative machinery to perform such identification efficiently?

What happens to procurement and the minimum support price system? Can procurement be thrown open completely to the private sector? Assuming that FCI's role is restricted to procurement for buffer stock purposes, how does one improve FCI's efficiency?

What happens to the present system of input (fertilizer, power, water, credit, seeds) subsidies in agriculture? True, they generally benefit better off farmers. Does this mean that one scraps all input subsidies? If not, and if subsidies are retained for poor farmers, is there any way to identify poor farmers objectively? Can this idea be implemented without leakage?

Should agriculture be exempted from direct (income) and indirect (excise) taxes?

Agriculture is constrained by various regulations like the Essential Commodities Act. These control production, marketing and distribution and various other activities. Should these controls continue? If they are removed, will dis-intermediation naturally take place? Or will these benefits accrue to millers, large farmers and larger corporate houses, if corporatisation of agriculture is permitted? Can IT be used to perform the task of dis-intermediation? What forms of corporate sector involvement are permissible? Will it also extend to banking and insurance? Will the land ceiling legislation continue? What forms can contract farming take and will there be a separate dispute resolution system for contract farming? Should futures markets be allowed?

What should be done about newer forms of technology, like genetically modified crops? Should technology choice be left to farmers? What can be done to improve testing and certification systems? Should product liability laws be tightened further? This is also related to the Prevention of Food Adulteration Act (PFA), where there is a multiplicity of standards, never enforced. While standards need to be harmonized, should they be mandatory or voluntary? What can be done to improve the record of prosecutions and convictions?

What should be India's stance in WTO negotiations? Should India accept lower bound rates for agricultural products, say 40 per cent? What happens to sectors like edible oils that are clearly uncompetitive? Is there a food security issue? Is there a possibility of monopolies in seeds and fertilizers?

### *1.2 Introduction*

Agriculture may account for only around 25 per cent of GDP (gross domestic product), but it accounts for around two-thirds of employment. Therefore, without improvements in agriculture, it is impossible to make a dent on poverty and unemployment. Uncorrected NSS (National Sample Survey) data for 1999-2000 show that 27.09 per cent of rural India is below the poverty line. Among major States, the figure is more than 40 per cent in Assam, Bihar and Orissa and more than 30 per cent in Uttar Pradesh and West Bengal. 27.09 per cent of India's population amounts to 193.2 million people. If 8 per cent rate of growth in GDP is required, the growth in agriculture must be at least 4 per cent, as projected in the Tenth Plan document.

### *1.3 Deceleration in Agricultural Growth in the 1990s*

Does the track record of Indian agriculture suggest that a 4 per cent rate of growth is possible? In constant (1993-94) prices, agriculture and allied activities grew at an annual average growth rate of 3.9 per cent between 1980-81 and 1991-92 and at 3.6 per cent between 1992-93 and 1999-2000. This is close to 4 per cent, but also suggests a deceleration in the 1990s. The deceleration becomes sharper if one considers only agriculture. Without the inclusion of allied (forestry, mining, fisheries) activities, agriculture grew at an annual average rate of 4.2 per cent between 1980-81 and 1991-92 and at an annual average rate of 3.7 per cent between 1992-93 and 1999-2000. Crop agriculture (minus animal husbandry and the dairy sector) grew at an annual average rate of 3.4 per cent between 1980-81 and 1991-92 and at an annual average rate of 2.2 per cent between 1992-93 and 1999-2000. There was some debate about the quality of the system of collecting agricultural statistics and about the extent of deceleration, but the conclusion that growth in the crop sector decelerated in the 1990s was unanimous. Within crops, the annual average rate of growth of 2 per cent for foodgrains between 1992-93 and 1999-2000 was only marginally more than the decadal (1991 to 2001) rate of population growth of 2.13 per cent.

This deceleration in rate of growth of crop output in the 1990s happened despite the historical discrimination against agriculture having been reversed. In the 1990s, the terms of trade moved in favour of agriculture and increases in prices of rice and wheat were more than general price increases. While the area under cereals may have declined a bit in the 1990s, that under rice and wheat increased. Are rice and wheat yield increases slowing down? Why are productivity increases slackening? In the 1980s, cost-reducing technical changes were a major factor behind production increases, accounting for 50 per cent of the increase in production. In the 1990s, the contribution of productivity enhancements to production increases has been less than 3 per cent.

There can be several possible answers. First, productivity increases may have slowed because of diminishing returns, with agriculture in Punjab and Haryana having become over-capitalized. Second, there is a regional dimension to this. Compared to the 1980s, regional growth in the 1990s has been less diversified. In the 1980s, availability of power, irrigation and infrastructure helped the spread of the Green Revolution to the Eastern Region. Because of power shortages, among other things, this osmosis has been less in the 1990s. Third, the adoption of the Green Revolution technology led to environmental and water degradation and may not only have contributed to higher unit costs, but also to a shift of R&D attention and over-cautiousness about matters concerning the environment. What is clear is an increase in output prices in the 1990s, but a simultaneous squeeze on agricultural profitability because of higher input costs. Fourth, there has been a deceleration in investments. While public investments in agriculture have declined, especially investments in research, private investments have not been able to compensate for the decline in public sector investments. Thus the burden of fiscal reform has been borne by agricultural investments, including expenditure on R&D. However, the point was also made that most of expenditure (90 per cent) is on salaries and very little is spent on actual research.

### *1.4 Diversification*

Agriculture is not just about food-grains like rice and wheat and there was some discussion about the extent to which diversification away from rice and wheat had taken place in the 1990s. For instance, the 4 per cent target rate of growth in agriculture can also be brought about through a 8 per cent or higher rate of growth in horticulture. While non-cereal and non-crop output has indeed grown, the diversification has not been enough, compared to targets. That apart, the growth in non-food and non-crop output was faster in the 1980s. In the 1990s, growth in animal husbandry, poultry, dairy, horticulture and fisheries slowed down in the second half of the 1990s. This is against the backdrop of income growth having led to a switch away from consumption of food-grains.

Why has this diversification slowed down, despite considerable value addition possibilities in food processing? The value addition in Indian agriculture is only 7 per cent, compared to 23 per cent in China and 100 per cent in developed countries. There are three generic sets of inter-related issues that can explain the constraints faced by agriculture - provision of services like irrigation, seeds, power, fertilizers, pesticides, water, credit and extension services, government pricing policies on inputs and outputs and issues concerning technology.

For examples, many policies on imports of sugar or cotton were completely *ad hoc*. Import cycles were therefore superimposed on usual agricultural cycles. This is also true to some extent of edible oils. *Ad hoc* policies also characterized exports, such as export bans on wheat and the East Asian slump led to a softening of global prices. Second, the State withdrew from spending on agriculture, without alternative institutional mechanisms being set up. There were no coordinated policies or crop adjustment programmes to enable the switch away from rice and wheat towards pulses, oilseeds or other crops. A Crop Adjustment Programme has now been proposed for Punjab. Third, diversification led to risk and uncertainty and in the absence of institutions, this was difficult to handle. Within public sector institutions, there was deterioration in management and monitoring norms. Hence, there are instances of adulterated fertilizers and seeds that are sub-standard. There is need for an independent body, outside the government, to which samples can be submitted for quality checks, encompassing inputs like fertilizers, insecticides, pesticides, feed and seeds. This work cannot be left to the extension departments of the States. Fourth, one should not forget that Indian agriculture is essentially a small holder agriculture and availability of credit has been a major constraint. In the 1990s, availability of credit for large farmers may have gone up, but that for small farmers declined. Had participatory institutions like cooperatives come into being, the problem would have been simpler. But farmers' organizations have not developed and the bad name for cooperatives has not helped. Producers' organizations need to be made more independent of the government and the new legislation is a step in the right direction.

There was agreement that the present system of expenditure on agriculture through input subsidies is inefficient and doesn't help poor farmers. User charges are not increased because of competitive populism. The existence of participatory institutions with decentralization will facilitate collection of right user charges and farmers (including poor farmers) are not averse to paying higher charges provided the service quality improves. Subsidies need to shift from inputs to investments like farm improvements, pumps and mechanization. The present system of subsidies focuses on the primary stage of processing and discourages value addition and encourages intermediation. Creation of rural infrastructure is not just about fresh infrastructure, but also about maintaining existing ones. Decentralization helps in this and can address the problem of an inability to increase the area under irrigation. If inputs need to be subsidized, it is possible to think of a system of input stamps that are given to targeted resource-poor farmers, instead of the present system of subsidizing inputs across the board. Capital costs can be reduced by creating and encouraging private service centres that lease out equipment on a first come first serve basis, instead of the present system, where farmers need to purchase the equipment. The government support and expenditure need not necessarily be fiscal, or certainly not in the form of current expenditure. There can be capital subsidies or expenditure on development of rural infrastructure or subsidies for marketing. Because risk management is a more serious concern for higher value added products, this too can be subsidized. There are some isolated examples of successful public-private partnerships, such as exports of grapes from Maharashtra and litchis from Bihar and these need to be generalized. Incidentally, there should be no objection to imposing an income tax on farmers, since it will be above a certain threshold level of income.

The present system of procurement needs to be discontinued and given its inefficiencies and lack of accountability, FCI (Food Corporation of India) needs to be restricted to buffer stock operations. FCI's inefficiencies are such that distributing food free costs less than stocking it and stocking costs account for 41 per cent of the present food subsidy. Because public stocks are high, private sector stocking operations have been squeezed. The private trade needs to be brought in and constraints to private sector operations removed. In so far as procurement for buffer stocking is concerned, minimum support prices should not be increased by more than what CACP (Commission on Agricultural Costs and Prices) recommends. Futures markets cannot work with administered prices.

India needs to have a common market in agriculture, but this has not yet happened and the market is fragmented. While the Essential Commodities Act (ECA) may have been amended, there continue to be restrictions through several Marketing Acts. There are too many statutes and orders and these have not been rationalized or harmonized. Nine different Ministries are concerned with food processing and there are 22 related Acts and Orders. Laws to enforce food standards should be unified and enforced. Exports also need to be freed up. Exporters should be allowed to buy from the farm-gate or from the market at minimum support prices and stocking and handling should be freely allowed. They should be encouraged to enter into long-term contracts (say 10 years).

Agro-industrialization is a necessary adjunct to agriculture, but there is no policy on this, or for that matter, on contract farming. Among other things, a complete absence of land records not only prevents the development of tenancy, it also prevents the development of contract farming. Land reforms have been driven by equity, rather than by considerations of efficiency. For example, consolidation of land holdings is important to exploit economies of scale, as has happened in Punjab. Land rights become complicated because of rights and sub-rights. However, it is possible to perform the consolidation on the basis of primary rights and legalize leasing of land. Land records will also make the credit problem easier to handle. Today, banks not only don't extend credit to small farmers, they don't extend credit to agri-businesses either. All reservations for the SSI (small-scale industry), connected with agriculture, also need to be scrapped. This will enable synergy between bankers, agro processors and farmers and permit the move towards higher value products. While there needs to be a public policy on biotechnology, information technology and ecology (biodiversity, land, climate, water), if the technology is not allowed to come in legally, it will come in clandestinely. Since technology is often area specific, this may not yield the best results. The use of IT (information technology) to facilitate dis-intermediation and agricultural development has also been inadequately explored. Why can't cyber-kiosks be managed by panchayats, providing information on output and input prices? Studies show that once a country crosses the per capita income threshold of 1000 US dollars, the demand for processed foods explodes. That needs to be facilitated through access to technology, including post-harvest technology, and agricultural policy should not be stuck in a time warp of being synonymous with a food-grains policy.

### *1.5 The Food Mountain*

The food mountain has short-term and long-term solutions.

In the short-term, it can be used to push the cause of education and literacy. For example, every BPL (below the poverty line) household can be given food (20 to 25 kilos per month) if children go to school. Stocks can be used for mid-day meals. The evidence shows that cooked meals for children attending school are preferable to dry rations, although some leakage has also been reported there. Food for Work programmes are possible for building rural infrastructure (such as rural roads), but this becomes a function of whether States have the requisite money. But conceptually, the idea should be to remove stocks to create assets.

Off-take through the PDS (public distribution system) is a function of prices and when prices were reduced, off-take increased. But because of mismanagement of the PDS and leakage, the PDS in its present form cannot be retained. The food subsidy and the PDS can only be revamped through a system of food stamps. This, together with reform of the procurement system, is the long-term solution to the food mountain problem.

Unfortunately, because most of agriculture is a State government subject, reforms are contingent on States taking appropriate action.

### *1.6 WTO Issues*

WTO's agricultural agreement has clauses on market access, export subsidies and domestic support. In addition, the agreements on trade-related intellectual property rights (TRIPs) and sanitary and phytosanitary measures also impinge on agriculture. The impression one forms is that WTO negotiations have been mishandled. Nor has a system of WTO-compliant subsidies evolved. India should argue that all subsidies need to be clubbed together, instead of being placed in separate boxes. Bound rates should not be lowered and anti-dumping and anti-subsidy duties or safeguard measures must be invoked in time. Imports should comply with standards and the TRIPs system needs to be strengthened. Negotiations should not be entered into without consulting experts from outside the government.

### *1.7 Epilogue*

The seminar on agriculture was held before information on the drought and its seriousness became evident. The seminar did raise questions about the reliability of agriculture-related statistics, such as production, yields or State-level investments. In addition, the drought raises questions about the quality of early warning systems (or their lack) and monsoon data and methods use to gauge impact of deficient rainfall on crops. There can also be questions about the efficacy of disaster management systems, which seem to be predicated on historical famine relief operations.

## 2. Rural Development

### *2.1 Initial Note*

Centrally sponsored schemes exist for rural roads (Pradhan Mantri Gram Sadak Yojana), rural housing (Indira Gandhi Awaas Yojana) and rural electrification (Pradhan Mantri Gramodaya Yojana). Where will resources for such centrally sponsored schemes come from? Do we need a multiplicity of centrally sponsored schemes? Do we need centrally sponsored schemes in these sectors at all? Or are these better left to States? How does one restore the fiscal health of States so that resources are freed up for social and physical infrastructure? To the extent centrally sponsored schemes continue, is it possible to impart greater accountability? At present, their success is judged through budgetary allocations and expenditure, not through tangible improvement in outcomes.

Similar points can be made about rural housing, rural sanitation, rural health-care and rural education. To what extent is private sector involvement possible? How does one handle the problem of user charges, irrespective of whether provisioning is public or private? Are the poor willing to pay higher charges, provided the quality of service improves? Is there a method of introducing subsidies if provisioning is private? Does government finance (through subsidies) have to be equated with government provisioning, or can the two be de-linked and competition introduced, even if there are subsidies?

How does one make schemes more accountable to users? Are local committees and decentralization the answer? Can decentralization help in maintenance of rural infrastructure, as opposed to creation of fresh infrastructure? Can decentralization help in identifying the poor and removing subsidies from those who don't merit them or are such local committees also subject to capture? Do Right to Information Acts help? What is the status of Right to Information Acts enacted by various State governments? Are clauses on information dissemination sufficiently transparent?

For many poor people, land is the only tangible asset. How does one develop land markets? How does one improve land records? Can IT help?

Rural poverty (the head count ratio) is more than 40 per cent (NSS, 1999-2000) in Arunachal Pradesh, Assam, Bihar, Manipur, Meghalaya, Mizoram, Nagaland, Orissa, Sikkim and Tripura. Other than Bihar and Orissa, there is thus a special problem in the North-Eastern States. How does one handle problems faced by these States?

Rural employment need not only be in agriculture. In fact, from 1994 to 2000, the Planning Commission's figures show that the annual growth rate of agricultural employment has been negative. How does one trigger employment creation in rural industries and allied services? What has been the success of central schemes specifically directed against rural unemployment? Why does the success vary widely across States?

### *2.2 Agricultural Development and Non-farm Employment*

Broad-based agricultural development is essential to ensure rural development. The diversification of the rural economy was fairly fast in the 1980s and the first half of the 1990s, but began to slow down during the second half of the 1990s. The reasons for this have already been mentioned in the section on agriculture. Suffice to say that the growth of non-food agriculture has also slowed down in the second half of the 1990s. This is despite the demand for food crops growing by 2 per cent, whereas the demand for non-food crops has been growing by 5 per cent. There has been a complete lack of coordination between credit, tariff and tax policies. Access to technology has been low and alternative distribution channels for marketing, seeds and technology have not evolved. Farmers' and producers' organizations remain weak, as do rules and organizations. Out of 100 million holdings in India, more than 80 million have less than 1 hectare of land. By 2020, the number of such marginal holdings will increase to something like 100 million. Policies cannot only be designed for richer farmers, those who number only 20 million holdings at the most. There have to be policies for the marginalized 80 million or 100 million holdings. Markets must be used and made to work for these. There must be technology for backyards. Even in areas like poultry, pig-rearing and shrimp farming, there tend to be economies of scale. So technology and appropriate diversification for small holdings is an issue.

Rural employment is not the same as farm-based employment and growth in employment will have to come from rural artisans and business and other services in rural areas. It is not true to say that two-thirds of the Indian population is employed in agriculture. There are States where the non-agricultural rural economy has grown. Gujarat, Karnataka, Andhra Pradesh and Haryana are examples. This has also happened to some extent in Punjab. The problem is that this transformation stopped in the mid-1990s.

In part, the answer lies in institutional reform of the cooperative sector. The 1 million self-help groups that exist are essentially for consumption or credit purposes. Because of institutional constraints and State intervention through laws and financial procedures that govern cooperatives, producers' cooperatives have not evolved.

Centralization and unnecessary State intervention is also evident in laws that govern forestry. Despite the 73rd and 74th amendments to the Constitution, village common land continues to be controlled by the revenue department and village forest land continues to be controlled by the forestry department. Legislatively, the present system cartelises and monopolizes the distribution chain. For example, in Orissa, under the law, tribals can sell minor forest produce only to sub-contractors who are approved by the forestry department. The farmer's share in the consumer's rupee must be increased by collapsing the distribution chain. The tariff protection on minor forest produce has also been completely warped, with 0 per cent tariff protection provided.

*2.3 Rural Infrastructure and Decentralization*

The percentage of population below the poverty line may be 26 per cent, but the percentage of individuals who are hungry (don't have two square meals per day as per the NSS questionnaire) has dropped from 19 per cent to 8 per cent. That's still 80 million people and the poverty problem is particularly serious for women-headed households. The question that then arises is, what forms of public policy and State intervention are necessary to provide food for the hungry? How can the PDS (public distribution system) be re-targeted and perhaps combined with employment schemes? The success of such schemes varies widely from State to State, depending on the efficiency of the administrative machinery. For instance, the success of the Employment Guarantee Scheme (EGS) in Maharashtra has not been replicated in every State. There is leakage in getting money across to the target beneficiary. Obviously, success is better when participants are involved in the process and self-selection is used as the norm.

There is the broader issue of providing physical infrastructure (rural roads, electricity, drinking water, irrigation, rural roads, housing) and social infrastructure (primary education, rural health care). It was agreed that the poor are willing to pay more for these services if the quality of provisioning improves. It was also agreed that the 45 Centrally sponsored schemes launched between 1950 and 1989 have rarely been successful. Their success has been measured not through improvements in outcomes, but through expenditure incurred. Much the same can also be said of government support through information and training institutions like village training centres and Krishi Vigyan Kendras. Professional competence has disappeared in these. Provided this can be changed, 15 million jobs a year can be created, leading up to the year 2020. These are jobs that will provide anything between Rs 10,000 and Rs 50,000 per month for rural households and are enough to provide livelihood and income in villages.

But there was some disagreement about the roadmap for providing solutions. At one extreme was the point of view that markets can be developed even for these sectors and private provisioning is the answer. In some parts of rural India, tuition fees charged by a government primary school are Re 1 per month, while fees charged by private schools are between Rs 30 and Rs 50 per month. However, poor people prefer to send their children to private schools because the quality of education imparted is better. NIIT's success in pushing computer education also bolsters the point. However, most people argued that private provisioning alone cannot be the answer. Moving along the continuum, there was the argument that government subsidies should only be for capital purposes and should be subsidies to producers, not consumers. However, this too was a minority view.

Most participants argued that government subsidies were necessary. However, this needs to be coupled with decentralization and should not amount to centralized, non-transparent, non-accountable and bureaucratized administration. Decentralized political reforms haven't taken place and because they were watered down, the 73rd and 74th amendments haven't lead to empowerment of people. Instead of being devolved through procedures laid down by State Finance Corporations, resources continue to be handed down through plan schemes. The sarpanch, rather than the village parliament (gram sabha) exercises effective authority and legislators, state bureaucracy and the sarpanch collude to siphon off resources. Lack of transparency and accountability facilitates this abuse. Gram swaraj cannot be this cosy relationship between the sarpanch and the BDO. Often, the sarpanch is also elected by the Election Commission, rather than by the villagers themselves. Experiments in Madhya Pradesh show how the system can be improved. A District Planning Act provides for planning by local governments and also institutes District Governments (headed by a Minister or MLA, with the District Collector as Member Secretary). Village resources are still controlled by the State. But village parliaments have been empowered to appoint local youth as village teachers and doctors. Such genuine decentralization and devolution of decision making, away from National and State capitals, will reform the present institutional mechanism and lead to genuine improvements in physical and social infrastructure. Incidentally, panchayats run by women tend to be outperform panchayats run by men.

This process will be facilitated if States implement Right to Information Acts and countervailing pressure is exerted by civil society, including NGOs. After all, half of India's districts have competent NGOs. Sustainable development from a village perspective requires land to be owned by the village. Industry can obtain such land on leases and approvals will be granted by village committees. This will facilitate the flowering of village industries, as has happened in China and provide employment outside of traditional agriculture.

Land records need improvement and land markets should be freed up. Once this is done, e-governance can improve, as has happened in some States. Cyber-kiosks (such as in Warana or Pravara) can be used to provide both economic (prices of outputs and inputs) and social (education and health) information, with the former flow used to cross-subsidize the latter.

## 3. Education

### *3.1 Initial Note*

Education needs to be divided into the separate heads of primary (secondary), technical and higher education.

Does making education a fundamental right (for children between the ages of 6 and 14) help? Are the goals of the Sarva Shiksha Abhiyan achievable? Clearly, at the primary school level, physical access to schools is not a serious problem, even in rural areas. What keeps children out of school then? Is there any substance to the argument that children are out of school because they have to work? Why are enrolment rates so low and why are dropout rates so high? What does one do about the gender bias?

What can be done to improve the quality of government-delivered primary education? How does one improve attendance of teachers, accountability and quality of infrastructure? What has been the success of central schemes like Operation Blackboard, Lok Jumbish or Sarva Shiksha Abhiyan? How has the Education Guarantee Scheme in MP worked? Does it have any lessons that can be replicated? Some research has been done on private budget schools, such as in Andhra Pradesh. What has been their track record and why do poor parents also send their children to such schools? How do these schools subsidize the poor? Why are there so many regulatory impediments to setting up such schools?

In addition to what has been said about primary education, are there any specific issues for secondary or senior secondary education? How has the literacy rate shot up from 52 per cent in 1991 to 65 per cent in 2001? Even if there are problems with the definition of literacy, this is a very sharp increase. What explains this improvement?

What should be the role of the UGC? Should there be changes in its present regulatory structure? Do scales of college and university teachers need to be centrally determined? Should private universities, including foreign ones, be allowed? How does one use IT and the Internet as an additional medium? Has the Open University system worked? Why should there be such large subsidies in higher education? Is it possible to hike fees, without depriving the poor of the right to higher education? Can scholarships and loan schemes be worked out? Will removal of subsidies affect India's R&D capabilities? In the presence of subsidies, can one handle the issue of subsidizing developed countries through the brain drain? Should there be an independent system of ranking colleges and universities? Should there be a common exam like the SAT to handle variations in quality across different boards? Are capitation fees an issue?

How has the AICTE's regulatory structure worked? There are allegations of corruption in the present system of recognition.

Why has the technical (vocational) training system not worked? Is there a lack of a coherent policy, since education spans different Ministries?

### *3.2 Primary and Secondary Education*

Although a view was expressed that education shouldn't be divided into compartments of primary, secondary, vocational or higher education and instead, an integrated view was necessary, most participants stuck to the division.

Many problems with the primary education system can be dated to the Education Commission of 1964-66. From the 1950s till then, the emphasis was on primary education and there was a belief that a single teacher or an unqualified teacher was better than no teacher at all. The Education Policy of 1966 and that of 1986 contradicted this earlier thrust and the emphasis shifted from quality to quantity. Since 1986, there has been a large increase in the number of single-teacher schools. Often such teachers have no training, no supervision and no qualifications. Under the Rajiv Gandhi Shiksha Mission, Madhya Pradesh and Rajasthan have schools with only 2 teachers, increased in 1992 to 3 teachers. Generally, multi-grade teaching has evolved in response to demographic causes, because it is not feasible to have more than a single teacher in remote locations. Are such teachers and such schools better than no teachers and no schools? Should primary education be for 5 years or 8 years? If the answer is 8 years, 32 per cent of children in upper primary schools are over-age. In that case, making education a fundamental right till the age of 14 makes no sense. The 93$^{rd}$ amendment, which conferred this right, also forgot about children under 6 years of age.

Over a period of time, education delivery has also become unduly centralized. Before 1947, education was controlled by the District Board. When districts were no longer in a position to bear the expenses, primary education became provincialized. State governments began to pay the salaries, procedures became centralized and transfers became State-wide. All decision making centralized in the Director of Public Instruction's (DPI) office. Instead, decisions and execution should be at the regional level. Today, no one is responsible anymore and the District Inspector system has completely broken down. The increase in literacy rates from 16 per cent in 1941 to 65 per cent in 2001 offers no room for complacency, since there are significant regional, gender and class cum caste biases. Despite several programmes, disadvantaged groups and women have not been able to take advantage of educational opportunities. SCs and STs account for 25 per cent of the population and 60 per cent of SCs are illiterate, with worse figures for STs. The socio-economic tensions that can result from such high dropout rates in disadvantaged groups can be enormous.

The critical question is, what keeps children out of schools? The national (Classes I-IV) drop-out rate is about 40 per cent and is correlated with poverty. The causation is however not very clear. Does education drive economic development or does economic development drive education? The poor have no economic stamina. They will not educate children unless they see economic returns quickly, after at most 5 years of schooling. Such education will be seen to have positive utility only when it leads to better jobs than what is possible to get without such education, that is, jobs that are better than manual labour. If the unemployment problem is to be addressed, semi-skilled non-agricultural employment needs to increase at 10 per cent a year. Currently, the education system does not prepare children for this kind of employment at all. The poor want education that has some demonstrated value. This is not simply a question of the curriculum, but is more often a question of how that curriculum is translated into practice.

There was some debate about whether the reason for low enrolments and high dropouts was fundamentally demand-constrained or supply-constrained. Clearly, supply seems to be a constraint because the poor seem to be willing to pay if the quality of education provided is good. In government schools, levels of literacy are low. After 4 years of schooling, children can't read or write. There is no independent assessment and testing has been abandoned, with an emphasis on automatic promotions. Government schools have low quality of educational infrastructure (proper buildings, roofs, toilets, playgrounds, drinking water) and facilities like availability of teachers and learning materials. Because government schools offer inferior quality, for those who can afford it, there has been a switch to private schools.

Some participants argued that injecting competition was the answer. For instance, subsidies to poor students could be in the form of vouchers and not to schools, so that students could take these vouchers to whichever school they wished to. This increases choice and competition. If there are grants to schools, these can be linked to performance. The setting up of private schools is still subjected to a licence permit raj and one should also give up the hypocrisy that education has to be non-profit. But the majority argued that private institutions are only likely to exist in high demand areas. That apart, the adjective private is a misnomer, since private schools also obtain subsidies from the government. Even in developed countries, only 5 per cent of primary education is through private schools and subsidies are common. In both Kerala and Himachal Pradesh, improvements in literacy have fundamentally been State driven. In areas where both private and public schools co-exist, twinning of schools through sharing of infrastructure is possible. If money is the issue, it is possible to impose a cess on private schools and use that to fund government schools. However, most participants argued that resources are not the issue. Rs 140,000 crores over the next 10 years is all that is required to ensure good quality primary education for everyone. This amounts to only 0.7 per cent of GDP. Resources are also not used efficiently in government schools. Wastage is huge and there is considerable scope for economy. Instead of giving up the government school system completely, the question really ought to be – how does one improve quality in government schools? How does one ensure that better students and those from higher socio-economic backgrounds are retained in government schools? However, this does not mean that the government alone has the right to determine quality of education. For example, under the 93rd amendment, there is no right to question the quality of education imparted.

Has the 93rd Constitutional Amendment, making education a fundamental right and providing teeth to Article 45 on the Directive Principles of State Policy, helped? This amendment emphasizes sharing of education-related responsibilities among various levels of government and devolves responsibility for primary education on Gram Panchayats. This should improve transparency and accountability, because Panchayats are answerable to the community through the Gram Sabha. A study by PRIA (Participatory Research in Asia) titled "Primary Education and Panchayati Raj Institutions" spanned 14 States and found that some of the euphoria was unwarranted. For instance, devolution to Panchayats has not really taken place and only soft powers have been given to Panchayats, with major decision making powers still with line departments. There is also overlapping of powers across three levels of Panchayats and adequate staff, with clear roles and responsibilities, have not been transferred to Gram Panchayats. There are multiple committees (under different Acts), so that the statutory and standing committees of Panchayats become non-functional. Politicization of Panchayats is also possible. As with Panchayats, there has probably been too much of euphoria about village education committees.

While the logic of accountability to local communities is unexceptionable, the system hasn't always worked that well. An inevitable criticism is, under the Education Guarantee System (EGS), teachers are paid low salaries and they are thus exploited. This is not a serious criticism, since minimum salaries can be prescribed and so can minimum qualifications. Teacher training is also critical and no use has been made of distance education to train teachers. Such teacher training that exists, is stuck in a World War I mindset. Ideally, teacher training should be through State Universities, rather than through IGNOU. The more serious criticism about schemes like the EGS is that the strategy is myopic, driven by financial considerations rather than considerations of quality. Because high salaries could not be paid, the EGS type system evolved. However, problems that plague regular schools also plague EGS type schools. If the EGS idea is generalized, what is the future of regular primary school teachers? External evaluations of such schemes in Madhya Pradesh and West Bengal have illustrated some of the problems. After 8 years of schooling in such schools, what happens to the children in Classes VI, VII and VIII? How will they be integrated and mainstreamed?

There was discussion about the utility of mid-day meal schemes, which also have positive effects on malnourishment. Surveys have shown that 89 to 90 per cent of children go to schools with no breakfast at all. Mid-day meal schemes can also help to reduce or eliminate social discrimination, such as taboos on eating together. The objection that teachers will refuse to cook is not a serious objection at all. Mid-day meals have a small impact on enrolment, but have a dramatic impact on retention. Admitted, there is leakage in mid-day meal schemes and there have been departmental inquiries against many teachers because of such misappropriations. But this does not negate the utility of the scheme. Incidentally, there is also a strong correlation between literacy and the percentage of primary school teachers who are women.

Some questions were also raised about the ideological orientation that has been sought to be given by the Centre or some State governments through the school system. Children pick up anti-female, anti-SC and anti-ST biases from school. Hindu-Muslims tensions are strengthened. In hostile environments, behavioural stereotypes tend to perpetuate themselves. There has been a deliberate campaign to show that every madrassa is ISI-funded and one of the challenges is to integrate madrassas into the standard school system. One participant also argued that perhaps the CBSE and State Education Boards could be disbanded, removing the corruption and licence raj type over-regulation, leaving schools free to set their own syllabi and medium of instruction. A common school-leaving examination and an external rating agency can ensure market-based determination of quality. The point was also made that teaching English at the primary level would make a vast difference.

### *3.3 Vocational Education*

A common and standard school education is an oxymoron and is the reason why vocational education has not taken off. Vocational training cannot be provided in standard schools because the variety of training is immense and no standard school can match it. Techniques change rapidly and no educational system can cope with such fast changes either. Expensive materials are also required for vocational training and regular schools cannot afford this. However, such materials are readily available in the work-place. Vocational training must also start to provide some income right from the start. This is required to induce the poor to train their children. The problem is that vocational training hasn't had sufficient flexibility. Therefore, all boys are taught carpentry or book-binding and all girls are taught tailoring, regardless of the demand for such jobs. The National Open School system can be strengthened to impart some flexibility. For example, up to Standard VIII, students can be encouraged to choose their own curriculum. One of the constraints with the present system is that students aged 14 and more cannot be admitted.

One possibility is to introduce sandwich programmes of academic courses in regular schools, alternating with apprenticeship training with relatively large employers. This can be instituted in Standards V-VIII. Students can be in pairs. This pair of students will alternate between regular schooling and working as an apprentice. That way, both the school and the employer will have a regular supply of children to be trained. Apprenticeships should carry a small stipend, so that there is an incentive for parents to retain their children in school. It is possible to link the stipend to the minimum wage rate. At least for the first five years. This scheme can be made mandatory on employers who employ more than 20 persons in semi-skilled jobs, with participation at the rate of one apprentice for every 10 semi-skilled employees employed. There can be an opt out option by paying a fee, which can then be used to reward those employers who offer extra apprenticeships. The State will naturally have the responsibility of transporting children from their homes to schools and workplaces.

### *3.4 Higher Education*

Educated unemployment is higher than uneducated unemployment, thus demonstrating that higher education has become somewhat irrelevant, with its unnecessary emphasis on a liberal education. Often, the marginal utility from liberal education is negative. There is a view that higher education is an inferior good and that the beneficiary should bear the cost. This is a debatable proposition. Even if the proposition is valid, the employer is also a beneficiary and should thus, also contribute to the cost. One way to ensure relevance is to insist that State funding will be linked to endowments higher educational institutions attract from employers.

There is a complete lack of data on higher education, including enrolment figures. All figures since 1990-91 are projections and part of the reason is that the UGC has not been computerized. Subject to this, figures show that the average enrolment in colleges is 500 and the average enrolment in universities is 2000. This shows that, on an average, there is enormous excess capacity and the rush is for good quality higher education, not higher education per se. Serious concerns were thus expressed about the regulatory role of the UGC and the AICTE, neither of which has been able to ensure quality. Meanwhile, private players, including foreign ones, have opted for back-door entry, in the absence of a clear, open and transparent policy. With expected pressures at the WTO for opening up higher education and resultant competition, it is necessary to completely revamp the regulatory role. Centralized regulation can be made weaker, with higher educational institutions free to set their own fees, salaries and syllabi. However, there must be proper disclosure norms and perhaps a system of external rating. Higher tuition fees will not deprive poor students from access to higher education. Through cross-subsidization, educational institutions can offer scholarships and also subsidize across disciplines or across departments. Loans are also possible. It is paradoxical that loans are available for studying in the United States, but not for studying in India.

## 4. Infrastructure

### *4.1 Initial Note*

Infrastructure needs to be first defined, because it covers a wide range of sectors – power, telecom, posts, roads, ports, railways, civil aviation and urban (or rural infrastructure).

A general problem is that of appropriate user charges. How does one only subsidize the poor and ensure that the non-poor pay economic costs? Can one solve the free rider problem? In what infrastructure sectors is private sector involvement possible and what forms can this involvement take? If the bulk of infrastructure has to be developed by the government, how does one solve the problem of rehabilitating Centre and State government finances? How should infrastructure development (public or private) be financed? What debt-equity combinations are possible?

What is the regulatory role of the State? What powers should regulatory agencies have? How should they be staffed and funded and are their recommendations binding? Can their decisions be challenged in courts? How do sectoral regulators mesh with competition law and the Competition Commission of India? Should consumer interests be the over-riding objective, or is there a trade-off with needs of developing the market? Is there a specific policy one adopts for mergers and amalgamations?

Specifically on power, how does one solve the distribution, metering and minimum charge problem, especially for agriculture? How does one bring down T&D losses? How does one rehabilitate SEBs? Should subsidies be routed through SEBs or should they come out of State government budgets? Are there any problems with the Electricity Bill? Should captive power plants be allowed? Are there any issues connected with trading power? Has enough attention been paid to demand management and is there an integrated energy policy?

Specifically on telecom, does government policy recognize convergence? Are there any problems with the Convergence Bill? How does the Convergence Commission of India mesh with the Competition Commission of India? How does one enforce the universal service obligations? Once a PSU is privatized and managerial control passes into private hands, should the government interfere with Board decisions?

On roads, the National Highway Development Project (NHDP) accounts for a very small percentage of India's roads. Most roads will have to be developed by States and local bodies. How does one finance this? How does one handle land acquisition and compensation problems? How does one handle public interest litigation?

On railways, how does one rationalize tariffs and bring back freight traffic to railways? How does one finance modernization and capacity expansion? How does one improve the safety record and reduce over-manning? How does one curb populist pressures to start fresh trains? Is the leasing idea workable for airports?

### *4.2 Types of Infrastructure*

The experience with infrastructure reform varies widely. How can infrastructure be defined? Are coal and steel infrastructure, as they have traditionally been assumed to be? The characteristic of infrastructure is that it is fixed in space and the value is determined by the location. Thus defined, each sector has a degree of infrastructure-ness. Generation, grids and roads are infrastructure. So are tracks. But rolling stock is not infrastructure. Part of the problem is that the policy does not differentiate according to the characteristics exhibited by a particular sector.

Many Second Five Year Plan arguments for State financing of infrastructure (scale economies, resource issues, management of finances) still continue to apply to infrastructure. Hence, no straight substitution of private financing for State financing is likely to be possible and State financing will not disappear. Since there are vulnerable interests, the State will have to play a major role in infrastructure development. Having said this, the objective should be to introduce competition, in whatever form possible. State financing need not be equated with State provisioning. One should note that government projects are often badly designed and the notion of opportunity cost of capital does not exist for the government.

Ninety-five to ninety-eight per cent of existing infrastructure is owned, managed and operated by the government. This can be taken out or extracted to improve efficiency. Telecom has been successfully extracted. Greenfield investments have been in the private sector and have overcome some initial problems in the transition from a licence fee to revenue sharing regime. In a few cases, pure privatization will be possible, with the government selling its assets. However, there will be a larger basket, where in the next 5 to 7 years, direct sales will not be possible. But this does not preclude commercialization. The question that arises in such situations is, what sort of framework is necessary and how does one make users pay? Third, there are areas like rural roads and primary education. Here, it is possible to hand over public assets (while retaining public ownership) to the private sector and buy services from the private sector, with appropriate payments being made. There are 9 such annuity roads in existence today. The quality of such privately built roads is better than publicly built roads, because the private enterprise knows it will have to maintain these roads, and costs are also lower. This can be interpreted as private financing of public infrastructure (PFPI) and the policy choice confronting the government is one of deciding what basket to put a specific project in. However, for PFPI to work, there has to be credibility about the government's ability to pay and this therefore impinges on governance issues. It helps if a specific cess can be earmarked to create a specific fund and more such dedicated funds are needed.

### *4.3 Experience with Infrastructure Reform*

The experience with infrastructure reform varies widely. Telecom has been relatively successful. The political economy has become easier to handle, because people can witness tangible results in the form of telecom rates, airfares, rail fares and housing rates dropping, thanks to greater competition. However, telecom, ports and civil aviation don't yet matter to most people. What matters is power and water and in these, there has been limited progress. Developing such infrastructure often requires a long-term view on the part of the establishment, which is usually missing because political entities tend to be short-term maximizers. To complicate matters further, there is an issue of Central versus State-level jurisdiction.

There has been some progress in road development, but other than power, ports and civil aviation are also in bad shape. In terms of speed of response, India has no time left, as infrastructure constraints impose severe transaction costs and these would have been more acute had GDP and manufacturing growth been higher than what it has been. There is no port strategy in place and it is a moot question whether India has 55 ports or 3 ports that work. Cities are in a state of governance collapse and municipal services are not available, although 3 urban funds have been mooted in this year's budget. Given the lack of governance at the local level, urban services have sometimes been privatized by the rich. Garbage collection is an example. But a lot of this privatization is technically illegal and is an option that is only available to the relatively rich. Some infrastructure improvements are linked to improving urban and rural governance and enhancing the role of panchayati raj institutions and urban local bodies. Ostensibly, there are 440 airfields, although few conform to quality and safety norms. On top of this, India tends to plan for shortages, not for more than the projected demand, which is the norm in other countries. Townships are also infrastructure. Why shouldn't FDI be allowed in the development of townships?

In many sectors, the macro policy and fiscal frameworks are in place. The problems lie elsewhere. Financial intermediaries have been badgered into playing a role. Although financial institutions have tended to retreat, banks have tended to come in more. However, two principal micro issues remain. First, infrastructure reform cannot be delinked from politics and in coalition politics, the bureaucracy tends to become risk averse. Bureaucratic decision making also leads to time dilations. Red lights are removed only in some States, where the Chief Minister tends to be dominant. However, even in such instances, there are problems if the infrastructure sector is in the Concurrent List. Second, there is a tendency to go after world class projects and this leads to world class costs as well. In part, banks and financial institutions have burnt their fingers with steel and oil projects and have become completely risk averse. This leads to lump sum turnkey contracts and multilateral funding forces more over-designing. Because the money has come in, discretionary special privileges and special treatment has been granted. Many such people who came in were financiers, with no particular expertise in developing that infrastructure sector. There are instances where BHEL was barred from bidding. Many State Highways require 2 lanes rather than 4 lanes and they can be built more cheaply with local contractors. Kutcha roads and irrigation networks are not capital intensive.

Regulation is an issue, whether there is a government monopoly or whether the public monopoly has been replaced by a local private monopoly. However, regulators are not truly independent and their recommendations are not mandatory. Independent regulators have become an employment avenue for ex civil servants, regardless of expertise and there is a multiplicity of regulators. Why should oil and gas, natural gas and power not have only a single regulator? Should there be a transport regulator or should there be a regulator for utilities?

### *4.4 The Power Sector*

In the power sector, despite attempts at reform, competition is now actually less. There are restrictions on trading. Approval has to be sought from a generating agency. Alternatively, power has to be sold to the single government monopoly and wheeling charges are imposed. Why does one have to sell to the grid? (The discussion did not bring in the new Electricity Bill.)

Seventy per cent of consumers (small domestic consumers, agriculture) consume power at less than the average cost of production and 40 per cent of consumers pay no costs at all. This cross-subsidy structure has been the bane of the power sector. While merit needs can indeed be supplied at lower than the average cost, this cannot be true of 70 per cent consumers. Small power stations, not large ones, are the direction for the future. Small plants have an advantage because it is possible to fragment markets automatically and power can move directly from pit heads to consumption heads. With smaller power stations and changes in the supply system, it is possible to earmark low cost supplies (hydel, existing thermal plants or new IPPs) for agricultural needs. One cannot wish away cheap power for agriculture. But who is this cheap power for and how is the system administered? It is necessary to measure entitlements and differentiate across different types of farmers. Except merit cases, power purchase should be delinked from the political economy and all new purchasers should be compelled to purchase power at marginal cost. Beyond a certain threshold level of consumption per month, there should be no subsidies. Since distribution is about billing and collection, it is possible to separate the supply function from the distribution function. For 11 KVA and below, it is possible to franchise out collection to local bodies like panchayats and this will bring down T&D losses. In urban areas, one can follow the cable operator model to make collection easier. The last mile problem can be solved if there is a framework for consumer protection and contract enforcement. Does targeting become easier if there are no subsidies at the pre-usage stage? Instead of a pre-usage subsidy, there can be a post-usage subsidy in the form of reimbursements on payments made. Billing on the basis of kilo-volt-amperes instead of billing on the basis of kilo-watts also encourages efficient consumption of energy. UP has successfully experimented with this idea for high tension consumers.

Since States are reluctant to reform, is it possible to link fiscal devolution to infrastructure reform? This has already been attempted in disbursements for roads and the same idea figures in the 3 urban funds mooted in this year's budget. Can this idea be used for power, such as through the accelerated power development programme, or will it lead to increased disparities among States? As a trigger for reform, should there be an Index of Infrastructure Development for different States?

## 5. Administrative Reforms

### *5.1 Initial Note*

The expression administrative reforms has to be defined, since it means more than reform of the civil services. On reforming civil services, recommendations were made by the Pay Commission and there are other recommendations in reports of the Expenditure Reforms Commission. The problem is that none of these recommendations (except hikes in salaries) were implemented. Do these issues need to be discussed again? Are downsizing, identification of the surplus pool and VRS feasible? Are contractual appointments, proper evaluation for vertical mobility, lateral entry into higher levels and consolidation of perks into gross emoluments possible? Do we need the present system of centralized recruitment on a large scale? Or can one think of a small and core centralized recruitment and larger recruitments at the State-level? Is it possible to insulate the civil services from political interference? Is it necessary to de-link revenue and judicial functions from administrative functions at lower levels?

Do we need so many Ministries and government departments? This is a State, as well as Central issue. Are reforms needed in the budget making process and accounting procedures? Do distinctions between revenue and capital expenditure and plan and non-plan expenditure need to continue?

How does one handle the problem of corruption in civil services? Does the CVC need to be strengthened? Are changes needed in the Prevention of Corruption Act? What about changes in Articles 12 and 311 of the Constitution?

How does the government become more accountable to citizens and business? Are changes in Secretariat procedures necessary? Are there adequate redressal mechanisms for grievances? Are there lessons from using IT to improve public governance, say in Bangalore? Are there examples from say, Bangalore or Hyderabad, where citizen action has made the government more transparent and accountable?

Why is the administrative law or subordinate legislation not readily available? Why is there so much discretion in interpreting these rules? Can these not be rationalized and unified so as to reduce discretion? Can they not be made publicly available? Are there lessons from States that have successfully reformed administrative law? Is there an Official Secrets Act issue?

Does administrative reform mean only the executive, or should one also talk about the legislature and the judiciary? Has civil society been able to exert countervailing pressure against inefficient functioning of these three organs of State? Should one discuss decentralization through panchayats and local bodies?

### *5.2 Governance*

The central theme of administrative reforms has to be improvements in governance. The basic problem of governance is an incapacity of the major institutions – the executive (political and bureaucratic), legislature (Parliament and State Legislatures) and the judiciary to manage the affairs of the State so as to provide a desired quality of life to India's citizens. Although self-curing by these three organs is unlikely, reforms must begin with the political institutions and encompass not only Cabinets (Union and State), but also the law and order machinery (the police), electoral reform (transparent funding of political parties and elections and audit of party funds), the federal system and decentralization. Within electoral reforms, there are also technical issues like changing the first past the post system and introducing proportional representation. It is estimated that complete decentralization from Centre to States and from States to local bodies will require resources amounting to 3 or 4 per cent of GDP. This can be raised through better tax compliance or slashing subsidies, which account for 15 per cent of GDP. The objective should be less government (reduce unnecessary controls), greater autonomy and power to citizens, greater competition in the provision of goods and services and decentralization following the 73rd and 74th amendments to the Constitution. There should be a Lok Pal Bill to prevent political corruption and redress citizen grievances. E-governance can facilitate the task of governance greatly.

Why is the political class so reluctant to accept this reform agenda, although reforms in governance should bring maximum payoffs? Why is civil service reform not part of the political agenda? Out of 28 million people employed in the organized sector, 20 million are employed in the government (including PSUs). Forty-five to fifty per cent of these are clerks, drivers and peons. How many of these 20 million are actively involved in the reform process? The figure will not be more than 5 or 6 lakhs. Downsizing may not be the right expression. But can these people not be re-deployed? It will of course be necessary to revamp old secretariat procedures. The interface between the citizen and the government exhibits traits of corruption and non-responsiveness. Birth certificates, death certificates, ration cards, caste certificates, all of these cannot be obtained without bribery. The concept of governance should be split up into two separate concepts, governance reforms that impinge on the productive sector (such as government monopolies increasing transaction costs for the private sector) and governance reform in relationship to the people. In the latter, new methodologies, new technologies and e-governance can be used to improve governance.

The broad agenda of governance may seem daunting, but it is possible to focus on a minimalist agenda - justice delivery, education, health care and sanitation. This is the least that the citizen expects from the government. India is falling far behind on the UN's Millenium Declaration targets. Only 3.2 per cent of GDP is spent on education, the figure for health is 0.9 per cent.

There are instances of best practices across Indian States. Karnataka has computerized 20 million land records through the Bhoomi Initiative. This has reduced delays, harassment and bribes. There is a pilot project in Tumkur, designed to improve government accounting systems. Countervailing pressure has been exerted by citizens and some States have passed Right to Information Acts. Citizens' Charters have also effectively been used in municipal governments. The question is, who will take this reform agenda forward?

# 2

## How is the State Functioning?

*A Comparative Analysis of Growth, Governance and Social Issues during the 8th and 9th Plan Periods*

DEBASHIS CHAKRABORTY

### Introduction

India has experienced an appreciable level of economic development over the plan periods. Presently, the country is going through the 10th plan, operational since 2002. The future growth potential of the country depends not only on the level of absolute development, but also on sustainable development. In terms of poverty alleviation, the idea is that the government objective should focus not only on upliftment of the poorer sections above the poverty line, but also rest on providing means for maintaining that status. The government seems to be catching up with this concept, as the recently released Planning Commission document – India Vision 2020 (2002), sets a target of enhancing the growth potential of various sectors by 2020. Poverty reduction, providing opportunity for the oppressed sections and sustainable development are the major goals specified in the document.[1]

While fulfillment of the goals targeted in that document is the need of the hour and highly commendable, a brief analysis of the economy towards sustainable development needs to be undertaken.[2] For this purpose, an evaluation of the performance of various sectors over the entire plan period is required. However, the current framework is too narrow for such a huge exercise and hence only a comparative analysis of the economy during the last two completed plan periods is attempted.

The analysis is organized along the following lines. First, the macro variables like GDP, savings trends and inflation are analysed.

Second, the performance of poverty alleviation and employment generation has been looked into. The sectoral growth trends and other related issues are discussed next. Similar exercise is followed for fiscal sector, social responsibilities, maintenance of law and order, infrastructure development and external trade scenario. Finally the paper sums up the findings.

It should be mentioned here that the analysis is not an exhaustive one for two reasons. First, a number of important sectors of the economy (e.g., the financial sector) have been excluded from the analysis. Second, for a couple of important variables (e.g., crime in law and order), the data are available only for the initial years of the recently concluded 9$^{th}$ plan period. However, from the time-trend it is unlikely that the conclusion would drastically change even with the completed data set. Therefore the current analysis, although indicative in character, highlights the major concern areas, which need to be addressed at the earliest.

## SECTION 1

## ECONOMIC GROWTH

### GDP

Sustaining high level of economic growth is always the topmost priority for a government, especially in developing countries. In terms of growth rate, the eighth plan period has remained the most successful era so far. While during most of the preceding plans, the economy experienced a double-digit growth rate in GNP, NNP and PCNNP; it reached an all-time peak during this period as seen from table 1.

It was expected that the ninth plan would be able to sustain this increasing trend and expand the growth potential further, build up on the solid foundation created during the earlier regime. However, not only has the expectation not been met, but also the growth rate registered an all time trough in the last twenty years (after the annual plan of 1979-80). The massive reduction in growth rate is likely to bear serious implications.

**Table 1**

*Average Annual Growth Rate during the Plans (current prices)*

*(Percentage)*

| | *GNP at factor cost* | *NNP at factor cost* | *Per capita NNP at factor cost* |
|---|---|---|---|
| First Plan (1951-56) | 1.8 | 1.5 | -0.3 |
| Second Plan (1956-61) | 9.5 | 9.4 | 7.3 |
| Third Plan (1961-66) | 9.6 | 9.5 | 7.1 |
| Three Annual Plans (1966-69) | 12.2 | 12.2 | 9.8 |
| Fourth Plan (1969-74) | 11.1 | 11.0 | 8.5 |
| Fifth Plan (1974-79) | 10.7 | 10.4 | 7.9 |
| Annual Plan (1979-80) | 9.4 | 8.3 | 5.7 |
| Sixth Plan (1980-85) | 15.2 | 15.1 | 12.7 |
| Seventh Plan (1985-90) | 14.4 | 14.2 | 11.8 |
| Two Annual Plans (1990-92) | 15.7 | 15.5 | 13.2 |
| Eighth Plan (1992-97) | 16.3 | 16.3 | 14.0 |
| Ninth Plan (1997-2002) | 11.1 | 11.3 | 9.2 |

Source: *Economic Survey (2002-03)*

Like the overall growth rate of GDP, the sectoral growth rates at factor cost have also remained at a low level during the ninth plan period as compared to the earlier span of time. The growth comparison across sectors is presented in table 2. Only in case of public administration, defence and other services, has there been an improvement in the sectoral growth rate. However, all other sectors, precisely agriculture and manufacturing, have registered a decline.

## Savings and Capital Formation

The high rate of domestic savings in India has remained a pillar of the vibrant monetary system. It is observed from table 3 that the level of domestic savings is declining during the 9$^{th}$ plan period. The situation is likely to worsen in the coming years since the growth rate of savings has also remained at a much lower rate during the 9$^{th}$ plan period. In addition, the government policy of reducing the interest rate on deposits might turn out to be counter productive - by reducing household savings, which constitute the main source.[3] Consequently, a similar declining trend has been noticed in case of capital formation. However, the situation is worse here, since the growth rate has become negative over the last couple of years.

**Table 2**

*Growth Rate of GDP at Factor Cost across Sectors*

*(Percentage)*

| | *Agriculture and allied sectors* | *Manufacturing* | *Trade, transport* | *Financing, insurance* | *Public administration, defence* | *Overall GDP* |
|---|---|---|---|---|---|---|
| 8th plan period | 4.63 | 8.04 | 8.83 | 7.98 | 5.09 | 6.69 |
| 9th plan period | 2.02 | 4.62 | 7.93 | 7.51 | 9.09 | 5.46 |

Source: Calculated from the time series data

**Table 3**

*Trends in Saving and Capital Formation*

*(Percentage of GDP)*

| | *Gross Domestic Saving* | | *Gross Domestic Capital Formation* | |
|---|---|---|---|---|
| | *Average level* | *Growth rate* | *Average level* | *Growth rate* |
| 8th plan period | 23.48 | 1.23 | 24.82 | 1.87 |
| 9th plan period | 23.22 | 0.87 | 24.02 | -0.44 |

Source: Calculated from the time series data

## Inflation

Inflation represents the rate of change in price level. While a moderate level of inflation is good for the economy, it acts as a retarding force at times, e.g., in the case of galloping inflation. The time trend of inflation based on WPI and CPI during the nineties is shown in the following diagram.[4]

**Diagram 1**

*Trend of Inflation during Nineties*

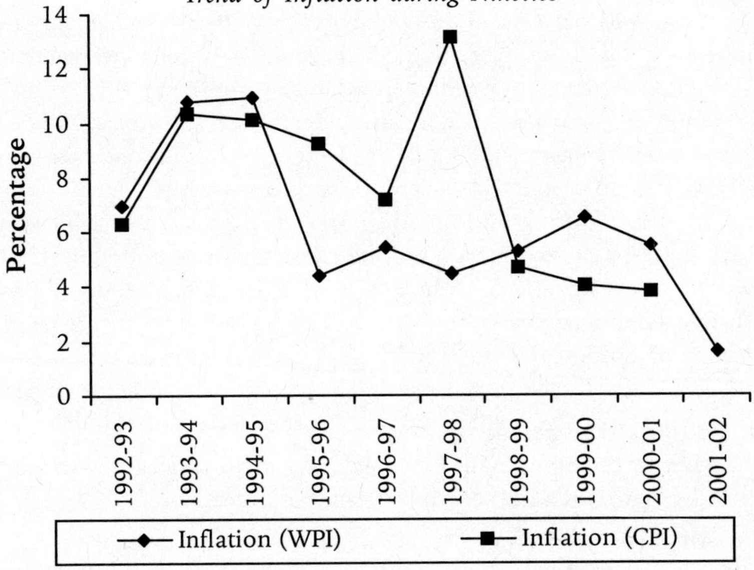


Source: *Economic Survey* (various issues)

During the early nineties, the inflation was at a high level, and the government was criticized on the ground of fiscal indiscipline. However, it declined to the normal level in the subsequent period, due to adoption of appropriate policies. During the $8^{th}$ plan the average inflation rate (based on WPI) stood at 7.7 per cent, as compared to 4.68 per cent prevailing in the $9^{th}$ plan. Inflation management during the $9^{th}$ plan, on the face of it, seems impressive. However, it has been pointed out by economists from time to time that this lowering tendency in inflation rate has nothing to do with macro management, but evolves out of slackness in demand and other factors. A brief account of the factors is provided in the following.

Firstly, the market structure in India in the post-liberalisation period has undergone a major change. The level of domestic competition has increased drastically, and in most of the cases is price-based rather than quality-based. This has maintained a downward pressure on price level.

Secondly, the three product groups – namely, primary, manufacturing and fuel products have a respective weight of around 22, 64 and 14 per cent in determination of WPI. The individual price movement of these over the period would help to understand the situation better. The primary products, comprising the essential commodities; and the manufacturing sector are showing stability in prices over the last couple of years, thereby causing a lower tendency in overall inflation. However, these groups experienced a high inflation rate during mid-nineties. The third group, which includes fuel, power, light and lubricants, and consists of energy products, falls within the purview of Administered Price Mechanism (APM). However, the domestic fuel prices are linked with international prices of crude oil, and the administered prices are adjusted in accordance with the global price change. The percentage change of this group has also remained lower in the last couple of years.

Thirdly, the stability in manufacturing sector prices reveals not a healthy sign, but slackness in demand and recession.

All these points taken together, the scenario is likely to raise alarm, rather than bring comfort. In short, the overall growth scenario during the 9$^{th}$ plan has remained bleak as compared to the 8$^{th}$ plan period.

## SECTION II

## POVERTY, FOOD SECURITY AND EMPLOYMENT

After macro management, the economic condition of people, namely poverty, needs to be focused. The concept of inequality is closely associated with that of poverty. The growth rate across the states has varied significantly in the nineties, paving the way for rise in inter-state inequality. While success stories in overall poverty reduction front are widely portrayed, a detailed analysis of the regional aspect of development opens up certain demanding issues. The resource-based economies, mostly located in the eastern and northeastern India are losing out.[5] These economies traditionally represent the less developed regions, and therefore, cumulative effect of underdevelopment might result there.

## Poverty

Poverty is a stark realty in our country and was always given special attention since Independence. However, the level of poverty the reduction over the last decade is the focus of the current analysis. The absolute level of poverty has declined from 39.4 per cent in 1987-88 to 37.1 per cent in 1993-94, which was in line with the ongoing pace of poverty eradication. The poverty estimate undertaken in 1999-2000 during NSS 55$^{th}$ round has shown a dramatic improvement, when the poverty ratio, as calculated on the basis of the survey, has declined to the level of 26.8 per cent. The result has been interpreted as a huge success of the poverty alleviation programme.

While poverty reduction over this period has been factually acknowledged by the economists, the new methodology employed in the 55$^{th}$ round received wide criticism. Since early 1950s, all NSSO rounds have assumed the reference period for consumption to be 'past 30 days', which has been revised in the 55$^{th}$ round. This time questions on consumption of clothing, footware, education (institutional) and durable goods were asked only for 'past 365 days' and for food, tobacco and intoxicants, all sample households were asked both the '30 day' and '1 week' estimates. Given this change, the NSS result is likely to be affected from two possible sources of bias. Firstly, there could be non-sampling biases in recall and response. In other words, there is a high probability that the households have multiplied the weekly expenditure by a simple factor of four to obtain their monthly expenditure. Secondly, there is almost definitely a sampling bias with respect to the under reporting of consumption by richer households.[6]

Even if the theoretical validity of this new methodology is accepted, the so-called success loses some of its credential due to the momentum effect. The poverty reduction has been much more intense in case of the progressive states as compared to the same in the relatively backward ones. For instance, the poverty level in certain big and populous underdeveloped states has not been reduced as per expectation and even witnessed a rise in inequality.[7] It is seen from table 4 that the poverty level in Assam, Madhya Pradesh and Orissa stood at a relatively high level after the 55$^{th}$ round, as they started from a lower level of development. In addition, although the poverty level has declined considerably for other states, it remained above the national average in case of populated states like Bihar, UP and West Bengal. Therefore, the reduction in poverty should be viewed in this light. Besides, a localization of poverty has also been noticed where poorer districts are concentrated around eastern and central India.[8]

## Table 4

*Percentage of Population Below Poverty Line*

*(Percentage)*

| *States* | *1983* | *1993-94* | *1999-00* |
|---|---|---|---|
| Andhra Pradesh | 28.91 | 22.19 | 15.77 |
| Assam | 40.47 | 40.86 | 36.09 |
| Bihar | 62.22 | 54.96 | 42.60 |
| Gujarat | 32.79 | 24.21 | 14.07 |
| Haryana | 21.37 | 25.05 | 8.74 |
| Himachal Pradesh | 16.40 | 28.44 | 7.63 |
| Jammu & Kashmir | 24.24 | 25.17 | 3.48 |
| Karnataka | 38.24 | 33.16 | 20.04 |
| Kerala | 40.42 | 25.43 | 12.72 |
| Madhya Pradesh | 49.78 | 42.52 | 37.43 |
| Maharashtra | 43.44 | 36.86 | 25.02 |
| Orissa | 65.29 | 48.56 | 47.15 |
| Punjab | 16.18 | 11.77 | 6.16 |
| Rajasthan | 34.46 | 27.41 | 15.28 |
| Tamil Nadu | 51.66 | 35.03 | 21.12 |
| Uttar Pradesh | 47.07 | 40.85 | 31.15 |
| West Bengal | 54.85 | 35.66 | 27.02 |
| All India | 44.48 | 35.97 | 26.10 |

Source: NHDR (2001)

## Table 5

*Poverty Estimates from Type 1 and Type 2 Schedules*

| *Round* | *Year* | *Rural* | | *Urban* | |
|---|---|---|---|---|---|
| | | *Type 1* | *Type 2* | *Type 1* | *Type 2* |
| 51 | July 94-June 95 | 41.2 | 22.8 | 35.5 | 18.3 |
| 52 | July 95-June 96 | 37.6 | 19.1 | 29.9 | 15.2 |
| 53 | Jan 97-Dec 97 | 35.9 | 20.7 | 32.3 | 17.8 |
| 54 | Jan 98-Jun 98 | 42.6 | 23.6 | 32.9 | 20.0 |
| 55[9] | Jul 99-Dec 99 | 27.6 | 24.8 | 25.2 | 23.4 |

Source: Sen (2000)

The notion of underreporting of expenditures gets manifested from the analysis provided in table 5. Sen (2000) has argued that in terms of income inequality, the 55$^{th}$ round has produced paradoxical results. Type 1 schedule has consistently exhibited greater inequality than by the type 2 schedule in all earlier rounds. However, this feature has not been observed in 55$^{th}$ round distribution, using the one week and 30-day recalls. On the contrary, both in rural and urban areas, the 55$^{th}$ round results by the two recalls are very close to each other. According to Sen it reveals that, consumption share of the bottom 40 per cent of the rural population by the one month recall of the 55$^{th}$ round would be overestimated by at least 5 per cent. In other words, it gives an impression that the margin of poverty alleviation is actually lower than the official estimate.

Another important lacuna in the claim of phenomenal poverty reduction deserves particular attention. Meenakshi and Vishwanathan (2003) have noted that while income poverty has gone down, calorie deprivation in rural India has sprung up. The decline in calorie intake in rural India, even if compared with a much older time frame, looks horrible, which amounts to approximately 70 calories per capita over the period 1983 to 1999-2000. More alarmingly, this is a general phenomenon in almost all major states, and true for even a green revolution state like Punjab. In addition, the percentage of persons consuming below 2400 calories per day has increased considerably in most of the states. The scenario is illustrated with the help of table 6.

## Food Security

The previous issue brings the concern on food security, i.e., availability of food to common people, forward. The average net production of cereals has not increased over the nineties, while public stock has increased considerably in the last couple of years. However, the later half of the nineties also witnessed a terrible mismanagement of this produced foodstuff. While a formidable section of the population is dying out of hunger, a mounting stock of foodgrains is rotting in FCI storehouses.[10] As seen from table 7, net availability of cereals is actually declining from 1997 onwards, i.e., since the initiation of 9$^{th}$ plan.[11]

## Table 6

*Some Summary Statistics on Calorie Intake and Poverty*

| States | Average calorie intake per capita per day (Kcal) | | Head count ratios (per cent consuming below 2400 calories per day | |
|---|---|---|---|---|
| | 1983 | 1999-2000 | 1983 | 1999-2000 |
| Andhra Pradesh | 2204 | 2021 | 68.5 | 80.7 |
| Bihar | 2189 | 2121 | 67.6 | 74.9 |
| Gujarat | 2113 | 1986 | 72.6 | 80.5 |
| Haryana | 2554 | 2455 | 54.1 | 55.1 |
| Himachal Pradesh | 2636 | 2454 | 44.5 | 56.5 |
| Jammu & Kashmir | 2569 | 2631 | 44.5 | 39.7 |
| Karnataka | 2260 | 2028 | 64.0 | 78.9 |
| Kerala | 1884 | 1982 | 81.5 | 81.2 |
| Madhya Pradesh | 2323 | 2062 | 62.5 | 78.4 |
| Maharashtra | 2144 | 2012 | 73.1 | 83.3 |
| Orissa | 2103 | 2119 | 70.9 | 74.6 |
| Punjab | 2677 | 2381 | 46.2 | 62.8 |
| Rajasthan | 2433 | 2425 | 54.2 | 56.7 |
| Tamil Nadu | 1861 | 1826 | 80.6 | 86.5 |
| Uttar Pradesh | 2399 | 2327 | 58.4 | 64.5 |
| West Bengal | 2027 | 2095 | 76.0 | 75.6 |

Source: Meenakshi and Vishwanathan (2003)

## Table 7

*Cereal Availability in the Nineties*

*(Grams per person per day)*

| Year | Net production | Net imports | Net change in public stocks | Net availability (1+2-3) |
|---|---|---|---|---|
| 1985-89 | 422.7 | 2.0 | -5.3 | 430.1 |
| 1990 | 456.9 | 0.3 | -5.0 | 452.1 |
| 1991 | 447.9 | -1.4 | 0.4 | 446.1 |
| 1992 | 446.8 | 1.3 | 4.2 | 443.8 |
| 1993 | 446.4 | 2.5 | 16.6 | 432.3 |
| 1994 | 456.3 | 0.2 | 16.6 | 439.9 |
| 1995 | 448.6 | -5.9 | -2.3 | 445.1 |
| 1996 | 451.7 | -6.9 | -11.7 | 456.4 |
| 1997 | 445.5 | -6.7 | -4.2 | 443.0 |
| 1998 | 455.3 | -4.7 | 11.0 | 439.6 |
| 1999 | 456.3 | -5.4 | 25.3 | 425.6 |
| 2000 | 452.7 | -5.2 | 30.7 | 416.8 |

Source: Deaton and Dreze (2002)

A comparison of plan periods will help to understand the last point better. The average level of net production of cereals increased from 422.7 grams in 7$^{th}$ plan to 449.96 grams in 8$^{th}$ plan period, i.e., increased by 6.44 per cent. The production also increased during the 9$^{th}$ plan period, but experienced a much smaller growth rate of 0.55 per cent. However, the availability of cereals, which reached a peak during the 8$^{th}$ plan, has declined during the 9$^{th}$ plan, and witnessed a negative growth rate.[12] The decline in public distribution operation has made things worse, which bears serious implications for people living under poverty line.

**Table 8**

*A Plan Wise Comparison of Net Availability of Cereals*

| | *Average level of net production (Grams per person per day)* | *Growth rate ( per cent)* | *Average level of net availability (Grams per person per day)* | *Growth rate ( per cent)* |
|---|---|---|---|---|
| 7$^{th}$ plan period | 422.70 | - | 430.10 | - |
| 8$^{th}$ plan period | 449.96 | 0.17 | 443.50 | 0.47 |
| 9$^{th}$ plan period (up to 2000) | 452.45 | 0.06 | 431.25 | -2.23 |

Source: Calculated from the time trend

To combat the concern over food security, in particular during the drought in 2001, two viable policy options came to the forefront. The first is providing food to the workers through 'Food for Work' programmes at various pockets in the country and the second is to provide mid-day meals to the school-going children. The idea was to provide cooked food (Mid-day meal) in the primary school premises. While the actual target would remain ensuring food security, this would also be instrumental in reducing the dropout rate.

The People's Union for Civil Liberties (Rajasthan) filed a writ petition in the Supreme Court in April 2001, demanding the immediate utilization of the country's food stocks for drought relief and prevention of hunger. The writ petition also urged the scope of this exercise not to be restricted to drought situations. The guiding motive of the petition was the general need to uphold "right to food", following from right to life (Article 21). The Supreme Court has responded positively to the writ petition. A brief account of the Supreme Court orders is provided in the annex. Although the court has asked the states to provide cooked mid-day meal to every child in the primary schools, unfortunately a number of states are yet to enforce it.[13]

## Employment

The sources of employment could be divided in two categories by structure, namely, in the organized and unorganized sector. The organized sector accounts for around 10 per cent of the total employment. Apart from open unemployment, disguised unemployment and marginal employment also characterize the scenario. It is seen from the latest NSS round that employment scenario has worsened, which bears serious implications for fulfillment of the sustainable development objective. The employment rate as obtained in 55th round (1999-2000) is shown in table 9:

**Table 9**

*Number of Persons Employed Per Thousand Workers*

| *Round* | *Year* | *Employed (All workers)* | | | | | |
|---|---|---|---|---|---|---|---|
| | | *Rural* | | | *Urban* | | |
| | | *Male* | *Female* | *Person* | *Male* | *Female* | *Person* |
| 55 | 1999-00 | 531 | 299 | 417 | 518 | 139 | 337 |
| 50 | 1993-94 | 553 | 328 | 444 | 520 | 154 | 347 |
| 43 | 1987-88 | 539 | 323 | 434 | 506 | 152 | 337 |

Source: *Employment and Unemployment, 1999-2000 (Key Results)*

It is evident from the table that employment rate has declined during the 9th plan, not only compared to the 8th plan, but also with respect to the 7th plan period. This dismal trend is more pronounced in the rural belt. The slackening of employment in the rural areas is obvious from the setback in agricultural growth rate as shown in diagram 3 later. Until and unless the issue of enhancing agricultural growth is properly addressed, the rural employment scenario is not likely to improve.[14]

A cross-state analysis on labour force participation is provided in tables 10 and 11, from which the slackening in overall employment rate during late nineties becomes obvious. In particular, from table 11 it is seen that the growth rate of employment increased only in case of Bihar and Punjab, which were at a fairly low rate during the earlier period.

## Table 10

*Persons in Labour Force (combined)*

*(Percentage)*

| *States* | *1983* | | | *1993-94* | | | *1999-2000* | | |
|---|---|---|---|---|---|---|---|---|---|
| | *M* | *F* | *P* | *M* | *F* | *P* | *M* | *F* | *P* |
| Andhra Pradesh | 89.7 | 58.1 | 74.1 | 87.8 | 60.3 | 74.2 | 85.1 | 54.2 | 69.9 |
| Bihar | 87.6 | 36.0 | 62.5 | 84.8 | 25.1 | 56.3 | 85.2 | 26.3 | 57.3 |
| Gujarat | 86.0 | 48.5 | 67.7 | 86.1 | 45.3 | 66.3 | 84.9 | 44.6 | 65.4 |
| Haryana | 84.1 | 32.0 | 60.0 | 80.9 | 39.0 | 61.5 | 77.4 | 27.4 | 54.2 |
| Himachal Pradesh | 86.7 | 67.3 | 77.1 | 87.1 | 69.2 | 78.2 | 81.7 | 63.4 | 72.5 |
| Jammu & Kashmir | 88.0 | 36.1 | 64.1 | 83.7 | 49.4 | 67.5 | 81.2 | 38.5 | 60.7 |
| Karnataka | 87.3 | 49.8 | 69.1 | 86.5 | 49.8 | 68.6 | 85.0 | 45.4 | 65.6 |
| Kerala | 82.7 | 47.0 | 64.3 | 82.2 | 35.0 | 57.9 | 80.8 | 35.3 | 57.4 |
| Madhya Pradesh | 88.6 | 58.1 | 73.9 | 87.1 | 53.4 | 70.9 | 84.6 | 50.7 | 68.3 |
| Maharashtra | 86.4 | 54.2 | 70.9 | 83.0 | 53.0 | 68.5 | 82.1 | 46.3 | 64.8 |
| Orissa | 89.0 | 39.6 | 64.6 | 85.4 | 42.9 | 64.5 | 84.1 | 40.6 | 62.6 |
| Punjab | 87.2 | 39.8 | 65.1 | 84.3 | 27.4 | 57.6 | 82.2 | 33.9 | 59.4 |
| Rajasthan | 87.3 | 59.1 | 73.9 | 85.5 | 57.2 | 71.9 | 82.6 | 50.2 | 67.2 |
| Tamil Nadu | 88.6 | 53.3 | 71.1 | 85.6 | 54.1 | 70.0 | 83.6 | 47.6 | 65.7 |
| Uttar Pradesh | 88.4 | 35.4 | 63.5 | 86.4 | 30.9 | 60.6 | 83.3 | 29.1 | 58.1 |
| West Bengal | 86.6 | 27.6 | 58.9 | 87.2 | 27.1 | 58.8 | 84.6 | 22.2 | 55.0 |
| India | 87.1 | 44.4 | 66.5 | 85.4 | 42.0 | 64.5 | 83.5 | 38.5 | 61.8 |

Source: NHDR (2001)

M – Male, F – Female, P – Persons.

## Table 11

*Growth Rate in Employment (combined)*

*(Percentage per anum)*

| *States* | *1983 to 1993-94* | | | *1993-94 to 1999-2000* | | |
|---|---|---|---|---|---|---|
| | *M* | *F* | *P* | *M* | *F* | *P* |
| Andhra Pradesh | 2.1 | 2.7 | 2.4 | 1.6 | 0.3 | 1.1 |
| Bihar | 1.8 | -1.7 | 0.9 | 2.3 | 3.0 | 2.5 |
| Gujarat | 2.4 | 1.6 | 2.1 | 2.1 | 2.2 | 2.1 |
| Haryana | 2.5 | 4.7 | 3.1 | 1.9 | -3.1 | 0.6 |
| Himachal Pradesh | 2.8 | 3.0 | 2.9 | 1.4 | 1.5 | 1.4 |
| Jammu & Kashmir | 1.7 | 5.9 | 2.9 | 2.2 | -1.2 | 1.1 |
| Karnataka | 2.2 | 2.4 | 2.3 | 2.0 | 0.8 | 1.6 |
| Kerala | 2.0 | -1.2 | 0.9 | 1.6 | 1.4 | 1.6 |
| Madhya Pradesh | 2.4 | 1.7 | 2.2 | 1.9 | 1.5 | 1.8 |
| Maharashtra | 2.1 | 2.3 | 2.2 | 1.8 | -0.2 | 1.0 |
| Orissa | 1.8 | 2.9 | 2.1 | 1.5 | 1.0 | 1.3 |
| Punjab | 1.8 | -1.4 | 1.0 | 1.5 | 6.1 | 2.6 |
| Rajasthan | 2.6 | 2.4 | 2.5 | 2.2 | 0.5 | 1.5 |
| Tamil Nadu | 1.6 | 2.0 | 1.8 | 1.4 | -0.3 | 0.8 |
| Uttar Pradesh | 2.3 | 1.1 | 2.0 | 1.8 | 1.4 | 1.7 |
| West Bengal | 2.4 | 2.1 | 2.4 | 1.6 | -0.8 | 1.1 |
| India | 2.2 | 1.7 | 2.1 | 1.9 | 0.9 | 1.6 |

Source: NHDR (2001)

M – Male, F – Female, P – Persons.

To make the analysis complete, the unemployment rate across the states during last two rounds is also provided in table 12. It is clearly seen from the table that the unemployment rate is on the rise in most of the states. However, the unemployment rate is not the ideal indicator, as it might lead to erroneous conclusions. For instance, the unemployment rate is highest in Kerala, which actually represents educated unemployment, and radically differs from the same prevailing in Bihar or Orissa.

## Table 12

*Comparison of Unemployment Scenario for 50th and 55th Round*

*(Per cent of labour force)*

| States | 1993-94 | | | 1999-2000 | | |
|---|---|---|---|---|---|---|
| | *Rural* | *Urban* | *Combined* | *Rural* | *Urban* | *Combined* |
| Andhra Pradesh | 0.5 | 3.2 | 1.1 | 0.7 | 4.0 | 1.4 |
| Bihar | 1.7 | 7.3 | 2.3 | 1.8 | 7.4 | 2.4 |
| Gujarat | 0.9 | 3.3 | 1.6 | 0.3 | 2.0 | 0.8 |
| Haryana | 1.2 | 2.7 | 1.6 | 0.8 | 2.7 | 1.2 |
| Karnataka | 0.7 | 3.7 | 1.4 | 0.7 | 3.4 | 1.4 |
| Kerala | 6.8 | 10.2 | 7.7 | 8.1 | 10.0 | 8.6 |
| Madhya Pradesh | 0.5 | 5.0 | 1.3 | 0.5 | 3.6 | 1.1 |
| Maharashtra | 0.8 | 4.3 | 1.9 | 1.4 | 5.7 | 2.9 |
| Orissa | 1.5 | 6.6 | 2.1 | 2.0 | 6.7 | 2.6 |
| Punjab | 1.3 | 3.4 | 1.9 | 1.8 | 2.8 | 2.1 |
| Rajasthan | 0.3 | 1.5 | 0.5 | 0.4 | 2.5 | 0.8 |
| Tamil Nadu | 1.3 | 4.9 | 2.4 | 2.0 | 3.8 | 2.6 |
| Uttar Pradesh | 0.7 | 2.9 | 1.1 | 0.8 | 4.1 | 1.4 |
| West Bengal | 1.8 | 7.9 | 3.5 | 2.7 | 7.6 | 4.0 |
| India | 1.2 | 4.6 | 2.0 | 1.5 | 4.8 | 2.3 |

Source: NHDR (2001)

Next an attempt is made for identifying the level of unemployment in the organized sector. Although there has been certain improvement in private sector employment generation, the benefit has been nullified by the dismal performance of public sector. It could clearly be seen from the following diagram that the overall growth rate of employment has remained negative throughout the 9th plan period.

**Diagram 2**

*Annual Total Employment Growth in Organized Sector*

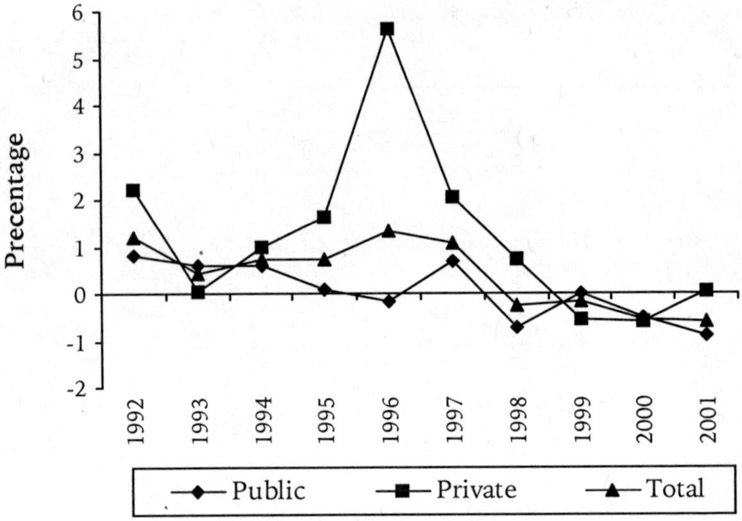


Source: Calculated from figures in *Economic Survey*

A brief overview of the scenario is shown with help of table 13. The average level of overall annual employment in the 9$^{th}$ plan is higher than in the 8$^{th}$ plan, thanks to employment growth in private sector during the initial years. However, the table suggests that growth rate of private sector employment is also drying up, and in the last couple of years, also witnessed negative growth.

**Table 13**

*Sector-wise Comparison of Employment Trends*

*(lakh)*

| | *Public Sector* | | *Private Sector* | | *Total* | |
|---|---|---|---|---|---|---|
| | *Average level* | *Growth rate* | *Average level* | *Growth rate* | *Average level* | *Growth rate* |
| 8$^{th}$ plan period | 193.75 | 0.38 | 80.39 | 2.10 | 274.24 | 0.88 |
| 9$^{th}$ plan period | 193.68 | -0.29 | 86.86 | 0.33 | 280.54 | -0.10 |

Source: Calculated from the figures in *Economic Survey*

During the 9th plan period the Prime Minister had promised that special programmes would be undertaken to generate new jobs for the poorer and deprived sections. Unfortunately, the promise is yet to be fulfilled.

## SECTION III

## SECTORAL TREND

The sectoral share of GDP in the three major categories is shown in the following table. It is seen from table 14 that the importance of agriculture in GDP is falling over the years, which has been compensated by the service sector. The proportional shares of agriculture, industry and services were 24.7, 26.4 and 48.8 per cent respectively in 2001. This is in direct contrast with the scenario in 1980 when agriculture was the principal contributor to GDP. The reversing trend was first noticed in 1990, when it was replaced by service sector at the top spot. While the growing importance of services in the economy could be interpreted as a sign of development, concerns about growth of the other two sectors still remain. Besides, the decline in share of GDP has not witnessed a commensurate fall in share of population dependent on agriculture.[15] In addition, services sector in spite of massive contribution in GDP, lacks high employment generating potential. Therefore, for proper upliftment of the population, the focus must be on agriculture and industry.

**Table 14**

*Contribution of the Sectors in GDP*

*(Percentage)*

| *Sector* | *1980* | *1990* | *2001* |
|---|---|---|---|
| Agriculture and Allied Sectors | 38.1 | 31.0 | 24.7 |
| Industry | 25.9 | 29.3 | 26.4 |
| Services | 36.0 | 39.7 | 48.8 |
| Total | 100.0 | 100.0 | 100.0 |

Source: *Economic Survey* (2002-03)

A sectoral analysis follows.

## Agriculture and Allied Sectors

From table 2, it has already been noted that agricultural GDP growth rate has, throughout the nineties, lagged behind the overall growth rate. Only during the first and the last year of the 8th plan and the last year of the 9th plan, this sector witnessed a growth rate higher than the national average. The plight of agriculture becomes obvious from diagram 3.

**Diagram 3**

*Comparison Between Agricultural and Overall Growth Rate*

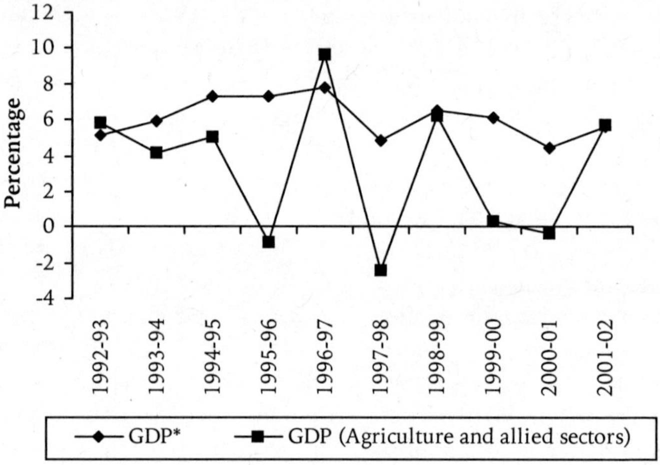


Source: *Economic Survey* (2002-03)
* - At 1993-94 prices

The major problem for Indian agriculture is that the sector is still dependent on monsoons for a good harvest. The growth of irrigation potential and the problems are discussed in the subsequent sections. The lack of irrigation facility in many places coupled with absence of a long-term focus on land fertility, has probably resulted a slackening trend in the level of productivity growth rate throughout the country. Even the green revolution states like Punjab and Haryana could not escape this trend.[16] The productivity levels for a number of principal crops are shown in table 15. While the absolute level of productivity still seems to rise, the growth rate is lagging far behind the same during 8th plan.

**Table 15**

*Productivity Trend for Principal Crops*

*(Kg/Hectare)*

| *Commodity* | *Productivity during 8th plan* | | *Productivity during 9th plan (4 years)* | |
|---|---|---|---|---|
| | *Average* | *Growth rate (%)* | *Average* | *Growth rate (%)* |
| Foodgrain | 1521.8 | 3.22 | 1629.75 | 0.43 |
| Rice | 1843.8 | 1.53 | 1932.00 | 0.49 |
| Wheat | 2490.0 | 2.36 | 2649.00 | 0.74 |
| Gram | 767.0 | 2.86 | 791.75 | -2.76 |

Source: Calculated from figures in CMIE (2002)

Give this scenario; a major boost for the sector was required through increased public spending. Unfortunately, the 9th plan period also witnessed a reduction in public expenditure on agriculture, the absolute value of which even dropped below the same during 8th plan. The details of agricultural investment and capital formation are shown with the help of table 16. In addition, the investment in agriculture as share in GDP also plunged by 0.3 per cent in the 9th plan period, as compared to earlier regime.

**Table 16**

*Gross Capital Formation in Agriculture (1993-94 prices)*

*(Rs. Crore)*

| *Year* | *Total* | *Public* | *Private* | *Per cent share* | | *Investment in agriculture as % of GDP* |
|---|---|---|---|---|---|---|
| | | | | *Public* | *Private* | |
| 1993-94 | 13523 | 4467 | 9056 | 33.0 | 67.0 | 1.6 |
| 1994-95 | 14969 | 4947 | 10022 | 33.0 | 67.0 | 1.6 |
| 1995-96 | 15690 | 4849 | 10841 | 30.9 | 69.1 | 1.6 |
| 1996-97 | 16176 | 4668 | 11508 | 28.9 | 71.1 | 1.5 |
| 1997-98 | 15942 | 3979 | 11963 | 25.0 | 75.0 | 1.4 |
| 1998-99 | 14895 | 3870 | 11025 | 26.0 | 74.0 | 1.3 |
| 1999-00 | 17304 | 4222 | 13082 | 24.4 | 75.6 | 1.4 |
| 2000-01 | 16687 | 3919 | 12768 | 23.5 | 76.5 | 1.3 |
| 2001-02* | 18057 | 4794 | 13263 | 26.5 | 73.5 | 1.3 |

Source: *Economic Survey* (2002-03)

* Quick Estimate

While private investment in agriculture in money terms is on the rise over this period, the increase is not substantial if viewed in real terms. Besides, the growth of private investment might not continue indefinitely due to the long-awaited reform in agricultural marketing and other restrictive regulations.

## Industry

### *Heavy Industry*

The heavy industrial sector showed a sign of stagnancy in recent years. For instance, the six infrastructure industries - electricity, steel, crude petroleum, petroleum refinery products and cement, are still showing trends of stagnation. The sector-wise annual growth rate of three major sectors and the overall growth rate is presented in table 17.

**Table 17**

*Annual Growth Rates of Industrial Production in Major Sectors*

*(Percentage)*

| *Year* | *Mining and Quarrying* | *Manufacturing* | *Electricity* | *Overall* |
|---|---|---|---|---|
| 1992-93 | 0.5 | 2.2 | 5.0 | 2.3 |
| 1993-94 | 3.5 | 6.1 | 7.4 | 6.0 |
| 1994-95 | 9.8 | 9.1 | 8.5 | 9.1 |
| 1995-96 | 9.7 | 14.1 | 8.1 | 13.0 |
| 1996-97 | -1.9 | 7.3 | 4.0 | 6.1 |
| 1997-98 | 6.9 | 6.7 | 6.6 | 6.7 |
| 1998-99 | -0.8 | 4.4 | 6.5 | 4.1 |
| 1999-00 | 1.0 | 7.1 | 7.3 | 6.7 |
| 2000-01 | 2.8 | 5.3 | 4.0 | 5.0 |
| 2001-02 | 1.2 | 2.9 | 3.1 | 2.7 |

Source: *Economic Survey*

The findings of table 17 are summarized in table 18. It could be seen that the average growth rate of all the sectors during the 9$^{th}$ plan lagged far behind the same prevailing during the 8$^{th}$ plan.

## Table 18

*Average Industrial Growth Rate during 8$^{th}$ and 9$^{th}$ Plan*

*(Percentage)*

| *Sectors* | *8$^{th}$ plan* | *9$^{th}$ plan* |
|---|---|---|
| Mining | 4.32 | 2.22 |
| Manufacturing | 7.76 | 5.28 |
| Electricity | 6.60 | 5.50 |
| Overall | 7.30 | 5.04 |

Source: Calculated on the basis of time series trend

In table 19, the growth rates of the industries by their use-based classification are provided. It is obvious from the table that growth rate during the 9$^{th}$ plan has been much lower across the sectors, barring the sole exception of capital goods industries. The index of industrial production also fluctuated over the 9$^{th}$ plan period, and declined during the last two years. The notion is reconfirmed from the summary statistics provided in table 20.[17]

## Table 19

*Growth Rates of Industrial Production by Use-based Classification*

*(Percentage)*

| *Year* | *Basic goods* | *Capital goods* | *Intermediate goods* | *Consumer goods* | *Index of Industrial Production* |
|---|---|---|---|---|---|
| 1995-96 | 10.8 | 5.3 | 19.4 | 12.8 | 13.0 |
| 1996-97 | 3.0 | 11.5 | 8.1 | 6.2 | 6.1 |
| 1997-98 | 6.9 | 5.8 | 8.0 | 5.5 | 6.7 |
| 1998-99 | 1.6 | 12.6 | 6.1 | 2.2 | 4.1 |
| 1999-00 | 5.5 | 6.9 | 8.8 | 5.7 | 6.7 |
| 2000-01 | 3.7 | 1.8 | 4.7 | 8.0 | 5.0 |
| 2001-02 | 2.6 | -3.4 | 1.5 | 6.0 | 2.7 |

Source: *Economic Survey* (2002-03)

## Table 20

*Average Industrial Growth Rate during $8^{th}$ and $9^{th}$ Plan*

*(Percentage)*

| *Sectors* | *$8^{th}$ plan (last two years)* | *$9^{th}$ plan (overall)* | *$9^{th}$ plan (last two years)* |
|---|---|---|---|
| Basic goods | 6.90 | 4.06 | 3.15 |
| Capital goods | 8.40 | 4.74 | -0.80 |
| Intermediate goods | 13.75 | 5.82 | 3.10 |
| Consumer goods | 9.50 | 5.48 | 7.00 |

Source: Calculated on the basis of time series trend

### Small Industry

The small industrial sector also suffered from the stagnating trend, just like heavy industries. As seen from table 21, the extent of stagnation in late nineties is obvious in terms of entry of new units, production, as well as export. This deceleration is acting as a retarding force on the employment generating capacity of this sector.

## Table 21

*Growth Trends in the Small-scale Sector*

*(Percentage)*

| *Year* | *Number of units* | *Production* | *Employment* | *Exports* |
|---|---|---|---|---|
| 1992-93 | 7.90 | 17.10 | 3.30 | 28.10 |
| 1993-94 | 6.20 | 15.50 | 4.00 | 42.30 |
| 1994-95 | 7.66 | 23.69 | 5.15 | 14.86 |
| 1995-96 | 3.88 | 21.34 | 4.13 | 25.46 |
| 1996-97 | 5.46 | 13.57 | 4.84 | 7.61 |
| 1997-98 | 5.03 | 12.33 | 4.50 | 13.23 |
| 1998-99 | 4.62 | 12.54 | 2.62 | 10.21 |
| 1999-00 | 4.29 | 10.03 | 4.03 | 10.66 |
| 2000-01 | 3.11 | 11.54 | 4.00 | 28.78 |
| 2001-02 | 3.91 | 8.03 | 3.55 | — |

Source: *Economic Survey*

To sum up, the lagging trend in the small-scale sector during the 9th plan period is illustrated with the help of table 22. The poor performance of the small-scale sector in the 9th plan becomes obvious from the table.

**Table 22**

*Analysis of the Small-sector over the 8th and 9th Plan*

*(Percentage)*

| *Year* | *Number of unit* | *Production* | *Employment* | *Exports* |
|---|---|---|---|---|
| 8th plan period | 6.22 | 18.24 | 4.28 | 23.66 |
| 9th plan period* | 4.19 | 10.89 | 3.74 | 15.72 |

Calculated on the basis of time series trend

* - upto 2000-01

## SECTION IV

## FISCAL ISSUES

### Budget Transactions

The major concern in the budget transaction is that, the proportion of non-developmental expenditure has increased monumentally over the last couple of years. The annual average of non-developmental expenditures has doubled over this span of time. It is also observed from table 23 that DE expressed as a percentage of NDE was much higher during the 8th plan, as compared to the 9th plan.

**Table 23**

*The Expenditure Pattern*

*(Rs. Crore)*

| *Account* | *8th Plan* | *9th Plan* |
|---|---|---|
| Non-Development Expenditure (annual average) | 91346.03 | 184166.36 |
| Developmental Expenditure (annual average) | 45944.76 | 83260.99 |
| Proportion of Development to Non-development expenditure ( per cent) | 50.95 | 45.29 |

Source: *Economic Survey*

In particular, the proportional pattern of NDEs in certain accounts deserves attention, as shown in table 24. It is seen that interest payment and administrative costs are on the rise steadily over the period. The expenditure on pension and other retirement benefits has also increased substantially. While subsidy to FCI is increasing in recent years, most of it is actually spent in maintaining the current stock and not for distributing foodgrains to the needy section of the population. However, important measures like social security and welfare, the benefits pertaining to the community, have actually been reduced.

**Table 24**

*Average Non-development Expenditures*

*(Percentage of total NDEs)*

| *Sector* | *8th plan* | *9th plan* |
|---|---|---|
| Interest payments | 48.06 | 48.53 |
| Administrative service | 5.93 | 6.48 |
| Pension & other retirement benefits | 4.23 | 6.48 |
| Subsidy to FCI | 5.42 | 5.56 |
| Social security & welfare | 0.36 | 0.33 |

Source: Calculated from data in *Economic Survey*

The compositional pattern for development expenditures is also worth mentioning. As seen from table 25, the plan outlay on two primary social sectors, education and health, has increased to some extent during the 9th plan as compared to the 8th plan. However, the practical experience suggests that a significant portion of these expenditures do not always reach the targeted population. On every other sphere, the developmental expenditure on important heads has been reduced. The low rate of employment growth is understandable from the reduction in labour and employment programmes. The stagnation in export growth rate is also obvious from the slackening in promotional campaigns. Worse, the prime objectives like enhancing the irrigation potential, rural developmental works, and welfare of backward classes failed to secure increased attention during the 9th plan.

## Table 25

*Average Annual Development Expenditure*

*(Per cent of total Development expenditure)*

| *Sectors* | $8^{th}$ *plan* | $9^{th}$ *plan* |
|---|---|---|
| Education, art and culture | 7.06 | 9.30 |
| Medical, public health, sanitation & water supply | 2.71 | 3.32 |
| Labour & employment | 1.06 | 0.99 |
| Public works | 1.04 | 0.80 |
| Foreign trade & export promotion | 1.55 | 0.91 |
| Irrigation (including major, medium and minor sources) | 0.28 | 0.27 |
| Rural development | 7.47 | 6.55 |
| Rural water supply schemes | 1.23 | 1.20 |
| Welfare of backward classes | 0.79 | 0.65 |
| Special Central assistance for SCs | 0.58 | 0.47 |

Source: Calculated from data in *Economic Survey*

In the following diagram, revenue deficit and fiscal deficit expressed as a percentage of GDP is shown. The revenue deficit, although increased in 1993-94, came down to 2.4 per cent in 1996-97, the terminal year of the $8^{th}$ plan. However, it remained above 3 per cent throughout the $9^{th}$ plan period. Similarly, fiscal deficit as a percentage of GDP was above 5 per cent in early nineties, and reached a peak in 1993-94. However, thanks to the strict management policies implemented, the deficit declined in the following period. It has remained at a high level in the last years of the $9^{th}$ plan, which probably has not attracted the requisite attention due to low inflation. The World Bank Study on *India Development Policy Review* has warned the government on managing the fiscal issues.

The levels of liabilities were also quite high in 1990-91, and increased during the early years of the $8^{th}$ plan up to 1993-94. However, the following period witnessed a decline up to 1998-99, but increased thereafter. Thankfully, this period has witnessed a decline in the level of outstanding external debt (the difference between internal and total outstanding liabilities), without which the situation would have been really troublesome. The steady rise in liabilities during the last phase of the $9^{th}$ plan, with no crisis comparable with that in 1991 around, gives a poor impression about fiscal management.

**Diagram 4**

*Expenditure as per cent of GDP*

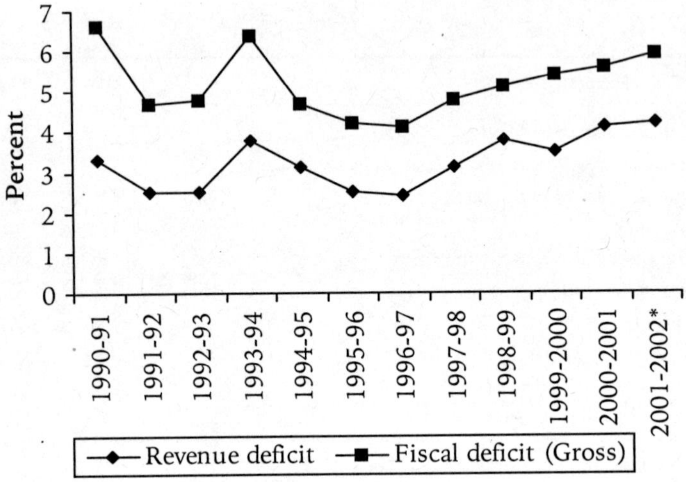


Source: *Economic Survey* (2002-03)

* - Provisional

**Diagram 5**

*Outstanding Liability as percentage of GDP*

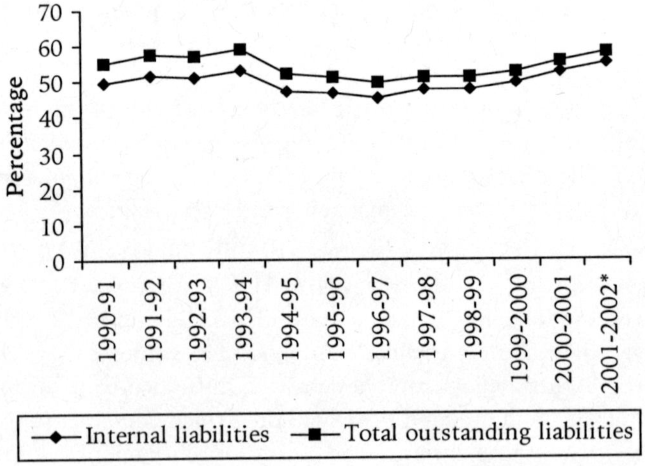


Source: *Economic Survey* (various issues)

* - RE

## Fiscal Overshooting and Expenditure Reform

While existence of huge deficit is a major problem, other problems also deserve similar concern. One particular problem is fiscal overshooting, i.e., the widening gap between the budget estimate and revised estimate. The problem has increased in recent years. In addition, the excessive non-planned expenditure of the government is also on the rise. The government appointed the Expenditure Reforms Commission in 2000 to take stock of expenditure in all ministries in a comprehensive manner. The commission so far has submitted reports on modification of expenditure on various issues, including fertilizer subsidy, optimization of staff strength, rationalization of structures of Ministry of Coal and Information and Broadcasting. In addition, the Commission has also recommended major policies for reduction in food subsidy. The Commission has stressed on avoiding unnecessary cost to government by overlapping of ministries. Although a number of recommendations have been implemented, others are still under consideration.

## Disinvestment Programme

One of the major criticisms against the fiscal adjustments undertaken during the 9$^{th}$ plan circled around the way in which the disinvestment programmes were undertaken. The decision for strategic disinvestment in loss-making PSUs was first considered during the 8$^{th}$ plan, and procedures were initiated in line with the recommendations of various government committees. In 1997 the Disinvestment Commission recommended 'Strategic Sale' in respect of 7 loss-making PSUs, namely - ITI, HTL, KIOCL, BALCO, ITDC, MFIL and BRPL. While disinvestment procedures have already been initiated, criticisms flowed from various quarters, on the way in which the programme is carried on.

The first and foremost criticism is about under-valuation of the companies to be sold. The disinvestment action was in the dust for nine months in case of BALCO, and the state government also raised voices on this issue. For BALCO, the government action has been criticized in the CAG report. Pointing to gross under-valuation, the CAG report states that the Government put up a reserve price of Rs. 514.4 crore for 51 per cent stake, whereas according to CAG, the reserve price should have been Rs. 558.64 crore.[18]

The second criticism, centers on the far-reaching consequences of under-valuation. The purchaser company, Sterlite, with an investment of just Rs. 550 crore, got control over a huge asset. The government stands to lose not only from the immediate loss from under-valuation of the controlling stake, but from future sales as well. Since Sterlite is controlling 51 per cent of the shares, no other company would be interested to purchase the large chunks of the stock remaining with the government at even the price being offered to Sterlite.

Thirdly, it has been alleged the valuation procedure that yielded this undeclared and abnormally low reserve price has neither been transparent, nor undertaken by qualified entities capable of valuing the plant and machinery of the company. The government decision to keep the reserve price a secret and declaring that the Sterlite bid was in line with the reserve price, seems unjustifiable. The government should have declared the minimum bid selected for consideration, based on its independently conducted valuation. This, coupled with the haste in which the entire exercise was undertaken, arouses suspicion.[19]

Similar disputes were generated during the disinvestment exercise for other PSUs as well. For instance, the ITDC Hotels, were also according to experts, been sold at throw-away prices and thereafter the purchaser has got back substantial portions of the paid amount, as post-closing adjustment. Adjustments on various grounds are often alleged to be non-developmental and utterly unprofitable. For instance, in case of Paradeep Phosphates, the tentative margin between the government refund to the purchaser and the realization from sale is pretty low. In case of VSNL, a huge surplus was left with the company to help its expansion or to provide benefits to the consumers. However, the purchasing company used this proceeds for other purposes. Therefore, while the urgency of the disinvestment programme in loss-making PSUs could not be undermined, the way this entire exercise had been undertaken so far during the 9$^{th}$ plan is hardly satisfactory.

## SECTION V

## SOCIAL SECTOR

The role of social capital is of prime importance in economic development. In the current context, the scenario in health and education are analyzed. In this section, the plan-wise comparison technique for key variables has not been strictly followed.

### Health

On the whole, the sector has fared quite well over the last decade, as negative factors like infant mortality rate, maternal mortality rate are down, and positive ones, e.g., number of hospitals, births attended by skilled personnel, life expectancy at birth etc. have improved. However, a couple of concern areas still remain. Although the overall performance of the country in the health front looks satisfactory, the success of a few states is still much lower as compared to the national average. For instance, in table 26 state-wise infant mortality rates are compared. The better and poorer performers are placed in the top and bottom panel respectively. It is clearly seen that the extent of reduction in IMR is much higher for a relatively developed state like Kerala, while the traditional poor performers like Orissa, Uttar Pradesh are far behind the national average.

**Table 26**

*State-wise Infant Mortality Rate*

*(Per thousand)*

| *State* | *1981* | *1991* | *2001* |
|---|---|---|---|
| ***States above national average*** | | | |
| Kerala | 54 | 42 | 16 |
| Lakshadweep | 132 | 91 | 30 |
| Maharashtra | 119 | 74 | 49 |
| Delhi | 100 | 54 | 51 |
| ***States below national average*** | | | |
| Bihar | 94 | 75 | 67 |
| Rajasthan | 141 | 87 | 83 |
| Uttar Pradesh | 130 | 99 | 85 |
| Madhya Pradesh | 150 | 133 | 97 |
| Orissa | 163 | 125 | 98 |
| **All India** | **115** | **77** | **71** |

Source: NHDR and *Economic Survey*

A similar experience is noticed in case of other indicators of health development. There exist wide inter-state disparities in maternal mortality rate, sex ratio, availability of health infrastructure in the rural belt and level of vaccination operations. Table 27 shows the extent of this disparity summarised from National Family Health Survey 1992-93 and 1998-99 for TT vaccination and births attended by professionals.

**Table 27**

*State-wise Disparity in Health Infrastructure*

*(Percentage)*

| *States* | *Births delivered in medical institutions* | | *Two doses or more of TT vaccination during pregnancy* | |
|---|---|---|---|---|
| | *NFHS 1992-93* | *NFHS 1998-99* | *NFHS 1992-93* | *NFHS 1998-99* |
| ***States above national average*** | | | | |
| Delhi | 44.3 | 59.5 | 72.5 | 84.8 |
| Goa | 86.8 | 90.5 | 83.4 | 86.1 |
| Kerala | 87.8 | 93.0 | 89.8 | 86.4 |
| Tamil Nadu | 63.5 | 79.8 | 90.1 | 95.4 |
| ***States below national average*** | | | | |
| Bihar | 12.1 | 14.7 | 30.7 | 57.8 |
| Madhya Pradesh | 15.9 | 20.4 | 42.8 | 55.0 |
| Orissa | 14.1 | 22.9 | 53.8 | 74.3 |
| Rajasthan | 11.6 | 21.7 | 28.3 | 52.1 |
| Uttar Pradesh | 11.2 | 15.7 | 37.4 | 51.4 |
| **All India** | **25.5** | **33.6** | **53.8** | **66.8** |

Source: NHDR (2001)

In order to improve the health scenario in general and to combat growing incidence of terminal diseases like AIDS, increased government expenditure has a crucial role. However, the government expenditure in the later half of nineties is showing a declining trend. According to the UNDP *Human Development Report*, the public expenditure on health has declined considerably over this period, and stood at 0.9 per cent of GDP in 2000.

## Education

On the educational front, two prime indicators of success have remained quite satisfactory, level of literacy has increased and drop-out rates have gone down. The women enrollment has also registered an increase during the last decade. However, the sector also suffers from the similar problem of divergence as well as continuance of backwardness, as noticed under health. For instance, from table 28, the performance of the relatively backward states could be noticed, where a formidable proportion of the population is still suffering from the darkness of illiteracy.

### Table 28

*State-wise Literacy Rate*

*(Per thousand)*

| *State* | *1971* | *1981* | *1991* | *2001* |
|---|---|---|---|---|
| ***States above national average*** | | | | |
| Kerala | 60.40 | 70.40 | 89.80 | 90.92 |
| Lakshadweep | 43.70 | 55.10 | 81.80 | 87.52 |
| Delhi | 56.50 | 61.50 | 75.30 | 81.82 |
| Maharashtra | 39.20 | 47.20 | 64.90 | 77.27 |
| ***States below national average*** | | | | |
| Orissa | 26.20 | 34.20 | 49.10 | 63.31 |
| Andhra Pradesh | 24.60 | 29.90 | 44.10 | 61.11 |
| Rajasthan | 19.10 | 24.40 | 38.60 | 61.03 |
| Uttar Pradesh | 21.70 | 27.20 | 41.60 | 57.36 |
| Bihar | 19.90 | 26.20 | 38.50 | 47.53 |
| All India | 34.45 | 43.57 | 52.20 | 65.38 |

Source: *Economic Survey* (2002-03)

Several other concern areas also deserve attention. For instance, the teacher-pupil ratio (expressed as pupils per teacher) in India as compared to the international standard, and the dropout rate is still high, the later being nearly 70 per cent. The introduction of cooked mid-day meal scheme as per the Supreme Court verdict is the need of the hour. A quick analysis of the gross enrollment ratio in India is provided in table 29. It could be seen that while gross enrollment ratio for primary education has increased during the 9th plan, it has gone down in case of upper primary. Hence although literacy rate as per the official definition has increased considerably, there is ample scope for questioning the increase in actual intensity of education.

**Table 29**

*Analysis of Gross Enrollment Ratio in India*

*(Per cent)*

| | *8th Plan* | *9th Plan** |
|---|---|---|
| Primary (I-V) | 86.68 | 93.10 |
| Upper primary (VI-VIII) | 60.68 | 58.37 |
| Elementary (I-VIII) | 77.42 | 80.22 |

Based on the time trend
* - first 4 years

In addition, the gender aspect of education is also showing an unhealthy trend. The female literacy rate is much lower than male literacy rate – the former being 54.16 while the later is 75.85, as per the 2001 census. Apart from this, the educational level of the backward segment, SCs and particularly, STs are much lower than the national average. Targeted programmes for these sections should immediately be initiated.

Another worrying issue needs to be mentioned. The number of schools per thousand population is quite low in India, and although on the rise in aggregate for upper primary, is actually falling for primary in a number of poor performer states. In other words, the expansion of educational infrastructure could not keep pace with the population growth rate. This coupled with the continued backwardness in poor performer states could result in further divergence. The scenario is explained with the help of table 30.

**Table 30**

*Number of Schools Per Thousand Population*

| *States* | *1982-83* | | *1992-93* | | *1997-98* | |
|---|---|---|---|---|---|---|
| | *P* | *UP* | *P* | *UP* | *P* | *UP* |
| Andhra Pradesh | 6.63 | 1.31 | 6.99 | 1.55 | 5.34 | 1.56 |
| Bihar | 5.68 | 2.30 | 4.88 | 2.24 | 3.97 | 1.92 |
| Karnataka | 5.08 | 4.83 | 4.44 | 5.40 | 3.82 | 6.61 |
| Kerala | 2.14 | 1.47 | 2.19 | 1.62 | 2.20 | 1.54 |
| Madhya Pradesh | 8.06 | 2.55 | 8.74 | 3.40 | 8.18 | 3.76 |
| Maharashtra | 5.17 | 3.45 | 5.22 | 3.98 | 3.97 | 3.68 |
| Tamil Nadu | 5.36 | 1.67 | 5.18 | 1.65 | 4.91 | 1.43 |
| West Bengal | 5.88 | 0.76 | 6.74 | 0.97 | 5.28 | 0.54 |
| All India | 5.70 | 2.44 | 5.75 | 2.69 | 5.04 | 2.75 |

Source: NHDR (2001)
P- Primary, UP – Upper Primary

## SECTION VI

## LAW AND ORDER

The maintenance of law and order has a special role to play in ensuring economic sustainability in long run. In addition, the persistence of good governance boosts the confidence of the international community in the domestic economy, which is reflected through the investment flow, both by governments as well as multinationals and private bodies. In addition, increase in social tension and inadequate governance results in a leakage of state resources and if measured in terms of expenditures, namely - man-day loss, deployment of police and special forces, property loss, cost of investigation and prosecution etc., it poses a huge burden on the exchequer (i.e., planned resources). Owing to this reason, the current section has been included in the analysis, although it does not come under the plan purview. The governance scenario in the last couple of years has not been appreciable and gathered criticism from various quarters. In many respect the situation has worsened as compared to the 8th plan. The specific areas of concerns are discussed in the following.

## Crime in General

The time series data on total number of cognizable crimes under IPC (Indian Penal Code) is provided in the following graph. It could clearly be seen from diagram 6 that the incidence of crime has increased sharply in the last couple of years.

**Diagram 6**

*Cognizable Crimes during the Last Decade*

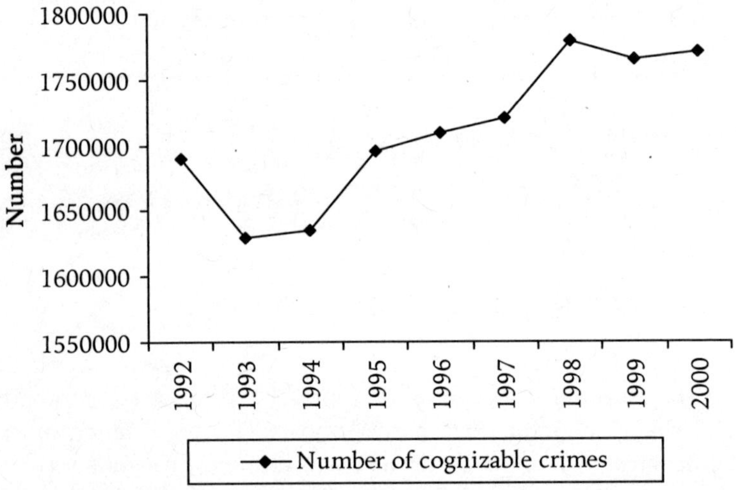


Source: *Crime in India* (various issues)

A close analysis of the series shows more interesting results, as summarized in table 31. The average level of total cognizable crimes during the 8th plan is considerably lower than the same under the 9th plan period (first 3 years). A similar result follows if the analysis is repeated with a comparable period. The growth rate of crimes is also quite higher during the 9th plan period.

**Table 31**

*Comparison of Crime Rate during 8th and 9th Plan*

| *Period* | *Total cognizable crimes under IPC* | |
|---|---|---|
| | *Average level (no.)* | *Growth rate (%)* |
| 8th plan period (full) | 1678056 | 0.38 |
| 8th plan period (first 3 years) | 1653628 | 0.16 |
| 9th plan period (first 3 years) | 1771509 | 0.99 |

Source: *Crime in India* (various issues)

## Crime against Women and Children

Crimes against the weaker sections, women and children, is also on the rise. The total registered crimes against women took a sharp upturn in the initial years of the 8th plan. However, the trend was curbed in the later years. The 9th plan witnessed a sharp increase in recorded crimes against women, and crossed the previous mark. In addition, the incidence of rape, has also increased rapidly over this period. It seems the 9th plan period was becoming increasingly unsafe for the womenfolk.

**Table 32**

*Plan-wise Comparison of Crime Against Women*

*(Number of cases)*

| | *Total crime against women (Average level)* | *Rape (Average level)* |
|---|---|---|
| 8th plan period | 105830 | 13871.2 |
| 8th plan period (first 3 years) | 97387 | 13060 |
| 9th plan period (first 3 years) | 136494 | 15705 |

Source: *Crime in India* (various issues)

A similar trend has been noticed in case of crimes against children, which is also on the rise, as evident from table 33 provided below. Strict and targeted action is the need of the hour and no further delays in this regard should be tolerated.

**Table 33**

*Plan-wise Comparison of Crime Against Children*

*(Number of cases)*

| *Duration* | *Total crimes against children (Average level)* |
|---|---|
| $8^{th}$ plan period (first 3 years) | 5146 |
| $9^{th}$ plan period (first 3 years) | 5256 |

Source: *Crime in India* (various issues)

## Crime against Oppressed Sections (SC/STs)

The crimes against the traditionally oppressed communities could be further subdivided on the basis of direction - SCs and STs. The average level of crimes against SCs witnessed an increase over 20 per cent, if the first two years of the $8^{th}$ and $9^{th}$ plans are compared. Similarly, the level of crimes against STs is also on the rise. It could be seen from the following table that crimes against STs during the first two years of the consecutive plans have increased by 12 per cent. The number of arrests under SC/ST (Prevention of Atrocities) Act in 2000 increased nearly by 9 per cent as compared to the earlier year, from 24568 in 1999 to 26773 in 2000.

**Table 34**

*Plan-wise Comparison of Crime Against Oppressed Sections*

*(Number of cases)*

| *(Average level)* | *Total crimes against SCs* | *Total crimes against STs (Average level)* |
|---|---|---|
| $8^{th}$ plan period (first 2 years) | 22232 | 3979 |
| $9^{th}$ plan period (first 2 years) | 26791 | 4460 |

Source: *Crime in India* (various issues)

## Corruption

The level of corruption could be considered as a bottleneck in the smooth functioning of the state machinery. Unfortunately, it is approaching an all time peak in the recent period. While on one hand, this increasing corruption is taking the share of public money allocated to the common people away, it is spreading gross inefficiency on the other. Analysing the total number of anti-corruption cases initiated during a particular year, it is seen that the 8$^{th}$ plan period has fared much better in this regard. In other words, the mishandling of public money is on the rise during the 9$^{th}$ plan.

**Table 35**

*Plan-wise Comparison of Anti-corruption Proceedings*

*(Number of cases)*

| *Period* | *Number of cases initiated during a year (Average level)* |
|---|---|
| 8$^{th}$ plan period (first 3 years) | 2022.00 |
| 9$^{th}$ plan period (first 3 years) | 2818.66 |

Source: *Crime in India* (various issues)

## SECTION VII

## INFRASTRUCTURE

The compliance of infrastructure level in a country with international standard is a principal prerequisite for development. Although governments have laid stress on these issues, the sector has a long way to go. The supply chain in India is one of the longest in the world and the trade potential of various sensitive products suffers heavily on this account. An analysis of the features of main infrastructure sectors during the last two plan periods is attempted in the following.

### Railways

The Indian railway was traditionally a major source of goods transport. However, the road sector is fast emerging as a strong competitor due to various procedural bottlenecks in railways and other related problems. The Indian Railways Report (2001), which outlined the reform agenda for this sector, raised concerns over this issue. Railways have a unique position as a major source of public as well as commercial transport in the Indian economy. Apart from that, raising connectivity of distant pockets with rest of the economy is equally important.[20] Unfortunately that role has not been fulfilled over the 9th plan period. The track enhancement programme, which grew at an annual average of 0.095 per cent over the 8th plan, was slackened and increased only by 0.080 per cent during 9th plan.

A more important concern centers on the issue of railway safety. All the Railway Safety Review Committees appointed so far have criticized the ongoing safety arrangements. The number of collisions, derailments and other accidents has been quite high in the last couple of years. For instance, the annual average of railway accidents during the 90s (1991-2000) stood at 464, as compared to 473 in 2001-02, the last year of the 9th plan. It could be seen from table 36 that although the number of derailments has declined in the 9th plan period as compared to the 8th plan, the number of deaths in derailment has actually gone up. In other words, the ferocity of the accidents has increased during the 9th plan. If all deaths taken together are considered, the performance of railways has marginally improved during the 9th plan period.

**Table 36**

*Average Level of Collisions and Fatalities in the Two Plan Periods*

*(Average annual incidence)*

| *Plan period* | *Derailment* | *Death in derailment* | *All deaths* |
|---|---|---|---|
| 8th Plan | 357 | 49.2 | 384.6 |
| 9th Plan | 309.6 | 54.4 | 384.0 |

Source: White Paper (2003)

## Road

The surface transport sector, although retaining importance in the recent period, lags far behind the desired level. The proportion of National highways as a proportion of total roads increased from 1.5 per cent during the 8th plan to 1.9 per cent in the 9th plan. Recently, during the 9th plan, the government has started implementing the first phase of the National Highway Development Project – which involves creation of the 'Golden Quadrilateral' by December 2003. The second phase would involve creation of the North-South and East-West corridors by 2007. While the project is ambitious, and very much likely to improve the scenario once in force, the immediate absence of feeder roads at important junctions is likely to compound the bottlenecks. The sorry condition of the state highways is another problem. The government promised to improve rural connectivity through 'Gram Sadak Yojona' in the last couple of years, which has also not been fulfilled.

## Irrigation

Given the dependence of the rural folk on agriculture as a means of livelihood, increasing the irrigation potential should be one of the prime objectives. Currently, out of 142.6 million hectares of net cultivated area, merely 57 million hectares (nearly 40 per cent) are irrigated. However, as already illustrated with the help of table 25, the expenditure on enhancing the irrigation potential is actually on the decline. So the situation might turn out to be severe for drought prone states like Orissa and Rajasthan. The states with low irrigation coverage are shown in the bottom panel of table 37. No particular special programme was initiated during the 9$^{th}$ plan to address these issues.[21]

### Table 37

*Gross Irrigated Area as % of Total Area (All crops – State-wise)*

*(Percentage of gross cropped area)*

| *States* | *Year* | | | | |
|---|---|---|---|---|---|
| | *1990-91* | *1992-93* | *1994-95* | *1996-97* | *1998-99* |
| ***States above national average*** | | | | | |
| Andhra Pradesh | 40.70 | 39.87 | 40.56 | 43.12 | 44.71 |
| Bihar | 39.98 | 54.50 | 44.61 | 45.99 | 47.27 |
| Haryana | 71.58 | 89.75 | 77.01 | 78.78 | 79.78 |
| Punjab | 94.05 | 94.58 | 95.14 | 94.07 | 92.24 |
| Tamil Nadu | 43.64 | 47.89 | 51.07 | 51.84 | 54.85 |
| Uttar Pradesh | 57.97 | 65.56 | 68.89 | 66.81 | 66.43 |
| ***States below national average*** | | | | | |
| Gujarat | 27.51 | 29.33 | 32.50 | 33.11 | 35.31 |
| Karnataka | 22.10 | 22.57 | 24.33 | 23.36 | 25.32 |
| Madhya Pradesh | 18.55 | 27.09 | 30.93 | 33.26 | 33.27 |
| Maharashtra | 15.18 | 15.51 | 15.81 | 15.41 | 15.45 |
| Orissa | 30.59 | 33.05 | 25.81 | 27.54 | 27.99 |
| Rajasthan | 24.00 | 27.20 | 28.53 | 32.58 | 31.81 |
| West Bengal | 22.06 | 22.38 | 28.57 | 27.50 | 26.81 |
| India | 34.03 | 35.99 | 37.56 | 38.66 | 39.22 |

Source: CMIE (2002)

## Electricity

In the power sector, the $9^h$ plan failed to make any particular impact. As seen from table 38, the growth rate of this sector has suffered massively during the $9^{th}$ plan, both in terms of installed plant capacity and gross energy generation. On the other hand, the distributional losses have almost doubled in this period. The financial performance has further worsened due to the failure in percentage recovery of costs during the $9^{th}$ plan period. The ongoing privatization exercise of the State Electricity Boards, at least in the short run, is yet to provide a sustainable solution to the problem.

**Table 38**

*Growth Trend for a Few Important Variables*

*(Percentage)*

| *Variables* | *$8^{th}$ Plan* | *$9^{th}$ Plan* |
|---|---|---|
| Installed plant capacity | 4.55 | 4.32 |
| Gross energy generation | 6.72 | 5.60 |
| Proportion of Electricity consumption by industry | 38.82 | 34.52 |
| T & D losses | 8.33 | 16.19* |
| Recovery as percentage of costs | 78.58 | 70.34 |
| Subsidy to sales revenue ratio (with cross subsidization)@ | 31.14 | 40.52 |

Source: Calculated from data in *Economic Survey* and Planning Commission (2002)

* - First three years

@ - The data for last couple of years of the $9^{th}$ plan are estimated

# SECTION VIII

# EXTERNAL TRADE

## Export and Import

Traditionally, India was never a major player in world trade. In 1990, India's share in world exports stood at 0.5 per cent. However, the role of exports became more important in the aftermath of economic liberalization initiated in 1991. During the $8^{th}$ plan, the export promotion strategy led the figure to increase to 0.6 per cent, which remained stagnant during the $9^{th}$ plan, in spite of a much more targeted approach followed. In addition, India's share in world export registered a decline for a couple of commodity groups over the later half of nineties, namely, spices, iron ore and concentrates, inorganic chemicals, essential oils and perfume materials, leather etc. In other words, these export items failed to capitalize on the improved market access resulting from the ongoing WTO negotiations.

The external trade scenario was quite gloomy in 1990-91, when the trade deficit was as high as US $ 5932 million. Thanks to the economic liberalization programme undertaken during 1991-92, an immediate export growth was noticed and the huge deficit came down. Throughout the 8th plan period, this export growth was sustained, resulting in a total trade deficit of US $ 17281 million over this period. On the contrary, the total trade deficit reached an alarming figure of US $ 42060 million over the 9th plan period. The deficit increased sharply after 1996-97, and reached a peak in 1999-2000. Although the level of deficit declined in 2000-01, it is showing a rising trend in the last two years. The trend is shown with the help of the following diagram. The deterioration in the balance of trade has probably not caught much public attention because of huge foreign currency reserves. The mounting trade balance is shown with the following diagram:

**Diagram 7**

*India's Mounting Trade Deficit*

(US $ million)

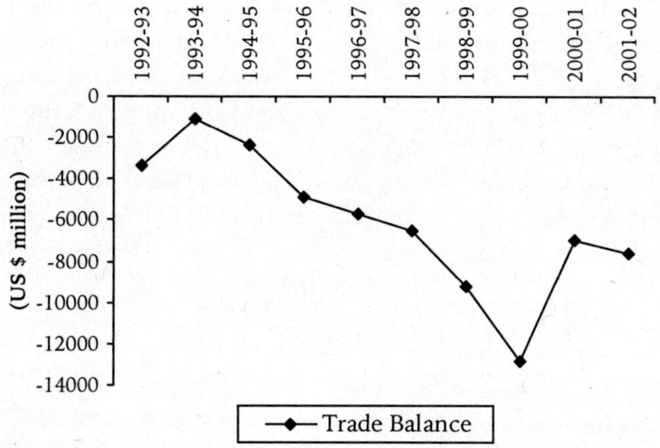

The value of exports originating from India has increased substantially over the last decade, from US $17865 million in 1991-92 to US $ 43827 million in 2001-02. However, a close analysis of exports reveals that the growth rate has flattened out in the recent period. Even worse, the absolute value of exports has also registered a decline twice in the recent past, namely in 1998-99 and 2001-02. Exports have increased at an annual average rate of 13.66 per cent during the $8^{th}$ plan period, as compared to a moderate 5.94 per cent growth rate over the $9^{th}$ plan period. The slackening of export growth during the $9^{th}$ plan period, although partly could be explained by the global depression, grossly results from the lack of desired emphasis on trade expansion. A timely export promotion strategy is the need of the hour.

In addition, the government, while hastily opening the domestic market to foreign companies, has probably lowered the tariff rate too much. On the agricultural front, for a large number of products, the applied tariff is much lower than the bound rate. This shows that the agricultural sector is not even getting the WTO compatible level of protection.

## Foreign Investment and FDI Inflow

The high rate of FDI inflow, materialized just after the liberalization exercise initiated in 1991, has declined massively in recent years, in spite of government efforts to boost it through certain procedural simplifications. During the $8^{th}$ plan a huge FDI inflow occurred when a number of developed countries entered into technical collaborations with Indian partners for getting the benefit of the large market. However, the same level of participation could not be sustained during the $9^{th}$ plan period, in spite of announcing special packages including opening of export processing zones. In particular, the absolute level of actual FDI inflow has declined twice during the $9^{th}$ plan period. The number of FDI approvals is also not increasing in the recent period.

## Table 39

*FDI Inflow and Growth Rate*

*(Rs. Crore)*

| *Year (Jan –Dec)* | *No. of FDI approvals* | *Amount approved of FDI* | *FDI inflow* | *Growth rate of actual inflow* |
|---|---|---|---|---|
| 1992 | 692 | 3888 | 675 | – |
| 1993 | 785 | 8859 | 1787 | 164.74 |
| 1994 | 1062 | 14187 | 3289 | 84.05 |
| 1995 | 1355 | 32072 | 6820 | 107.35 |
| 1996 | 1559 | 36147 | 10389 | 52.33 |
| 1997 | 1665 | 54891 | 16425 | 58.09 |
| 1998 | 1191 | 30814 | 13340 | -18.78 |
| 1999 | 1726 | 28367 | 16868 | 26.44 |
| 2000 | 1726 | 37039 | 19342 | 14.66 |
| 2001 | 1982 | 26875 | 19265 | -0.39 |
| 2002 | 1966 | 11140 | 21286[@] | 10.49 |

Source: *Economic Survey* (2002-03)
@ - January - August

The fact that Mauritius is the largest source of FDI inflow into India also raises the suspicion that a large chunk of this money is tripped into India through some vicious means. Besides this, the nature of FDI coming in these days also needs to be focused. Most of FDI in the manufacturing sector has come into consumer products, e.g., cars, two-wheelers, consumer durables, food products, apparel etc. A similar trend has been noticed in case of services, which has witnessed entry of foreign banks, new insurance companies, and global management consultancy and accountancy firms. While these changes are also welcome, FDI in recent years has contributed next to nothing for fixed investment, exports, and technological modernisation. In addition, a sizable chunk of the inflow reaching the Indian market is spent in merger and acquisition activities. However, foreign investment, which suddenly dropped in the early phase of the 9$^{th}$ plan, has increased considerably over the last couple of years, as seen from diagram 8. However, it is worth noting that the investment level during the 9th plan could never match the peak achieved during the 8th plan period.

**Diagram 8**

*Foreign Investment Inflow*

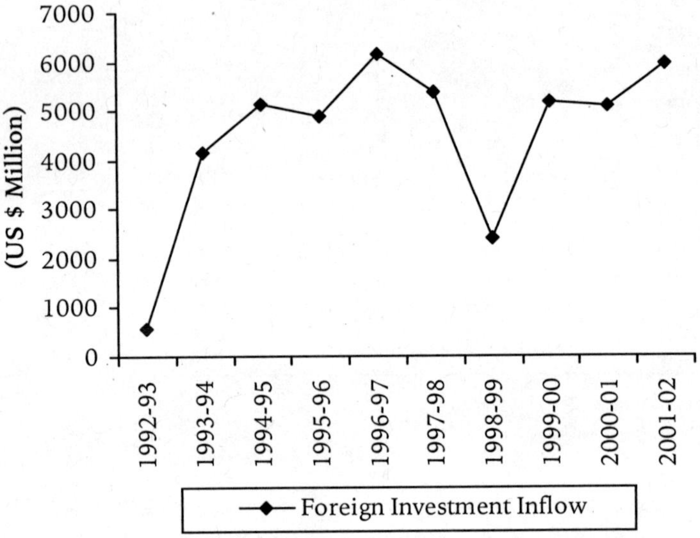


Source: *Economic Survey* (2002-03)

## Foreign Exchange Reserve

The rate of foreign exchange reserve growth has been much higher during the 9th plan period, as seen from diagram 6. While the policymakers could feel comfort, concerns have been raised by various quarters that this does not represent actual growth. While some of the inflow represents real investment, a significant portion actually comes from arbitrage by NRIs to take advantage of the high domestic interest rates and reverse hawala transactions.

**Diagram 9**

*India's Foreign Exchange Reserves*

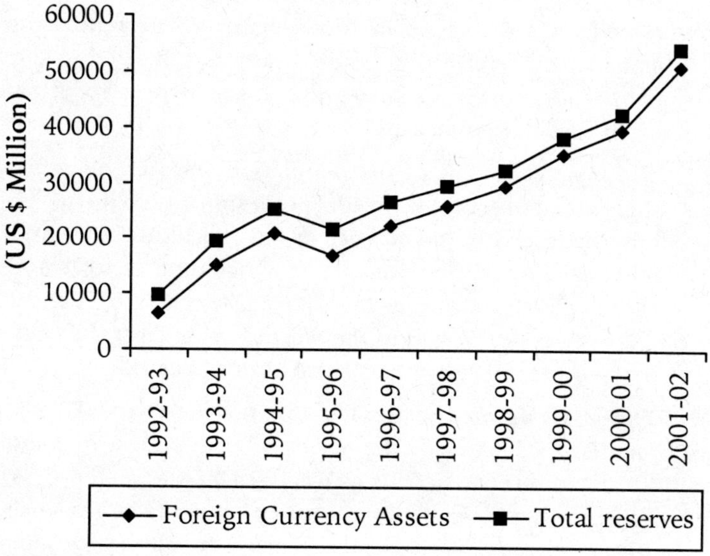


Source: *Economic Survey*

## Conclusion

So far the analysis concentrated on relative performance of various sectors of the economy during the last two completed plan periods. The findings suggest that although in an absolute sense the growth performance of the 9th plan might seem impressive, a comparison with the 8th plan brings out a number of concern areas. Suitable policy initiatives must immediately be focused to recover the growth rates of various sectors of the economy, as well as the overall growth rate. In addition, lowering the gap between the states in social sectors must be accorded highest priority. The broad findings are summarised in the following:

1. The overall growth rate and levels of savings and capital formation are lower during the 9th plan as compared to earlier periods. While inflation rate is within controllable limits, this is likely to be due to other factors rather than appropriate macro management.

2. Although poverty rate during the 9$^{th}$ plan is lower, the change in methodology makes the new results not strictly comparable with results obtained in earlier rounds. Besides, concerns are raised over the issue of food security. The reduction in employment levels during the 9$^{th}$ plan as compared to the 8$^{th}$ plan is also likely to bear grave consequences for a major section of the population.
3. The major segment of the population stays in villages, and therefore poverty alleviation programmes would never be fully successful in the absence of the agricultural growth. It is observed that the performance of agricultural sector has been alarmingly worse during the 9$^{th}$ plan in comparison with the 8$^{th}$ plan period. To add to the worries, a similar result follows both in case of heavy and small-scale industries.
4. The analysis on the fiscal front reveals that NDEs have increased substantially during the 9$^{th}$ plan period. In addition, fiscal and revenue deficits as well as liabilities are on the rise, which in the absence of any national crisis (e.g., the crisis of 1991) suggests fiscal mismanagement. In addition, a number of DEs were reduced proportionally in government expenditure, bearing serious consequences for future development. Fiscal overshooting has become a major problem. The procedures followed in the disinvestment programme have also gathered much criticism in the last couple of years.
5. The social sectors, namely, health and education have done reasonably well at the overall level. However, the persistence of underdeveloped pockets is a major area of concern. In addition, the reduction in level of expenditure in the health sector is likely to be a major setback.
6. On the governance front, the 8$^{th}$ plan period has fared much better than the 9$^{th}$ plan period. The situation has worsened for a number of fields, namely, overall crime rate, crime against women and children, atrocities against backward classes, and level of corruption investigations. The decline in governance level might act as a major hindrance to sustainable economic development.

7. The infrastructure level, although in absolute sense has improved during the 9th plan period, suffered from several bottlenecks. While a couple of these problems were inherited from the 8th plan, they actually magnified during this period. The expansion programme of railways has been lower, power sector was in turmoil, pace of irrigation expansion suffered from cut in funds, and road sector suffered from the lack of smooth connectivity.

8. The external sector has shown slackness in export growth rate and a mounting trade deficit. The economy could not fully reap the benefits of WTO accession in the external front, while the high applied-bound rate gap for a number of agricultural products suggests that the required protection is not always being extended to domestic producers. While FDI, foreign investment, and foreign exchange reserves increased during the 9th plan, questions were raised on their composition.

# Annex 1

*Status and Supreme Court Orders on Mid-day Meals*

## Status of mid-day meals in different states of India as on July 1, 2003

*Full Implementation*: Cooked mid-day meals are being implemented in all districts of Andhra Pradesh, Chattisgarh, Madhya Pradesh, Gujarat, Kerala, Rajasthan, Karnataka and Tamil Nadu.

*Partial Implementation*: So far, mid-day meals are being provided only in tribal blocks of Maharashtra and Orissa. West Bengal has initiated the programme in 4 poor districts, Uttaranchal in the capital district and Punjab in one block per district.

*No Implementation*: Mid-day meal programme is not being implemented at all in Assam, Bihar, Jharkhand, Uttar Pradesh and Haryana. Some of these states, however, are in the process of introducing mid-day meals, if only on a pilot basis.

## Supreme Court Orders

The broad verdicts passed at various dates in the Supreme Court hearings on the right to food (PUCL vs Union of India and others) Case are presented in the following.

## Order of May 2, 2003

- SGRY scheme to be doubled for an interim period of three months (May - July).
- Famine codes will be binding in the months of May, June and July. However, if better measures are incorporated in other schemes, these may be implemented instead.
- Government of India to clarify its response to the Abhijit Sen Committee report by August 8, 2003.
- Government of India has to evolve a system of ensuring that all poor families are identified as BPL.
- Licences of ration shop dealers to be cancelled if they (i) do not open on time, (ii) overcharge, (iii) retain ration cards, (iv) make false entries in BPL cards, or (v) engage in black marketing.

- BPL households are to be permitted to buy grain in instalments.
- The following groups to be given *Antyodaya* cards:
  1. Aged, infirm, disabled, destitute men and women, pregnant and lactating destitute women;
  2. Widows and other single women with no regular support;
  3. Old persons (aged 60 or above) with no regular support and no assured means of subsistence;
  4. Households with a disabled adult and no assured means of subsistence;
  5. Households where due to old age, lack of physical or mental fitness, social customs, need to care for a disabled, or other reasons, no adult member is available to engage in gainful employment outside the house; and
  6. Primitive tribes.
- States that have not implemented the order on mid-day meal scheme to immediately start providing mid-day meals in at least 25 per cent of the districts (with priority to poorest districts).

## Order of October 29, 2002

- The hearing on 29th October, 02 resulted in the clarification of some points pertaining to the previous orders. The Supreme Court reaffirmed the previous orders and issued some of the following broad points as the order.
- Chief Secretaries will be held responsible if starvation deaths are established in their states.
- Each state will appoint one officer as an assistant to the commissioner.
- One last chance is given to the states to take up the publicity of the orders and translation them.

## Order of May 8, 2002

- The *gram panchayats* shall frame employment generation proposals in accordance with the SGRY guidelines... These proposals shall be approved and sanctioned by the *Gram Panchayats* and the work started expeditiously.

- The respondents shall focus the SGRY programme towards agricultural wage earners, non-agricultural unskilled wage earners, marginal farmers and in particular, SC and ST persons whose wage income constitutes a reasonable proportion of their household income and to give priority to them in employment, and within this section shall give priority to women.
- GoI shall release money entitlements under the different employment generation schemes to each State on schedule, provided that utilisation certificates have been provided by the states certifying that the funds have been used for the specified purpose.
- The *gram sabhas* are entitled to conduct Social Audits into all Food/Employment schemes.
- *Gram Sabhas* are entitled to monitor the implementation of the various schemes and have access to relevant information.
- In view of the grievance that the identification of BPL families is not being done properly the central... and the state governments are directed to clarify the issue and work out a policy for...
- The respondents shall ensure that rations shops remain open throughout the months during fixed hours the details of which will be displayed on the notice board.

Dr. N.C. Saxena and Mr S R Sankaran are appointed as commissioners of the Court to redress complaints that have not been resolved by the Collectors and the Chief Secretary. They can take the help of NGOs and individuals to help them monitor the implementation of the court's orders.

## Order of November 28, 2001

*TPDS*

- It is the case of the Union of India that there has been full compliance with regard to the allotment of foodgrain in relation to the TPDS. However, if any of the States gives a specific instance of non-compliance, the Union of India will do the needful within the framework of the Scheme.

- The States are directed to complete the identification of BPL families, issuing of cards and commencement of distribution of 25 kgs. grain per family per month.
- The Delhi Govt. will ensure that TPDS application forms are freely available and are given and received free of charge and there is an effective mechanism in place to ensure speedy and effective redressal of grievances.

*Antyodaya Anna Yojana*

- It is the case of the Union of India that there has been full compliance with regard to the allotment of foodgrain in relation to Antyodaya Anna Yojana. However, if any of the States gives a specific instance of non-compliance, the Union of India will do the needful within the framework of the Scheme.
- We direct the States and the Union Territories to complete identification of beneficiaries, issuing of cards and distribution of grain under this Scheme latest by 1st January, 2002.
- It appears that some *Antyodaya* beneficiaries may be unable to lift grain because of penury. In such cases, the Centre, the States and the Union Territories are requested to consider giving the quota free after satisfying itself in this behalf.

*MDMS*

- It is the case of the Union of India that there has been full compliance with regard to the Mid-Day Meal Scheme (MDMS). However, if any of the States gives a specific instance of non-compliance, the Union of India will do the needful within the framework of the Scheme.
- We direct the State Governments/Union Territories to implement the Mid-Day Meal Scheme by providing every child in every Government and Government assisted Primary Schools with a prepared mid-day meal with a minimum content of 300 calories and 8-12 grams of protein each day

of school for a minimum of 200 days. Those Governments providing dry rations instead of cooked meals must within three months [February 28, 2002] start providing cooked meals in all Govt. and Govt. aided Primary Schools in all half the Districts of the State (in order of poverty) and must within a further period of three months [May 28, 2002] extend the provision of cooked meals to the remaining parts of the State.

- We direct the Union of India and the FCI to ensure provision of fair average quality grain for the Scheme on time.
- The States/Union Territories and the FCI are directed to do joint inspection of food grains. If the food grain is found, on joint inspection, not to be of fair average quality, it will be replaced by the FCI prior to lifting.

*NOAPS*

- It is the case of the Union of India that there has been full compliance with regard to the National Old Age Pension Scheme. However, if any of the States gives a specific instance of non-compliance, the Union of India will do the needful within the framework of the Scheme.
- The States are directed to identify the beneficiaries and to start making payments latest by 1st January, 2002.
- We direct the State Govts./Union Territories to make payments promptly by the 7th of each month.

*Annapurna*

- The States/Union Territories are directed to identify the beneficiaries and distribute the grain latest by 1st January, 2002.

*ICDS*

- We direct the State Govts./Union Territories to implement the Integrated Child Development Scheme (ICDS) in full and to ensure that every ICDS disbursing centre in the country shall provide as under - Each child up to 6 years of age to get 300 calories and 8-10 grams of protein; Each adolescent girl to get 500 calories and 20-25 grams of protein; Each pregnant woman and each nursing mother to get 500 calories & 20-25 grams of protein; Each malnourished child to get 600 calories and 16-20 grams of protein.

- Have a disbursement centre in every settlement.

*NMBS*

- We direct the State Govts./Union Territories to implement the National Maternity Benefit Scheme (NMBS) by paying all BPL pregnant women Rs. 500/- through the Sarpanch 8-12 weeks prior to delivery for each of the first two births.

*NFBS*

- We direct the State Govts./Union Territories to implement the National Family Benefit Scheme and pay a BPL family Rs. 10,000/- within four weeks through a local Sarpanch, whenever the primary bread winner of the family dies.

*Other*

- We direct that a copy of this order be translated in regional languages and in English by the respective States/Union Territories and prominently displayed in all Gram Panchayats, Govt. School Buildings and Fair Price Shops.
- In order to ensure transparency in selection of beneficiaries and their access to these Schemes, the Gram Panchayats will also display a list of all beneficiaries under the various Schemes.

**Order of September 17, 2001**

- States & Union Territories who, according to the learned Attorney General, had not identified the below poverty line families under the Antyodaya Anna Yojana, to identify, we are not satisfied that any such exercise in the right earnestness has been undertaken.
- The Food for Work Programme in the scarcity areas should also be implemented by the various States to the extent possible.

## Order of July 23, 2001

- In our opinion, what is of utmost importance is to see that food is provided to the aged, infirm, disabled, destitute women, destitute men who are in danger of starvation, pregnant and lactating women and destitute children, especially in cases where they or members of their family do not have sufficient funds to provide food for them.
- By way of an interim order, we direct the States to see that all the PDS shops, if closed, are re-opened and start functioning within one week from today and regular supplies made.

Source: www.righttofood.com

## Notes

1 The document puts two major goals as to bring millions of families above the poverty line by 2020 and to bring the poverty ratio to 13 per cent and to generate nearly ten million new employment opportunities per annum, especially for those in the lower income groups.

2 The recent India Development Policy Review of World Bank was critical about the slackening rate of economic growth, persistence of poverty and growing regional and urban-rural disparities. The study also voiced concerns that the current rate of progress is insufficient to meet the Tenth Plan targets.

3 The interest rate has been reduced a couple of times after the $8^{th}$ plan period. Although the guiding motive was to help the manufacturing sector, so far no special investment boom, owing to reduction in interest rate, has been observed.

4 The WPI and CPI based inflation rates are provided for financial and calendar year respectively.

5 Bhandari and Khare (2002)

6 Sen (2000)

7 It has been pointed out by Deaton and Dreze (2002) that the data obtained by using the newer methodology also leads to a wrong notion about persistence of inequality. They found that "The direct use of the unit record data in the $55^{th}$ Round, with no adjustment, shows a substantial reduction in inequality within the rural sector of most states, with little or no increase in the urban sectors. With the correction, we see that within state rural inequality has not fallen, and that there have been marked increases in within-state urban inequality."

8 A detailed analysis of India's poorest districts has recently been performed by Debroy and Bhandari (2003). The study has shown that among 69 poorest districts, 26 are located in Bihar, 13 in Uttar Pradesh, 10 in Jharkhand, 10 in Orissa, 6 in Madhya Pradesh, 3 in Arunachal and 1 in Karnataka.

9 For $55^{th}$ round, the result for 30 day recall for food is given in type 1, which is not strictly comparable with the same under the four earlier rounds. The result from the 7 day recall is given in type 2.

10 The policy followed so far has been criticised by the Committee on Long-Term Grain Policy (2002). The Committee remarked, "These stocks are deteriorating because of shortage of storage space, but to hold these the Centre is spending more than what it expends on Agriculture, Rural development and on Irrigation and Flood control taken together." Similar concerns have been raised by other economists from time to time.

11 A similar declining trend is noticed for pulses as well.

12 The Human Development Report (2003) noted that the proportion of undernourished people which stood at 25 per cent in 1990-92 came down only by 1 per cent in 1998-2000.

13 For successfully enforcing food security, at least for the undernourished pockets, incorporation of a national Employment Guarantee Act would be useful. Mander, Dreze and Vivek (2003) have shown that the estimated cost of such a scheme, along the same lines as Maharashtra's 'Employment Guarantee Scheme', would not be a major burden on the state exchequer.

14 For a detailed analysis on rural employment in the nineties, see Chadha and Sahu (2002).

15 According to the 1991 Census data, around 65 per cent of the total workforce is dependent on agriculture as a means for livelihood. Although the complete results of Census 2001 are yet to be published, it seems, the trend has not changed drastically.

16 See Sidhu (2002).

17 After 1995-96, the relative weight of these industries in determination of overall industrial growth rate has been changed. Therefore, for conducting the analysis with a comparable data set, only the last two years of the $8^{th}$ plan have been considered.

18 BALCO, although suffering from procedural bottlenecks and lack of managerial autonomy, was a profit making PSU with an extremely low debt to equity ratio. The government had gone out of its way to sell 51 per cent of its share against the recommended level of 40 per cent.

19 Although bids were invited following official procedures, the valuation of the firm, the setting of the reserve price and the acceptance of Sterlite's bid were finished too soon.

20 It has been pointed out by Debroy and Bhandari (2003) that connectivity has a major role to play in eradication of backwardness.

21 Recently, the Tenth Five Year Plan (2002-07) has targeted 15 million hectares of rain fed land under various watershed development programmes.

## References

Bhandari, Laveesh and Khare, Aarti, (2002), "The Geography of Post-1991 India Economy", *Global Business Review*, July-December.

Centre for Monitoring Indian Economy Pvt. Ltd. (CMIE), (2002), Economic Intelligence Service, *Agriculture*, December.

Chadha, G. K., and Sahu, P. P., (2002), "Post-Reform Setbacks in Rural Employment: Issues that Need Further Scrutiny", EPW, May 25-31.

Deaton, Angus and Dreze, Jean, (2002), "Poverty and Inequality in India: A Re-examination" EPW, September 7.

Debroy, Bibek, and Bhandari, Laveesh, (2003), *District Level Deprivation in the New Millennium*, Konark Publishers, New Delhi.

Human Rights Watch, (2003), "Compounding Injustice: The Government's Failure to Redress Massacres in Gujarat", Vol. 15, No. 4 (C) – July, New York

Mander, Harsh, Dreze, Jean and Vivek S., (2003), "Freedom from Hunger and Fear: Priorities for Action", RGICS Agenda for Improving Governance Series – XV.

Meenakshi, J. V., and Vishwanathan, Brinda, (2003), "Calorie Deprivation in Rural India, 1983-1999/2000", EPW, January 25.

Ministry of Finance and Company Affairs, "Economic Survey", Government of India (various issues)

Ministry of Railways (Railway Board), (2003), Government of India, "White Paper on Safety on Indian Railways", April.

National Crime Records Bureau, *Crime in India*, Government of India (various issues)

NSSO, (2000), "Employment and Unemployment in India : 1999-2000 – Key Results", Ministry of Statistics and Programme Implementation, Government of India.

Planning Commission (Power & Energy Division), Government of India, (2002), "The Working of State Electricity Boards & Electricity Departments", May.

Planning Commission (2002), *National Human Development Report 2001*, Government of India.

——— (2002), "Report of the Committee on India Vision 2020", Government of India, December.

Sen, Abhijit, (2000), "Estimates of Consumer Expenditure and its Distribution: Statistical Priorities after NSS $55^{th}$ Round", *EPW*, December 16.

Sidhu, H S., (2002), "Crisis in Agrarian Economy in Punjab: Some Urgent Steps", *EPW*, July 27– August 2.

3

# A Review of Administrative Reforms in India[1]

RAHUL MUKHERJI

This paper has been written as a policy paper designed to read between the lines of various reports of the Government of India. The idea was to discern the Government's own thinking on reforming its administration. I deal with five broad issues. The first is the concern that the administration may lose the much-needed insulation from the political system. The second is the concern that lack of accountability in administration, which is structural, is eroding performance. The third is the issue of corruption, which is intimately related to the problem of over regulation. The fourth and related concern is the problem of over manning and the need for rightsizing. Last but not the least, I review the initiatives taken by the Government to bring the citizen closer to the administration.

## 1. Politicization and Integrity

A bureaucracy is supposed to uphold the high standards of integrity insulated from political considerations. Politics is often particularistic and swayed by narrow corporate, caste, class, or regional interests. Administration needs to be fair. A significant challenge before the Indian administrative system is the lack of autonomy of the bureaucracy from the executive.

When the executive works for particularistic gain, it is tough for the officer to remain honest. A local MLA can take issue with an official on a land title document. A minister in the state may interfere with a District Collector on a personnel decision. A Central Minister may get his contract through. On the other hand, when the executive works for non-partisan and clearly defined goals, the administration is able to perform well. Success stories include, M.G. Ramachandran's

Noon Meal Program, refugee relief in 1971 (Indo Pakistan War) and in the 1980s (Sri Lanka crisis), and the Kumbh Mela (Krishnan and Somanathan, 2001, pp. 23, 26-27).

There are officers with a higher or lower propensity to remain honest. According to a senior officer involved with the training of recruits at the Lal Bahadur Shastri Academy of Administration, on an average, 20 per cent of the officers may be of high integrity, 20 per cent may be easily corruptible, while 60 per cent may be sitting on the fence. A system that promotes corruption is likely to be at least 80 per cent corrupt while that which promotes integrity, could be 80 per cent honest. The trick is to get the system to promote integrity rather than depend on altruism for promoting honesty.

*Transfers*

The ability of the political executive to transfer officers arbitrarily has increased the play of politics and particularism in administration. With the expansion of the functions of the All India Services, the number of positions at the senior level have proliferated. The norm of equal pay and responsibility has suffered due to this. It has become easy for the political executive to punish officers at the senior level with great ease by posting him to an equivalent posting with less responsibility. A senior government servant reported that the frequency of transfers was a good indicator of the level of governance in a particular state.

The ability of the executive to transfer officials enables the executive to punish disobedient officials. Lack of a stable tenure robs the ability of officials to perform a task. M. Shankarnarayanan, a celebrated Chief Secretary of Karnataka, was transferred to Gulbarga as Secretary, Hyderabad Karnataka Development Board in 1990. A state government officer not belonging to the state civil service and with little administrative experience secured posting as a District Magistrate in a district where his family had caste and political backing. This appointment facilitated the eruption of communal violence that took months to bring under control (Krishnan and Somanathan, 2001, pp. 30-33).

The Government of India took note of the problem of arbitrary transfers at a very early day and age. Paul Appleby, the noted American scholar of public administration and the inspiration behind the Indian Institute of Public Administration, noted in 1956 that rapid transfers had the effect of robbing the administrative leadership of knowledge and experience (Appleby, 1956, p.27).

The Fifth Pay Commission noted the gravity of this problem and suggested detailed guidelines by each department as part of a comprehensive transfer policy. There should be the conception of a normal tenure of 3 to 5 years. Premature transfers need to be on sound grounds. Detailed reasons must be given and the officer should have the right to appeal against such decisions. Decisions on transfers without a change in incumbency of the Prime Minister (PM) or the Chief Minister (CM) should be taken after a thorough examination by the Civil Services Board.

The Civil Services Board at the Centre should comprise a retired Judge of the Supreme Court or a High Court, a prominent person in public life, and the Cabinet Secretary. At the state level, the first two positions need to be jointly decided by the CM and the Leader of the opposition, while the Cabinet Secretary's position in the Board could be replaced by the Chief Secretary. For each premature transfer, the Secretary Personnel will have to submit a detailed explanation to the Civil Services Board. If the Board does not accept this transfer request, it needs be tabled before the House in the next session (Government of India, 1997, pp. 215-220).

The Conference of Chief Ministers of May 27, 1997 modified the Fifth Pay Commission's recommendations, seeking to secure power to the political executive. The CM would appoint top positions like the Chief Secretary, the Director General of Police and the Chief Conservator of Forests. The Civil Services Board would recommend transfers of officers of the level of Joint Secretary or above, and, Heads or Additional Heads of Departments, Divisional Commissioners, Financial Commissioners, District Magistrates and Superintendents of Police. The Chief Secretary would be the Chairman of the Civil Services Board. The second member would be the Additional Chief Secretary, the Chairman of the Revenue Board or the seniormost financial commissioner. The Member-Secretary would be Secretary Department of Personnel and Training (Government of India, 1997, 57-58).

The difference between the recommendations of the Fifth Pay Commission and the Conference of Chief Ministers is stark. There was no mention of a normal tenure by the Chief Ministers. The top positions were sought to be made fully subservient to the political executive. No participation from the judiciary or civil society was suggested in the Civil Services Board, which was to be entirely constituted by the top bureaucracy.

Even the agreement of the Chief Ministers has not been implemented by the states. Assam, Gujarat, Haryana, Jammu & Kashmir, Karnataka, Tamil Nadu, Tripura and West Bengal have merely issued orders outlining a transfer policy of the government. Only Karnataka, Nagaland and Uttar Pradesh (UP) have set up institutions equivalent to the Civil Services Board in the Centre (Government of India, May 2002, pp.9-10,25). The present Government in UP is notorious for frequent transfers despite the setting up of a Board. The World Bank has threatened to withdraw funding from development projects in UP unless it does something about frequent transfers (Tripathi, September 27, 2002, pp. 34-37).

Veteran administrator P.K. Dave has noted that the lukewarm response of the CMs to a transfer policy that would ensure stability. Western democracies generally set standards that they meet before deciding a premature transfer. The civil society may need to intervene. When public consciousness about maladministration and its developmental consequences is heightened, people will demand administrative reforms through the democratic process (Dave, 2001, pp. 111-114).

Karnataka has initiated exemplary best practices worthy of emulation. The State Government's Governance Strategy Document notes that between 2000/01 and 2001/02 the number of transfers came down from 50,029 to 16,830. According to an executive order of November 21, 2001, cadre management authorities will affect transfers only between April and May of the year. The transfers will be kept to the bare minimum, not exceeding 5 per cent of the cadre strength. There is a public database on the transfers of civil servants (vsb.kar.nic.in/dpar/dpar.html), which is being updated every 6 months (Governance of Karnataka, 2002, pp. 4-5).

## 2. Accountability and Efficiency

Paul Appleby noted in 1956 that it was very tough to attribute responsibility in the Indian administrative system. Individual responsibility was tough to pin down when there were convoluted notions of Parliamentary responsibility, Cabinet responsibility, and, an excessive reliance on procedure and cross-reference (Appleby, 1956, p. 7). The issue of administrative accountability was discussed again in a seminal paper of the Economic Administrative Reforms Commission chaired by L.K. Jha (Government of India, 1983). Between 1956 and 1983 the burden of unaccountability began to weigh heavily on the administration's performance.

The EARC noted that the multi-dimensional development process involved a large number of agencies. Targets for each organization were not well defined. Limits to authority were emphasized through audit and other administrative procedures. Accountability was stressed through procedural norms rather than on the basis of the performance of a task (Government of India, 1983, pp. 3-4).

The EARC urged the administration to move from a negative conception of accountability to a positive conception of accountability. This would involve responsibility for results rather than subservience to procedure. The administrative task at hand would have to be clearly specified with delineation of responsibility, delegation of powers, target-setting, performance appraisal and rewards (Government of India, 1983, p. 2). Each ministry or department should be encouraged to set targets. It should share the targets with the rest of the Government, with periodic reports to the Cabinet. The Secretary would be responsible for the ministry as a whole, while the Joint Secretary, Director and Deputy Secretary could look after specific issue areas. Proper delegation with responsibility would reduce administrative delays (Government of India, 1983, pp. 7-11).

A variety of procedures obscure accountability. Career assessment is impressionistic and general. The Report suggested the need for more objective criteria emphasizing the task at hand. The stability of tenure was stressed as being key to performance. Officials, especially those at the senior level, needed some time before they could make an impact in terms of the set targets. Ex-post audit questions, vigilance and CBI often created more problems for achievers than helped to curb corruption (Government of India, 1983, pp. 12-13). I have discussed challenges to the stability of tenure in the previous section. I will come back to performance appraisal and unnecessary procedure in a subsequent section.

The EARC noted the confusion created by inter-departmental and inter-ministerial involvement in projects, making it tough to attribute responsibility to a particular agency. When a subject concerns more than one ministry, Rules of Transaction of Business 4(1) ensure that no order can be issued till all the ministries concur. Even Cabinet committees become powerless when one or more of the ministries concerned are not prepared to concur with the ministry substantively responsible for the task. It opined that specialized agencies should only concern themselves with broad guidelines and not with implementation (Government of India, 1983, pp. 14-15).

The EARC suggested a matrix approach to committees. Like the District Collector who coordinates the functions of different projects, the Secretary of the lead ministry should chair the relevant committee. The Commission noted that on industrial approvals alone, there were nine committees meeting once a fortnight or week. There were many other statutory and non-statutory committees or boards, making it impossible for the Secretary to attend to all these. It was suggested that many of these committees could be fixed at the level of Joint Secretary, with decision-making authority to the lead ministry. If inter bureaucratic fights were tough to resolve, these should go the Cabinet Secretary in the Centre or the Chief Secretary in the state. Similarly, inter-ministerial disputes should be resolved at the level of the Chief Minister in the states or the Prime Minister in the Centre (Government of India, 1983, pp. 14-17).

The Fifth Pay Commission repeated the advice of the EARC. On the issue of vigilance, it wanted the Central Anti-Corruption Bureau out of the CBI and under the charge of the Vigilance Commissioner. Elections being at root of political corruption in India, it recommended a National Election Fund. It emphasized target-oriented accountability and suggested a reduction in bureaucratic discretion to the minimum. Such discretion was at the root of corruption in the bureaucracy (Government of India, 1997, pp. 206-214).

The Fifth Pay Commission recommended that the criteria for an officer's appraisal be changed from the qualitative and vague notions "outstanding", "very good", "good", or "poor" to a 10-point scale. A score of less than or equal to 6 should have adverse consequences for promotions. The adverse report should be reported to the officer concerned with suggestions for improvement. If the Report was completely inconsistent with the previous years, then the officer had the right to get transferred. Confidential reports (CRs) of the past five years alone should be considered alongside a quinquennial review, which would provide for an appreciation of the broad career trajectory (Government of India, 1997, 182-187).

A large number of innovations are possible through administrative creativity. Anil Lakhina transformed his collectorate into a client-oriented bank teller type system. T.V. Antony spearheaded Tamil Nadu's family planning program. The total literacy program in Ernakulam was an innovation by an IAS officer. The privatization of sewage pumping stations in Madras Metrowater was an innovation by two IAS officers (Krishnan and Somanathan 2001, pp. 40-41).

The pertinent advice of these Commissions notwithstanding, responsive administration has been difficult because of the bias in favor of the status quo due to procedures, vigilance, lack of rewards, and, political interference. Paul Appleby had noted that auditors knew very little about good administration. An Undersecretary knew more about a department than the entire office of the Comptroller and Auditor General of India (CAG) [Appleby, 1956, p. 27]. More recently, the Fifth Pay Commission also noted that audit should be more geared towards the achievement of goals rather than towards respecting unnecessary procedure (Government of India, 1997, Ch. 24).

Entry is meritocratic, but promotions are largely based on seniority. Even the Fifth Pay Commission, which came out with important policy recommendation only superficially dealt with the issue of exemplary reward for merit. It promised two assured promotions for Groups B, C, and D, and, three for Group A services (Government of India, 1997, pp. 188-202). Meritocracy could be exphasized through more rigorous evaluations after 15 and 25 years of service.[2]

Officers of integrity and purpose must be honored. Britain uses the Knighthood with great effect to honor its worthy subjects. India does not have prestigious awards to reward its civil servants. The Centre rarely rewards officers with titles of prestige such as Padma Bhushan (Krishnan and Somanathan, 2001, p. 47). The Report of The Core Group noted that a lot needed to be done to bolster the system of rewards initiated by the Centre and the states. Punjab, Rajasthan, Maharashtra, Uttar Pradesh, Tamil Nadu and Andaman & Nicobar

Islands have instituted awards (Government of India, 2002, pp. 9, 24-25).

### 3. Corruption

A regulated economy with an excessive role for the Government and discretion to the administration promotes corruption. The Commission on the Prevention of Corruption chaired by Santhanam produced important findings. It noted the scope for abuse in every sphere regulated by the Government. Discretion was at the root of the problem.

The Commission pointed to corruption with concrete examples. Low paid officers were likely to be more corrupt. It recommended that housing for income-tax, customs and excise officials in the metros was a must, if they were to remain honest. It noted that the private sector had fallen pray to the regime of controls. FICCI did not even respond to the Commission's request for help (Government of India, 1964, pp. 44-47). Construction projects of the Public Works Department earned executive engineers and lower officers about 7 per cent to 11 per cent of the project cost (Government of India, 1964, p. 10). The Commission's recommendations led to the creation of the office of the Central Vigilance Commissioner. The Commission could not get the vigilance process to cover the political class (Maheshwari, 1981, pp. 35-39).

The Commission observed that Article 311 rendered excessive security to the Indian public service official. The official had the right to be informed about the charges and the evidence leveled against him. He could write a statement against these charges at his convenience. The official could first have his case heard by the Public Service Commission, failing which he could move the courts. The Commission noted that this had made it extremely tough to hold an official accountable for an offense against the private citizen (Government of India, 1964, pp. 34-35).

The Fifth Pay Commission recommended measures that would discourage corruption through the electoral process. It sought to strengthen the vigilance process. And, in order to check the negative nexus between politicians, public officials, business and criminals, it suggested the Lok Pal Bill (Government of India, 1997, pp. 206-214).

States that have reported strengthening their vigilance process include, Karnataka, Kerala, Maharashtra, Nagaland, Uttar Pradesh and West Bengal. The Lok Pal Bill was introduced in Parliament in August 2001. Assam, Andhra Pradesh, Bihar, Gujarat, Himachal Pradesh, Karnataka, Madhya Pradesh, Maharashtra, Orissa, Punjab, Rajasthan, Uttar Pradesh and the National Capital of Delhi have set up the corresponding institution of *Lok Ayukta* (Government of India, 2002, p. 8-9).

## 4. Rightsizing

Excessive regulation is a burden on the exchequer for two principal reasons. First, over regulation promotes inefficiency because some services like luxury hotels, telecommunications, among others, are best provided by the private sector. The profit motive and the regulated market do a good job of service delivery. Second, if public officials engage in tasks that are best performed by the private sector, then the government is unlikely to be able to afford so many officials. The previous section noted how over regulation and discretion in public office has promoted corruption.

The Commission on the Prevention of Corruption had opined that reducing the size of the government was good for reducing corruption. It suggested that the government should be allowed to retire some officers at the age of 50, after 25 years of service. A committee of two secretaries and with the Central Vigilance Commissioner as chair should be allowed to review the cases of all officers who had crossed the age of 50. At that time, the Central Government could not take action regarding the termination of tenure without the agreement of the respective state governments. The Commission thought that this was unreasonable because many officers at the Centre had been away from their respective states for prolonged periods (Government of India, 1964, pp, 39-41).

The Fifth Pay Commission made a significant statement in favor of rightsizing. Some functions belong to the Government, some to the private sector, and others to the mixed economy. Defense, atomic energy, space, railway infrastructure, and security for defense installations provide examples of services that the private sector would not easily invest in. To the mixed economy belonged services like road, rail, air transport, telecom, banking, insurance, power, medical education, courier, defense aircraft and coins. These were areas where the government in cooperation with the private sector could best serve the government. Finally, many goods and services needed to be corporatized. Ordinance factories, telecom factories, and most public sector units were worthy candidates (Government of India, 1997, 122-125).

Reduction in manpower through better manpower management was suggested. It gave examples of how ministries could be merged into one by following an interesting methodology. It opined that the Central core subjects should be the last candidates for downsizing. If a core ministry in the Centre was also a core ministry in the states, this called for downsizing in the state. Auxiliary subjects were good candidates for downsizing. The Department of Administrative Reforms could be merged with the Cabinet Secretariat. Organizations like the Delhi Milk Scheme, the National Dairy Development Board, and the Central Institute of English were better off being autonomous. Ordinance factories were better off as pubic sector units rather than being run directly by the Ministry. It suggested that levels in the bureaucracy should be reduced to six.[3]

The Pay Commission recommended *level jumping*. A file need not be screened by any greater than three levels in order to ensure speedy disposal. Level 1 could comprise of Deputy Secretary or Under Secretary; level 2 could be Joint Secretary, Additional Secretary or Secretary; and, level 3 could be anything higher than that. Two people within the same level were to be dissuaded from looking at the same file. Another efficiency promoting recommendation was to replace a section with a desk. Each desk could have two officers, and two multi-skilled assistants. The executive assistant could look after noting, filing, styling and stenography. A multi-skilled office attendant could take up various other tasks. Third, office automation would enhance efficiency (Government of India, 1997, pp. 122-136, 146-149).

There has been some research, but little action implementing these initiatives. The Department of Administrative Reforms and Personnel Grievances (DARPG) studied 10 ministries for the purpose of downsizing. The DARPG's work on downsizing (except the Department of Commerce) was completed between 1999 and 2001. It recommended the abolition of 8000 posts, winding up 13 organizations and restructuring 24. The Expenditure Reforms

Commission submitted 10 reports by September 2001. It looked at 36 ministries, and, recommended the reduction of 20,000 posts in the main ministries and another 100,000 posts in attached and subordinate offices. A voluntary retirement scheme has been announced and a Division of Retraining and Redeployment has been constituted (Government of India, 2002, p. 10). The DARPG is less aggressive than the Finance Ministry in the area of rigthsizing. Moreover, the Fifth Pay Commission's recommendation of merging ministries seems to have gotten lost somewhere.

The Government of Karnataka has succeeded in some financial control with the fiscal deficit coming down from 4.5 per cent of the gross state domestic product (GSDP) in 2000/01 to 4 per cent of the GSDP in 2001/02. A Fiscal Responsibility Act has been passed. The Government has taken the decision to close, privatize or disinvest at least 10 public sector units. Various activities are being outsourced to the private sector. The Transport Department is considering outsourcing activities like issuance of fitness certificates and learner's license, registration of non-transport motor vehicles, and tests of eligibility for a driving license (Government of Karnataka, 2002, pp. 1-3,6).

## 5. Citizen Concerns

A number of initiatives have been taken to bring the government close to the people. These initiatives include citizen's charters, the redressal of public grievances, the review of administrative laws, devolution of powers, and, the right to information. India resides mostly in villages, towns and cities outside Delhi. If states do not take an active initiative in these areas, the citizen's plight will not improve.

Inspired by the British initiative of 1991, the DARPG wished to gift Indian citizens with *Citizen's Charters,* ensuring government service accountability by setting standards for various services. It was to be a $50^{th}$ birthday gift to the nation from the Government. Standards would be displayed and readily adhered to. There would be officials responsible for upholding these standards. If response was not adequate, three would be a grievance redressal procedure with the possibility of compensation. Standards would be set and reviewed periodically (Government of India, 2002, p. 2-3).

Some progress has been made. 68 organizations of 17 Central Government Ministries issued Citizen's Charters by May 2002. 23 States and Union Territories had issued about 470 Charters (Government of India, 2002 B, 28-29). Andhra Pradesh is taking the responsiveness of government services seriously (see http://www.aponlive.gov.in). In Karnataka, the Stamps and Registration Department, the Transport Department, and a few others have released charters. The Police Department is ready with a charter (Government of Karnataka, 2002, p. 6).

The Fifth Pay Commission had made recommendations about *public grievance redressal,* drawing from the insights on accountability made by the Economic Administrative Reforms Commission in 1983. It was important to record the grievance and fix responsibility. The grievance should keep traveling up the hierarchy until it gets redressed. There should be a senior officer at level of Secretary, looking after public grievances. If the grievance is not addressed, it should travel to the top officer. The aggrieved party should be allowed to make a public presentation before the Sarvochha Lok Adalat. Secretary, Public Grievance, should have the right to access any file from any ministry and could seek appointment with the Cabinet Secretary or the PM to give him the required edge in decision-making (Government of India, 1997, pp. 157-161).

The public grievance redressal mechanism was strengthened in the Centre with the appointment of a Director of Public Grievance in every ministry, department and organization. Guidelines were developed and e-monitoring was encouraged. A Directorate of Public Grievance was set up in the Cabinet Secretariat to look into individual complaints pertaining to 16 ministries in 1988. In 1988, a Standing Committee of Secretaries to Government of India was constituted under the Chairmanship of the Cabinet Secretary, to address the public grievance redressal mechanism at the Centre.

Some organizational innovations have been initiated in the states. Madhya Pradesh, Tamil Nadu and Uttar Pradesh have monitoring arrangements in the Chief Minister's Secretariat. Andhra Pradesh, Assam, Haryana, and Madhya Pradesh have special programs to take administration to the people. There is a Public Grievance Commission in the National Capital Territory of Delhi and a separate department in Assam and Madhya Pradesh (Government of India, 2002 B, pp. 29-30).

Many of our laws have outlived their time. A Commission was set up under the Chairmanship of P.C. Jain to review steps taken by different ministries and departments for ascertaining the *efficacy of various administrative laws* and regulations. The Commission was to identify proposals for amending laws and regulations, which have an intersectoral impact. It was also to make suggestions about the repeal and amendment of dysfunctional laws.

The Report submitted on September 30, 1998, suggested that expeditious amendments be carried in respect of a critical list of 109 laws. There was need to unify and harmonize laws and statutes that related to domestic and foreign investors and consumers. There were specific proposals on regulating housing and real estate, company law, banking, foreign direct investment, industry, consumer affairs, health, environment, labour, income-tax excise & customs, exim policy and procedural issues, and power. There was need to take a more exhaustive look at the laws affecting the poor and the system of alternate dispute resolution (Government of India, 1998).

The Government of India constituted a committee under Secretary, Personnel, for monitoring the implementation of these recommendations. The Commission reviewed 2500 laws, recommended the repeal of about 1400 and amendments to about 241 laws. 393 laws were repealed till May 2002. 37 acts had been amended and 18 were pending in the Parliament (Government of India, 2002 B, pp. 30-32).

Citizens have the *right to information* that must legitimately be in the public domain. The Freedom of Information Bill was introduced in the Parliament on July 25, 2000. It proposed to suitably amend the Official Secrets Act and the civil servant's conduct rules. Goa, Karnataka, Maharashtra, National Capital Territory of Delhi, Rajasthan and Tamil Nadu have legislated on the right to information. Andhra Pradesh, Assam, Tripura, Maharashtra and UP had decided to legislate. Information facilitation counters outside the security perimeter have been set up in Arunachal Pradesh, Assam, Madhya Pradesh, Kerala and UP. Madhya Pradesh has set up information kiosks under the *Gyandoot* scheme. Andhra Pradesh, Assam, Karnataka, Pondicherry and UP have set up their web-sites. Andhra Pradhesh's www.aponline.gov.in is probably the most innovative web-site.

Institutional innovations apart, the most important transformation concerns the psyche of sharing information. When I approached the

DARPG for public documents on Administrative Reforms, I was requested by the Additional Secretary to meet with the concerned Director. The concerned Joint Secretary never returned my calls. The Director shared only some documents in the public domain, and denied access to some others that I requested. I obtained these public documents from outside. The DARPG finally shared some documents only after senior officers (not in DARPG) indicated that these documents could be rightfully procured.

*Devolution and decentralization* has been sought by providing constitutional status to the $73^{rd}$ and $74^{th}$ amendments to the constitution. Most states and union territories have made the necessary changes to their legislation. Elections have been held everywhere except Arunachal Pradesh, Jharkhand, Uttaranchal, Punjab, Pondicherry and Chandigarh. 3.4 million people's representatives have been elected at all levels. As for local bodies, elections are being held regularly everywhere except Bihar and Pondicherry. All states have transferred a number of subjects to Panchayati Raj institutions.

The State Finance Committees of most states (except Bihar) have given their reports (Government of India, 2002, pp. 5-6). To give one example, Karnataka was proud to proclaim that it increased the level of untied grants to the *gram panchayats* from Rs. 2 lakhs to Rs. 3.5 lakhs. These funds would be disbursed on an incentive based system designed to encourage them to mobilize resources (Government of Karnataka, 2002, p. 4).

## 6. Summing Up

Politicization, accountability, corruption and over manning are the fundamental problems facing the administrative system. If these are addressed, many of the citizen's concerns will automatically be addressed. The ingenuity of the government lies in its ability to self reflect and introspect into its problems and come up with good answers. The tragedy is that implementation has been lacking.

Adhoc transfers are an easy way for the executive to intervene in the affairs of the administration without rhyme or reason. The problem was noted by Appleby in 1956 and received elaborate treatment in the Report of the Fifth Pay Commission in 1997. Yet, when the Chief Ministers sat down to recommend action in 1997, they watered down the proposals of the Fifth Pay Commission and did not push implementation.

The need to move from procedural to result oriented accountability was noted by Appleby in 1956, by the Economic Administrative Reforms Commission in 1983, and, by the Fifth Pay Commission in 1997. Citizen's charters and the public grievance redressal mechanism are based on the need for better accountability where the citizen meets government. Much will depend on how far the different states take accountability to the citizens. If devolution of powers to the *Panchayati Raj* institutions and municipal bodies works well, this may promote accountability.

The work of the Commission on Corruption (1964) notwithstanding, corruption in high places remains a problem. While the Commission's valuable gift in the form of the CVC has produced results, the political class is still not under its supervision. Retiring corrupt and inefficient officials early was a task undertaken by the Commission on Corruption as well as the Fifth Pay Commission. There seems to have been much research, but little action on reducing the size of the government.

The right to information is an important right. It will promote accountability within the administration. Right to information acts are being legislated by various state governments. It also needs to be internalized by the officials. Public officials must serve and feel accountable to the citizens. An administration that treats citizens as subjects not worthy of much attention can hardly be expected to provide meaningful public services.

## Notes

1. The author thanks Bibek Debroy, Devesh Kapur, P.L. Sanjeeva Reddy, K.P. Krishnan, V.K. Agnihotri, Vikram K. Chand, Vatsala Vatsa, Shilpa Modi, and, the library staff of the Indian Institute of Public Administration for their generosity. Information contained in this paper is a function partly of the state's propensity to share its progress with administrative reforms.
2. Somanathan and Krishnan suggest that the UPSC selection board could consist of eminent people from the academia and the corporate sector. After reviewing the officer's written material, integrity, and familiarity with subjects of the officer's concern, some officers should not be promoted to the next grade, and, a certain proportion of them could be retired at age 50 (2001, pp. 45-46). Interestingly, the commission on investigating the problem of corruption chaired by Santhanam in 1964 had also discussed ways in which some officers could be retired early (1964, pp. 39-41).
3. These include top executive, senior executive, executive, supervisory staff and support staff

## References

Appleby, Paul. H (1956), *Report on India's Administrative System* (New Delhi: Lok Sabha Secretariat).

Dave, P.K. (2001), "The Citizen and the Administration," in V.A. Pai Panandiker and Subhash C. Kashyap, eds., *Political Reforms: Asserting Civic Sovereignty* (New Delhi; Konarak).

Government of India (2002), *Report of the Core Group on Administrative Reforms in Government* (New Delhi & Mussoorie: Department of Administrative Reforms and Public Grievances and The Lal Bahadur Shastri National Academy of Administration).

———. (2002 B), *Department of Administrative Reforms and Public Grievances: Through the Ages* (New Delhi: Department of Administrative Reforms and Public Grievances - Ministry of Personnel, Public Grievances and Pensions).

———. (1998), *Report of the Commission on Review of Administrative Laws Volume 1* (New Delhi: Department of Administrative Reforms and Public Grievances - Ministry of Personnel, Public Grievances and Pensions).

———. (1997), *Report of the Fifth Central Pay Commission Volume 1* (New Delhi: Ministry of Finance).

———. (1997 B), *Action Plan for Effective and Responsive Government: The Conference of Chief Ministers - May 24, 1997* (New Delhi: Department of Administrative Reforms and Personnel Grievances - Ministry of Personnel, Public Grievances and Pensions).

———. (1983), *Accountability* (New Delhi: Economic Administrative Reforms Commission Report No. 29/Phase I).

———. (1964), *Commission on the Prevention of Corruption* (New Delhi).

Government of Karnataka (2002), *Governance Strategy and Action Plan in Karnataka - 2002* (Bangalore: Department of Personnel and Administrative Reforms).

Krishnan, K.P. and T.V. Somanathan (2001), "Civil Service: An Institutional Perspective," *Conference on Public Institutions in India* (Cambridge, MA: Weatherhead Center for International Affairs - Harvard University).

Maheshwari, Shriram (1981), *Administrative Reforms in India* (New Delhi: Macmillan).

Tripathi, Purnima (2002), *The States* (New Delhi: Frontline) September 27.

# 4

## Administrative Reforms in India

AMIR ULLAH KHAN

"In spite of numerous attempts at reform, the administration tends to be hierarchal and status-bound...the administrative system must reflect an individual's contribution to the human welfare and economic gain...it is well-known that knowledge has been growing faster than our ability to handle it. Administrators lag behind in the situation they are supposed to administer. If a large promotion of investment we have made under the Plans remains unutilized, the cause is to be found in administrative shortcomings."

– Late Indira Gandhi,
*Former Prime Minister of India*
*(Convocation speech, Roorkee University, 1967)*

"People often perceive the bureaucracy as an agent of exploitation rather than a provider of services."

– Atal Bihari Vajpayee,
*Prime Minister of India*

### Introduction

In developing societies that are predominantly agrarian and industrially backward, there abound several scarcities. They also are typically "soft states" that are unable to effectively enforce reform. But by far the biggest problem they face is by way of weak and inefficient administrative structures. Riddled by corruption and apathy, public officials lack knowledge and skills. Political surveillance and control further undermines a sense of public accountability amidst various charges of collusion between politicians and government servants. This problem has only accentuated following decolonialisation and the extensive role governments took on for themselves. This wide jurisdiction has ensured a great concentration of powers with officials and has severely hampered private enterprise and the ability of the people to solve their own problems.

In August 2002, the *UN Human Development Report* rated China 96 while India was at 124. This ranking translates into the following: one fourth of India's population lives below the poverty line, one third is illiterate, nine out of ten households in rural areas don't have access to toilets, one of six villages is yet to get electricity, and two out of five don't get drinking water. And this is despite the fact that India has the largest number of civil servants in the world today (1.9 crore). Two of every three workers in the organized sector work for the government and the total salary bill of government employees — state, centre, and public sector enterprises — is over Rs. 70,000 crore.[1]

- Two of every three workers in the organized sector are employed by the Government.
- Average per capita emolument of a public-sector employee is Rs. 1,66,592, while the per capita income of the country is Rs. 22,000.
- In the past three decades, while the consumer price index has gone up by 998 per cent, salaries to employees of public sector enterprises have gone up by 2,714 per cent.
- In 87 of the 256 PSUs, the equity investment has been completely eroded by accumulated losses. The net worth of these companies in March 2000 was a negative Rs. 31,841 crore.
- Accumulated losses of public-sector enterprises in 1999-2000 were Rs. 52,550 crore.

Not only is this huge sum of money spent wastefully, it also translates into little delivery. An example will illustrate this unsustainable situation: In the 2002-03 budget, the government allocated Rs. 13,670 crore to the Rural Development Ministry. Its allocation for just the wages of the Central Govt. employees is Rs. 17,861.57 crore, for allowances it is Rs. 12,460.44 crore and for travel expenses, Rs. 1,268.05 crore. A total of 31,589 crore rupees.

The central theme of administrative reforms has been improvement in governance. Over the decades, there have been attempts to stem the root in the 'steel frame'. However, all such initiatives have been met with resistance from politicians and bureaucrats. Things have only worsened. There has been resistance not only at the level of quantity but also quality. For example, the IAS has seven decision-making layers to deliver. Moreover, in today's context, we need specialists, and not generalists.

In August 1997, the *Fifth Pay Commission* agreed to hike salaries only if the government cut decision-making layers from seven to three, slashed staff by 30 per cent across 10 years and abolished 3.5 lakh vacant posts. The recommendations were ignored, but the babus got the biggest ever hike. In September 2001, the *Expenditure Reforms Commission* recommended the abolishing of vacant posts, rightsizing, introduction of technology and freezing of new recruitments. In contrast, this year the employee strength is expected to rise by 21, 142 to 33,42,645 and costs from Rs. 30,055. 61 crore to Rs. 31,589 crore.[2]

Last year, the Public Affairs Centre, Bangalore, and ORG-Marg surveyed 37,000 households in 24 states to focus on the five basic public services in which the government has invested thousands of crores, including drinking water, health and sanitation, education and child care, the public distribution system (PDS) and road transport. Their findings:

- Only 13 per cent of the users are satisfied with doctors and paramedics.
- Less than 10 per cent are content with the PDS system.
- Barely 16 per cent are satisfied with teachers.
- Just 5 per cent are satisfied with sanitation levels in schools.
- Only a fifth are satisfied with the public transport system.

Unfortunately, most attempts to trim the bureaucracy have been unidirectional. The initiatives have focused only on the strength-and-cost argument. The crux of the problem is the architecture of the Government. What should the Government intervene in — should it bake bread and run hotels too? Analysis would reveal that if the Government privatizes, and not disinvests, it could instantly bring down the number of ministries by 11. What is the point of having ministries like coal, shipping, broadcasting or civil aviation in this day and age? The best way is to demarcate public services like health, education, and infrastructure and to privatize the rest. In the Anglo-Saxon democracies and tiger economies of East Asia, there are less than a dozen critical ministries. The Government should exit business and function as a provider of social infrastructure.

## Administrative Reforms since Independence

*"Our patterns of administration were drawn or designated at a time when the government's main business was to keep law and order. They are inadequate for the challenge we face today. What we need, therefore, is revolution in the administrative system without which no enduring change can be brought about in any field."*

Late Indira Gandhi, former Prime Minister
*(Replying to a debate in the Lok Sabha, 1966).*

The expression 'administrative reforms' goes beyond the reform of the civil services. Administrative reforms are mainly concerned with the systems, procedures, processes, methods and techniques of administration at the national, state and local levels to bring about administrative efficiency and improvements. The term is applied to improvements in executive machinery, ranging from fundamental realignments in the governmental structure to relatively minor changes in the methods of conducting ministerial or departmental working. The aim of such reforms is to make available to the citizens a clean, efficient, and result oriented administrative set-up.[3] Some of the modern advocates of reforms are of the opinion that administrative reforms are synonymous with the rationalizing process that has started with the bureaucratic revolution.[4]

Since Independence, there have been covert and overt changes in administration. The need arose for administrative reforms as people became more aware and aspirations increased. Also, there was an enormous increase in the scale of the governmental operations. There was a sudden shortage of topnotch British officials and some Muslims opted to go to Pakistan. All these developments necessitated appropriate administrative readjustments.[5] As a result, the Indian Administrative Service (IAS) replaced the old ICS. Also, other new services were created such as the Indian Police Service, Indian Foreign Service, the Central Services, and the Central Secretariat Service, among others.

In 1949, N. Gopalaswamy Iyenger was asked to review the working of the central government. His committee dealt with organizational changes such as the total number of departments to be created, new groupings of ministries and departments and improvement in methods of financial control.

In 1951, the Planning Commission set up the *A D Gorwala Committee* to find out whether the administrative machinery was adequate and sufficiently equipped to meet the requirements of planned development. Gorwala recorded that the public was experiencing delay in execution, and that there was lack of integrity and undue interference and corruption and lack of involvement of officials. He recommended a reorganization of the government for greater speed, efficiency, effectiveness, and responsiveness. He even suggested that a minister and a secretary be appointed solely for pursuing administrative reforms and its promotion.

In 1953, Paul Appleby, an American Professor of Public Administration, who surveyed and reported on administrative reform in India at the invitation of Nehru, gave his second report. He suggested the setting up of an O&M (Organization and Methods) Division in the Government of India. This division was intended to initiate and sustain a concerted effort to improve efficiency in all walks of administration. This was accepted and an O&M Division was established, which was located in the cabinet secretariat. The O&M Division was converted into the Department of Administrative Reforms in 1964 to meet a range of varied and complex problems of administration. It looked into economy and office procedures, and the organization and systems of selected public agencies. Similar departments were created in the states too.

In 1970, the Department of Personnel was constituted on the recommendation of the *Administrative Reforms Committee* 1966. In 1973, this department was merged with the existing Department of Administrative Reforms to constitute the Department of Personnel and Administrative Reforms. It continued under the Prime Minister until it was shifted to the Ministry of Home Affairs. Today, it is known as 'Department of Personnel, Public Grievances and Pensions.'

Paul Appleby was impressed with the Government of India's efforts to achieve development through democracy. However, he suggested methods to modernize office work. In 1956, he proposed to streamline a number of areas: organization and work procedures in public sector enterprises; recruitment; relations between the administration and (a) Parliament, (b) Planning Commission, and (c) Comptroller and Auditor General.

Apart from these suggestions, all Five-Year Plans have suggested administrative reforms under various heads such as securing integrity, preventing corruption, promoting efficiency, among others.

## Major Suggestions for Reforms

Among the 20 committees and commissions set up since Independence in India to look into administrative reforms, some of the major ones are:

1. *Second Central Pay Commission:* It made significant suggestions on promotion by merit, drawing of administrative personnel from as wide a field as possible, and having technical departments headed by technical officers.
2. *Krishnamachari Report on Indian and State Administrative Services and Problems of District Administration:* The report underlined the need for improving the training of the IAS officers.
3. *Santhanam Committee Report on Prevention of Corruption (1966-67):* The Committee examined the organization and working of the Vigilance Units in Central Ministries and Departments, suggested steps for checking corruption, examined and suggested changes in conduct rules applicable to Government servants. As a result of its recommendations, the Central Vigilance Commission was set up by the Government of India.
4. *Administrative Reforms Commission 1966-70 (ARC):* This report had 20 volumes with a total of more than 580 recommendations on various aspects of administration including the machinery of the central government, Centre-state relations, personnel administration, and redressal of grievances.

The ARC suggested seven major areas for consideration:

- A more rational distribution of work in the secretariat and among the executive agencies; a regrouping of subjects
- Improving coordination
- Reduction in agencies and staff
- Strengthening top management

- Reduction in levels of consideration to reduce delays and promote quick decision-making; adoption of desk officer system
- Integration of the secretariat with field agencies
- Delegation of powers

The other salient features of the ARC included:

- A unified pay structure (of 20-25 grades) on the basis of job evaluation
- Promotion from within the ranks
- Tightening of parliamentary control for ensuring accountability

The *Third Pay Commission,* which the Government of India appointed in 1970, submitted its report in two volumes in 1973. The Commission was to give consideration to the principles which should govern the structure of emoluments and conditions of service of Central Government employees and to formulate measures which should be taken to change the structure of emoluments and service conditions. The Commission rationalized the pay scales of different categories of employees and made recommendations pertaining to working hours, holidays, overtime allowance and other welfare measures.

The Union Public Service Commission appointed a committee known as the *Kothari Committee on Recruitment and Selection Methods* in 1976. On the recommendation of the Committee, it was decided that there would be a combined examination for all India services and the Central Group A Services of non-technical fields.

The other important Committees on administrative reforms have been the *National Police Commission* (1977), the *Ashok Mehta Committee on Panchayati Raj Institutions* (1977), the *Economic Reforms Commission* under L.K. Jha (1981), the *Eighth Finance Commission* headed by Y.B. Chavan (1982), the *Sarkaria Commission* (1983).

In different states in India, administrative reforms were also suggested. For this, some state governments constituted an Administrative Reforms Committee, such as in Kerala in 1958. The Committee suggested measures for

- Improving the administrative machinery to enable it to cope with development activities;
- Promoting better coordination;
- Facilitating expeditious dispatch of government work;
- Enhancing the democratization of the organs of the government to promote effective participation of local self-governing institutions.

The main recommendations of the Kerala Administration Reforms Committee were as follows:

- Panchayats should be made the basic units of administration and there should be greater delegation of executive responsibility to them;
- Women should be represented on the taluq council, by co-option if not election;
- Constitution of district development councils should be considered;
- More delegation of powers to be made to the departments;
- O & M Division to be constituted;
- Secretariat work to be confined to framing of policies;
- Laying down rules and principles of procedure, financial control, work connected with legislation, general direction, and evaluation.

In 1965, the Vellodi Committee on Kerala Administration also made several recommendations on the introduction of *Panchayati Raj* institutions, the secretariat administration, and matters covered earlier. Many of the recommendations have been carried out. Other state governments like West Bengal have also had a committee on administrative reforms (1982).

In early 1975, two eminent administrators L.P. Singh and L.K. Jha prepared for the prime minister a note on improving administrative efficiency. The 20-point administrative reforms plan discussed the following issues:

- Improving work conditions and office environment
- Need to enforce punctuality and discipline

- Introduction of O&M to minimize delays, assessment of staff requirements, house-keeping and staff welfare
- Decentralization of legal advice
- Training
- Need to set up administrative tribunals
- Analysis of matters taken to court
- Problems in matters of recruitment to be taken up with the Union Public Service Commission

## Issues in Administrative Reforms Today

In 1963, A.H. Hanson — a scholar of planned economy, visited India. When he took a look at the ground reality, he became baffled enough to ask: "The men are able, the organization is adequate, the procedures are intelligently devised. Why then have the plans since 1956 so persistently run into crises?"

If Hanson were here, he would ask the same question today. The reason is most of the reforms, recommended since the 1950s and 60s, have remained only on paper. For example, none of the recommendations, except hike in salaries, have been implemented despite so many recommendations made by the *Pay Commission* and *Expenditure Reforms Commission*. Therefore, the urgent questions that need to answered in this regard are:

- Are downsizing, identification of the surplus pool and the Voluntary Retirement Schemes (VRS) feasible? Are contractual appointments, proper evaluation for vertical mobility, lateral entry into higher levels and consolidation of perks into gross emoluments possible? Or can one think of a small and core centralized recruitment and larger recruitment at the State-level? Is it necessary to de-link revenue and judicial functions from administrative functions at lower levels?
- Do we need so many ministries and government departments? This is a State, as well as Central issue. Are reforms needed in the budget making process and accounting procedures? So distinctions between revenue and capital expenditure and plan and non-plan expenditure need to continue?

- How does one handle the problem of corruption in civil services? Does the CVC need to be strengthened? Are changes needed in the Prevention of Corruption Act? What about changes in Articles 12 and 311 of the Constitution?
- How does the government become more accountable to citizens and business? Are changes in Secretariat procedures necessary? Are there adequate redressal mechanisms for grievances? Are there lessons from using IT to improve public governance, say in Bangalore? Are there examples from say, Bangalore or Hyderabad, where citizen action has made the government more transparent and accountable?
- Why is the administrative law or subordinate legislation not readily available? Why is there so much discretion in interpreting these rules? Can these not be rationalized and unified so as to reduce discretion? Can they not be made publicly available? Are there lessons from States that have successfully reformed administrative law? Is there an Official Secrets Act issue?
- Does administrative reform mean only the executive, or should one also talk about the legislature and the judiciary? Has civil society been able to exert countervailing pressure against inefficient functioning of these three organs of State? Should one discuss decentralization through *panchayats* and local bodies?[6]

## Conclusion

The reform agenda can successfully work if the basic form of the Government is changed into two simple layers: policy and execution. For example, between them, the Central and State Governments spend roughly Rs. 42,000 crore annually on direct poverty alleviation. If this sum were disbursed directly among the five-crore-odd poor families in the country, they would each get Rs. 800 per annum, lifting them out of poverty. Clearly the theory of percolation is overtaken by the evaporation through the layers. There is no justification for parallel empires governing poverty eradication both at the Centre and the States, and for the replication of apparatus in state capitals and district headquarters. The Maharashtra Government, for instance, has transferred 22 critical functions from the state capital

Mumbai to the districts successfully. More could be done if *panchayats* are empowered, as has been tried in Madhya Pradesh.

Arguably, no system can be sustained if the execution is immune from accountability. Using a combination of modern management practices, information technology and transparency, the Government must set targets of efficiency — be it the issue of ration cards and passports or the clearances the citizen seeks. Andhra Pradesh Chief Minister N. Chandrababu Naidu holds weekly videoconferences on targets. Such management tools should be used to control the delivery systems.

In India, the mere fact of being employed by the Government affords immunity from accountability. This is totally unacceptable. There are provisions that govern civil servants on what they should not do, but none on what they should do. Very simply, there is a crying need to legislate efficiency benchmarks. The first step should be to abolish the immunity afforded by the concept of a public servant and introduce accountability.

### Getting it Right

* Privatize — not disinvest — state-owned enterprises, both at the Centre and in the states. Demarcate public services like health, education and infrastructure and privatize the rest.
* Abolish civil aviation, textiles, coal, mines, heavy industries, information and broadcasting, petroleum and natural gas, chemicals and fertilizers, food processing, communications, shipping and IT ministries. Also decentralize. There is no justification for rural development ministries both at Centre and in the states.
* Implement the Fifth Pay Commission's recommendations in their entirety. Abolish 3.5 lakh vacant posts, slash number of employees by 30 per cent and reduce decision-making layers from seven to three.
* Ensure accountability by punishing non-performing civil servants and rewarding doers.
* The Government needs to be professional. Abolish the IAS and introduce specialists for each ministry.

Source: *India Today*, September 2, 2002

The best way to do this may not be through legislation alone, but by ensuring people's participation. It is accepted wisdom that dissemination of information curbs discretionary practices that lead to corruption. Besides, transparency improves efficiency. Empowerment through right to information is a good beginning, but is not enough. The problem with the right to information strategy is that information would still need to be asked for.

Last year, the Rural Development Department wanted to set up bulletin boards in every village and *taluka* to inform people of the disbursal of funds under Central schemes. This would encourage citizens to question both babus and elected representatives. It is an idea worth initiating as a pilot case and then enlarging through legislation from the *panchayat* level to the Centre. Every decision must be communicated in real time using IT and media. This will spur accountability and trigger public participation.

The simple truth is that without people participation no system, however well designed, can deliver consistently. Therefore, large-scale computerization holds the key to effective implementation of administrative reforms.

# APPENDIX

- *Karnataka Administrative Reforms Commission, Interim Report,* Jan 2001
- *K. Santhanam Committee Report,* 1969
- *The Vellodi Report, The Administrative Reorganization and Economy Committee, 1965-67*
- *V.T. Krishnamachari Report, Indian and State Administrative Services and Problems of District Administration, August, 1962*
- *Government of Kerala Report, Chairman — E M S Nambudripad, July 1958*

## Karnataka Administrative Reforms Commission Interim Report Jan 2001

### Summary of Recommendations

- File Processing
- Rationalisation of Staff
- Reduce File Pendency
- Reduction of Meeting
- Rationalisation of Secretariat Departments
- Delegation of Powers
- Revision of the Secretariat Manual of Office Procedure
- Human Resource Development
- Introduction of Information Technology & Office Automation
- Office Modernisation
- DPAR & Finance Department
- Lack of Courtesy in dealing with the Public
- Grievances Redressal
- Non-Availability of Officials
- Reorganisation of District Offices
- Revenue Department

- Agriculture Department
- Forest Department

## Decentralisation

*Planning under Decentralisation*

- Every *Gram Panchayat* must be given matching grants equivalent to the resources collected, and fifty per cent of this amount must be spent on the social sector. Some differentiation may be shown between *Gram Panchayats* by categorizing them into different groups, given them weightage accordingly. The criteria so developed should be applicable for the *Gram Panchayat* and not for the district as a whole since even within a district there would be vast differences amongst villages. The criteria should be objective; the process of devolution of funds should be transparent. The criteria should be based on the Human Development Indicators, Infant Mortality Rate, Maternal Mortality Rate, Literacy Levels etc.
- Job chart of every village level functionary must be made available to every *Gram Panchayat* member.
- Even where the *Gram Panchayat* comprises of more than one village the *Gram Sabha* is called for all the villages at the same time. Such a type of meeting does not encourage participation and is wasteful. It would be better if a *Gram Sabha* is convened for each hamlet.
- Holding *Gram Sabha* meetings must be made compulsory. If the meetings are not held, there should be on devolution of funds to the gram panchayats. In an order issued in 1999, the department has made the Taluka Executive responsible for deciding the dates for the gram sabha in consultation with the President of the *Gram Panchayat*. The Secretary of the *Gram Sabha* has to prepare the agenda notes and make them available to the villages on a payment of Rs. 1-000 per copy. Instead of decentralizing the powers to call for the *Gram Sabhas* have been taken away from the *Gram Panchayat* and given to the *Taluk Panchayats*.

- Powers to convene the *Gram Sabhas* must be given to the *Gram Panchayats* only.
- The frequency of calling village level workers to *taluk* must be reduced.
- All the posts at the village level, must be made district cadres wherever they have not been made so far. This would not apply to honorary workers like the anganwadi workers.
- Action plan must be finalized by the end of May or June every year.
- Some lump sum grant should be given to the districts which the district could operate in the State list.
- Planning at all levels under the *zilla panchayat* system is a mere formality. Proper training must be given to all the officials, non-officials on how to utilize the various human development indicators for planning at the district level.
- The number of meetings at the *zilla panchayat* level must be reduced. On an average, every Chief Executive Officer is either chairman or member of about 52 committees. Most of these committees have to meet either monthly or quarterly. Such meetings take away much of the time of these officers and leave them with less time to actually tour and inspect the work. This applies also to other district level officers.
- Several of the State sector schemes which ought to be implemented at the district level itself should be transferred to the *zilla panchayats*.

## K. Santhanam Committee Report, 1969

### General Recommendations

8.1 We have made some detailed and specific recommendations in regard to the following:-

1. Directorate General of Supplies and Disposals.
2. Directorate General of Technical Development (Formerly Development Wing).

3. Import and Export Organisations.
4. Central Public Works Department.
5. Income-tax Department.
6. Customs and Central Excise Department.
7. Central Corporate Undertakings.

Recommendations in regards to these are in Annexure VII to XIII

8.2 We had dealt with preventive measures in Section 6 and have also made various suggestions in different parts of this report. We would like to deal with certain other matters of general importance in this Section.

8.3 We find that the Ministry of Home Affairs had examined the procedure to be adopted in dealing with anonymous complaints and issued comprehensive instructions on 27th July, 1962. The instructions issued strike a balance between the view that anonymous complaints should be ignored and the view that they should not be ignored.

8.4 We examined the procedure followed in regard to placing a Government servant under suspension. The relevant rules relating to control and discipline enabled the Central Government to place a Government servant under suspension in cases where

i. A disciplinary proceeding against him is contemplated or is pending; or
ii. A case against him in respect of any criminal offence is under investigation or trial.

There was some doubt regarding the point whether a member of All India Service could be placed under suspension when a disciplinary proceeding against him is contemplated. That doubt has been removed by certain recent judicial pronouncements. In our recommendations regarding control and discipline rules we have recommended suitable provisions. By another judgement pronounced in November, 1963 the Supreme Court declared that the power to suspend, as an interim measures, a member of the former Secretary of States Services vests only in the Central Government.

8.5 Placing of an officer under suspension has certain financial and other implications. We consider that some of the circumstances under which it would be appropriate to place a Government servant under suspension are —

1. Cases where investigation whether by the Police or departmental authorities, has commenced regarded —
   (a) any offence or conduct involving moral turpitude;
   (b) corruption; embezzlement or misappropriation of Government money; possession of disproportionate assets; misuse of official powers for personal gain;
   (c) serious negligence and dereliction of duty resulting in considerable loss to Government;
   (d) allegations which, if proved, may result in dismissal, removal or compulsory retirement;
2. Wherever continuance in office will prejudice the investigation trial or an inquiry (e.g. apprehended tampering...........)
3. Servant for offences which, if proved are likely...... In his conviction and consequent dismissal, removal or compulsory retirement from public services;
4. Desertion of duty;
5. Refusal or deliberate failure to carry out written orders of superior officers;
   1. Where continuance in office is likely to subvert discipline in the office in which the public servant is working.

8.6 We recommend the following procedure relating to (a) granting sanction to prosecute a Government servant where such sanction is required under any provision of law; and (b) the manner of dealing with petitions for withdrawal of prosecutions already launched.

8.7 As regards the first, a procedure was settled in 1949 according to which in cases investigated by the Special Policy Establishment and in which the sanction has to be accorded by the Central Government the Ministry of Home Affairs issues the sanction after obtaining the concurrence of the Ministry which controls the service to which the public servant proposed to be prosecuted belongs. The substantive decision whether sanction should be accorded or not is taken by the administrative Ministry. It has now been provided that in all such cases the Central Vigilance Commission will advise the Ministry of Home Affairs whether sanction should be accorded or not. The power to accord such sanction has also been centralized and vested in the Ministry of Home Affairs. This new procedure will remove many of the difficulties that arose under the previous procedure.

8.8 But the more difficult question is the manner of dealing with requests for withdrawal of prosecutions already launched. There are no judicial pronouncements which furnish a guide regarding the principles that should be observed in such matters. It is not difficult to visualise cases where the question of continuing or withdrawing a prosecution may assume deserved or underserved importance. It is also likely that various pressures may operate. We consider that it would not be desirable to leave such matters in a vague state of affairs. In our opinion some of the principles that should be observed are:-

(1) when once a case is put in a court it should be allowed to take its normal course,

(2) if in any case it becomes necessary to consider a petition that

    (a) the court has not commenced recording evidence;

    (b) it is clear from the records that the competent authority had not examined that merits of the case before according sanction; and

    (c) facts have come to light which would show that no offence had been committed by the accused.

But we would like to reiterate that departure from the normal principle of not entertaining petitions for withdrawal of prosecution after sanction has been accorded or the case has been put in court should be exceptional.

8.9 We have examined the question whether a Government servant who has been convicted by a court of law should immediately be dismissed from service on such conviction, or the Government should wait till he has executed his remedies available under the law by way of appeal or revision. According to instructions now in force, he should be dismissed immediately on his conviction. But where the advice of the Union Public Service Commission is required to be taken the latter prefers to wait till the final termination of the proceedings. It is obvious that a public servant who is convicted by a court cannot be allowed to function in his post. He has, therefore, to be removed from service or at least placed under suspension. No uniform rule without exceptions can be laid down. If the Government is legally advised then dismissal is certainly the best course. It may save the Government the subsistence allowance that has to be paid during suspension. On the other hand, if the legal advice is that there is a reasonable chance of the appeal being allowed, to continue that suspension would be preferable because in case the public servant succeeds in appeal he will have to be restored and paid his full salary and allowances.

In this connection we would suggest that the question of consulting the Union Public Service Commission in respect of Government servants who have been convicted by courts of law may be re-examined. While in departmental proceedings, which are of a quasi-judicial nature. Consultation with the Union Public Service Commission is a valuable safeguard the verdict of court of law is final so far as the Government is concerned unless it is reversed by a higher court. Therefore in all cases of conviction, we recommend that the consultation may be dispensed with.

8.10 We found that in the Directorate General Supplies and Disposals, the O&M Unit of the Directorate had undertaken a post-facto scrutiny of disposed of files to find out the nature of mistakes or irregularities that have occurred. We consider that this experiment could usefully be adopted in other organisations which deal with grant of contracts and licences, permits assessment, collection and refund of taxes, etc.

8.11 Misutilisation and trafficking in licences has become a scandal. We were informed that except certain categories of import licences granted under the Export Promotion Schemes licenses are not transferable. Frequently enough licensees commit a breach of the conditions of non-tranferability and proper utilization. Systematic efforts should be made to discover such breaches. We therefore, recommend that there should be a machinery for verification whether the conditions of the licenses are fulfilled.

8.12 One of the point mentioned to us with same emphasis was that in matters of giving contracts for construction and supplies that decisions should be taken by a committee and not by individuals if the amount involved is large, say rupees one lakh or more obviously this practice could also apply to grant of different kinds of licences. While the suggestion appears at first sight, attractive, there are two difficulties, viz: (1) possible blurring of responsibility and (ii) the committees being dominated by one forceful personality. We are of the opinion that in each department which has to deal with such matters, an attempt should be made to classify those matters which are best left to a committee for decision and those which are better left to be decided by individual officers.

8.13 Another matter that was brought to our notice was that undue secrecy in transacting Government leads to 'sale of information'. The extent to which secrecy should be observed is a question that could be answered only by each possible transaction of Government business should be open and in accordance with declared principles and procedures and there should not be any undue secrecy.

8.14 The Government gives grants to many non-official institutions engaged in social, literary, artistic or cultural activities. This form of assistance is certainly desirable, but at the same time care should be taken to see that the bodies and associations which take such grants functions properly. They should be asked to send their annual reports and audited accounts and some responsible officers should place on record that the grants had been utilized for the purpose for which they were made.

## The Vellodi Report, The Administrative Reorganization and Economy Committee, 1965-67

### Summary of Recommendations

*Panchayats*

1. The following considerations should weigh with Government in the context of introduction of *Panchayati Raj*:

   (a) The lowest unit of administration should be the *Panchayat*, identical with a Revenue Village

(b) The *Panchayat* should have well-defined functions and adequate resources to discharge them.

(c) *Panchayat* should link up with the subdistrict unit, which should take in a whole number of *Panchayats*.

(d) The democratic body at the sub-district level should have real powers.

(e) The nature of the democratic body at the district level should be decided on pragmatic rather than on theoretical grounds.

2. A fresh delimitation of *Panchayats* to make them co-terminous with existing revenue villages is not desirable, since delimitation of *Panchayats* has been completed only recently.

3. There is no need to accept the existing *Panchayats* as units of resurvey; the unit should be one, is most convenient from the technical angle; if the size of a *Panchayat* has to be altered in future, the portion added on or taken away should be whole number of the unit re-survey.

4. All existing *Panchayats* as also the Municipal and Corporation areas should be notified as Revenue Villages.

5. The Guruvayoor Township be deemed as part of the nearest village for general administrative and revenue purpose; for functions of local self-government it should retain its status as a Township.

6. There is no need to integrate the village staff and the *Panchayat* staff in the proposed set-up.

7. The village and *Panchayat* Officers in the new unit should be housed in the same building.

8. The revenues of the *Panchayat* should be collected by the *Panchayat* should be collected by the *Panchayat*'s staff; the Village Officers should collect land revenue and other dues to Government as at present.

9. *Panchayat* may utilize the services of Village Officers for the collection of their own revenues under Section 75 of the *Kerala Panchayats Act,* 1960.

10. Collectors have to be brought squarely into the picture of *panchayat* administration.
11. All District Collectors should be notified as Directors of *Panchayats* in their respective Districts.
12. All Revenue Divisional Officers should be notified as Deputy Directors of *Panchayats* in their respective Divisions.
13. The Directorate of *Panchayats* and its regional offices be abolished.
14. The District *Panchayat* Officers and subordinate staff should continue in their present form.
15. District *Panchayat* Officers should function as Personal Assistants to the Collectors in the *Panchayati Raj* wing which should be organized in all Collectorates.
16. The Directorate of Municipalities should be abolished and District Collectors should be notified as Directors of Municipalities in their respective Districts.
17. The staff of the Directorate and the regional officers of the Department of *Panchayats* and the staff of the Directorate of Municipalities should be distributed among the Collectorates.
18. *Panchayats* and Municipalities should be administered by the Agriculture and Rural Development Department at the Government level.
19. All mandatory functions under Section 57(1) of the Act should be undertaken by the *Panchayats*; the mandatory functions under Section 57(1) should not be abridged.
20. The list of discretionary functions in Appendix 111 should be notified immediately as mandatory.
21. Wherever such discretionary functions are now being discharged by departmental funds should be transferred to *Panchayats* and the concerned departmental officers made functionally responsible to the *Panchayats*.
22. In the circumstances that exist in the State at present, it would not entrust primary education to the *Panchayats*.
23. Government should go slow in the matter of entrustment of agency functions to the *Panchayats*.

24. Effective functional committees should be constituted in the *Panchayats* and the services of retired officials, technical men etc., should be untilised for the purpose.

25. If *Panchayats* should become effective units of local self-government their resources should be adequately built up.

26. Basic tax collected from all *Panchayat* areas should be treated as a common pool and distributed among *Panchayats* as following:-

    a) Grant towards meeting a part of the establishment charges should be given to all Third Grand Panchayats subject to the following:

       (i) the staff engaged should conform to the pattern approved by Government.

       (ii) the payment should be limited to the amount by which actual expenditure on establishment charges exceeds 25 per cent of the annual income of the *Panchayat* (excluding grants, loans and contributions).

    b) Grants should be given to *Panchayats* whose total annual income (including the establishment grant) is below Rs. 20,000 the quantum of grant being the difference between the total annual income and Rs. 20,000.

    c) The remainder of the basic tax should be distributed to all *Panchayats* on the basis of population, a suitable per capita rate to be determined for this purpose.

27. Section 67 of the *Panchayats Act,* 1960 should be suitably amended for the disbursement of grants to *Panchayats* on the above basis. When basic tax is made over to *Panchayats,* the payment of grants, *ad hoc,* should cease.

28. Transfer of departmental funds to *Panchayats* for the performance of departmental *Panchayats* for the performance of departmental functions should be outside the basic tax grants.

29. Surcharges on stamp duty should continue to be a source of revenue for *Panchayats*.

30. The collection of their own revenues by *Panchayats* is not quite satisfactory; as a mechanism to improve the collection of *Panchayat* revenues, Government may prescribe suitable provisions to with-hold part of the admissible basic tax grant, if the *Panchayat*'s collection of its own revenues falls below 75 per cent of the demand.

31. The collection of *Panchayats* revenues should be constantly watched and systematically reviewed by the Revenue Divisional Officers and the District Collectors.

## Administrative Efficiency

127. Responsibility at every level has to be clearly laid down; job-charts should be issued for all categories of officers; to make a quantitative evaluation of work possible, targets should be prescribed wherever the work done would lend itself to such prescription; yard-sticks should be devised to assess the exercise of control over subordinate officers by District Officers; Heads of Departments should be personally responsible for adherence to time-schedules etc. in Plan implementation.

128. Further powers to Heads of Departments and subordinate levels to the extent mentioned in Appendix VII should be delegated; Government should refuse to interfere in the area of delegated authority; when non-exercise of delegated authority is seen, a serious view of the concerned officer's conduct should be taken; when such non-exercise is a continuous course of conduct, the concerned officer should be found unfit to hold-his post and remove.

129. Urgent steps should be taken to prepare detailed questionnaires, Department-wise, so that a review of work done in each Department's subordinate officers and its evaluation are possible.

130. Prescribed scales of inspection should be scrupulously followed; advance programmes of inspections by officers should be obtained by the next higher level and the programmes of inspections watched and reviewed.

131. A time limit of one m should be fixed for submission of rectification reports and there should be a follow-up inspections, soon after receipt of rectifications reports.

132. An Inspection Register should be maintained by all Departments and Officers in which Inspecting Officers can enter remarks during "cursory" inspections.

133. The defects in touring mentioned in 7.11 should be remedied; hit and run type of touring should be discouraged; a halt-march ratio should be prescribed for all categories to touring officers; tour programmes of inspecting officers should be so staggered that an inspecting officer does not visit the same officers or institution close on the heels of another.

134. Manuals should be prepared immediately for Departments which do not have them; draft Manuals of some Departments pending with Government should be approved and issued without delay; preparation of manuals should not be held over till after the unification of laws in the component parts of the states.

135. Conferences are useful, but have to be properly planned; decisions taken at conferences should be considered as authority to take consequential action.

136. All Heads of Departments should scrutinize their lists of periodicals and weed out obsolete and unnecessary items.

137. A simple system of Office procedures well knit and free from loop-holes, which cuts down delays and unproductive work to the minimum, should be devised by the O&M wing.

138. Supervisory staff should sit and work with the staff; Heads of Office should walk around the office and see how work is being carried on.

139. Canteen attached to offices should be "out of bound" to clerks except during meal time. If meals are served in canteens at a fixed hour of the day, a tea/coffee trolley should be brought around to the rooms where the clerks sit and work.

140. Every office of any importance should have a Reception Room with a telephone; the receptionist should have a

thorough knowledge of the office and should be able to give useful and correct information to visitors.

141. The workload for a clerk in the office of a Head of Department should be fixed as 10 currents per day; for a clerk in a Regional or District Officers it should be 12 currents a day and for a clerk in a sub-District office, 15 currents.

142. On the basis of the workload suggested above, a permanent overall reduction of 5 per cent in the number of clerks would be possible; the strength of clerks in each office should be refixed on the basis of the yard-sticks indicated.

143. In all offices where the strength of peons is 5 or more, one fifth of the total strength should be retrenched.

144. The ratio for supervisory ministerial officers vis-a-vis clerks, should be 1:8 in the office of the Heads of Departments, 1:10 in Regional and District Officers and 1:12 in Sub District officers. The ratio in the Secretariat should be refixed as 1:6.

145. It is desirable to have a leave reserve of 5 per cent of the cadre strength for categories in which even short leave vacancies cannot be left unfilled without detriment to work and where filling up of such vacancies takes time.

146. Persons who take earned leaves for a minimum period of not less than a month should be allowed to surrender an equal period of earned leave if admissible and get leave allowance for the leave surrendered.

147. Government should impress on all officers the importance of proper record management.

148. The machinery for anti-corruption work and Vigilance is adequate; however, significant results cannot be achieved unless Heads of Departments realize that the fight against corruption has to be incessantly carried on by the Departmental agencies themselves. Vigilance Officers of Departments should be well acquainted with relevant decision of Courts, apart from the Rules themselves.

149. To ensure speed and better results in the conduct of anti-corruption work, the recommendation made in para 7.35 should be implemented.

150. Public relations work should make greater impact on the rural population; at the Block-level the work should be done by the Extension Officers for *Panchayats*.
151. Government should examine whether the two monthly magazines issued by the Department of Public Relations serve any useful purpose.
152. Public relations work, to be successful, has to be anticipatory in character.
153. Proper training should be given to Public Relations Officers.

## V.T. Krishnamachari Report, Indian and State Administrative Services and problems of District Administration, August, 1962

## Urban Bodies and *Panchayati Raj* Institutions and Other Special Problems

### 2. Urban and Rural Administration

Plan of social and economic development of rural areas have to be linked up closely with those of adjoining urban areas. There has to be continuous coordination in respect of programmes of agricultural production, planning of markets and communications, education, water supply, medical relief etc. Para 1.

Medium and large towns and cities have to be administered as separate units with their own bodies. The arrangements for establishing close relationships between municipal and rural institutions provided under the *Panchayat Raj* legislation enacted so far in the form of representation for municipal bodies in *panchayat* samitis and zila parishads and constitution of joint committees are indicated in Statement X. Para 2.

The following approach is suggested in devising suitable arrangements for joint planning and coordination at each level without resorting to any amendments in the legislation at this stage.

1. Towns with small population which have their own *Panchayats* may be represented on the *panchayat* samitis. Frequently towns with population upto 10,000 fall within this group.

2. In the case of urban bodies constituted for small towns such as the headquarters of block, tahsils, etc. joint committees of these bodies and *panchayat* samitis may be established.
3. Coordination with large and medium sized towns in a district such as district headquarters can be achieved at the level of the zila parishads by means of joint committee or mutual representation or cooperation of members of committees dealing with different subjects.
4. Systematic regional planning is needed for cities with a population of 100,000 or more and a suitable joint machinery should be set up in which the cities and rural areas represented.
5. The district planning committees should be reconstituted with representatives of the zila parishads, the municipal councils and the district officers to see that (1) arrangement are made for preparing a district plan in which both rural and urban plans are shown together with their interrelations.

## Additional Requirements and Methods of Recruitment of I.A.S Officers

The I.A.S cadre has risen from 803 in 1948 to 2147 on 1st January, 1962. The increased tempo of economic and social developments in the Third and Fourth Five Year Plans will necessitate further increase in the cadres for which careful estimates should be made.

Review of the future requirements of I.A.S officers made by the Ministry of Home Affairs early in 1961 indicated that the total strength of the Services which was 2036, based on 1015 senior posts under the State Governments and 404 senior posts at the Centre (Statement 11) would have to be increased to 2400 by the end of this Third Plan comprising of 1162 senior posts under the States and 463 senior posts at the centre.

State Governments have generally agreed with the assessment made by the Ministry of Home Affairs. The total strength of the cadre on 1st July, 1962, was 2252 (Statement 111). Taking into account the increases anticipated in the cadres of States, the total strength would reach the figure of 2400 by the end of the Third Plan period as estimated by the Ministry of Home Affairs.

The number of posts to be filled through direct recruitment by April 1966 is estimated as 525.

It is recommended that appointment of 115 candidates may be made to IAS/IFS every year during the next 4 years on the basis of the annual competitive examination for making up the shortages in the IAS cadres. This can be done without impairing the efficiency of the Services.

In view of the difficult position regarding availability of IAS officers the recommendation of the Second Pay Commission for raising the age of superannuation may be accepted. Pending such re-examination, IAS officers who are capable of efficient services may be continued in services or re-employed on a basis similar to that now adopted for scientific and technical officers.

## Government of Kerala Report

Chairman — E M S Nambudripad, July 1958

### Summary of Recommendations

*The Panchayats*

1. *Panchayats* should be made the basic units of administration at the village level.
2. The functions of *panchayats* may be divided into three categories:-
   (i) Those in respect of which they would have full devolution of powers;
   (ii) Those for which the *Panchayats* will function with executive delegation of powers as agents of Government; and
   (iii) those in respect of which the role of *Panchayats* will be mostly advisory.
3. There should be one *Panchayat* for each revenue village but where the population is less than five thousand, two or more villages may be conveniently combined.
4. Where the population is above 25000, the question of converting the unit into a Municipality may be considered,

provided the area is small, compact and has distinct urban characteristics. "Townships" may be formed in places which are distinctly urban, but have small population and area.

5. *Panchayats* should be constituted on the basis of direct election by adult franchise of one member for approximately one thousand voters. One women member may be co-opted by the *Panchayat* if no woman is elected. But there is no need for co-option for any special groups or organisations.
6. *Panchayats* should have functional committees for different subjects consisting both of *Panchayat* members and others who are interested in public welfare. There could also be ward committees for each ward in the *Panchayat*.
7. The provisions regarding mandatory functions in the Kerala *Panchayat* Bill may be accepted. Registration of birth and deaths may also be included among the mandatory functions.
8. In the exercise of these functions the *Panchayats* should have sufficient administrative powers to accord sanctions etc.
9. In the field of 'social services programmes' and 'development work' the *Panchayat* should function with executive responsibility as agents of Government.
10. In the field of education, Government-owned primary schools should be maintained and run by the *Panchayats*.
11. In the field of health the *Panchayats* should have the responsibility to maintain and run the rural dispensaries, primary health centres, child welfare centres and the maternity homes.
12. When new institutions are opened in the village, as many of them as possible, should be entrusted to the *Panchayats*.
13. It will be the responsibility of the *Panchayats* to formulate the programme of development work and to implement as many of them as would lie within their sphere.
14. There should be a continuous search to effect greater and greater delegation of executive responsibility to the *Panchayats*.

15. The village revenue establishment may form part of the *Panchayats* and the *Panchayats* may be made the agents for the collection of land revenue.
16. 50 per cent of the basic tax collected by the *Panchayats* may be allotted to them and the remaining 50 per cent of the total for the State may be distributed to the *panchayats* on the basis of needs.
17. The same revenue staff now attending to the collection of revenues should continue to do so in the new set up also. The present Village Officer may function as the Revenue Officer of the *panchayat* and the village Assistant or the Manon as the Revenue Assistant.
18. The work of the revenue staff will as now be inspected, supervised and reviewed by Tahsildars and the higher officers.
19. There is no need for continuing the conventional hereditary system of village officers now prevalent in the Malabar area.
20. In order to link the *Panchayats* organically with extension and development work, each *Panchayat* may be given the services of a Gram Sewak who will function as its extension and development assistant.
21. For the proper exercise of these mandatory functions, the *panchayats* may be assigned the sources of revenue listed in the Draft Kerala Panchayat Bill.
22. For implementing the functions in respect of which the Panchayats will be given executive responsibility specific grants for each subject should be made which will be equivalent approximately to the amount of expenditure that would have been incurred by Government.
23. The *Panchayat* budget would be scrutinized by the Tahsildar before it is approved by the *Panchayat*. Once the *Panchayat* has accorded sanction to the Budget, it should not be required to send it to higher authority for approval.
24. If the *Panchayat* persistently defaults in its functions, the Collector should have the power to supersede it or to withdraw from it such of the functions as in respect of which the default has occurred.

25. The *Panchayats* will have to employ their own staff for performing their mandatory functions.
26. The *Panchayat* Executive Officers, Revenue Officers, Revenue Assistant, the Gram Sewak, the Health Assistant, and the staff of the institutions which will be transferred to the maintenance of the *Panchayats* may be recruited on the basis of a district cadre and their pay and allowances may be borne by the State.
27. A certain amount of administrative control over the staff should be vested with the *Panchayats*.
28. The powers of the *Panchayats* and the departmental officers over the staff should be clearly defined and there should be no room for conflict between the two.
29. There will be a complete re-shaping of the pattern and mobility of staff in the *Panchayats* and in the Revenue and the Local Bodies departments.
30. Village Courts should be formed by nomination from a panel of names suggested by the *Panchayats*.
31. There is no need to appoint a legal member to these courts.
32. The powers proposed to be vested in the Village Courts under the Kerala Village Courts Bill are adequate and may be accepted.

## Notes

1. Aiyar, Shankar (2002) "Can we Reform Babudom," *India Today,* September 2, 2002.
2. Budget 2002-03.
3. Singh, Hoshiar and Mohinder Singh (1989) *Public Administration in India: Theory and Practice,* New Delhi: Sterling Publishers.
4. Gerlad E. Caiden has defined administrative reform as "the artificial inductment of administrative transformation against resistance." John Montgomery defines administrative reform as a "political process designed to adjust the relationship between a bureaucracy and other elements in a society or within the bureaucracy itself in order to change the behaviour of the public service." According to Professor Maheshwari, administrative reform seeks to apply new ideas to administration, and thus, entails values.
5. Ramachandran, Padma (1996) *Public Administration in India,* New Delhi: National Book Trust.
6. These questions were raised during a series of seminars under *Agenda for Improving Governance* (2002) by the Rajiv Gandhi Institute for Contemporary Studies.

# 5

## Suggested Agenda for Administrative Reforms

JAYAPRAKASH NARAYAN

> 'India has the potential to show the fastest growth over the next 30 to 50 years. Growth could be higher than 5 per cent over the next 30 years and close to 5 per cent as late as 2050 if development proceeds successfully............While growth in the G6, Brazil, Russia and China is expected to slow significantly over the next 50 years, India's growth rate remains above 5 per cent throughout the period. India's GDP outstrips that of Japan by 2032......India has the potential to raise its US dollar income per capita in 2050 to 35 times current levels.'
>
> **Goldman Sachs**,
> *Dreaming With BRICs: The Path to 2050,*
> *Global Economics Paper No: 99.*

There is a "feel good" factor that characterizes the assessment of the Indian economy today. The possibility of stupendous economic growth has become a regular feature in the media. The way we formulate our economic policy will determine whether India will achieve stupendous economic growth as is being portrayed. However, failure to improve our governance process will certainly make it impossible for us to achieve higher growth rates. We need to remember that the economic growth rate of a country is not merely a product of economic policies and productive capacity of its industry and agriculture. The economic growth rate of a country is also contingent on the way it governs itself. The collapse of erstwhile Soviet Union bears testimony to this fact. This, combined with the experience of the transition countries, demonstrate that corruption and mis-governance are increasingly acting as impediments to growth. Let me throw in a few more examples:

- The *"Anti-Corruption in Transition: A Contribution To The Policy Debate,"* a survey by World Bank and EBRD in 2000 has demonstrated that bribes were acting as regressive tax amounting to 5 per cent of the revenue for small firms, 4 per cent of revenue for medium firms and 3 per cent for large enterprises in East Europe. It is pertinent to ask an important question here, can an economy prosper if corruption acts as a regressive tax?

- A study by Tanzi and Davoodi titled *"Corruption Growth And Public Finances,"* observed that one point increase in corruption reduced the ratio of direct taxes to GDP by 1.8 percentage points, while the indirect taxes fell by 1.2 percentage points to GDP. Further, individual income taxes declined by 0.63 per cent of GDP with one point increase in corruption.

While the above examples pertain to the impact of corruption on the economy, there is a growing problem of organized crime impacting the growth in the economy. Many transition countries and economies of developing countries are increasingly becoming hostage to the activities of organized crime. The recent stamp scam in our country is also a pointer in this direction. In a well-functioning democracy, the political process ought to find answers to such governance problems. It is through the process of elections that a democratic choice is exercised on solutions to be adopted for various governance problems. Every election holds a promise for peaceful change. People in India have been voting for change time and again. But the political process is locked into a vicious cycle, and has become a part of the problem. There are six factors complicating the political process, perpetuating the status quo. First, election expenditures are large, unaccounted and mostly illegitimate. For instance, expenditure limit for assembly elections in most major states was Rs. 6,00,000 until recently, when it was revised to Rs. 1 million. In reality average expenditure in most states is several multiples of this, sometimes exceeding Rs. 10 million. Most of this expenditure is incurred to buy votes, bribe officials and hire musclemen. Such large, unaccounted expenditure can be sustained only if the system is abused to enable multiple returns on investment. Rent seeking behaviour is therefore endemic to the system.

Most of this corruption is in the form of control of transfers and postings, which in turn sustains a system of retail corruption for a variety of routine services, regulatory functions and direct transfer of resources through government programmes. Large leakages in public expenditure, and collusion in contracts and procurement are extremely common. The economic decision-making power of the state is on the wane as part of the reform process. But as the demand for illegitimate political funds does not decrease, corruption shifts to the core areas of state functioning, like crime investigation. Robert Wade studied this phenomenon of corruption, and described the dangerously stable equilibrium that operates in Indian governance. This vicious chain of corruption has created a class of political and bureaucratic 'entrepreneurs' who treat public office as big business.

Second, as the vicious cycle of money power, polling irregularities, and corruption has taken hold of the system, electoral verdicts cease to make a difference to people. Repeated disappointments made people come to the conclusion that no matter who wins the election, they always end up losing. As incentive for discerning behaviour in voting has disappeared, people started maximizing their short-term returns. As a result, money and liquor are accepted habitually by many voters. This pattern of behaviour is responsible for converting politics and elections into big business. As illegitimate electoral expenditure skyrocketed, the vicious cycle of corruption got further strengthened. With public good de-linked from voting, honesty and survival in public office are further separated.

Third, this situation bred a class of political 'entrepreneurs' who established fiefdoms. In most constituencies, money power, caste clout, bureaucratic links, and political contacts came together perpetuating politics of fiefdoms. Entry into electoral politics is restricted literally, as people who cannot muster these forces have little chance of getting elected. While there is competition for political power, it is often restricted between two or three families over a long period of time; parties are compelled to choose one of these individuals or families to enhance their chances of electoral success. Parties thus are helpless, and political process is stymied. Absence of internal democratic norms in parties and the consequent oligarchic control has denied a possibility of rejuvenation of political process through establishment of a vicious cycle.

Fourth, in a centralized governance system, even if people wisely use the vote, public good cannot be promoted. As the citizen is distanced from the decision-making process, the administrative machinery has no capacity to deliver public services that are cost-effective and of high quality. A climate that cannot ensure better services or good governance breeds competitive populism to gain electoral advantage. Such populist politics have led to serious fiscal imbalances.

Fifth, fiscal health can be restored only by higher taxes, or reduced subsidies or wages. The total tax revenues of the union and states are of the order of only 15 per cent of GDP. Higher taxation is resisted in the face of ubiquitous corruption and poor quality services. Desubsidization is always painful for the poor who do not see alternative benefits accruing from the money saved by withdrawal of subsidies. A vast bureaucracy under centralized control can neither be held to account, nor is wage reduction a realistic option.

Sixth, elected governments are helpless in changing this perilous situation. As the survival of the government depends on the support of legislators, their demands have to be met. The legislator has thus become the disguised, unaccountable executive controlling all facets of government functioning. The local legislator and the bureaucrats have a vested interest in denying local governments any say in real decision making. The vicious cycle of corruption and centralized, unaccountable governance is thus perpetuated.

This vicious cycle of corruption and centralized, unaccountable governance can be addressed effectively through various reform measures listed as follows:

## I Electoral Reforms

*a) Candidate Disclosure*

The March 13 Supreme Court (SC) verdict on candidate disclosures declared Section 33B of the *"Representation of the People (3rd Amendment) Act, 2002 (Amendment Act)"* illegal, null and void, and reiterated its earlier judgment on May 2, 2002. On May 2, the SC held that citizens have the fundamental right to know the antecedents of candidates for elective office, as part of freedom of expression guaranteed under Article 19(1) of the Constitution. But Section 33A of the Amendment Act provided for disclosure of only part of the criminal record. No other disclosure including assets and liabilities of candidates was required.

Section 33 (B) specifically sought to nullify the Court judgment of May 2, by declaring, "Notwithstanding anything contained in any judgment, decree or order of any court or any direction, order or another instruction issued by the Election Commission, no candidate shall be liable to disclose or furnish any such information, in respect of his election, which is not required to be disclosed or furnished under this Act or the rules made thereunder". It is this provision whose constitutionality was challenged. The Supreme Court on March 13, 2003 declared that obtaining relevant information about the candidates is indeed a fundamental right under Article 19 (1), and as the Parliament had no power to make such a law abridging fundamental rights [Article 13 (2)], such a law is void.

With the final judgment of the Supreme Court in place, disclosures are now mandatory and irreversible. The Election Commission has issued a revised notification removing the power of Returning Officers rejecting nominations on grounds of false information.

The key provisions of the legislation include candidate's disclosure of his/her:

1. Criminal antecedents
2. Assets and liabilities
3. Educational qualifications

It has been proven by *Lok Satta*'s activism that civil society groups, with media support, by publicizing information and putting pressure on the political parties, can improve candidate choice in the long-term. *Lok Satta*'s experience shows that major parties will refrain from nominating new candidates with criminal record, provided people's movements are strong enough to make candidate choice a key issue. Along with weeding out the criminal elements from politics, the reform efforts should also focus on providing legitimate resources for political activity.

*b) Political Funding Reform*

Accountable and legitimate political party expenditure and campaign finance is at the heart of the fight against corruption. A law to this effect having far-reaching consequences has seen the light of the day. The Election and Other Related Laws (Amendment Bill, 2003) (Funding Reform Bill) was a crucial change proposed in the Indian electoral process. *Lok Satta*, CSDS and *Lok Niti* had been advocating funding reform and direct state funding in elections. The May-June 2001 issue of *Lok Satta Times* examined the issue of political funding and detailed proposals had been put forward for reform. Presentations were made to ministers, leaders of opposition and key officials. Except for public funding, most of the key provisions proposed by civil society groups found place in the Bill introduced first in Lok Sabha on 19$^{th}$ March, 2002, and the revised Bill was introduced in Parliament on 13$^{th}$ May, 2003, after incorporating changes recommended by the Parliamentary Standing Committee on Home Affairs. The Election and Other Related Laws (Amendment) Bill, 2003 (Bill No. 18 of 2003) was approved by both Houses of Parliament in August 2003, and became law in September with the assent of the President. The law accomplished the following objectives:

First, it removed the loophole inserted in 1974 with respect to election expenditure ceiling in the form of explanation 1 under Section 77 of the Representation of the People Act, 1951. In a brazen display of dishonesty and political chicanery, the law was amended in 1974, and all expenditure incurred or authorised by a political party or by any other individual or body of persons or association was exempted from election expenditure ceiling. This amendment made a mockery of the election expenditure limits, and most parties and candidates violated the spirit of the law with impunity. This legal infirmity now stands removed by Section 4 of the new law, whereby only the travel expenditure incurred by leaders of political parties is exempt from election expenditure limits. For recognised political parties, the number of leaders whose travel costs are exempt is limited to forty, and for other parties, to twenty. By any standard, this is a reasonable exemption. Now, all other election-related expenditure incurred by a party, or person will be counted for ceiling purposes and shall not exceed the limits imposed by law – currently Rs. 10,00,000 for Assembly constituencies and Rs. 25,00,000 for Lok Sabha in major states.

Second, full tax exemption to individuals and corporates on all contributions to political parties is a strong incentive for open contributions to political parties. Parties need money for organization and mobilizing public opinion, and to compete in the marketplace of ideas. Candidates need money to get themselves known and to reach out to the voters and communicate effectively. Our failure to evolve rational incentives for political funding has severely distorted the electoral process. Parties and candidates have habitually abused their political clout to extort money, and the license-permit raj of the past gave ample opportunities for unaccounted resource mobilization. This ambivalence led to several flip-flops in the past. The Companies Act was amended in 1960 allowing corporate contributions to political parties. But in 1969, at the height of the license-permit raj, such contributions were prohibited.

Then in 1985, Rajiv Gandhi government amended the law again, permitting companies to contribute up to 5 per cent of their average three years net profits for political purposes. However, in the absence of tax incentives, most companies preferred to fund parties clandestinely for a variety of reasons – on account of the ubiquitous black economy, for fear of retribution from rival parties, and as a bribe or extortion money for favours received or anticipated, or avoiding harassment. For the first time, the law now provides for full tax exemption to individuals and corporates for all contributions to registered political parties. Sections 80 GGB, and 80 GGC have been inserted to this effect. Considering this, the tax incentive provided by the recent law is a vital step in encouraging open and accountable funding of parties in the long run.

Third, as a corollary to the previous provision, all contributions of Rs. 20,000 and above must be disclosed by the party to the Election Commission, and such information will be in the public domain. This would ensure accountability and curb the inflow of black money in politics.

Fourth, indirect public funding to candidates of recognized political parties – including free supply of electoral rolls (already in vogue), and such items by the Election Commission as are decided in consultation with the Union government.

Fifth, equitable sharing of time by the recognized political parties on the cable television network and other electronic media (public and private). This is by far the most far-reaching reform from a long-term perspective. The recognized parties will now get free broadcasting time in all electronic media. If the Election Commission applies this provision creatively, not only will parties get free time, but we can have exciting debates between candidates and parties. This has the potential to transform the nature of political campaigning, and will reduce campaign costs dramatically. In one stroke, parties in India have been given a powerful platform to reach voters free of cost.

However, some issues still remain. There are no penalties for donors for non-disclosure of funding. Auditing by a chartered accountant from a panel approved by CAG has been deleted (from the earlier draft). Direct public funding to candidates or parties, if implemented, would promote performance-based candidates and parties. The vibrant functioning of political parties is also contingent on the internal democracy of the political parties and the effectiveness of anti-defection provisions.

*c) Political Party Reform*

Political recruitment has suffered a great deal, and bright young people are no longer attracted to politics. Centralized functioning of parties is imposing an enormous burden on leadership to manage the party bureaucracy, leaving little time for evolving sensible policies or governance. Party leaders are helpless in candidate selection, and the choice is often between Tweedledum and Tweedledee. An important reform to improve the quality of politics and restore credibility would be a law to regulate political parties' functioning, without in any way restricting leadership choice and policy options. A law needs to be enacted to regulate political parties in four key aspects.

Membership and disciplinary action would be a crucial focus area ensuring internal party checks. Leadership choice by regular, secret, democratic ballot is the second key feature. This will be accompanied with formal processes to challenge the party leadership without fear of retribution. The third suggested reform would be transparency and public auditing of party funds and expenditure. Finally, choice of candidates for elective office to be decided by members or their elected delegates through secret ballot. The provisions can be similar to Article 21 of the German basic law and federal law to regulate parties.

*d) Strengthening Anti-Defection Provisions*

The provisions of the Tenth Schedule essentially disqualify a member elected on a party symbol if he voluntarily gives up membership of that party, or if he votes, or abstains from voting in the legislature contrary to any direction ('whip') issued by his party.

But, if one-third of the members or more stray from the party line, and claim that the legislature party has split, and they constitute a new group, then disqualification does not apply. The presiding officer of the house concerned is the final authority to determine disqualification. All disqualification proceedings are deemed to be proceedings of the legislature under Articles 122 and 212, and therefore no court shall have any jurisdiction in respect of such matters.

However, anti-defection provisions failed to prevent defections. The only novel feature now is that individual defections invite disqualification, while collective defection is perfectly legitimate and is amply rewarded! As a result splits are engineered, and constitutional coups are planned with meticulous precision, and careful conspiracy. Several parties 'split' even in Parliament, and as the JMM case testifies, the defecting members benefited immensely.

The 1997 case of defections from BSP in UP proved how partisan speakers could actually create new arithmetic while applying anti-defection provisions! Twelve of the 69 legislators of BSP violated party whip, and in a perverse order, speaker Kesari Nath Tripathi refused to disqualify them, though they clearly constituted less than a third of the legislature party. The matter went to courts, and died a natural death as their lordships could not come to a conclusion before the expiry of the term of the house on the weighty issue of what number constituted a third of 69! Recently in January 2003, the roles are reversed, and Mayawati engineered defection of 8 MLAs in the 23 member Congress legislature party, and the same speaker Kesari Nath Tripathi recognized them as a separate party, instead of disqualifying them!

There is however one major unintended consequence of anti-defection provisions. The intention was to prevent change of power in gross violation of popular mandate. But in effect, violation of party whip on any vote attracts disqualification. Party legislators who may honestly differ on a piece of legislation are now forced to submit to the will of the leadership. The ill-conceived legislation on Muslim women's maintenance after the Supreme Court verdict in the Shah Bano case is one sad example. If the Congress MPs had freedom of choice, that Bill would never have become law. That folly, and the resultant outcry forced the party to overcompensate to appease the enraged public. Unlocking the gates of the disputed structure in

Ayodhya, the '*silanyas*' under the watchful eye of Buta Singh, the then Home Minister, and the launch of the 1989 election campaign from Ayodhya with the promise of *Ramraj* – all these followed. The rest is history. An even more shameful episode is the direction issued by the Congress party to its MPs not to vote on the impeachment proceedings against Justice Ramaswamy in 1991. Consequently, judicial accountability collapsed, and eventually power of appointment of judges has been usurped by the judiciary!

In an effort to rectify the above distortions, the Cabinet's proposed legislation not only makes it mandatory for all those switching political sides – whether singly or in groups – to resign their legislative membership and seek re-election, but also bars legislators from holding, post-defection, any office of profit. For added measure, it puts limits on the size of ministries. Under the proposed changes, applicable both to Parliament as well as state assemblies, the strength of a council of ministers cannot exceed 15 per cent of the size of any legislature. Now that the Cabinet has decided to act, the opportunity must be utilized to remove the distortions in our party system. While defection by one or many should incur disqualification, three safeguards are needed to ensure healthy parliamentary debate, and curtail autocratic tendencies of party bosses.

First, party whip, and disqualification for violation must apply only for a vote affecting the survival of government – money bills, and confidence or no-confidence motions. On all other issues, members should have freedom of vote. Second, there should be recognition of legitimate splits in a party. If party bosses are utterly autocratic, or if their policies are blatantly unconstitutional, then the members must have an opportunity to rebel, and even split the party. On such occasions, the split should first take place in the party fora in a transparent and public manner after a statutory notice of, say at least a month, and after the members or delegates are allowed a free vote. A resultant split in the legislature wing should be recognized irrespective of the proportion the splitting members constitute. Third, past evidence clearly suggests that a partisan presiding officer loyal to the government cannot be trusted with the power to decide on disqualification. That power rightfully belongs to the Election Commission. Parties would do well to act with foresight and make the EC the final authority on all such matters. If these safeguards are incorporated, the new amendment will be a huge step forward in eliminating horse-trading and promoting clean politics.

Apart from the above mentioned amendments to the Indian Constitution, simple measures such as making the Post Office a nodal agency for electoral registration will go a long way in strengthening our democracy by substantially reducing polling irregularities.

*e) Eliminating Polling Irregularities*

There is evidence to suggest that the electoral rolls are severely flawed, and false voting by impersonation is rampant. As a result, many decent candidates are at a disadvantage, when compared to those who muster money and muscle power, and with trained cadres. The compensatory errors of rival candidates neutralize each other, and the final outcome is usually unaffected. However, given the local electoral compulsions in a flawed system, the parties are forced to look for 'strong' candidates who can manipulate the polling process, thus undermining and discrediting democracy and governance.

Simple procedural improvements will substantially ensure the purity of elections. A small yet significant step to facilitate increased access and more transparency is to use the existing post offices as nodal agencies for voter registration. Let us examine some figures to gain more clarity into the problem. About 15 per cent of rural electoral rolls and 40 per cent of urban rolls are defective. And last but not the least, voter registration is inaccessible to the people. Incorporating the existing post office as nodal agency is the best solution. Without any massive capital re-allocation, the change would bring the government at the citizen's doorstep.

Display and sale of rolls of local polling stations, sale of statutory forms; receipt and verification of applications for additions, deletions and changes for a fee (if EC accepts the procedure) can all be easily accomplished. Registration of new voters and changes at post offices with provision for appeal (if EC accepts and rules are amended) could also be done. The Election Commission (EC) could also assist during revision of rolls by verifying addresses etc. (if EC seeks it). The issue has been pending for over two years. Limited changes are expected soon. Presently, the EC and Postal department have agreed to incorporate post offices in a phased manner. Finally, actual registration at the post office would involve a change in the rules.

Another effective reform would be to make re-polling mandatory whenever tendered votes (proof of rigging by impersonation) exceed a fixed percentage (say 1 to 2 per cent) of votes polled in a polling station. This will significantly reduce the incentive for rigging. Compulsory voter photo-identity cards issued to all voters would be an effective mechanism to check bogus voting. These measures will cleanse the electoral process substantially. However, to reduce the role of caste and religion in politics or to relegate the primordial politics into the background, there is a need to usher systemic changes such as proportional representation and in ensuring direct election of Head of Government in States and Local Governments.

*f) Proportional Representation*

The first-past-the-post (FPTP) system that India has adopted led to several distortions, given the passage of time and ingenuity of legislators. Politics of fiefdom at constituency level has forced the parties to rely on local strongmen. As a result, the political parties and independent candidates have astronomical election expenditure for vote buying and other illegitimate purposes. This has led to a significant weakening of the party platform and ideology, reducing elections to private power games. In many states, national parties have been marginalized, where their voting percentage falls below a threshold. Following from this, regional parties have occupied center stage in several pockets, holding larger interests at ransom.

All these failings find expression in bigger and long-term predicaments. The inability of all political parties to attract and nurture best talent is the primary issue. Difficulties of minority representation leading to ghetto mentality, backlash, and communal tension form another facet of the problem. Lastly, leadership is undermined by permanent reservation of constituencies (or regular rotation) in order to provide fair representation to SCs. The solution to this flawed system is adoption of a mixed system of election, combining FPTP system with proportional representation. This will be broadly based on the German model. The key features of the suggested system are as follows:

- The overall representation of parties in legislature will be based on the proportion of valid votes obtained by them.

- A party will be entitled to such a quota based on vote share only when it crosses a threshold, say 10 per cent of votes in a major state, and more in minor states.
- 50 per cent of legislators will be elected from territorial constituencies based on FPTP system. This will ensure the link between the legislator and the constituents.
- The balance 50 per cent will be allotted to parties to make up for their shortfall based on proportion of votes.

  eg 1): If the party is entitled to 50 seats in legislature based on vote share, but had 30 members elected in FPTP system, 20 more will be elected based on the party list.

  eg 2): If the party is entitled to 50 seats based on vote share, but had only 10 members elected in FPTP system, it will have 40 members elected from the list.
- The party lists will be selected democratically at the State or multi-party constituency level, by the members of the party or their elected delegates through secret ballot.
- There will be two votes cast by voters - one for a candidate for FPTP election, and the other for a party to determine the vote share of the parties.

It needs to be remembered that PR system can be effective only after internal functioning of political parties is regulated by law. Otherwise, PR system will give extraordinary power to party leaders and may prove counterproductive. However, the PR system has one more advantage, which needs to be reiterated. PR system, more than FPTP system, ensures better representation of women in legislatures.

*g) Enhancing Women's Representation*

There is overwhelming demand for fairer representation to women under the current FPTP system. Women are moving in the direction of near equal participation in only a handful of countries, such as Germany, Sweden, Norway, Denmark and Finland. In these societies, women have begun to seriously alter the very nature of politics, making enduring and substantial gains in every field. However, in all other countries, including the supposedly advanced democracies of western Europe and North America, where women exercise certain freedoms and have acquired the wherewithal for economic independence, female presence in legislatures remains small and relatively insignificant.

In India, the problem for women is more serious for several reasons. The participation of women in politics has declined both in quality and quantity. The representation of women in Lok Sabha has basically remained stagnant. Pervasive gender discrimination has resulted in sidelining even veteran women politicians. Also, the few women in leadership positions have not been able to encourage the entry of greater numbers of women in electoral and party politics, and are an ineffective majority within their own respective political groupings.

The $85^{th}$ Constitutional Amendment Bill introduced in Lok Sabha in December 1999 is both controversial and flawed. Reservation of constituencies with rotation of seats is both unpopular with legislators, and impractical. Such rotation will mean unseating of most incumbents in every election, leading to several problems. The elected women representatives will be unable to establish a political base. Proxy women candidates (family members and close confidants of incumbents) will become a dominant feature, leading to tokenism without empowerment. If an incumbent is sure to lose the constituency in rotation, there will be no incentive to perform well.

It becomes clear how the Bill proves to be counter-productive. An alternative Bill has been scripted to do away with the flaws in the existent Bill. It should be made mandatory for political parties to nominate women candidates in a third (or any other proportion prescribed by law) of the constituencies. Constituencies will not be reserved, and there will be no rotation. Each party will determine its nominees taking into account its own compulsions and local political realities. Certain checks within the system would ensure effective implementation. First, in order to ensure that parties put up women candidates in all regions and sub-regions in fair numbers, and do not nominate them only in weak constituencies, a group of constituencies (say, three parliamentary constituencies for State Assembly; and the State for Lok Sabha) shall be the unit for women's nomination. Second, if the number of women candidates of a party falls short of the prescribed percentage, for the shortfall of every woman candidate, two male candidates of the party shall lose the party symbol.

### *h) Direct Election of Head of Government in States and Local Governments*

The other systemic reform that is needed to isolate the executive from unwanted influences, as has been pointed out, is to ensure direct election of Head of Government in States and Local Governments.

As election costs have skyrocketed, candidates spend money in anticipation of rewards and opportunities for private gain after election. Legislators perceive themselves as disguised executive, and chief ministers are hard pressed to meet their constant demands. Postings, transfers, contracts, tenders, tollgates, parole, developmental schemes, and crime investigation - all these become sources of patronage and rent seeking. No government functioning honestly can survive under such circumstances. While the legislators never allow objective and balanced decision-making by the executive in the actual functioning of legislation, their role has become nominal and largely inconsequential. This blurring of the lines of demarcation between the executive and legislature is one of the cardinal features of the crisis of our governance system.

Therefore, separation of powers, and direct election are necessary in States and local governments. At the national level, such a direct election is fraught with serious dangers. Our linguistic diversity demands a parliamentary executive. Any individual seen as the symbol of all authority can easily become despotic, given our political culture. But in states, separation of powers poses no such dangers. The Union government, Supreme Court, constitutional functionaries like the Election Commission, UPSC, and CAG, and the enormous powers and prestige of the Union will easily control authoritarianism in any state. This necessitates adoption of a system of direct election of the head of government in states and local governments. The fundamental changes suggested find mention as under:

The legislature will be elected separately and directly, while the ministers will be drawn from outside the legislature. The legislature will have a fixed term, and cannot be dissolved prematurely except in exceptional circumstances (sedition, secession etc.) by the Union government. The head of government will have a fixed term, and cannot be voted out of office by the legislature. Any vacancy of office will be filled by a due process of succession. The elected head of government will have no more than two terms of office. Even though these changes may not be panacea to all evils in the present structure of legislature and executive, it will certainly encourage more healthy and vibrant democracy and democratic processes. Further, clear delineation of functions between Union and States, and among various tiers of local governments is also a necessary condition for a vibrant democracy. It is only a true federal structure that can ensure unity in this multi ethnic and multi religious society.

## II. Federalism and Local Governments

There is a need to ensure periodic review of the Seventh Schedule to facilitate changes in the Union-State jurisdiction to suit the requirements of changing times. Clearer separation of powers between Union and States can be effected by further subdividing list III subjects (concurrent list), and providing for demarcation with minimal overlap. Special powers would be given to the Union to preserve unity and national integrity. Terrorist offences, inter-state trade, inter-state water resources, protection of linguistics and other minorities, equal employment and educational opportunities' provision across all regions would be key areas where Union will adjudicate.

Fiscal devolution forms a critical aspect of federalism. The Finance Commission would devolve the fiscal package and ensure that it is non-discretionary. Centrally sponsored schemes would be abolished, instead lumpsum grants would be given to States, with the exception of a few critical areas. These being population control, critical health schemes, national testing board for comparing educational standards, central fund for improving access to judiciary and enhancing judge:population ratio, fund for expansion and modernization of police forces.

A re-look at the All India Services is due, given the passage of time and the changing scenario. Creation of an Indian Judicial Service would ensure higher standards of recruitment and impartiality in trial courts. This will also serve as recruiting ground for higher courts. The practice of nominating governors needs to be abolished. Governors would either be directly elected chief executives, or the state legislature and local governments would elect a constitutional head of state (on par with the President).

In the area of legislative jurisdiction, the governor's power to reserve a Bill for President's assent under Article 200 needs to be done away with, or severely limited (by fixing a time limit of 60 days for President's assent or otherwise). For effective decentralization of power, Article 243 must be amended making it mandatory for the States to transfer to local governments the subjects listed under Eleventh and Twelfth Schedules. Local government subjects ($11^{th}$ Schedule and $12^{th}$ Schedule) to be incorporated in the Seventh Schedule, giving such division of powers a mandatory status. Strengthening of local governments is very important as it ensures a link between votes and public good, between taxes and services, and between authority and accountability. Access to justice can also be ensured through decentralized judicial apparatus. Creation of *Sthanika Nyayalayas*, for a population of 25,000 in rural and 50,000 in urban areas with summary procedures will result in speedy dispensation of justice. There are various other judicial reforms, which need to be implemented in right earnest.

## III. Judicial Reforms

People have great respect for the judiciary, and in general our faith in the judiciary has been vindicated as rule of law has become integral to our democratic process. But a series of events in recent years rudely awakened us out of this complacency. The failure of Justice Ramaswamy's impeachment proceedings in Parliament on partisan and extra-judicial considerations, for all practical purposes, proved that errant judges cannot be removed. And then in a perverse interpretation, the Supreme Court effectively held that in matters of judicial appointments, the opinion of the Chief Justice is more or less final and binding. The judiciary appoints itself, and cannot be removed by anyone. This self-perpetuation and unaccountability created a Mullah Raj! Such a state of affairs is clearly unacceptable in a democracy. The consequences are predictable. A string of scandals – alleged involvement of judges in corruption in the public service commission in Punjab, Shamit Mukherjee's complicity in the DDA scam, and brow beating of journalists who wrote about the Karnataka scandal – exposed and embarrassed the judiciary as never before. The contempt powers invested in the judiciary, making the judge complainant, prosecutor and judge, further undermined notions of accountability. The abnormal pendency of cases (25 million) in various courts made justice expensive and delayed. The incomprehensible procedures made it inaccessible to most ordinary people. Thanks to failure of the justice system, rough and ready justice for a price has become the norm. There are increasing concerns about falling standards of probity in judiciary too. Ceaser's wife, alas, is no longer above suspicion!

Several aspects of the judicial system have to be restructured, making it more relevant and to enhance its functionality. To start with, instituting a National Judicial Commission that would have the powers of appointment and removal of higher judiciary. The Venkatachaliah Commission recommended a five-member committee, with three senior-most judges, Law Minister and one person nominated by the President in consultation with the Chief Justice. The government's proposal is very similar, except the fifth member is a nominee of the Prime Minister. The committee on judicial accountability, a body of independent jurists, suggested a NJC with five retired judges - a member each nominated by the Supreme Court, High Courts, government, opposition and Bar Council. In a democracy, we cannot completely delink the NJC from the political process. Public interest may be best served if the government has two nominees, the opposition and the judiciary. Such a collective body must function independently and its decision must be final. Such a committee must notify the names for consideration and hold public hearings, so that known corrupt or incompetent persons cannot be nominated to high judicial office through secret deals. There are far too many undesirable appointees already, who do no credit to our constitutional offices. The NJC must also be empowered to remove a judge after due enquiry by a committee of peers. Given the failure to remove a single judge under Articles 124 and 217 of the constitution, we need a simpler, transparent and effective mechanism to remove errant judges, but with adequate safeguards. Finally, contempt powers of judges are anachronistic in this day and age. That even truth is no defence in contempt proceedings is a mockery of justice and fairness. In fact, the ordinary law of civil or criminal defamation is adequate to deal with any transgressions. Only weak institutions need crutches like contempt powers. Our judiciary is strong enough to preserve its dignity and protect its independence without draconian powers.

Given the number of pending cases and monumental delays associated with courts, appeals to higher courts must be limited to constitutional matters and writs (to be heard by the Supreme Court). Guaranteed right to time-bound justice is central to the idea of the judiciary. There must exist time frames within which the cases must be disposed. Hearing of criminal and civil cases will not exceed one and two years respectively. In case of appeals, the time frame for criminal and civil cases will be six months and a year respectively. Further, substantial amendments to the Civil Procedure Code are suggested to facilitate speedy trials. A first step in speeding up the procedure would be making the confessions before a police officer admissible as evidence. Further, our adversarial criminal justice system inadvertently encourages and rewards cheating and other unsavoury practices in order to 'win' the case. When evidence before the court is all that matters and the judge is more a passive umpire and not an active seeker of truth, the lawyers have a field day. It is the reputation and skill of the advocate, not the merits of the case or truth, which often lead to 'victory'. Therefore, careful tutoring of witnesses, inducements, and involved arguments have become acceptable practices over a period of time. This can be supplemented by a shift from adversarial system of criminal justice to the inquisitorial system. Formulation of a new Police Act would ensure a separate, independent police force for crime investigation in each state, insulated from political vagaries. An independent prosecution commission to supervise the police force could address the issue of policing the police.

While efficient judiciary and police are necessary for enforcing the rule of law, there is also a need to have strong institutional mechanisms to curtail unlawful behavior of persons manning the state apparatus.

## IV. Self-correcting Institutional Mechanisms

A democracy must be truly practicable and transparent. For this, a right to information law must be in place. It would make transparency and accountability more than just catchphrases. Institution of the Lok Pal is another step towards ensuring transparent governance. It must be handed over substantive powers and adequate autonomy. The directions of the Lok Pal would be binding.

An independent CVC to control corruption; removal of single directive to ensure impartial and independent enquiry would be crucial checks for maintaining functional democracy. The "Single Directive" (SD) policy, which earlier made it mandatory for the CBI to seek prior permission of the government to investigate corruption and prosecute senior civil servants, is given a firmer footing by incorporating it in the new legislation. This was done contrary to the earlier Supreme Court (SC) ruling that the SD is illegal as it is discriminatory in nature and blurs the distinction between decision-making officers and other civil servants. The SC again sought the government's explanation for retaining the provision in the CVC Act. Defending the inclusion of the SD in the CVC Bill, the Union Minister for Law, Arun Jaitley, argued that this enabled bureaucrats to exercise their discretion without fear of harassment by malicious investigations. This is exactly the argument that bureaucrats employ to defend the Directive, which they portray as a necessary protection against an investigating agency more than capable of misusing its powers. But in reality, SD has only helped shield many corrupt civil servants. The party in power habitually protects its cronies, and upright public servants are sometimes harassed for being 'inconvenient' and 'obstructive'. It is indeed a startling admission by the civil servants and politicians that crime investigation agencies can be manipulated to settle scores with political opponents. That being the case, what faith can citizens have in the crime investigation and governance process? The solution lies in separating the crime investigation process from political control and placing it under quasi-judicial control. In addition, prior permission of an independent collegium (say CVC) for investigation and prosecution will give the required protection to honest civil servants. Similarly, Constitutional functionaries are to be independently appointed. This could be modeled after the appointment of Judicial Commission by a collegium.

It becomes imperative to have effective checks against abuse of constitutional offices. This could be accomplished by specifying a category of constitutional offences along with the ensuing penalties. It must also provide for an independent mechanism to investigate such offences. The idea of Citizen's Charters must be realized and would list out and provide for all Union services. The procedure for obtaining these services is to be clearly laid down and made as simple as possible for easy access by the citizens. There must exist clearly earmarked areas of responsibility, making the Charter user-friendly. The Charter must also provide for well-defined and measurable performance standards, enabling ease in citizen appraisal of services. Finally, there must be compensation to the citizen for every day's delay in provision of services.

The key requirements to enforce accountability are plurality of civil society institutions and citizen assertion. We need to create enabling climate for citizen activism through the following measures. A citizen-friendly central cooperative law that is liberal in its postulates and effectively implementable would be a step in this direction. Contributions to non-profit organizations must enjoy full income-tax exemption to promote civil society institutions that can voice citizens concerns. Societies and trusts must be freed of all fetters and controls to encourage vibrant democracy.

## V. Civil Service Reforms

In the area of civil service reforms, the issue of public appointments (postings) is central. Key postings, if recommended by Civil Service Boards, would ensure the impartiality of the decision. Following which, the government will choose one appointee chosen by the Civil Services Board. A subject committee of Parliament would confirm the appointment through public hearings. Once appointed, the functionary would have guaranteed tenure of three years with provisions for removal or transfer only on grounds of proven incompetence or corruption. An amended Article 311 then could be applied only for the purposes of removal and dismissal. The court's jurisdiction would be prohibited except on grounds of equality before law.

## VI. Conclusion

The above-suggested agenda, because of its huge scope and implications, might deter some of us from action. But the complexities of the problems should not cloud our thinking and should not deter us from advocating sensible solutions. Any serious reform advocacy must be based on clear thinking, rational analysis, and sensible goals. Opportunities will always knock at the doors, and once the goals are clear, it becomes easier to design campaigns and activities to suit the requirements. A vibrant and informed civil society, media exposure and "political will" to enforce these governance reforms are the vital inputs. And it is only when we assert our rights that we can transform our procedural democracy into a substantive democracy. Eric Shaub aptly sized up the crux of the matter when he said, "Our democracy is 'out of shape' because we don't 'exercise' our rights." The systemic overhaul, suggested here, might not be an overnight phenomenon. Short-term gains will lead to long lasting successes for democracy. The light of passing ships might prove enticing, but it's the constant light of the distant star that must navigate the course of governance reforms.

# 6

# Concept and Practice of Administrative Reforms in Indian States

P. S. A. SUNDARAM

## Concept of Good Governance

The period since 1950s to the present has witnessed a conceptual movement from government-centric notions of public administration to a broader view of governance. This coincided with the recognition of the critical role of government and the role of the effective state in important publications like the *World Development Report* of 1997. Governance is distinct from government, and is the process through which various stakeholders articulate their interests, exercise their rights, and mediate their differences. This realisation coincided with the shift to ideals of new public management such as customer focus, quality services, performance orientation, flexible and autonomous management, decentralisation, deregulation, market testing, competition and alternative service delivery. This change reflects an ideological shift common to different donor agencies, but the exclusive focus of good governance on the principles of new public management is alleviated in developing countries by a belief in democracy, peace, rule of law and social justice. UNDP advocates the principles of accountability, transparency, predictability, participation, decentralisation, equity, effectiveness and efficiency. The Government of Andhra Pradesh has adopted the concept of SMART (Simple, Moral, Accountable, Responsive and Transparent) government as part of its vision for 2020. Similar policies have been outlined by the governments of Kerala, Madhya Pradesh, Orissa and Karnataka. Whatever the label, good governance is closely associated with public policy and development economics as the Tenth Plan document is careful to emphasise.

In a large and diverse country like India, with inherited traditions of administration and rigid rules, good governance would focus as much on the primary responsibilities of law and order, revenue and swift dispute resolution as on meeting the challenges of liberalisation and globalisation. The principle of subsidiarity (doing things at the level at which they can best be done) would become critical in the framework of 73rd and 74th Constitutional amendments.

The *National Human Development Report* of the Planning Commission for the year 2001 provides an illuminating list of achievements and challenges in different fields of governance, economic, political and civic. The report points out that the determining factor for successful development outcomes and reducing poverty is not the availability of funds alone, but institutional capacity to formulate viable and need-based schemes with efficient and responsive delivery systems. The priority areas are identified as: devolution of powers and resources to elected local bodies; civil service reform; enforcing incentive and disincentive structures to ensure accountability; procedural reform in all areas of public interface; and empowerment of women and marginal groups.

There is a growing realization within government as, well as major donor agencies, about the virtue of comprehensive intersectoral governance reform programs at the state level. Administration in India is seamless, not the least because of uniform civil service systems and common personnel regulations applicable to and enforced by the departments in charge of finance and personnel departments. All the development sectors suffer from common problems of functional overlaps, centralization, weak monitoring and coordination, overstaffing, skill gaps, corruption, poor budgetary management and unresponsive delivery systems. Administrative reform is thus a theme and tool that penetrates all the social and infrastructure sectors. The Approach Paper for the Tenth Plan reiterated the link between fiscal reforms and improved governance in terms that resonate with statements by the World Bank and other donor agencies in their papers on country strategy and structural adjustment.

Annex 1 describes the initial efforts for administrative reform and the work of successive committees and commissions, including the Administrative Reforms Commission. Annex 2 describes the recent initiatives of central and state governments and the approach towards administrative reform in the Five Year Plans, including the Tenth Plan.

## Process and Direction of Reform

Civil service reform is often identified with the cost-containment measures of personnel retrenchment and real-wage reduction for fiscal reasons (this is implied in the TOR of the Expenditure Reforms Commission, 2001 and this explains much of the suspicion attached to "civil service reform" in employee unions and the hidden resistance of the functional services). Reduction of fiscal deficit certainly demands containment of the runaway growth in salary and pension expenditure, which often accounts for more than 100 per cent of own revenues in many states. However, while the cost-containment dimension is important, administrative reform is much more than staff freeze and indiscriminate abolition of posts. The goal of government employment and wage policy is neither to minimize employment nor to compress wages, but to achieve a workforce with the size, skill mix, motivation, professional ethos and accountability necessary to: provide quality public services; reduce transaction costs for the private sector; design and implement economic policy; execute budgets and investment projects; preserve key assets of society; and facilitate institutional development throughout the economy.

As part of *long-term measures,* each ministry and agency could be required to submit a concrete restructuring plan consisting of a statement of objectives; strategies for achieving these objectives; a staffing program; a timetable; simple indices of administrative performance; training needs; and financial requirements. Once the plan is approved after full discussion at the highest level, and irreversible initial steps toward its implementation have been taken, the ministry or agency in question can freely recruit *from other ministries;* resume normal wage increases and promotions; have its reasonable financial needs met; and move up to the new salary scale established in the meantime. Such a process would create incentives for all government entities to improve their organization and operations as fast as possible in order to be allowed to "move up" to the new flexible structure, and for individual employees to join the more dynamic government entities. Along with this, ministries could think of radical ways to depart from conventional methods of providing education or health care based on staff and buildings and examine whether fully subsidized services are not in fact crowding out alternative quality providers.

Civil society organizations recognize that, notwithstanding many examples of successful interventions of NGOs or the private sector in service delivery, the government remains the dominant provider which also determines the rules of the game. Measures for administrative reform are therefore critical to success of economic and social goals.

## Reform Initiatives in Selected States

India is a Union of 28 states and 7 union territories. The Ninth Plan stresses the concept of cooperative federalism, whereby the states would have the freedom not only to determine their own priorities, but also the modalities of public intervention and provision of goods and services. The political changes in the 1990s, variations in levels of growth and human development indices, and huge fiscal deficits in the states have made the quality of states' own economic and social management and public administration a more important determinant of growth and pro-poor performance. Both the central government and donor agencies like the World Bank recognized that it was critical to accelerate state reforms by local partnerships and structural adjustment loans and MOUs of state governments with the Central Finance Ministry.

Although the thrust for civil service reform in the states was sparked by the unsustainable increase in salary and pension cost and growth of personnel at all levels, a number of states developed a broader reform agenda. Comprehensive strategies for reforming governance were announced by UP, AP, Karnataka, Gujarat, Orissa, Maharashtra, Kerala and Madhya Pradesh, based on widespread consultation and reports of administrative reform commissions/task forces. MP and Kerala are carrying district and village level government to the logical end by devolving powers and resources and by reducing the dominance of line departments over schemes and staff. The packages of structural loans concluded by the World Bank for AP, UP and Karnataka (and proposed for Orissa) envisage milestones for fiscal and governance reform, which are consistent with medium term goals of reduction of fiscal deficit and workforce size. Orissa's White Paper on Public Expenditure Management and Administrative Reforms is perhaps the most forthright statement on the perilous state of finances and the factors leading to administrative collapse and outlines a set of bold measures for fiscal reform and more responsive and open administration with people's participation.

The two major components of the reform in AP and Karnataka are: a) simplifying, redefining and rationalizing government's role to focus on the most critical public goods and services, and b) enhancing accountability, responsiveness and transparency with which the government and its agencies perform this role. Underlying this (although not much elaborated), is the strengthening of the core functions of law and order, dispute resolution and sustaining the legal and administrative framework for the economic and social activities of business and citizens. The link between administrative reform and poverty reduction and improved access to services is clearly recognized in the White Paper of Orissa and policy statements from Kerala and MP. The support for decentralization is muted in AP, while it is strident in MP, Kerala and Karnataka.

The objectives of administrative and civil service reform were similar in other states, and the thrust areas that are being pursued with varying degrees of emphasis are:

- Public enterprise privatization and restructuring;
- Ensuring affordability of civil service, by pursuing well-sequenced options for downsizing, retrenchment and redeployment of redundant staff, weeding out incompetent staff and attractive schemes of voluntary retirement;
- Enhancing productivity of the civil service and rationalizing the mission and organizational goals by functional reviews, deregulation, restructuring and privatization of public enterprises, and encouragement of public-private partnerships;
- Devolution of functions and resources to elected local bodies;
- Promoting accountability, transparency and responsiveness of public agencies by installing a regime of citizen-friendly services and access to information through decentralization, citizens' charters, effective redress of grievances, right to information, laws for transparent procurement, electronic governance, user consultation, and empowerment of user groups in areas like the management of education, health, use of water, forest and natural resources;

- Strengthening meritocracy and motivation by sound human resource management practices and database, reduction and monitoring of transfers through transparent guidelines and civil service boards, merit-based recruitment, improved performance assessment, operating a regime of rewards and sanctions for performance and the implementation of a well-designed action plan to train all employees at different stages of the career; and
- A vigorously pursued anti-corruption agenda.

Electronic governance is an intrinsic part of increasing efficiency and transparency in government and governments signaled this through flagship activities such as CARD in AP, multi-utility centers for one-stop-nonstop service such as *E-seva* in AP, *Bhoomi* in Karnataka, *Gyandoot* in MP, SETU in Maharashtra and the counter services in municipalities like Vishakapatnam and Mumbai. Demand-led goals of increased accountability and responsiveness, as well as e-governance, are seen as dependent on the reengineering of procedures and organizational structures as well as focused measures like *Janmabhoomi* to take administration to the people and change employee attitudes. However, in the absence of a clear road map and overarching strategy for e-governance, sector level successes in areas like land records in Karnataka do not add up to a coherent program.

Despite the announcement of impressive reform packages and the achievement by individual states in different areas, the performance has not been uniform across sectors in the reforming states. The defining task of redefining goals and reorganizing government departments and machinery has been taken up in stop-go fashion. This is partly due to the pulls of political forces and vertical hierarchies in administration and the ineffectiveness of central coordinating systems. The law on right to information is not credibly enforced in a number of states and much useful information is not in the public domain. The report of the core group of administrative reforms in 2002 refers to islands of success in the midst of generally lackluster progress in citizens' charters. The group notes that e-governance is yet to take root in the absence of process reengineering and change of mindset. Performance has been more sustained and better linked with fiscal goals where a government like AP has installed a strong unit within government to oversee the process, with intellectual support from a think tank like the centre for good governance. Senior officials recognize that complex exercises like functional reviews and organizational restructuring would need to be undertaken with clear outcomes in view, along with strategies to neutralize opposition from vested interests.

Political instability and regime change have been major factors in the difficulty of sustaining the momentum of improvements in states like UP. The credibility of the reform agenda in public perception has been dented by the persistence of inefficient and unresponsive services even in states like Karnataka. The transfer policy in Karnataka is among the most transparent and aimed at stability of tenure; but even there, the officers in higher levels have been subject to arbitrary transfers and short tenures. The reform agenda has not had significant effect on the resistance of ingrained tendencies for centralization and departmental hierarchies to organizational restructuring and devolution of powers and staff to elected local bodies. The demotivating factors for good performance continue to operate, such as secretive and subjective systems of performance assessment, liability of officials to premature transfers, poorly codified cadre rules, weak systems of establishment control and sanctions, insufficient recognition and reward of merit, unsatisfactory human resource database, poor work environment and inadequate opportunities for upgrading skills and knowledge. Corruption continues to be a major problem. There is inadequate capacity within secretariat to obtain and use well-researched advice and to monitor the governance reform process. There is a tendency to overstress the outputs of computerization at the expense of process reengineering and organizational backstopping.

The above list of unfinished tasks underscores the fact that governance reform is a long haul and requires sustained political support, bureaucratic stamina and dedicated and well-equipped support systems.

## Implications of Citizen-centered Administration

There is an increasing tendency in central and state governments to advance demand-driven approaches to problems of governance through citizen action, to increase accountability of public agencies and to cultivate the receptiveness of government agencies to citizen-led initiatives. While not rejecting the role of government, the initiative provides a corrective to the dominant supply-side approach to governance, which focuses exclusive attention on the reform of public sector institutions and civil service. The objective is to restore public trust in the capacity of government to deliver services equitably and efficiently. The initiative resonated strongly with the statement of chief ministers in the conference on effective and responsive administration, which was convened by the Prime Minister in May 1997. While not going overboard on civil society or government agencies to drive development, rebuilding partnerships between citizens and government means working on both sides of the equation — that is, going beyond 'civil society' or 'state-based' approaches, to focus on their intersection, through new forms of participation, responsiveness and accountability.

Where large and unresponsive public agencies have a monopoly over many services, voice mechanisms for improved accountability are more important than exit. Report cards (pioneered by the Public Affairs Center in Bangalore), citizens' charters and budget analysis offer means of supplementing the traditional accountability and oversight mechanisms in ways that place a premium on transparency, participation and support from civil society. At the micro level, the report card became a meaningful platform for the citizens in Bangalore to enter into dialogue with service providers. This was demonstrated by the experience of many citizen networks in the city such as CIVIC and Committee of Bangalore Resident Associations (COBRA) the multi-stakeholder forum called the Bangalore Agenda Task Force and the new initiative called PROOF (Public Record of Operations & Finance). The work of the NGO centers for budget analysis coincided with the advocacy interest of diverse groups, be it social audit or greater allocation of funds for schemes benefiting the poor. A leading example in the use of Budget and Financial Analysis tool for transparency is the campaign of Mazdur Kisan Sakti Sanghathan (MKSS) of Rajasthan for right to information and public records of expenditure and the conduct of *Jan Sunwai*.

There has been a flurry of legislation since 1997 for right to information in different states such as Tamil Nadu, Goa, Maharashtra, Karnataka, Madhya Pradesh, Delhi and Rajasthan, while legislation is contemplated in AP, UP, Orissa and Punjab. By all accounts, the Maharashtra law is considered to be the most progressive. However, the progress on operationalization of law is slow. Reformers within government and activists acknowledge that the legislation is only as good as it is implemented, and that the citizens continue to be affected by secrecy and obfuscation of public agencies. Efforts such as those of the Commonwealth Human Rights Initiative and *Parivartan* are needed for the evaluation of the experience of state laws and to generate debate on their credible implementation.

Piloting and scaling up deregulation, people-centered practices and citizens' charters call for reengineering of processes, amendment to rules, simplifying and consolidating licenses, and breaking down departmental walls and communication barriers on the basis of systematic study and consultation of stakeholders and field staff. Process reengineering has to precede computerization in many cases, as demonstrated in the case of the reforms in registration and *SETU* citizen information centers in Maharashtra, the CARD and *E-Seva* in AP, FRIENDS in Kerala and *Bhoomi* in Karnataka. There are good examples of such sustainable system reforms based on consultation with citizen groups and experts, as exemplified by the Mumbai master plan and development control rules, slum rehousing, low cost sanitation, rural water supply, and single window systems for industry and public offices in Karnataka and Punjab.

Structural adjustment programs and fiscal corrective measures have to be conveyed in meaningful terms to diverse sections of society including the poor and marginal groups — such as the reordering of expenditure to improve services and allocations for non-salary components of education and health. The consultation on the Orissa White Paper led to remarkable feedback from the people on cutting down bloated bureaucracy and focusing on areas of human development. There is reluctance among states in general to engage in frank dialogue with all stakeholders on the process of fiscal and administrative reform and to remain content with posting papers on the web site. It is possible to elaborate institutional reforms in terms that address people's need for responsive and accountable bureaucracy — reforms in areas such as stability of tenure, performance assessment, enforcement of a regime of incentives and sanctions, weeding out incompetent persons, prosecuting the corrupt etc., Recognition of people's concerns would help to prioritize areas for reform in personnel management.

Citizen-centered initiatives go beyond legislation for right to information and require partnerships at city and district level for service delivery and program implementation. The Mumbai Urban Transport Project has led to the unique partnership with a slum dweller's association and SPARC for participatory relocation. A similar partnership on slum sanitation in Mumbai and Pune, and beneficiary-driven rural water supply, has raised the credibility of government programs with poor and marginal citizen groups. The Mumbai Municipal Corporation is engaged in a growing partnership with PRAJA and other groups for enforcing citizens' charters and an on-line grievance redress system. These are pointers to the opportunities to explore the scope for participatory governance and empowerment of citizen groups in different sectors and levels of administration in ways that need not be threatening to political leadership.

## ANNEX 1

### *Initial Effort Towards Reform*

The movement towards administrative reforms in India has been ceaseless, punctuated by the impatience of successive Prime Ministers with the rigid and unresponsive ways of bureaucracy. The central government commissioned studies and reports by retired civil servants like Gopalaswami and Gorwala in the early 1950s to advise the government on reforms in existing organization and systems. The Planning Commission has been advocating the importance of reforms in administrative procedures and civil service from the First Plan onwards. Paul Appleby, the noted public policy expert, submitted two highly influential reports in 1954 and 1956 on administrative reform at the instance of the then Prime Minister. The central department of administrative reforms was set up in 1964 to look at the scope and areas of continuous improvement in administration, economy and work practices in all departments.

A milestone in the history of administrative reform in India was the establishment of the Administrative Reforms Commission in 1966 (ARC.1969) and its reports on diverse aspects of central, state and local administration. The most important reports were a) Machinery of Government and Procedures of work and b) Personnel Administration. It advocated a rational pay structure and unified grading system that would truly reflect the actual responsibilities borne in each job. The Commission recommended the division of senior positions into eight functional groups and the appointment to these positions through a process of selection from all the services. It recommended lateral entry into public services from universities, industrial concerns and non-profit agencies. The Commission recommended excellent principles for creation and expansion of organizations, which were unfortunately not followed by central ministries.

As Indian administration is seamless and individual departments are governed by common rules and procedures, as well as a common civil service, sector policies are influenced for good or worse by administrative changes. Committees, which were set up for generic reforms or sector policy, made significant recommendations to improve administration in one or more sectors. The Santhanam Committee on Prevention of Corruption (Ministry of Home Affairs, 1962) commented on preventive aspects of corruption, reducing controls and discretionary powers and swifter punishment of offenders within the system. The report led to the establishment of the Central Vigilance Commission and departmental vigilance establishments. The Economic Administrative Reforms Commission submitted separate reports in 1983 on accountability, improved decision making within the secretariat and reforms in civil service.

The National Police Commission inquired into all aspects of police administration in 1977. It was the first to deal with the vexed issue of political interference in the placement and promotion of police officers. The Commission recommended the establishment of State Security Commissions under the chief minister to lay down policy guidelines for transfers, to hear appeals against premature transfers, and to regulate service conditions of police officers.

The impetus for reforms did not come solely through expert committees and commissions. Many recommendations on streamlining administration were made by conferences of chief secretaries and conferences of officials in charge of different sectors. Successive Central Pay Commissions have recommended improvements in the civil service system and measures to improve its productivity. The report of the Administrative Reforms Commission of 1969, and other reports of the experts and commissions set up by the central government, influenced state governments in their nascent state of public administration. In addition, the administrative reform committees set up by many states, from 1948 onwards, suggested reforms in the administrative system. The state pay commissions also made several recommendations. The Tamil Nadu High Level Committee on Administrative Reform and Preventing Corruption (Tamil Nadu, 1997) made several recommendations on reforms in systems and procedures, right to information and civil service. Box 1 givens a profile of recommendations made by ARC and some state reform commissions.

## BOX 1

### *Recommendations of State Administrative Reform Committees and Others*

The major recommendations of the state administrative reform committees, chief secretaries, and the study report of the ARC include:

- The need to assign to the chief secretary a position of pre-eminence and power, and to strengthen his secretariat for effective policy analysis and follow-up;
- The need to preserve the critical role of the district collector in all activities, including development;
- Need to bifurcate development and revenue administration, and making the *zilla parishad* the executive body in the PRI system;
- Phased merger of the secretariat departments and directorates, and streamlining present relationships between the two;
- Officer-oriented pattern of work and staffing in government offices, delayering and level jumping to expedite decision-making, simplification of financial and departmental procedures, reduction of paper work;
- Greater delegation of authority to the lower levels of administration and promoting coordination;
- Need for State government to identify special areas at the cutting edge level like police stations, block office and hospitals for improvements in public satisfaction and efficiency through simplification of procedures, organizational changes, attitudinal changes and training;
- Rationalization of forms and returns as regards their simplification or abolition, combination with other departmental forms, frequency of renewal, number of copies and ease of submission;
- Introduction of modern office equipment and computers as aids to administration, services to people and speed of decision-making;
- Relieving senior officers of heavy preoccupation with the burden of routine, massive paper work, conferences and meetings, and
- Various personnel management issues.

Important recent reports include those of the Karnataka Administrative Reforms Commission (2001), Kerala Administrative Reforms Committee (2001) and the report of the one-man Committee on Good Governance in Maharashtra (2000). AP government followed up a report of the task force on good governance by constituting a Cabinet Sub Committee on Administrative Reforms, which has initiated comprehensive improvements in administration. Orissa government constituted a task force on governance and civil service reform and arranged for widespread discussion of the report of the task force.

Besides these committees, there are reports of committees and experts in different states relating to individual sectors and departments, such as the reports of state finance commissions, committees on district administrations, taxation inquiry committees, GVK Rao report on *panchayati raj* in Karnataka, Sabhanayagam report on revenue procedures in Tamil Nadu, and several reports on local government in Kerala. The dissemination of these studies would throw light on the directions of departmental reforms in different states.

# ANNEX 2

*Recent Initiatives in Administrative Reform*

## Recent Initiatives of Central Government

Significant milestones in the last five years have been the 1997 report of the Fifth Central Pay Commission (FCPC), the Conference of Chief Ministers on Effective and Responsive Administration in May 1997 and the thrust for good governance contained in the Approach Paper for the Tenth Five Year Plan and the main Plan document itself.

The last five years witnessed major initiatives of state governments such as the release of vision documents (such as AP, Gujarat), announcement of policies for governance and civil service reform (AP, Karnataka, UP, Orissa and Kerala), legislation for right to information (Karnataka, MP, Goa, Rajasthan, Tamil Nadu and MP), electronic governance and various schemes for responsive and citizen-centered service delivery. All these developments coincided with the blossoming of governance policies and interventions by major donor agencies like the World Bank, Asian Development Bank, UNDP, DFID UK and USAID.

FCPC enunciated an efficiency program of how to redefine the goals of government, contract out certain non-core activities and develop partnerships between government, industry and NGOs. The Commission suggested ways to change work methods and work environment, bring about autonomy, transparency, productivity and equity in the system, reduce paperwork, and introduce automation and information technology. The Commission made proposals for manpower development to enable government to attract and retain the best talent in administration and follow new methods of recruitment including lateral entry and contract employment. Finally, FCPC examined various options of optimizing the size of the government machinery, especially in the organized services, railways, posts and telecommunications, ways to restructure departments and ministries, and to control the workforce.

## Action Plan for Effective and Responsive Administration and Later

The period following the 1996 General Elections found all major political parties agreed on the need to implement an agenda of accountable, transparent, responsive, participatory, decentralized and honest governance. The Action Plan, adopted in the Chief Ministers' Conference on Effective and Responsive Administration in May 1997, envisaged concerted action by central and state governments, in collaboration with stakeholders in civil society, in the following three broad areas:

i) Making administration accountable and citizen-friendly

ii) Ensuring transparency and the right to information; and

iii) Tackling corruption, cleansing and motivating the civil services.

The conference was followed by countrywide efforts for citizen-friendly government such as the formulation of citizens' charters, more effective measures for the redress of public grievances, devolution of powers and resources to elected local bodies and the widespread use of computers in the cause of service delivery and speedier decision making[1].

Legislation for freedom of information was enacted by Karnataka, Goa, Tamil Nadu, Maharashtra, Rajasthan and Delhi, while the central government introduced a Bill in Parliament. Many states like Rajasthan, UP, MP and Assam issued instructions to provide easy access of people to records of local bodies and development departments. Participation and user empowerment became the centerpiece of service delivery, implementation of schemes for poverty reduction and management of natural resources as typified in user committees for water and forests as well as the provision of education and health services.

Central and State Governments have realized that overregulation and excessive laws, monopoly character of most public services and the complex and secretive processes of decision making led to harassment and opportunities for corruption. The Prime Minister observed that people perceive the bureaucracy as an agent of exploitation rather than as a provider of service. Concerted efforts were made by central and state governments for the simplification of existing laws, regulations and procedures, repeal of obsolete laws, reform of laws operating against the weaker sections, and steps to reduce the time and cost of disposal of cases in civil and criminal courts. This was built into policies for deregulation of business and economic activity. A Commission on Administrative Law, appointed by the Prime Minister, submitted a comprehensive report in 1998. This was followed by the repeal of about 400 laws and amendments to 55 laws, besides major new laws on information technology, patents and fiscal transparency by ministry level efforts for legal reform. A number of states like UP and Rajasthan set up similar committees for legal reforms or deregulation. Central task forces in 2000 gave recommendations on subjects like service litigation, appointment of senior officers, disciplinary and vigilance proceedings and recruitment rules. The core group on AR notes that significant progress in legal reform has been made only by Gujarat, Karnataka and West Bengal.

At the level of civil society, industry associations and the Task Force set up by the Prime Minister have come out with agenda for good governance, which emphasize the role of civil service reform, deregulation, electronic governance, increased accountability and responsiveness of administration.

Following reports of expert groups or internal dialogue, steps for improving the performance and integrity of civil service were considered by central and state governments such as a code of ethics, mechanisms to ensure stability of tenure, streamlining departmental inquiries and vigilance proceedings and improved systems of performance assessment. The central Ministry of Personnel proposed to build capacity through an effective training plan to meet the needs of employees, with AP providing the model.

## Approach in the Five Year Plans

The documents released by the Planning Commission on the Five Year Plans and the mid-term appraisal reflect the consensus in National Development Council (composed of the central ministers and state chief ministers). The Approach Paper for the Tenth Plan (*ibid*) reiterated the link between fiscal reforms and improved governance in terms that resonate with statements by the World Bank and other donor agencies. The paper advocated a redefinition of the role of government in the center and states to reflect the reordering of priorities in functions and expenditure. It outlined an ambitious civil service renewal programm aimed at improved public satisfaction and strengthening delivery institutions, district administration and the village panchayats. The stress would be on maximizing development outcomes and effectiveness of service delivery rather than development funding.

The Commission declared that the states would neither be able to end the fiscal crisis nor restore growth, unless they addressed the problems of governance and falling standards of integrity and significantly redirected and improved administration. The collapse of ethical standards was seen by the Commission as related to fiscal indicipline and populist administration. The Commission has been using the levers of regular and contingent assistance to states to enforce elements of good governance such as rightsizing of civil service, stable tenure for program managers and district officers and genuine strengthening of elected local bodies.

## Notes

1. Programs to take administration to the people include: Andhra Pradesh (*Janmabhoomi* and *Prajalu Vaddaku Palana*), Assam (*Raijor Padulit Raijor Sarkar*), Haryana (*Sarkar Apke Dwar*), Madhya Pradesh (*Gram Sampark Abhiyan*), Maharashtra (*People's Sovereignty Day & Headquarters Day*), Rajasthan (*Prashasan Gaon Ke Sang*) and Tamil Nadu (*Manu Veedhi Thittam*).

# 7

## E-governance

*Government Initiatives in India*

P.D. KAUSHIK

The advent of Information Technology (IT) as a highly leveraged enabling tool for delivery of services in the public and the private sector has by now been universally accepted. This has redefined the fundamentals of delivery systems, which has the potential to change the institutions as well as the mechanisms of delivery of services forever. It is in this context that e-governance or Smart Governance has emerged on the scene. The objective of achieving e-governance goes far beyond mere computerisation of stand alone back office operations in the government departments. It essentially means to change the management processes of government operations. This implies a new set of responsibilities for the executive, legislature and the citizen. The effort should aim to bring about a social catharsis that needs to be orchestrated in a comprehensive, concerted and planned fashion.

### E-governance

The definition of e-governance goes beyond the application of IT in government functioning. It implies a completely new definition and concept of public governance. E-governance is defined as digitisation of government information and online transaction of public services. In other words, it implies electronic delivery of public services between government and its citizens. Others use the term e-governance as an extension of e-commerce to government procurement and see it as Business-to-Government (B2G) transactions. Application of Electronic Data Interchange (EDI) in trade facilitation agencies, like Customs, has been promoted as e-governance by multilateral agencies like the United Nations Conference on Trade and Development (UNCTAD) and World Trade Organisation (WTO).

E-governance implies action and commitments of the State and its agencies at two levels, namely —

- Involves the promotion and adoption of Information and Communication Technologies (ICT) in the day to day government functioning; and
- Commitment to use ICTs for government business, citizen interaction, and most importantly for development.

**INFOCID- A single window service for citizens in Portugal**

- Single source of information for the citizens
- Optimising resources of multiple organisations
- Create economies of scale for information producers and distributors
- Inter-governmental participation
- Public networks

Good or smart governance, although not clearly defined, implies transparency in government decision making, clear rules and procedures, and civic participation in the process. IT-enabled government processes embody these principles, which significantly improves the possibility of empowering the citizens and promote development and strengthening of democracy.

In this regard, the Government of India defines e-governance as using IT to bring about Simple, Moral, Accountable Responsible and Transparent Governance or SMART Governance[1]. Other international bodies observe e-governance as an opportunity to harness ICTs to- (a) improve the efficiency and effectiveness of the 'executive functions' of government, including the delivery of public services; (b) enable governments to be transparent to citizens and businesses, giving access to more of the information generated by the government; and (c) facilitate fundamental changes in the relationships between the citizen and the State, and between Central and State governments, with implications for the democratic process and structures of government.

Thus, e-governance encompasses a wide variety of IT-enabled government services, both in terms of adoption of ICTs in government processes and use of e-commerce in government purchasing and delivery systems. Introduction of ICTs has made significant contribution in the achievement of good governance goals. E-governance makes governance more efficient and more effective, and brings about other benefits too. The three main contributions of e-governance are:

- Improving government processes (e-administration);
- Connecting citizens (e-citizens and e-services); and
- Building external interactions (e-society).

Most developing countries are confronting two challenges in establishing e-governance within their government operations. First, the strategic challenge of e-readiness, and second about the tactical challenge of closing design. Heeks (2001), among others, has highlighted a vision for managing change in government processes. Although, computerisation in government is not a new phenomenon, the old model was based on IT automating the internal workings of government by processing data. But the new model is one of ICTs supporting and transforming the external workings of governance by processing and communicating data. Based on the new model, e-governance should be viewed to encompass all ICTs, but the key innovation is seamless flow of information through computer networks – from Intranets to the Internet – creating a wealth of new digital connections:

## E-governance: Digital Connections

- Connections within government – permitting 'joined-up thinking'.
- Connections between government and NGOs/citizen groups– strengthening accountability.
- Connections between government and business/citizen groups – transforming service delivery.
- Connections within and between NGOs – supporting learning and concerted action.
- Connections within and between communities – building social and economic development.

As a result, the focus grows from just parts of e-administration to also encompass e-citizens, e-services and e-society. The new systemic approach has experienced a paradigm shift from the past, the old models held IT isolated from the mainstream of reform, or held IT as the objective of reform. The new model brings information systems (IS) to the heart of reform. In real terms, the central role for ICTs is based on the premise that as governance becomes information-intensive, ICTs become an integral part of more and more governance initiatives. ICTs are also recognised as a fundamental lever of change. IT is no longer isolated on the sidelines.

A much broader definition of e-governance encompasses an integrated role for ICTs in governance, which means using ICTs as a strategic tool to good governance. ICTs are no longer seen as an end in themselves and they are seen to work only as part of a wider systemic 'package'. Overall, e-governance is the ICT-enabled route to achieving good governance, which may also imply as 'i-governance' or integrated governance – since it integrates both the processing and the communication technologies. It integrates people, processes, information, and technology in the service of achieving governance objectives.

## E-governance: Development & Systemic Improvement in Processes

Government costs too much, delivers too little, and is not sufficiently responsive or accountable to its people. Good governance reforms aim to address these shortcomings. E-Governance offers a way forward, helping improve government processes, connect citizens, and build interactions with and within civil society. At root, it has the power of ICTs, which provide three basic change potentials for good governance for development:

- *Automation*: replacing current human-executed processes, which involve accepting, storing, processing, outputting or transmitting information. For example, the automation of existing clerical functions in government offices.
- *Informatisation*: supporting current human-executed information processes. For example, supporting current processes of decision making, communication, and decision implementation.
- *Transformation*: creating new ICT-executed information processes or supporting new human-executed information processes. For example, creating new methods of public service delivery.

These change potentials bring in five fundamental benefits to governance for development. Gains from IT-enabled government usually comprise of efficiency gains and effectiveness gains. The benefits of e-governance are:

*Governance that is cheaper*: producing the same outputs at lower total cost.

*Governance that does more*: producing more outputs at the same total cost.

*Governance that is quicker*: producing the same outputs at the same total cost in less time.

*Governance that works better*: producing the same outputs at the same total cost in the same time, but to a higher quality standard.

*Governance that is innovative*: producing new outputs.

These are the direct and objective benefits. ICTs have the capabilities of bringing in many others benefits in indirect forms. For example, use of ICTs in government can bring benefits both internally and externally, for instance providing benefits such as better staff motivation or greater political control or an improved public image. On the other external front, by delivering cheaper, better services to those who critically depend on government services. Besides, indirect benefit of e-governance could also be demonstrated as catalysing the local IT industry; which can bolster foreign investment. Contrary to popular perception, e-governance does not cover e-commerce and e-business applications that focus solely or mainly on the private sector. Nitro (2000) highlights three main domains of e-governance, namely

- *Improving government processes*: e-Administration
- *Connecting citizens*: e-Citizens and e-Services
- *Building interactions with and within civil society*: e-Society

These focal domains particularly address the problems of the government, which suggests that government is too costly, too inefficient and too ineffective; too self-serving and too inconvenient; and too insular.

**Focal Domains for E-governance Initiatives**

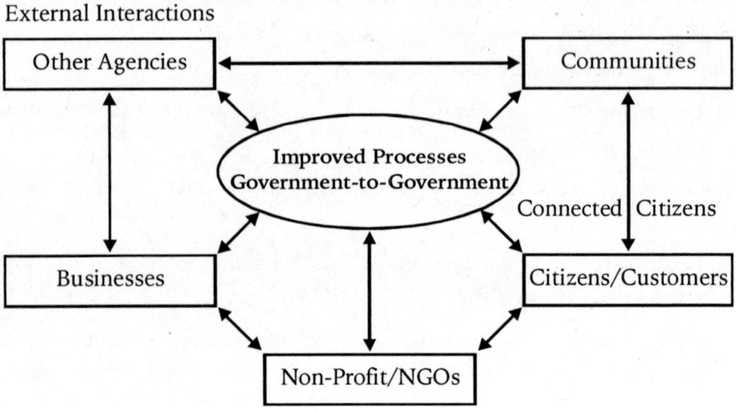


*Source*: Heeks (2001)

## E-administration: Improving government processes

Such initiatives deal particularly with improving the internal workings of the government. They include:

*Cutting process costs*[2]: improving the Input/Output ratio by cutting financial costs and time. Computerisation replaced higher human costs with lower ICT costs to support efficiency and productivity improvements. Informatisation also supports decisions and implementation in downsizing or rightsizing exercises. The rationale is to address the large size of government expenditure and the inefficiency in many of its operational processes. For example, the Election Commission of India has computerised the complete voter list (all Indian citizens above the age of 18) and issued voter cards, which is also treated as a proof of residence by other governmental agencies. Likewise, the Income Tax authorities have issued PAN Number for keeping a computerised record of income tax payees in the country (online income tax return filing is likely to commence.

*Managing process performance*[3]: planning, monitoring and controlling the performance of process resources (human, financial and other). Informatisation supports this by providing information about process performance and performance standards. The rationale is to make more efficient or effective use of process resources. For instance, the

Government of India has recommended an allocation of 2-3 per cent of annual budget in computerisation in all Ministries and Departments. Likewise, the Government has directed each Department/Ministry should form a standing panel of IT consultants for seeking advice on various technical issues. Strengthening of the Department of Administrative Reforms and Public Grievances, the Government has identified specific areas of concerns at which the Department of Administrative Reforms and Public Grievances could look at- Redesigning the Manual of Office Procedures, Cyber laws and their implementation, and 'Content' Organisation.

*Making strategic connections in government*[4]: connecting arms, agencies, levels and data stores of government to strengthen capacity to investigate, develop and implement the strategy and policy that guides government processes. Examples of such connections are central-to-local, ministry-to-ministry, executive-to-legislature, and decision maker-to-data store. Automation and informatisation support this by digitising existing information channels. Transformation supports this by creating new digital channels. The rationale is to provide clearer direction for Central and State government processes and to provide for a more evidence-based approach to policy and process. For instance, there was a recognition of the issue in the Government of India that formulation and implementation of sustainable development strategies were hampered by lack of adequate information, and that much of the data underlying this information lay scattered in many different organisations. Therefore, Prime Minister constituted a Task force on IT to formulate an ICT-enabled National Agenda, particularly linking a set of key national government, local government and public sector research institutions. The recommendations helped in charting the basic framework of action for the government to connect leading decision-makers with valuable Web-based data resources on sustainable development. In addition to raising the profile of sustainable development with policy makers, the framework has also helped bring faster and more information to the process of strategic environmental decision making.

*Creating empowerment*[5]: transferring power, authority and resources for processes from their existing locus to new locations. Typically that transfer is to lower, more localised levels of the government may be viewed as decentralisation. Transformation supports this by creating new information flows to decision-makers and process implementers in new locations. The rationale is to reduce the costs and increase the speed of processes and decision making and to create more flexible and responsive processes. There are various pilot projects launched by the State governments to bring information closer to the local decision-makers (details are given in State Government e-governance initiatives).

Traditionally, ICTs have been used within government in 'automation' mode, replacing clerical labour processes with their digital equivalent. These are essential building blocks for e-governance. In the North, replacing costly workforce with cheap ICTs may considerably cut operational costs, although there is evidence that productivity gains are somewhat limited. However in developing countries, replacing low wage workforce with expensive ICTs is unlikely to be justified on financial cost grounds. As time replaces costs as a more critical global resource, ICTs ability to increase process speed provides some justification for automation in the third world countries.

From this base of automation, there are three e-administration trends at work in developing countries, namely ICTs are spreading up the organisation, increasingly supporting the work of operational and tactical managers and recently, beginning to touch the working lives of legislators, politicians and other senior public officials. As the change potential of ICTs increases, they deliver ever-greater benefits and enable ever-greater changes in the process of government.

## E-citizens and E-services: Connecting Citizens

Connecting citizens' initiatives deal particularly with the relationship between government and citizens, either as stakeholders from where the government derives its legitimacy, or as customers who consume public services. These initiatives may well incorporate the process improvements as identified in e-administration. However, they also include a broader scope, such as:

*Talking to citizens*[6]: providing citizens with details of government activities. It relates to certain types of accountability, making public servants more accountable for their decisions and actions. Informatisation and transformation support this by providing the new information flows from government to citizens on which accountability depends. The rationale is to increase the pressure on staff to perform well and to improve public understanding of government. One of the initiatives is the Government of India's web site, which is operated and maintained by the National Informatics Centre- http://goidirectory.nic.in. This provides a wide variety of information at various Ministeries and Department levels. The NIC network has connected all the district centres in India for seamless flow of information from districts to regional and national headquarters.

*Listening to citizens*[7]: increasing the input of citizens into government decisions and actions. This could be flagged as either democratisation or participation. The main potential is for informatisation and transformation to support this by providing new information flows from citizens to government. The rationale is to make public decisions more responsive to citizens' view or needs. Various government web sites under the NIC seeks public opinion on variety of strategic issues. For instance, the Indian Parliament web site (http://parliamentofindia.nic.in) puts all the pending bills on their web sites for greater transparency and at the same time seeks suggestions from the general public and members of the civil society to file their views on the pending bills.

*Improving public services*[8]: improving the services delivered to members of the public along dimensions such as quality, convenience and cost. This uses all the potentials of ICTs to deliver the informational components of public services to citizens in digital form. The direct rationale is clear from the definition, but there is also an indirect rationale of saving opportunity cost for citizens in terms of time and money that would otherwise be captured by inefficient service delivery. For instance, Causelists (http://causelists.nic.in) are scheduling of cases to be heard by the courts on the following day. The Causelists of the Supreme Court and many other High Courts are available on NIC Web Servers. As the Supreme Court of India and all the 18 High Courts and their 10 Benches are fully computerised, all these courts generate Daily and Weekly Causelists from the computer servers installed by NIC. The Causelist application is the backbone application of all courts as no court can function without that day's Causelist. Hence this has become near time critical application in all the Courts. Immediately after generation of the Causelist, most of the courts cyclostyle the stencils cut from the printers attached to the servers for generating thousands of copies running into a few lakhs of pages every day. Due to this reason, the courts take a lot of time for generation and supply of the Causelists to the advocates at their offices or residences. Usually the advocates receive the cyclostyled copies of a day's Cause List not before 8 PM. Some High Courts send the Causelists data on a floppy to the Printers for printing thousands of copies. This process costs each High Courts lakhs of Rupees every year. By making the Causelists available on Internet, no High Court is incurring any expenditure, as they are using the already available infrastructure and the Software of NIC. Likewise, *e-seva, Gyandoot, Aapki Sarcar- Aapke Dwar,* etc. are variety of government initiatives launched at State Government level for improving public access to government services. All such initiatives are at pilot level, which needs to be expanded to national level.

All such initiatives rely on the new connectivity via computer networks offered by ICTs, they are all relatively new inclusions within e-governance. They are representatives of the new possibilities offered by e-governance for development. They also represent something of a further agenda of ICT-enabled governance, besides e-administration. The chronology starts with *publishing* (delivering data to citizens), then moves to *interaction* (delivering data to citizens and receiving data from citizens), then moves to transaction (undertaking other government processes online).

Although such initiatives are rare in developing economies, yet even very basic publishing activities can have significant effects on the quality of life of common man. Lack of information to citizens often leads to corruption and rent seeking. Putting such information on the Web directly attacks information monopolies and its effects. Putting government forms can also have a strong disintermediating effect – cutting out the middlemen and public servants, who may illegally charge citizens for access to such forms. But middlemen cannot be completely eliminated in the new paradigm for governance because in the new medium certain intermediaries act as catalyst in the operational processes. Realistic e-governance for development projects will have to identify and nurture such intermediaries. They may be existing professionals (e.g. accountants for online tax systems; notaries for online registration systems); or public servants (e.g. in call centres or in one-stop-shop government offices); or NGOs and community-based organisations (e.g. staffed community telecentres);

or private sector organisations (e.g. cybercafes or info-kiosks); or other public institutions. The *Gyandoot* case provides an example – the entrepreneur running the online kiosk frequently goes online on behalf of his/her clients, helping cross the cognitive gap between cyberspace and life in an Indian village.

## E-society: Building Interactions

Such initiatives deal particularly with the relationship between public agencies and other institutions (public agencies, private sector service providers, non-profit and community organisations) and with the relationship between civil society institutions. As with citizen connections, these initiatives may well incorporate the process improvements in government day to day functioning. However, building interactions between civil society and public institutions also include a broader remit:

*Working better with business*[9]: improving the interaction between government and business. This includes digitising procurement from and services to business to improve their quality, convenience and cost. This uses all the potentials of ICTs to deliver the informational components of public services to business in digital form. It also includes digital support for opening up government to business through outsourcing and other public—private partnerships. The direct rationale is to drive costs down and quality up within government, but there is also an indirect rationale of improving the efficiency and responsiveness of local business. For instance, both business and Government in India were concerned about the delays and corruption associated with customs and importation. An ICT-based system (http://dgft.nic.in8100/iec) was introduced to address these concerns. Importers create a single electronic declaration, which is processed to calculate payments due and to undertake risk analysis, which identifies shipments that may require physical inspection. The online system has allowed a move to cashless procedures in which verification of duty/tax payment is sent electronically from authorised banks to Customs. The verification is automatically reconciled against processed declarations and a release order is then issued. The release order is sent electronically to the Customs warehouses that hold shipments. The result is a much faster service for business.

*Developing communities*[10]: building the social and economic capacities and capital of local communities. This uses the potential of ICTs to strengthen current information connections and to build new information connections within communities and between communities and other institutions. The rationale is to improve the wealth-creation potential and quality of life of community members. For instance, the *Gyandoot* project (www.gyandoot.com) in Madhya Pradesh set up 31 Internet-connected kiosks in villages in a district of central India where 60 per cent of the population live below the poverty line (earning less than US$1 per day). Each kiosk was initially funded by the local government committee. It is run by a local young entrepreneur along business lines: fees are charged for the services provided. Government-related services include online application for government certificates; online filing of complaints; printing of land records (which are held online and which all farmers need every season to obtain bank loans); and access to information on government welfare and related schemes. Other community development services include: access to agricultural produce prices; an auction site for sale/ purchase of land, equipment and animals; online discussion forums; and e-mail. In the first year of operation, the kiosks were used on tens of thousands of occasions. Proven benefits include better prices for agricultural produce; easier sales of other items; faster reactions to complaints or problems (e.g. an outbreak of cattle disease); and improved knowledge and skills within the communities served.

*Building partnerships*[11]: strengthening institutional relationships has two strategic issues. First, building government partnerships, strengthening relations between government and other institutions such as NGOs or international organisations. Second, building civil society partnerships focussing on strengthening relations between the institutions of civil society, such as between NGOs. This uses the potential of ICTs to strengthen current information connections and to build new information connections between institutions. The rationale is to create a strong economic, social and political 'fabric' within society. For instance, Civil society in India has networked with government in establishing public-private partnership at local level. *Drishtee* (www.drishtee.com) and *TARAhaat* (www.tarahaat.com) are two successful examples of civil society networks tying up with government to set up public private partnerships in rural India.

E-society, at least relating to communities or to other non-governmental institutions, has been a focus for recent donor-funded 'e-development' initiatives because such initiatives operate at the institutional rather than individual level, and because they operate somewhat independently of the red tape of government. There has also been a strong e-development interest in government-disintermediating service delivery initiatives. These seek to deliver education and health advisory and other information-intensive services direct without state intervention. Other components of e-society – typically those relating to government links – have been rather more neglected. Thus, as with citizen-focus projects, the opportunity has yet to be fully grasped to use the new connectivity to help refocus the state from an internal, self-serving view to an external, nation-serving view.

## Overview of E-governance Initiatives in India

The first and foremost example of e-governance initiative in India with wide ramifications, especially on the life of common man, was the computerised railway reservation system in the Indian Railways. As discussed above highlighting the wide scope of e-governance, the Government of India has launched variety of initiatives at various levels of governance, of which some are related to e-administration especially observed at the Ministerial level and some at State level. Nevertheless, there are scores of other forms of e-governance initiatives launched under private-public partnership, especially seen in connecting citizens and building interactions within society.

## National Level

*Five Year Perspective Plan:*

- The Government has already approved the policy of allocation of 2-3 per cent of Budget for IT. A system of monitoring the allocation, which each Ministry/Departments has made in their Annual Plan should be introduced.
- Due to limitation of resources the whole exercise of computerisation has, necessarily, to be phased, to cover various areas of Government operations. In order to have an impact of use of IT in Government for citizen service, those services

which have a direct interface with the public should be taken up for computerisation on a priority basis.

- Five years from now, majority of the transactional services will be provided by way of Internet. Net-based banking comes at only 10 per cent of the operating costs of conventional banking practices and services. As banks are going to play a key role in IT enabled public services involving electronic money transactions we feel that cooperative banks should consider NET-Banking in a big way.

*Intranet/Internet:*

- Government should have an Intranet for ensuring smoother flows of data, communications and access to information by different Ministries and Departments. It should be made mandatory for all Ministries and other Departments to put as much information as possible on to the Intranet but in a manner in which searches can be made easily.
- Transactions between various departments of the government of India and other Government organisations should be networked so that a substantial part of transfer of files and paper can be replaced by an intranet within the Government.
- All departments & agencies to ensure that they operate web sites that provide upto date information, forms, leaflets etc.
- E-mail to be incorporated into the normal range of contact methods and departments & agencies will implement arrangement for rapid response to e-mail queries.
- Service-wide guidelines and practices to be adopted regarding content format and presentation for web sites and inter-departmental group to be established to deal with these issues.
- Ministry of Information Technology (MIT) should bring out periodic bulletins on the Pilot project implementation in order to facilitate dissemination exchange of information.
- There should be a single web based front-end for all government services to the public.
- To use Internet and WWW based applications, Domain Name standardisation of various states must be done as it is available for various countries.

*Leasing of Computers:*

The introduction of computers in every Department/Ministry of Central and State Governments and their sub-ordinate organisations would require huge investments for the purchase of hardware and software. One way to possibly reduce the cost would be for the Government to enter into arrangements for leasing of computers. This would reduce the initial heavy capital investments. If it were combined with provisions for upgradation by periodic replacement, it would have the added benefit of keeping up with the changes in technology. The Finance Ministry can substantially bring down the lease charges by extending the concession under the Income Tax Act, so that any investment made in IT systems would be eligible for 100 per cent depreciation in the first year itself. The leasing companies can be persuaded to provide these systems at an interest rate of 12 per cent (if not less) which would be an attractive rate of interest. Once this is done the departments could proceed with the leasing of computes in a big way. There are already a number of agencies such as Infrastructure Leasing and Financial Services (ILFS) and Infrastructure Development Finance Corporation (IDFC) and other financial institutions which would be in a position to fund the leasing to the departments.

*Use of local languages:*

The access of information must be permitted in the language most comfortable to the public user, generally the local language. There are already existing technologies such as GIST and language software by which transliteration from English into other languages can be made.

*Spreading Awareness:*

Perhaps the most important aspect of computerisation and spreading of IT is bringing a change in the mindset of the government servants who have been accustomed to work only in the manual mode. It is necessary to train all employees in basic computer usage. The government is actively organising workshops and seminars for spreading computer literacy at all levels.

*Issuing Indicative Guidelines:*

An Inter-departmental group under the Department of Administrative reforms can be formed to prepare common guidelines on different aspects of acquiring IT items, evaluating execution of such contracts etc.

*Infrastructure for IT:*

The Government of India is aiming at creation of the infrastructure for Information Technology in the entire country by building National Information Infrastructure (NII), State Information Infrastructure (SII) and Local Information Infrastructure (LII).

*Information Kiosks:*

Communication of data to public i.e accessibility and retrieval of data by public through citizen I.T. interface (Information Kiosks) in Public Places such as shopping centers, post office, railway station, libraries. PCOs (Upgraded to manned public access terminals) selected STD/ISD booths at prominent places can be converted into information Kiosks.

*Cyberlaws:*

Cyberlaws should be made available to the public as early as possible so that the IT systems and information documents stored in the systems will have the same legal validity as the documents stored today on paper. The Government of India has enacted the IT Act 2001 in this regard and it is the government's first step towards making cyber laws for the country.

*Identification of Government Certification Authorities:*

Certification Authorities provide digital certificates that help create an online identification and security system for the Internet allowing individuals, corporations and government organisations to conduct transactions and communications with full security and confidence. Some of the Certificate-enabled applications are online banking, cyber-shopping, electronic data interchange (EDI), secure Electronic mail, government applications and services, online health services etc. Hence steps have been taken to identify such Certification Authorities.

*Standardisation:*

E-Governance demands standards in all areas. Some of the key areas are:

- Data encoding (ISCII or UNICODE)
- Application logic for common horizontal applications
- User interfaces
- Data dictionaries

Many a times, different user groups develop similar applications and there is no possibility of interaction between these functions within the organization or with outside agencies. It is possible to develop these functions as sharable across systems, languages, platforms and operating systems by developing them as reusable Components. The Government of India has constituted an expert group in the MIT to look into the issues of standardisation, independent of the User interfaces.

**E-governance: Identification of Government Departments with Citizen Interface**

Government of India has identified specific departments that have frequent interaction with the public in order to introduce the use of IT for effective government-citizen interface. Listed below are a few such departments:

*Public Grievances*: Electricity, Water, Telephone, Ration Card, Sanitation, Public Transport, Police

*Rural Services*: Land Records, Below Poverty Line (BPL)/EWS Families

*Police*: FIR Registration, Lost and Found, Valuables, Persons, Dead Bodies

*Social Services*: Pension, Old Age, Widows, Exgratia Scheme, Acquisition/Rehabilitation & Compensation, Registration of Licences and Certificates, Ration Cards, Birth Certificates, Death Certificate, Domicile Certificate, Caste/Tribe Certificate, Arms Renewal, Registration of Documents, School Registration, University Registration, Motor Vehicle Registration, Driving License

*Public Information*: Employment Exchange Registration, Employment Opportunities, Examination Results, Hospitals/Beds Availability/Services, Railway Time Tables, Airline Time Tables, Road Transport Time Tables, Charitable Trusts, Government Notifications, Government Forms, Government Schemes

**Contd. ...**

*EWS Services*: Civil supplies, Old Age Pension, Widow Pension, Handicapped Pension/Services, Ex Gratia Payment

*Agriculture Sector*: Speeds Information, Pesticides, Fertilizers, Crop disease, Weather Forecast - short range/District wise, Market Price

*Utility Payments/Billing*: Electricity, Water, Telephone

*Commercial*: Taxation & Return Filing, Income Tax, Corporate Tax, Custom Duty, Central/State Excise Duty, Sales Tax, House Tax, Property Tax, Octroi, Road Tax, Company Returns

*Government*: Electronic Procurement, Education University Model for E-Governance

While initiatives have been emanating from various directions, they are often at cross-purposes and so repetitive and wasteful. The National Task Force has also made several recommendations in this regard. Considerable progress has been done in making e-governance a reality in India.

## E-governance: An Overview of Ministries and Department

The fundamental responsibility of the government is to introduce computerisation at Ministry and department level in order to imbibe a culture of e-governance in the country. Considerable work has been carried out at various Ministries/Departments level. Almost all Ministries and Department have their web pages on the NIC web site displaying objectives, responsibility, contact person, etc. Besides, all the major Ministries/Departments display their policy and other decisions on their web sites. Few ministries/departments have launched their electronic newsletter for widespread awareness of their operations. Following is an update on e-governance at various Ministry and Department levels.

*Ministry of Chemicals & Fertilizers (http://chemicals.nic.in & http://fertilisers.nic.in)*

The IT Plan for the Department was prepared about two years ago and the implementation has been phased over a period of five years. The hardware required for the Sections and the Senior Officers was procured in 1999 itself. All officers up to the level of Section Officers have been connected to LAN. In-house Training Courses were organised by NIC for all the officials on Windows 98, Office 97, Internet browsing and E-mail. A web site of the Department has also been launched, which was inaugurated in January, 2000. The information required for updating the site is collected on the 5th of every month and passed on to NIC's main server machine. The Department is also operating a Facilitation Centre for providing information required by general public. The Department is maintaining database on production Monitoring for the Chemicals and Petrochemicals on the Server machine installed at the NIC-C&PC Monitoring cell. To implement the paperless office concept, the Office Procedure Automation (OPA) package has been put into use and its implementation is reviewed periodically. All the officers of the Ministry have been provided e-mail accounts for effective communication. It is also proposed that the PSU's/Organisation/ Attached Office of this department should have a VSAT connectivity for online communication both ways. The Department's IT plan is periodically reviewed by Secretary to ensure speedy implementation and to finally achieve the objective of integrating itself with the other Ministries/Departments through e-governance.

*Ministry of Civil Aviation (http://civilaviation.nic.in)*

Ministry of Civil Aviation is using IT extensively in their office and necessary infrastructure has been set up with the help of National Informatics Centre. Connectivity with various Government Departments is available including Internet connectivity, E-mail, video conferencing etc. They have some packages like Office Procedure Automation (OPA), Parliament assurances, Monitoring System, Parliament Questions and Pay roll etc. Through OPA, they have computerized the files & receipts handling and monitoring system since 1993. They have set up a Facilitation Counter where information required by public is disseminated.

*Ministry of Defence (http://mod.nic.in)*

The department of Defence deals with three Services and with Inter-Services organisations. It is responsible for the Defence Budget, establishment matters, Defence policy, matters relating to Parliament, Defence cooperation, and coordination. With the usual computerisation of the Ministry an d launching of the web site, the Ministry has put on its web site defence tender notifications for incorporating greater transparency. Besides, computer education and training has become an integral part of resettlement and welfare scheme for defence forces personnel.

*Ministry of Disinvestment (www.divest.nic.in)*

The Ministry has a bi-lingual web site, putting all the guidelines on disinvestment, list of PSUs approved for disinvestment, procedures, etc. on its web site for making the process of disinvestment transparent. It has also commenced with the rapid computerisation programme in order to improve its functioning.

*Ministry of Environment & Forests (http://envfor.nic.in)*

Ministry of Environment & Forests has launched their web site where information/status on important matters e.g. environment and forest clearance is also available online. The Ministry is also in the process of setting up a LAN in the Ministry and also drawn up IT Plan for the Ministry.

*Ministry of External Affairs (http://meadev.nic.in)*

The Ministry has put on government online international project of G-8 countries, Visa regulations of major countries (15). It has implemented back office automation activities, which have Citizen Interface, RPO & E-mail project. Eight regional passport offices have been fully computerized and networking between them is complete. The Ministry has launched its own web site with the assistance from NIC displaying necessary rules and regulations for passport and other outside travel formalities. The electronic passport application form and passport application online query system is also operational now.

*Ministry of Finance (http://finmin.nic.in)*

In the Department of Economic Affairs, Ministry of Finance, following steps have been taken to accelerate the usage of Information Technology. Besides, usual computerisation and LAN and WAN connectivity to all officers, a Facilitation Centre had been setup for the department for dissemination of the information to general public. The status on the "Electronic Governance for the usage of Information Technology" in respect of Aid Accounts and Audit Division, under various aspects in as under- Identification of functional areas of immediate concern with respect to Electronic Governance. All the work activities of this office, namely maintenance of loan-wise accounting, draw down of external assistance committed by various donors, debt service payment, budget preparation with regard to external assistance, amenable to complete computerisation. Web site for Ministry of Finance has been created three years ago and is being updated regularly. Computerisation activities in the Ministry of Finance started nearly 12 years back with installation of the Commonwealth Secretariat Debt Record Management System (CS-DRMS) package. Subsequently, some more standalone application packages were developed both in-house and by NIC. It has since been decided to develop an Integrated Computerised System (ICS) by setting up a Common Data Base (CDB). For this purpose, A.F. Ferguson & Co. have been appointed as Consultants. The work is being done in 2 phases. Phase I which comprised setting up of various masters, screens for capture of various transactions etc. has been completed. Phase II of the system which will provide solution to various other work activities like ACA releases, Budget preparation, finalisation of External Assistance Brochure etc. will be taken up. Besides, the monthly utilisation statement of External Assistance and quarterly status of External Debt (on Government account) have been put on the Internet through NIC. Some excerpts of External Assistance Brochure 1997-98 have also been disseminated for DEA users and also for public domain.

This Ministry has consistently taken initiatives in the use of information technology for delivering end results in terms of approval to the company, maintenance of approval records, compilation of ECB debt statistics etc. The ECB Division is using PCs right from the level of dealing assistants for processing the proposal and for correspondence with corporates. It is also maintaining an in-house database where the details of ECB proposals from the date of receipt of application up to the final disposal of the proposal are properly maintained. Under the existing arrangement, this Division is maintaining a data bank where year-wise details of ECB approval, taken on record of loan agreement out of current year of approval as well as the total taken of record are being maintained for the last three financial years (including the current one) at any point of time.

The details are available for an individual corporate and sector-wise consolidated details are also being maintained.

While interacting with the major international rating agencies, E-mail facility is the main source of communication. Through this facility, this Department as a nodal agency is continuously interacting with rating agencies like M/s. Moody's Investor Service, M/s. Standard & Poor's etc. on a day to day basis. This has ensured the smooth transfer of message/information without any substantial time lag. This has also helped in developing a better understanding with the rating agencies, which is one of the factors influencing the rating decisions for the Sovereign.

*Ministry of Health (http://mohfw.nic.in)*

Besides, the usual computerisation and launching of its web site informing about key policies and programmes of the Ministry, it has also commenced an information education and communication scheme. The department of ISM & H has evolved IEC Scheme with the objective to create awareness among the general masses about the various pathies, their cost effectiveness and the availability of the herbs used for prevention and treatment of common ailments by using various media channels, including networks.

*Ministry of Home Affairs (http://mha.nic.in)*

Ministry of Home Affairs has successfully completed the ongoing Ministry computerisation project. It has also set up its web site and put up the controversial POTO legislation for greater transparency and wide spread awareness. Besides, its web site also informs about various rules and procedures for foreigners and tourists. Even to keep up pace with development in e-commerce, its web site displays various tender notifications issued by subordinate police organisations, etc.

*Ministry of Labour (http://labour.nic.in)*

Besides, usual computerisation, the Ministry has set up an IT Committee to formulate and recommend the computerisation proposals in consultation with users. The committee also monitors the implementation of approved projects and helps in removing the bottlenecks, if any. Keeping the rapidly changing nature of IT in mind, the Ministry is formulating a conceptual plan for implementing Integrated Labour Information System consisting of interrelated segments like, Social Security, Industrial Relations, Employment and Manpower, Industrial Safety and Health. Recruiting Agents Database is being maintained on the Ministry of Labour web site with query facilities for public access regarding emigration. An Industrial Relation System integrated with chief Labour Commissioner (Central) and Central Government Industrial Tribunals (CGITs) will be the next area providing FOC database access to public and data capture at the point of origin. Other areas for web enabled systems are to be identified and prioritized in consolation with MOL Organisation Heads and Bureau Heads. The other initiatives of IT in some of Ministry of Labour Offices and Organisation are as follows: The Employees' Provident Fund organisation has already computerised and its field offices and the Employees' PF and Pension Schemes are operated on computerised systems with on-line subscribers' database. It is planning restructuring and IT driven functioning with the help of MIT and NIC, EPFO plans. The Employees' State Insurance Corporation has been successfully running Computerised System in its Headquarters Dispensaries, Medical Stores and Regional Offices in coordination with NIC. It is in the process of creating data based of Insured Persons in its field offices.

The Labour Bureau is maintaining its own web site on NICNET with regular updation of Labour Statistics like Customer Price Index Numbers that is accessible to the public. This web site is linked to the Ministry's web site. It is upgrading its Infrastructure regularly with higher level of computerisation. The V.V Giri National Labour Institute is also maintaining its own web site with linkage of the Ministry of Labour web site. The chief Labour Commissioner (Central) office has also created the computer infrastructure in its head offices and field offices. The trade union membership verification system is at present operational in CLC(C) Hqrs. It is planned to decentralised processing at Hqrs. The Directorate General of Factory Advisor Service & Labour Institutes and Directorate General of Mines Safety and Health, have computer infrastructure and are operating on computerised system. They are augmenting their IT resources. Further to improve the quality of IT services from this Ministry, individuals Bureau Heads have been instructed to submit revised IT plans based on working group on IT.

*Ministry of Law*

Ever since NIC took up computerization of courts, many applications have been computerized which have impact on masses i.e. litigants. Following are some of the applications which have been successfully implemented at Supreme Court and 18 High Courts and these applications have either direct or indirect impact on the masses.

*List of Business Information System* (LOBIS): It is about scheduling of cases to be heard by the courts on the following day. It enabled the Registries of Supreme Court and High Courts in eliminating manual process of Cause List generation thus any manipulation by vested interests. These databases contain details of fresh cases, disposed and pending cases. It is the backbone application of every Court.

*Filing Counter Computerization*: In the Supreme Court of India and all High Courts fresh cases are filed only before the computerized Filing Counters. As the advocates stand in queue for Filing cases before the counters, the data entry Operator enters preliminary details required for Registration such as Party names, advocate details, etc. The computer terminal at the query counter is used to attend to the quarries of the litigants on the spot. The defects, if any, are listed out and handed over to the litigants/advocates for rectification. Time limitation is also checked by the system automatically.

*COURTNIC*: This is about providing Supreme Courts' pending case status information to litigants/advocates on any node of NICNET. COURTNIC answers about two hundred queries of litigants/advocates per day all over the country on the status of their pending cases. It is available on nominal charges. Primarily COURTNIC information is available in all NIC-High Court Computer Cells and in some District Court. It has been in use since 1993.

*JUDIS*: NIC has brought out Judgement Information System (JUDIS) consisting of complete text of all reported judgement of Supreme Court of India from 1950 to 1998. The Judgements of 1999 onwards are available on Internet. JUDIS-CD is available on a Membership basis for Rs. 6000/-. It is marketed by NICSI. (http://judisi.nic.in).

*Supreme Court's Pending Cases on IVR*: Interested litigants and advocates can find out the status of their cases pending in Supreme Court on telephone by making use of Interactive Voice Response

System (IVR) free of charge. For accessing this, the phone nos. are: 011-4362062, 4360112.

NIC took up computerisation of all 18 High Courts and 9 Benches on the lines of Apex Court's Computerisation. NIC implemented the List of Business Information (LOBIS) in all High Court Courts. Some of the High Courts' Cause List are also available on Internet. Many possible applications in all High Courts have been computerised. Most of the High Courts have opened query counters along with Filing Counters for providing pending cases information to the litigants and advocates. Lately NIC took up the computerisation of all 430 District Courts in the country on the lines of High Courts Computerisation Project.

*Ministry of Parliamentry Affairs (http://mpa.nic.in)*

Ministry of Parliamentary Affairs has put in considerable efforts in the e-governance. They are in the process of computerisation the working of the Ministry. They will seek the expert advice of the department in application of IT in efficient Governance after completion of computerisation in the Ministry.

*Ministry of Power (http://powermin.nic.in)*

Ministry of Power has taken the some initiatives in relation to IT Governance and delivery of services/schemes through use of Information Technology. A new plan scheme involving a budget of Rs. 1 crore for remaining years of the 9th plan has been introduced from this year. The details of the scheme have been finalised which envisages procurement of hardware/software providing training to the officers/staff of the Ministry etc. The Ministry of Power also has a web site, which has been functioning since 1996. All policy initiatives taken by the Ministry are available on the web site. Separately, the web site also has detailed information on the organisational structure of the Ministry, important notifications issued, especially those related to private power projects, status of reforms/restructuring programmes in various states etc.

*Ministry of Surface Transport*

Besides, the computerisation in the Ministry, the ministry has launched Project on Development of Automatic Vehicle Counting,

Classification and Axle Load Weighing System for Highway Applications, Project on Intelligent Transportations System for Indian Conditions, etc. It has also constituted a Committee for implementation of the scheme for Ancillary Development related to shipbuilding and ship repair. It has also initiated Networking of the Lighthouses for DGLL and Introduction of Vessel Traffic Management System (VTMS) service in the Gulf of Kutch.

*Ministry of Textiles (http://texmin.nic.in)*

The Ministry of Textiles has set up a Task Force on IT to formulate the methodology of introducing IT in different aspects of textile sector. They have taken initiative to set up a computer communication network for all its offices at state levels. As part of recommendations of IT Task Force, all related offices are taking up initiatives to establish e-mail facility for communication. Web site on Internet is being installed in the Ministry as well as its attached/subordinate offices. Economic Research and Market Intelligence Unit (ERMIU) has been set up at Office of Textiles Commissioner, Mumbai for collection and dissemination of information on production, designs, fashion etc. As recommended by IT Task Force, all offices and subordinate organizations are directed to take up in house computerization for implementation of MIS in routine working.

*Ministry of Tourism (www.tourismofindia.com)*

The Ministry has created a thematic CD-ROM on important monuments. It has also installed Data base driven visitor query system at all the Tourist Offices. It has put up computer based tourist information kiosks at airports, railway stations, bus depots, tourist offices etc. One type of kiosk shall have a multimedia content providing information in an entertaining way and the other on Geographical Information System (GIS). It is also developing MIS packages for various Divisions and subordinate offices.

*Department of Agriculture*

The Department of Agriculture and Cooperation under Ministry of Agriculture has initiated specific programmes for strengthening of Information Technology in the Agriculture Sector. For instance, the Ministry has created an IT Division and its web site is operational since 1999 at the following address http://www.nic.in/agricoop. DAC HQs and most of its attached and subordinate offices have been declared Y2K compliant. A central sector scheme for strengthening IT apparatus in the DAC HQs. has been approved. Under the scheme, IT tools are being provided to all the offices in DAC; Under the aforesaid scheme, an Early Warning System is being established to monitor agriculture on real time basis directly from the fields by use of IT applications. Video Conferencing facilities have been established in the DAC HQs. with the help of NIC. Officers are now using e-mail in their day-to-day working and the DAC has also been given the centralised e-mail address: agrindia@krishi.delhi.nic.in. Software programs are being developed keeping in view the functional needs of various divisions. An independent computer training room has been set up where training is available on all working days during working hours to all officers and staff as per their needs and convenience. A central sector scheme for strengthening Information Technology and their horizontal and vertical networking with the DAC HQs is under consideration and the proposal has been referred to Planning Commission. A centrally sponsored scheme for strengthening and promoting informatics in agriculture in the States is also separately under consideration.

*Department of Commerce (http://commin.nic.in)*

It is a part of Ministry of Commerce and Industry. Department of Commerce has been quite active in computerisation of key departments, especially in terms of government-to-business contact area. As discussed earlier, computerisation of Director General Foreign Trade Office has brought relief to number of exporters and imorters and has been instrumental in trade facilitation. Besides, its official web site has emerged as a great resource for all WTO matters. It has also come up with an electronic newsletter, name WTO Focus for researchers and policy makers, as part of infusing greater transparency in government decision making.

*Department of Posts (www.indiapost.org)*

The Department of Posts has undergone a sea change in terms of computerisation, for instance computerisation in Post Office, front offices, Money order services, postal life insurance, etc. It also proposes to connect Postal Directorate at Delhi, the N.E. postal circle and the Assam postal, circle with internet as the link network, and computerisation of international mail and airlines accounts.

The IT initiatives in the Ministry has been limited to merely computerisation of Ministry and subordinate offices. Besides, some Ministries and Departments have launched their web sites for greater transparency. However, as part of the government drive towards e-governance, the Central Government has to cover lot of areas for building an adequate platform for seamless interface between government-to-citizen contact. As discussed earlier in e-governance for development, in many strategic areas like connectivity (connecting remote markets), standardisation, cyberlaws, etc. The major limitation that the Ministries and other Government Departments are likely to face is the changes in management processes in decision making. For instance, the departments identified by the Task Force on IT for better government-to-citizen contact have yet be fully computerised to take up the next phase of higher platform catering to complex computerised back-end activity via online requests. Without appropriate computerisation and policy intervention in strategic areas, G2C will remain an elusive dream for quite some time.

## State Level

During the last few years there has been major initiatives by different State Governments towards ushering in IT and its tools in the functioning of Government. The emphasis has been on providing better services to citizens and in improving the internal productivity. It has been widely accepted that IT implementation in State Government is the most difficult process and hence requires careful planning and formulation of strategies for effective implementation. The experiences of individual States in this regard need to be understood and shared to evolve meaningful strategies.

The first point to be noted is the need to use *local languages in the IT implementation process*. It is imperative to note that, particularly because of the work done by C-DAC (MIT) and various Indian Institute of Information Technology (IIIT), the technology is now very much locally available. This by itself could give a major boost to IT implementation efforts in the States. Here, a focused effort would have to be made in improving the technologies for transliteration. Similarly, efforts are on for *perfecting the OCR technology for local languages*. This is critical as an effective OCR technology is required to convert the data that is scanned and stored in local languages into meaningful and workable databases. This could also help in substantially simplifying the efforts at content generation and data warehousing.

The second point to be noted is on the scope of *IT implementation within Government*. Most States have focused on computerisation of individual activities per se. This leads to mere automation of the existing manual work and could lead to a situation where an activity done by 20 persons would get done by 20 computers and 20 persons on implementing IT. Of late, the fallacy of such an approach is being realised. The emphasis currently is on conducting system studies to understand the work flows involved in each of the activities and attempt computerisation of such work flows. This results in certain levels of simplification & rationalisation and even an improvement in productivity. However, here also the basic issues involved in delay and red tapism within Government are not adequately addressed. Even in computerisation of work flows, there will be a need to update the data periodically. In the event of each individual completing the work assigned to him, even in the present system delays would not have occurred. In this context, it is clear that *substantive administrative reforms would have to precede attempts at e-govemance*. In other words, the emphasis will have to be on simplifying procedures, rationalising processes, restructuring Government and then use IT to institutionalise such changes. It is in these circumstances that attempts at e-govemance based on *creative and effective uses of relational databases* needs to be attempted.

## E-governance Initiatives in States

The first element of such initiative will be to define a uniform citizen code at the national level. Once this is done each state may be asked to arrange its databases with one field earmarked for this code. This would facilitate easy retrieval of data and integration of databases at any point of time. The second element of such initiative would be to ensure that the databases that are going to get generated as part of the census operations may also be digitised and made available for building up citizen databases. This would possibly require amendments to the census act and it is suggested that a thorough study may be made to identify the uses of such data in building up comprehensive databases immediately. Another element that needs to be effectively addressed is the issue pertaining to dissemination of information gathered through our investments in science and technology. A case in point is the information collected by remote sensing which could be of immense use in estimating the availability of resources and qualitatively alter the planning process. An effort to identify similar repositories of data and information relevant for providing better services to citizens through e-governance and a strategy for the desegregation of such data and its dissemination needs to be urgently formulated.

*Andaman & Nicobar (http://andaman.nic.in)*

It is a remotely located state in Bay of Bengal. The State Government has commenced computerisation of key departments. It web site attempts to promote the state as a tourist destination to the outside world. the official web site lists out rules and procedures of obtaining permissions for water sports like scuba diving, foreign yachts, etc. The schedules of charter flights and ferry service timings are also put on the official web site. Most government forms are put online as part of the citizen's charter. The official web site also allows online booking of rooms at various hotels in the Andamans.

**Telemedicine**

Telemedicine consists of customised medical software integrated with computer hardware, along with medical diagnostic instruments connected to the commercial VSAT (very Small Aperture Terminal) at each location. Generally the medical record/history of the patient is sent to the Specialist Doctors, who will in turn study and provide diagnosis and treatment during video-conferencing with patient's end.

*Andhra Pradesh (www.andhrapradesh.com)*

The Andhra Pradesh government's e-governance initiative is best known for APSWAN (Andhra Pradesh State Wide Area Network), a state-wide network for voice, data and video communication, which is the basic information highway for improving government-citizen and government-industry interface. In subsequent phases, APSWAN would be extended to all 'mandal' headquarters, other towns and eventually, to all villages. Prior to this, one of the first projects effectively taken up towards the implementation of e-govemance was by the state's Department of Registration. It provides an easy and transparent process for registering and documenting immovable property.

**_e-Seva_ : E-governance initiative of AP Govt**

*e-Seva* provides a one–stop venue for services of various state and central government departments through an easy access through a chain of computerized Integrated Citizen Service Centres (ICSCs) and through the Internet i.e. www.esevaonline. com. *e-Seva* covers various departments of both State Government and Central Government.

- ICSCs operates from 9-AM to 7-PM on all working days and is open on Sundays and Second Saturdays also 9.00 A.M to 3-00 PM.
- Electronic queuing system and efficient transaction of business reduces waiting time
- Any service at any counter in the center Any service at any center at any place in the city
- Distribution of centers in all major areas surrounding the city and likely to expand to other parts of the state
- At present there are 18 *e-Seva* centers spread across Hyderabad and Secunderabad

Perhaps the most daunting task for the Andhra Pradesh government was the compilation of the socio-economic classification of the state's residents and the preparation of a database of land records. These are the first stepping stones towards the issuance of multipurpose identity cards that would ensure better targeting for poverty alleviation programmes. Popularly known as the 'IT project focussed on the common man', TWINS enables the citizens of Hyderabad and Secunderabad to access select services and information on Departments of the State and Central Governments. This is done by accessing integrated citizen service centres (ICSCs). The ICSC is a one-stop shop for key citizen services - such as payment of electricity, water and sewage bills, property tax, registration and issuing of birth and death certificates and many more. The government has also initiated the Secretariat Knowledge Information

Management System with a view to exploit the power of computer networks, automate workflow in the Secretariat and provide effective tools for performance evaluation. The Andhra Pradesh Planning Department has put together a sophisticated Geographical Information System (GIS) which captures inputs from remote sensing satellites to create thematic data on road networks and community infrastructure.

*Bihar (http://bihar.nic.in)*

Bihar Government is keen to promote IT culture through out State in order to benefit the mass through this technology. Some of the major computerization activities carried out by the State government with the technical support from National Informatics Centre, includes computerisation of statewide transport, treasury, GDP Office, commercial tax system, Bihar State Electricity Board, etc. Besides all these, Bihar State Unit has successfully computerised the elementary education under HRD Department. Created an MIS of 2 lacs of school teachers including Primary and Middle. Completed the 6th All India Census in the record time. There are many other state Govt. Projects such as Land Records, Health, Commercial Tax, Science & Technology, Bihar State Electricity Board etc. as well as central Govt. Projects such as Central Excise, ROC, Provident Fund Organisation etc. which as been accepted, maintained and computerisation plan are initiated. National Informatics Centre has also developed a computerised system to keep track of distribution of food grains, sugar, kerosine oil etc. in the state of Bihar. The system also takes care of district level requirement of allotment of such commodities dealer wise on the basis of rationing units.

*Chandigarh (http://chandigarh.nic.in)*

Project Telemedicine interconnecting three premier medical institutes i.e. PG1-Chandigarh, AIIMS-Delhi and SGPG, Lucknow using ISDN for tele-dignosis, tele-consutation and tele-education, each of which in turn will be connected with one medical college has been initiated.

*Chattisgarh (http://chattisgarh.nic.in)*

The government plans for State-wide Geographical Information System GIS to be set up through ISRO which brings the state's entire 20,000 villages into digital domain. All villages and towns will be connected through wireless solutions, connecting them with CHOICE centres (Chattisgarh Online Information System for Citizen Empowerment).

*Dadra Nagar Haveli*

Ongoing project in the Union Territory is computerisation of government offices. It has yet to launch its official web site.

*Delhi (http://delhigovt.nic.in)*

The Delhi Government is playing an active role in (a) Promoting IT for masses (b) Ushering E-Governance (c) Creating an atmosphere conductive for the growth of IT Industry & IT Infrastructure. Besides, the usual computerisation of government offices and departments, Delhi Government has launched its official web site. All important government forms are available online. With a view to bring in a culture of openness and transparency, the Government of Delhi has enacted the Delhi Right to Information Act, 2001. It would help the citizens in getting the required information as a matter of right barring certain areas. The government also plans to start a "Teach the Teachers" programme for upgrading the IT knowledge and skills of teachers on a regular basis. A Spcecial Cell will be set up in State Council for Education, Research and Training to work out details of this programme. The government intentds to take up training of at least 10 per cent of teachers in higher Secondary Schools during 2000-01. There shall be an incentive scheme to attract teachers to this programme and to encourage them to complete it successfully.

*Goa (http://goagovt.nic.in)*

The State Government has issued a notice to all its departments to computerise the activities of their departments by using various operating systems, software programmes to ensure compatibility, seamless transfer of data and information, etc. It has also directed government departments to send in proposals for e-governance for better government to citizen contact[12].

*Gujarat (http://gujarat.nic.in)*

Gujarat was in the limelight when it introduced the smart card-based driving license project. Each of the 22 Regional Transport

Offices (RTOs) of Gujarat was equipped with state-of-the-art enrolment and issuance centres. The government has also implemented a state-wide WAN (Wide Area Network) project that connects its various office complexes and corporations and supports services like voice, data and video traffic. The network provides a backbone for connectivity to any LAN establishment throughout the state.

Gujarat's State Road Transport Department's 'computerised check posts' project has reduced corruption at the 10 octroi posts to zero and has enhanced revenue earnings. The Government has also used IT to handle its recurring problem of natural disasters creatively. The communication systems are being so designed as to remain unaffected during emergency situations. The Vadodara Model District Project put in place at a cost of just Rs 1.22 crores set its own benchmark. The project involved software development and training for the entire staff, and connected 64 nodes in the Collectorate with 13 nodes in as many block towns in the state.

The Government has already launched a comprehensive information technology policy and a new corporation viz. Gujarat Information Technology Ltd. has been launched. Mega infocity project is coming up near Gandhinagar and will boost the software industry and generate vast employment opportunities. An ambitious project of Info-tower, set up by the GNFC in Ahmedabad is having all infra structural facilities including connectivity to the entrepreneurs in the field of information technology. Gradually all the district headquarters will be linked up with the secretariat in Gandhinagar with E-governance Network. So far 1,00,000 government employees have been imparted the computer training. As per the plan chalked out by the information technology department over 2,00,000 educated young persons will be given training and employment opportunities in this sector.

*Haryana (http://haryana.nic.in)*

The State Government has instituted an Information Technology initiative fund with an initial corpus of Rs 10 crore for e-governance and to promote the IT in the State. It would also be utilised for developing replicable and reusable models of e-governance, IT innovations in administration, re-engineering and IT supported resource optimisation.

**Public-Private Partnership: Drishtee at Sirsa**

*Drishtee offers e-governance, education and health services through a software package which facilitates communication and information interchange within a localised intranet between villages and a district centre. The objective of the project has been to establish community-owned, innovative and sustainable IT projects in the most poverty-stricken and tribal dominated rural areas throughout India. The projects seek to use IT for rural people causing a shift in the government's delivery apparatus – to serving villagers directly rather than through civil servants.*

*The objective of Drishtee is to create a sustainable model of rural distribution and promotion of consumer goods and basic services, and then replicate these information islands and interconnect them. The services it enables include access to government programs and benefits, market related information, and private information exchanges and transactions. Using a tiered franchise and partnership model, Drishtee is capable of enabling the creation of approximately 50,000 Information Kiosks all over India within a span of six years. These kiosks would potentially serve a market of 500 million people, with aggregate discretionary purchasing power of Rs. 100 billion (Rs. 10,000 crores). In less than two years, Drishtee has successfully demonstrated its concept in over 90 kiosks across five Indian states, namely Madhya Pradesh, Rajasthan, Punjab, Haryana, and Uttar Pradesh.*

A corpus fund of Rs 5 crore for the seting up of an Indian Institute of Information Technology (IIIT) at Gurgoan. An ultra-modern cyber city in Gurgoan near Indira Gandhi International Airport is being setup to provide employment opportunities to five lakh persons and make an impact of Rs. 15,000 crore on the economy of the State.

*Himachal Pradesh (http://himachal.nic.in)*

NIC established State as well as District Centers, by installing Computer Systems and providing Satellite-based Computer Communication Network (NICNET). The 11 District Centres have been provided with IP-Advantage (IPA) VSAT for NICNET connectivity, by installing a 1.2m Dish antenna for the purpose, for Internet and Email services through the DNS). These 11 district centres are also provided with a telephone line each, for extending the NICNET connectivity further to outside users on Dial-up Line. The

Himachal Pradesh Govt. has also launched its official web site, giving details about tourist destinations, policy programmes, etc. It has been also instrumental in putting up exclusive web pages fore each district. It is in the process of implementing wide-scale computerisation programme in all the government departments, for instance tourism, excise and taxation, industries, law and justice, rural development and panchayati raj, police, health, revenue and finance, etc.

*Jammu & Kashmir (http://jammukashmir.nic.in)*

This state has been strife with insurgency and terrorism for the last two decades. The IT initiatives of the state government are still in infancy. Only few government departments have been able to implement the computerisation programme of the Central Government. However, the State Government has launched it official web site giving all the necessary details about the State, for instance fact sheet, who's who, tourist destinations, etc. There is also and added facility for the people to get in touch via e-mail with the Chief Minister.

The State Government plans to promote IT in a more aggressive manner in the state by implementing wide-scale computerisation in the government departments at the district level. It also plans to use IT-enabled services for government-to citizen contact. Some private initiatives in education have been launched by NGOs by using multimedia techniques, but it is still in experimental stages.

*Jharkhand (http://jharkhand.nic.in)*

It is a new state carved out Bihar. The State Government has commenced with the computerisation of government departments. It has also launched its official web site to add greater transparency in the government operations. Government policies, who's who in the state and other wide variety of information are put on the official web site.

*Karnataka (http://karnataka.nic.in)*

The Karnataka Government has embarked upon an ambitious e-governance programme to make its citizen interface (especially in revenue, land registration and civic utilities) more transparent and friendly. Within the government, the most commendable work has been done by the Department of Treasuries, which completed the installation of 250 VSATs to capture every single transaction at all district and taluk treasuries. The government also proposes to have an optic fibre running across the state, linking all the 70-plus engineering colleges, ITI's and other technical institutions. It has computerised the Education Department to enable monthly reviews, recruitment, posting of teachers, and online counselling.

**_Bhoomi_ : Computerisation Of Land Records**

All 17 million land records of 67 lakhs land owners in 177 taluks of Karnataka will be computerised. As on now 125 *taluks* in the state has been computerised & working on-line. This system works with the software called "*BHOOMI*" built fully in-house by NIC, Bangalore. Computerisation of Land Records in entire Karnataka will be completed by March 2002. This scheme is largely funded by Government of India, some components in this scheme are funded by State Government. Once this scheme has been operationalised in the *taluks*, the manual RTCs will be considered as illegal. *Bhoomi* software authenticates users on their fingerprint. This ensures that no body can hack the system by imitating other users. This software also has the provision of scanning of original mutation orders of revenue inspectors (who is the authorised person to pass orders in the mutations in the field) and notices served on interested parties. *Bhoomi* directly impacts 6.7 million farmers across Karnataka. The programme, in simple terms, is the computerisation of 20 million records of land ownership in Karnataka's farming community. Any farmer in the state can today get a copy of the Record of Rights, Tenancy and Crops (RTC), a critical document of ownership required to avail bank loans, for a user charge of Rs.15.

All the farmer has to do is go to the *Bhoomi* centre at the sub-district office and obtain the required document, be it the RTC, a mutation extract for a piece of land that has been sold or a title deed. Before *Bhoomi*, the process took weeks and was riddled with corruption. Farmers claimed they had to pay anywhere between Rs.100 and Rs.2,000 in bribes to officials. What's more, the project has already started earning large revenue for the state – as much as 7-7.5 million Rupees every month. The software also includes the biometrics aspect, which records and identifies the fingerprint of the official who would be entering the change of ownership or sale of any piece of land in the state.

The Department of Information Technology and Rural Development & Panchayat Raj Department have conceived an IT training scheme called "Yuva.com" has been conceived by the Department of Information Technology and Rural Development & Panchayat Raj Department. This scheme is for the rural youth. Under this scheme, training centres will be established in each of the 225 assembly constituencies over the next twelve months. These centres will train about one lakh educated unemployed youth in IT related services. The private sector will participate in setting up and running these centres.

*Kerala (http://goidirectory.nic.in/kerala.htm)*

The Government of Kerala is making an impact in the public life with a series of e-governance initiatives aimed at bringing the most transparent and efficient governance to each citizen's doorstep. A series of departmental workshops with service organisations initiated to assess the employee's perceptions and apprehensions about IT implementation in Government and also in identifying the preparatory work to be carried out for a smooth transition to e-govemance. Two to three nodal officers identified by each Department who would champion the cause of IT within the department provided with a two-phased orientation programme in collaboration with major IT companies. Individual Government departments empowered with flexibility to outsource hardware procurement, systems study, software development and training to reputed total solution providers (TSPs), without going through complicated procurement procedures.

The CARD project of Andhra Pradesh has been adapted in the registration department. Five sub-registrar's offices in the Thiruvanthapuram district are being computerised under the direct supervision of the IT Department. A successful computerisation model evolved in the Office of the Controller of Entrance Examinations, which is fully computerised and equipped with software developed to facilitate the on-line admission to almost 25 different professional colleges and around 100 courses, matching the individual's choices with the availability of seats. Besides, a unique networked project for the establishment of a computer information network covering all the sub districts/blocks, as part of the larger objective of inter connectivity of all tiers of Government, connecting 152 development blocks in the state has been completed. This project will help in developing an effective information dissemination system at the block level and would facilitate monitoring of development projects undertaken at the block level. The government network was planned for the State with a view to provide transparent and effective administration at the block level. The first phase of the project for networking all the sub-treasuries in the State has been completed with five sub-treasuries and the extension counters in Thiruvananthapuram district being linked online. The second phase would test the capability of the VSAT architecture for networking. Even on completion of the first phase, the implications on proper resource planning at the Government level are fairly obvious. The project for linking the sub-offices, checkposts and other main nodes of commercial taxes department has completed the stages of systems study, techno-economic clearance and final tendering.

The Computer Server of the FRIENDS Centre will be linked to the server of the concerned departments for updation of data on a real time, once the computerization of the departments are completed. Until then, FRIENDS Centre shall work on the principle of "Collect and Remit" and "Receive and Forward" methods to offer public services like KSEB Bill Payments, KWA Bill Payments, Property Tax, Professional tax, Traders License Fee, Building Tax, Basic Tax, Revenue Recovery, Fee for new ration card, time vehicle tax, etc. Various other services which work on "Check and Confirm" mode - such as KSRTC Express Reservation service, booking/reconfirmation of Indian Airlines/ Air India, KTDC hotel reservation etc, can be added in future.

*Lakshadweep (http://goidirectory.nic.in/lakshadweep.htm)*

The State Government has embarked on ambitious plan of training of Officers and staff in basic concepts of computer and applications. Besides, the government has computerised selected departments for providing better access to citizens, especially services like ship ticketing, accounting system contingent bills, Electricity Billing System, Voucher Compilation for PAO, Entry permit Holder Information System, etc.

*Madhya Pradesh (http://mpgovt.nic.in)*

The State government is one of the first states to use IT for connecting the government with local masses. Government has identified Gwalior, Indore, Jabalpur and Raipur to come up as IT cities in the State. The State Government had launched a unique Government to Citizen initiative, popularly known as Gyandoot. It plans to build on this experiment to other districts of Madhya Pradesh.

**Towards G2C: *Gyandoot***

The *Gyandoot* project was launched on January 1, 2000 with the installation of a low cost rural Intranet covering 20 village information kiosks (*Soochanalayas*). Later, 11 more kiosks were set up. Kiosks were set up in villages that hold weekly markets in tribal areas, or are located on major roads. Each kiosk caters to about 25 to 30 villages. The entire network of 31 kiosks covers 311 *Panchayats* (village committees), over 600 villages and a population of around half a million (nearly 50 per cent of the entire district). Kiosks have been established in the *village Panchayat buildings*. They have dial-up connectivity through local exchanges on optical fibre or UHF links. The server hub is a Remote Access Server housed in the computer room in the District *Panchayat*. User fees are charged at the kiosks for the services provided. Local rural youth act as entrepreneurs, running these information kiosks along commercial lines. At the inception of the project it was decided that further expansion of kiosk centres will take place only when local youth come forward to start new centres as private enterprises.

**Services offered:**

*Prevailing rates of prominent crops at the local and other recognized auction centres* around the country are available on-line for a nominal charge of Rs. 5. The volume of incoming agricultural produce, previous rates, etc., are also provided on demand. *Copies of Land Records:* Documents relating to land records including khasra (record of rights) are provided on the spot at a charge of Rs. 15. All of the banks in the district have agreed to accept these kiosk documents. Approximately 0.2 million farmers require these extracts at every cropping season to obtain loans from banks for purchasing seeds and fertilisers. *On-line Registration of Applications*: Villagers had to make several visits to the local revenue court to file applications for obtaining income/caste/ domicile certificates. Now, they may send the application from a kiosk at a cost of only Rs. 10. Within 10 days, notification about the readiness of the certificate is sent via e-mail to the relevant kiosk. Only one trip is needed — to collect the certificate. *On-line Public Grievance Redress:*

**Contd. ...**

A complaint can be filed and a reply received within 7 days for a cost of Rs 10. These can include complaints regarding drinking water, quality of seed/fertilizer, scholarship sanction/disbursement, employee establishment matters, functioning of schools or village committees, etc. *Village auction site:* This facility began in July 2000. It makes auction facilities available to farmers and villagers for land, agricultural machinery, equipment, and other durable commodities. One can put one's commodity on sale for a charge of Rs. 25/- for three months. The list of salable commodities can be browsed for Rs. 10/-. *Transparency in government:* Updated information regarding beneficiaries of social security pension, beneficiaries of rural development schemes, information regarding government grants given to village committees, public distributions, data on families below the poverty line, etc. are all available on the Intranet, which makes the government functioning more transparent.

On-line matrimonial advertisements, information regarding government programs, a forum for school children to ask questions, ask an expert, e-mail (free for information on child labor, child marriage, illegal possession of land belonging to Scheduled Tribes, etc.) Some kiosks also have added *photocopy machines, STD PCO, and horoscope services*. In January 2000, the first month of operation, the kiosk network was accessed 1,200 times for a variety of services. That number reached nearly 9,000 in July. During the first 11 months, the 31 *Gyandoot* kiosks were used nearly 55,000 times

*Maharashtra (http://goidirectory.nic.in/maharashtra.htm)*

The Government of Maharashtra, recognising connectivity as an important tool for successful e-governance, took up the task of connecting 3,000 offices through a network. It aims to further the reach of the network to the 'sub-taluka' level. The government has gone for a district Wide Area Network (WAN) which links the 3,000 district offices. Further, the government's Stamps and Registration Department has undertaken extensive computerisation and is supported by comprehensive training modules for its staff. The state, with the aid of Computer Maintenance Corporation (CMC), undertook the task of developing software for the State Excise Department and creating basic awareness amongst employees.

**Warana Wired Villages Project (Maharashtra)**

By participating in a government project to plug 70 villages into the Internet, Warna's sugar cane farmers are among the first in the country to embrace the high-tech wave. Before the advent of the Warna Wired Village Project, farmers had to travel several hours to the cane crushing factory. Once there they would wait for hours as the crop was weighed and crushed, along with hundreds of tons of produce from other farmers. Only after this process was completed did farmers find out how much money their harvest had earned. In fact, all details about the sugar industry were available only at the factory. But now the farmers — who all belong to a co-operative that buys their sugar cane and then gives them an equal profit share — can get their information at a computer kiosk in his village. With computers in all the villages, the farmers are linked to a central network. Suddenly, connectivity is changing a centuries-old way of life.

The $600,000 network was funded by the central government, and provides 70 villages with computers. Through the network, farmers get a daily weather report, learn what fertilizer to use, and access the sale price of several other crops, which helps them decide what to plant next. Soon, they will be able to use the network to diagnose crop diseases.And they have no desire to keep the advancements secret; they want the 700 million Indians who live in the countryside to also have access to computers, believing it will help raise living standards across India as others discover the economic benefits of high-speed information.

*Orissa (http://orissa.nic.in)*

The Orissa Government deployed information technology towards the planning and development of land. The Bhubaneshwar Development Authority (BDA) has set up kiosks at its office that map the city using a GIS. This has made life easier for citizens as they can check on existing schemes for housing, commercial and industrial projects without depending on middlemen. Citizens can also get accurate information on rates, vacancies and administrative procedures. Satellite earth station is functional for giving data connectivity to IT companies, launching of Internet services introduced by DOT for general public, Orissa Centre of IBM Software imparting high-end software training, B.Sc (Hons), Computer Science courses introduced in six Govt. colleges, etc.

*Pondicherry (http://pondicherry.nic.in)*

The State Government has initiated steps to impart IT training by educational institutions and to make the Govt. machinery citizen friendly by facilitating transparency and efficiency. Besides, computerisation of government offices, it also provides facilities in the outlying regions with Internet facilities. The Pondicherry Engineering College is identified to establish a city centre to provide a permanent training facility under which computers will be purchased and given by the Government. The Engineering College will undertake the maintenance and training of staff. It has also set up a separate police-net for networking of all Police Stations, VAST facility in the assembly building with provision for Internet and E-mail, etc. The State Government also plans to set up a Software Technology Park.

*Punjab (http://punjab.nic.in)*

Punjab has announced its IT policy and plans to establish software technology parks in the state. Panchkula has emerged as a hub for IT industry. Punjab Government has also launched a wide spread computerisation programme of government departments and other state bodies. So far the e-governance initiative focussing of G2C has been experimental stages in few districts.

**Tarahaat: Public-Private Initiative at Bhatinda**

*Tarahaat.Com*, a project to provide online services to a large number of rural communities in north India, has been promoted by Development Alternatives (DA), a Delhi-based NGO. Pilot projects are in place at several locations in Bundelkhand, M.P., and Bhatinda, Punjab. While the project will provide a menu of services similar to other rural ICT projects, its current business model requires influx of capital before it becomes self-sufficient. One of the more innovative aspects of the project is its highly interactive and graphics-intensive interface system which allows semi-literate and neo-literate users enhanced access products and services. DA is an internationally-acclaimed voluntary group working on the issues of development, environment, technology and governance. The group has an experience of over two decades of using modern

**Contd. ...**

science for the benefit of the economically backward sections of the Indian society. Its primary task is to design new ways to create jobs for people in villages and towns. It does so by designing better technology, better ways to revive our forests, rivers and soils, and better systems of governance in our communities.

TARAhaat.com is the website developed by DA, and is focussed on the theme of connecting the Indian villager to the rest of the world. The design of the site has been kept simple to be handled even by a young child or an illiterate person. For a few rupees, the citizen can use a computer at a TARAdhaba to find out the crop prices at a faraway mandi, print out a map of her land or find a bridegroom for his daughter. TARAhaat.com covers a wide range of services, which include: E-News, E-Commerce, E-Governance, E-Education, E-Health, E-Entertainment. The website uses vivid illustrations and minimal text. For example, a walking, talking postman on the site informs the user that this is the link from where an email can be sent or received. Similarly, illustrations mark the links for health (hospital), administration (local government office), transport (a moving bus) and other links.

*Rajasthan (http://goidirectory.nic.in/rajasthan.htm)*

The State Government has launched Vikas Darpan – GIS based Planning & Decision Support System covers 40000 Tehsils on about 200 demograph and socio-economic indicators. Rajasthan's Department of Information Technology has developed a state-wide intranet called 'rajSWIFT. This system uses the Internet to facilitate online data, text and email communication between the Office of the Chief Minister and the 32 District Collectors. RajNIDHI, a web-enabled citizen-service information kiosk framework, is a modern, transparent and responsive system. The government aims to provide greater transparency in government-citizen interactions through projects such as 'Aarakshi' (which provides field officers with online information on criminals); computerisation of the Ajmer Collectorate (including grievance monitoring systems); computerisation of hospitals; computerisation of the Registration and Stamps Department; and networking of the Secretariat.

*Sikkim (http://goidirectory.nic.in/sikkim.htm)*

The Sikkim Government plans to provide connectivity in the state with help of Telstra V. Comm, which will provide VAST connectivity in Industrial Growth Centre/Technology Park. It also plans to set up a R&D unit in Sikkim House, New Delhi and a 128 kbps VAST link for global connectivity supplementing present ERNET VAST bandwidth.

*Tamil Nadu (http://goidirectory.nic.in/tamilnadu.htm)*

Tamil Nadu is now firmly established as a major player in India's IT scene. A NASSCOM study in 1998 has rated Chennai as the best possible location for investment in the software industry. As part of government's commitment to the growth of the IT industry in the State, the Tamil Nadu Government was one of the first to announce a comprehensive Information Technology Policy in 1997. As a consequence of all these innovative efforts, software exports from the State have increased from just Rs. 37 crores in 1995-96 to nearly Rs. 1,900 crores in 1999-2000. As a major initiative for the development of IT infrastructure in Tamil Nadu, the Government of Tamil Nadu has promoted "TIDEL Park", the largest, most advanced facility of it kind in India through the joint efforts of two of its Public Sector Undertakings, namely TIDCO and ELCOT. The TIDEL Park has facilities specifically designed to meet the need of the IT Industry including international data connectivity, uninterrupted power, fully automated building maintenance system operation, maintenance of facilities by international experts and a world class working ambience.

The Government of Tamil Nadu, in order to restore the faith of citizens in the efficacy of the government, undertook projects like STAR (Simplified and Transparent Administration of Registrations across Tamil Nadu); SCHOOL (which aims to take computer literacy to 1300 high secondary schools); computerisation of land records (in order to eliminate corruption in the department); and computerisation of the Transport Department (which maintains an accurate historical data of over one crore vehicles and drivers). In addition, tele-medicine has met with tremendous success - it allows doctors in remote areas to consult experts on special cases. A Tamil Internet Research Centre has also been set up for funding projects promoting the use of Tamil on the internet to maximise access to citizens.

### G2C: Sustainable Access in Rural India (SARI)

Pathinettangudi some 35 km from Madurai, which presents the look of just another underprivileged village. However, a silent IT revolution is brewing in the tiny hamlet where the illiterate farm workers use webcams, voice mail and e-mail regularly. Similar is the communication technology spread in at least 30 other villages around Pathinettangudi, paving the way for the caste-conscious Melur to become the first cyber taluk in the country— courtesy the Sustainable Access in Rural Internet (SARI) project.

- They can download application forms for caste, birth and death certificates, and simply forward it through e-mail to the tahsildhar. The acknowledgement is received within hours and the certificate issued in a week.
- Voice mail, chatting and e-mail.
- A large number of youth in Melur taluk are employed in the Middle East. Their dear ones are no longer scared of ISD bills. It's just Rs. 25 an hour to see their wards live on screen through the interactive webcam.
- Online clarification of agricultural queries from the Madurai Agriculture College and the Research Institute of the Tamil Nadu Agricultural University which is providing free counselling.
- Villagers get close-up colour pictures of their eyes examined by specialists in the Aravind Eye Hospital in Madurai and fix up appointments for surgeries.
- They are planning to provide online train, air and bus ticket booking.
- Free consultancy on veterinary sciences is also on the anvil.

'Public Access Internet Kiosks' have been established in 30 villages under the SARI project in association with "n-logue". This government-public-private-institution partnership programme also involves IIT Chennai, the Massachusetts Institute of Technology and the Harvard University. The technology provides highspeed Internet wireless access to more than 1,000 systems within a radius of 25 km radius. The kiosks have been established by individuals who took the risk of investing Rs. 50,000 in computer and multi-media and other accessories. Now

**Contd. ...**

the owners, who have installed the user-friendly Tamil softwares 'Padhami', 'Padhakkam' and 'Minnal', make an average income of Rs. 2,500 a month and the patronage is growing steadily. As of now, a chunk of villagers in these 30 villages have e-mail identities, which they use for seeking assistance from the Government under various schemes. The SARI project has evoked excellent response from the Government and the public.

*Uttar Pradesh (http://up.nic.in)*

The government proposes to undertake "Project Allahabad" to make Allahabad a Smart District. In the first phase of IT initiatives, the government plans to provide IT enabled services in select departments like Land, Revenue, Sales Tax, Transport, Rural Development, etc. It also plans to establish a Hi-tech Habitat at Greater Noida.

*Uttaranchal (http://uttaranchalassembly.org)*

It is newly carved state out of Uttar Pradesh. The State Government has taken adequate steps to computerise government departments and various State Bodies. It has launched its Vidhan Sabha web site for infusing greater transparency in legislative body functioning. The state is poised for implementing broader IT-enabled initiative for wider reach. The State Government plans to replicate the Gyandoot project in the State. Some NGOs have shown interest in spreading IT for the masses, but it is still in proposal stage.

*West Bengal (http://westbengal.nic.in)*

The Department of Information Technology has been set up recently in the State and IT has been identified as one of the thrust areas of development. The State government plans to introduce E-Governance in administration, ensure transparency and speed in providing information to the citizens through improved services, construct infrastructure and create an enabling atmosphere to set up IT industry, etc. In the present socio, economic and cultural environment it is not possible for IT to reach each citizen immediately. However, the elected Municipalities and the Panchayati Raj Institutions, which are essentially a part of the decentralised system, is likely to play a big role in taking IT to the masses in the future.

*Seven Sisters of the North-East*

The seven sisters comprise – Arunachal Pradesh, Assam, Manipur, Meghalaya, Mizoram, Nagaland and Tripura. Focus of the north-eastern states is on computerisation of government departments. But their respective web sites aims to present each state as a tourist destination. Few states have also launched IT-enabled initiatives to connect the government with people. For instance, Tripura Government has launched its official web site at: tripura.nic.in.It is in the process of further improvement of the site. The Government has also taken up the programme of training its officers and staff in basics and slightly more advanced concepts of computing. Some of the major IT projects at the implementation stage are Computerisation of Taxes, Computerisation of Treasuries and an Intranet for the State in various departments. In addition to these projects, the system study is being done for the Transport MIS, Computerisation and Information System for Rural Infrastructure. The Government has also opened an Information-cum-Facilitation Centre(IFC) in the State Secretariat. This centre provides basic information on the activities of the various government departments of Tripura and uses a Database at the back-end to respond to all queries that may come up. This centre is also linked to the Internet so that information can also be got on national and global aspects.

Besides, the respective State governments are also attempting to promote local products from their cottage industry in the global market. Wood and wood products are commonly available on most of the official web sites. It will be some time before the respective State Governments initiate any specific G2C IT-enabled initiative in the region.

*Few Public-Private Initiatives: Government to Citizens (G2C)*

In recent times, wide variety of pilot projects in e-governance has been launched at district level for seamless flow of information between government and citizens. Some are exclusively sponsored by the local State Government tying with civil society, and few initiatives are launched by civil society for the local community with services ranging from education to government services like driving licences, birth and death certificates, below poverty line certificates, old age pension, etc. Following are some of the successful e-governance initiatives for improving the quality of life of the people in rural areas.

## Telemedicine Service in Pune Primary Health Centers

Those living in interior Pune villages will now be able to avail expert medical council well within their means, thanks to a unique telemedicine program. The Pune district administration has teamed up with www.doctoranywhere.com and Tata Council for Community Initiatives (TCCI) to launch a telemedicine service from a government primary healthcare center (PHC). The service will reduce the traveling time and expenditure of the poor villagers. The villagers rush to big cities to meet specialist doctors. Since their relatives often accompany the patients, the cost mounts up. The service launched at three primary health centers is targeted at the rural masses.

The telemedicine project will ultimately connect all the PHC's in the district. In the first phase, three PHC's in Wagholi, Chakan and Paud regions would be linked with the district administration of Pune and the specialists. Suresh Ramu of doctoranywere.com says most PHC's were operational from the premises of the district administration run schools and most schools had computers that could be used to provide this service. Ten specialists (two each from each category) have been chosen from dermatology, nephrology, neurology, cardiology and gastroentrology. Doctors at the PHC's will refer complicated cases to the specialists in major cities who in turn will give their advice within 24 hours. The TCCI has donated three Pentium computers for the pilot project. The district administration will provide computers to other PHC's.

## Smart Cards by SKS

Swayam Krishi Sangam (SKS) is a Micro Finance Institution (mFI) operating in the drought-prone Medak District of Andhra Pradesh, with an aim to reach out to another 100 poorest districts of India. One of the biggest challenges facing any mFI is the high cost of delivering microfinance. It is estimated that even the most efficient mFIs spend 35 per cent to 51 per cent of its average loan outstanding on operating costs. SKS' Smart Card Project is an initiative that seeks to provide such a solution.

*SKS Smart Cards: How it works?*

Each SKS staffer has a palm-pilot sized Hand-Held Terminal (HHT). The HHT downloads the collection information from the branch office computer, so no manual collection sheet is required. In the village, each member has a Smart Card, which functions as an "electronic passbook" that electronically holds member information and a record of transactions. During the weekly center meetings, client Smart Cards are sequentially inserted in the HHT and transactions are updated both in the Smart Card and the HHT. The HHT also prints receipts so members have a printed record of their transactions. At the end of the day's center meetings, the staff person simply uploads the information from the HHT to the branch computer, and all transaction information is transferred and all accounts are updated.

## Challenges to E-governance for Development

The success stories cited above are the exception rather than the rule for two reasons. First, most developing countries have only undertaken a limited number of e-governance initiatives. This mainly relates to a lack of e-readiness. Second, most e-governance initiatives that are begun currently fail. Surveys of e-governance initiatives in developed countries are rare, a shortcoming that needs to be addressed. Even donors, who should be committed to monitoring and evaluation, rarely seem to produce reports. From the material that is available, two main types of e-governance failure can be identified.

In some cases, there is the *total failure* of an initiative never implemented or in which a new system is implemented but immediately abandoned. For example, India's Indira Gandhi Conservation Monitoring Centre was intended to be a national information provider based on a set of core environmental information systems. Despite more than a year of planning, analysis and design work, these ICT-based systems never became operational, and the whole initiative collapsed shortly afterwards (Puri *et al* 2000).

Alternatively, there is the *partial failure* of an initiative in which major goals are unattained or in which there are significant undesirable outcomes. For example, the Tax Computerisation Project in Thailand's Revenue Department set out seven areas of taxation that were to be computerised. At the end of the project, only two areas had been partly computerised, and five others were not operational (Kitiyadisai 2000).

One type of partial failure that particularly seems to affect e-governance initiatives is the *sustainability failure* of an initiative that succeeds initially but then fails after a year or so. An example is the creation of a set of touch-screen kiosks for remote rural communities in South Africa's North-West Province. These were initially well received. However, the kiosks' lack of updated or local content and lack of interactivity led to disuse, and the kiosks were removed less than one year later (Benjamin 2001). Sustainability question marks also hang over some of the case studies cited above.

As noted, these are only glimpses of evidence about the prevalence of such failure. A few surveys have been conducted. Use of ICTs for health reform in South Africa's public sector: widespread partial failure of high cost systems with little use of data (Braa & Hedberg 2000).

Use of ICTs in the Thai public sector: 'failure cases seem to be the norm in Thailand at all governmental levels' (Kitiyadisai 2000). Donor-funded public sector ICT projects in China, all were found to be partial failures (Baark & Heeks 1999). World Bank-funded public sector ICT projects in Africa: almost all were partial – often sustainability – failures (Moussa & Schware 1992). Likewise, independent reports on ICT use in the public sectors of individual developing countries find failure to be the dominant theme (World Bank 1993; Oyomno 1996). Lately, the two public-private initiatives in India, namely the TARAhaat and Drishtee, were closely studied and the study revealed strategic weakness in their business models and operational strategy (Kaushik & Singh, 2002). It is important to acknowledge that developing countries are not alone in suffering high levels of failure with e-governance initiatives. However, they do face a particular set of constraints that arise from two related challenges: lack of e-readiness and large design reality gaps.

## Conclusion

Thus, in simple terms e-governance is giving citizens the choice of when and where they access government information and services. Putting the citizen at the centre of government means taking a delivery channel view. This would mean using more and more use of convergent technologies in many of the government functions. There is tremendous importance for rules and procedures in the government. Unless the records are kept properly, accessing information and tracing the precedents becomes time consuming and this is one of the reasons for the delays in government administration. Secondly, rules and procedures lead to enormous red tape and delay and this in turn leads to corruption. Today, we find that the present paper based system is very time consuming and inefficient. The rules, procedures can be made transparent to the citizens, information can be made freely available to the citizen, trace precedents faster and in short, improve the pace of effectiveness of governance by using Information Technology. A 'joined up' government-community-citizen infrastructure has its own significance. A strong and effective information chain, comprising a choice of practical, accessible and manageable channels of communication has a dual benefit. Citizens enjoy a fast and convenient 'service', whilst government not only becomes more integrated into the community itself, but can focus its resources where they are needed most. Moreover, a culture of self-service enables citizens to 'help themselves' wherever possible, saving time and money for all concerned.

In the ultimate analysis, the electronic governance wave has started worldwide. With the technologies to implement electronic governance already available, managerial issues are of key importance. Change in the mindset of the people particularly at the top levels in the bureaucracy and policy making is important because it is they who provide the leadership. This change in the mindset can be brought about by focused organization development interventions and training programmes. Once this is done, there should be a corresponding trickle down effect right through the spectrum of government. The future is e-homes with e-services at the doorsteps.

For more information, following web sites can be used to provide information on such initiatives.

http://www.mit.gov.in/

http://egov.mit.gov.in/

http://www.undp.org.in

http://www.developmentgateway.org/

http://www.digitalgovernance.org/

http://www.partners.panasia.org.sg/

**Some Success Stories**

http://gyandoot.net

http://www.blonnet.com/

http://www.indiachi.com/

http://www.andhrapradesh.com/

http://www.tiruvaruronline.com

http://himachal.nic.in/lokmitra2.htm

http://www.bangaloreit.com/html/egovern/egovern.htm

http://www.rajcomp.net/

## Notes

1. As given by the Ministry of Information Technology, see at (http://mit.gov.in)
2. IDSC (2000)
3. Ntiro (2000)
4. SDNP (2000a)
5. Benjamin (2001)
6. World Bank (2000a)
7. Microsoft (2000)
8. World Bank (2000b)
9. Bhatnagar (2001)
10. Bhatnagar & Vyas (2001)
11. SDNP (2000b)

## References

Benjamin, P. (2001) 'Community development and democratisation through information technology: Building the new South Africa'; in *Reinventing Government in the Information Age*, R.B. Heeks (ed.), Routledge, London, 194-210.

Bhatnagar, S.C. & Vyas, N. (2001) *Gyandoot: Community-Owned Rural Internet Kiosks*, World Bank, Washington DC http://www.worldbank.org/publicsector/egov/gyandootcs. htm.

Braa, J. & Hedberg, C. (2000) 'Developing district-based health care information systems'; in *Information Flows, Local Improvisations and Work Practices*, Proceedings of the IFIP WG9.4 Conference 2000, Cape Town.

Heeks, R.B. (2001) *Building e-Governance for Development*, i-Government paper no.12, IDPM, University of Manchester http://www.man.ac.uk/idpm/idpm_dp.htm.

IDSC (2000) *Civil Information Systems: The National ID Number*, IDSC, Cairo.

Kaushik P. D. & Nirvikar Singh (2002) 'Information Technology and Broad Based Development: Preliminary Lessons from North India".

Kitiyadisai, K. (2000) 'The implementation of IT in reengineering the Thai Revenue Department'; in *Information Flows, Local Improvisations and Work Practices*, Proceedings of the IFIP WG9.4 Conference 2000, Cape Town.

Microsoft (2000) *IEC of South Africa wins Computerworld Smithsonian Award*, Government News, 28 June, Microsoft Europe, Reading.

Moussa, A. & Schware, R. (1992) 'Informatics in Africa: lessons from World Bank experience', *World Development*, 20(12), 1737-1752.

Ntiro, S. (2000) *e-Government in Eastern Africa*, KPMG, Dar-es-Salaam.

Oyomno, G.Z. (1996) 'Sustainability of governmental use of microcomputer-based information technology in Kenya'; in *Global Information Technology and Socio-Economic Development*, M. Odedra-Straub (ed.), Ivy League Publishing, Nashua, NH.

Puri, S.K., Chauhan, K.P.S. & Admedullah, M. (2000) 'Prospects of biological diversity information management'; in *Information Flows, Local Improvisations and Work Practices*, Proceedings of the IFIP WG9.4 Conference 2000, Cape Town.

SDNP (2000a) *SDNP China Helps to Implement Agenda* 21, UNDP, New York http://www.sdnp.undp.org/it4dev/stories/china.html.

——— (2000b) *SDNP Honduras: Civil Society's Information System*, UNDP, New York http://www.sdnp.undp.org/it4dev/stories/honduras.html.

Ugandan Parliament (2000) *The Uganda Parliamentary Technical Assistance Project*, Uganda Parliament, Kampala http://www.parliament.go.ug/UPTAP.htm See also http://www.crosswinds.net/~usaid/cp2000.html.

World Bank (1993) *Turkey: Informatics and Economic Modernization*, World Bank, Washington DC

——— (2000a) OPEN: *Seoul's Anticorruption Project*, World Bank, Washington DC http://www1.worldbank.org/publicsector/egov/seoulcs.htm.

——— (2000b) *Chilean Tax System Online*, World Bank, Washington DC http://www1.worldbank.org/publicsector/egov/chile_taxcs.htm.

# 8

## Reforming Infrastructure

*Survey of Recommendations of Select Committees*

DEBASHIS CHAKRABORTY

### Introduction

The role of infrastructure development has a unique position in the economic growth of a country. In India, since the initiation of the economic reform in 1991, several policies have been undertaken by the Government to improve the infrastructure scenario. In addition, Government of India has appointed several commissions, taskforces and working groups in this regard from time to time. In general, all these committees recommended for a limited role of the Government, concentrating on regulatory issues, and more active participation of the private sector to meet the investment requirement. Although a couple of the recommendations provided by the committees have been implemented, a number of policy recommendations are yet to be addressed.

In the current analysis five sub-sectors within the infrastructure sector, namely, telecommunication, roads, ports, power and railways are selected. A brief survey of the policy recommendations provided by various committees for each of these sub-sectors is presented in the following. At the end of each sector, the reform measures initiated, or under consideration in the recent period, are mentioned in brief. The Government reports considered here are mentioned at the end.

Apart from the sector-specific measures, improving the framework in general could also play a major role in revitalising reform measures. The Expert Group (1996) on infrastructure explored these issues, and strongly recommended reforms in capital market, regulatory framework and fiscal field, side-by-side with the sector-specific measures.

**Recommendations of the Expert Group (1996)**

- Government intervention to ensure meaningful commercialisation of projects through capital market reform; through provisions of fiscal incentives; reform of insurance, provident and pension funds; strengthening of forex market, facilitate external commercial borrowing; and debt market reforms.
- Regulatory reform for enhancing coordination between various infrastructure sectors, introduction of an autonomous regulatory body in each sector, enactment of quick dispute settlement mechanism, removal of existing guidelines on FIIs to increase investment, implement necessary changes in legislation etc.
- Fiscal reform to provide incentive for investing in infrastructure projects.

In the following portion, the sub-sectors are arranged in decreasing order of the intensity of their reform measures undertaken. The telecommunication sector comes first, since so far, it has witnessed implementation of maximum number of reform policies. It is followed by Road Transport and Port Sector, both characterised by a limited liberalisation exercise, and slow beginning of private sector participation. The power sector comes next, where the reform measures are still in the implementation or consideration stage. The railway sector comes at the end owing to the near absence of reform measures undertaken.

## Telecommunications

### *Sector Profile*

The telecommunication sector in India is the 14$^{th}$ largest in the world. However, the sector suffers from a very low penetration rate.[1] In addition, the market is characterised by presence of excess demand. In order to grow in the technologically advanced world of twenty-first century, a balanced growth strategy for telecom sector is required with significant private sector participation.

The Expert Group (1996) identified that the existence of low teledensity in India is an advantage, since there is no possibility of earlier technologies becoming obsolete, and opined that if the sector could grow at a rate of 20 per cent for next five years, it would rank among the six largest networks in the world. However, substantial investments and policy reforms were recommended for this purpose.

The total fund requirement for provision of basic and cellular mobile telecom services over the 10-year period (1996-2006) was calculated to be Rs. 1915 billion, and private sector was expected to contribute a significant proportion of it. The reform measures recommended by the Expert Group are presented below:

**Policy Reform**

The Expert Group suggested that for the sake of long-term balanced growth, the Government should not view this sector as a source of additional general resource mobilisation. The future licensing and taxation policies should be framed keeping this in mind. The Expert Group held the view that corporatisation would help DoT to utilize its vast asset base in effective generation of the massive funds required for fulfilling its growth requirement. With this view, the following policies were suggested:

- The inter-circle long distance services should be opened to the private sector by 2001.
- Strengthening DoT to withstand competition from private entrants by allowing greater flexibility at management level. Ideally DoT should be corporatised as India Telecom at the earliest. This would help the DoT to effectively leverage its vast asset base to meet the huge requirement of funds for growth.
- To provide effective autonomy at the regional level, it is desirable to structure India Telecom as a holding company, with regional subsidiary companies and other functional subsidiaries such as a separate long-distance service company.

Regarding MTNL operation, the Expert Group opined that since considerable disinvestment has already taken place, it should continue as a separate corporation. Keeping the experience of MTNL and DoT for running such huge network, the future reform agenda was outlined as follows:

- Further privatization of MTNL must be considered.
- MTNL may form joint ventures with various companies for offering value-added services in order to complement its own skills in areas like marketing.

- After establishment of India Telecom, MTNL and DoT should seek global presence through investments in joint ventures with telecom companies abroad for provision of telecom services in other countries.

**Tariff policy**

The present policy of cross-subsidisation benefits the local tariff at the cost of the international and domestic long-distance calls. To reach a more rational situation, the Expert Group recommended:

- Introduction of a more cost-oriented tariff structure.
- Initiating a tariff study, which would be instrumental in formulating a tariff structure reasonable and affordable to consumers, and provide an implementation plan to induce competition, without ignoring Government's social welfare plans.

The telecom network in India is the $14^{th}$ largest in the world. In order to become a global player, the working group concluded that investment in developing manufacturing capabilities is need of the hour. This would take care of future domestic requirements as well as the export sales. The following policies are suggested in this regard:

- Rationalisation of import tariff should be extended to components and inputs required by domestic manufacturers to encourage domestic production.[2]
- Import duties for network elements for cellular mobile services and handsets are around 50 per cent, whereas the domestic production of these items is significant, resulting in higher service charge. Rationalization of import tariff would help in reduction of cost of service provided.

**Legal and Regulatory Reform**

In order to implement the reform agenda efficiently, the following reforms in the legal framework were recommended by the Expert Group:

- A new and forward-looking legislation should replace the Indian Telegraph Act 1885, which would reflect current status of the telecom sector with appropriate emphasis on government policies.

- For successful operation of TRAI, the 3-member apex body needs to be supported by a team of highly qualified professionals, drawn from both within and outside the government.[3]
- TRAI should ensure that the interconnectivity between networks of different operators remains seamless as far as the consumers are concerned, and the agreements should be legally, commercially, and financially sound to support private sector entry.
- Adequate care be given to the increasing complexity of the tariffs and access charges as the number of service providers increase.

**Funding Issues**

For sustained investment in the sector, a thorough funding policy needs to be worked out. Keeping this in mind, the following measures were suggested:

- Government should adopt liberal policy guidelines and directives to encourage long-term investments (both domestic and foreign) in this sector. New sources of long-run funds are to be created and suitable instruments need to be explored in this regard. Sector-specific guidelines and entitlement limits for external commercial borrowing are also necessary.
- The proceedings of large amounts of funds in the form of license fees, duties and taxes are to be deposited in a newly created Infrastructure Fund. The fund should provide debt and participate in equity of various infrastructure projects. The telecom sector could be given the first option to utilize a certain portion of the fund.

The portion of the funds coming to telecom sector could be utilized for the following purposes, as recommended by the Expert Group (1996):

- Providing equity and long-term debt funds to all players of the sector, administered by IFDC with transparent government guidelines.
- Providing resources for evaluation of the new emerging technologies and their relevance in the Indian context.

- Providing funds for addressing the needs of technical manpower training of both existing employees of the DoT as well as of future personnel.
- Providing funds required for the initial establishment of the TRAI and specialised training for its personnel.
- Funding initial investments required to create an information superhighway in the country.

**Future Implementation Issues**

In addition to the focused and target-specific recommendation, the Expert Group also suggested a few policies to improve inter-governmental coordination.

- With emergence of newer technologies, the traditional boundary between telecom, broadcasting and computer technology is dissolving. Therefore, a broader regulatory body would be required in future to address issues like airwave regulation, which does not fall under TRAI.
- Presently, Ministry of Communications & Technology Information, the Department of Telecom and the Department of Information Technology are responsible for three sub-segments. Formation of a highest-level inter-ministerial body to formulate national policy on information technology, which would be binding on these three ministries/departments, was strongly recommended.
- A long-term Implementation Monitoring Group should be created to ensure that the recommendations accepted by the Government are effectively implemented.

*National Telecom Policy*

During the early years of reform, the NTP (1994) was formulated, which welcomed the participation of private investment in this sector. A number of value-added services were opened up to private investment in July 1992. However, in 1999, a second NTP has been introduced, which recognized that some of the objectives of NTP 1994 have not been fulfilled. Broadly, NTP 1999 recommended the following policy measures:

- Separation of policy and licensing functions of DoT from the service provision functions.
- Allowing the various service providers to freely operate and provide service facility within their area of operation.
- Indian telecommunications system continued to be governed by the provisions of the Indian Telegraph Act (ITA, 1885) and the Indian Wireless Act (IWA, 1933). Keeping the substantial changes taken place since liberalization, ITA should be replaced with a more forward-looking act.

*Recommendations of the Working Group (2001)*

In recent period, a Working Group (2001) on Telecom Sector was set up by the Department of Telecommunications, which recommended strong emphasis on the following issues in the Tenth Five Year Plan (2002-2007) period:

- Rural Telecom Development
- Private Investment Promotion
- Telecom Equipment Manufacturing
- Research and Development
- Improvement of Customer Services

*Various Committees appointed by TRAI on Focused Area of interest*

In subsequent period, a number of committees were formed by TRAI to recommend path of reform on various sectors. A brief summary of their recommendations are provided below:

## Table 1

*The Recommendations of various Committees on Telecom policy*

| No. | Committee | Recommendation |
|---|---|---|
| 1 | Basic Service Licenses (2002) | The committee recommended grant of licenses for Basic Service Operators in 15 Vacant Circles. The number of players and their mode of selection will be recommended by TRAI in a time bound manner in order to eliminate non-serious players. Regarding six Circles, where private operators have already been licensed, it was recommended that while in the interest of introducing effective competition, these six Circles also may be opened to free competition like the other 15 Circles at the same point of time. In the interest of maintaining an economic level playing field, some justified relief be extended to the existing Basic Service Operators. |
| 2 | Growth of Internet in the country (2002) | The committee recommended establishment of a National Internet Exchange of India (NIXI) under the umbrella of an Industry representative neutral body. Government should encourage usage of internet in rural belt through various policies. ISPs have already been granted income tax exemption under Section 80(1)(A), and additional concessional duties including those relating to custom duties etc. should also be made applicable. ISPs should also be given the status of Infrastructure Industry. Taxation on Internet Services needs to be rationalized to prevent multiple taxation. TRAI should rationalize tariffs for the domestic leased line. |
| 3 | Opening up of Internet Telephony (2002) | The committee recommended Internet Telephony may be introduced with effect from 1st April, 2002 i.e. date of opening of the ILD sector for private participation. The committee also addressed the issues of quality of service and fixation of tariff rate. |
| 4 | Licensing issues relating to Public Mobile Radio Trunking Service Providers (PMRTSPs) (2001) | The present service area of the PMRT service operators in all metros as well as the cities has been found to be rather small and, therefore, too restrictive to meet the needs of customers subscribing to the PMRTS. Hence TRAI recommends redefinition of 'Metropolitan Cities' and 'Other Areas' and also some enlargement of the service area of the PMRT Service providers available for this service. Although TRAI held the view that the market is self-limiting and will determine the number of players, it acknowledged the need of |

| | | |
|---|---|---|
| | | eliminating non-serious players through certain screening mechanism. Lack of interconnectivity with PSTN and inter-site connectivity is yet another reason which has limited the value of the service for the users and has been a restricting factor in its growth. TRAI recommended removal of these restrictions to improve the utility and acceptability, although the interconnectivity granted would neither be unconditional nor unlimited in nature. |
| 5 | Introduction of competition in National Long Distance Communications (1999) | The committee recommended free competition with open entry subject to pre-qualification and performance obligation. In line with NTP 1999 resale was allowed for domestic telephony, but only when the market matures. Hence, resale of NLD services was recommended only after 3 to 4 years of the opening up of the market. No formal license is required for Category I Infrastructure Providers. They may simply be required to register with an appropriate authority. However, Category II Infrastructure Providers may be licensed on simple terms and conditions. The duration of license for the provision of NLD service was recommended for an initial period of 20 years from the effective date, which would be extendable by additional periods of 10 years thereafter. A restructuring of tariff rates was also recommended. |
| 6 | Opening of the International long Distance Service (2001) | The committee recommended open Competition in the International Long Distance Service sector, i.e., there need be no ceiling on the number of operators. License may be issued to all operators who meet pre-qualification criteria. The committee addressed the issues of eligibility criteria, entry fees, and revenue sharing in details. |

## Table 2

*Relaxations Granted to Attract FDI*

| *FDI Slab* | *FDI Upper Limit* | *Categories coming under the FDI Slab* |
|---|---|---|
| 1 | 100% | • Manufacturing of telecom equipment<br>• Internet services (not providing international gateways)<br>• Infrastructure providers (Category I)<br>• E-mail services<br>• Voice mail services |
| 2 | 74% | • Internet services (providing international gateways)<br>• Infrastructure providers (Category II)<br>• Radio Paging services |
| 3 | 49% | • National long distance services<br>• Basic telephone services<br>• Cellular mobile services<br>• Other value added services |

## Table 3

*Fiscal Provisions for the Telecommunications Sector in Budget 2001-02*

| *Tax type* | *Fiscal Provision* |
|---|---|
| Direct Tax | • The five year tax holiday and 30 per cent deduction which was available to the telecommunications sector till 31st March, 2000 was re-introduced retrospectively for the units commencing operations on or before 31st March, 2003 for the next 5 years. These concessions were also extended to the Internet Service Providers and broad-band networks.<br>• All surcharges (13 per cent and 17 per cent) payable by corporates and non-corporates removed except surcharge of 2 per cent for financing National Calamity Contingency Fund.<br>• The dividend tax has been brought down from 20 per cent to 10 per cent. |
| Customs Duty | • Customs duty on specified products has been brought down along with removal of the surcharge of 10 per cent.<br>• Concessional rate of 5 per cent customs duty applicable/ admissible to specified equipments and parts thereof for basic telephones, cellular, radio paging, V-SAT PMRTS, and Internet services has been extended up to 2002. |

Source: Working Group on Telecom Sector (2001)

*Measures to Attract Private Investment*

Apart from this, the following policies are being implemented to attract investment:

- Allowing additional foreign investment through holding/ investment company
- Automatic approval for technology fee up to US $ 2 million, royalty to 5 per cent for domestic sales and 8 per cent for exports in telecom manufacturing (higher amount through specific approvals)
- Allowing full repatriability of dividend income and capital invested in the telecom sector

However, the actual private investment in telecom sector is yet to match its full potential. The investment has mainly come in the area of the cellular mobile telephone service, which accounted for about 27 per cent of the total investment through FDI. The basic telecom service could attract only about 5 per cent of the total FDI. It has also been noted that the domestic capital markets have not been tapped extensively and the bulk of the external resources have been obtained from the financial institutions. The category-wise FDI inflow is provided in the annex 1.

*Present Scenario: Reforms in the Telecom Sector in the Ninth Plan*

- An independent regulatory authority called Telecom Regulatory Authority of India (TRAI) was set up in 1997.
- A new policy for Internet Service Providers (ISPs) was announced in 1998 opening the area to private sector providers. The policy was promotional in nature. ISPs have been allowed to set up International Internet Gateways both satellite and landing stations for Submarine Cable systems.
- Migration from the regime of fixed licence fee to a new regime of revenue share was permitted in August, 1999.
- The regulatory mechanism has been further strengthened through the TRAI (Amendment) Act, 2000. The Act provides for establishment of a separate dispute settlement mechanism called Telecom Dispute Settlement and Appellate Tribunal.

- National Long Distance Service was opened for competition in August, 2000.
- Corporatisation of DoT into a public company called Bharat Sanchar Nigam Ltd. from 1st October, 2000.
- Videsh Sanchar Nigam Ltd. (VSNL) and HTL limited have been disinvested.

In addition, several reform measures have been taken in the field of information and broadcasting as well.[4]

**Policy Highlights During 2001-02**

- National Long Distance sector opened for unrestricted entry with announcement of guidelines for licensing NLDO operators.
- Multiple Fixed Service Providers licensing guidelines were announced.
- ISPs have been allowed to set up International Internet Gateways both Satellite and Landing stations for submarine optical fibre cables.
- Licenses for Voice Mail/Audiotex service will be granted, on non-exclusive basis, SDCA (Short Distance Charging Area) wise. Licence fees and entry fee will be zero.
- Wireless in Local Loop (WLL) has been introduced for providing telephone connections in urban, semi-urban, and rural areas promptly.

Source: Compiled from Annual Report, DoT (2001-02)

## Roads

### *Sector Profile*

The roads in India from administrative point of view come under four categories, National Highways, State Highways, District Roads and Village Roads. The responsibility of development and management of the first one lies with Central Government, while the other three rests on the State Governments. From 1951 to 1994, the average yearly growth of road traffic grew in the order of 8 to 10 per cent. Unfortunately, the main road network comprising National and State Highways could not keep pace with the traffic growth. In 1996, out of the total 165,000 Km length of National and State Highways, 2 per cent, 34 per cent and 64 percent in terms of length was four-lane, two-lane and single-lane respectively.[5]

This transport bottleneck has put a heavy cost on the transport sector. The commercial vehicles are able to run only at an average speed of 200-250 km per day, as compared to 500-600 km per day in developed countries. Existence of congested sections, railway crossings, octroi posts, poor condition of the road[6], safety and pollution etc. further compound the problem. This led the Expert Group on Infrastructure to suggest, creation of a 20-year master plan for development of these roads. The investment requirement for development of National, State and Supernational Highways would be Rs. 320 billion from 1996-97 to 2000-01 and an additional Rs. 630 billion between 2001-02 to 2005-06. An additional fund of Rs. 205 billion was required for the maintenance of roads. The recommendations of the Expert Group regarding various issues are presented in the following.

*Source of Financing*

Identifying suitable and stable source of financing the huge investment requirement of this sector was given a high importance. The Expert Group pointed out that all over the world, four sources are used to build up good infrastructure, namely,

- Allocations from the existing user tax collected as part of general revenue.
- Creation of an earmarked fund through levy of specific user tariffs.
- Development and maintenance of highways on 'user pays' basis by raising commercial loans.
- Private sector participation.

However, in India only the first source is explored. Now, given the mammoth requirement of funds for developmental and maintenance work, the participation of private sector is a necessity both in case of Central and State Highways.[7] Hence, in order to tap resources, and given the massive backlog of previous years, the Expert Group recommended that appropriate policies must be formulated to attract resources from all possible sources, public and private, domestic and foreign.

*Policies for Highway Development*

- Creation of a Highway Development Fund as an assured extra-budgetary source for funding highways.

- Borrowing money from the market to develop highway and repay later with the proceedings of toll tax, coupled with tapping private managerial and entrepreneurial skill was suggested.
- Development and maintenance of supernational highway, improvements on existing highway through private sector or through collaboration was given special importance.
- Setting up of a Highway Infrastructure Saving Scheme (HISS) in the pattern of National Saving Scheme (NSS) was recommended to provide assured funds to commercial roads. The withdrawals from the scheme will be recouped out of toll revenues. Furthermore, the resolution on the Central Road Fund passed by Parliament in 1988 should be implemented.
- The mammoth fund requirement of the sector has to be met. But, given the limitation of Government fund, alternate sources have to be worked out. For instance, the Expert Group encouraged to view various taxes, which are currently levied on motor vehicles of different types, the use of fuel in transportation etc., as charges for road usage. Substantial proportion of such revenues, if not all, should be earmarked for road development.

*Development Strategy*

- Priority must be given to reconstruction of weak and distressed bridges and major missing bridges. Improvement has been initiated in National Highways by dividing the network in high, medium and low traffic zones. A similar approach should be followed for State Highways.
- Corridor development should form the basis of highway strategy. Based upon the traffic volume to be served and related considerations, improvements have to be planned in the form of expressways, widening to four-lanes, construction of paved shoulders and strengthening of pavement etc. for a period of 20 years. The projects need to be taken up accordingly in stages and in order of priority.

- A central body like a Roads Board should be established to ensure coordinated development of the trunk route system. The roles of the Central and State Government need to be clearly defined.

*Maintenance and Management of Highways*

- Modern maintenance and management systems have to be implemented.
- Maintenance deports should be established all along the highway network.
- Maintenance activities should be contracted out in a gradual manner.
- Management of Highways should include control of traffic as well as highway land, *viz.*, maintenance of right-of-way, prevention of encroachment on highway land, regulation on construction along highway within a defined width, removal of bottleneck etc.

*Highway Improvement Strategy*

- Four-laning of some of the existing highways through 'public toll roads' method should be adopted. Funds could be borrowed from World Bank or ADB for this purpose. Local funds could be raised from financial institutions, and the Government, which would be repaid from the toll revenue.
- Traffic on existing roads as well as newly constructed ones should be charged.[8]

*Institutional Needs*

A Roads Board should be set up at national level with the following three tasks, while establishment of similar boards is also encouraged at state level:

- Planning and implementing the highway programme in a time-bound and proposed manner.
- Mobilizing the required private funds from domestic and international markets.
- Maintaining and managing the National and State highway networks.

*Comprehensive Guidelines for Highways*

- Guidelines and procedures must be laid down for approval of private sector projects, clearly indicating the nature of clearances required and the authorities to be approached.
- A central legislation in the form of a Highway Act has to be enacted where issues like smooth running of traffic, quick attention to maintenance, speedy help to drivers, efficient traffic management, removal of encroachment etc. would be duly addressed. The idea of assignment of these functions to private parties also needs to be focused.

A Taskforce on Integrated Transport Policy (2001) appointed by the Planning Commission also recommended a number of policies for the development of road sector, which were broadly in line with those of the Expert Group.

*Recommendations of the Taskforce*

- Upgrading high-density corridors both in terms of carpet width and riding quality, keeping in view the parallel programme of Railways.
- Serving Ports and industrial centres through spur connection.
- Assigning higher priority to removal of existing deficiencies in the road network *vis-à-vis* network extension.
- Developing Asian High Network in order to exploit trade and other possibilities with neighbouring countries.
- Modernizing high-density corridors through introduction of new technology in the design, engineering and construction methods.
- Encouraging use of new materials for road construction and award of big road contracts on turnkey basis and use of machines to improve quality and speed of construction particularly for development of HDCs.
- Introducing and encouraging low tare weight and heavy haul multi-axle vehicles through suitable fiscal measures.
- Reducing octroi and sales tax barriers to facilitate flow of road transport.

- Encouraging private sector participation in construction of by passes, bridges and short stretches carrying heavy traffic. Under BOT concept, direct tolling, viewed mainly as a user charge, to be replicated on selected stretches of National Highways. Mechanism of shadow tolls/annuity to be used mainly for maintenance and road construction projects on experimental basis.
- Utilizing budgetary resources to leverage private investment for improving the viability of projects.
- Evolving a system of user charges to be used as an important source of revenue for road construction in future.
- Reducing exhaust emission from automobile engines by-stricter emission norms, improved petroleum fuel supplies and shift to less pollutant alternate fuel.

*Present Scenario*

The Government, keeping the long-term development of the transport sector in view has initiated a number of policy measures. The measures as obtained from the Annual Report of Ministry of Road Transport and Highways are summarized below:

- Central Road Fund has been revamped by creating a cess of Rs. 1 per litre on petrol and diesel. A central Road Fund Act (2000) has been enacted in December, 2000. Rs. 5800 crores has been provided in the 2000-01 budget for development and maintenance of the roads in the country.
- four-laning of 42 km and two-laning of 860 km of National Highway have been completed by January 2001, and further upgradation of a considerable portion of the remaining highway is expected to be accomplished soon.
- To attract private sector participation, FDI upto 100 per cent is allowed in road sector, with total foreign equity upto Rs. 1500 crores. In addition, two concession agreements have been finalised, one for major projects costing more than Rs. 100 crores, and the other one for minor projects, costing upto Rs. 100 crores.
- Around 20 projects have been initiated involving an investment exceeding Rs. 1000 crores, and toll is being collected from 11 of them.

- Projects on National Highway development funded by World Bank, Asian Development Bank, and Japan Bank for International Cooperation are on the way.
- Two major projects on National Highway development are currently in progress. The first one intends to connect the golden quadrilateral, the four metros, Delhi, Mumbai, Calcutta and Chennai. The second one, North-South, East-West Corridor intends to connect Porbandar to Silchar, and Srinagar to Kanyakumari. The projects are expected to be completed by December 2003, and December, 2007 respectively.

## Ports

### *Sector Profile*

The port sector consists of 11 major ports and 139 intermediate and minor ports. The responsibility of development and management of major ports rests on the Central Government and the State Government looks into the remaining ones. Although most Indian ports operate at more than 100 per cent capacity utilisation, they are operationally inefficient when compared to other ports in Asian Region. For instance, indicators like berth occupancy, Average Ship Turn Around (ASTA), Average Ship Berth Output (ASBO), labour and equipment productivity in Indian ports are far less impressive as compared to Asian standard. The low productivity in Indian Ports originates from various factors like operational constraints, frequent breakdown of cargo-handling equipment, inadequate dredging and container-handling facilities, inefficient deployment of port equipment, lack of proper coordination in entire logistic chain etc. The problems are further compounded by absence of modern technologies.

Port traffic consists of overseas and coastal traffic. The overall port capacity has to be increased considerably in the next ten years, given the expected increase in traffic over this period. The Expert Group on infrastructure estimated the investment requirement of this sector to be Rs. 250 billion over this period, significantly higher in comparison with actual expenditure of just under Rs. 16 billion during 1992-96. This led the Expert Group to conclude that resources either have to be generated internally, or from other sources. The recommendations of the Expert Group are presented in the following:

*Commercialization*

The major ports are in a shabby condition and needs a massive inflow of funds. Measures must be implemented at the earliest in order to achieve:

- Upgradation of the handling technology
- Modernization of the equipment and management
- Raising adequate resources, both for the creation of additional port facilities and to improve existing ones.

This requires pursuance of a completely new approach, where commercialization, liberalization, privatization and modernization of port administration have to be used in combination as strategies. The required investment could be achieved through adoption of innovative methods as recommended by the Expert Group:

- Autonomous port authorities should operate on commercial lines, which would enable them to raise resources from primary market by way of equity and debt and from FIs.
- Port authorities could service the debt obligations and pay a reasonable return to investors on equity on the basis of the existing tariff level.

*Immediate Actions*

While, the commercialization exercise will remain in force, the Expert Group recommended implementation of certain actions on an urgent basis for improving the health of the sector, as summarized below:

- Granting more power to the port trusts to facilitate speedy creation and operation of assets. Presently, the port trusts have power to incur expenditure upto Rs. 50 million only. On the contrary, PSEs having a gross block of over Rs. 2 billion entering into MoUs have power to incur expenditure of additions, modifications, and new investments upto Rs. 500 million. In case of expenditure on replacement and renewal of assets, the limit is further extended to Rs. 1000 million. The same relaxation should be provided to major port trust boards.

- Projects to be executed through private participation involving no investment by port authority need not require the approval of Expenditure Finance Committee or Public Investment Board.
- Port authorities should have the autonomy to create necessary technical posts required for modernization.

*Private Sector Participation*

In order to bring about a quantitative and qualitative improvement in port infrastructure, competition within private sectors, for instance, in various cargo-handling activities, could play a vital role. Private participation was permitted through Port Trust Act, 1963, and amended in 1992, 1993 and 1995 for issuing guidelines for land management in ports, which attracted a limited inflow of private investment in ports.

In order to boost the investment further, the expert group urged leasing out of berths and other existing assets to private sector on the basis of cost efficiency. This recommendation goes one step ahead of the Standing Committee on Transport and Tourism recommendation, which suggested private participation to be restricted only for creation of additional capacity.[9]

*Technical Upgradation*

In the competitive world, the success of the ports depends on the facilities that it could provide to the business community. The expert group suggested that in order to reach the international standard, the Indian ports have to implement the following policies:

- Technological upgradation
- Mechanical cargo handling
- Initiation of computer-based cargo and customs clearance system.

*Labour Policy*

A labour resistance in the initial period of reform is expected as the modernization and restructuring of ports would require reallocation of labour, capital and management. The pace of reform should not be halted by this initial protest, as the restructuring will result in a better management and skill upgradation of the workers in line with new needs.

The existing pay structure also should be reformed. The system should move to a piece-based wage structure instead of the monolithic pay structure currently in force. This incentive structure is expected to foster efficiency and innovation at the lowest level.

*Area Management*

The port authorities have a vast urban land area. This could be optimally utilized through an area rejuvenation programme for facilitating the required restructuring. This requires an integrated and comprehensive approach, possibly through an appropriate institutional framework.

*Operational Efficiency*

While the government could retain the controlling stake, privatization of certain services could be implemented. Various activities like cargo handling, storage, warehousing, customs clearance, security and administration could individually be considered as separate profit centres, and appropriate policies should be worked out for commercialization and allowing private sector participation in each case. The Expert Group opined that it might be better to make the ports work as corporate entities with administrative independence and the ability to raise finances for development.

*Long-term Planning*

The Indian ports need to develop with a 15-20 years planning horizon, and achieve the following goals:

- Developing some of the ports as megaports operating as the warehouse for the Indian subcontinent.
- Developing at least two ports for this purpose, one each on the west and east coasts.
- The optimal economic size for cargo handling for a port is around 70 to 100 million tonnes by world standard. This should be the targeted size of the megaports.

*Decentralisation*

The multiple regulatory and commercial functions undertaken by the Port Authorities is not viewed as transparent by the private sector. This might act as a major hindrance to private investment. Therefore, the Expert Group recommended that:

- While the commercial operation of the ports be entrusted to existing port authorities with adequate autonomy, a separate regulatory authority should be set up to deal with issues relating to pricing and conditions which will govern private sector participation and operations and maintenance of the port assets. The regulatory authority should have due representation from Port Authority, Ministry of Surface Transport, Ministry of Industry and Commerce, and various industry associations.
- In order to facilitate the duel purpose of setting the Regulatory Authority and ensuring private participation, the Expert Group recommended necessary amendments in the Port Trust Act.

*Recommendations of the Taskforce*

The Taskforce on integrated transport policy (2001) has suggested the following policies for viable operation of the ports:

- Adoption of a strategic approach in order to explore inter-port complementarities.
- Enhancing port productivity by developing a series of specialized minor ports, along the coastline in order to divert traffic from the congested major ports.
- Establishing two modern gateway/trans-shipment ports in Mumbai and Chennai and provide for inter-modal linkages through efficient rail/road services between two ports namely JNPT and Chennai so as to facilitate movement of large trans-shipment containers.
- A sharper focus on port technology ensuring compatibility with development in shipping.
- The pricing policy of port services should ensure adequate returns and enhance productivity of ports. Cross subsidization needs to be phased out.

- Introducing organizational changes in the form of corporatisation for efficient management, institutional funding and attractive private and foreign collaborative ventures.
- Making Tariff Authority for Major Ports (TAMP) as appellate body.

*Present Scenario*

The present Government policy on port operation has allowed private sector participation through various policies. The reform initiatives, obtained from the Ministry web-site, are briefly mentioned below:

**Identified Areas of Participation through Joint Venture**

- Construction of new port facilities within the existing port.
- Improving productivity of an existing port facility by upgrading and/or improving managerial practices (entire terminal meant for a particular commodity could be given for running it as a common user facility), and/or
- Development of a new port.
- Any combination of the three above

*Conditions for Entering into Joint Venture*

- The major ports would provide financial support, ensure availability of port assets at agreed terms, and provide services such as experts, water front, pilotage, conservancy, and safety, in lieu of agreed terms and return over the period of collaboration.
- The period of collaboration will be upto 30 years. Upon expiry of the period, the port related assets would revert back to the Major Port Trust in accordance with conditions of Agreement.
- The Joint Venture arrangements can be finalized without tender.
- The Joint Venture will require approval from Central Government.

*Regulatory Framework for Private Sector Participation*

- Although the ports continue to maintain their regulatory role under Major Port Trusts Act, 1963, for the purpose of fixing and revising port tariffs an independent Tariff Regulatory Authority has been set up. The tariff so fixed would be ceiling (upper limit) and both the private entrepreneurs and the ports would be free to charge any tariff less than such notified tariff.

- The port should ensure that private investment does not result in the creation of private monopolies, and that private facilities are available to all users on equal and competitive terms. However, in the case of berths constructed or taken on lease by private entrepreneurs, they would be permitted to give priority berthing to their own ships and they would service other ships on a first come first served basis.
- The private entrepreneurs will be obliged to protect the national interests like national security whenever necessary and required, and also honour priority berthing orders of Central Government, in this regard. The private entrepreneurs will also abide by the various statutory requirements on the protection of the environment; anti-pollution measures, safety, conservancy, etc, and also abide by the directives issued by the Government/Port in this regard from time to time.
- The ports with the approval of the Central Government will take steps to frame regulations under relevant sections of Major Port Trust Act consistent with the guidelines to enable private sector participation in Port Sector.

Till such regulations are framed, cases will continue to be governed by these guidelines.

*Areas of Privatisation*

The following areas have been identified for participation/investment by the private sector. These are indicative in nature and individual ports can expand the scope of activities after prior consultation with Central Government.

- Leasing out existing assets of the Port.
- Construction/creation of additional assets, like construction and operation of container terminals, bulk break bulk, multi-purpose and specialized cargo berths, Warehousing, Container Freight Stations, storage facilities and tank farms, Cranage/

handling equipment, Setting up of captive power plants, Dry docking and ship repair facilities etc.

- Leasing of equipment for port handling and leasing of floating crafts from the private sector.
- Pilotage.
- Captive facilities for port based industries.

There is no legal bar to private sector participation in port facilities as per the provisions of the existing Major Port Trusts Act, 1963. However, the Port Trust Board considers all the proposals on a case-to-case basis on merits. Private participation is allowed on the basis of open competitive bidding. The tenders would be based on two-cover system consisting of technical and price bids. For the sake of transparency, after the issue of tender document, the port may arrange one or more pre-bid conferences for clarifications, if necessary.

*Labour Policies*

Before privatising an existing port facility, the ports should examine:

- Whether the labour force is likely to be rendered surplus afterwards.
- Possibility of re-deploying and re-training such surplus labour.
- After the above exercises, the port should identify the labour which has to be necessarily taken over with the facility and clearly bring it out in the tender document, so that the intending bidders (private sectors) are aware of the liability.
- No retrenchment should be done without the concurrence of labour and should only be in accordance with Industrial Disputes Act/relevant labour laws. However, voluntary retirement should be encouraged.
- The lessee would be bound by all the labour laws of the country.
- Conditions of service of transferred labour, if any, would not be inferior to what they enjoyed before.

**Table 4**

*Private Sector/Captive Port Projects Approved so far*

| No. | Port | Project | Capacity (Million Tonnes) | Project Cost (Rs Crores) | Name of Party |
|---|---|---|---|---|---|
| 1 | JNPT | Container Terminal | 6.00 | 800.00 | P&O. The project is under completion |
| 2 | JNPT | Liquid cargo | 4.50 Berth | 200.00 | BPCL & IOC agreement is under finalisation and to be executed soon |
| 3 | Kandla | 5th Oil Jetty | 2.00 | 221.00 | IFFCO. Completed |
| 4 | Kandla | Oil Jetty at Vainar | 15.00 | 600.00 | Essar Oil Ltd. Agreement finalised |
| 5 | Kandla | Two Virtual Jetties | 2.00 | 30.00 | IOC & HPCL. Completed |
| 6 | Mormugao | Off Shore Stockyard and Berth | 5.00 | 300.00 | Mormugao Martina |
| 7 | Tuticorin | Container Terminal | 3.60 | 100.00 | PSA Corporation. Under Completion |

Source: www.ipc.nic.in

In addition, nine projects at various ports are under consideration. When implemented, the financial problems of the ports are likely to come down.

*Formation of Standing Committee*

Cases have been reported where entrepreneur come up with innovative proposals for creation of facilities at ports, which have not been conceived by the Port Trusts. In such cases, a decision needs to be taken as to how to proceed with such unsolicited innovative proposals. In order to evaluate such innovative proposals and to see whether they should be proceeded with, a Standing Committee is set up with representations from port authorities and concerned ministries.

## Power

*Sector Profile*

The power sector in India is characterized by predominance of the government sector, where the central and state electricity departments jointly account for over 95 per cent of generation, transmission and distribution capacity in the country. The State Electricity Boards, the major players responsible for power sector development accounts for 61 per cent of country's generation, 70 per cent of transmission in terms of ckt.kms., and almost 100 per cent of distribution capacity. The success of the sector could be highlighted by the instance of increased installed capacity from 1362 MW to over 100,000 MW since independence and electrification of more than 500,000 villages accounting for 86 per cent of the total. However, one of the less impressive characteristics of power sector in the country is chronic shortage with poor and erratic quality of supply. In addition, the annual per capita consumption is among the lowest in the world.[10] To add to the worries, SEBs are presently in a poor financial health.[11]

To improve the situation of this sector, various committees had been appointed over the period, and all of them have recommended thorough reform in transmission and distribution of power. The analysis could start with the recommendations of the Expert Group on Infrastructure (1996). The Expert Group expressed grave concern over the prevailing scenario, and opined that a total investment of nearly Rs. 5000 billion over the period 1996-2006 is required for the improvement of this sector. The broad reform policies recommended by the Expert Group are the following:

*Price Reform*

The Expert Group opined that the existing uneconomic consumer pricing structure is causing lot of problems and suggested a thorough reform through the SEBs. The following policies were recommended to get over the problems:

- Adoption of a cost-based pricing system for each consumer segment in a phased manner through a 10 per cent increase in average tariff per annum net of inflation.
- Providing meters at consumer ends or at an intermediate distribution point to tackle the problem of indiscriminate use.
- Developing institutional means to determine targeted consumer groups, to whom subsidization could be extended.
- Setting up an independent regulation of prices with provision for price reform to be balanced by improvement in quality of service, technical as well as commercial.

*Regulatory Reform*

The excessive centralization of the power sector in India causes a lot of procedural hassles. To curb these problems, a regulatory reform was recommended on the following fields:

- Autonomy to regulatory agencies both at State and Central level.
- The regulatory reform at the State level should cover consumer tariffs, overseeing the public and private undertakings at equitable terms, monitoring service standards and approving projects below the threshold specified for central clearance.
- The Central regulation must focus on bulk generation and inter-state transmission tariffs, approvals for larger projects, and enforcing the right of access to the inter-state and inter-region network.

*Private Participation in Power Sector*

The government control over the power sector has failed to solve the problems inherent in the system. The Expert Group noted that the need to encourage private participation in power sector has been recognized, as the current government policy permits 100 per cent foreign-owned companies to set up power projects of any capacity and type and repatriate profits. Greater flexibility has also been extended to price arrangements for thermal and hydro-electric generation. The policy has resulted in signage of a large number of MoUs. However, to convert these MoUs in actual investments, a balanced power purchase agreement should be in force. The Expert Group pointed out two problems, which are standing in the way:

- Issues specific to the MoU route.
- Problems relating to the Sector itself.

The Expert Group suggested that in order to strengthen the negotiating positions of the SEBs, the operation should be carried on in a transparent manner so as to obtain public acceptance, with two key policies:

- Identifying a pre-determined benchmark price per unit of energy.

- Arriving at an unambiguous political mandate to secure the target price or break off negotiation.

Given the non-transparent nature of the existing bidding procedure for approvals from the point of public acceptance, the Expert Group recommended the following:

- Constitution of a Central Electricity Regulatory Commission, an autonomous approval agency setting its own policies, and operating outside Government control and would consist of members of Central Electricity Authority.

*Restructuring of State Electricity Boards*

The financial conditions of the SEBs are in a very sorry state. Delay in addressing this issue would cause a dampening effect on private investment into transmission and distribution and underutilization of generation capacity respectively. This led the Expert Group to recommend the following reform agenda to be pursued:

- Restructuring the SEBs into compact, viable, corporatised units, where the functions of generation, transmission, and distribution would be adequately separated.
- Transferring some of the CEA's functions to high-powered Regional Electrical Authorities.

*Other Recommendations*

The Expert Group also recommended a number of general suggestions for speedy implementation of the process of commercialization:

- Replacement of the Plant Load Factor (PLF) yardstick by Plant Availability.
- Adoption of 'time-of-day' pricing and introduction of 'power pooling' arrangements.
- Evolution of a medium-term fuel strategy.

*Settling the Dues of SEBs*

In order to settle the monumental dues of the SEBs, an Expert Group (2001) was appointed, which presented a scheme to ensure payment of current dues in future. The Expert Group's recommendations include a package of incentives and disincentives linked to commercial discipline and initiation of a process of reforms. The main features of the scheme recommended by the Expert Group are as follows:

- For the States participating in the scheme, 50 per cent of the surcharge/interest on delayed payments could be waived. The rest of the dues amounting to the full principal amount as well as the remaining 50 per cent of the interest/surcharge, aggregating Rs. 33,600 crore should be securitised through bonds issued by the respective State Governments. Taking all the factors[12] into account, the total securitisation under this scheme is estimated to be around Rs. 35,000 crore.
- The bonds should be issued through the RBI at a tax-free interest rate of 8.5 per cent per annum. The term of the bonds should be structured to achieve a moratorium of 5 years on repayment of principal with the entire principal being repaid between the 6th and 15th year. These bonds should be identical to bonds issued in connection with the market borrowings of State Governments, with the attendant discipline in repayments. The bonds will be subject to lock-in restrictions that will allow release of only 10 per cent of the bonds in the secondary market each year.
- For ensuring timely payment of current dues in future, defaults in current payments for power/fuel should attract a graded reduction in the supply of power from central power stations and in coal supplies. Where such defaults exceed 90 days from the date of billing, the Ministry of Finance should recover these dues through adjustment against releases due to them from the Centre.[13]
- In order to initiate steps towards reform of the sector, the scheme requires SEBs to accept reform-based performance milestones such as setting up of SERCs, metering of distribution feeders and improvement in revenue realization. The milestones should be specified in the MoUs to be signed with the Ministry of Power.

- The States should be offered incentives for complying with the scheme. If SEBs do not default on their current dues and adhere to the performance milestones, CPSUs should pay them, during the first four years commencing from 1.4.2001, bi-annual cash incentives equal to 2 per cent of the value of bonds. Further, if SEBs open and maintain LCs till the end of December 2001, CPSUs should pay them a one-time cash incentive equal to 2 per cent of the value of bonds. These incentives could add upto Rs. 6,300 crore. In addition, States undertaking reforms should also be assisted through APDP grants and discretionary allocation of power.

*Present Scenario*

Two Government Reports, namely, *Major Initiatives for Power Sector Development* (2001), and *Blueprint For The Power Sector Development* (2002), along with *Annual Report of Ministry of Power* (2001-02) describe the recent status and the future growth plans being implemented by the Ministry of Power. The major initiatives taken by the authority and the future agendas as portrayed in these three Government documents are given below.

**Capacity Addition**

Based on projections made by the 16$^{th}$ Electric Power Survey conducted by Central Electric Authority, Ministry of Power is preparing plans to generate an additional capacity of 100,000 MW by the end of XI-th plan.[14] In order to achieve the target, special emphasis has been given to thermal and hydro projects, stepping up nuclear power generation, increase in non-conventional energy sources, improving end-use efficiency, and increase in private sector participation.[15] The private sector participation in power sector could be ensured by distribution reform. Several policies that has already been implemented are presented in the following:

- The Electricity (Supply) Act, 1948 was amended in 1991 to promote private investment in generation and is quite successful in drawing private investment.[16]
- Foreign investments are now allowed in generation, transmission, and distribution and granted automatic approval (RBI route) without limit for Hydro-electric Power Plants,

Coal/Lignite based thermal power plants, and Oil/Gas based thermal power plants.

- Competitive bidding has become mandatory for power projects.
- Standard PPAs and fuel supply agreements are created to facilitate Independent Power Producers (IPPs). An IPP can also go for the fuel of its choice.
- Regulatory Commissions have been notified/set up in about 15 States (details in annex 2) to undertake independent tariff determination and tariff rationalization.
- Recently, FDI in power trading has also been allowed in order to develop a market for power.
- Exemptions from ICB route are granted to a few categories of initiatives in order to reduce project cost.[17]
- The policy announced in 1991 envisaged that, an amount not exceeding 40 per cent of the total outlay for private sector units may come from Indian Public Financial Institutions (IPFIs). This ceiling has since been removed, but with a stipulation that considering the need of maximizing financing from external sources and prudential norms exercised by IPFIs, allowing a higher domestic debt component for projects which are developed based on indigenously sourced plant and equipment, would be more desirable.

**Private Investment in Transmission**

The Ministry of Power's plan to double the generation capacity by 2012 requires an investment of Rs. 200,000 crores, of which, private sector is expected to contribute a sizable proportion. The Law was amended in 1998 to permit private investment in transmission and detailed guidelines were issued in January 2000 regarding the process for attracting private investment in transmission projects. However, the level of private investment in transmission so far failed to match the expectations. The Ministry of Power is reviewing the need of further institutional changes required in order to ensure greater inflow of private investment within the framework of the regulated transmission sector.

**The main causes behind low private investment in Power sector**

- The foremost problem due to which many projects have been unable to achieve financial closure in spite of progressing well on other fronts, remains the poor financial health of the State Electricity Boards (SEBs), who do not have the financial capability to support more than a few projects in terms of regular reimbursement of bills, opening of letters of credit and escrow accounts.
- A bankable escrow cover has been sought by almost all the IFIs financing IPPs. The states do not have sufficient escrow space to accommodate all the IPPs. Difficulties have been witnessed in identifying the quantum of escrow capacity available with the states. In several cases, the escrowable capacity identified by the state governments has not been accepted by the financial institutions. The inability of the state governments to accommodate all the IPPs for allocation of escrow cover has also led to litigation by some of the IPPs.
- The delay in non-finalization of various contracts such as Power Purchase Agreement, Fuel Supply Agreement and Fuel Transportation Agreement etc. acceptable to all the concerned parties.
- Court cases in the form of Public Interest Petitions etc.

Source: Annual Report of the Ministry of Power (2001-02)

**Demand Side Management**

To improve the quality and reliability of power supply, a massive upgradation and strengthening of the distribution[18] system is proposed to implement, which include installation of meters and capacitors at all levels, reconfiguration of feeder lines and transformers to make the system less LT oriented, installation of smaller size energy efficient distribution transformers, re-conductoring of over-load stations, development of digital mapping of the entire distribution system etc.

In order to reduce the cost of power, and to promote end use energy efficiency, the government has proposed to adopt the following policies:

- Rationalization of Tariff and Price
- Energy Audits in Industry
- Increasing Efficiency in Agriculture
- Facilitating use of Energy Efficient Household Appliances
- Focus on time of day metering and pricing

### Financial Crisis in State Power Sector

All the three Government reports expressed grave concern over the poor financial performance of the SEBs. The table provided below clearly shows that the commercial losses of the SEBs are gradually increasing over the period and that puts immense pressure on the respective State Government.

The loss in incurring transmission and distribution activities is further aggravated by theft and wrong classification.[19] Hence, the state governments were asked to reduce loss in these accounts in a time-bound programme by adopting the following measures:

- By completing 100 per cent metering by December, 2001.
- By conducting regular energy Audit at all levels.
- By strengthening and upgrading Sub-transmission and distribution system by taking Sub-station as a unit on priority basis.
- By installing suitable Management Information System (MIS) for effective energy accounting.
- By achieving commercial viability in distribution in 2-3 years through creation of profit centres with full accountability, handing over local distribution to panchayats/local bodies and privatization of distribution.

### Alternate Payment Security Mechanism

In view of the current policy, against giving counter guarantees and pending fructification of reform measures, the Ministry has taken steps to set up alternate payment security mechanism for the investors as an interim resource mobilization strategy. The mechanism has been evolved in consultation with leading financial institutions like IDBI, ICICI, SBI Caps etc. on the basis of a memorandum of agreement/understanding to be signed with the reforming States wherein the States agree on milestone based package of reforms like restructuring of SEBs, setting up of SERCs, reduction in T&D losses, 100 per cent metering, improvement in PLF, energy audit etc. This would bring about improvement in revenue collection and financial health of the SEBs and enable them to provide escrow before the commercial operation date of the power project.[20]

## Table 5

*Commercial Losses of SEBs*

*Rs. (Crore)*

| *Year* | *Total Revenue* | *Revenue Expenditure* | *Gross Operating Surplus* | *Depreciation* | *Net Operating Surplus* | *Total Interest Payable* | *Commercial Profit(+) /Loss(-)* |
|---|---|---|---|---|---|---|---|
| 1996-97 (Actual) | 52567.42 | 44508.29 | 8059.13 | 4840.85 | 3218.28 | 7892.59 | -4674.31 |
| 1997-98 (Actual) | 59620.68 | 53250.66 | 6370.02 | 5199.94 | 1170.08 | 8768.03 | -7597.95 |
| 1998-99 (Actual) | 66475.06 | 61068.07 | 5406.99 | 5465.18 | -58.19 | 10450.56 | -10508.75 |
| 1999-2000 (provi.) | 75095.42 | 74952.49 | 142.93 | 5897.59 | -5754.66 | 9333.48 | -15088.14 |
| 2000-01 (RE) | 84015.73 | 84751.09 | -735.36 | 6139.42 | -6874.78 | 10918.94 | -17793.72 |
| 2001-02 (AP) | 92817.71 | 97691.84 | -4874.13 | 7090.54 | -11964.67 | 12872.55 | -24837.22 |

Source: Planning Commission (2002)

### Restructuring the SEBs

The restructuring of the SEBs, a much awaited reform agenda, is being pursued by the Ministry of Power by not following a unique model, rather States are encouraged to initiate reform in the way that suits them best within the available options. Seven States, Orissa, Haryana, Andhra Pradesh, Karnataka, Uttar Pradesh, Rajasthan and Delhi have already enacted their reform laws and unbundled their SEBs. Madhya Pradesh has passed its reform laws while Gujarat has drafted its legislation. Reforms in Orissa have progressed the farthest with privatisation of all distribution companies in the State. The reform status of SEBs across the states is given in annex 3.

**Electricity Bill, 2001**

The Electricity Bill 2001, which responds to a number of recommendations by various committees, has been introduced in Parliament in August 2001. The Bill seeks to replace three existing acts, viz., the Indian Electricity Act, 1910, the Electricity (Supply) Act, 1948 and the Electricity Regulatory Commissions Act, 1998. The Bill stressed upon the following issues:

- The Central Government to prepare a National Electricity Policy in consultation with State Governments.
- Thrust to complete the rural electrification and provide for management of rural distribution by Panchayats, Cooperative Societies, non-Government organizations, franchisees etc.
- Generation being delicensed and captive generation being freely permitted. Hydro projects would, however, need approval of the state government and clearance from the Central Electricity Authority.
- Transmission Utility at the Central as well as State level, to be a Government company – with responsibility for planned and coordinated development of transmission network. Provision for private transmission licensees. Open access in transmission from the outset with provision for surcharge for taking care of current level of cross subsidy with the surcharge being gradually phased out.
- Distribution licensees would be free to undertake generation and generating companies would be free to take up distribution licensees.
- The State Electricity Regulatory Commission is a mandatory requirement.
- Provision for licence free generation and distribution in the rural areas.
- The SERCs may permit open access in distribution in phased with surcharge for current level of cross subsidy to be gradually phased out alongwith cross subsidies and obligation to supply.
- Provision for payment of subsidy through budget.

**Contd. ...**

- For rural and remote areas stand alone systems for generation and distribution would be permitted.
- Trading is being recognized a distinct activity with the safeguard of the Regulatory Commissions being authorized to fix ceilings on trading margins, if necessary.
- The State Governments have flexibility to unbundle the SEBs or continue with them as distribution licensees and State Transmission Utility.
- The Bill does not prescribe any model of reform, instead provides flexibility to the State Government to choose the model suiting to their conditions.
- Metering of all electricity supplied made mandatory.
- An Appellate Tribunal to hear appeals against the decision of the CERC and SERCs.
- Provisions relating to theft of electricity made more stringent.

Source: Annual Report, Ministry of Power (2001-02)

**Tackling the Supply Bottlenecks**

To get over the shortage of power problem, the indigenously available resources in isolated pockets has to be optimally utilised through enhanced inter-regional transfer of power. A National Grid will be developed by creation of "Transmission Highways" which would be capable of evacuating bulk power from large sized thermal and hydel power stations located in Eastern, Northern and North-Eastern Regions to the major load centres in the Northern, Western and Southern Region. It is expected that the total inter-regional power exchange capability will be increased to 8,000 MW and 30,000 MW by January 2004 and end 2012 respectively.

*Status of Reforms & Restructuring in Power Sector*

Central Electricity Regulatory Commission formed under the provisions of Electricity Regulatory Commissions Act, 1998 has been made fully functional. The Commission has passed orders on Availability Based Tariff and has also brought out terms and conditions for determination of tariff. Eighteen States have issued tariff orders. Several states are also progressing on the path of reform. In order to bring in focused approach to addressing the problems specific to States, the Government of India has been encouraging States to sign MoUs. So far, twenty States have signed Memorandum of Understanding (MoU). The MoUs affirm joint commitment of the two parties to undertake reforms. In reciprocation of the commitment made by States to undertake reforms in a time bound manner, the Government of India has been extending support and assistance to the State Governments on the following:

- Provision of additional power through allocation of additional power from Central Generating Stations, development of new generating capacity through CPSUs, and support for enhancement of generating capacity in the State sector.
- Provision of necessary inter-State transmission lines and commitment to have PGCIL take up some identified intra-State lines.
- Provisions of additional financing by PFC in relaxation of standard requirements.

The details of the reforms undertaken are shown in the annexes 2 and 3.

## Railways

### *Sector Profile*

Railways in India holds a unique position in terms of integrating the nation through the huge transportation network. However, in the later part of the 1990s, the railways have begun experiencing a financial crisis. The crisis originated due to a number of reasons. First of all, the policy of subsidisation of passenger traffic put a heavy financial burden on the central exchequer. On the other hand, in freight transport segment, over the last decade, the proportionate transportation through rail has gone down for almost all commodities. The major problems of the sector are identified as lack of flexibility in pricing, high costs of internally sourced products and services, investments in non-remunerative projects etc. Rising employee costs, poor productivity, and declining budgetary support in recent years, have further compounded the problem.

The aforesaid problems became particularly staggering in the 1990s, and the financial position of IR reached to a trough, when it failed to pay a dividend to the government on its past investment for the first time in 17 years. Therefore, to suggest a way out of this problem, an Expert Group was appointed, which submitted its report in 2001. The report suggested that the solution lies in modernization of IR to meet the need of the growing economy through expansion of capacity. In addition, given the shrinking government funds, the report suggested that new investments need to be financed on a commercial basis. The Expert Group recommended policy reform in following areas:

*Long-Term Traffic Growth Patterns*

The Expert Group finds that the policy to subsidize passenger traffic led to charging higher tariff on freights, which in turn leads to lowering of business opportunity. Hence, a significant change in IR's policy towards freight traffic must be undertaken to boost business. The observations of the Expert Group are provided below:

- By merely providing physical capacity sufficient to meet the demand, an annual growth rate of 5 per cent for freight traffic could be achieved. However, a major organizational restructuring along with modified pricing strategy would result in a higher growth rate.
- A significant improvement in freight services was strongly recommended.[21]
- Implementation of appropriate measures to capture back the lost bulk freight and carry a greater proportion of non-bulk freight would raise the freight revenue by an average of 6.9 to 7.2 per cent per year for the next 15 years.
- Revenue from passenger traffic could also be expanded through greater availability of services to upper class services and tariff rebalancing in accordance with elasticities of demand.[22]
- With tariff rebalancing over the next 5 years, passenger revenues can grow by about 8.6 per cent per year; whereas the same would grow at 7.5 per cent without tariff rebalancing per year both in real terms.

*Revenue Generation from Freight Traffic*

In order to generate the growth impetus, the Expert Group strongly recommended that a strategic high growth policy must be followed in order to boost earning from both freight and passenger traffic. The policy of constantly raising freight rates over the years has been counter-productive for business. In this light, the following policies were strongly recommended:

- No further real increase in freight rates.
- To encounter the competition from the road transport segment, special attention must be paid on commodities drifting away from railways, improvement in freight train speeds, upgrading the rolling stock in order to reduce cost of maintenance as well as number of break downs, elimination of road crossings etc.
- Sector-specific investment for a few commodity groups like finished steels, and cement movement in bulk, incorporation of special wagons and handling arrangements were also recommended.
- Finally, in order to experience a coordinated growth between road and railways, establishment of two or more additional container depots in each industrially advanced state and at least one container depot in all other states were recommended.

*Revenue Generation from Passenger Traffic*

The Expert Group recommended the following suggestions in order to exploit the revenue potential of the passenger segment:

- Introduction of new trains and services will be of much help. The process has already begun.[23]
- In line with the elasticities of demand, an annual adjustment of about 10 and 8 per cent increase in second class sleeper fares and ordinary fares respectively should be undertaken on a continuous basis for about five years assuming about 6 per cent annual inflation over the period.
- During the same period, in line with the demand elasticities, an annual increase around 1-2 per cent in upper class fares was assumed to increase the revenue.[24]
- The fare restructuring has to be accompanied by tangible improvement in service.

After restructuring of prices, the ratio of second class and AC first class fares would be around 1:9, much similar to the 1:9.6 ratio suggested by the Railway Freight and Fare Committee (1993). Similar price restructuring was recommended for sub-urban fares as well. The Expert Group foresaw the expected annual revenue growth to be around 7.5 per cent at constant prices, if all these measures are undertaken.

*Reduction of Cost*

Citing the findings of a study conducted by RITES for the Railway Board, the Expert Group stated that any modernization exercise would require an accelerated reduction of the excess manpower without delay.[25] The Expert Group recommended reduction of at least 20 per cent of the existing employees through spinning off of ancillary activities and also a well-designed VRS scheme, in addition to normal retirements, in next 5 to 7 years.

*Targeted Investment*

The Expert Group identified the investment requirement of IR to be Rs. 130,000 crores, 160,000 crores and 200,000 crores for realizing low growth, medium growth and strategic high growth respectively.

Now, in order to generate the massive investible fund for strategic high growth, IR has to reduce cost on a massive scale and become commercially viable in 7 years.

During the period, extensive government support in terms of devolution of some portion of pension liabilities, compensation for investment and losses incurred, is extremely important for the sector.

In addition, IR must generate some internal fund through asset sales of about Rs. 500 crore in each of the first 5 years.

Apart from this, the faulty planning procedure resulting investment in projects of low priority and doubtful return, increasing bottlenecks, etc. requires a special attention. Too many funds have been tied in gauge conversion, and creation of new lines, and suitable policies has to be adopted in this regard.

The Expert Group recommended closure of non-remunerative lines in order to free resources to be efficiently utilized elsewhere.

*Corporatisation of Indian Railways*

The Expert Group has recommended a plan for corporatisation of Indian Railways:

- Institutional separation between social obligation and performance imperatives, to improve the declining performance of IR is a much-needed step. This would confine the policymakers to determine the policy, regulators to fix the competition rules and pricing strategy, and management to manage the system, and remuneration would be clearly linked with performance indicators.[26]
- Commercialization exercise rather than privatization is the ideal solution. The restructuring would involve re-organization of the rail system into its component parts, spinning off non-core activities, and adoption of commercial accounting performance management systems.
- The distancing with government should be done in such a way that railways could ultimately evolve in India into a broad-based industry with multiple-players and multiple-owners. This commercialization should be undertaken through extensive corporatisation by following an outward-looking, business-oriented, and customer-driven principle.

This would involve re-organization of core transportation network into key components; freight, passenger, sub-urban, fixed and shared infrastructure and others. Although these different units would function with greater autonomy, they will be held responsible for a balanced score-card of commercial performance measures. The additional steps recommended were:

- Before corporatisation, the accounts of Indian Railways should be brought into company format, in accordance with Company's Act 1956.
- Following the success of a few foreign countries in usage of financial and non-financial information in management decision-making is also recommended and incorporation of IT based MIS system is suggested for that purpose.

### *Changes in Legislation*

When the broad framework of the restructuring is finalized, a special task force has to be set up in order to frame a suitable legislation for the new organizational framework. The main objective of the legislation would be the following:

- Corporatising Indian Railways.
- Revamping the Railways Board.
- Redefining the relation between Government and the revamped Indian Railway Executive Board.
- Providing tax exemption during the transitional period of 5 to 7 years.
- Permitting private participation in railway operations.
- Facilitating the induction of personnel from outside railways.
- Ensuring incorporation of the social obligation of the government in the new legislation through subsidization in social areas to extent of available funds, and setting a social safety net to take care of the surplus labour.

The new organizational structure as proposed by the Expert Group requires establishment of the following agencies:

- The IR has to be transformed into Indian Railways Corporation (IRC), which would be governed by a reconstituted Indian Railways Executive Board (IREB). IRC will be an independent, corporatised, customer focused and financially viable organization, concentrating on core activities, run along commercial principles and abide by the standard corporate accounting principles.
- Overall, the IREB will be responsible for the restructuring process, and the leader of each business unit would be responsible for their unit's performance. It will comprise qualified persons including representation from private sector business community.
- An Indian Rail Regulatory Authority (IRRA) has to be constituted which would distance IRC from Government, and regulate IRC's activities as a monopoly supplier, particularly, the tariff policies.

The Government under the new framework has been assigned the following responsibilities:

- Setting policy direction.
- Constituting IRRA and IREB.
- Implementing changes in the structure according to its vision.
- Providing adequate funding to railways for fulfilling the well-defined social obligations.
- Appoint/dismiss people holding key responsibilities in IRRA and IREB according to their performance.

The Expert Group suggested a period of 3-5 years to redesign the legal framework for incorporating the changes suggested in the Report and expressed optimism that if the road map for corporatisation is initiated immediately, Railway Budget could be abolished by 2002, which would serve as a potent signal of the change in attitude.

*Recommendations by the Taskforce*

The Task force on Integrated Transport Policy (2001) commented that the emphasis will have to shift from merely providing transport infrastructure and services to technological upgradation and modernization of the same in order to ensure mobility and not only accessibility. The thrust will have to be on provision of improved high quality services with minimum use of cross subsidization and emphasis on achieving optimal inter modal mix with appropriate pricing and user charges policy and through injection of competitive impulses. The recommendations of the Task force for improving the standard of railway service were:

- Regaining its share in freight traffic through qualitative capacity augmentation aided by corrective pricing policies and organizational change.
- Focusing on technology upgradation and modernization.
- Augmenting capacity on the saturated high-density routes and replace over aged assets, facilitating reduction in asset failure, improvement in productivity and enhancing safety of rail operations.
- Reducing speed differentials between freight and passenger services.

- Improving coach and freight car designs as well as pay load to tare ratios for freight, mechanize track maintenance and adopt latest state-of-the-art locos.
- Organizationally spliting the existing six manufacturing units into independent profit and cost centres.
- Improving self-financing capability through marked reduction in the extent of subsidization of passenger traffic.
- Focusing on creation of rail hubs with sufficient warehousing capacity to accelerate the programme of containerization.
- Enlarging the scope of private sector participation gradually in acquiring rolling stock through innovative leasing schemes.
- Setting up an independent regulatory authority for fixation of taxes and freights.

*Railway Safety*

It has been argued that in a sub-continental country as large as India with its widespread railway infrastructure (the second largest in the world), certain accidents are unavoidable. However, proper precautionary measures could keep that possibility at the minimum level. The Expert Group (2001) commented that proportion of expenditure on repairs and maintenance has been declining steadily over the years.[27] Some staggering features of railway safety are provided in annex 4. Post-Independence, four high-level committees, namely, Kunzru Committee (1962), Wanchoo Committee (1968), Sikri Committee (1978), and Khanna Committee (1998), were constituted to scrutinize various facets of the Indian Railways, all of which emphasized the need to improve safety measures. In the current context, the recommendations of the Khanna Committee, which submitted its report in 1999, are discussed below:

*Developing Research and Safety Organizations*

The Khanna Committee (1999) assigned the *Research, Designs & Standards Organization (RDSO)* the following responsibilities:

- Playing the role of facilitator by seeking active collaboration of industry, Institutes of technology and other specialist agencies for developing technologies.

- Identifying new technologies that can most suitably be adopted by IR and thereafter associate manufacturers and technical institutions in developing and upgrading these technologies in a time bound programme.
- Quickly establishing links with such institutions and strengthening them through exchange of ideas on technical, operating issues, new technologies, etc.
- Functioning as the sounding board as also the guide on various safety issues agitating the Zonal Railways.
- Conducting detailed investigations into systems failures in accidents, analysis of long-term trends of accidents, human factor issues, and complex technical problems, such as rail-wheel interaction, safety tolerances, etc.

For better functioning of *Commission of Railway Safety* (CRS) the Khanna Committee recommended the following:

- For restoring public confidence, all CRS inquiries should be made public and transparent and the inquiry reports should be made available to the public immediately after finalization. However, the IR Act needs to be suitably amended to ensure that such transparency does not result in unnecessary litigation or harassment of railwaymen. A clause could be included in the relevant laws that no railway servant can be prosecuted without the sanction of the authority competent to appoint him or a higher authority. Further, it should be stipulated that the Commissioner of Railway Safety or any other investigating authority who has powers of a civil court for conduct of enquiries cannot be called as witness or for examination by any court in cases which arise from investigation done by them. Finally, the report and the findings of the CRS should not be allowed to be used as evidence.
- Making railwaymen from other disciplines directly associated with train operations such as Mechanical, Traffic, Signal and Electrical, eligible for posting in CRS.
- Relieving CRS of the function of approving new designs of rolling stock before they are pressed into service, requiring deletion of Section 27 of the Railway Act, 1989.

- Finalization of conclusions and recommendations of serious accident inquiry reports should be adopted after discussions in a Board consisting of at least two Commissioners, preferably with different professional backgrounds. At least one Deputy Commissioner and two senior inspectors should assist each Commissioner, and preferably they should have different professional backgrounds.

*Restructuring the Safety Organization*

In order to develop a group spirit, it is necessary that all departments of Indian Railways must feel equally part of the safety department and should contribute their expertise to furtherance of safety objectives. It could be mentioned that the Sikri Committee (1978) had recommended that the Safety Organization be manned by officers from any of the major five departments, namely, Operating, Civil Engineering, Mechanical Engineering, Signal & Telecommunication and Electrical Traction, who are mainly concerned with safety in train operations, but this recommendation was not accepted by the Ministry of Railways. The broad recommendations were:

- Safety Department on IR should be made broad based and suitable officers from Traffic, Civil, Mechanical, Signal and Electrical Engineering Departments should be posted as Safety officers at all levels.
- The Chief Safety Officer should be given the status of PHOD and the incumbent should have worked successfully as DRM.
- There should be four officers of Deputy HOD rank (from departments other than that of CSO) reporting to him.
- A similar pattern should be adopted on the Divisions where the DSO should invariably be in JA grade. He should have Assistant/Senior Scale officers reporting to him.
- All safety officers should have a minimum tenure of three years.
- Each safety group should have transport available for surprise checks.
- Experience as DSO/CSO should be necessary for promotion to PHOD/GM.
- Concept of safety audits should be introduced on IR.

*Present Scenario*

The present scenario in Indian Railways is obtained from the Annual Report of Ministry of Railways (2000-01) and the Status Paper (2002). The major initiatives to make Railways commercially viable and to improve safety, already undertaken and on the process of implementation, are presented in the following:

**Reduction in Staff Strength**

Indian Railways had been restricting the intake of fresh manpower since the beginning of the last decade. It has, between 1991 and 2001, reduced the staff strength from 18.07 lakhs (as on 31.3.91) to 15.45 lakhs (as on 31.3.2001) – reduction of 2.62 lakhs. In August 2000, Ministry of Railways have issued directives to all zonal railways for restricting the fresh intake of staff to 1 per cent in case of Operational categories and 0.5 per cent in other than Operational categories (excluding compassionate appointments).[28]

**Safety and Renewal of Assets**

- As a follow up of recommendations of the Khanna Committee, a Special Railway Safety Fund amounting to Rs.17,000 crores has been formed for replacement of overdue renewal assets by the end of 10th Plan. While Rs.5,000 crores will be contributed by Railways through Safety surcharge imposed on passenger traffic, the balance Rs.12,000 crores will be provided by the General Exchequer.
- To improve the crash worthiness of coaches, coach interiors are being re-designed with improved fittings and features, which would reduce impact of the accident. Simultaneously, the coach body will be re-designed to absorb more impact, so as to keep the passenger-carrying areas intact.
- Anti-collision Device based on Satellite-based Global Positioning System has been designed to prevent collisions between trains. The system is undergoing extended field trials on the Railway to test its efficacy.

**Measures being Implemented for Improving Safety**

The status report (2002) has pointed out the following measures in the process of implementation for improving safety conditions:

- Replacing over-aged assets where the exercise is overdue.
- Extending Track circuiting facility to cover the entire network in a phased manner.
- Adopting auxiliary warning system for giving advance warning of signal aspect to drivers.
- Incorporating long-welded rails to reduce chances of sabotage.
- Incorporating state-of-the-art ultrasonic flaw detection of track and rolling stock system.
- Replacing level crossings by road over bridges/road under bridges.
- Upgrading rolling stock and consequently improving the reliability of assets.
- Introducing efficient Anti-Collision Device.

**Policies to Improve Efficiency and Financial Strength**

The following measures are being implemented in order to improve the financial strength of Indian Railways:

- Initiation of new marketing schemes to attract additional traffic.
- Setting up of non-lapsable safety fund for liquidating arrears of asset renewals and investment in safety enhancement projects.
- Rationalizing fare and freight rates.
- Funding of projects by innovative schemes including participation of State Government, private sector and funding of projects of national importance through the General Exchequer.
- Rationalizing allocation of resources for projects in different states.
- Focusing on safety including introduction of Anti-Collision Device, crashworthy coaches and longer rail panels, etc.
- Formulating passenger business strategies, through introduction of Jana Shatabdi; augmentation of capacity of sub-urban systems; training of frontline railway staff; computerisation of unreserved ticketing; and computerised Passenger Reservation System at all district headquarters.

- Concentrating on administrative reforms, including decentralization and delegation of powers to field officials.
- Formulating policy to strengthen the Golden Quadrilateral and its diagonals for running of freight trains at 100 kmph and construction of mega bridges.
- Using Information Technology for improving efficiency and making the organization customer-focused.
- Creating focused business organizations, such as Indian Railway Tourism and Catering Corporation (IRCTC), RAILTEL Coporation of India Limited (RCIL) and the proposed Land Development Authority.
- Signing of MoU with NTPC for setting up of dedicated power plants for generating power for captive use of Railways' traction requirement.
- Providing warehousing facilities through CWC and private freight terminals.

# Bibliography


### *Telecommunications*

- "The India Infrastructure Report: Policy Imperatives for Growth and Welfare", Expert Group on the Commercialization of Infrastructure Projects, (1996)
- "Report of the Steering Committee on Communication and Information for the Tenth Five Year Plan (2002-2007)", Planning Commission, Government of India (May, 2002)
- "Report of the Working Group on Telecom Sector for the Tenth Five Year Plan (2002-2007)", Government of India, Department of Telecommunications, Ministry of Communications (April 23, 2001)
- National Telecom Policy (1999)
- National Telecom Policy (1994)
- "Recommendations on Basic Service Licenses", Telecom Regulatory Authority of India, (2002)
- "Report of Taskforce on Growth of internet in the country", Telecom Regulatory Authority of India, (September 9, 2002)
- "Recommendations on Opening up of Internet Telephony", Telecom Regulatory Authority of India, (February 20, 2002)
- "Recommendations of TRAI on licencing issues relating to Public Mobile Radio Trunking Service Providers", Telecom Regulatory Authority of India, (PMRTSPs) (March 2, 2001)
- "Recommendations on introduction of competition in National Long Distance Communications", Telecom Regulatory Authority of India, (December 13, 1999)
- "Recommendations on opening of the International Long Distance Service", Telecom Regulatory Authority of India, (November 12, 2001)
- Annual Report, Government of India, Ministry of Communications and Information Technology, Department of Telecommunication (2001-2002)
- Annual Report, Telecom Regulatory Authority of India (1999-2000)

### *Road*

- "The India Infrastructure Report: Policy Imperatives for Growth and Welfare", Expert Group on the Commercialization of Infrastructure Projects, (1996)
- "Taskforce on Integrated Transport Policy, Planning Commission", Government of India, (October, 2001)
- Annual Report, Ministry of Road Transport and Highways, Government of India (2000-01)

### *Port*

- "The India Infrastructure Report: Policy Imperatives for Growth and Welfare", Expert Group on the Commercialization of Infrastructure Projects, (1996)
- "Taskforce on Integrated Transport Policy", Planning Commission, Government of India, (October, 2001)

### *Power*

- "The India Infrastructure Report: Policy Imperatives for Growth and Welfare", Expert Group on the Commercialization of Infrastructure Projects, (1996)
- "Major Initiatives for Power Sector Development", Ministry of Power, Government of India (May, 2001)

- "Blueprint for Power Sector Development", Ministry of Power, Government of India (August, 2001)
- "Annual Report of the Ministry of Power" (2001-02)
- "Annual Report on the Working of State Electricity Boards and Electricity Departments (2001-02)", Planning Commission, Power and Energy Division, Government of India (May, 2002)
- "Report of the Expert Group, Settlement of SEB Dues", Planning Commission, Government of India (May, 2001)

*Railways*

- "The Indian Railways Report, Policy Imperatives for Reinvention and Growth", Expert Group on Indian Railways, (2001)
- "Railway Fare and Freight Committee Report", Ministry of Railways, Government of India, 1993
- "Report of the Railway Safety Review Committee" (1999)
- "Taskforce on Integrated Transport Policy, Planning Commission", Government of India, (October, 2001)
- "Status paper on Indian Railways, Issues and Options", Government of India, Ministry of Railways (May, 2002)
- Annual Reports and Accounts, Government of India, Ministry of Railways, (2000-01)


## Annex 1

*Actual Inflow of FDI in Telecom Sector from August 1991 to November 2001*

| *No.* | *Service* | *Rs. (Million)* | *Percent* |
|---|---|---|---|
| 1 | Basic Telephone Service | 3937 | 4.85 |
| 2 | Cellular Mobile Telephone Service | 22154 | 27.27 |
| 3 | Radio Paging Service | 910 | 1.12 |
| 4 | E-Mail Service | 688 | 0.85 |
| 5 | VSAT Service | 281 | 0.35 |
| 6 | Cable TV Network + Internet | 746 | 0.92 |
| 7 | Satellite Telephone Service | 481 | 0.59 |
| 8 | Radio Trunking Service | 71 | 0.09 |
| 9 | Manufacturing and Consultancy | 7677 | 9.45 |
| 10 | Holding Companies | 44016 | 54.19 |
| 11 | Other value added Services | 2 | 0.00 |
| 12 | Automatic Route | 262 | 0.32 |
| | Total | 81224 | |

Source: Annual Report, Department of Telecommunications (2001-02)

## Annex 2

*Independent Regulatory Commissions for Power*

Reform of the Power Sector would be greatly aided by the establishment of independent regulatory agencies responsible for setting tariffs and regulating power purchase agreements. Accordingly, the Government of India has enacted Electricity Regulatory Commission Act, 1998 for setting up of independent regulatory bodies viz. The Central Electricity Regulatory Commission (CERC) and the State Electricity Regulatory Commissions (SERCs) at the Central level and State level respectively. These regulatory bodies would primarily look into all aspects of tariff fixation and matters incidental thereto.

*Central Electricity Regulatory Commission* (CERC) was constituted on 2-7-1998 at the Central level and its conduct of Business Regulation notified on 26-4-1999. CERC is in operation.

Nineteen States viz. Orissa, Haryana, Andhra Pradesh, Uttar Pradesh, Karnataka, West Bengal, Tamil Nadu, Punjab, Delhi, Gujarat, Madhya Pradesh, Arunachal Pradesh, Maharashtra, Rajasthan, Himachal Pradesh, Assam, Chhatisgarh, Kerala and Uttaranchal have either constituted or notified the constitution of State Electricity Regulatory Commission (SERC). SERCs of Orissa, Andhra Pradesh, Uttar Pradesh, Maharashtra, Gujarat, Karnataka, Rajasthan, Delhi, Madhya Pradesh, Himachal Pradesh and West Bengal have issued tariff orders.

The States of Orissa, Haryana, Andhra Pradesh, Uttar Pradesh, Karnataka, Rajasthan, Madhya Pradesh and Delhi have enacted their State Electricity Reforms Acts which provide, inter-alia, for unbundling/corporation of SEBs, setting up of SERCs etc. The SEBs of Orissa, Haryana, Andhra Pradesh, Karnataka, Uttar Pradesh and Rajasthan have been unbundled/corporatised. The unbundling of Delhi Vidyut Board (DVB) is under active consideration of the Delhi Government.

Source: Planning Commission (2002)

# Annex 3

*Status of Reforms in States*

| No. | State | Status of Reform |
|---|---|---|
| 1 | Andhra Pradesh | • SERC constituted, functional, two tariff orders issued.<br>• Reform Law enacted, SEB unbundled.<br>• Distribution Privatisation strategy being finalised.<br>• MoU signed with Government of India. |
| 2 | Arunachal Pradesh | • SERC notified (yet to be constituted). |
| 3 | Assam | • Single member SERC constituted<br>• MoU signed with Government of India |
| 4 | Bihar | • MoU signed<br>• Tariff revised by SEB |
| 5 | Chattisgarh | • MoU signed with Madhya Pradesh adopted. |
| 6 | Delhi | • SERC constituted, functional.<br>• First tariff order issued.<br>• Reform Law enacted, DVB to be unbundled.<br>• Committed to Distribution privatisation.<br>• REP for Distribution privatisation issued. |
| 7 | Goa | • MoU signed with Government of India |
| 8 | Gujarat | • SERC constituted, functional, first tariff order issued.<br>• Reform Law approved by Government of India and introduced in the State Assembly<br>• MoU signed with Government of India |
| 9 | Haryana | • SERC constituted, functional, two tariff orders issued.<br>• Reform Law enacted, SEB unbundled.<br>• MoU signed with Government of India. |
| 10 | Himachal Pradesh | • One Member HPSERC constituted. Member appointed w.e.f. 6/1/2001.<br>• First tariff order issued.<br>• MoU signed with Government of India. |
| 11 | Jammu and Kashmir | • Government of J&K has appointed Administrative Staff College of India as consultant conducting reform studies.<br>• Reform Law has been passed |
| 12 | Jharkhand | • MoU signed with Government of India. |
| 13 | Karnataka | • SERC constituted, functional, first tariff order issued.<br>• Reform Law enacted, SEB unbundled.<br>• MoU signed with Government of India. |

| | | |
|---|---|---|
| | | • Distribution privatisation to be completed by Dec. 2001 as per MoU signed with Government of India. |
| 14 | Kerala | • MoU signed with Government of India<br>• SERC constituted |
| 15 | Madhya Pradesh | • SERC constituted<br>• First tariff order issued.<br>• Reform Law passed by the Assembly and notified.<br>• MoU signed with Government of India. |
| 16 | Maharashtra | • SERC constituted, functional, two tariff orders issued.<br>• MoU signed with Government of India. |
| 17 | Orissa | • SERC functional, four tariff orders issued.<br>• Reform Law enacted, SEB unbundled.<br>• Distribution Privatised<br>• MoU signed with Government of India. |
| 18 | Punjab | • SERC constituted. Chairman, Members appointed. |
| 19 | Rajasthan | • SERC constituted, functional, two tariff orders issued.<br>• Reform Law enacted, SEB unbundled.<br>• One generation, one transmission & three Distribution companies created.<br>• RFP for Distribution privatisation to be issued by July, 2002.<br>• MoU signed with Government of India |
| 20 | Tamil Nadu | • SERC constituted.<br>• MoU signed with Government of India |
| 21 | Uttar Pradesh | • SERC constituted, functional, two tariff orders issued.<br>• Reform Law enacted, SEB unbundled.<br>• Distribution privatisation strategy to be finalised<br>• MoU signed with Government of India |
| 22 | Uttaranchal | • MoU signed with Government of India |
| 23 | West Bengal | • SERC constituted.<br>• First tariff order issued.<br>• MoU signed with Government of India. |
| 24 | Nagaland | • Have shown willingness to constitute Joint Electricity Regulatory Commission. |
| 25 | Meghalaya | |
| 26 | Mizoram | |
| 27 | Manipur | |
| 28 | Tripura | |
| 29 | Sikkim | |

Source: Planning Commission (2002)

## Annex 4

*Staggering Features of Railway Safety*

- Organisationally, Railway Board has a Safety Directorate headed by an Executive Director. At Zonal and divisional levels also, there are earmarked officers dealing with safety. However, while a few items of works could be identified as specific to safety, Railway safety aspects are generally germane to many activities including repair/maintenance/renewal etc. of permanent way/ rolling stock/signals etc. Funding-wise, too, only 13 specified items including automatic warning systems, road/foot, over/ under bridges etc., are funded from a separate head DF-IV. For the rest, individual departments bear responsibility for safety aspects including funding in their own areas. At the Board level, the Safety Directorate is more concerned with accidents, their enquiries, analysis and follow-up. It does not really function as the nodal agency for over-all safety performance.

  Thus there is no clear responsibility centre. Apart from the expenditure incurred under DF-IV (Rs.464.30 crores during 1993-94 to 1997-98, against allotment of Rs.548.15 crores), it is not possible either to identify the funds committed to safety. Overall, the expenditure under DF-IV during 1993-94 to 1997-98 came to just 1.76 per cent of the total plan expenditure. (Paras 3 and 4)

- There was under-reporting of cases of accidents by Zonal Railways to Railway Board. Out of 14,000 accidents during 1993-94 to 1997-98 (3,782 consequential and 10,218 miscellaneous), only 3,157 accidents (22.55 per cent) were reported to Railway Board. In turn, Railway Board reported 2187 accidents (15.62 per cent) to the Parliament in Appendix 1 to their annual reports on safety performance of Indian Railways. Three Railways in particular (Southern, Central and Western) actually reported between 10 and 20 per cent of the cases to the Board. Incidentally, the same 3 Railways accounted for over 67.18 per cent of the total accidents. (Para 5)

- Commissioners of Railway Safety (CRS) are supposed to enquire into all the serious accidents. Yet, out of 2,274 serious accidents reported during the period of review, only 126 (5.54 per cent) were enquired into by Commissioners of Railway Safety. (Para 8)

- Status of 4 important safety aids, identified by different Committees over the last 20 years, was checked by Audit. None of these has been fully implemented. Out of 1,529 stations re-

Contd. ...

quired to be track circuited on A and B routes on 8 Zonal Railways, till 31 March 1998, track circuiting has been completed only on 911 stations and on 234 stations (218 stations on Central Railway and 16 stations on Southern Railway), the work has not been taken up at all. Similarly, the provision of Auxiliary Warning System (AWS) on trunk routes with speed level of 100 kmph and above has not even been taken up in 5 Railways. In 1 Railway (Eastern), the project has been scrapped. In 2 others (Central, Western), there has been very limited implementation. Another recommendation related to provision of radio communication between trains and control centres. In 2 Railways (Eastern, Northern), the system has not been provided at all. In the others, there has been some implementation, but to a rather limited extent. On this, the Railway Board had decided (1995-96) to go in for Universal Emergency Train Radio Communication System and sanctioned 19 works, but these stand frozen. The fourth safety aid was Remote Controlled Train Activated Automatic Warning devices at unmanned level crossings. These have not been installed at any of the 1707 unmanned level crossings on A and B routes. Incidentally, during 1993-94 to 1997-98, 581 deaths (24.70 per cent of total deaths) had occurred at unmanned level crossings on A and B routes. [Para 9.1 (a) to (d)]

- In regard to staff in the 'safety category', on an average 8.07 per cent vacancies existed during the period of review. The shortage was more acute at 11.20 per cent in the Drivers category, and was rather severe in 3 Railways (Northern 20.52 per cent, Northeast Frontier 18.28 per cent and Western 16.05 per cent). Such shortage naturally would tend to enhance the degree of overtime hours of running duty by drivers. In 9 Zonal Railways in 21.89 per cent trips of drivers, the duty hours exceeded 10 hours. [Para 9.2 (a) and (b)]
- Similarly, there has been substantial shortfall in training of 'Safety category staff'. In 11 Zonal Training Centres and 33 divisional training schools test-checked in audit, on average, shortfall was 30.80 per cent and 19.08 per cent respectively with reference to the number of staff required to be trained. The situation was no better in regard to safety camps. In 6 Zonal Railways, as much as 25.76 per cent of the staff required to attend these camps remained absent. [Para 9.2 (c)]
- Study of 1327 accident cases on 8 Zonal Railways indicated that around 30 per cent were due to equipment failure related to rolling stock and permanent way. It was also seen that in

**Contd. ...**

87 sections (of 29 Divisions in 8 Railways), the actual line utilisation was 116 per cent of the charted line capacity. Such excess utilisation leads to more stress and also non-availability of blocks for maintenance. Infact, in 9 Railways, only 42.22 per cent of the stipulated block hours could be provided for maintenance. Further, in 18 divisions test checked on 8 Zonal Railways, 8,758.68 kms of track were not replaced with higher standard rails. It resulted in 144 speed restrictions (77 on South Central Railway and 37 in North Eastern Railway) and 61 accidents (59 on North Eastern Railway).[Para 10 to 10.1 (c)]

- Out of 9631 rail fractures and 4628 welded fractures that were reported on 9 Zonal Railways during 1993-94 to 1997-98, 61.78 per cent rail fractures and 40.54 per cent welded fractures occurred on South Eastern Railway alone. Despite the need to detect flaws in rails in time, the only one SPURT car available was used to the extent of only 48.31 per cent of effective machine days available. [Para 10.1 (d)]
- 64.06 per cent of wagons/coaches [3,86,293 out of 6,03,023 rejected by the Neutral Control Wing (NCW)] were passed locally by Railway Administration on 8 Zonal Railways without final clearance of NCW. The failure to adhere to the prescribed procedure was very pronounced in 3 Railways (100 per cent on Central Railway 91.89 per cent on Southern Railway and 89.24 per cent on Eastern Railway). [Para10.2 (b)]

Source: Khanna Committee Report (Part II), Chapter 3

## Notes

1 The Expert Group (1996) pointed out that the penetration ratio is 1.3 per 100 population, whereas the world average is over 10.

2 This is in compliance with the National Telecom Policy objective of ensuring that India emerge as a major manufacturing base and an exporter of telecom equipment.

3 The professionals are to be selected from fields like law, economics, technology, finance, accounting or business administration. The stuff should be trained quickly in regulatory matters.

4 For example, the instance of allowing all TV Channels and Indian News agencies to uplink from India, and allowing Indian Companies to set up uplinking hubs (teleports) could be cited.

5 Expert Group on Infrastructure (1996).

6 The economic losses due to the bad condition of the road are estimated to be of the order of Rs. 200 to Rs. 300 billion per anum.

7 The investment requirement of the private sector in Rs. 330 billion and Rs. 300 billion respectively in case of National and State Highways over the 10-year period (1996-2006)

8 The National Highway Act (1956) already provides an enabling provision in this regard.

9 Expert Group on Infrastructure (1996).

10 The annual per capita consumption is 350 kwh in India, among the lowest in the world.

11 With the commercial losses of SEBs touching Rs. 24,000 crores in 2000-01, and heavy overdues to PSUs, Railway and Coal companies in the order of Rs. 45,000 crores, their inability to clear the due is effectively preventing investment (public and private) in the sector, even in the aftermath of economic liberalisation.

12 The factors include, additions arising out of conversion of old bonds, as well as incentives for better managed SEBs, to be partly offset by reductions resulting from settlement of disputes etc.

13 The Expert Group recognised that such adjustments from the State Governments' accounts would be an exceptional measure which should not normally be resorted to, but hoped that given the circumstances prevailing in the power sector, such a measure is needed in the interim before longer term efforts to reform bear fruit.

14 Given the existing capacity of 100,000 MW, this would double the generation capacity of the country and supposed to ensure 'Power to all' by 2012.

15 A large number of power plants have become very old, and 170 and 35 thermal and hydel power plants respectively are identified by CEA to be in need of renovation and modernisation. A new Accelerated Power Development Programme (APDP) has been taken up from 2001 with a budgetary allocation of Rs. 1000 crores to take up these activities.

16 Since 1991, 26 projects involving a capacity of 5000 MW have been commissioned and another 20 projects with a capacity of around 6000 MW are under various stages of Construction. Overall, 57 private projects with a capacity of around 29500 MW have received Techno-Economic Clearance (TEC) from CEA.

17 Annual Report (2001-02), Ministry of Power, pp. 44, Government of India.

18 According to the Blueprint for Power Sector Development, all the districts in the country will have a detailed distribution improvement plan. The Ministry/CEA will help the States in capacity building measures in areas related to technical and commercial activities as well as planning and deployment of personnel. Assistance would also be provided to SEBs to improve their accounting practices.

19 Based upon the calculations, the Blueprint for Power Sector Development pointed out that mere prevention of theft alone can lead to mobilisation of over Rs. 20,000 crores annually.

20 Infact, 16 states have already entered into such MoUs. A system of monitoring the performance in the Ministry has been introduced. Major Initiatives for Power Sector Development, Ministry of Power, Government of India (2001)

21 The Expert Group cited that Services Sector already accounts for 48 per cent of GDP, and every increase in GDP will require faster bulk transport services. Then IR has to compete with other modes of transport, to sustain traffic volumes.

22 As estimated by the Expert Group.

23 The examples of new class of service such as Second Class A.C. 2 tier and Chair Car, and new trains such as Shatabdi Express have been mentioned in the Report.

24 It was assumed that the capacity would be updated regularly to meet the enhancement in the demand generated.

25 The report concluded that excess manpower could be more than 25 per cent of the total workforce.

26 The Expert Group also expressed their discontent over the current promotion scheme.

27 The strain on the IR's resources has also prevented adequate investment in track renewals and other safety related areas.

28 Status paper on Indian Railways, Issues and Options, Government of India, Ministry of Railways (May, 2002)

# 9

# Water Management in India

## *Policy Issues*

MOHAMMED SAQIB

India faces an increasingly urgent situation in water resources. The finite and fragile water resources are stressed and depleting while various sectoral demands are growing rapidly. The historical situation in which relatively plentiful water resources have been used primarily for irrigated agriculture, with demands in other sectors insignificant relative to other resources available is changing rapidly and will continue to do so in foreseeable future. The composition of change in the demand is resulting from rising incomes, urbanisation and rapid industrialization. Industrial needs will be high economic priority; agriculture, with two-thirds of production dependent on irrigation and accounting for 83 per cent of consumptive water use continues to remain crucially dependant on water. Conflict between sectoral uses, domestic, agriculture, industry, energy, ecological, flood control, navigation fisheries, recreation and other uses, is already a serious problem.

Water is becoming an increasingly scarce resource, yet it continues to be used inefficiently on a daily basis in all sectors. In recent years, there has been realization and policy pronouncement regarding the need to address these problems, however the policies have yet to be translated into action. The present institutional arrangements including central, state and local institutions and both formal and informal structures do not enable comprehensive water allocation, planning and management. Existing organisations lack capacity in key management areas as well as effective mechanism for implementation. Appropriate economic incentives for efficient water use and conservation are lacking on various levels, thereby impacting negatively on water provisions and usage in these sub-sectors. The absence of appropriate direct water pricing, and lack of adequate application of other economic and financial incentives at the sub sector level have also served as an obstacle to the smooth transfer of water between sectors and state. Moreover supporting technological and informational system to enable effective planning and management of water is also very weak.

## Introduction

Water has been and will play an important role in the development of a country or nation or a region. There are predictions that future wars will be fought on water issues, stemming out of the social conflicts over sharing of scarce water sources. It is said that 21st century will decide the powerful nations on the basis of availability of water to a particular nation. Already different States in India have been at loggerheads over the sharing of river waters necessitating the formation of five water tribunals. Internationally, many countries, India included, have simmering conflicts with their neighbouring countries over sharing of water.

Water resource development and management is a fundamental requirement in the developmental process. It influences economic development, employment, agriculture, housing, health and numerous other sectors. Everywhere development of water resources takes place in a context of limited funds, competing priorities, human resources and other institutional limitations, and social and political systems that both shape it and determine its eventual success. Both fiscal and human/institutional resources are in short supply in India. One of the most important sectors for development has been the provision of potable water supplies, sanitation, transportation, irrigation and power. Improvements in these areas are essential to food security and to promoting health for the general population. Major water supply and sanitation facilities, especially those serving urban areas and economic centers, form part of the national infrastructure like roads and electricity. In rural areas improving water supplies is intrinsic to community development.

Increase in population for example, can far outstrip development of facilities so that even after many years of investment, the absolute number of people unserved may be about the same. This is particularly seen in mega cities and huge urban agglomerations.

What is to be done? How can we balance the many conflicting interests involved in water allocation? How can we protect the environment? How can we prevent waste and encourage behavior that supports sustainable use of our water resources? How can we provide an equitable distribution system? These are some of the questions that make water one of the hottest environmental issues today.

## Water Resources

### *World Scenario*

World oceans cover about three fourth of earth's surface. According to the UN estimates, the total amount of water on earth is about 1400 million cubic kilometer (m.cu.km.) which is enough to cover the earth with a layer of 3000 meters depth. However the fresh water constitutes a very small proportion of this enormous quantity. About 2.7 per cent of the total water available on the earth is fresh water of which about 75.2 per cent lies frozen in Polar Regions and another 22.6 per cent is present as ground water. The rest is available in lakes, rivers, atmosphere, moisture, soil and vegetation. What is effectively available for consumption and other uses is a small proportion of the quantity available in rivers, lakes and ground water. The crisis about water resources development and management thus arises because most of the water is not available for use and secondly it is characterised by its highly uneven spatial distribution. Accordingly, the importance of water has been recognised and greater emphasis is being laid on its economic use and better management.

Although water is a renewable resource, supplies are limited and finite. Only 3 per cent of Earth's water supply is fresh water. Total usable supply of fresh water is over 4 million cubic kilometers. Ground water makes up over 95 per cent of Earth's usable fresh water supplies. About 90 per cent of the world's population gets its water supplies from river basins. Two or more countries share more than 200 rivers, and more than 40 per cent of the worlds' population relies on water originating in a country other than their own.

Despite its availability, water is not evenly distributed or used around the world. More than 1.2 billion people do not have access to adequate and safe water supplies. The average efficiency of irrigation systems is less than 40 per cent. More than 60 per cent of the water delivered never reaches the plant, or more than twice as much is delivered than is necessary. Water is a critical element in sustaining eco-systems and bio-diversity. Wetlands (lakes, ponds, etc.) sustain one third of all endangered and threatened species. Over 50 per cent of the world's wetlands have been lost or degraded through dams and canal projects, agricultural development, urbanization, and contamination. Of the 8.5 million sq. kms. of wetlands worldwide, only two per cent are protected under the Convention on Wetlands of International Importance Especially as Waterfall Habitats (The Ramsar Convention).

Analysing the country-wise geographical area, arable land and irrigated area in the World, it is found that among the continents largest geographical area lies in the Africa which is about 23 per cent of the world geographic area. However, Asia (excluding erstwhile countries of USSR) with only 21 per cent of world geographical area has about 32 per cent of world's arable land followed by North Central America having about 20 per cent of World's arable land. Africa has only 12 per cent of world's arable land. It has been seen that irrigated area in the World is about 18.5 per cent of the arable land in 1994. In 1989, 63 per cent of world's irrigated area was in Asia, whereas in 1994 this percentage has gone upto 64 per cent. Also 37 per cent of arable land of Asia was irrigated in 1994. Among Asian countries, India has the largest arable land, which is close to 39 per cent of Asia's arable land. Only United States of America has more arable land than India.

*Indian Scenario*

There is a general feeling that India with mighty rivers like the Ganga, the Brahmaputra, the Krishna, the Godavari, and the Narmada etc. has abundant water resources. But it is realised that this impression is not correct. The availability of water in India is:

- Annual precipitation 4000 Billion Cubic Meters (b.cu.m.)
- Available surface water 1869 b.cu.m. (46.7 per cent)
- Utilisable water resources 690 b.cu.m. (36.9 per cent)
- Utilisable ground water 432 b.cu.m.

Thus, the total water resource available for utilization including ground water is only about 1122 b.cu.m. Only 28.3 per cent of the water derived from rainfall can be utilised. The position in some of our largest river basins is worse. For example in the Brahmaputra basin, which contributes 629 b.cu.m. of surface water of the country's total flow, only 3.33 per cent i.e. 21 b.cu.m. is utilizable. With the increasing population as well as all round development in the country, the utilization of water has also been consequently increasing at a fast pace. In 1951, the actual utilization of surface water was about 20 per cent and 10 per cent in the case of ground water. In 1997-1998, the country used about 57.8 per cent (329 b.cu.m.) of utilizable quantum of surface water and about 53.2 per cent (230 b.cu.m.) of the ground water.

## Surface Water Resources

The annual precipitation including snowfall, which is the main source of the water in the country is estimated to be of the order of 4000 cu.km. For the purpose of rainfall, country has been divided into 35 meteorological sub-divisions. The Resources potential of the country, which occurs as natural run off in the rivers is about 1869 cu.km. As per the basin wise latest estimates of Central Water Commission, considering both surface and ground water as one system. Ganga-Brahmaputra-Meghna system is the major contributor to total water resources potential of the country. Its share is about 60 per cent in total water resources potential of the various rivers. Based on 1991 census, the per capita availability of water works out to 220 cubic meter (cu.m.). Due to various constraints of topography, uneven distribution of resource over space and time, it has been estimated that only about 1122 cu.km. of total potential of 1869 cu.km. can be put to beneficial use, 690 cu.km. being due to surface water resources. Again about 40 per cent of utilisable surface water resources are presently in Ganga-Brahmaputra-Meghna system. In majority of river basins, present utilisation is significantly high and is in the range of 50 per cent to 95 per cent of utilisable surface resources. But in the rivers such as Narmada and Mahanadi percentage utilisation is quite low. The corresponding values for these basins are 23 per cent and 34 per cent respectively.

The distribution of water resources potential in the country shows that as against the national per capita annual availability of water of 2208 cu.m. the average availability in Brahmaputra and Barak is as high as 16589 cu.m. while it is as low as 360 cu.m. in Sabarmati basin. Brahmaputra and Barak basin with 7.3 per cent of geographical area and 4.2 per cent of population of the country has 31 per cent of the annual water resources. Per capita annual availability for rest of the country excluding Brahmaputra and Barak basin works out to about 1583 cu.m. Any situation of availability of less than 1000 cu.m. per capita is considered by international agencies as scarcity conditions. Cauvery, Pennar, Sabarmati, East flowing rivers and West flowing rivers are some of the basins which fall into this category.

*Rainfall*

Rainfall in India dependent in differing degrees on the Southwest and Northwest monsoons, on shallow cyclonic depressions and disturbances and on violent local storms which form regions where cool humid winds from the sea meet hot dry winds from the land and occasionally reach cyclonic dimension. Most of the rainfall in India takes place under the influence of South West monsoon between June to September except in Tamil Nadu where it is under the influence of Northeast monsoon during October and November. The rainfall in India shows great variations, unequal seasonal distribution, still more unequal geographical distribution and the frequent departures from the normal. It generally exceeds 1000 mm in areas to the East of Longitude 78 degree E. It extends to 2500 mm along almost the entire West Coast and Western Ghats and over most of Assam and Sub-Himalayan West Bengal. On the West of the line joining Porbandar to Delhi and thence to Ferozpur, the rainfall diminishes rapidly from 500 mm to less than 150 mm in the extreme west. The Peninsular has large areas of rainfall less than 600 mm with pockets of even 500 mm. The estimate of aerial average rainfall is subjective depending on the method adopted.

*Rivers*

India is blessed with many rivers. As many as 12 of them are classified as major rivers whose total catchments area is 252.8 million hectare (m.ha.). Of the major rivers, the Ganga-Brahmaputra Meghana system is the biggest with catchment area of about 110 m.ha which is more than 43 per cent of the catchment area of all the major rivers in the country. The other major rivers with catchment area of more than 10 m.ha are Indus (32.1 m.ha.), Godavari (31.3 m.ha.), Krishna, (25.9 m.ha.) and Mahanadi (14.2 m.ha.). The catchment area of medium rivers is about 25 m.ha and Subernarekha with 1.9 m.ha. catchment area is the largest river among the medium rivers in the country.

## Water Bodies

Inland Water resources of the country are classified as rivers and canals; reservoirs; tanks and ponds; beels; oxbow lakes; derelict water; and brackish water. Other than rivers and canals, total water bodies cover an area of about 7. m.ha. Of the rivers and canals, Uttar Pradesh occupies the first place with the total length of rivers and canals as 31.2 thousand km, which is about 17 per cent of the total length of rivers and canals in the country. Other states following Uttar Pradesh are Jammu & Kashmir and Madhya Pradesh. Among the remaining forms of the inland water resources, tanks and ponds have maximum area (2.9 m.ha.) followed by reservoirs (2.1 m.ha.).

Most of the area under tanks and ponds lies in Southern States of Andhra Pradesh, Karnataka and Tamil Nadu. These states along with West Bengal, Rajasthan and Uttar Pradesh, account for 62 per cent of total area under tanks and ponds in the country. As far as reservoirs are concerned, major states like Andhra Pradesh, Gujarat, Karnataka, Madhya Pradesh, Maharashtra, Orissa, Rajasthan and Uttar Pradesh account for larger portion of area under reservoirs. More than 77 per cent of area under beels, oxbow, lakes and derelict water lies in the states of Orissa, Uttar Pradesh and Assam. Orissa ranks first as regards the total area of brackish water and is followed by Gujarat, Kerala and West Bengal. The total area of inland water resources is, thus, unevenly distributed over the country within five states namely Orissa, Andhra Pradesh, Gujarat, Karnataka and West Bengal accounting for more than half of the country's inland water bodies.

## Ground Water

Ground water is an important source of irrigation and caters to more than 45 per cent of the total irrigation in the country. The contribution of ground water irrigation to achieve self-sufficiency in food grains production in the past three decades is phenomenal. In the coming years the ground water utilization is likely to increase manifold for expansion of irrigated agriculture and to achieve national targets of food production. Although the ground water is annually replenishable resource, its availability is non-uniform in space and time. Hence, precise estimation of ground water resource and irrigation potential is a pre-requisite for planning its development.

A complexity of factors, hydrological and climatological, controls the ground water occurrence and movement. The precise assessment of recharge and discharge is rather difficult, as no techniques are currently available for their direct measurements. Hence, the methods employed for ground water resource estimation are all indirect. Ground water being a dynamic and replenishable resource, is generally estimated based on the component of annual recharge, which could be subjected to development by means of suitable ground water structures.

The first attempt to estimate the ground water resources on scientific basis was made in 1979. Agriculture Refinance and Development Corporation (ARDC) constituted a High Level Committee known as Ground Water Over Exploitation Committee. This Committee recommended definite norms, for ground water resources computations. Based on these norms the State Governments and the Central Ground Water Board computed the gross ground water recharge as 46.79 m.ha.m. and the net recharge (70 per cent of the gross) as 32.49 m.ha.m. This committee had however recommended that the methodology be revised with increasing availability of data to make it more scientific.

*Future Demand*

The food requirement of the growing population will be about 450 million tons in 2050 as against the present highest food grain production of around 198 million tons. Two-third of this is obtained from irrigated food grain production areas. Thus, irrigation requirements of the country are likely to share a major chunk even in the future. Even with the full development of the estimated ultimate irrigation potential of 139.89 million hectares by 2050 AD only 65 per cent of net sown area will receive irrigation, and the balance 35 per cent will still depend on vagaries of the monsoon. Consequently, irrigation will continue to be a bulk consumer of water. Thus there is a need for conservation of water. In the hydrological sense, water conservation means improving the dependability of the water through augmenting additional resources through storage of rainwater in reservoirs, ponds, lakes, shallow and deep ground water or in the soil moistures. A present day definition may also include the conservation of water as defined above in both qualitative and quantitative assessment. As of now, the storage capacity created in the country is about 50 per cent of the ultimate possibility.

## Future Water Demand

The population of India is estimated to reach between 1.5-1.8 billion by the year 2050. The UN agencies have put the figure at 1.64 billion. It is now generally accepted that the countries with annual per-capita water availability of less than 1,700 cubic meter ($m^3$) are water stresses and less than 1000 cubic meter water annually by 2050 to be above the water stress zone and 1,650 b.c.m. to avoid being a scarce country. The average annual surface water flows in India has been estimated as 1869 b.c.m of which only 690 b.c.m. can be utilized if appropriate storages can be treated. The reason for this vast difference between potential (1869 b.c.m.) and the conditional availability (690 b.c.m. if it can be stored) has been well recognized as the monsoonic climate, besides topographical and geological limitations.

In addition to surface water, there is the groundwater resource. Its potential has been estimated as 432 b.c.m. including recharge due to canal irrigation. This means that the total water availability would be 2301 b.c.m in 2050 or the per-capita availability of 1403 cubic meter. The country will be water stressed even if the total available water is taken into account. For feeding a population of 1.64 billion, nearly 450 million tones of food grains would be required in 2050, production of which would be a gigantic task considering the constraints being faced in the irrigation sector.

Access of safe drinking water is still a distant reality for most of the population, especially in rural areas. It is estimated that half of the population in the country may be living in urban areas by the year 2050. Most of these urban areas will have multiple water related problems. The above problems faced by the country in the area of water resources development and management necessitate conservation measures to meet the demands for irrigation in arid and drought prone areas and in water deficit basins and to meet the requirements of domestic water supply in the ever expanding urban areas and for industry.

## Conservation Strategies

Process of conservation may be synonymous of preservation against loss or waste. Technically, conservation of water implies the same meaning in a much wider perspective. Briefly stated it means putting the water resources of the country for the best beneficial use with all the technologies at our command.

Water conservation basically aims at matching demand and supply. The strategies for water conservation may be either demand oriented or supply oriented and/or management oriented. The strategies may vary depending upon the use of water — domestic, irrigation or industrial.

## Development of Resources

### *Completion of ongoing projects*

A large number of river valley projects, both multi-purpose and irrigation have spilled over from one plan to another plan mainly because of financial constraints and problems relating to land acquisition, forest clearance and rehabilitation of affected persons. As a result, a huge amount of investment already made on these projects has not yielded any tangible result. About 162 Major projects, 240 Medium projects and 74 Extension, Renovation and Modernisation (ERM) of old projects are spilling over to the Ninth Plan.

### *Better Irrigation Practices*

On farm irrigation, the practices prevailing in the country result in wastage of water leading to poor irrigation efficiency. The absence of field channels forcing adoption of field irrigation adds to the problem.

### *Sprinkler and Drip Irrigation*

Improved methods of irrigation, like sprinkler and drip, are being recommended for achieving higher irrigation efficiencies. Sprinklers tend to irrigate more uniformly than gravity, systems and, therefore, efficiencies average about 70 per cent.

### *Use of Saline Water for Irrigation*

Saline water is widely available but rarely used for agriculture because it restricts plant growth and yield. Salt resistant varieties of crops have also been developed in recent times.

*Long Distance Transfer of Water*

Transfer of water from surplus basins by creating storage at appropriate locations and inter-linking various systems is yet another strategy for increasing the benefits considerably.

## Constitutional Framework

The constitutional provisions in respect of allocation of responsibilities between the State and Centre fall into three categories: The Union List (List-I), the State List (List-II) and the Concurrent List (List-III). Article 246 of the Constitution deals with subject matter of laws to be made by the Parliament and by Legislature of the States. As most of the rivers in the country are inter-State, the regulation and development of waters of these rivers, is a source of inter-State differences and disputes. In the Constitution, water is a matter included in Entry 17 of List-II, i.e. State List. This entry is subject to the provision of Entry 56 of List-I i.e. Union List. The specific provisions in this regard are as under:

*Article 246*

1) Notwithstanding anything in clauses (2) and (3), Parliament has exclusive power to make laws with respect to any of the matters enumerated in List I in the Seventh Schedule (in this Constitution referred to as the "Union List").
2) Not withstanding anything in clause (3), Parliament, and, subject to clause (1), the legislature of any State also, have power to make laws with respect to any of the matters enumerated in List III in the Seventh Schedule (in this Constitution referred to as the "Concurrent List").
3) Subject to clauses (1) and (2), the Legislature of any State has exclusive power to make laws for such State or any part thereof with respect to any of the matters enumerated in List II in the Seventh Schedule (in this Constitution referred to as the "State List").
4) Parliament has power to make laws with respect to any matter for any part of the territory of India not included in a State notwithstanding that such matter is a matter enumerated in the State List.

*Article 262*

In case of disputes relating to waters, Article 262 provides:

1) Parliament may, by law provide for the adjudication of any dispute or complaint with respect to the use, distribution or control of the waters of, or in, any inter-State river or river valley.
2) Notwithstanding anything in this Constitution, Parliament may, by law provide that neither the Supreme Court nor any other court shall exercise jurisdiction in respect of any such dispute or complaint as is referred to in Clause (1).

*Entry 56 of List I of Seventh Schedule*

Entry 56 of List I of Seventh Schedule provides that "Regulation and development of inter-State rivers and river valleys to the extent to which such regulation and development under the control of the Union are declared by Parliament by law to be expedient in the public interest".

*Entry 17 Under List II of Seventh Schedule*

Entry 17 under List II of Seventh Schedule provides that "Water, that is to say, water supplies, irrigation and canals, drainage and embankments, water storage and water power subject to the provisions of Entry 56 of List I".

As such, the Central Government is conferred with powers to regulate and develop inter-State rivers under Entry 56 of List I of Seventh Schedule to the extent declared by the Parliament by law to be expedient in the public interest.

It also has the power to make laws for the adjudication of any dispute relating to waters of Inter-State River or river valley under Article 262 of the Constitution.

*The River Boards Act, 1956:* was enacted under Entry 56 of List I of the Constitution for the establishment of River Boards for the regulation and development of Inter-State River and River valleys. Central Government has however not been able to constitute any River Board under this Act so far. Moreover the role of the River Boards as envisaged in the said Act is only advisory in nature. The

National Commission for Integrated Water Resources Development Plan has recommended to repeal the Act and enact new Act called Integrated and Participatory Management Act.

*National Water Policy:* A comprehensive policy framework is needed to ensure an integrated approach to water resource development, with rational and equitable allocation of resources, and giving priority to the poor and unserved. Effective policy frameworks recognize the longer-term perspective of water as a finite and vulnerable resource, and address the whole water cycle. They also observe key behavioral roles at all levels. An effective policy framework should also include the establishment of standards and targets, as well as a system to monitor and use them as indicators for planning and management purposes. A national water sector strategy should state the government's objectives and the methods to be employed to achieve them. It will include investment and project development guidelines, which should aim to ensure that the development of water supply reflects considerations of water resource management and environment, such as equitable distribution of water resources and the prevention of pollution.

## Inter-State Water Disputes

Most of the major rivers in India are inter-State in character, having catchments/water sheds in two or more States. Often, water disputes arise amongst the basin States with regard to the use, distribution or control of the water in respect of many inter-State rivers or river valleys or in the interpretation of the terms of any agreement relating to the use, distribution or control of such water or in the implementation of any such agreement or in the levy of any water rate in contravention of various prohibitions.

## Constitutional Provisions: Resolution of Inter-State Water Disputes Through Negotiations

Following actions/steps are being undertaken so that inter-State disputes are resolved for optimum development of water resources:-

i) encouraging bilateral/trilateral agreements among the basin States.

ii) Enacting Legislations to constitute Corporations/Boards for development of river basins.

iii) Securing basin development through Inter-State Agreements on particular projects.

iv) Setting up of Joint Control Boards.

v) Arranging consensus in Zonal Councils on vexed non-technical, administrative issues.

*Tribunals*

The Central Government has set up five Inter-State Water Disputes Tribunals so far, namely

i. Godavari Water Disputes Tribunal (April, 1969)

ii. Krishna Water Disputes Tribunal (April, 1969)

iii. Narmada Water Disputes Tribunal (October, 1969)

iv. Ravi and Beas Waters Tribunal (April, 1986)

v. Cauvery Water Disputes Tribunal (June, 1990)

While the first three Tribunals have already given their final awards, the remaining 2 Tribunals are still adjudicating the issues referred to them.

## Sarkaria Commission's Recommendations in respect of Inter-State River Water Disputes and on the Proposed Amendments in the Inter-State Water Disputes Act, 1956

It is generally observed that the Tribunals set up for resolving inter-State issues take considerable time to give decision/awards. The matter received attention of Sarkaria Commission. The Sarkaria Commission in its report at Chapter XVII on Inter-State River Water Disputes has recommended that:

i) Once an application under Section 3 of the Inter-State River Water Disputes Act (33 of 1956) is received from a State, it should be mandatory on the Union Government to constitute a Tribunal within a period not exceeding one year from the date of receipt of the application of any disputant State. The Inter-State River Water Disputes Act may be suitably amended for this purpose.

ii) The Inter-State Water Disputes Act should be amended to empower the Union Government to appoint a Tribunal, suo-moto, if necessary, when it is satisfied that such a dispute exists in fact.

iii) There should be a Data Bank and information system at the national level and adequate machinery should be set up for this purpose at the earliest. There should also be a provision in the Inter-State Water Disputes Act that States shall be required to give necessary data for which purpose the Tribunal may be vested with powers of a court.

iv) The inter-State Water Disputes Act should be amended to ensure that the award of a Tribunal becomes effective within five years from the date of constitution of a Tribunal. If, however, for some reasons, a Tribunal feels that the five years period has to be extended, the Union Government may on a reference made by the Tribunal extend its term.

v) The Inter-State Water Disputes Act, 1956 should be amended so that a Tribunal's award has the same force and sanction behind it as an order or decree of the Supreme Court to make a Tribunal's award really binding.

The erstwhile Sub-Committee of the Inter-State Council considered these five recommendations. The Sub-Committee accepted four out of five recommendations. The remaining one recommendation against para 17.06.01 of Sarkaria Commission's Report was accepted with a minor modification. The time frame specified for constituting a Tribunal by the Union Government was increased from one year to two years. The Inter-State Council in its meeting held on 15.10.96 generally endorsed the recommendations. However, in view of the reservations expressed by some of the Chief Ministers, it was decided that they would convey their reservations to the Inter-State Council Secretariat so that their views could be further considered by the Standing Committee of the Inter-State Council.

Taking into account the views of the State Governments and that of the Ministry of Water Resources, the Inter-State Council Secretariat prepared a consensus paper on the recommendations of Sarkaria Commission which was deliberated upon during fifth meeting of the Standing Committee of Inter-State council held on 10.11.97 under the chairmanship of the Union Minister of Home Affairs. Based on the recommendations given by the Inter-State Council on Sarkaria

Commission's Recommendation a bill for amending the Inter-State Disputes Act 1956 was introduced in Lok Sabha on 7.3.2001. The Bill was passed in Lok Sabha on 3.8.2001 and Rajya Sabha on 11.3.2002 and received the assent of the President on 28.3.2002.

## Pricing of Water

There are wide variations in water rate structures across states and the rate per unit volume of water consumed varies greatly for crops. In some states the irrigation charges vary from project to project depending on the mode of irrigation. The rates vary widely for the same crop in the same state depending on irrigation season, type of system etc. There are no uniform set principles in fixing the water rates and a multiplicity of principles are followed such as recovery of cost of water, capacity of irrigators to pay based on gross earning or net benefit of irrigation, water requirement of crops, sources of water supply and its assurance, classification of land linked with land revenue system and combination of various elements. In some states water cess, betterment levy, etc. are also levied. According to the Report of the Committee on Pricing of Irrigation Water of the Planning Commission of 1992 water rates are a form of users charge and not a tax and hence users of public irrigation must meet the cost of the services.

Irrigation is one of the key inputs for crop production and hence pricing of this input is one of the first steps and integral component in the process of rationalizing the totality of the price structure and raising the efficiency of water use. The under pricing of water adversely affects the availability of resources for the management of irrigation systems. Inadequate allocation for maintenance and repairs acts as a direct consequence of the poor financial position of the states and is responsible for the low, possibly deteriorating quality of services. This means that potential increase in productivity which new technology makes possible cannot be realized in full. A revision in the level and structure of water rates is thus necessary in the interest of both efficiency and equity. The revision should be such as to achieve full cost recovery in due course and in the process promote saving, create disincentives for wastes and thereby enable the service area to be expanded and a more reliable service assured. Revision of water rates should go hand in hand with measures to improve the quality of services and to keep a check on costs. In the light of a detailed assessment, rates for non-agricultural uses of water such as domestic and industry should also be revised so that the cost are fully recovered and arrangements should be built into supply contracts for ensuring full and prompt recovery of dues. Cost recovery should be the main consideration for rate determination. Rates should be based on operation and maintenance norms and capital charges (interest and depreciation).

Water rate is charge levied for supply of water from a public or private system for its proper and beneficial use. But the study reveals that there is considerable diversity in the system of levying water rates by different States/UT's in the country. For example, no water rate is levied for agricultural purposes in most of the North-East States except for Manipur whereas in the State of Orissa a flat basic compulsory water rate is charged for the staple crop (Paddy) in respect of lands coming under the command of Major and Medium Irrigation Projects irrespective of the fact that water is taken or not for the other crops, crop-wise rates are levied. In West Bengal water is supplied only on pre-payment basis as far as Minor Irrigation Schemes are concerned. There is yet another system in the States of Andhra Pradesh, Karnataka, Tamil Nadu and Union Territory of Pondicherry where water rate and land revenue are inseparable in respect of irrigated lands coming particularly under command of older systems of irrigation. In these States lands are classified as 'Wet' and 'Dry' depending upon their getting or not getting water from a recognised Government source. Wet and Dry lands are assessed differently for land revenue. Wet assessment is higher as compared to the Dry assessment and difference between the two is attributed to water rates.

In the States which charge water rate for agricultural purposes, rates are in general levied on the basis of area irrigated except for the Tubewell irrigation where the levy is based on number of hours of watering or volume. But there is no uniformity as regards to how these two important factors are taken into account by States in fixing water rates. However, the rates for perennial and defussal crops are higher than those for other crops. In some States differentiation is also according to sources of irrigation as is the case in the States of Bihar, Haryana, Punjab, Rajasthan and Uttar Pradesh. Within a State, the rate is uniform for a given class of irrigation source. In some States special purpose cesses are also levied on irrigated area/crop over and above water rates. This system is in practice in the States of Andhra Pradesh, Haryana, Karnataka, Kerala, Maharashtra and Tamil Nadu etc.

There is also no uniformity as regards to principles considerations adopted by the States in fixing of water rates. Some of the important factors which are generally taken into consideration are Crop Water requirement, assuredness of supply of water, paying capacity of the farmers based on net/gross value of agricultural produce, cost of supply of water, recommendation of Irrigation Commission etc. But there is no uniformity or consistency as regards to how these factors are employed in fixation of rates by different States/UTs.

So far as irrigation projects in the public sector are concerned, sale of water for irrigation constitutes the major portion of Gross Receipts from them. The various committees/groups constituted for suggesting ways and means to improve financial performance of projects have emphatically recommended for restructuring of the irrigation water rates in the country. Some of the committees, which have dealt with the irrigation water rates and related subjects, are enumerated below:

1. Maharashtra State Irrigation Commission, 1962
2. Nijalingappa Committee, 1964
3. Second Irrigation Commission, 1972
4. National Commission on Agriculture, 1976
5. Water Rates Review Committees/Boards appointed by the perspective State Government such as Gujarat, Madhya Pradesh etc.
6. Public Accounts Committee, 1983
7. National Conference of Irrigation and Water Resources Ministers, 1986
8. Jakhade Committee on Operation & Maintenance of Irrigation Projects, 1987
9. National Water Policy, 1987
10. Successive Finance Commissions (5th to 9th Commission)
11. Vaidyanathan Committee on Pricing of Irrigation Water, 1991.

The Group of Officers set up by the Planning Commission in October, 1992 further studied the Vaidyanathan Committee recommendations. The Group in its report in December, 1994 recommended that the irrigation water rates should cover the full annual operation and maintenance cost in phases in next 5 years period. Irrigation being the State subject, the recommendations of the Group along with the report of the Vaidyanathan Committee was sent in February 1995 to all the States/UTs for further action. The States have started taking action on the recommendations of the Vaidyanathan Committee. The States which have recently revised their water rates are: Andhra Pradesh (January 1997), Bihar (November 1995), Haryana (September 1995) and Maharashtra (July 1994). The Government of Tamil Nadu has set up a Committee on Irrigation Water Pricing which has already made suggestions towards revision of water charges and these are under consideration of the State Government. Revision of water rates in Rajasthan is also on anvil.

## Irrigation Sector

India's irrigated agriculture sector has been fundamental to India's economic development and poverty alleviation. Some 28 per cent of India's GDP and 67 per cent of employment is based on agriculture, and in turn, irrigation is the base for about two-thirds, possibly more, of total agricultural output. The rapid expansion of irrigation and drainage infrastructure has been one of India's major achievements. From 1951 to 1997, gross irrigated area (including double cropping) expanded four fold from 23 million ha to 90 million ha. Coupled with introduction of associated high yielding varieties and fertiliser, the high productivity and reliability of irrigated lands enabled the "Green Revolution" commencing in the 1960s. As a result India has moved from the specter of food imports to self-sufficiency, food exports and progressively more diversified production.

The major expansion of irrigated area has occurred on all fronts. Major and medium surface schemes have increased more than three fold from 1951 to 1997, while ground water irrigation, largely private investment, has expanded seven fold. The ground water irrigation comprises 39 per cent of irrigated area, canal irrigation 47 per cent and other irrigation mainly tank 14 per cent.

## Issues in Irrigation

The main issues facing India are related to public sector managed surface irrigation system. These are physical, institutional and financial constraints. Common physical constraints include, inadequate maintenance, resulting in progressive deterioration of the surface irrigation system and poor water management due to ineffective control structures for surface irrigation and inappropriate incentives for ground water use. The institutional constraints pertain to public sector management without accountability to the farmers. There is no direct link between the irrigation service provided, revenues generated, expenditures and staff incentives. The main financial constraints are, very low water charges, requiring continual subsidisation by state government and weak revenue generation. There are no incentives for efficient water use.

The physical, institutional and financial problems which affect the Indian irrigation sector are operationally inter related. From the policy reform perspective, it is a kind of vicious circle, where different facets of irrigation problem interact with each other.

The poor quality of the irrigation service serves as a starting point. Combined with inadequate agriculture technology, it leads to low yield and then low incomes, which in turn leads to farmers' dissatisfaction with the irrigation system. Under this system water rate revisions are resisted, leading to low cost recovery and political pressure not to pay for the service. Low cost recovery, in turn, is linked to under funding of the operation and maintenance of the conveyance systems and compounded by the inappropriate structure, policies and staff skills, closes the circle by poor service quality.

The key need is to change the incentives structure, both at the level of government and farmers. At present neither has the incentive to change. For government, the lack of accountability to the client means that all incentives are internal, and there is no external incentive to be cost efficient, to be financially self-sufficient, to improve the quality of services, or to link up other government services, private sector or civil society. For farmers also there are no incentives to improve the service as they are detached from decision-making and feel they have little influence. Their only leverage is through political pressure resisting to pay for surface water irrigation and electricity charges for ground water pumping.

There is a need to evolve some incentive structure for government as well as farmers. There is a need to bring farmers into the management of irrigation system and to create client driven pressure on the service provider to improve performance. There is also a need to change the role, structure and financing of the Irrigation Department, to become fully accountable to the farmers, and funded by the farmers, so that farmers are in the driving seat. There is also need to upgrade the irrigation service and agriculture extension, so that benefits from institutional and financial change can be realized.

Thus any agenda for reform should aim to tackle, (i) Institutional reforms to involve farmers and restructure Irrigation Departments to be commercially operated autonomous entities (ii) restoring the sectors financial viability and cost effectiveness including private sector financing; and (iii) improving technical performance through upgrading irrigation system and agriculture extension.

## Groundwater

Groundwater is extremely important for India. This is the source of drinking water and food security for more than a billion Indians. The groundwater is source of 80 per cent water for domestic use in rural areas and around 50 per cent of water for urban and industrial uses. Over the last three decades, the rapid expansion in use of groundwater primarily for irrigation has contributed significantly to agriculture and economic growth.

Groundwater irrigation potential, the number of wells, and the number of energized pump sets have grown exponentially since 1950s. With more than 17 million energized wells nationwide groundwater now supplies more than 50 per cent of irrigated area and, due to higher yields in groundwater irrigated areas, is central to a significantly higher proportion of total agricultural output.

The rapid development in groundwater, however, has had a price. In many arid and hard rock zones increases in overdraft areas and associated water quality problems are emerging. Sustainability of the groundwater has become an issue because of over drafting. The need is to shift the emphasis from development or additional extraction activities to management. The emphasis on management needs does not imply that groundwater resources in India are fully developed.

Additional extraction could still be supported in a few localities. However, focus on development activities most now be balanced by a management mechanism to achieve a sustainable utilisation of groundwater.

Since most groundwater development has been accomplished through private investment of millions of farmers, government needs to play the appropriate role in various activities in the sector where private is unlikely to play any role. Protection of drinking water sources, pollution control, groundwater recharge, and environmental concerns such as overdraft and associated water quality problems are the key issues of concerned. Moreover, in many areas, modern agricultural practices have caused extensive water contamination with pesticides and salinisation of soils and groundwater. Mining and industry have caused localized water contamination with industrial chemicals and metals. In certain areas, there is pollution in groundwater, attributed to natural geological conditions, like arsenic in West Bengal, and fluoride in several parts of the country. Fluorosis is a major problem in Andhra Pradesh.

## Water, Health and Environment

One of today's main environmental concerns is pollution — pollution from agriculture, industry, from urban growth, and from water development projects such as dams and reservoirs. Contaminated water supply is the major cause of disease in the developing countries. Human activities have had devastating impacts on aquatic ecosystems — damaging fisheries, coral reefs, wetlands and watersheds. Each year as many as four million children die because they lack clean water and effective sanitation. The amount of wastewater has doubled between 1980 and the year 2000. In 1993, the Ministry of Environment and Forests had proposed a major plan to clean the extremely polluted stretches of 13 major rivers in the country at a cost of Rs. 1,115 crores.

Untreated wastewater and unmanaged solid waste not only spread disease and create squalid conditions in urban slums, they also contaminate the rivers and ground water on which the cities depend. There are widespread problems with unsafe drinking water and discharge of untreated sewage. Mega cities release huge amounts of wastewater, often the result of inefficient usage, into the existing water channels, thus polluting the freshwater channels. Technology offers the opportunity to harness this water, at a cost.

## Water Quality Issues

Contamination can enter the water bodies through one or more of the following ways:

- Direct point sources: Transfer of pollutants from municipal industrial liquid waste disposal sites and household hazardous waste and refuse disposal sites.
- Diffuse agricultural sources: Wash off and soil erosion from agricultural lands carrying materials applied during agricultural use, mainly fertilsers, herbicides and pesticides.
- Diffuse urban sources: Run off from city streets, from horticultural, gardening and commercial activities in the urban environment and from industrial sites and storage areas.

## Rivers

### *Change in Physical Characteristics*

Temperature, turbidity and total suspended solids (TSS) in rivers can be greatly affected by human activities such as agriculture, deforestation and the use of water for cooling. For example, the upward trend in soil erosion and the related increase in TSS in rivers can be seen in most of the mountainous regions in India.

### *Contamination by Faucal and Organic Matter*

In India faucal contamination is still the primary water quality issue in rivers, especially where human and animal wastes are not adequately collected and treated. Although this applies to both rural and urban areas, the situation is probably more critical in fast-growing cities. The release of untreated domestic or industrial wastes (high in organic matter) into rivers results in a marked decline in oxygen concentration (sometimes resulting in anaerobic conditions) and a rise in ammonia and nitrogen concentrations, downstream of the effluent input. The most obvious effect of the release of organic matter along the length of the river is the depletion of oxygen downstream of the discharge as shown by the so-called 'oxygen-sag curve' which plots dissolved oxygen concentration against distance. Industrial activities which discharge large organic loads include, pulp and paper production and food processing: faecal matter affects the use of water for drinking or bathing, as well as ecological health of river.

*Toxic Pollutants: Organics and Heavy Metals*

Organic pollutants (mostly chemicals manufactured artificially by man) are also becoming an important water quality issue. They enter rivers as:

- point sources directly from sewers and effluent discharges (domestic, urban and industrial sources)
- diffuse sources from the leaching of solid and liquid waste dumps or agricultural land run off
- indirectly through long-range atmospheric transport and deposition.

Uncontrolled discharge of industrial wastewater often causes pollution due to toxic metals. Other sources of metal pollution are leachates from urban solid waste landfills and mining waste dumps.

Rivers such as the Yamuna, which pass through large towns and cities, are often badly affected with organic pollutants. Another example is that of Damodar River which is polluted with heavy metals arising mostly from electroplating, tanning and metal based industries.

*River Eutrophication*

During the 1950s and 1960s, eutrophication (nutrient enrichment leading to increased plant arid algae growth) was observed mostly in lakes and reservoirs. Since the 1970s the increasing levels of phosphates and nitrates entering rivers, particularly in developed countries were largely responsible for eutrophication occurring in running waters. In India isolated reports have appeared for some river reaches especially in plains around agriculture tracts of land.

In small rivers eutrophication is said to promote macrophyte (large plants) development, whereas in large rivers phytoplankton (algae) are usually mere dominant than macrophyte. In such situations the chlorophyll concentration of the water may reach extremely high values due to the fact that this pigment is present in all plants.

Eutrophication can result in marked variations in dissolved oxygen arid pH throughout the day. The changes in water quality caused by eutrophication can be a major cause of stress to fish due to the release, at high pH, of highly toxic gaseous ammonia and depletion of oxygen after sunshine hours.

*Salinisation*

Increased mineral salts in rivers may arise from several sources:

- pollution by mining waste waters
- pollution by certain industrial waste waters
- increased evaporation in the river basin (mainly in arid and semiarid regions)

Industrial and mining waste pollution results in increase in specifications. Evaporation however, increases the concentration of all specifications.

## Groundwater

*Unsewered Domestic Waste*

Under certain hydrogeological conditions, unsewered domestic waste can cause severe groundwater contamination by pathogenic bacteria, nitrate and other pollutants. Unsewered waste normally means septic tanks or pit latrines of the ventilated, dry or pour-flush types. There are important differences between the two in relation to the risk of groundwater contamination. Septic tank soakaways discharge at a higher levels in the soil profile than pit latrines and such conditions are preferable as far as the elimination of bacteria is concerned. Pit latrines are often deep excavations (to allow a long useful life) and the soil may be entirely removed thus offering less opportunity for bacterial death. Further the loading from septic tank soakaways is likely to be less than for some of the pit latrine types. Septic tanks are lined and their solid effluent of high nitrogen content is periodically removed, whereas most pit latrines are unlined and the solid material remains in the ground. The impact of unsewered domestic waste is felt particularly in relation to the contamination of groundwater drinking water supplies. In India, the percentage of sewered population is nearly negligible in most of the rural areas and is quite meager (0 to 50 per cent) in most medium and small towns. As a result, the contamination of groundwater by pollution from unsewered areas is one of the most important environmental problems facing the country.

*Disposal of Liquid Urban and Industrial Waste*

Methods of wastewater disposal include infiltration ponds, spreading or spraying onto the ground surface and discharge to stream or dry streambeds, which if not carefully regulated may provide a rapid pollution pathway to underlying, shallow aquifers. In some areas, deep soakaways or abandoned wells are used for the disposal of liquid domestic, industrial or farming wastes into aquifers. Lack of monitoring, supervision or management adds to the problem.

Even if the intention is to dispose of the waste at depth, improper sealing or corrosion of well linings often produces leaks and subsequent pollution of the shallow groundwater which is used for water supplies. In urban areas covered by sewerage systems, an economical and common, method of partial treatment of sewage is wastewater stabilization by retention in shallow oxidation lagoons before subsequent discharge into rivers or onto land for irrigation systems. These lagoons are often unlined and, if constructed over coarse-textured soils, may have high rates of seepage loss. Further, the use of such effluent in irrigation may also lead to similar problems. Most of the unplanned industrial complexes and scattered industrial units in urban areas and the agricultural-related industries in remote villages are good examples of this type of pollution.

*Disposal of Solid Domestic and Industrial Waste*

The most common method of disposal of solid municipal waste in India is by deposition in landfills. In order to minimise the impact of such landfills on groundwater quality and the environment in general it is necessary to properly design and build these facilities to prevent pollution and put in place strict management controls to ensure they are operated correctly. Unfortunately this is rarely done as few towns and industries in the country make the necessary effort to ensure that their solid waste is treated or disposed of in a proper manner.

The principal threat to groundwater comes from inadequately controlled landfills where leachate generated from the fill material is allowed to escape to the surrounding and underlying ground. The chemical composition of such leachate depends on the nature and age of the landfill and the leaching rate. Most leachates emanating from municipal solid wastes are not only high in organic content but also contain some toxic material. Leachates from solid wastes of industrial origin, however, often contain a much higher proportion of toxic constituents, such as metals and organic pollutants.

*Cultivation with Agrochemicals*

Agricultural land use and cultivation practices have been shown to exert major influences on groundwater quality. Under certain circumstances, serious groundwater pollution can be caused by agricultural activities, the influence of that may be very important because of the large areas of aquifer affected. Of particular concern, in India, is the leaching of fertiliser chemicals (e.g. nitrate) and pesticides from regular intensive cultivation of crops. The impact of cultivation practices on groundwater quality is greatest, as are most anthropogenic effects, where relatively shallow, unconfined aquifers are used for potable supply.

In India, a high proportion of the rural population in agricultrual areas obtain their domestic water supplies from shallow, private bore holes, which suffer the impact of nitrate pollution to a much greater extent than the deeper, public supply aquifers utilised for urban water supply. These deeper acquifers can also be affected by nitrate contamination although this pollution often takes much more time to percolate to these depths.

Much less attention has been given in this country to the leaching of pesticides from agricultural land to the underlying groundwater in spite of the dramatic increase in the use of pesticide formulations over the last years. There are currently few laboratories with the capability of analysing pesticides.

*Salinity from Irrigation*

Increasing salinity resulting from the effects of irrigated agriculture is one or the oldest and most widespread forms of groundwater pollution. It is caused by the dissolved salts in irrigation water being deposited following evaporation of the water. The addition of further excess irrigation water merely leaches salts from the soil and transfers the problem to the underlying groundwater.

*Mining Activities*

A range of groundwater pollution problems can be associated with mining activities. The nature of the pollution depends on the materials being excavated and extracted. Both surface and underground mines usually extend below the water table and often dewatering is required to allow mining to proceed. The water pumped either directly from the mine or from specially constructed boreholes, may be highly mineralised and its usual characteristics include low pH (down to pH3) and high levels of iron, aluminium and sulphate. Disposal of this mine drainage effluent to surface water or groundwater can cause serious impacts on water quality for all uses. Pollution of groundwater can also result from the leaching of mine tailings and from settling ponds and can, therefore, be associated with both present and past mining activity.

*Geological Formations*

Groundwater in certain geological formations may not be of desired quality for specifc uses. Naturally occurring fluorides, arsenic and salinity are known to adversely affect the quality of water for drinking water supplies.

*Lakes and Reservoirs Pollution Pathways*

The following pathways, in addition to the ones mentioned above, assume special significance in the case of lakes and reservoir pollution:

- Riverine sources: pollutants in solution in the inflow or absorbed onto particulate matter, or both. The cumulative input is the sum of contaminants from all of the rivers draining the watershed into a lake.
- Groundwater sources: groundwater systems polluted from point and diffuse sources (noted above) flowing into rivers, and directly into lakebeds.
- Atomspheric sources: direct wet and dry atmospheric deposition of contaminants to the lake surface and wash off of similar pollutants from the land. This latter process is defined as secondary cycling.

In addition to the above, lakes serve as traps for pollutants carried by rivers and groundwater draining the watershed. The pollutant concentration in the lake usually builds up due to evaporation of water from the lake's surface unless there is a natural flushing with good quality water.

*Eutrophication*

Simply speaking, eutrophication is the biological response to excess nutrient input to a lake. The production of biomass and its death and decay results in a number of effects, which individually and collectively result in impaired water use. The most important of these effects are decreased dissolved oxygen levels, release of odorous compounds (e.g. $H_2S$) and siltation. Many important lakes in India (e.g., Hussein Sagar (Hyderabad), Nainital (Uttar Pradesh) and Dal (Jammu and Kashmir) have reportedly progressed to advanced eutrophication levels.

*Lake Acidification*

One of the major issues related to lakes in particular, and to freshwaters in general, is the progressive acidification associated with deposition of rain and particulates (wet and dey deposition) enriched in mineral acids. The problem is characteristic of lakes in specific, regions of the world, which satisfy two major critical conditions: the lakes must have soft water (i.e. low hardness, conductivity and dissolved salts) and be subjected to 'acid rain'. To date, lake acidification has not been reported as a problem in India.

*Bioaccumulation and Biomagnifications*

The processes of bioaccumulation and biomagnifications are extremely important in the distribution of toxic substances (discharged in waste effluents) in fresh water ecosystems. The concentration of pollutants within the organism due to bioaccumulation and biomagnifications depends on the duration of exposure of the organism to the contaminated environment and its tropic level in the food chain. Several fold increases in trace contaminant concentrations have been commonly observed in lakes and estuarine environments.

## Urban Water and Sewage Problem

The rapid pace of urbanisation, industrialisation as well as agricultural activities have made environmental pollution a growing concern globally. Off all the receptor systems exposed to the contaminants, groundwater has received little attention in the past because of the common belief that groundwater was pristine.

Groundwater Pollution is usually traced back to four main origins industrial, domestic, agricultrual and over exploitation. The last category mainly accounts for seawater intrusion. Studies carried out in India reveal that one of the most important causes of groundwater pollution is unplanned urban development without adequate attention to sewage and waste disposal. Industrialisation without provision of proper treatment and disposal wastes and affluent is another source of groundwater pollution. Excessive application of fertilizers for agricultural development coupled with over-irrigation intrusion due to excessive pumping of fresh water in coastal aquifers are also responsible for groundwater pollution.

With the declared objectives of providing at least the basic amenities there has been a tremendous development in India, in the agriculture and industrial sector, with concomitant pressure on the fresh water resources. The waste generated by anthropogenic activities has not only polluted the environment as a whole but had a particular detrimental effect on the quality of aquatio-envison too. Lechates from compost pits, animal refuse of garbage dumping grounds nutrient enriched retrun irrigation flows seepage from septic tanks, seepage of sewage etc. has adversely affected the goundwater quality in several parts of India. The rate of generation of wastewater in India during 1981 was estimated to be 74,529 million litres/day i.e about 27 km annually, which poses a perennial danger to the potable groundwater resource. The gravity of situation can be judged from the act that in spite of sewage treatment plant, Delhi discharged 100 million gallon of untreated sewage into the Yamuna. The problem is likely to compound further with increasing rate of wastewater generation which is estimated about $40km^3$ (110,000 million litre/ day) annually by the year 2000 when the population is estimated to be around one million. Solid waste disposal is also not lagging behind in adding to groundwater pollution problem. With increase of human and livestock population the quantum of waste produced has increased tremendously. The estimated annual waste production from these sources is around 2000 million tons (Vimal & Tala Shikar, 1983). Studies on chemical composition of ground water in phrestic zone have revealed that in many cases an anomalously high concentration of Nitrate Potassium and even phosphate (total phosphate) are present in contrast to their virtual absence or low concentration (No. 3 and K less than 10 mg/l) in semi-confined and aquifers. Unsystematic use of synthetic fertilizers coupled with improper water management practices have resulted in deterioration of groundwater quality in many parts of the country.

In case of industrial units, effluent in most of the cases are discharged into pits, open ground, or open unlined drains near the factories, thus allowing it to move to low lying depressions resulting groundwater pollution. The industries which are burgeoning at terrifying fast rate, daily produce about 55000 million $M^3$ of wastewater per day, out of which 68.5 million $M^3$ is discharged into river streams. Thus the magnitude of damage caused to our water resources can be estimated from the fact that about 70 per cent of rivers and streams in India contain polluted water.

The incidence of grounwater pollution is highest in urban where large volume of waste are concentrated and discharged into relatively small areas. The groundwater contamination, however, is detected only some time after the subsurface contamination begins.

Thirteen states in India have been identified as endemic to flurosis due to abundance in natural occurring fluoride bearing minearls. These are Nalgonda, Rangaraddy district in A.P., Banskatha, Kutch, Amroli in Gujarat, Hissar, Kaithal, Gurgaon in Haryana, Augul Bolengir, Phulbani in Orissa, Bhatinda, Sangrur in Punjab, Ajmer, Bikaner, Pali, Nagur, Sirohi in Rajasthan, Chengalpatti, Madurai in Tamilnadu, Unnao in U.P., Karnataka, Madhya Pradesh, Maharashtra, Bihar and Delhi. There are nearly half million people in India suffering from ailment due to excess of fluoride in drinking water. In some villages of Rajasthan and Amroeidities in Gujarat level of the fluoride goes up to 11.0 mg/lt.

Though iron content in drinking water may not affect the human system as a simple dietary overload, but in the long run prolonged accumulation of Iron in the body may result in homochromatosis, where tissues are damaged. In some districts of Assam (Barpota, Darrang, Kamrup, Sonipni) and Orissa (Balasore, Cuttack, Puri) groundwater have high iron content ranging from 1 to 10 mg/l.

A total of 10,6019 sq. km area (about 31 per cent) of Rajasthan comes under Saline groundwater in the state of this 88675 sq. km area falls in western Rajasthan of Ganganagar, Barmer, Bikaner, Churu and Jaisalmer districts. The electrical conductivity of groundwater in western Rajasthan is over 8 ds/cm and in eastern Rajasthan over 6 ds/cm. Vast low lying alluvial tract from North-Western part of Banaskantha district through the Western part of Mashing and Ahmedabad districts western and north-eastern parts of Surendranagar district, Southern part of Ahmedabad and South-Western part of Kheda district is underlain by saline groundwater (EC 3.46 ds/cm). Groundwater in Sangrur, Bhatinda, Ferozpur and Faridkot districts have on high as 11.30 ds/cm salinity. Groundwater is saline in almost the entire Bhakra canal and the lift canal system of Southwestern part of Haryana. About 3766 sq. km. area in Haryana is underlain by saline groundwater (EC 6 ds/cm).

Arsenic in groundwater have been reported in a range (0.05-3.2) mglp in shallow aquifers from 61 block in 8 districts of West Bengal namely Malda, Mushirbad, Nadia, North and South 24 Pargana, Bardharnan, Howrah and Hugli.

The demand for water supply and sanitation in urban areas for both domestic and industrial use is huge and increasing rapidly. To date the supply of these services are inadequate. Quantities of water delivered are insufficient and service is unreliable, requiring consumers to make alternate arrangements which are more costly in terms of time and money. Low quality of service is endemic, resulting in deleterious impacts on consumers. The reason for inefficient services is financial non-viable status of service providers without extensive subsidies.

## Conclusions and Suggestions

Water is becoming a major issue of concern for India. The current approach emphasizes development of water resources and construction of new infrastructure under a top down, supply oriented and fragmentary framework. There are various policy pronouncements but hardly any action. Present institutional structure is not good enough to tackle the problem. Existing organizations lack capacity in key management areas. The incentives to users for efficient use of water are not there and create negative impact on water usage. There is no appropriate direct water pricing system and lack of other economic and financial incentives and weak infrastructure leads to additional problem in smooth transfer of water between sectors and states.

The fundamental reforms are required in how water is captured, allocated between sectors, delivered to users and managed. There are two broad issues that need addressing if constraints are to be overcome. First solution must be found to improve resource allocation and management, both between competing inter-sectoral uses between states sharing the same river basin. Second, reforms to improve service delivery in the water sub-sector i.e. irrigation, urban/ rural water supply, sanitation must be implemented.

Resolving India's water resource management problem is not easy. It is a multidimensional and complex issue involving users from different sectors with different needs and with multi-layered levels of social organisations and public administration each acting in its own interest. Thus a comprehensive approach is required combining policy, institutions, pricing and technology. The role of government needs to be reoriented from provider and financier to facilitator and enabler. The improvement in the policy, legislative and regulatory framework is also required.

## Notes

• I am grateful to Prof. Bibek Debroy for his guidance and comments on the paper. I would also like to thank Rajiv Nagpal and Mukesh Krishna Lath for sharing their field experiences on water issues in Rajasthan.

## References

Dhawan, B.D. (1990), *Studies in Minor Irrigation with Special Reference to Groundwater.* New Delhi: Commonwealth Publishers.

Government of India, (1991), "Status of Groundwater Pollution in India, Central Groundwater Pollution Directorate, Ministry of Water Resources.

——— (1992), *National Policy Statement for Abatement and Pollution,* New Delhi, Ministry of Environment and Forest (MoEF).

——— (1992), *Report of the Committee on Pricing of Irrigation Water* (The Vaidyanathan Committee Report). New Delhi: Planning Commission.

——— (1996), *Report of the Ninth Plan Working Group on Major and Medium Irrigation Programmes,* New Delhi: Planning Commission.

——— (1997), *Approach Paper to the Ninth Plan.* New Delhi: Planning Commission.

——— (1997), *Report of the Sub-Committee on irrigation for the Indian Water Resources Sector Review,* New Delhi: Central Water Commission.

Indian Water Resource Society, (1997), *River Basin Management: Issues and Options,* Theme Paper Water Resource Day. New Delhi.

Mathur, O.P. (1993), *The State of India's Urban Poverty,* New Delhi: National Institute of Public Finance and Policy.

Roy, B.K. (1991), *Water Availability in India'* Water Resources Development, Vol. 7, No.2 June.

Singh, C. (1992), *Water Law in India,* New Delhi: Indian Water Institute.

World Bank, (1991), *India Irrigation Sector Review.* Washington: Agriculture and Water Division, South Asia Dept 2.

——— (1993), *Water Resources Management,* A World Bank Policy Paper. Washington, D.C.

# 10

# Reform Agenda for Agriculture

C.H. HANUMANTHA RAO

## Introduction

### *(a) The Setting*

The incentive framework for Indian agriculture improved considerably as a result of trade and exchange rate liberalisation and a significant reduction in the protection to domestic industry, following economic reforms introduced in the country in the early nineties. The terms of trade for agriculture have improved and there has been a record rise in agricultural exports. On the whole, farmers' expectations have been aroused for better prospects from the opening up of the economy. This is reflected in a big rise in private investment in agriculture in the nineties. The full benefits for agriculture from the macroeconomic reforms introduced so far can be expected to materialise, in course of time, when reforms directly affecting agriculture such as removal of restrictions on domestic trade and processing, stepping up public investment in agriculture, reforms in the management of infrastructure, etc., are put in place. Indeed, the slowing down of agricultural growth in the post-reform period, despite favourable macroeconomic environment, is explained by the neglect of such reforms directly affecting agriculture.

This note seeks to spell out such a reform agenda.

### *(b) The Objectives of Reforms*

The basic objectives of reforms in agriculture should be: First, stepping up agricultural growth to at least 4 per cent per annum to sustain the overall growth rate in GDP at a high rate, say, 8 per cent. Second, diversifying agriculture with a view to promoting, among other things, the growth of rural non-farm sector such as agro-processing, thus facilitating a significant shift of labour force from agriculture to non-agriculture. Third, increasing application of cost-reducing technologies for making agriculture competitive. Fourth, reducing rural poverty and inequality through broad-based growth of agriculture by reducing disparities between different regions and classes of farmers and by strengthening the role of women in farming. Fifth, protecting environment by reversing the on-going degradation of natural resources like land and water and by preventing the excessive chemicalization of agriculture.

Reforms needed for achieving these objectives are outlined below within the framework of a two-pronged strategy to improve the performance of agriculture: (a) To release the initiative and enterprise of farmers and the private sector in general by removing restrictions on agricultural trade, processing, etc., and (b) To facilitate adequate supply response to the incentives so created by strengthening infrastructure, agricultural research and extensions and delivery of credit, while protecting environment.

## I. Removal of Restrictions on Domestic Trade and Processing

*(a) Removal of Restrictions*

The prevailing restrictions on domestic trade and processing of agricultural commodities are inherited from the post-war, pre-green revolution era of shortages. With the achievement of self-sufficiency in foodgrains, increasing trend towards diversification of agriculture, globalisation of trade and W.T.O commitments, such restrictions on movement, storage and processing have outlived their utility and have become counter-productive, denying fair prices to producers as well as to consumers and inhibiting much needed investments in the technological upgradation and modernisation of processing, storage and marketing.

The Essential Commodities Act (ECA), Agricultural Produce Marketing Act, the Small Scale Industry reservation, and so on, need to be thoroughly reviewed and revamped with a view to abolishing all legal impediments under these Acts that restrict the entry of big private sector, including FDI, in marketing, storage and processing. For example, agro-processing, including the processing of groundnuts and mustard oilseeds now reserved for SSI, need to be liberalised. Major investments in these sectors will emerge, if legal environment provides the private sector a level playing field *vis-à-vis* cooperatives and public sector concerns. It is essential to facilitate the emergence of vertical integration between farmers, processors and retailers to facilitate high value addition in agriculture. To ensure that food safety laws are duly enforced, and Sanitary and Phyto-Sanitary (SPS) standards adopted, it is desirable to promote large processing facilities with state-of-the-art technology.

While revamping these Acts, care has to be taken to see that some of the positive features in them are retained and strengthened. Given unscrupulous practices by certain sections of traders and middlemen, some regulations, including regulated markets, are necessary. Further, in states such as Punjab and Haryana, markets and road infrastructure were developed through taxes collected via APMC Acts. However, there is a need to rationalise these taxes. For example, Commission Agents' charges could be removed and *Mandi* fees could be waived when processors buy directly from the farm gate (such as through contract farming) and commission charges not levied.

*(b) Minimum Support Prices and Public Procurement of Foodgrains*

The mounting stocks of foodgrains with the FCI are explained by the steep rise in procurement prices (acting as minimum support prices), and the open ended procurement by the FCI even when market conditions were adverse. A good part of the large amounts of grain procured is off-loaded at a price almost half its 'economic cost'. Such market operations at huge discounts drove out the private sector from grain trade, and consequently government is saddled with even more stocks.

In principle, since MSP is intended to provide an element of insurance against precipitous fall in prices, it should preferably be based on the average paid-out cost, while the procurement price should be set by the market conditions in competition with the private trade. However, sudden and drastic changes in the existing system of pricing and procurement of foodgrains carry the risk of undermining food security so assiduously built over a long period. In the medium term, therefore, the objective should be to consolidate the food security achieved so far and simultaneously move towards diversification of agriculture in consonance with the changing demand and resource endowments.

Towards this end, the government should, as a rule, accept the recommendations of the Commission on Agricultural Costs and Prices (CACP) while deciding the level of MSP. Moderation on the price front for foodgrains by tilting the relative prices in favour of non-foodgrains needs to be combined with vigorous non-price interventions for making the cultivation of non-foodgrains attractive to farmers such as through research and extension, infrastructure development for agro-processing and marketing, and measures for promoting exports. Since diversification leads to risk and uncertainty for higher value added products, their risk management can be subsidised. In the meantime, the foodgrain surpluses available with the FCI provide an opportunity to generate rural employment for productive works like watershed development, afforestation and for building up other community assets. They should also be used for providing mid-day meals to the children in schools for improving their nutrition and reducing drop-out. Over and above this, the BPL (below the poverty line) families, whose children go to school, can be compensated for their children's earnings foregone by giving them 5 to 10 kgs. of grain per month free, so as to induce them to send their children to school.

A major element in the new dispensation should be to allow the private sector to operate in the market without any restrictions in terms of the movement of grain, stocking limits, levy to the government agencies, exports, etc. This necessitates that the public agencies (FCI) should not be reimbursed for their losses due to their open market operations (beyond what is absolutely necessary on account of the maintenance of buffer stocks and the operation of the PDS) at a price much below their cost. Otherwise the private sector will be driven out of the market. An alternate system of storing in warehouses by providing credit to farmers, say, upto 70 per cent of the value of the stocks stored, could be considered.

It would be good to encourage vertical integration even in the foodgrain sector. The freedom to operate warehouse receipt system, direct buying from the farmers by the private companies (without recourse to commission agents), rationalising the purchase tax on grains, *mandi* tax etc., would encourage private companies to invest in the development of the grain markets, storage and processing of grain.

### *(c) Trade and WTO Related Issues*

There is a need to formulate a consistent policy for export of agricultural products and processed agro-products in which the country has a comparative advantage. Most agricultural commodities (cotton, onions, sugar, etc.) continue to be under severe export controls and quotas. These destroy any chance of building up a sustained international market. Exporters should have the freedom to enter into long-term contracts. They should be allowed to buy from the farm-gate or from the market at minimum support prices and stocking and handling should be freely allowed.

India should argue at the WTO that all the subsidies need to be clubbed together, instead of being placed in separate boxes (green, blue, amber), as some of the developed countries have been claiming large exemptions by using such provisions and also by interchanging subsidies shown from one box to the other. India would not be adversely affected if these are clubbed together, as the aggregate measure of support (AMS) to Indian agriculture is still well below the *de minimis* of 10 per cent. This position would be reinforced if, as India has been arguing, the AMS is calculated as the sum of product-specific and non-product-specific support, as the former is significantly negative in the Indian case. Moreover, input subsidies to the resource poor farmers are exempt from reduction commitments even now under the WTO provisions. If India avails of this, the non-product specific support may come down to less than half of what is being shown today. Bound rates should not be lowered and anti-dumping and anti-subsidy duties or safeguard measures must be invoked in time. Imports should comply with standards and the TRIPs system needs to be strengthened.

## II. Agricultural Research and Extension

### *(a) Agricultural Research*

India is endowed with one of the most advanced agricultural research systems among the developing countries in terms of scientific skills as well as its reach, even though a great deal of restructuring is needed for its efficient functioning. Indian farmers, despite low literacy levels, have responded exceptionally well to the opportunities opened up by new technologies. Also, frontier technologies like biotechnologies remain under-exploited in the country. Therefore, the returns from investment in agricultural research and extension in the country can be expected to be very high, relatively quick, and assured.

The existing public outlay on agricultural research and education stagnating around 0.3 per cent of agricultural GDP in the country is too meagre and needs to be stepped up substantially. At the same time, there is considerable potential for raising the effectiveness of these outlays by re-ordering the priorities in agricultural research and re-defining the relative roles of public and private sectors in research and extension.

There is a need for a shift away from individual crop-oriented research focused essentially on irrigated areas towards research on crops and cropping systems in the drylands, hills, tribal and other marginal areas. In view of high variability in agro-climatic conditions in such unfavourable areas, research has to become increasingly location-specific with greater participation or interaction with farmers. Greater attention to research on horticultural products that are land-saving as well as water-saving, animal husbandry and dairying integrated with crop production, and on small ruminants can benefit resource-poor farmers and women, besides being environmentally sustainable.

Progress in post-harvest technology is essential to promote value addition through the growth of agro-processing industry. Economies of scale can be exploited through the food park concept. Agricultural diversification necessitates subsidizing risk management, and private sector involvement in agro-processing opens up opportunities for sharing risk with the farmers through contract farming. However, steps have to be taken to ensure contractual obligations, for example, when market prices are higher than contractual prices.

Private sector participation in agricultural research, extension and marketing is becoming increasingly important, especially with the advent of biotechnology and protection being accorded to intellectual property. However, private sector participation tends to be limited to profitable crops and enterprises undertaken by the resources-rich farmers in well-endowed areas. Public sector research has to increasingly address the problems facing the resource-poor farmers in the less-endowed regions.

*(b) Extension*

The existing Travel and Visit (T&V) system of extension is top-down in its approach, has a narrow focus in so far as it is oriented to individual crops grown in favourable areas, offers very little scope for the initiative and participation by the farmers and is also not accountable to them. Further, the squeezing of assistance to states by the central government for extension services has led to the virtual breakdown of extension machinery in the states. As a result, farmers are becoming increasingly dependent upon the private sector for extension services. In the absence of public regulation of such services, the resource-poor and gullible farmers are becoming victims of exploitation by the unscrupulous traders and money lenders interested in selling spurious material.

There is, therefore, an immediate need for revamping and revitalising the existing agricultural extension system in the country, so as to conform to the new priorities in agricultural research, with adequate financial support from the centre and the states. The main ingredients of this reform should be: (1) Active involvement of farmers through user groups and Self Help Groups (SHGs), and accountability to them; (2) Enabling participation by the private sector, farmers' associations and the NGOs, to complement public services, by putting in place an independent regulatory body, to which samples can be submitted for quality checks, encompassing inputs like fertilizers, pesticides, and seeds; (3) Increasing use of media and Information Technology, including cyber kiosks, to disseminate the knowledge on new agricultural practices and the information on output and input prices for improving the effectiveness of agricultural services in general. The use of information technology will reduce the requirement of a large number of extension workers at the block level and would indeed complement, to a considerable extent, the services rendered by the extension workers in remote areas; (4) Building gender concerns into the system, for example, by manning the extension services predominantly by women in hill and tribal areas where farming is managed essentially by women; and (5) Capacity building of extension functionaries and farmers, among other means, through distance education.

## III. Management of Infrastructure

### *(a) Exploiting the Available Irrigation Potential*

Public investment in basic infrastructure, especially roads, irrigation and power, where private sector is still reluctant to enter, will have to be stepped up. Government programme on highways and rural roads has made some progress, but major institutional and price reforms are required in irrigation and power sectors to raise efficiency, and generate resources at least for the proper upkeep and maintenance of the systems.

Nearly 40 per cent of the available irrigation potential of 58.5 million hectares from major and medium irrigation projects in the country still remains to be exploited. Over 400 such projects were in the pipeline at various stages during the Ninth Plan period. When these on-going projects are completed, bulk of the remaining irrigation potential would have been exploited. Decline in public investment and the thin spread of resources over a large number of projects are responsible for the delay in the completion of these projects. This underlines the need for stepping up public investment for the speedy completion of the on-going major and medium irrigation projects by the states, as the latter account for over 95 per cent of public investment in irrigation in the country. The resource-poor states in the eastern and central regions account for the bulk of the irrigation potential remaining to be exploited. There may, therefore, be a need for special central assistance to enable such resource-poor states to speedily execute the on-going irrigation projects.

Thanks to the easy availability of power in large parts of the country for pumping water for irrigation, as much as 78 per cent of the available potential of 81.4 million hectares from minor irrigation sources, consisting predominantly of ground water resources, has already been exploited. However, further progress towards the exploitation of the remaining potential hinges on the availability of electric power for pumping water in the eastern states where as much as 75 per cent of their ground water potential still remains to be exploited.

*(b) Raising Water-Use-Efficiency*

Since water-use-efficiency for irrigation is very low in the country, achievement of water security depends not only on the exploitation of the remaining potential but increasingly on the efficient and productive use of available irrigation water. There exists a vast gap now between the knowledge available for improving water-use-efficiency and its actual application in the country. This is explained by the lack of incentives to follow improved practices under the existing system of management and pricing of water. However, reforms in management and pricing are inter-linked as farmers would be willing to pay higher charges only if the efficiency of services improves.

Involvement of user-farmers in the management of irrigation systems at various levels is accepted the world over as an effective alternative to the present system of management by the government, as well as to privatisation. Participatory Irrigation Management (PIM) being experimented in the country towards this end has thrown up certain useful lessons.

Unwillingness to devolve adequate powers to the Water Users' Associations (WUAs) and insufficient infrastructure for capacity building at grass roots level have inhibited the participation of user-farmers and impeded the growth of leadership at the local level. India has been very much lagging behind several South East Asian countries in respect of coverage by WUAs as well as effectiveness of their performance. Therefore, there has to be a vigorous drive towards the empowerment of Water Users' Associations in the country by putting in place an adequate infrastructure for capacity building.

*(c) Input Subsidies and Pricing of Irrigation Water and Rural Electricity*

The rising subsidies on irrigation water from canals and on electricity for pumping water have benefited the large farmers as well as the consumers at large on account of the food security achieved and the decline in the relative prices of foodgrains for quite some time. However, these subsidies caused severe deterioration of the systems due to the neglect of their maintenance in addition to becoming fiscally unsustainable. Further, they have led to the highly wasteful use of canal water, ecological degradation from waterlogging, salinity and pollution, excessive consumption of electricity, and overdrawal of groundwater resulting in the shortage of drinking water in several parts of the country. There is, therefore, an immediate need to reverse this process.

Awareness on the part of the farmers about the harmful consequences of rising input subsidies and their cooperation in pricing the inputs on a volumetric basis is essential for making the change-over politically feasible and sustainable. A possible solution is to evolve a system where the village communities develop a stake in the conservation of resources. As an experiment, Water Users' Associations and *Panchayati Raj* Institutions (PRIs) can be fully empowered and induced to charge and collect water and electricity rates from the farmers on the basis of the volume of actual consumption where metering is possible, or, on the basis of the quantities of water received or electricity consumed as estimated by the farmers' associations where metering is uneconomical or otherwise infeasible. In such situations, *Panchayats* can regulate the cropping pattern and the use of water for raising water-use-efficiency and productivity. The revenues so collected should be allowed to be retained partly or wholly by the WUAs under the aegis of *Panchayats* for maintenance and development of irrigation and rural electricity services. Since agricultural income has not been taxed, this should be made the fiscal domain of PRIs through a land-based tax.

Where found necessary, a subsidy at a flat rate, say, on the estimated consumption of electicity on holdings upto one or two hectares, can be given to all the farmers or only to the small and marginal farmers, requiring them to pay for the extra consumption. This would have the merit of providing relief to a large number of deserving farmers in a manner that is politically feasible, even as there would be an incentive to conserve electricity and water.

In situations where volumetric pricing is not practicable, farmers have to be charged for water and electricity at a flat rate, say per horse power of electric motor, by announcing a time-frame of 2 to 3 years, where phased increase in tariffs would be linked to improvements in supply. However, care has to be taken to ensure that high flat rates do not result in a small number of affluent farmers cornering water and selling it to the small and marginal farmers at very high rates. Pumping and selling water by PRIs and a subsidy on investment in wells for the resource-poor farmers may promote competition by increasing the number of wells.

The prevailing heavy subsidy on nitrogenous fertilizers perpetuates inefficiencies in the domestic fertilizer industry. The benefit flowing to the farmers and consumers of food is illusory, as it is leading to the degradation of soil on account of excessive chemicalization and adverse NPK ratio. As in the case of water and electricity discussed above, a fixed quantity of fertilizers sufficient for one or two hectares may be subsidised for all the farmers, if necessary through a system of input stamps, requiring them to purchase the remaining quantities in the market at the going rates. Although income support is the best form of support for marginal farmers, perhaps routed through PRIs, it may not be administratively workable. Also, considering the incentives needed for input intensification, there is a need to continue with the present system of input subsidies for marginal farmers.

## IV. Credit Reforms

About 60 per cent of the credit requirements of farmers are now met by the institutional sources, and the remaining 40 per cent by informal sources like money lenders who charge very high interest rates. However, small and marginal farmers (less than 2 ha.), including tenants, who account for nearly 80 per cent of holdings and one-third of area operated, depend far more heavily on informal sources. Among the formal credit institutions, the commercial banks have emerged as a major player in agriculture credit (about 50 per cent) followed by cooperatives (about 43 per cent) and RRBs (about 7 per cent).

In the post-reform period, despite the rise in capital-intensity of agriculture in the wake of its diversification, and despite broadening the definition of 'priority sector' by adding a number of activities hitherto financed outside the priority sector, the direct agriculture advances by the commercial banks declined to 11-12 per cent of net bank credit as against the original target of 18 per cent. The position is much worse in the eastern and north-eastern states, even though the commercial banks are saddled with excess liquidity. The Rural Infrastructure Development Fund (RIDF), started a decade ago presumably as a temporary measure to provide infrastructural support to agriculture in lieu of its falling share in commercial bank credit, seems to have been turned into an easier route for meeting part of the stipulated obligations. In the process, individual needs of the farmers for investment and production credit are not being adequately met. This declining priority to agriculture is apparently explained by the efforts on the part of the banks to reduce 'transaction costs' and minimise 'risks'. Nothing short of a major change in the mind-set, and a new code informed by social purpose, initiated and monitored by the authorities in the banking system, can remedy the situation.

The share of Cooperative Banks in the institutional credit for agriculture and allied activities has declined from 45 per cent in 1996-97 to 41 per cent during 2000-2001. Under the prevailing economic scenario of liberalization and globalisation, the cooperatives have to be strong enough to compete in the open market. They may need to be assisted in recapitalisation and also by substantially increasing the quantum of refinance by NABARD. Also, the proposals initiated by the Centre for amending the cooperative laws of the states with a view to inject professionalism, autonomy and transparency in the functioning of these societies need to be followed up expeditiously.

Kisan Credit Scheme, aimed at providing adequate and timely support to the farmers from the banking system in a flexible and cost effective manner, does not seem to be succeeding in its avowed purpose because of various stipulations and restrictions. Its operation seems to be limited to only fertilizers from fixed shops. A more farmer friendly credit card system needs to be operated so as to realise the objectives of the scheme.

High value agriculture needs higher working capital and also entails higher risks. Facilitating credit through processors, input dealers, NGOs, etc. that are vertically integrated with the farmers, including through contract farming, for providing them critical inputs or processing their produce, could increase the credit flow to agriculture significantly. These dealers/processors can act as non-banking financial intermediaries, who can get refinance from the banking sector and can give loans to agriculture, and bear the risk of default. Such arrangements would reduce transaction costs and ensure good recovery. Policy changes are needed to facilitate such intermediation by freeing up interest rates within a band.

Self-Help Groups of women for providing micro-credit have been a success story in the country. Such households being essentially landless, credit by SHGs has been confined mainly to activities falling outside agriculture. However, their experience does point to the promise that groups comprising small and marginal farmers hold, especially women farmers, in managing credit for land-saving activities like animal husbandry, dairying, horticulture, agro-forestry, etc., provided there are contractual arrangements with dealers and processors for the provision of inputs and services for marketing. As capital assets of these farmers are limited, community/group collateral and the produce on farmers' land, including that of tenants, should be considered as collateral in granting credit.

## V. Measures to Conserve Land and Water Resources

### *(a) Watershed Development*

The experience from the on-going watershed development programme for drought proofing of rain-fed agriculture by conserving land and water resources has been encouraging. The single most important factor accounting for the positive impact of this programme is community participation and decentralization of programme administration made possible under the new guidelines. Yet, the present level of participation is inadequate for sustaining this development, especially in areas where the programme has proceeded too fast by fulfilling the targets for completion of works without the required institution-building and leadership formation at the grass roots level. The coverage has, nevertheless, to expand through increased outlays, as only about 25 per cent of around 107 million hectares of degraded land in the country is estimated to have been treated so far.

Certain policy changes are needed for the movement to become self-sustaining as and when the assistance under the current officially sponsored programme ceases. The foremost among these requirements being institution-building and leadership formation, it calls for empowering people inhabiting the watersheds by delegating authority to their committees and user-groups. Mobilizing adequate contribution from the land owning households on a regular basis for the maintenance of assets created, and ensuring equitable benefits to weaker sections, especially the landless poor, are essential for sustaining the movement. The second major task is creation of awareness and capacity building through training at various levels by entrusting this to an autonomous nodal agency at the national level and by guaranteeing adequate funding. Third, a major shift is needed in the existing policy for dryland or rain-fed agriculture by according greater priority to agricultural research and extension, supply of inputs, infrastructure development like roads and marketing and price and credit policies. Because of the emerging shift of consumer demand towards water-saving products which also have a good export potential, greater priority to dryland agriculture can provide the necessary incentives to the local communities to sustain their interest in the conservation of land and water resources and indeed for easing pressure on such resources.

*(b) Joint Forest Management (JFM)*

JFM is a programme for the regeneration and conservation of forest resources in partnership with the local people consisting largely of tribal population. This programme has, on the whole, made a much better impact in a relatively short period when compared to the watershed development programme. Apart from the absence of problems arising from individual property rights as in areas under watershed development, the returns to the participating farmers from the regeneration of forests are quick and assured. Also, the institutions of forest dwellers, especially of tribals, are conducive to community participation.

For these reasons, JFM, as the centre piece of forest development funded by the Government of India and the donors, holds a great promise. Some of the major problems still to be addressed are: permitting JFM in good or high productivity forest areas, encouraging profitable enterprises like agro-forestry, increasing the participation of women, greater security to the poorer segments of the participants, reorganising self-initiated.

*(c) Hill and Tribal Areas*

The protection of fragile ecology of hills requires a major shift from short duration crops like foodgrains to forestry, animal husbandry, pasture management and horticulture. This calls for effective interventions by way of research and extension, and development of transport and marketing infrastructure. Since farming is done essentially by women in hill areas, greater interaction with them would be necessary for developing technologies and programmes suited to these areas. Also, access to technology, inputs and credit has to be ensured predominantly through women extension workers.

Although tribal areas in general are endowed with high rainfall and plentiful groundwater resources, agricultural productivity is very low on account of traditional technology and low input use. Further, even though the incidence of poverty among tribals is much higher than the average, they have a better access to land when compared to the poor in general. There is, therefore, considerable potential for raising agricultural productivity and reducing poverty in tribal areas through the development of well irrigation, provision of appropriate technology and inputs. As in hill areas, women play an important role in agriculture in tribal areas. Direct access to inputs and services for them needs to be ensured through women extension workers. Tribal and hill areas including North-East have a comparative advantage in organic farming because of lower use of chemical inputs. This profitable avenue should be exploited through appropriate policies.

*(d) Flood-Proofing of Flood-Prone Agriculture*

About 4 per cent of the crop area in the country, located mainly in the eastern states, is affected by recurring floods. The traditional land use and cropping patterns are closely adapted to the seasonal flooding cycle, emphasis being on flood management rather than on flood control as such. Farmers usually harvest bumper rabi crops in the post-flood season, thus compensating kharif losses to some extent. The strategy for flood proofing through embankments, dams, sluices, etc., combined with the use of high yielding varieties for irrigated rabi crops have led to significant and positive changes in the farming systems, diversified employment opportunities and better food security. In the light of this experience, research has to be designed to adjust cropping systems to the flooding cycle, harvest flood water for irrigation in the post-flood season and to evolve yield-raising technologies.

## VI. Land Ceiling and Tenancy Laws

In view of the continued pressure of population on land, it may not be advisable to remove, at the present juncture, the ceiling on the ownership of agricultural land. Ceiling on the ownership of land has in general made land market favourable to the small and marginal farmers who can augment their ownership as well as operational holdings. However, tenancy laws guaranteeing security of tenure and prescribing the rental share have led to the growth of concealed tenancy which discourages investment by the tenants and restricts the flow of credit to them. Since each tenants are in any case paying market rents, liberalization of tenancy laws can help to increase their employment and income by augmenting their operational holdings, stepping up investment and getting better access to credit and inputs.

## Conclusion

It is clear from the above that the role of government by way of public policies, programmes, and investment is going to be extremely important. Success depends crucially on effective governance at the grass roots level, as many of these programmes are going to be location specific. Interaction with farmers is essential for ensuring relevance and quality of the programmes designed, and accountability to them is necessary for effective implementation. The key to the success is the effective functioning of the *Panchayati Raj* Institutions as enjoined by the 73$^{rd}$ and 74$^{th}$ amendments to the Constitution. As it is, most state governments have been reluctant to transfer functions, finances and functionaries to the *Panchayats,* as indicated in the Eleventh Schedule to the Constitution. Major initiatives are needed from the Center to persuade the States to devolve these powers and, if necessary, bring about consensus for directly transferring from the Centre to the *Panchayats* resources allocated to schemes falling under the subjects listed in the Eleventh Schedule.

# 11

## Social Sector Schemes

### *A Brief Review*

D. SHYAM BABU

Though there is no precise definition available for 'Social Sector', traditional welfare activities aimed at helping the poor and disadvantaged, and in general enhancing human development are called 'Social Sector'. The social sector is the concern of all the tiers of the government — from the Centre at the national-level to the *Gram Panchayat*.

Soon after independence, the nation's attention was drawn by the problems related to mass poverty, illiteracy and regional disparities in terms of socio-economic development. Moreover, socio-economic discrimination and exclusion perpetuated on some sections, especially the Scheduled Castes and Scheduled Tribes, and women had created an imperative to adopt a development model that would find solutions to these problems. Centralised planning through the Planning Commission, setup in 1950, was to be the agent of change and development.

During more than fifty years of development experience, India has created a huge administrative machinery and nearly 500 'schemes' and 'programmes' for the overall development of the country. And the 'social sector' has been the main focus of the government.

In the fiscal 2001-2002, the expenditure on the entire social sector at national level accounted for 1.8 per cent of the Gross Domestic Product (GDP) at market prices. Total central plan outlay on major schemes of social sector was Rs. 24,809 crore, out of the total outlay of Rs. 1,00,100 crore. This means nearly one-fourth (24.78 per cent) of the plan budget is spent on the sector.

Most of this money is being spent by the states or local bodies — who are the implementing agencies. In addition to this, states too spend considerable amounts on social sector but figures for the same are not available. Though states have their own schemes or programmes, most social sector schemes are 'centrally sponsored' in that they are devised and funded by the central government. At least in two occasions, a state scheme was found to be good and later adopted by the Centre. One is the 'Employment Guarantee Scheme' initiated by Maharashtra in the 1970s and the other is the 'Education Guarantee Scheme' of the Madhya Pradesh in the nineties.

All the schemes initiated at the national level are administered by the concerned ministries such; as the Ministry of Rural Development, Ministry of Urban Development and Poverty Alleviation, Ministry of Social Justice and Empowerment, Ministry of Human Resource Development, Ministry of Tribal Welfare, etc. Specifically, the Ministry of Statistics and Programme Implementation monitors all central schemes costing Rs. 20 crore and above. The ministry has a division to monitor the Twenty Point Programme (TPP)[1].

The Twenty Point Programme, unveiled in 1975 and revised twice in 1982 and 1986, is an umbrella programme on *inter alia* attack on rural poverty; rainfed agriculture; irrigation; land reforms; health; drinking water; family planning; education; SC/ST welfare; women/ youth development, etc. All the schemes that fall in one or the other points of the TPP-86, though they came into existence much later (such as Sampoorna Gramin Rozgar Yojana) are treated as part of the programme.

According to the *Economic Survey 2001-2002*[2], the following areas fall under social sector:

1. Social Services:
   a. Education, Sports & Youth Affairs;
   b. Health and Family Welfare;
   c. Water Supply, Sanitation, Housing and Urban Development;
   d. Information & Broadcasting;
   e. Welfare of SCs/STs and Other Backward Classes;
   f. Labour, Employment and Labour Welfare;

   g. Social Welfare and Nutrition;

   h. North-Eastern Areas;

2. Rural Development;
3. Basic Minimum Services (BMS) including Slum Development;
4. Pradhan Mantri Gramodya Yojana (PMGY) and Pradhan Mantri Gram Sadak Yojana (PMGSY).

Considerable progress has been made by India in terms of human development. For example, poverty has come down by half from 56.44 per cent in 1973-74 to 26.10 per cent in 1999-2000. Similarly, there has been improvement in other aspects, too. Life expectancy has increased to 65 years and mortality rates have come down. There has been spectacular progress in eradicating illiteracy. At the time of independence, India's literacy rate was a mere 12.10 per cent; now it stands at 65.38 per cent.

*Major Employment Generation and Poverty Alleviation Programmes*[3]

- *Jawahar Gram Samridhi Yojana* (JGSY): Introduced in April 1999, restructuring the Jawahar Rozgar Yojana. Centre contributes 75 per cent of funds and States 25 per cent and implemented by the Gram Panchayats for "creation of durable productive community assets" and to generate "wage employment for the rural unemployed poor."
- *Swarnjayanti Gram Swarozgar Yojana* (SGSY): Initiated in 1999, it is the new version of Integrated Rural Development Programme (IRDP), Development of Women and Children in Rural Areas (DWCRA), Training of Rural Youth for Self Employment (TRYSEM), Million Wells Scheme (MWS), etc. SGSY "covers all aspects of self-employment like organisation of rural poor into SHG (Self-Help Groups) and their capacity building, training, planning of activity clusters, infrastructure development, financial assistance through bank credit, subsidy and marketing support, etc." Centre-State share of funding: 75:25.

  According to Dr. Rohini Nayyar, "the objective of SGSY is to bring the existing poor families above the poverty line in three years by providing them income-generating assets through a mix of bank credit and Government subsidy. The SGSY is a credit-cum-subsidy programme, with credit as the critical component and subsidy as a minor and enabling element."[4]

- *Employment Assurance Scheme* (EAS): Started in 1993 and now being operated in all the 5448 Rural *Panchayat Samitis*, the EAS targets "drought prone areas, desert areas, tribal areas and hill areas." Centre-State share of funding: 75:25.
- *Sampoorna Grameen Rozgar Yojana* (SGRY): It provides "wage employment in rural areas as also food security, along with the creation of durable community, social and economic assets." EAS and JGSY are scheduled to be integrated into the SGRY. Centre-State share of funding: 75:25.

  Rohini Nayyar says that the "programme is self-targetting in nature. While providing wage employment, preference is to be given to women, members of SC/ST and parents of child labour withdrawn from hazardous occupations".[5]
- *National Social Assistance Programme* (NSAP): Started in 1995, the NSAP is a 100 per cent Centrally Sponsored Scheme and aims to accord "social assistance benefit to poor households affected by old age, death of primary bread earner and maternity care." It has three components: 1) National Old Age Pension Scheme (NOAPS); 2) National Family Benefit Scheme (NFBS); and 3) National Maternity Benefit Scheme (NMBS).
- *Pradhan Mantri Gramodaya Yojana* (PMGY): Introduced during 2000-2001, the PMGY concentrates on "five critical areas, i.e., health, primary education, drinking water, housing and rural roads."

  i. *Pradhan Mantri Gram Sadak Yojana* (PMGSY): Launched in December 2000, the PMGSY is to provide "road connectivity through good all-weather roads to all rural habitations with a population of more than 1000 persons by the year 2003 and those with a population of more than 500 persons by the year 2007."

  ii. *Pradhan Mantri Gramodaya Yojana (Gramin Awas)*: To be implemented on the lines of Indira Awas Yojana to ensure "sustainable habitat development at the village level and to meet the growing housing needs of the rural poor."

iii. *Pradhan Mantri Gramodaya Yojana (Rural Drinking Water Project)*: Desert Development Programme and Drought Prone Areas Programme should have a minimum of 25 per cent of the total allocation devoted to "projects/ schemes for water conservation, water harvesting, water recharge and sustainability of the drinking water sources."

- *Swarna Jayanti Shahri Rozgar Yojana* (SJSRY): Started in 1997, the SJSRY aims at urban poverty alleviation. It has two components: 1) Urban Self-Employment Programme and 2) Urban Wage Employment Programme. Centre-State share of funding: 75:25.
- *Indira Awaas Yojana* (IAY): The IAY stipulates the construction of houses, free of cost, to the poor and also in the improvement of unserviceable *kutcha* houses to semi-*pucca* houses.
- *Samagra Awaas Yojana* (SAY): Started as a pilot project in 1999-2000, the SAY is to ensure "integrated provision of shelter, sanitation and drinking water. The underlying philosophy is to provide for convergence of the existing housing, sanitation and water supply schemes with a special emphasis on technology transfer, human resource development and habitat improvement with people's participation."
- *Food for Work Programme:* Started in February 2001, the programme "aims at augmenting food security through wage employment in the drought affected rural areas in eight states" (Gujarat, Chattisgarh, Himachal Pradesh, Madhya Pradesh, Maharashtra, Orissa, Rajasthan and Uttaranchal). "The Centre makes available appropriate quantity of foodgrains free of cost to each of the drought affected states as an additionality under the programme."
- *Annapurna*: Started in 2000 as a 100 per cent Centrally Sponsored Scheme, "it aims at providing food security to meet the requirements of those senior citizens who, though eligible for pension under the National Old Age Pension Scheme, are not getting the same. Foodgrains are provided to the beneficiaries at subsidised rates..."

- *Krishi Shramik Samajik Suraksha Yojana:* Started in 2001, it is a social security scheme for agricultural labourers on hire in the age group of 18 to 60 years.
- *Shiksha Sahayog Yojana:* It gives 'educational allowance' of Rs. 100/- per month to the children of parents living below the poverty line for their education from the 9th to 12th standard.

## Towards Centralisation

One aspect that is striking is that the Centre has come to assume more responsibilities in the social sector because of the centralised planning. Most of the social sector subjects are included in the state's list under the Seventh Schedule in the Constitution. 'Planning' ('Economic and Social Planning') itself is to be found in the Concurrent List. According to Ajit Mozoomdar:

> If the constitutional distribution of functions had to be followed in allocating planning responsibilities, only broad indicative planning would have been feasible, since the exclusive responsibility of the Centre was restricted only to small parts of the productive sectors of the economy, namely mines and minerals, railways, ports and shipping, post and telecommunications, banking and insurance. The states' exclusive areas of responsibility cover many more sectors including agriculture, irrigation, power and roads, besides health and education, urban development and all forms of social welfare[6].

Mozoomdar also highlights the fact that, under the constitutional scheme, States ended up with more responsibilities and the Centre with more resources. But the centralised planning created the requirement to transfer funds to the States. "Until the Third Plan the central financing power was used in the form of scheme-by-scheme allocations to the States. This proved to be increasingly unworkable as well as contentious, and was replaced by block loans and grants to the States."[7] The 'block' transfers of plan funds — in itself a contentious issue — where by "the Planning Commission proposing new investment programmes to be included in the state plans but to be financed wholly or partly by additional assistance from the Centre." The block transfers system has come to be known as the Centrally Sponsored Scheme (CSS).

During the last three decades, the CSS have increased manifold. They in fact doubled only in the 1990s. By the end of the last decade, there were nearly 250 (as per some estimates, 327[8]) CSSs. The

*Approach Paper to the Tenth Five Year Plan (2002-2007)* mentions that "the share of the CSS in the plan budget of the Central Ministries has now increased to 70 per cent against 30 per cent in the early 1980s[9].

## Critique of Centralisation

- ***Ramakrishna Hegde***: " I can understand 'central schemes' and that also to a limited extent. There are central universities. And there are central research institutes. This I can understand. But I could not understand what they actually meant by centrally sponsored schemes for the people of this country."[10]
- ***A.K. Anthony***: Centrally-sponsored schemes had been launched indirectly by 'encroaching' upon Additional Central Assistance (ACA), a good portion of which was costly to the State. He said that the ACA for basic minimum services had been converted into 'de facto' centrally-sponsored schemes under the Prime Minister's Rozgar Yojana, for which sanctions had to be obtained from Central Ministries even on rural housing and roads and, he asked, "was it not odd when the Constitution itself had assigned these responsibilities to local Governments?"[11]
- **Chandrababu Naidu**: The over centralised planning process for state plans under the elaborate procedures established by the Planning Commission is too rigid, elaborate, cumbersome, unnecessary and counterproductive. The States are unable to reflect their priorities in the plan.

  Centrally sponsored schemes (CSS) should be abolished. The money presently earmarked for CSS should be transferred to states as untied grant as part of tax devolution. States are in a better position to design and implement schemes reflecting local needs, priorities and problems.

  The role and responsibilities of the Planning Commission should be downsized. The Commission should be restricted to giving loans for specific projects to be negotiated by each State under a World Bank/IMF type arrangement. The quantum of loans and their terms will be determined by the nature of the project as also the specific economic and financial circumstances of the State much like under the IMF regime. The terms and conditions of loans in various sectors could be used by Centre to signal national priorities.[12]

## CAG Comments

The Comptroller and Auditor General of India studied the implementation of the 'Centrally Sponsored Schemes' and came to the following conclusions:[13]

- Inability of the Union ministries to control the execution of the schemes... the programmes continued to be executed in uncontrolled and open-ended manner without quantitative and qualitative evaluation of delivery.
- The controlling Union ministries confined their role to the provision of budget and release of the funds... rather mechanically.
- The ministries were unable to ensure correctness of the data and facts reported by the state governments. Overstatement of the figures of physical and financial performance by the state governments was rampant.
- The ministry was more concerned with expenditure rather than the attainment of the objectives. Large parts of funds were released in the last month of the financial year, which could not be expected to be spent by the respective state governments during that financial year.
- The 'state governments' attitude to the execution of the programmes was generally indifferent... Misuse of the funds provided for vulnerable sectors and sections of the society was rampant.... The controlling Union ministries had no clue to such misuse.
- Nobody could be held responsible for shortfall in performance, poor delivery of output, wanton abuse of the authority to misuse the funds provided for succor to the victims of calamity, economic upliftment of the poor Scheduled Tribes, eradication of Malaria, sheltering from the suffering of repeated droughts, etc.

The Planning Commission, in its analysis, highlighted the following problems:[14]

- There are too many schemes to be monitored, the Divisional Commissioner, Kanpur identified 167 schemes being run at the block level...It was impossible, he felt, for the BDO to keep effective control on their proper execution.
- A number of plan schemes are in operation with similar objectives targeting the same population... For every new scheme, there is a tendency to develop new implementation machinery at the national, state and district levels. There are schemes that are no longer productive, but still continue. All this calls for a lot of consolidation and convergence.
- Ministries are hesitant to monitor state sector schemes, although it may have important bearing on the sector with which the central Ministry is concerned... If financial monitoring is weak, the impact of funds on performance is hardly studied, and sustainability is never questioned!
- Delayed evaluation serves little purpose, as officers have a short time perspective. Independent assessment by academics that is not sponsored by Ministry ever reaches the Ministry.
- There is unwillingness to accept poor performance, for fear of being questioned by Parliament or adverse press publicity. Senior officers feel that they would be taken to task if failure were admitted. Hence, a vested interest develops up at the top to conceal shortcomings, and not encourage independent evaluation.
- Most schemes follow a blue print and top-down approach, with little flexibility given to field staff. Any change in the scheme requires approval from GoI which is time consuming.
- States do not release the counterpart funds in time, leading to uncertainty about the availability of funds at the field level. Even the release of GoI funds to the field is held up for several reasons. First, the states have to get legislative approval for GoI schemes, which takes time. Second, states do not attach importance to spending on CSSs, and thus are in no hurry to sanction expenditure. And third, fiscal problems at the state level force the states to divert GoI funds for paying salaries.
- Much time is spent by state government officials in collecting district, and sometimes block level information, and little in

analysis. Officers at all levels spend a great deal of time in collecting and submitting information, but these are not used for taking corrective and remedial action, but only for forwarding it to a higher level, as they have no power to change the nature of CSSs.

- Little time is left for officers to initiate reforms or change schemes. With the best of commitment, it often takes two years to get a scheme changed.

## Restructuring CSSs

The NDC (National Development Council) Committee on Transfer of Centrally Sponsored Schemes (CSS) met on August 21, 2002 under the Chairmanship of Deputy Chairman, Planning Commission. The representatives of the states and concerned central ministries were apprised of the exercise that had been undertaken for the Tenth Five Year Plan in the Planning Commission to identify the Centrally Sponsored Schemes that could be transferred to the States, weeded out and merged. There were 360 CSS in existence prior to the exercise with a Ninth Plan Outlay of about Rs. 99,000 crore. Out of these, 49 CSS have been identified for discontinuation and 161 CSS would be merged into 53 Centrally Sponsored Schemes (CSS). Nine CSS have been identified for transfer to the States. As a result of this exercise, 194 CSS would be in operation in the Tenth Plan. The meeting also discussed how to promote greater interaction amongst the Planning Commission, the Central Ministries and the State Governments for efficient utilization of funds and effective implementation of CSS. "The States also opined that the guidelines of the CSS were quite rigid and did not take into account the regional variations and priorities of the State Governments, as such, there is a need to introduce greater flexibility in the guidelines of the CSS."[15]

## Outlays and Expenditure on Social Services[16]

(Rs. Crore)

| *Plan Period* | | *Welfare of SCs, STs and OBCs* | *Social Security & Welfare, Women & Child Development (WCD)* | *Women & Child Development (WCD)* |
|---|---|---|---|---|
| First Plan | Outlay | 39.00 | 5.00 | * |
| (1951-56) | Actuals | 30.00 | 1.60 | |
| Second Plan | Outlay | 90.00 | 29.00 | * |
| (1956-61) | Actuals | 79.00 | 13.40 | |
| Third Plan | Outlay | 114.00 | 28.00 | * |
| (1961-66) | Actuals | 99.14 | 19.14 | |
| Annual Plan | Outlay | 62.00 | 12.08 | * |
| (1966-69) | Actuals | 68.49 | 7.38 | |
| Fourth Plan | Outlay | 171.29 | 41.38 | * |
| (1969-74) | Actuals | 141.00 | | |
| Fifth Plan | Outlay | 227.89 | 63.53 | * |
| (1974-78) | Actuals | 226.00 | | |
| Annual Plan | Outlay | 99.09 | 20.11 | * |
| (1978-79) | Actuals | 99.94 | | |
| Annual Plan | Outlay | 98.84 | 18.32 | * |
| (1979-80) | Actuals | 86.40 | | |
| Sixth Plan | Outlay | 1,479.00 | 150.00 | * |
| (1980-85) | Actuals | 1,480.00 | | |
| Seventh Plan | Outlay | 3,206.55 | 799.97 | * |
| (1985-90) | Actuals | 3,567.60 | | |
| Annual Plan | Outlay | 1,039.98 | | * |
| (1990-91) | Actuals | 838.75 | | |
| Annual Plan | Outlay | 752.22 | * | |
| (1991-92) | Actuals | | | * |
| Eighth Plan | Outlay | 7,266.26 | 375.00 | 2,010.00 |
| (1992-97) | Actuals | 293.43 | | 3,359.81 |
| Ninth Plan (1997-2002) | Outlay | 16,999.93 | 7,810.42 | |

Note: *: Included in Social Security & Welfare and Women & Child Development.

### *The Tenth Plan Approach to Social Sector*[17]

- SGSY should be transformed into a micro-finance programme to be run by the banks and other financial institutions, with no subsidy.
- Funds to *gram sabhas* should be extended only when the people contribute, either in cash or in kind, say 15 per cent in normal

blocks and 5 per cent in tribal/poor blocks. This will instill a sense of ownership in the community.

- There should be single wage employment programme to be run only in areas of distress. The focus should be on undertaking productive works and their maintenance, such as rural roads, watershed development, rejuvenation of tanks, afforestation, irrigation and drainage. The payment of wages should be mainly in the form of foodgrains with some cash component. This will improve self-targetting.
- Rural development funds should also be used for enhancing the budgetary allocation of successful rural development schemes that are being run by state governments, or for meeting the state contribution for donor assisted programmes for poverty alleviation.
- Grassroot women's groups should be empowered and encouraged to implement selected poverty alleviation schemes, particularly food-for-work schemes in areas affected by natural disasters.
- Special efforts should be made to strengthen the economy of the marginal and small farmers, forest produce gatherers, artisans, unskilled workers etc. The poor should not merely benefit from growth generated elsewhere, they should contribute to growth.
- Special efforts must be made to encourage development of tiny and village industries suited for rural areas to provide non-farm employment in rural areas.

## Report of Working Group on Strengthening Monitoring and Evaluation System for the Social Sector Development Schemes in the Country.[18]

*Summary of Recommendations*

1. Professionals need to be associated with the monitoring team to raise the quality of monitoring and evaluation of social sector programmes. Economists, engineers, sociologists and accountants should form part of monitoring teams.

2. For effective monitoring, diversion of staff sanctioned for monitoring to other divisions/sections of the Ministries and the State Governments should be stopped.
3. It is desired that District Collector, who is responsible for implementing social sector programmes in a district, should have minimum stay of three years in district so that he concentrates fully on the implementation of social sector policies and programmes.
4. Delivery system designed for the social sector schemes should provide for inherent monitoring system envisaging transparency in discussing reactions, clarifying doubts, etc. through face to face communication, strengthening the understanding and motivation of field workers at the village level through training and appropriate incentives with promotional opportunities should also be ensured.
5. Micro level planning may be strengthened. Individual and family based plans need to be formulated keeping in view, their distinct interests and talents.
6. Currently, follow-up action by the functionaries at grass root level leaves much to be desired. They focus more on the achievement of allocated financial and physical targets. What is urgently required is to make them pay attention to the actual outcome benefits derived by the beneficiaries.
7. Under social sector programmes, like, Jawahar Gram Samridhi Yojana, Swarnjayanti Gram Swarojgar Yojana, Employment Assurance Scheme etc. creation of assets takes place through construction of roads, watersheds, *panchayat ghars*, etc. The programmes have not earmarked funds for maintenance of these assets. Moreover, there has been no monitoring by the Ministries and the State Governments of the conditions of such assets created through implementation of social sector programmes. There is a need to have an effective monitoring of the conditions of the assets created.
8. The air of secrecy that very often prevails in Government functioning needs to be lifted if monitoring of programmes is to be effective. There is a need to share information and make the system more transparent. Transparency would facilitate

faster reforms and make the administration more responsive and performance orientated.

9. Accountability in the monitoring process is very weak. The fear of adverse remarks has prevented officials from reporting poor performances. Concealment of shortcomings and manipulation of data have been resorted to, to cover poor performance. Due to concealment of weaknesses in programmes, appropriate corrective actions are not taken.

10. Corrective measures suggested by the monitoring and evaluation units should be monitored to improve the implementation of the programmes. Each State should constitute a committee headed by the Chief Minister or the Chief Secretary to monitor and review the follow-up action on the monitoring and evaluation reports.

11. Preparation of social maps (i.e. poverty, illiteracy, inverse sex-ratio, morbidity, malnutrition etc. severally and by super-imposition) – scheme-wise and their integration (on selective basis) for visual effect and scrutiny by the lay public and elected representatives for debate, discussion, verification and validation, need to be introduced to improve monitoring of social sector programmes.

12. Generalized objectives of all programmes and schemes being implemented need to be broken down into specific goals from the point of view of evaluation and monitoring. Care should be taken to see that the evaluation and monitoring groups take note of them from the data generated by other agencies, both official and non-official, in the same or allied sectors. Primary data generated by different agencies should be used to cross-check the progress as well as the impact of these schemes.

13. Rationalization of objectives, specification of goals/sub-goals, their operationalisation in terms of variables, preparation of a base-line/preparedness profile, identification of target group, existing or new organisation of people at the local level, process of intervention or service delivery, beneficiary and citizen participation, change over time in the socio-economic status of target groups (outcome/impact), conflicts and their resolution during implementation of a scheme, bottlenecks

and their correction, transparency of results and future leads, comparison of this data with those of other schemes in terms of opportunity, access, input, use, client satisfaction, social environment and strains, cost-effectiveness, created assets infrastructure/equipment and impact etc. should deserve attention.

14. The State Plan Division of the Planning Commission, who recommends release of funds to the States and Union territories should, before releasing funds in a financial year to the States, thoroughly monitor and evaluate the programmes implemented by the State in the preceding year to a financial year. Similarly, the other Sectoral Divisions of the Planning Commission should thoroughly monitor and review the performance of the administrative Ministries before recommending release of funds to the Ministries for a particular scheme. Moreover, these Divisions should also monitor and ensure that the plan goals formulated by the Governments are being achieved through the implementation of social sector schemes.
15. Performance-based system of releasing funds to States needs to be in place if monitoring is to play a role in improving implementation of social sector schemes. Release of funds must be linked with performance in the field.
16. To improve flow of information to the monitoring agencies statutory provisions requiring Ministries/States to supply the requisite information to them may be envisaged. This would ensure that monitoring units get the required information and time is not wasted in collecting data from the Ministries/ States on the schemes being implemented by them.
17. To make monitoring of the social sector programmes/anti-poverty programmes more meaningful, the expenditure incurred on each programme by the implementing agencies should also be monitored so that the unit cost of delivery is ascertained and comparison between States and various implementing agencies can be worked out. The monthly ranking of the State Governments in effecting delivery of the programmes should also take into account their unit cost.

18. It is suggested that all the social sector schemes before the start of the Tenth Plan should be reviewed by the Planning Commission. Schemes which have become outdated or schemes which are duplicate in nature being implemented by more than one Ministry for the same goals should be scrapped/amalgamated. We should have very few schemes in the social sector so that their monitoring and evaluation can be done focally and thoroughly.
19. For successful implementation of social sector programmes, participation of various stakeholders is essential. Widespread awareness about the programmes among the voluntary agencies, groups of beneficiaries, etc. would be desirable. The top down approach in Planning and Implementation has led to formulation of schemes without assessment of the need of the people.
20. States should delegate more powers to the *Panchayats* for successful implementation of the programmes at the village/block level. Monitoring should be made an essential feature in the working of these local bodies, which would ensure that programmes are implemented properly. These bodies may be made accountable for monitoring all programmes in their respective areas.
21. Participation of Subordinate and attached Ministerial Institutions, Non-Governmental Organisations, Universities and Research Institutions in formulation and monitoring of programmes may be encouraged. They may be allowed to contribute their views in designing the programmes which they have reviewed. Importance may be attached to monitoring reports of these bodies by the various ministries/departments of the Government.
22. The tentative targets for the programmes should be fixed by the respective ministries by the end of March preceding the onset of the financial year so that the State Governments can further work out and plan their actions to achieve the Statewise/District-wise/Block-wise and Village level targets. The targets should be realistic and match with the financial allocations made to the States/UTs. Moreover, the final targets for the States and the UTs should be confirmed and conveyed

by the administrative ministries by 31$^{st}$ May of the financial year. In no case, the final targets should be revised and changed to suit the achievement of the States for the various programmes.

23. Scientific method is central to all innovation and progress. This essentially means experimentation, i.e., ceaseless trial and many an error. If we punish honest error sooner rather than later, all efforts for improvement will also cease. This is one of the major maladies of our delivery systems.

24. Re-orientation of present monitoring system from quantitative to qualitative has to be made in order to capture the complete picture of development in the social sector. Development of appropriate indicators is necessary for making the impact of a programme visible in various stages of the programme cycle. Indicators should comprise input indicators, output indicators and impact indicators. Each social sector needs to develop appropriate indicators to assess the qualitative changes made by different programmes.

25. Training should be made an important organisational aspect of monitoring development. All staff should be adequately trained, particularly in modern methods of information-management. Training in information technology significantly raises the computer capabilities of monitoring staff. Training of monitoring officials should be a mixture of training in technology as well as in aspects of general management. It is suggested that in the 10$^{th}$ Plan a training institute on monitoring and evaluation should be set up at the national level.

26. Increase in the number of social sector schemes being implemented by the Ministries/State Governments has given rise to the need to have effective information system to monitor these programmes. Use of computers in information management has, therefore, become essential. Use of information technology would speed up information between field units and the nodal Ministries, thereby improving the monitoring of the programmes. Investment in development of computer network and training of staff in the use of IT needs to be given continued importance during the 10$^{th}$ Plan period.

27. Effective monitoring depends on timely and correct information flow from the primary source to the monitoring unit. To enable a speedy flow of information, network covering all the villages and blocks of the country needs to be developed.
28. Data collection on paper formats has to be replaced by computerised formats to enable instant data transmission and bring down time spent in entering data into computers. Computer compatible formats have to be designed so that information can be transmitted instantly.
29. Introduction of hand held computer (Palmtop) to monitoring units in the field to improve data collection and transmission may be actively considered to improve monitoring at the grassroots level.
30. Local participation in monitoring and evaluation is suggested to counter the traditional top down approach to monitoring and evaluation. It has been seen that the traditional approach does not give a clear picture of the various schemes and projects being monitored. The conventional monitoring techniques have proved costly and ineffective in terms of measuring and assessing programme achievements. Bottom up strategy that employs participatory methodologies should be encouraged.
31. The decentralization of planning envisaged with the implementation of the 73$^{rd}$ and 74$^{th}$ Constitution (Amendment) Acts empowering *Panchayats* and local bodies must be implemented in letter and spirit. These bodies must be actively involved in the planning, designing and monitoring of all programmes at the grassroots level for better delivery.
32. *Panchayats* and urban local bodies may be empowered to plan, implement, supervise and coordinate subjects falling in the 11$^{th}$ Schedule of the Constitution.
33. To ensure monitoring at the grassroot level, *Panchayats* and local bodies need to be in existence. Elections to these bodies should be held timely and fairly.
34. To strengthen participatory monitoring at the grassroot level, Non-Governmental Organizations may be included in the

monitoring process. Official recognition may be granted to reports submitted by these bodies. Funding of these bodies to undertake monitoring may be made a regular feature by ministries involved in social sector programmes.

35. It is high time that the huge expertise and academic manpower available with universities, research institutions, etc. are utilised for monitoring the social sector programmes. Professionals/academics from various fields should be involved in designing the monitoring systems and carrying out evaluation studies. Research in social sector programmes may be encouraged in these institutes. Monitoring and evaluation studies carried out by the universities/institutes should be funded by the concerned ministries/State Governments.

36. To have an effective monitoring and evaluation system it is necessary that a Central Institution to coordinate between the different agencies should be in place. Presently, monitoring is being done by the nodal ministries, Planning Commission, Ministry of Statistics & Programme Implementation and monitoring bodies at the State level. There is no coordination among these various monitoring bodies. Reports and evaluation studies done by various monitoring bodies are not shared among themselves.

37. The existing arrangement of setting targets by the Planning Commission and release of funds by the Ministry of Finance has led to confusion among most ministries. Targets are fixed without taking into consideration the funds available for the programmes. This has led to ministries/States not achieving their targets due to paucity of funds. A suitable mechanism may be evolved to ensure that adequate funds are made available for achieving the targets.

38. The State Governments should have review committees at state, district and block levels to assess the performance of the social sector programmes.

39. Review of all programmes through monitoring should be made compulsory before Annual Plan meetings. Each programme should be properly evaluated before the new budget estimates for these programmes are approved.

## Conclusion

If the preceding analysis, instead of bringing some clarity, leads to more confusion, it is because of the way the social sector has evolved over the decades into what it is today. It is a sector of probably a dozen areas split into hundreds of schemes, funded mostly at national level and implemented at several layers of governance. There is a clear divorce of authority from accountability. First, there is too much centralization of financial powers in the hands of the Centre. Second, in exercising its financial clout, the Centre may formulate or 'sponsor' schemes but it is in no position to monitor them. Third, states regard central assistance inadequate and more often divert the funds for book-keeping, thus defeating the purpose of these schemes. Fourth, though there is consensus over the existing corruption, mismanagement, diversion of funds, etc., nobody is held accountable. Fifth, public disinterest due to obvious reasons, and local politics and prejudices are depriving the system of participatory character.

The system could have withstood one or two of the above lacunae but it is afflicted with all of them and much more. A clear picture may emerge only after the ongoing restructuring of social sector schemes is completed. However, the exercise appears to be falling short of the much-needed overhaul. Therefore, even after the 'restructuring', there are bound to be significant problems with the sector. The issue is also intrinsically linked with federalism and democratic decentralisation. Nothing concrete is happening with regard to these two areas, though it is almost ten years since the 73$^{rd}$ and 74$^{th}$ amendments to the Constitution were enacted.

## ANNEXURE

### *The Most Upto-Date List of the Centrally Sponsored Schemes (CSS)*

| *Sl. No* | *Name of the Centrally Sponsored Schemes (CSS)* |
|---|---|
| | **Department of Agriculture, Cooperation & Extension, MINISTRY OF AGRICULTURE** |
| 1. | Assistance to Cooperatives of Weaker Sections |
| 2. | Assistance to Women Cooperatives |
| 3. | Special Scheme for SCs and STs |
| 4. | Reclaimation of Alakli (Usar) Soils |
| 5. | Oilseeds Production Programme |
| 6. | National Pulses Development Programme |
| 7. | Oil Palm Development Programme |
| 8. | National Wasteland Development Project for Rainfed Areas |
| 9. | Improvement of Crop Statistics (ICS) |
| 10. | Timely Reporting of Estimates of Area & Production of Principal Crops |
| 11. | Establishment of an Agency for Reporting of Agricultural Statistics (EARAS) |
| 12. | Crop Estimation Survey on Fruits, Vegetables & Minor Crops |
| 13. | Livestock Census |
| 14. | Accelerated Maize Development Programme |
| 15. | Assistance to Cooperative Credit Institutions in Under-Developed States & Special Areas (Non-Overdue Cover) |
| 16. | Agricultural Credit Stabilisation Fund |
| 17. | Assistance to Cooperative Marketing, Processing, Storage in Under-Developed States and UTs |
| 18. | Share Capital Participation in Cooperative Sugar Factories |
| 19. | Share Capital Participation in Cooperative Spinning Mills (Growers) |
| 20. | Sustainable Development of Sugarcane-Based Cropping System |
| 21. | Integrated Cereals Development Programme in Rice-Based Cropping System Areas (ICDP-Rice) |
| 22. | Integrated Cereals Development Programme in Wheat-Based Cropping System Areas (ICDP-Wheat) |
| 23. | Integrated Cereals Development Programme in Coarse Cereal—Based Cropping System Areas (ICDP-Coarse Cereals) |
| 24. | Special Jute Development Programme |
| 25. | Intensive Cotton Development Programme |
| 26. | Technology Mission for Cotton Development |
| 27. | Balanced & Integrated Use of Fertilizers |
| 28. | Promotion of Agricultural Mechanisation among Small Farmers |
| 29. | Integrated Programme for Development of Spices |

30. Integrated Development of Cashewnet
31. Use of Plastics in Agriculture
32. Soil Conservation in Catchment of River Valley Projects
33. Integrated Watershed Development in Flood-Prone Rivers

---

**Department of Animal Husbandry and Dairying, MINISTRY OF AGRICULTURE**

---

34. Progeny Testing Programme
35. Extension of Frozen Technology
36. National Bull Production Programme
37. Assistance to States for Feed Fodder Development
38. Professional Efficiency Development
39. National Ram/Buck Production Programme
40. Development & Preservation of Pack Animals
41. Assistance to States for Integrated Piggery Development
42. Freshwater Aqua-culture
43. Fish Harbour facilities at Minor Ports
44. Integrated Brackish Water Development
45. Development of Coastal Marine Fisheries
46. Welfare of Fishermen
47. Improvement of Slaughter Houses
48. Establishment of Carcass Utilisation Centres/Flaying Units
49. National Project on Rinderpest Eradication
50. Systematic Control of Animal Diseases
51. Foot & Mouth Disease
52. Animal Diseases Surveillance
53. Integrated Sample Surveys for Estimation of Major Livestock Products

---

**Department of Higher & Secondary Education, HRD MINISTRY**

---

54. Environment Orientation to School Children
55. Improvement of Science Education in Schools
56. Assistance to NGOs for Strengthening of Hostel Facilities for Girls
57. Integrated Education for Disabled Children
58. Education Technology
59. Computer Education in Schools (Class)
60. Vocationalisation of Education
61. Promotion of Yoga

---

**Department of Elementary Education, HRD MINISTRY**

---

62. Strengthening of Administrative Structure
63. Nutritional Support to Primary Education (Mid-Day Meals)

64. (I) Post Literacy and Continuing Education
(II) Special Programme for Eradication of Illiteracy
65. Appointment of Urdu Teachers
66. Operation Blackboard
67. Teacher Education
68. Non-Formal Education (Elementary)
69. Rural Functional Literacy Project
70. Appointment of Hindi Teachers

**Department of Family Welfare**

71. National Family Welfare Programme

**Department of Food & Consumer Affairs**

72. Purchase of Mobile Vans/Trucks
73. Construction of Godowns

**Department of Health**

74. National Malaria Eradication Programme
75. National Leprosy Eradication Programme
76. National TB Control Programme
77. National Programme of Prevention of Blindness
78. National AIDS Control Programme
79. Assistance for Augmentation of Drug Testing Facilities in the States (Strengthening of State Drug Analytical Laboratories)
80. Drug Inspectorate Staff in Various States/UTs (Strengthening of State Drug Control Organisations)
81. Financial Assistance to the States for Strengthening Food Testing Laboratories
82. Assistance for Upgradation of Post Graduates
83. National Guineaworm Eradication Programme

**Department of Industrial Development**

84. Growth Centres Schemes
85. Transport Subsidy Scheme
86. Capital Investment Subsidy Schemes (North East Region)
87. Interest Subsidy Scheme (North East Region)

**Department of Justice, Law & Company Affairs**

88. Development of Infrastructural Facilities for the Judiciary
89. Setting up of Special Courts for Trial of Offences under the Narcotic Drugs and Psychotropic Substances Act, 1955 (NDPS)

### Department of Youth Affairs

90. Establishment and Development of Mounteneering Institutes
91. National Service Scheme (NSS)
92. Games and Sports in Colleges and Universities

### Department of Women & Child Development

93. Indira Mahila Yojana
94. Integrated Child Development Schemes (ICDS)
95. World Bank-Assisted ICDS Projects
96. Rural Women's Development and Employment Project
97. National Resource Centre for Women

### MINISTRY OF COMMERCE

98. Export Promotion Industrial Park

### MINISTRY OF ENVIRONMENT AND FORESTS

99. Seed Development Agencies
100. Paryavaran Sudhar Pariyojana — Environment Improvement and Dissemination Schemes
101. Fuel Wood/Fodder Projects
102. Aerial Seeding
103. Non-Timber Forest Produce including Medicinal Plants
104. Promotion of Construction of Common Effluent Treatment Plants (CETP) for Clusters of Small Scale Industrial Units
105. Industrial Pollution Control Projects
106. Biosphere Reserves
107. Conservation and Management of Mangroves
108. Conservation and Management of wetlands
109. Ganga Action Plan Phase-I
110. Ganga Action Plan Phase-II
111. National River Action Plan
112. Association of Scheduled Tribes and Rural Poor in Regeneration of Degraded Forests
113. Introduction of Modern Forest Fire Control Methods
114. Development of National Parks and Sanctuaries
115. Project Tiger
116. Beneficiary-Oriented Scheme for Tribal Development
117. Eco-development around Sanctuaries and National Parks including Tiger Reserves
118. Project Elephant
119. Integrated Afforestation and Eco-development Project

120. Taj Protection Mission

**MINISTRY OF LABOUR**

121. World Bank-Aided Schemes
122. Rehabilitation of Bonded Labour

**MINISTRY OF NON-CONVENTIONAL ENERGY SOURCES**

123. National Programme on Improved Chulha
124. Institutional/Community Biogas Plant Programme
125. Integrated Rural Energy Programme
126. National Project on Biogas Development
127. Solar Photovoltaic Lantern/Domestic Lighting Programme
128. Small Hydro Power Programme

**MINISTRY OF POWER**

129. Inter-State Transmission

**MINISTRY OF RURAL DEVELOPMENT**

130. Rural Water Supply Programme
131. Rural Sanitation Programme
132. Jawahar Gram Samrighi Yojana (Earlier JRY)
133. Employment Assurance Scheme
134. Indira Awas Yojana
135. Strengthening of State Training Centres
136. Strengthening of Extension Training Centres
137. Roads in Special Problem Areas
138. National Social Assistance Programme
139. Drought-Prone Area Programme
140. Desert Development Programme
141. Computerisation of Land Records
142. Strengthening of Revenue Administration and Updating of Land Records
143. Swarnjayanti Gram Swarozgar Yojana (Earlier IRDP, etc.,)
144. District Rural Development Agencies (DRDAs) Administration

**MINISTRY OF SOCIAL JUSTICE AND EMPOWERMENT**

145. Scheduled Caste Development Corporation
146. Boys Hostels for SCs
147. Boys Hostels for STs
148. Girls Hostels for SCs
149. Girls Hostels for STs
150. Book-Banks for SC/ST Students

151. Coaching and Allied Scheme
152. Post-Matric Scholarship for SC/ST Students
153. Pre-Matric Scholarship for Children of those Engaged in Unclean Occupations
154. Ashram Schools for STs
155. Grants to Tribal Research Institutes and Award of Research Fellowships
156. National Scheme of Liberation and Rehabilitation of Scavengers
157. Implementation of the Protection of Civil Rights Act, 1965 and SC/ST (Prevention of Atrocities Act), 1989
158. Employment of Handicapped
159. Scheme of Prevention and Control of Juvenile Social Maladjustment
160. Post-Matric Scholarships for OBCs
161. Pre-Matric Scholarships for OBCs
162. Hostels for OBC Boys and Girl Students
163. Residential Schools for OBC Boys and Girl Students

---

**MINISTRY OF SURFACE TRANSPORT**

---

164. Economic and Interstate Importance (E&I):
    a) Inter-State Roads/Bridges;
    b) Roads/Bridges of Economic Importance
165. Inland Water Transportation Schemes Implemented by the States

---

**MINISTRY OF TEXTILES**

---

166. Schemes for Handloom Export
167. Project Package — All States and North East
168. Handloom Development Centres/Quality Dyeing Units
169. Welfare Schemes: Workshed cum Housing
170. Group Insurance
171. Thrift Fund
172. Loans to State Governments (for Handloom Weavers)

---

**MINISTRY OF URBAN AFFAIRS AND POVERTY ALLEVIATION**

---

173. Urban Low Cost Sanitation Scheme for Liberation of Scavenges
174. Accelerated Urban Water Supply Programme for Towns with Population less than 20000
175. Integrated Development of Small and Medium Towns
176. Mega-City Scheme
177. Contribution to National Capital Region Planning Board
178. Contribution to Urban Transport Consortium Fund
179. Swarna Jayanti Shahri Rozgar Yojana (Earlier NRY+UBSP+PMIUPEP)

---

| MINISTRY OF WATER RESOURCES | |
|---|---|
| 180. | Command Area Development Programme |
| 181. | Central Loan Assistance to Government of Assam |
| 182. | Rationalisation of Minor Irrigation Statistics |
| 183. | Flood Proofing Programme in North Bihar |
| 184. | Critical Anti-Erosion Works in Coastal States |
| 185. | Raising and Strengthening of Embankments along Kosi and Gandak |

Note: Courtesy Dr. Rohini Nayyar, Adviser (Rural Development) Planning Commission, New Delhi

## Notes

1 *Annual Report 2001-2002*, Ministry of Statistics and Programme Implementation (New Delhi: Government of India, 2002), p. 3. and *Monthly Progress Report, April-2002: The Twenty Point Programme-1986*, Ministry of Statistics and Programme Implementation (New Delhi: Government of India, 2002)

2 *Economic Survey 2001-2002* (New Delhi: Government of India, 2002), pp. 234-268.

3 The entire section has been taken from *Economic Survey ibid.*, pp. 243-4.

4 Rohini Nayyar (unpublished).

5 *Ibid.*

6 Ajit Mozoomdar, "The Rise and Decline of Development Planning in India", in Terrence J. Byres, ed., *The State and Development Planning in India*, pp. 99-100.

7 *Ibid.*

8 Mamata Singh, "Govt may eliminate 900 central sector schemes", February 2, 2002, www.rediff.com. (http://www.rediff.com/money/2002/feb/02bud.htm). According to the article, there are 900 central schemes, distinct from the CSSs.

9 *Approach Paper to the Tenth Five Year Plan (2002-2007)* (New Delhi: Planning Commission, Government of India, September 2001), p. 49.

10 Ramakrishna Hegde, "Local-Self Government in Karnataka: Planning From Below", in Malcolm S. Adiseshiah *et al*, *Decentralised planning and Panchayat Raj* Proceeding of the D.T. Lakdawala Memorial Symposium held on September 24, 1992 (New Delhi: Concept Publishing Company for the Institute of Social Sciences, 1994), p. 20.

11 CM seeks lower interest rates, *The Hindu* September 2, 2002. (http://www.hinduonnet.com/thehindu/2001/09/02/stories/0402211d.htm).

12 From the Speech at the Meeting of the Inter-State Council in 1997. (http://www.andhrapradesh.com/apwebsite/ourcm/speech_interstatemeeting.html)

13 Cited in the *Approach Paper to the Tenth Five Year Plan (2002-2007)* (New Delhi: Planning Commission, Government of India, September 2001), pp. 47-49. [The CAG's criticisms are taken verbatim.]

14 *Ibid.*

15 Meeting of the NDC Committee on the Transfer of Centrally Sponsored Schemes (CSS), see http://planningcommission.nic.in/neaug.htm#aug8

16 *Indian Planning Experience: A Statistical Profile* (New Delhi: Planning Commission, 2001), p. 178.

17 *Approach Paper to the Tenth Five Year Plan (2002-2007), pp.29-30.*

18 Source: http://planningcommission.nic.in/reports/peoreport/peo/wrkg_strnthing.pdf [Taken verbatim.]

# 12

## The State of India's Education

### *A Survey of Literature*

PAROMITA SHASTRI

Education strengthens the multiple dimensions of freedom from fear and freedom from want. The Constitution of India (1950) says: "The State shall endeavour to provide within a period of ten years from the commencement of this Constitution, for free and compulsory education for all children until they complete the age of fourteen years." Over half a century later, India still has half of its children, around 83 million, out of school. Even if we take into account the official enrollment figure of 109 million of 1995-96, there are still 50 million children out of school, most of them in the six states of Bihar, Madhya Pradesh, Uttar Pradesh, Rajasthan, Andhra Pradesh and West Bengal. This is despite two national policies on education in 1968 and 1986, but it took 46 years after independence to introduce a law to make education a fundamental right for children up to 14 years. In November 2001, Parliament passed the 93$^{rd}$ amendment ensuring all children from age 6-14 in classes I-VIII, the right to elementary education.

But the gap between children's rights and ground realities remains vast. Even as a child's right to education is now justiciable, we are still very far from the goal of Universal Elementary Education (UEE), the latest deadline for which is end of Tenth Plan. The World Conference on Education for all, held at Jomtien, Thailand, in 1990, called for universal access to and completion of primary education by the year 2000. The Special Session on Children in United Nations General Assembly in May 2002 has further extended the commitment and committed "high priority to ensuring by 2015 that all children have access to complete primary education that is free, compulsory and of good quality". The Tenth Plan programme for UEE, *Sarva Shiksha Abhiyan,* marks the goal of Universal Primary Education (6-10 years) as 2005 and that of UEE as 2010. The nation has also set itself a deadline for achieving full literacy by 2005. This would mean covering all children of 6-14 years either through the school system or by non-formal methods with comparable standards. It would also mean the acquisition of functional literacy by more than 100 million adults of 15-35 years.

The government says that to implement the goals of UEE or education for all (EFA), which were also the goals of the Ninth Plan, it would require an extra 0.5 to 1 per cent of India's GDP every year for the next five years, money that will be certainly difficult to obtain. Against the world average of 5 per cent, India currently, and very inefficiently, spends about 3.4 per cent of GDP on education. By contrast, China has achieved much more by spending only 2.6 per cent of its GNP. Only 16 per cent of its population aged 15 years and above is illiterate as against India's 43 per cent.[1] Among states, expenditure on education ranges around 2.5 per cent of SDP, with a few exceptions (Kerala spends 6 per cent). Plan funds take care of most of the spending on education, and half of this is devoted to elementary education, where delivery and utilisation of funds have often been compared to carrying water in a leaking bucket. As of now, even the implementation of the 93rd constitutional amendment is being delayed ostensibly because of funds crunch. There have been several estimates of the total funds required to give education to all[2] from time to time, including simulation studies by the World Bank.[3] According to latest estimates, by the *Tapas Majumdar Committee* in 2001, assuming 1996 prices, an extra spending of Rs. 14,000 crore every year is needed for 10 years to achieve UEE. This will involve raising the education budget to 6 per cent of GDP, which the committee feels is easily achievable and will just need tightening expenditure. But since India has ratified international treaties like the Convention of the Rights of the Child, which define the child as one up to 18 years, this estimate will easily balloon.

**How much for Education for all**

What does the government actually need to achieve its goal of universal elementary education? There have been several such estimates, and some notable efforts to summarise India's initiatives and issues on the economics of education include those by J.G. Tilak and several other studies by the National Institute of Educational Planning and Administration (NIEPA). The M.R. Saikia Committee, 1997, which looked into the feasibility of making education a fundamental right, reported an average expenditure per student in classes I-VIII in 1995-96 to be Rs. 948 per annum. It recommended an additional investment of Rs. 40,000 crore in the next five years to ensure education for all children out of school. According to the Tapas Majumdar Committee (2001), at 1996 prices, an extra spending of Rs. 14,000 crore every year is needed for 10 years. This will involve raising the education budget to 6 per cent of GDP but won't actually require much hardship. To take one example, minimising subsidies that don't actually benefit the poor will release money to raise the education budget.

As a result, even as we have implemented one part of the promise, a significant part may remain unfulfilled for quite some years. Close to 90 per cent of schools in India are government schools where fees are waived till the upper primary level, yet education is not free. In his preface to the Pratichi Trust Education Report, Nobel Laureate Amartya Sen says: "In effect, successful primary education has ceased to be free, and this is nothing less than a violation of a basic right guaranteed by the Constitution. It is also an immensely discriminating system, in which the foundational principle of equal entitlement to primary education is violated, against the interests of children from the poorer and less privileged families." It would be pertinent here to remember that in 1930, Mahatma Gandhi had warned against a British system of education saying that if such a system was continued, it wouldn't be possible to achieve universal primary education even in the next 100 years. He said: "This poor country of mine is ill able to sustain such an expensive method of education, our state would revive old village school master and dot every village with a school both for boys and girls..."

All this is not to undermine the importance of what has been achieved. Our elementary education system is the second largest in the world with 150 million children of 6-14 years enrolled and 3 million odd teachers. There are close to 9 lakh educational institutions of all kinds. This shows reasonable progress compared to the situation right after independence, when there were 1.4 lakh primary schools, 12,899 middle/secondary schools, 20 universities and 591 colleges. Enrollment in primary schools was only 36 per cent of the school-going population of 6-11 years. Literacy was 16.67 per cent. The education system was beset with many problems — few institutions, regional imbalance, gender disparities, absence of vocational and technical education, lack of uniform curricula and emphasis on English education. But increasingly, Indian policymakers have had to run faster to keep up with even this modest rate of progress. Despite an increase in literacy to 62 per cent, in absolute numbers India still accounts for one-third of the world's illiterates. While the world is talking of a minimum of 10 to 12 years of education for all, India continues to struggle with five years of primary schooling and a little over two-thirds of our children complete that basic cycle.

There is also a raging debate about the desirability and efficacy of the education system that has evolved in the past 40 odd years. As educationist Yash Pal said recently[4]: "Education does not comprise only of textbooks that are read to the class by teachers. That is the least important component. Education is a transaction between the teacher and the student and building on the unexpected entanglements with the environment and the unpredictable mind of the young."

Several committee and commissions that have gone into education from time to time have found that lack of political will and the rigidity of the bureaucracy are the major stumbling blocks to providing an education that is relevant, meaningful and convergent with broader development issues. In April 2000, the World Education Forum was convened in Dakar, Senegal, to review the achievements of the last decade and find out how far the Jomtien commitments had been met. The India Report was not only viewed as a stocktaking exercise, but also as a base for future planning. The report identified the following goals: a holistic view of basic education with greater linkages between pre-school, primary, non-formal and adult education;

improved access for deprived sections; quality improvement; community participation and involvement of NGOs; decentralisation in education management and increasing financial support. In the nineties, the findings of most review committees and village-people surveys point to the fact that these goals could never have been or can be at all achieved in the present government school and curriculum-led framework. The consensus seems to be that there is an urgent need to radically change the orientation, contextual framework and priorities of the Indian education system.

But first, the history. After independence, the government convened two conferences in January 1948 — the Conference of the Central Advisory Board for Education (CABE) and an All India Conference of Provincial Ministers of Education. However, it was clear that achieving the goal of universal education in a decade was too ambitious. The sixties finally saw significant work and exchange of radical ideas on education. The Kothari Education Commission (1964-66) was appointed with the mandate to advise on the national pattern of education and on the general principles and policies for the total development of education. Below are its main recommendations:

1. Work-experience and social service should be introduced as integral parts of general education at more or less all levels of education.
2. Secondary education should be vocationalised.
3. Mother-tongue has a pre-eminent claim as medium of instruction at school and college stages. Moreover, the medium of education in school and higher education should generally be the same. The regional language should, therefore, be adopted as the media of education in higher education.
4. The teaching and study of English should continue to be promoted right from the school stage. English will serve as a link language in higher education for academic work and intellectual inter-communication.
5. The Central and State Governments should adopt measures to introduce education in moral, social and spiritual values in all institutions under their control.

6. Secondary schools should be of two types, including high schools providing a course for 11-12 years.
7. Education, as distinguished from pedagogy, should be recognised as an independent academic discipline.
8. Duration of training courses should be two years for primary teachers who have completed the secondary school course. It should be one year for the graduate students.
9. Science and mathematics should be taught on a compulsory basis to all pupils as a part of general education during the first ten years of schooling.
10. No single stage of education need be designated as basic education, but its essential principles should be retained to guide and shape the educational system at all levels.
11. External examinations should be improved by orienting question papers to objectives rather than to acquisition of knowledge, by improving the nature of questions, adopting scientific scoring of scripts.
12. Internal assessment should be comprehensive and evaluate all aspects of student growth.
13. Some centres of advanced study and a small number of major universities should be set up with the view to achieving highest international standards.
14. Education for agriculture, and research in agriculture and allied sciences should be given a high priority in the scheme of educational reconstruction.
15. The Ministry of Education, in collaboration with the Asian Institute of Educational Planning, should undertake studies of educational planning in the different states and conduct intensive courses for training the personnel involved in the planning process at different levels.
16. Universities, professional organisations, and teaching colleges should be deeply involved in a periodical evaluation of all major programmes included in the Plan and in the development of a large-scale research programme.

The findings of the Kothari commission as well as the report of the committee of MPs on higher education (1963) which went into the feasibility of the commission recommendations, threw up the first National Policy on Education (NPE) on July 24, 1968. The policy resolution called for a transformation of the system of education, linking it more closely with the lives of the people, continuous efforts to expand educational opportunities and raising of the quality of education at all stages. It emphasised the development of science and technology and on qualitative moral and social values, gave importance to work experience, social and national services as an integral part of education, and advocated expansion of education through part time, distance education and vocational studies.

However, it was clear that in a vast and plural country like India that was committed to a participative democracy as a way of life, the national system of education would have to be:

- highly decentralised with the involvement of the Central and State Governments, local authorities at district levels and local communities,
- highly deconcentrated by making due provision for the autonomy of universities (which should share it with the Departments and Colleges) and for adequate freedom to schools and teachers to experiment and innovate, and
- highly diversified and elastic to suit the immense variations between the different parts of the country and the specific needs of different social groups.

Apart from the NPE, there was also the long-term perspective of educational development (1966-86) prepared by the Education Commission. But the educational performance did not show any improvement because there were several weaknesses in the National Policy on Education (1968) and because the major recommendations of the Education Commission that could have made an impact on the overall situation were totally disregarded. Consequently, in 1978, the Ministry of Education and Social Welfare requested Prof. J.P. Naik of the Indian Council of Social Science Research and former member Secretary of the Education Commission, to undertake a review of the implementation of the NPE. Naik's 1979 report said that "it'd be incorrect to describe the existing educational system as an instrument for educating the people; the evidence clearly shows that it's more appropriately designed for not educating them." It found that despite its efforts, India had merely managed "a large-scale linear expansion of the formal education system created by the British." Naik regretted that India had appointed a University Education Commission in 1948, a high-level Technical Manpower Committee in 1949, and a Secondary Education Commission in 1952, an English — as medium of instruction committee in 1954, Assessment Committee on basic education in 1956, and so on, but so far, no Elementary Education Commission.

The Naik report found the education system to be not only ineffective but retrograde too. It said that about 60 per cent of the people (age 10 and over) were still illiterate and had received none of the benefits of this vast educational system. About 20 per cent of the children, mostly the lowest of the low, were completely by-passed by the formal system of education. Of those children that entered the schools, nearly half dropped out by class V and nearly three-fourths dropped out by class VIII; only about 15 per cent reached class XII, and less than one per cent managed to obtain the first degree. The system accorded very low priority to programmes such as adult or non-formal education to benefit the masses especially the poor. On the other hand, it gave high priority and invested the bulk of its resources in secondary and higher education that help mostly the top 30 per cent of the people.

As a result, the eighties saw the education system getting more decentralised with states and local bodies having a greater say in policy and implementation. Such a system also became necessary after it was decided that primary education ought to get the greatest priority for the nation to have a strong base in education. After the Eighth All India Conference on Educational Statistics held in Udaipur in September 1980, a High Level Committee under S. Ramamoorthi was set up to look at the entire educational statistical system and make a perspective plan for its improvement and utilization in policy making. Its recommendations vastly strengthened and gave a new look to education statistics in India.

The subject of education continued to be on the State List till 1976 when, through the $42^{nd}$ Amendment, it was brought on the concurrent list. Constitutional Amendments further contributed to educational development by strengthening *Panchayati Raj* Institutions to support development of education at the grassroot level. The States began to have greater responsibility towards the primary and the secondary education sectors but were poor in terms of both human and financial resources. However, the Centre enjoys a powerful position in deciding the educational agenda and the State do not have control over quality and character of education. In 1985, the integrated Ministry of Human Resource Development was set up, to help build the country's human resources, looking beyond economic indicators like growth and gross national product and to bring about a coordinated integrated approach to all programmes related to human resource development. At the same time, the government reviewed the education system and initiated a national debate on education. Based on the suggestions received, a new National Policy on Education (NPE) 1986 and its Programme of Action, 1992 were prepared in consultation with the State Governments and adopted by Parliament.

The NPE 1986 made concurrency workable. While outlining a meaningful partnership between the Centre and the States, it placed on the Centre the responsibility of ensuring the national and integrated character of education, maintaining quality and standards, requirements for advanced study, international aspects of education, cultural and human resource development. Another significant aspect of the policy was the greater concern for the empowerment of women, and access to education to disadvantaged sections of the society, educationally backward minorities and the disabled. Most important, the Policy gave added impetus to the launching of a large-scale programme of non-formal education, boldly acknowledging that the school system cannot reach all children. In order to nurture rural talent, it suggested the establishment of *Navodaya Vidyalayas* (model schools) with residential facilities. It also called for greater rigour and discipline in academic pursuits, autonomy and accountability, experimentation and innovation, nurture of excellence and modernisation of process at different levels of education.

It was for the first time in the NPE 1986, that stress on Early Childhood Care and Education (ECCE) was laid out in black and white, even though India's first national children's project ICDS (Integrated Child Development Scheme) had been started in the seventies. Conceptually, the NPE, a sound and forward-looking document, recognised quality as a major factor and the need to make education relevant to the life contexts of both children and adults. It also redefined learning in an empowering context, and advocated changing curricula and texts to address the life and living concerns of the disadvantaged.

This policy document was reviewed by the Ramamoorthy Committee, which submitted its report in December 1990 on alternative modalities of implementation. The N. Janardhana Reddy Committee set up by the CABE again reviewed the Policy in 1992. The Committee recommended a revision of the programme of action and laid special emphasis on education for women's equality, education for SCs/STs, and educationally backward minorities. The NPE and its POA (programme of action) were adopted in 1992. The new amended policy said: "The main task is to strengthen the base of the pyramid, which might come close to a billion people at the turn of the century. Equally, it is important to ensure that those at the top of the pyramid are among the best in the world."

This was just the beginning of a huge churning in the education system, one of which was the open school system advocated by the Planning Commission's Core Group (Chitra Naik Committee) Report on Open Learning in February, 1992; the EFA Summit Framework for Action 1993; and CABE's (G. Ram Reddy Committee) Report on Distance Education in February, 1994. But the self-questioning was prompted most by the National Advisory Committee set up by the HRD Ministry under Prof. Yash Pal to advise the Government on improving the quality of learning while reducing the burden on school students. In its historic report in 1993, the committee said: "Our committee was concerned with one major flaw of our system of education. The flaw can be identified briefly by saying that a lot is taught, but little is learnt or understood." The committee also made specific prescriptions on how the huge course content of subjects like social science could be trimmed and rationalised.

It was a follow-up to the Yash Pal report that the World Bank — sponsored District Primary Education Programme (DPEP) was introduced in selected districts in an attempt to solve this problem. DPEP tries to make education child-centred (instead of examination-centred), experiential (instead of theoretical) and activity-oriented (instead of examination-oriented). Though critics say it's success has been mixed, the programme has emerged as one of the major vehicles for UEE as well as for international assistance for basic education and is operational in 271 districts in various states. The programme is based on principles of decentralisation and community initiative and has as focus area, low female literacy districts. It was also in 1993 that the Supreme Court clearly declared education a fundamental right. Deciding the Unnikrishnan vs. State of Andhra Pradesh case, the court said: "Though the right to education is not stated expressly as a fundamental right, it is implicit in and flows from the right to life guaranteed under Article 21."

**Miles to go**

The sixth All India Education Survey (1995) is still the latest source of data, other than the census, for the education department. Its main findings were:

- 94 per cent of rural population was served within one km by primary (grades I-V) stage and 85 per cent within 3 km by upper primary (grades VI-VIII) stage.
- Of the total 8,22,486 schools, 70 per cent were primary and 20 per cent upper primary schools.
- Of the total 15,39,06,057 pupils enrolled in all the schools, 63 per cent and 22 per cent were enrolled at primary and upper primary stages respectively. 41 per cent of the total enrolled children were girls.
- 66 per cent of the total 6,36,38,488 girls enrolled were in primary and 22 per cent were in upper primary.
- Of the total 41,97,555 teachers, 38 per cent and 27 per cent were employed in primary and upper primary schools respectively.
- 84 per cent of the primary and 89 per cent of the upper primary schools had pukka and partly pukka buildings.

Over the eighties and nineties, a number of other programmes were begun involving both the Union Government and the States. These are Operation Blackboard, Non-Formal Education, establishment of District Institutes of Education and Training (DIETs), National Literacy Mission, Scheme of Nutritional Support to Primary

Education (Mid-day Meals), Mahila Samakhya Project under which free education is provided to girls in Kendriya Vidyalas and Navodaya Vidyalayas, etc. Among the more important are:

- "Operation Blackboard" is working since 1987-88 and aims at qualitative improvement of primary schools by providing two reasonably large all-weather rooms along with separate toilet facilities for boys and girls, at least two teachers, one a woman, and provision of essential teaching and learning material.
- The 1995 National Programme of Nutritional support to Primary Education, popularly known as the Mid-day Meal Scheme, is also a major intervention for increasing enrolment and retention in schools and curbing child labour. Under this, cooked meals are supposed to be served in schools but states have the flexibility to distribute foodgrain at the rate of 3 kg per child per month.
- For those out of school, the Programme of Non-formal Education, started in 1979, now extends to urban slums, tribal areas, hilly and desert areas with a special emphasis on working children in 21 States. These are managed mostly by NGOs with a core strategy to mobilise the village community to take responsibility for the education of their children.

Non-Formal Education (NFE) was proposed as far back as the Kothari commission to address the problem of the reach of primary school and impart education that would have a flexible approach and be relevant to the local context. The intention was not only to get to the untapped but also to ensure their re-entry into the formal system. Local language and teachers, use of teaching learning materials, flexible calendar and school timings, etc. were an important part of NFE. However, though the concept is innovative, the support system comprises teachers who are less qualified or trained. Instead of being a bridge course to help children who are out of school into the formal school system, NFE is now increasingly being seen as a parallel system of school education for children who cannot reach formal schooling that is either getting too expensive or remote. In fact, nearly 20 years of effort and money spent on providing Non-Formal Education (NFE) to out-of-school children have brought no lasting benefits, according to a CAG report recently tabled in Parliament. It said non-enrolment of children in NFE centres, as per the norms of the scheme, deprived 43.59 lakh children of its benefits during 1995-96 to 1999-2000. A number of "half-hearted measures," lack of community support, large-scale mismanagement of resources, and inadequate strength of networks are the main reasons for the programme's poor performance.

**An Experiment in Bengal**

Endowed with Nobel Prize Funds awarded to Amartya Sen, the Pratichi Trust was recently established, and a team of Pratichi researchers (Kumar Rana, Abdur Rafique, and Amrita Sen Gupta) reported on their village surveys in West Bengal which brought out the deteriorating trend of educational performance in West Bengal. The Pratichi study confirmed the problems with teacher performance (absenteeism, social distance from students, unionism, and "economism"), weak parental participation, and rapid growth of private tutors. The recent establishment of less formal system called Sishu Siksha Kendras (SSK) seems constructive, but the consequent dual systems threaten to polarise academic achievement among the rich and poor. Private tutors help children whose families can afford the extra cost, but the practice also reduces reform pressures on the public sector. The consequent disparities between class, caste, and gender are significant and perhaps growing. In West Bengal, once under-paid teachers have witnessed significant compensation adjustments, to monthly levels of Rs. 5,000 to 10,000. Teachers, however, lack support systems — refresher training, curricular revitalisation, and teacher-parent committees.

As a result, the government decided to launch the Sarva Shiksha Abhiyan (SSA). The SSA, the umbrella scheme for the elementary education sector, is the government's latest move towards improving the performance of the school system and to provide community-owned quality elementary education. All existing schemes are now a part of SSA except for the externally assisted programmes that will continue till their terms come to a close. The targets are: All children complete 8 years of schooling by 2010, focus on elementary education of satisfactory quality, and universal retention by 2010. The SSA has completed a year but major concerns remain. They include unqualified teachers, inferior quality education and, in some places, emphasis on literacy rather than on education. It is also seen as a mere conglomeration of existing schemes with nothing new to offer. The Human Resource Development Ministry has now come out with a report outlining an 'Education Guarantee Scheme and Alternative and Innovative Education,' where the concept of para-teachers was mooted.

Worse still is the fact that formal schooling is seriously affected. The Tenth plan promised an extra Rs. 10,000 crore annually but the actual disbursal is a meagre 10 per cent of this. A major chunk of the resources was meant for energising the formal education system as per the Tapas Majumdar Committee. Unfortunately, most state governments are submitting proposals for inferior options. According to HRD Ministry figures studied by the World Bank[5], education spending as a share of SDP increased in eight states and decreased in nine over 1990-9. Even as a share of total spending, it increased in only 5 states and went down in 12 in that period. What is also left unexplained is what constitutes "free" education. While government schools did not charge tuition fees, households incurred substantial direct costs of education (towards textbooks, uniforms and so on), which in turn was an important reason for the non-participation of children from poor families. Universal enrollment of children and their subsequent retention cannot be ensured unless education of a satisfactory quality was imparted. With reference to the scheme of deploying Shikshakarmi or para-teachers, the committee pointed out that there was no substitute for fully qualified and properly paid teachers. It clearly maintained that it was opposed to a national programme of deployment of para-teachers.

If fact, latest surveys find that NGO initiatives under non-formal education touch barely less than 5 per cent of primary enrollment. These have also been restricted to out-of-school and working children. In fact, there may be only around six organisations that have been able to genuinely partner the State in improving the quality of education — Lok Jumbish, along with Digantar and Sandhan Shodh Kendra in Rajasthan, Ekalavya in Madhya Pradesh, the Rishi Valley Rural Education Centre in Karnataka, and Pratham in Mumbai. A little elaboration of the pioneering Hoshangabad Science Teaching

Programme (HSTP), which came to be known as the Ekalavya project, is necessary here.

The HSTP was developed in the seventies well within the framework of the system of school education in Madhya Pradesh and with the approval, cooperation and assistance of successive governments at costs that were almost ridiculously low. As they went along, they developed expertise in writing new kinds of textbooks, training teachers through short-term refresher courses, publishing magazines for children and for teachers, and devising toolkits at a fraction of prevailing costs. In course of time, a social science component was also developed based on the same principle of proceeding from the familiar to the abstract rather than the other way around. By 2001, the HSTP was operative in 1000 schools in 15 districts and one lakh children were its beneficiaries. However, the Madhya Pradesh government has recently stopped the programme after surveys found little improvement in literacy in Hoshangabad, triggering much protest from all corners. The state government's own Education Guarantee scheme too has had significant impact on raising literacy.[6]

**Are unaided schools better?**

Convincing evidence of government failure to optimise education spending comes in the form of successful private schools in most states, including those in Kerala. A World Bank study of urban schools in Uttar Pradesh shows that because private unaided schools have management and budgetarial autonomy and can choose a mix of options appropriate to local conditions, they often fare better than private aided schools and which don't have budgetarial autonomy. The worst, as it found in Tamil Nadu, was the situation in government schools, where efficiency of expenditure was lower than in private aided schools. The study concludes that closer supervision of teachers and greater commitment to high student results, might help government schools to boost their own performance.

The other example recently cited by Amartya Sen in his introduction to the Pratichi education report is that of West Bengal's cost-effective and quite successful experiment with Shishu Shiksha Karmis. However, even Sen notes that "the students receive far less support in the SSKs than in primary schools, and some of these gaps can be reduced, without overturning the cost-effectiveness of SSKs. The reliance on SSKs should not reduce the recognition of the urgency of reforming and enhancing the main avenue of primary education, viz. primary schools."

After over five decades of educational development, the Indian state is at the crossroads, deliberating and dithering over policies that have finally produced a system that is clearly far from inclusive and all-encompassing and not embracing all its people and barely adequate to throw up occasionally a few brainy students nurtured by essentially expensive, private initiatives. According to Anil Sadgopal, eminent educationist, the precise point at which the Indian state jettisoned its constitutional obligation was at the 1990 Jomtien Conference. He resigned from the Acharya Ramamoorthi Commission protesting against the government's backtracking on the goal of universalisation of elementary education. According to him, before the Jomtien Conference, the Government of India felt answerable to the Constitution on the subject of education. After Jomtien, it has felt answerable to the forces of globalisation. The huge emphasis in the eighties on the national literacy missions was intended to keep India's labour "competitive", without raising the educational level so as to make for real improvement in productive skills, he adds. In fact, the 1994 Arun Ghosh Committee to evaluate the Total Literacy Movement rejected the NLM's claims of "total literacy" as false and unreliable. It recommended "the target approach of achieving "total literacy" should be given up...A success rate of 55-60 per cent among identified non-literates should be considered to be a good success rate." Also, "there should be a second cycle of literacy campaigns in low literacy/ difficult areas after another round of motivational campaigns so as to reinforce the achievement of the first cycle of the literacy campaigns and also achieve substantial results." This was the first acknowledgment of the gigantic dimensions of the problem of 'left-outs' or the 'residual illiterates'. The other problems highlighted were the "fragile" attainment of literacy, increasing bureaucratisation of the programme and inordinate delays between phases.

The strategy for the 1990s was aimed mainly at primary education as also linking the different stages of education across generations and programmes of education with national concerns such as health, environment etc., through collaboration between different departments of the government. By and large, this seems to have been a failure, even though schools dot the countryside and early childhood care centres mushroom in the cities. The biggest proof of this is that dropout rates remain high. At the primary level, there is much higher enrolment but close to 40 out of 100 children still drop out of school, while the upper primary level it is stagnant at 55 per cent. A line from the Yash Pal Committee Report (*Learning without Burden,* 1993) may be relevant here, "a significant fraction of children who drop out may be those who refuse to compromise with non-comprehension..."

The final big denouement came in 1999 in the form of the Public Report on Basic Education for India (PROBE), whose findings showed that except in Himachal Pradesh, precious little had changed in primary education. Supported by the Center for Development Economics (India), it was a survey carried out from September to December 1996, covering school facilities and a sample of 1376 households, in 234 villages of Bihar, Madhya Pradesh, Rajasthan, Uttar Pradesh and Himachal Pradesh. The five states covered by the survey account for 40 per cent of India's population and more than half of all out-of-school children. The study found serious weaknesses in public schooling, disturbing trends toward privatisation and commercialisation, and consequent fragmentation of educational systems. Overall, PROBE found many general misconceptions about the poor and education, including a false belief that poor parents don't care about educating their children, that children aren't in school because they are working, that elementary education is free, and that schools are available and functioning.

It is another matter that parents do not always have much faith in the system's ability to impart such education, says PROBE. In Uttar Pradesh, all parents thought education was important for boys, and 92 per cent said it was so for girls. However, in rural India sending a child to school on a regular basis requires a great deal of effort on the part of the child and his or her parents. Cost may be prohibitive, there may not be a functioning school within walking distance, the child may face a hostile environment at school, lack of support and progress at school may sap the morale of parents and children. If fact, PROBE found that the expectation of two reasonably large, weather-safe rooms for primary schools remained unrealised in most schools. Most schools are held outside, in rented rooms, or in crumbling structures with leaking roofs, bad lighting, few resources, poor teachers, and conditions of social discrimination.

Teaching activity is of short duration; teachers arrive late and leave early. No teaching aids were used; curriculum would be alien and textbooks absent with the child. No craftwork or colour or music, little physical activity, gender bias and quiet discrimination against children of disadvantaged background.

**Positive PROBE**

Educational performance cannot be delinked from development and economist Jean Dreze points out that Himachal Pradesh's superior performance may be due in part to the egalitarianism of earlier land reforms. The PROBE report found that Himachal, which is very close to universal primary education, serves as an inspiring example of change and improvement in the schooling system. The contributing factors are: exceptionally high parental motivation for education, social consensus that education is of vital importance, low gender bias, supportive attitudes for children and teachers, good school environments, well-maintained records, motivated teachers and concern for children.

Even though there has been little change in the state of India's schooling system in the last few years, says PROBE, a few interesting experiments to help improve education have taken place. Notable among them are the school mid-day meal program, the Shikshak Samakhya (joyful learning program) and the volunteer teacher scheme. All across the country, alternative schools, private schools, and non-formal schools run by NGOs have sprung up to meet the demand for education as an attempt to make up for unsatisfactory government schools. But can all this be a substitute for government-funded schools?

If any single factor can make the difference between a poor school and a successful school, says PROBE, it is the commitment and initiative of the teacher. However, the state of teachers in India is very poor. The rural primary teachers bear the burden of education in complete isolation with very little support. The rural teacher is also expected to perform other functions such as census taking, etc., which take time away from teaching. Teachers often have very low academic qualifications and no training. Another problem is the lack of female teachers in India. Only 31 per cent of teachers are women, compared to 51 per cent in the developing world as a whole. Finally, there are simply not enough teachers to go around.

Another factor that PROBE found to be discouraging children and teachers is the unfriendly and unimaginative curriculum. Teaching continues to be completely out of context and is only geared towards scoring in conventional written examinations. But, argues PROBE, the current situation in education management makes it difficult to reform a system that operates with top-down management style from the national government down to the rural level, and gives the impression of a rigid bureaucracy, unresponsive to the real needs of teachers and children. Classroom realities are out of focus and the preoccupation instead is with holding the administrative fort and fulfilling official directives. Teachers are not respected or listened to, the school inspection system is inept and ineffective, and there is a huge lack of understanding school teacher occupies the lowest position in the hierarchical administrative structure and is expected to and training about education at every level.

As the PROBE report also proves, the strongest criticism against central policy on education and its implementation has centered on discrimination among categories of students. The amended NPE 1992 had said: "The concept of a National System of Education implies that, up to a given level, all students, irrespective of caste, creed, location or sex, have access to education of a comparable quality." But little seems to have changed from what J.P. Naik said in 1965 trying to answer the question, "Who has benefited most from the expansion in education that has been achieved in the post-Independence period? He wrote: "...the largest beneficiaries of our system of education are boys, the people of the urban areas, and the middle and the upper classes. Educational development, particularly at the secondary and higher stages, is benefiting the 'haves' more than the 'have-nots'."

According to Prof. Yash Pal[7] "This is largely a system where education is believed to be a commodity to be delivered to children.

The examinations, including the CBSE and the State Boards, are largely concentrating on the storage capacity of minds for information, dead or alive. There is a madness on the part of parents, students and teachers to 'train' children like race horses to get that last 1 or 2 per cent. This pleases the enormously lucrative industry of tuitions and coaching in which a large fraction of the teachers from schools are also involved. All this is socially discriminating to a high degree. Students are under high pressure, to an extent that the joy of acquiring knowledge is often extinguished. The stress levels reach a point where children suffer from cortexial elimination. After a while even the child's brain shuts down the processing circuits that have not been used for a long time. Scientific temper, wondering and dreaming become useless "out of course" activities. Our examination system does not distinguish between fertile knowledge and barren information." Yash Pal's views are echoed by Sen. He says[8]: "There is an urgent need for taking class divisions more seriously and also insisting on the exercise of responsibility by public servants who serve the underdogs of society. The overarching need is to overcome the rigid barriers of class divisions that blight the basic rights of children from economically and socially disadvantaged backgrounds."

It would be interesting here to observe what the children themselves have to say about the education that they get in schools. It is one group that the government has curiously never tried to learn from. HAQ Centre for Child Rights, a Delhi-based NGO, did a survey for the India Alliance for Child Rights for the UN Special Session where about 65 children from all over India had collected. Among other issues highlighted in the box above, children emphasised a lot that all children must be given equitable education. They felt that whether the child gets admission in a government, private or public school, the curriculum should be the same. The above clearly brings out that even the children are aggrieved at the iniquities in the system. Clearly, to close the gap between tall promises and small achievements, the future of education in India will have to be driven by bold state policies and a great deal of public pressure.

**What Children Want**

Does the government know what these little minds want? A Delhi-based NGO, HAQ did a survey for the India Alliance for Child Rights for the UN Special Session where about 65 children from all over India had collected. Children felt that

- Education today must be accessible and equal with same curriculum for all children.
- Non-formal classes must not exist, as it is convenient for parents but not good for children. It is an easier option for parents to send their children, especially girls, for the two-hour class so that they can come back and work at home.
- Every school must have basic amenities like toilets, electricity, water, fans and qualified good teachers. Classes should not be overcrowded.
- Incentives like mid-day meal should be provided in all schools.
- Schools must be inspected from time to time and teachers who are not performing must be punished.
- Age group for formal schooling should be between 3-18 years.
- Adult education should also get top priority as well as vocational training institutes. It's only when parents are educated that they understand the value of children's education.
- Children who are weak in studies should be given a chance to study too.

## Prominent Committees on School Education in India

1. Committee on Secondary Education in India, 1948.
2. Committee on the Ways and Means of Planning Educational Development in India, 1948.
3. Committee on the Relationship between State Governments and Local Bodies in the Administration of Primary Education, 1951.

4. Secondary Education Commission, 1952-53.
5. Committee to Examine the Problem of Instruction at the University Stage and Recommend the Ways and Means of Securing Adequate Proficiency in English, 1954.
6. Study Team on General Education, 1955.
7. Assessment Committee on Basic Education, 1956.
8. Committee on Rural Education, 1957.
9. Committee on General Education, 1958.
10. National Committee on Women's Education, 1958.
11. Committee on Religious and Moral Instruction, 1959.
12. Committee on Differential Curriculum for Boys and Girls, 1961.
13. Committee of Members of Parliament on Higher Education, 1963.
14. Education Commission, 1964.
15. Committee of Members of Parliament on Education, 1967.
16. Review Committee on Future Development of National Council of Educational Research and Training, 1968.
17. Committee on the University Grants Commission, 1974.
18. National Review Committee on Higher Secondary Education with Special Reference to Vocationalisation, 1977.
19. Working Group on Universalisation of Elementary Education, 1977.
20. Committee to Review the Educational Statistics in India, 1982.
21. National Commission of Teachers, 1983-85.
22. Committee to Review the 1986 National Policy of Education, 1990.
23. Committee on Minimum Levels of Learning at Primary Stage, 1990.
24. Core Group on Open Education in Planning Commission, 1991.
25. Advisory Committee to Suggest Ways to Reduce Academic Burden on School Students, 1992.

26. Expert Group on Evaluation of Literacy Campaign in India, 1994.
27. CABE Committee on Distance Education, 1994.
28. Committee on Mid-day Meals, 1995.
29. Committee of State Education Ministers to Examine Implications of Making the Right to Free and Compulsory, Elementary Education a Fundamental Right, 1997.
30. Committee on Cost of Universalisation of Primary Education, 2001.

## Notes

1. *World Development Report*, 2002, The World Bank.
2. Tilak, J.B.G, *Economics of Inequality in Education*, New Delhi, Sage Publications, 1997.
3. The World Bank, Primary Education in India, 1997.
4. Yash Pal's letter of 1 July, 2002 to Digvijay Singh, Chief Minister of MP, about the closure of the Hoshangabad programme.
5. *Primary Education in India, ibid.*
6. Anita Sharma.
7. 2002 letter *ibid.*
8. *Pratichi Education Report 2002.*

## References

Drèze, Jean and Sen, Amartya (1995): *India: Economic Development and Social Opportunities.* OUP, New Delhi.

Gandhi, M.K. (1962): *The Problem of Education.* Navodaya, Ahmedabad.

Ghosh, Arun (1987): *Tyranny of Education System*, Economic and Political Weekly, Vol. 22, No. 38.

Ministry of Education (1964-66): *Report of the Education Commission.*

Ministry of HRD (1986): *National Policy of Education.*

——— (1993): *Education for All: The Indian Scene, Widening Horizons.*

——— (1992): *National Policy of Education 1986 — Programme of Action.*

——— (1993): *Report of the CABE Committee on Decentralised Management of Education.*

——— (1993): *Report of the Group to Examine the Feasibility of Implementing the Recommendations of the National Advisory Committee.*

——— (1994): *Development of Education in India, 1993-94.*

——— (1995): *Treading the Uncharted, Country Report on Innovative and Non-Traditional Approaches in Education*, Second Ministerial Meeting, Bali.

——— (1995): *DPEP Overview.*

——— (1996): *Education and National Development: Report of Education Commission.*

——— (1998): *Analysis of Budgeted Expenditure on Education, 1994-95 to 1996-97*, New Delhi.

——— (2000): *Education for All: The Challenge of Universal Primary Education*, Consultation Document, March 2000.

Naik, J.P. (1965): *Educational Planning in India*, Allied Publishers, New Delhi.

——— (1975): *Elementary Education in India: A Promise to Keep*, Allied Publishers, New Delhi.

NCAER (1994): *Non-enrolment, Drop-out and Private Expenditure on Elementary Education: A Comparison Across States and Population Groups.*

NCERT (1991): *School Education in the 1990s: Problem and Perspectives.*

——— (1995): *Sixth All-India Education Survey.*

NIEPA (1990): *Education for All by 2000: Indian Perspective*, New Delhi.

——— (1992): *New Economic Policy and Financing Education*, New Delhi.

——— (1994): *Resource Requirement in Education in India — Implication for the Tenth Finance Commission.*

NSSO (1993): *Results in Participation in 16 Major States Sarvekshana 55th and 56th Issues*, Ministry of Planning/Department of Statistics.

Operations Research Group: *Final Reports on Evaluation of Non-formal Education Programme Reports for West Bengal, (1994) and Lok Jumbish (1996)*, New Delhi.

Pal, Yash (1993): *Learning Without Burden: Report of the National Advisory Committee*, New Delhi, Ministry of HRD/Department of Education.

Tilak, Jandhyala B.G. (1987): *Economics of Inequality in Education*, New Delhi, Sage, 197p.

——— (1996): *How Free is "free" Primary Education in India? Part I and II.* Economic and Political Weekly, Vol. 31, Nos. 5 and 6, p275-282, 355-366.

The World Bank (1997): *Primary Education in India, India*, 1997.

**Table - 1**

*Resource requirements, Availability, and Financing gaps for Expanded and Better quality Primary Education, India 1996-2007 (in Rs. million at constant 1993 prices)*

| *Indicator* | *2000* | *2003* | *2007* |
|---|---|---|---|
| ***Maintaining the existing system*** | | | |
| Teachers' salaries | 90074 | 101319 | 118530 |
| Incentives | 1447 | 1447 | 1447 |
| Textbooks and material | 1447 | 1447 | 1447 |
| Subtotal | 96570 | 104213 | 121423 |
| ***Expanding coverage*** | | | |
| School construction | 12128 | 12128 | 12128 |
| Salaries for new teachers | 15772 | 28387 | 49814 |
| Textbooks and instructional material | 325 | 520 | 780 |
| Incentives | 487 | 780 | 1170 |
| Subtotal | 28712 | 41814 | 63891 |
| ***Improving quality*** | | | |
| Rehabilitation of classrooms | 4052 | 4052 | 4052 |
| Water and toilets | 3115 | 3115 | 3115 |
| Classroom instructional materials | 1006 | 1171 | 1392 |
| School instructional materials | 1006 | 1171 | 1392 |
| In-service teacher training | 1158 | 1258 | 1391 |
| Subtotal | 10336 | 10766 | 11341 |
| ***Financing*** | | | |
| Total resources required | 132015 | 156793 | 196655 |
| Total resources available | 100399 | 122305 | 159121 |
| Financing gap | 31616 | 34488 | 37534 |

Source: *Primary Education in India*, The World Bank, 1997.

## Table - 2

*State-wise Gross Enrolment Ratios (%): 1986-87 and 1993-94*

| State | *Primary Level* | | | | *Upper Primary* | | | |
|---|---|---|---|---|---|---|---|---|
| | *Girls* | | *Total* | | *Girls* | | *Total* | |
| | *1986-87* | *1993-94* | *1986-87* | *1993-94* | *1986-87* | *1993-94* | *1986-87* | *1993-94* |
| Andhra Pradesh | 80.01 | 86.50 | 92.03 | 93.27 | 24.75 | 39.89 | 34.55 | 49.20 |
| Arunachal Pradesh | 78.10 | 119.87 | 94.70 | 130.96 | 26.89 | 48.43 | 34.43 | 55.95 |
| Assam | 81.21 | 86.57 | 90.10 | 92.88 | 39.15 | 48.59 | 45.09 | 53.37 |
| Bihar | 52.77 | 53.16 | 79.13 | 73.06 | 16.12 | 19.86 | 29.93 | 32.87 |
| Goa | 127.22 | 102.68 | 133.13 | 104.26 | 96.07 | 93.74 | 103.18 | 99.58 |
| Gujarat | 95.31 | 96.42 | 107.86 | 105.65 | 44.15 | 56.73 | 54.77 | 67.74 |
| Haryana | 77.61 | 80.58 | 87.35 | 83.78 | 39.89 | 58.36 | 59.31 | 68.56 |
| Himachal Pradesh | 92.59 | 100.17 | 99.41 | 110.13 | 64.79 | 85.58 | 79.28 | 100.02 |
| J & K | 67.25 | 56.19 | 79.96 | 71.71 | 41.73 | 41.32 | 56.62 | 55.69 |
| Karnataka | 98.69 | 114.09 | 108.33 | 119.23 | 41.83 | 59.31 | 51.49 | 66.95 |
| Kerala | 104.59 | 95.33 | 105.67 | 96.14 | 88.09 | 100.48 | 88.28 | 100.55 |
| Madhya Pradesh | 76.33 | 86.54 | 96.86 | 97.98 | 24.24 | 39.43 | 43.79 | 54.96 |
| Maharashtra | 107.22 | 114.65 | 116.7 | 118.76 | 51.71 | 72.96 | 64.84 | 81.58 |
| Manipur | 86.91 | 127.64 | 93.50 | 131.88 | 52.99 | 75.18 | 60.49 | 76.89 |
| Megahalaya | 107.08 | 136.72 | 108.61 | 134.29 | 49.20 | 53.77 | 51.51 | 53.76 |
| Mizoram | 118.45 | 146.35 | 122.53 | 152.13 | 56.78 | 80.82 | 57.12 | 79.59 |
| Nagaland | 103.92 | 99.92 | 107.76 | 101.73 | 37.39 | 51.23 | 41.64 | 49.87 |
| Orissa | 81.87 | 87.08 | 96.24 | 100.57 | 29.60 | 38.65 | 40.32 | 50.00 |
| Punjab | 92.85 | 81.42 | 95.08 | 84.60 | 54.15 | 60.97 | 60.19 | 65.62 |
| Rajasthan | 50.62 | 58.46 | 80.31 | 85.10 | 16.24 | 23.40 | 38.96 | 46.24 |
| Sikkim | 115.83 | 126.84 | 127.72 | 132.74 | 50.83 | 71.74 | 55.90 | 73.18 |
| Tamil Nadu | 120.02 | 136.1 | 122.44 | 143.50 | 63.41 | 92.74 | 73.97 | 103.38 |
| Tripura | 112.73 | 119.92 | 124.17 | 126.73 | 49.95 | 60.57 | 57.99 | 65.87 |
| Uttar Pradesh | 50.33 | 59.53 | 69.29 | 75.69 | 23.09 | 31.29 | 40.61 | 46.62 |
| West Bengal | 70.17 | 97.71 | 78.86 | 104.15 | 32.48 | 45.17 | 41.01 | 53.05 |
| A & N Islands | 85.52 | 123.42 | 91.72 | 132.24 | 77.91 | 106.35 | 83.52 | 114.08 |
| Chandigarh | 79.44 | 94.46 | 80.55 | 96.24 | 75.67 | 99.67 | 73.60 | 98.16 |
| D & N Haveli | 107.45 | 97.36 | 123.18 | 113.15 | 36.16 | 43.07 | 43.79 | 57.14 |
| Daman & Diu | 149.30 | 90.85 | 157.19 | 90.89 | 85.12 | 82.45 | 97.40 | 87.78 |
| Delhi | 90.21 | 112.19 | 91.58 | 110.17 | 79.37 | 113.27 | 79.88 | 111.26 |
| Lakshadweep | 138.96 | 154.04 | 144.87 | 146.75 | 76.56 | 102.82 | 87.62 | 121.5 |
| Pondicherry | 115.95 | 114.11 | 118.94 | 117.62 | 72.17 | 111.64 | 79.73 | 110.20 |
| All India | 77.55 | 85.02 | 91.69 | 95.90 | 35.03 | 47.91 | 47.95 | 59.07 |

Source: NCERT, 1992 and 1995.

## Table - 3

*Out-of-School Children at All India Level: 1993-94*

(Based on NCERT Data)
(Figures in Million)

| *Age-group* | | *Age-specific Popu-lation* | *Enrol-ment* | *Adjusted Enrol-ment (@15%)* | *Out-of-School Children* | *%* | *NER %* | *GER (%)* |
|---|---|---|---|---|---|---|---|---|
| 6-11 (I-V) | | | | | | | | |
| | Boys | 62.12 | 55.61 | 47.27 | 14.85 | 40.44 | 76.09 | 89.52 |
| | Girls | 57.68 | 42.13 | 35.81 | 21.87 | 59.56 | 62.08 | 73.04 |
| | Total | 119.8 | 97.74 | 83.08 | 36.72 | 100.00 | 69.35 | 81.59 |
| 11-14 (VI-VIII) | | | | | | | | |
| | Boys | 31.87 | 20.63 | 14.54 | 14.33 | 45.71 | 55.04 | 64.73 |
| | Girls | 28.43 | 13.42 | 11.41 | 17.02 | 54.29 | 40.13 | 47.20 |
| | Total | 60.30 | 34.05 | 28.94 | 31.35 | 100.00 | 47.99 | 56.47 |
| 6-14 (I-VIII) | | | | | | | | |
| | Boys | 93.99 | 76.24 | 64.81 | 29.18 | 42.87 | 68.95 | 81.11 |
| | Girls | 86.11 | 55.55 | 47.22 | 38.89 | 57.13 | 54.84 | 64.51 |
| | Total | 180.10 | 131.79 | 112.03 | 68.07 | 100.00 | 62.20 | 73.18 |

Note: Totals may not tally due to rounding of figures.

Source: NCERT (1995) and MHRD (1997).

## Table - 4

*Projection of Additional Enrolment Required in 2001 to achieve UEE from 1993-94 level*

*(Figures in Million)*

| *Age-group* | *Age-specific Population 2001* | *Adjusted Enrolment: 1993-94 @15%* | *Additional Enrolment Required* | | *Net Additional Children Required to Enrol* | *Percentage Increase from 1993-94 Level* |
|---|---|---|---|---|---|---|
| | | | *Within Age-group* | *Outside Age-group* | | |
| **6-11 Years** | | | | | | |
| Boys | 60.42 | 47.27 | 13.15 | 1.97 | 15.12 | 27.19 |
| Girls | 57.84 | 35.81 | 22.03 | 3.30 | 25.33 | 60.12 |
| Total | 118.26 | 83.08 | 35.18 | 5.27 | 40.45 | 41.39 |
| **11-14 Years** | | | | | | |
| Boys | 38.50 | 17.54 | 20.96 | 3.14 | 24.10 | 116.82 |
| Girls | 35.97 | 11.41 | 24.56 | 3.68 | 28.24 | 210.43 |
| Total | 74.47 | 28.94 | 45.52 | 6.82 | 52.34 | 152.82 |
| **6-14 Years** | | | | | | |
| Boys | 98.92 | 64.81 | 34.11 | 5.11 | 39.22 | 51.44 |
| Girls | 93.81 | 47.22 | 46.59 | 6.98 | 53.57 | 96.43 |
| Total | 192.73 | 112.03 | 80.70 | 12.09 | 92.79 | 70.41 |

Source: NCERT

## Table - 5

*Drop-out Rate at the Elementary Level (%)*

| *States/UTs* | *Boys* | *Girls* | *Total* |
|---|---|---|---|
| Andhra Pradesh | 71 | 77 | 74 |
| Arunachal Pradesh | 70 | 71 | 70 |
| Assam | 70 | 70 | 70 |
| Bihar | 76 | 82 | 78 |
| Goa | 12 | 24 | 18 |
| Gujarat | 55 | 65 | 59 |
| Haryana | 23 | 36 | 29 |
| Himachal Pradesh | 26 | 33 | 29 |
| J & K | 33 | 42 | 37 |
| Karnataka | 58 | 67 | 62 |
| Kerala | 2 | 0 | 1 |
| Madhya Pradesh | 54 | 67 | 59 |
| Maharashtra | 49 | 57 | 53 |
| Manipur | 31 | 35 | 33 |
| Megahalaya | 83 | 84 | 84 |
| Mizoram | 72 | 69 | 71 |
| Nagaland | 67 | 67 | 67 |
| Orissa | 65 | 72 | 68 |
| Punjab | 39 | 42 | 40 |
| Rajasthan | 74 | 81 | 76 |
| Sikkim | 78 | 76 | 77 |
| Tamil Nadu | 31 | 42 | 36 |
| Tripura | 74 | 73 | 73 |
| Uttar Pradesh | 47 | 55 | 50 |
| West Bengal | 71 | 75 | 73 |
| A & N Islands | 25 | 29 | 27 |
| Chandigarh | 14 | 6 | 10 |
| D & N Haveli | 52 | 69 | 60 |
| Daman & Diu | 3 | 17 | 9 |
| Delhi | 2 | 2 | 2 |
| Lakshadweep | 38 | 53 | 45 |
| Pondicherry | 6 | 13 | 10 |
| All India | 58 | 63 | 60 |

Source: NCERT

# Table - 6

## *Education for All: Basic Indicators*

| State/UT | Literacy Rate (15+), 1991 | Literacy Rate (15+), 1997 | GER (ECCE), 1990 | GER (ECCE), 1997 | % of Habitations Accessed to Primary Schools within 1 km. 1993-94 | % of Habitations accessed to Upper Primary Within 3 km. 1993-94 | Ratio of Primary to Upper Primary Schools, 1998-99 | % of Female Teachers: Primary Level, 1998-99 | Pupil-Teacher Ratio (Primary Level), 1998-99 | Average No. of Teachers in Primary Schools, 1993-94 | Gross Intake Rate (Primary), 1997-98 | Net Intake Rate (Primary), 1997-98 | Gross Enrolment Ratio (Primary), 1998-99 | Net Enrolment Ratio (Primary), 1998-99 |
|---|---|---|---|---|---|---|---|---|---|---|---|---|---|---|
| Andhra Pradesh | 38 | 47 | 7.49 | 13.3 | 97.51 | 74.45 | 5.95 | 34.09 | 46 | 2.2 | 142.6 | 83.1 | 90 | 69 |
| Arunachal Pradesh | 38 | 54 | 38.2 | 71.6 | 90.69 | 73.22 | 3.92 | 25.74 | 38 | 2.2 | 104.4 | 60.9 | 97 | 69 |
| Assam | 50 | 73 | 10.11 | 12.8 | 89.02 | 88 | 3.69 | 27.88 | 35 | 2.4 | 120.8 | 75 | 109 | 98 |
| Bihar | 35 | 44 | 5.75 | 8.1 | 94.32 | 88.24 | 3.9 | 19.19 | 63 | 2.1 | 108.5 | 65.7 | 76 | 76 |
| Goa | 72 | 84 | 24.74 | 16.5 | 95.83 | 90.49 | 10.63 | 69.18 | 21 | 2.8 | 115.1 | 67.1 | 86 | 61 |
| Gujarat | 66 | 63 | 16.35 | 16.7 | 98.32 | 92.3 | - | 49.8 | 51 | 2.3 | 128.1 | 46.1 | 118 | 86 |
| Haryana | 49 | 57 | 10.14 | 29 | 97.17 | 89.17 | 5.74 | 50.13 | 46 | 3.3 | 97.3 | 69.2 | 84 | 73 |
| Himachal Pradesh | 57 | 72 | 13.49 | 17.1 | 87.68 | 92.41 | 6.5 | 39.93 | 30 | 3 | 103.1 | 44.7 | 90 | 68 |
| J & K | NA | 51 | NA | 13.5 | 93.75 | 90.76 | 3.38 | 37.2 | 30 | 1.9 | 99.7 | 58.2 | 67 | 55 |
| Karnataka | 51 | 53 | 20.51 | 36.5 | 97.15 | 89.11 | - | 43.62 | 32 | 2 | 135.6 | 92.8 | 113 | 89 |
| Kerala | 88 | 91 | 10.59 | 17.5 | 83.54 | 89.59 | 2.28 | 70.73 | 29 | 7.6 | 83.6 | 52.5 | 90 | 72 |
| Madhya Pradesh | 40 | 50 | 8.57 | 15.6 | 94.75 | 72.04 | 4.11 | 28.93 | 44 | 2.5 | 107.8 | 62.7 | 102 | 88 |
| Maharashtra | 60 | 69 | 14.36 | 27.6 | 96.22 | 84.25 | 1.88 | 50.26 | 36 | 3.3 | 125.3 | 79.2 | 113 | 84 |
| Manipur | 57 | 71 | 38.81 | 125.5 | 95.26 | 90.39 | 4.08 | 34.57 | 19 | 3.5 | 96 | 55.9 | 86 | 68 |

(Contd...)

| State/UT | Literacy Rate (15+), 1991 | Literacy Rate (15+), 1997 | GER (ECCE), 1990 | GER (ECCE), 1997 | % of Habitations Accessed to Primary Schools within 1 km. 1993-94 | % of Habitations accessed to Upper Primary Within 3 km. 1993-94 | Ratio of Primary to Upper Primary Schools, 1998-99 | % of Female Teachers: Primary Level, 1998-99 | Pupil-Teacher Ratio (Primary Level), 1998-99 | Average No. of Teachers in Primary Schools, 1993-94 | Gross Intake Rate (Primary), 1997-98 | Net Intake Rate (Primary), 1997-98 | Gross Enrolment Ratio (Primary), 1998-99 | Net Enrolment Ratio (Primary), 1998-99 |
|---|---|---|---|---|---|---|---|---|---|---|---|---|---|---|
| Megahalaya | 49 | 68 | 129.38 | 91 | 94.01 | 81.46 | 4.95 | 46.98 | 39 | 2.1 | 129.8 | 75.6 | 93 | 50 |
| Mizoram | 82 | 95 | 51.38 | 52.9 | 95.27 | 89.47 | 1.68 | 48.73 | 24 | 3.9 | 171.4 | 99.9 | 114 | 73 |
| Nagaland | 59 | 83 | 136.99 | 143.9 | 93.36 | 70.13 | 3.13 | 40.81 | 20 | 4.9 | 110.8 | 64.5 | 94 | 59 |
| Orissa | 46 | 47 | 7.81 | 21.2 | 96.13 | 91.73 | 3.49 | 24.77 | 37 | 2.4 | 114 | 69.8 | 91 | 70 |
| Punjab | 53 | 60 | 10.72 | 16.3 | 99.17 | 86.71 | 5 | 62.59 | 42 | 3.5 | 86.1 | 50.2 | 82 | 71 |
| Rajasthan | 36 | 49 | 10.86 | 14.9 | 93.05 | 76.68 | 2.37 | 30.66 | 44 | 2.7 | 163.3 | 95.3 | 97 | 72 |
| Sikkim | 51 | 76 | 60.31 | 72.6 | 85.95 | 83.84 | 3.82 | 45.46 | 18 | 5.1 | 146.8 | 85.5 | 113 | 61 |
| Tamil Nadu | 57 | 65 | 5.9 | 11.8 | 99.43 | 85.55 | 5.57 | 41.45 | 39 | 3.8 | 127 | 97.2 | 109 | 85 |
| Tripura | 57 | 71 | 66.07 | 83 | 86.79 | 92.8 | 4.99 | 22.9 | 21 | 4.5 | 104 | 60.6 | 88 | 80 |
| Uttar Pradesh | 39 | 49 | 5.52 | 8 | 85.64 | 80.89 | 4.57 | 25.27 | 42 | 3.5 | 86.4 | 39.3 | 62 | 47 |
| West Bengal | 56 | 69 | 9.24 | 16.3 | 91.94 | 87.66 | 18.2 | 23.2 | 52 | 3.3 | 140.8 | 82.1 | 92 | 56 |
| A & N Islands | 68 | 97 | 66.27 | 64.8 | 81.16 | 82.96 | 3.69 | 47.27 | 20 | 4 | 81.2 | 47.3 | 87 | 64 |
| Chandigarh | 75 | 79 | 38.54 | 40.6 | 93.33 | 96.97 | 1.41 | 92.31 | 26 | 9.4 | 106 | 61.8 | 80 | 60 |
| D & N Haveli | 36 | 49 | 22.24 | 32.3 | 88.82 | 89.58 | 2.67 | 32.26 | 45 | 1.6 | 108.8 | 63.4 | 96 | 70 |
| Daman & Diu | 66 | 84 | 35.92 | 49.9 | 100 | 100 | 2.41 | 60.23 | 49 | 6.6 | 140.2 | 81.7 | 99 | 74 |
| Delhi | 72 | 82 | 25.48 | 29.9 | 88.19 | 98.75 | 4.45 | 63.59 | 38 | 11.2 | 99.4 | 57.9 | 89 | 68 |
| Lakshadweep | 78 | 94 | 51.05 | 109 | 100 | 100 | 4.75 | 41.72 | 25 | 13.6 | 48.8 | 28.4 | 105 | 73 |
| Pondicherry | 70 | 87 | 50.15 | 40 | 97.08 | 95.1 | 3.33 | 60.9 | 26 | 5.3 | 107.2 | 62.4 | 94 | 74 |
| All India | 49 | 57 | 10.33 | 16.9 | 93.03 | 87.91 | 3.3 | 34.55 | 42 | 2.9 | 116 | 67.5 | 90 | 71 |

Source: Arun Mehta 2000.

# 13

## A Note on Educational Policy for India

P.V. INDIRESAN[1]

This paper presents a strategy to: (a) empower poor parents to send their children to schools for long years; (b) induce employers to support education with hands-on vocational training and by patronising academic programmes, and (c) match higher education to the needs of the economy, and thereby, make it purposeful, remunerative and affordable.

Among others, this paper suggests the following strategies to obtain universal functional and computer literacy, and economically fruitful education of high quality:

1. Modify the Food-for-Work programme to provide food, fuel, and water to poor parents of children attending schools.
2. Combine single-teacher schools in a cluster of villages, and replace them by one large multi-teacher school.
3. Transfer vocational training to the work-place, and organise it as a sandwich with academic schooling.
4. Get employers to support academic programmes by contributing an education cess in proportion to their wage bill.
5. Offer successful students education vouchers to help them pursue studies further.
6. Save on higher education costs by restricting it to the numbers needed in the economy.
7. Liberalise private institutions on condition they keep average fees within set limits, and thereby, ensure that rich students cross-subsidise poor ones.
8. Enhance the reputation and influence of teachers and educational institutions by granting them autonomy, and by

using academic grades as the sole criterion for shortlisting candidates for admission to higher courses and for job selection.

9. Free restrictions on individual fees charged by private educational institutions so long as their average is within specified limits.
10. Make computer literacy and proficiency in the English language universal.

This paper deviates at times from conventional wisdom. That is both an advantage and a disadvantage. It is a disadvantage because every deviation has to be checked and tested carefully. It is an advantage because it opens avenues for change, which we need badly to ensure rapid progress.

Thomas Sowell[2] has postulated two kinds of Vision — the Constrained and the Unconstrained. The Unconstrained Vision assumes that existing constraints are not critical, that desired ideals can be achieved, and that all needed inputs can be found. The Constrained Vision assumes that immediate goals should be set within the limits set by existing constraints. The Unconstrained Vision is based on ideology, which is generally treated as sacrosanct. Advocates of Unconstrained Vision are idealists with fixed views. Being idealists, they are often intolerant of any deviation from the chosen path. The Constrained one operates on a paradigm that is accepted only to the extent it is useful, and is discarded once it ceases to be useful. Its advocates are, therefore, pragmatic, and willing to experiment with change.

Conventional wisdom in India is based on the best practices prevalent all over the world. That is idealistic. Hence, it is a case of Unconstrained Vision. That is the strength of our conventional wisdom as well as its weakness. Today India should adopt not exactly the present policies of developed countries (however good they may be) but should also consider what they did when they were poor like us, were growing the way we are at present.

This paper has adopted the Constrained Vision with an aim to find implementable solutions. It is not offered as a substitute for the conventional wisdom of Unconstrained Vision but as a supplement to it. Some of the strategies suggested here are controversial. Even then, they may at least deserve to be tested experimentally for their validity.

## 1. Status of Education in India

According to a report of the Brookings Institution, increases in knowledge contributed one and a half times what capital did to the growth of the United States in the mid-Twentieth century. No corresponding study appears to have been made for India. Yet, comparing the spate of failed public enterprises, and the number of sick industries in the private sector on the one hand with the exceptional success of the software industry and of NRIs on the other, it is probable that education has contributed even better than capital both to India's growth, and to its growth potential.

The *National Human Development Report* estimates that 40 per cent of the children drop out by the end of Class V, and 57 per cent by Class VIII. Even in Delhi, the richest city in the country, 15 per cent of the children drop out by Class VIII. However, there are practically no dropouts in Kerala. Surprisingly, West Bengal has one of the highest dropout rates in the country, next only to Bihar and almost comparable with it.

According to the UNDP's *Human Development Report 2002*, as a proportion of GNP, Sri Lanka invested 3.4 per cent in education and India 3.2 per cent. However, adult illiteracy rate in Sri Lanka was 8.4 and in India 42.4. Bihar spends 4.5 per cent of state GDP on education but its illiteracy rate is 65 per cent. That is the case even though 85 per cent of the rural children are within 500 metres of a primary school. Evidently, neither lack of funds nor of schools can be the cause of India's poor performance; chronic inefficiency must be the reason.

At the highest levels, there is a false notion that we have one of the largest number of scientists in the world. The actual figure is, there are 158 scientists and engineers in R&D per million of population in India; developed countries have typically 3000 of them, about twenty times more.

## 2. Weaknesses of the Indian Education System

According to currently accepted theory, as propounded by Gordon, there are eight types of intelligence — factual, numerate, linguistic, athletic, artistic, analytical, intuitive, and emotional. Students differ widely in their aptitude for these eight categories. Yet, school education is uniform for all types of students. There is no provision to address and promote their separate and differing aptitudes.

Educationists have made liberal studies as the core of education. However, the number of students and parents who are interested in pure scholarship are few. Overwhelming number of students and parents invest in education only to get lucrative jobs, that too in the organised sector — defined as those organisations that employ ten or more persons. Unfortunately, the organised sector accounts for only 7 per cent of the workforce. Hence, though their average wage is 3-4 time higher than those in the unorganised sector, numerically, the opportunities the organised sector offers is meagre.

Over 75 per cent of the jobs are in the field of agriculture and handicrafts. The *National Human Development Report* estimates that educated farmers are 7-8 per cent more productive than uneducated ones. Productivity in handicrafts too is low, and offers subsistence wages only. As the organised sector offers 300-400 per cent more, the marginal benefits of education in farming and traditional crafts does not enthuse people. Nor is education considered useful in their case because, traditionally, both have managed all along without formal schooling. Hence, those who see no avenue of employment other than agriculture or traditional crafts, are not interested in formal education. On the other hand, those who go after a smattering of education are unwilling to accept such employment; they want something better, preferably white-collar jobs. For them, returns to education are often far below expectations. They are liable to suffer from the Eliza Doolittle (the heroine of Bernard Shaw's *Pygmalion*) Syndrome: Education makes them unemployable.

Poverty too must be considered a contributory factor for our poor performance. According to national statistics, 5.4 per cent of children in the age group 5-14 years are at work to earn a living. In the age group 10-14 years, the percentage must be even higher. As they have chores to do at home, many more children drop out. However, it is difficult to say whether poverty is responsible for poor performance in education or poor organisation of education is the cause of our poverty. The student to teacher ratio in Primary schools is 42, and definitely higher in rural schools. In that situation, it is likely that many children drop out because the attention they get in school is poor. Many poor parents have obviously decided that they get little benefit from schools, particularly single-teacher schools.

In the Indian tradition, education was imparted in a *gurukul*, or by following in the footsteps of the parent, or by apprenticeship to competent artisans. That ensured close ties between the teacher and the taught, preservation of traditions, and informal social security too. It also led to conservatism, resistance to change, and indifference to innovation. Thus, India produced no new technologies in the Middle Ages the way the Chinese did, nor has India progressed the way Westerners have in the past four centuries. At the same time, concern is increasing that positive values of our traditional culture have eroded, national pride has given way to slavish imitation of the West, discipline has become a bad word, and licentiousness rampant. In other words, we are witnessing a cultural hiatus.

Though, India's expenditure on education, at 3.2 per cent of GNP, is substantial, funds available for instructional facilities are far below international levels. The root of the problem lies in the extreme disparity between the wages in the organised and the unorganised sectors. In the United States, Mr. Alan Greenspan, the Chairman of the FED is paid $130,000 a year, about four times the national per capita income. In India, as a proportion of per capita income, even elementary school teachers are paid more. For that reason, salaries gobble up 98 per cent or more of the primary school budget leaving next to nothing for essential non-salary investment and expenditure. Until such extremely high wages fade away in the organised sector, and they come closer to international practice, education will remain beyond the reach of the poor.

### 3. Political Interference and Public Apathy

Education has always been a politically charged process. In India, political parties depend on vote banks for survival — mainly the illiterate and slum dwellers. It is probably not an accident that governments get rarely re-elected in educationally advanced states like Kerala and Tamil Nadu, while Bihar and West Bengal — the two states with the highest dropout rates — have a tradition of re-electing the same politicians. Hence, there is a vested interest among political parties to perpetuate illiteracy (and slums too). Unless politicians see an advantage in increasing literacy, the progress in education will be slow. At the other end, there is a populist fervor in favour of expanding higher education without limit. There is considerable political pressure (connived at by the self-interest of the teaching profession) to lower standards without limit merely to promote new colleges. That is how a new college is being added every two days. That expansion too is unhealthy because it is unrelated both to the economic needs of the market and to the intellectual abilities of the students admitted.

Government policy is, in a way, a reflection of the lukewarm interest in education shown by the people themselves. In India, 3.9 per cent of the Personal Final Consumption Expenditure goes for beverages, *pan*, alcohol, and tobacco, and only 2.3 per cent is spent on education. That glaring disparity is an indicator of the lopsided priorities of our people.

There are nearly 5 million teachers in the country. Their salaries are relatively high, several times the national average wage. Hence, once selected, they are catapulted to the top ten per cent of the country's population. Many political parties have found that appointments of teachers are a lucrative source of political patronage. Due to their interference, the most qualified are not allowed to teach, and no discipline can be enforced on those that have been appointed. As teachers are the intellectual seeds of the next generation, the resultant loss of quality affects societal, cultural, and economic progress for generations to come.

At the same time, thanks to their substantial numbers, governments have found in teachers a convenient resource for election work, public awareness programmes for family planning, and many other such irrelevant chores. It would be better to draft postal employees for such work; postal officials have closer contacts with people than teachers have, and are more familiar with the local people than teachers are. However, the post office has few women employees.

## 4. Compulsory Liberal Education

Knowledge has infinite dimensions. Cultures vary. Yet, even in the liberal environment of the United States, there are governments that seek to force one stream of thought on impressionable minds. That is a universal, age-old threat to academic freedom.

Political populism and intellectual liberalism favour universal liberal education without reference to future employment opportunities. It is now the accepted Conventional Wisdom that every child must undergo ten years of compulsory education. Logically, compulsion of any type is unsatisfactory because it requires the Big Brother for enforcement. In this case, what should we do to parents who will not send their children to schools? Will sending them to prison make the situation of the child better? What should we do to a child who insists on playing truant? How much, and what kind of punishment can be imposed on a child? What should we do with schools where no qualified teacher is willing to serve?

Much of our Conventional Wisdom is composed of borrowed feathers, often devised by aping the West the way it is today. We would be well advised to look also at what the West did when it was as poor as we are today. For instance, the West has made child labour an over-riding issue, forgetting that its own prosperity today is founded on child labour of past years with children ill treated to the extent of being chained to machines. In the United States, which is in the forefront of the war against child labour, 58 per cent of the children live in broken families. As a consequence, the US suffers from unprecedented levels of juvenile delinquency, even murders by children. In contrast, children of carpet weavers become responsible, law-abiding citizens. Yet, the US and several countries of the West have imposed sanctions on products produced by child labour. Should we then prohibit goods manufactured by single mothers abandoned by heartless lovers?

On the one hand, we see children who take to apprenticeship early becoming responsible citizens. On the other, many with long years of compulsory education become problem cases. Hence, the case against child labour is not as watertight as we have been made to believe. There are three basic issues here: Should a child learn only in a classroom, or can it acquire useful life skills in the workplace, and whether learning in the workplace is synonymous with ill treatment? Here is a typical conflict between the Unconstrained and the Constrained Visions: In the world of the Unconstrained Vision ten years of classroom education is sacred, and no reduction is admissible. In the Constrained Vision, schooling is only as good as the good it does. It needs to be supported only as long as it is useful.

This is also a chicken and egg problem: Which comes first, prosperity or ten years of compulsory education? Few are aware that leprosy was as widespread in the nineteenth century Europe as it is in India today. It vanished from Europe not because of better medicines but because of better environment and nutrition, which in turn was the result of economic prosperity. Hence, faster economic development may be a better solution to the problem of child labour than compulsory education. Unfortunately, even prosperity is no solution to truancy. Only good parents can help. Hence, we need both the prosperity of the West, and the family solidarity that India has. In other words, we may copy the West but should do so without letting family values go astray in the manner West has done.

Well-intentioned government moves are known to go awry. The present Labour government in the U.K. has decided that up to 50 per cent of the students should join universities. To meet that objective, it has modified the grading system with the result there is now little discrimination between good and poor students. Apart from fall in academic standards, universalisation of higher education has lowered academic discipline: few institutions are able to enforce rules for attendance, time limits for completing a course. If that is the case in a rich country like the UK, the problems in India are likely to be greater.

## 5. Issues to Consider

If primary education is to become universal, it should be universally worthwhile. To attract the destitute poor, it should not only be free but financially rewarding too. Higher education too should be worthwhile. As time is money, the longer the time spent on education, the higher should be the reward in some form or other. That reward need not necessarily be higher income (labourers in the US shipyards earn more than university professors). Other kinds of rewards are fulfilment of Maslow Needs, better security, higher status, greater autonomy, or opportunity to take on more interesting pursuits.

The overwhelming majority of students are interested only in securing lucrative careers and not a liberal education. Even the *Taitteriya Upanishad* exhorts *kushalam na pramaaditavyam* (do not neglect welfare). Hence, education should lead to good living. It can be liberal, but cannot neglect employable skills. Only the rich (and ascetics) can seek knowledge as an end in itself.

Prolonged beyond reason, education makes people unemployable in the manner forcefully brought out by Bernard Shaw in his play *Pygmalion*. Few are as frustrated as the educated unemployed. History has shown repeatedly that, if not suitably employed, educated youth become a tinderbox. They have often brought down governments violently. Hence, access to higher education must be selective. It should be confined (a) to the numbers the economy needs, or (b) to those who will bear the full cost of their education, and hence, will not be a burden on the economy.

Disparities in educational attainments — rich-poor, rural-urban, male-female, upper caste-lower caste, and North and East-South and West — are increasing. Political fashion is to target directly the afflicted, to provide them subsidies. That is charity, a tribute to the heart but not to the head. A wiser course would be to train them to earn more. Charity is often ineffective too, because what is meant for the disadvantaged is captured by the privileged. That kind of misappropriation is unlikely to occur in the case of public goods, which are, by definition, designed and meant for everyone. Thus, well-selected public goods, like quality schools, health services, public housing, connectivity, and information services, that serve one and all can mitigate the handicap of individual disparities even better than targeted subsidies.

A simple arithmetic will show how. Consider a highly unequal society where the top one per cent of the population earns a hundred times the bottom one per cent. If the state provides public goods worth ten units for each, the combined private plus public income will have a ratio of 110 to 11 — a not unacceptable figure. Hence, enhancing public goods is a good way of mitigating disparity, in many ways better than targeted subsidies, which have a tendency to go astray. Conversely, whatever may be the remedial action taken, disparities will persist so long as the supply of public goods is poor or improperly distributed — like building expensive flyovers in cities and leaving villages with no roads.

General economic prosperity too helps. By Engel's Law, as average incomes increase, the rich will spend more and more on luxury goods. Hence, the disparity in the expenditure of essential goods — be it food or clothing, or education — decreases. Thus, few middle class parents will deny their children the best education they can afford. However, even if the rich send their children to expensive schools, they may not necessarily educate them well. Children benefit best from education only when parents can afford to send them to good schools and in addition, they encourage children to study and discipline than when they do not. Hence, income alone is not enough; a family's culture that values educational discipline is equally important. That is why lower middle class children often outperform children from rich families.

In other words, disparities can be better minimised through ways that are not direct, not necessarily obvious. For instance, the rural-urban divide is essentially the result of the poor (often non-existent) connectivity of rural areas. Hence, it can be mitigated better by improving rural connectivity than by targeting rural schools. Gender disparity would diminish if schools were given toilets, and homes had water taps close by. Likewise, the regional disparity between the states of the North and the East and those of the South and the West is purely a matter of politics. In this case, political reform is the best remedy. No form of direct educational intervention is likely to succeed in this case; any additional resource that may be provided to schools is liable to be misused. Hence, good education does not depend on education policy alone; it requires integrated development too.

Similarly, the rich-poor divide throws up intriguing possibilities. Rich parents often get round admission requirements by patronising private institutions. Generally, that is considered unethical. Hence, restrictions are placed on the admission of rich students who pay large sums of money. That merely pushes them to foreign universities, wastes precious foreign exchange without stopping them from being admitted to higher education. Hence, it is illogical to deny the rich the freedom to use their wealth (even waste it) to educate their less-than-able children abroad. It is also good policy to educate well the children of the rich, and the powerful too, than suffer later on the consequences of their ignorance.

Private universities in the US have resolved this problem of the rich-poor divide well. Reputed private institutions, like Harvard and MIT, allow relatively easy entry to the rich but take adequate precautions to check that they do not turn away any meritorious student for want of money. Few people are aware that these private institutions subsidise, on an average, two-thirds of the cost of education. They even give free education to brilliant but poor students. They ensure that no bright student is turned away by adhering to a simple rule: keep average student-cost within twenty per cent of that in reputed state universities. It should be worthwhile to follow their example; let private institutions charge as they like, provided the average fee is within acceptable limits. If that precaution is observed, for every rich student admitted, there will also be a poor but bright one. That is a better system than keeping fees uniformly high, and expecting poor students to take loans to pay high fees.

There is a view that higher education is an "inferior good" in the sense it offers private benefit through better careers for the students. Therefore, it is argued, the students should pay for the cost of their education. By the same token, higher education offers private benefit to employers too. Hence, employers too should be made to pay. They should also be given incentives to pay. One such incentive is a voice in the administration of the institution they support. To that extent, the tight control the government exercises at present over educational institutions should be relaxed in favour of donors.

Except in the case of economic disparity, all governments in India have used reservation as a universal panacea to counter disparities. Reservation is a one-sided contract: it confers privileges and demands no obligations whatever in return. For that reason, it has become a hindrance to social harmony. Matters will improve, and existing animosity against reservation will decrease substantially if the beneficiaries are expected to at least attend classes regularly, which many of them do not.

Even otherwise, reservation is losing its sheen. Until recently, 80 per cent of educated employment was in the government sector. With increasing privatisation, that share will dwindle. Alarmed by this trend, some have advocated extending Reservation Policy to the private sector also. That poses two problems. One, backward classes no longer command the goodwill they used to do. However powerful they may have become, they will face violent resistance if they try to extend reservation to the private sector. Two, reservation lowers the quality of higher education, and reduces global competitiveness. Hence, extending reservation further may provide backward classes 80 per cent of the top jobs in a poor economy but not real prosperity. Therefore, we need a better solution than reservation to empower the backward classes to compete with others.

A study in Tamil Nadu has shown that three castes, Nadars, Goundars, and Naidus, who have taken to businesses have prospered and also become highly literate, besides taking to higher and professional education. Three other castes — the Mukkulathors, Vanniars, and Dalit — who took to caste politics, remain far less developed and educated. In one case of Dalits, in Sathur, a thousand Dalit families started small match factories. They are now a confident lot. They do not allow Dalit leaders to create tension between them and other communities. The moral: Those who fight for benefits from the government become government-dependent. As the government cannot help them much, they get frustrated. On the other hand, those who concentrate on self-reliant businesses prosper and become responsible citizens too.

The United States has tried Affirmative Action instead of Reservation to help backward communities. Reservation insists on rigid quotas while Affirmative Action offers flexible handicaps. Neither has proved satisfactory because a new divide — between brilliant and ordinary students — is created. Few in India bother about this divide. For instance, the Indian Council of Social Science Research (ICSSR) will fund no studies on brilliant students, but only those on disadvantaged ones. The Approach Paper on the Tenth Plan has a section on backward sections of the society but not a word on encouraging brilliant youth. All fast developing nations (particularly, China, Singapore) are proud of their brilliant students, but India is uncomfortable with them, consider it a social sin and political *hara-kiri* to encourage good performers from the upper castes. Time has come to inquire whether, irrespective of parentage, brilliant youth should have a place or not under the Indian sun.

In recent years, an uncharacteristically aggressive form of Hinduism has erupted. That has its roots in unequal laws that favour minorities and discriminate against Hindus. The concept of minorities itself is misleading. Brahmins are less in number than Christians, Brahmins and Banias put together are fewer than Muslims. Yet, Brahmins and Banias, are deemed the majority when it comes to conferring minority privileges, and yet, accused of being an anti-social minority whenever they do well. It appears that it is best for justice to be blind. Whatever privileges are considered desirable for minorities should therefore be extended to all groups, including Hindus. That will take nothing away from the minorities and cut at the root of a dangerous form of communalism.

## 6. A Vision Statement

Vision Statements help frame clear policies. Such statements should be specific to avoid ambiguity. As they should endure for a long time, they should avoid details of merely current concern.

The *Taitteriya Upanishad* enjoins on students to be socially responsible by being generous in six different ways. It also exhorts them to take care of their own welfare. Cardinal Newman in his Convocation Address to Oxford University emphasised that the objective of education is to train youth to conduct themselves in a gracious manner. Francis Bacon transformed Western society by emphasizing the importance of accepting as true only that which can be experimentally verified. The period of European Renaissance is a saga of intellectual courage. Combining these time-tested ideas, an educational vision should address social, economic and, of course, intellectual concerns. Then, we may consider a Vision Statement for education on the following lines:

*The education system will train youth in social skills to make them good citizens of the nation and of the world. It will implant curiosity to experiment with change. It will inculcate intellectual courage to search for truth without fear of consequences. It will create wealth for each and every individual by matching, on the one hand, the differing skills/aptitudes of individual students, and on the other, the multitude of needs of the economy.*

## 7. A Set of Objectives and Strategies for Each

Based on these arguments, the following Objectives for Indian education and strategies in each case are suggested:

*a. Impart skills to match the kind of jobs the national economy needs and the capabilities and aptitudes of individual students.*

In this case, students should have the freedom to excel where their talents are greatest, and have the freedom to drop out of topics of no interest to them. Hence, there should be a wide variety of courses, and at the same time, as far as possible, all courses should be elective; no course should be compulsory. It may be worthwhile to have different types of schools even to cater to different tastes. Only then can the best match be devised to cater to varied talents and interests of students.

Logically, education will match job opportunities only when employers are drafted into the education process. That may be done in two ways: one, institute sandwich courses that alternate between classroom instruction and workplace training; two, allow active participation of employers in the management of educational institutions.

Sandwich courses may be instituted from the middle school level onwards with students spending alternate weeks in the classroom and in the workplace. If they are arranged in pairs, both the school and the employer will have continuous supply of children to be trained. These sandwich programmes could be at three levels and organised in parallel with middle, secondary, and higher secondary schools for job entry at ages 14, 16, 18 years respectively. In order to provide social status to these courses, they may be arranged to culminate in degree courses in Technical Arts that will focus more on practical skills than on theoretical studies.

This proposal conflicts with the current policy of having a minimum of ten years of schooling and academic education. In this connection, we should ponder (a) whether state governments can afford that many years of compulsory education, and (b) even if the government does so, whether our poor can afford to keep children in schools that long. Here is an eternal conflict between what is desirable and what is doable. As late as the early 1960's, Britain had the Plus Eleven system by which at age 11 years, children were streamed: academically good ones went to grammar schools, and the rest to vocational ones. At that time, Britain was far richer than what we are today. The issue is whether we should follow what Britain and other countries are doing today, or what they did when they were not all that wealthy.[3]

We should also enquire whether vocational training and child labour are identical. Who become better citizens: the ones who learn a trade willingly, or the ones who are compelled to attend uninteresting classes? It should be noted that vocational training insists on skills of acceptable and usable quality. In contrast, academic education tolerates less than minimum knowledge and accepts low pass standards, lowered further by grace marks — a situation entirely unacceptable in skill training. Here are two fundamental issues: Are ten years of academic schooling so sacrosanct that (a) that many years of academic schooling should be made compulsory in spite of increasing incidence of educated unemployment (and indiscipline too), and further (b) whether no alternative of vocational education should be permitted, and early vocational training should be prohibited outright.[4]

In order to make vocational training feasible, employers who employ more than 20 persons in semi-skilled jobs may be asked, by statute, to offer one apprenticeship for each set of 10 semi-skilled employees and pay a stipend that will not be less than the cost of food, fuel, water, and cost of travel to school/workplace. In return, they may be entitled to low-cost credit linked to the amount of stipends they pay. That is not illogical: For any firm, the number of apprenticeships, it is willing to support, is an indicator of its potential for growth.

At the college level, a balance between the numbers educated and that needed by the economy can be ensured in three ways: One, the number of students admitted in any course in any college may be linked to, and limited by the number that secured gainful employment in the previous year. Alternately, employers may be charged the cost of the final year of study (in return for a voice in the choice of electives and topics of dissertation). The government contributes a matching grant that will meet the cost of one more year. Then, the students will have to pay for the remaining one-third of the cost if all students are employed but much more when admissions are excessive. Then, the market will indicate how many graduates will be needed in each specialisation. Students too will have exact information of the market value of the course they study, and admissions will tend to follow market demand.

Professionally-oriented programmes, on the lines the Army provides at the Indian Military Academy and the Indian Railways does in Jamalpur, offer a third model. The recruitment takes place at the Plus Two stage itself, and college education guarantees a lifelong career. This model may be useful to overcome the shortage of good candidates for teaching and research — traditionally, the path towards social and economic advancement for poor but bright youth.

*b. Quality education should be economical enough to be affordable by all including the poor.*

The Food-for-Work programme may be modified as a Food-for-Education programme where parents get free grain every day their children attend school. (It would be worthwhile to include fuel and water too. That will relieve many a girl child from the daily chore of fetching them, and enable them to attend school.)

Every child might get, right at birth, education vouchers in terms of school years. The value and the duration of the vouchers may be upgraded each time the student shows progress. At the minimum, vouchers will be for five years of elementary education. Thereafter, students will get entitlements for further study either in the academic stream, or in the vocational stream, according to their aptitude and choice.

Single teacher schools rarely offer quality education, and the sufferers are invariably the rural poor. For that reason, instead of taking schools (even if they are under-equipped) to where students reside, students might be encouraged to travel at least to the next village, and get an opportunity to study in better endowed, higher quality schools. Then, 50,000 multiple teacher schools (with at least ten teachers each) would replace (at any rate supplement) 500,000 single teacher schools. Such concentrated schools can be better endowed, better maintained, and better regulated. Children are likely to find such better endowed schools more attractive even if they have to travel some distance. Clustering appears to be unavoidable if we want to ensure universal computer literacy — only in that case we offer computer access to all children.

Clustering of schools in this manner will be objected on the ground that girls will not be allowed to travel outside the village.[5] That fear is confined to some parts of the country only. In most parts, it is a common sight for girls walking along roads for miles to go to schools. At least in such regions, clustering of schools may be attempted. Critics who object to clustering of schools insist also on ten years of compulsory education. Is it possible to provide that many years of education in every hamlet, which normally have single teacher schools? Quality education in tiny schools is too expensive to combine ten years of schooling with a separate school for every village. Even if the cost is affordable, is it possible to persuade well-trained, competent teachers to live in villages, or at least, commute there every day?

Without universal computer literacy, we cannot survive in the Twenty-First century. There is next to no hope of achieving it in single-teacher schools. For that reason too, clustering is necessary.

Modern technology allows the lessons given by the ablest teachers to be cheaply reproduced and broadcast widely.[6] That makes Operation Blackboard passé. In future all classes should be equipped with TV screens to reproduce lessons recorded in the best-equipped schools in the district. That will greatly minimise the disparity between schools with good teachers and those who cannot afford them.

The study of English is the most prominent divide between the rich and the poor. The rich-poor divide will not fade away unless all children, however poor, can study in English. Video lessons will be particularly useful in the teaching of English. Many critics forget that for many villagers, particularly tribals, the official state language is as alien to them as English is[7].

c. *Financial allocation, both by the governments and by the public, should be adequate and properly balanced between salary and non-salary expenditure.*

By statute, the salary budget of any educational institution should not exceed a specified proportion of the total. That is the only way to ensure that instructional facilities are not sacrificed to pay teachers more.

Finding additional finance for high quality instructional facilities is a problem for cash-starved governments.[8] In this respect, the cess on diesel for improving national highways offers a lesson. For various reasons, people are suspicious of taxes appropriated to the Consolidated Fund and evade them as much as possible. On the other hand, they cooperate better and offer little or no opposition in the case of cess earmarked for worthwhile objectives. As in the case of the cess on diesel, the public may welcome a 3-5 per cent cess on wages (including stipends for apprentices at the rate of one apprentice for every ten employees) if that is (a) reserved for contributions to local schools, and (b) is spent in a transparent manner only for enhancing infrastructure and instructional facilities, and not for raising wages further.

It is best to index college fees to the fees paid by the student at the school level. That will ensure that rich students pay high fees while the predominantly poor, who attend state funded schools, pay only nominal amounts.

On the lines of Harvard and other reputed private universities, only the average charged by a private institution will be regulated but no restrictions will be placed on the admission of students, or on the individual fee paid by them. The emphasis on average fee will ensure that rich students are balanced by brilliant ones. That will also minimise the corruption that prevails in private professional colleges.

d. *Impart liberal education to meet the social skills and cultural values needed for good global and national citizenship.*

Even though vocational training has been strongly advocated, liberal studies should by no means be neglected. That is why sandwich courses have been suggested, in place of fulltime vocational training. By definition, liberal studies involve multiple views of the same issue. Hence, it is undesirable to have textbooks written by central agencies; it is better to leave their preparation to individual scholars with different attitudes. For the same reason, it is desirable to decentralise examinations and certification to permit the full diversity of our cultures to be propagated by some one or other. As a further exercise in promoting and preserving diversity, students should have a multiple choice for the schools they attend. Further, all professional courses must have a significant component of liberal education. (The IITs have about ten per cent weightage for humanities).

At the college level, pure liberal education, not linked to employment, is a luxury both for the individual and for the society. Normally, that should interest the rich, or those that make teaching such courses, or treat marriage as their career. Hence, except for those who want to teach, liberal education unrelated to employment should be limited to those who are prepared to meet the most.

When, in this manner, state support is restricted to the numbers that are absorbed by the economy, the government should have enough money to raise instructional facilities to international standards.

e. *Help the disadvantaged without hurting standards, particularly standards of evaluation.*

The policy of reservation has blocked most intellectual arteries of the country. We need a bypass badly to help bright youngsters without hurting the others. Then, university courses may be divided under two categories, Pass and Honours. Honours Courses will be designed to challenge brilliant students, and the Pass courses will be simple enough to be handled by others. Pass Courses will concentrate on processes to consider the question "what". Honours Courses will delve into basic principles, and concentrate on the question "why".

Examination systems should naturally be made simple for Pass Courses. In their case, there may be no secrecy about question papers either for admission tests or for final examinations. Students may be asked to answer a set of questions, which the students themselves pick by lots, from a pre-disclosed Question Bank. That will ensure that the students have studied all of them. Then, there will be no surprises, nor complaints about question papers being "out of syllabus". As different students will have different questions to answer, even copying will become impractical. Those who cannot answer such open question papers satisfactorily will have to quit (or pay the full cost of instruction to continue).

On the other hand, examinations for Honours students should be open-ended, set to be competitive at the global level. They will test the ability to innovate, to apply basic principles to work through situations with insufficient data — the way it is in real life. Those who cannot cope at this level will drop down to a Pass Course programme.

Honours courses will normally lead to careers in teaching and research. Such careers may not attract higher salaries but will enjoy better perquisites, the way dons in Oxford and Harvard do.

f. *Inculcate intellectual self-confidence to experiment with new ideas, and be unafraid of change.*

As a rule, innovative thinking is encouraged when experimental learning overrides rote learning, and projects/dissertations are emphasised over conventional classroom instruction.

The current system of examinations does not encourage (actually discourages) innovation and experimentation which requires a different form of evaluation altogether. At least in Honours Courses, evaluation should be linked to creative projects rather than on traditional paper and pencil tests. As a corollary, grading should be internal, not external. That is the practice in the IITs, and in universities the world over. A case can be made even for abolishing the mass examinations conducted by state and central boards, and by universities. It would be better for school boards (and universities) to grade institutions and not the students.

At present, educational institutions are completely de-linked from the real world of work. It is fashionable to treat employers as malefactors who exploit labour rather than as benefactors who create wealth. Instead of treating employers as outcasts, they may be made active participants in social development. They may be given a voice in the management of local schools — limited to the extent they contribute financially. In that case, the idea of the educational cess suggested above may receive good support.

Employers may also be encouraged to suggest suitable classroom projects and topics for dissertation for students. That will help schools to link instruction to real-life problems.

g. *Effective steps should be taken to minimise disparities between rich-poor, rural-urban, state-state, male-female, and between forward castes and backward ones.*

Disparities are rarely remedied by targeting them directly. It is better to correct the environmental flaws that lead to such disparities. For instance, improving rural connectivity is the best way to minimise the rural-urban divide. Several measures advocated here tackle the rich-poor divide. However, the greatest rich-poor divide is in the study of language: rich children study English, poor ones are confined to vernacular languages. Universalisation of the teaching of English is a must to bridge the rich-poor gap.[9]

The inter-regional divide between Northern/Eastern India and the Southern/Western parts is the result of bad politics, and bad politicians are at the root of the problem. Politicians may be induced to take greater interest in social welfare and development if the Constituency Fund each legislator gets is linked to the Human Developement Index in their constituency. (It is possible to devise simple, transparent methods to obtain an equivalent of HDI at the constituency level).[10] It may even be the rule that those from the bottom 10-20 per cent constituency will not be eligible to become ministers! Such innovations will yield better results than pouring money into bottomless pits.

The caste divide too is political. With increasing privatisation and globalisation, employment in the government sector will become less and less in the future. In order to counter that decrease in reserved posts, backward castes should be encouraged to engage in trade and business. In the future, giving them subsidised credit to start their own business may help them more than outright reservation in college courses. It would be a good idea to have reservation in elite schools rather than in colleges. In that case, admission to colleges may be based on Positive Affirmation where handicaps are given but no quotas are fixed. That way, children from disadvantaged groups will get (a) a head start and (b) learn to face competition in course of time.

Gender divide, at the primary level, may be minimised if poor families are guaranteed fuel and water, which girls are expected to fetch. Total absence of toilets in village schools deters girls from going to schools. Mandatory construction of girls' toilets (and their proper maintenance) will improve girls' attendance substantially. At higher levels, glass ceilings cause gender disparities. There is no simple way to crack them. Tax incentives for employing women in executive positions may open up more avenues for women, and induce more girls to shift from soft to hard options at the university level. Motherhood too is a handicap for women. Women need a break in their careers when they have to look after young children. For that purpose, they may be given several years leave without the penalties of break in service. Further, the years they lose in bringing up children may be compensated by raising their retirement age by the same number of years. Medically, such an extension can be justified as women live longer.

h. *Education can only be as good as the respect teachers and institutions get. Over-centralisation has destroyed the respect for both. Their traditional autonomy to decide what to teach, whom to teach and who will teach should be restored.*

Teachers and educational institutions perform two basic functions: One, instruct; two, evaluate. The respect they command from students and their parents depends largely on how well they instruct. The respect they command from the establishment is set by the value attached to their evaluation. When American universities admit Indian students, they depend almost entirely on student grades and teacher reports. That adds prestige to those teachers and to the institutions too. Normally, in India, we ignore altogether the evaluation done by the educational system. The political and legal environments in India are such that it is impractical to rely entirely on such evaluation for final selection, as American universities do when they admit our students. Yet, the evaluation done by the educational establishment may be made the sole determinant at least for shortlisting. That will generate respect for both education and for teachers.

For instance, consider the case of admission to the IITs. Each school board may be given a quota for shortlisting depending on the performance of students from that board in the IIT in the previous years. The IITs will then have relatively few students to evaluate. They can, therefore, use comprehensive tests to identify those with the best aptitude. At the same time, grades in higher secondary examinations will acquire value, and student discipline in those classes will improve. Similar formulae may be adopted in other institutions too for short-listing candidates either for admission, or for recruitment by major employers (civil services for instance). Then, the self-image and public reputation of schools and colleges will rise. (The reputation of the Thomason College, now re-named IIT, Roorkee, was at its peak when its graduates were automatically inducted into the Engineering service.)

The IITs enjoy considerable academic, administrative, and financial autonomy. They can finalise the admission of students and the recruitment of faculty without reference to the government. Once the budget is allocated, they can operate them without seeking any kind of government approval. These freedoms have helped a great deal in making the IITs as good as they are. Although many college teachers are opposed to autonomy, the kind of autonomy that the IITs enjoy should be allowed in as many institutions as possible. Past experience has shown that educational institutions without such autonomy do not invest or operate their resources efficiently. Hence, the Central Government should avoid aiding any non-autonomous institution, and leave their management and financing to state governments.

Even the best of institutions can make mistakes in faculty recruitment. That is why American universities give tenure only after seven years of service, and then too, selectively. In India, the period of probation is one year only, too short a period to assess the worth of a faculty member. In any case, terminating probation is virtually unknown. We would do well to adopt the American system of non-tenure contract appointments for as long as seven years. In that case, the reward package and the prerequisites should be so much more attractive than in other professions to attract brilliant youth.

i. *Organise continuing education such that everyone is up to date with employable skills throughout their career.*

All employees may be entitled, by law, to have, say, 2-3 weeks' paid training programmes, every year. Those programmes may be designed either to enhance existing skills, or to impart new ones to empower workers in sunset institutions to transfer to sunrise ones.

## 8. Discussion

Government institutions are bound by rules and by precedence; private ones by short-term results. Both ways, innovation is precluded. Thus, lack of interest in experimentation, and the absence of curiosity about the unknown, distinguishes us from the more successful cultures of the West and the Far East. We excel in analysis but fall flat when it comes to embarking on novel solutions. In general, we are so fearful of change that we dread exploring uncharted paths. We look at every door as half closed and not as half open. Hence, the country is short of innovation, nowhere more so than in the education policy. For that reason, in our country, most policy recommendations are strong on analysis but fall short of making a break with the past.

At first sight, innovation will appear impractical. However, like birds that soar in the sky, and are yet bound to earth, good innovations soar high in imagination and are yet founded on solid ground. We are generally poor in sensing that strong but invisible link between imaginative ideas and its down-to-earth roots. We do not have the patience to wait for nebulous ideas to become usable products, nor the courage to invest time and money for the purpose. That is why infant mortality of innovations is high in India. Lack of self-confidence, and lack of interest in experimentation are the root causes for this malaise. Not for our policy makers the words of Robert Frost:

*Two roads diverged in a wood, and I,*
*I took the one less travelled by,*
*And that has made all the difference.*

Our policy makers shudder to tread the less travelled path, or make a difference. As the poet, Tennyson has warned:

*And God fulfils Himself in many ways,*
*Lest one good custom should corrupt the world.*

So, we need to change all the time lest any one good custom extended beyond reason will corrupt us. Hence, the purpose of this paper is not to arrive at agreed solutions but to induce policy maker to give up old ways that have become corrupted by over-use, and experiment with newer and better ones.

Modern scientific spirit is based not on ideology but on the concept of the paradigm. Scientists treat the paradigm, so long as it rules, with as much respect as the faithful venerate ideology. However, because of their Constrained Vision, scientists are ever suspicious of the paradigm they use. Their constant endeavour is to disprove, not prove, the hypotheses that define the paradigm. Once that base is eroded, the scientist discards the old paradigm and moves on to a new one that performs better than the old one. In contrast, in their Unconstrained Vision, ideologists assume that their ideas and ideals are not only perfect, but eternal too. They seek to transform the world and make it follow the bounds of ideology, not the other way round. Such idealism is necessary but only within limits. That is why pragmatic Constrained Vision too is needed in practice.

For decades, we have been ruled by ideology as a matter of faith. That has left us poor. Hence, let us instead try a dose of pragmatism. Let us experiment with change with the clear understanding that there will be freedom to change what we change.

## Epilogue

No proposal, nor hypothesis, can be accepted as valid unless and until it is verified as correct by experiment. The proposals made in this paper are no exception. In particular, the following hypotheses require verification.

a. Clustering of schools will attract better teachers, inculcate better discipline, provide better education, and reduce dropout rates.

b. Food, fuel, and water for education will induce the poor to send children to elementary schools.

c. Sandwich courses in association with employers will induce poor parents to continue to educate their children beyond the primary stage.

d. Video lessons from reputed teachers, combined with computer literacy and proficiency in English will empower poor students to compete with rich ones.

e. Autonomous colleges with admissions linked to employment can improve quality and will also reduce the financial burden on the government.

Provided, all these educational reforms are instituted as an integral part of the overall economic development of the community.

The experiment may be tried out in a few selected rural development blocks. The blocks may be allocated Plan investment at the per capita average of the Five-year plans of the Centre and the state. Likewise, employment too at the per capita average for the Central and state governments may be allocated. With this foundation, the scheme will aim to reduce school dropout rates to less than ten per cent up to the tenth standard level by improving connectivity, health services, and other infrastructure facilities as an integrated package of development.

In other words, resource constraints are taken as given, and pursuit of education is voluntary. Within those constraints, children will be induced to study for ten years.

For comparison, compulsory ten years of schooling may be experimented within conventional schools. Additional resources as required may also be granted. Comparing the results will set at rest controversies better than acrimonious debates.

## Notes

1. The author is grateful to Professor Anil Sadgopal, Sri Anil Bordia and Dr. Bibek Debroy for their critical comments. However, opinions expressed in this paper are my own.
2. *A Conflict of Visions: Ideological Origins of Political Struggles*, Quill, New York, 1987.
3. The separation of bright students into grammar schools was abandoned in the 1960s and all state-aided schools were forced to become "comprehensive" due to a fear that streaming adversely affected children from poor families who, it was felt, would not be able to compete with upper class students at the tender age of eleven. After forty years, it is now argued that the result has been the exact opposite. According to the *Economist* (Dec 5, 2002). "The abolition of grammar schools is probably one reason why recent figures suggest that social mobility in Britain has slowed: Many of the best state-funded schools chose to go private as a result, so the gap between rich and poor people's education widened.... Of the 100 schools that get the top A level grades now, only two are comprehensives: they rank 96th and 99th. Compared with children who grew up in the 1960s and 1970s, those who grew up in the 1980s had less chance of being more successful than their parents..... The answer is not to tweak the system when people are 18, but to provide them with better education earlier on. The government needs to re-create something like the grammar schools, to let down for the next generation the ladder up which this generation of top people climbed."
4. According to the *Times of India*, November 14, 2002, two doctors and twenty engineers were among the 13,500 applicants for temporary clerical posts. That is symptomatic of increasing educated unemployment in the country.
5. As a remedy, bus transport between nodal villages where cluster-school is located and adjacent villages may be established. That will help not only the girls but the rural economy as well. An investment of Rs. 10,000 crores on buses, and a similar additional amount to upgrade rural roads should cover 80 per cent of the villages. Installing transport system will be cheaper and more viable than trying to enforce hundreds of thousands of teachers to commute to small villages, or reside there.
6. The distribution of these lessons can be left to private enterprise, with the state providing only the capital equipment. Ten units in each of 50,000 schools will cost barely Rs. 1000 crores as capital costs. A set of CD ROMs for all ten classes could be purchased for Rs. 100,000, (a total of Rs. 5000 crores for all 50,000 schools). Even if both viewing equipment and CD ROMs are replaced every three years, the annual cost will be Rs. 2000 crores only. The cost of buildings and electricity is extra. The cluster approach is both economical, and necessary for quality maintenance too. If computers are installed in every village, cost will increase ten times, and the system will not be maintainable because it is difficult to get maintenance technicians to keep track in all remote villages. There is also a risk that in small villages, local leaders will grab the equipment for their personal use. That risk is less in the cluster approach.
7. As Nocholas Kristoff explains in the *New York Times* of November 22, 2002, "the long-run competitive challenge we Americans face from China will have less to do with its skylines, army or industry than with its Super Kids, who though their first languages are Mandarin Chinese and Shanghainese, they could rattle off answers to equations faster than I could even in English." Time we wake up!
8. Salaries are higher than what the economy can afford. That imbalance is a significant part of the problem. The difficulty may become manageable if salaries are determined by the market and not by politics.
9. Cuba raised literacy levels in one go by carrying out a campaign the way we have done in the case of smallpox. It should be possible to raise literacy rates above 90 per cent within one year by raising a voluntary army to fight illiteracy. Such a short but massive campaign may work better and may cost less than the sub-optimal techniques we are using currently. Computer techniques are now available to make people functionally literate within 60 hours of instruction.
10. For instance, the amount a legislator gets may be linked to (a) direct taxes collected, and (b) number who have passed the Tenth standard examination.

# 14

## The Health Status of Indians

*A Perspective*[1]

LAVEESH BHANDARI • AARTI KHARE

This paper seeks to present a perspective on the wide range of health issues facing India. It does so using information from many different sources. The key insights arising from such an analysis are:

- There is large heterogeneity in the requirement of health care.
- This care has to be made accessible at a low cost.
- Needs and requirements are changing rapidly with economic growth and shifts in demographic pattern.

Therefore, health policy should be one that smoothly changes its character with time. All of this, in the belief of the authors, can best be achieved through a strong reliance on private initiative – be if for profit or non-profit, and not by an over-dependence on public modes. The health policy for India should be one, therefore, that encourages the entry of all types of care providers, services, product suppliers, into the health care sector.

### 1. Introduction

This paper reports the generic health status of the people of India. The health status of a society is a function of many factors – economic status, climate, living conditions and habits, availability and quality of health care, all play an important role. Most of these factors have contributed to the poor health conditions in India.

According to the *Human Development Report-2001*, India ranks among the lowest 40 countries in terms of its general human development indicators. Of the many measures that contributed to

India's poor showing, health indicators were among the lowest. This is not surprising given high poverty levels by any standards and a climate that is conducive to the birth and spread of disease vectors. However, within India there are large differences. Many states of India have been making consistent progress in achieving better living conditions for their residents. Though at an overall level, India performs extremely poorly, there are many parts of India that are much better (and worse) off.

**Table 1**

*Mortality and Life Expectancy for Indian States and Comparable Countries*

| *States and Comparable Countries* | *Under 5 mortality (Per '000) 1998-99* |
|---|---|
| Kerala | 19 |
| **Mauritius** | **19** |
| **Argentina** | **22** |
| **Guatemala** | **53** |
| Maharashtra | 58 |
| Tamil Nadu | 63 |
| West Bengal | 68 |
| Karnataka | 70 |
| Punjab | 72 |
| Haryana | 77 |
| **Bolivia** | **84** |
| Gujarat | 85 |
| Andhra Pradesh | 86 |
| Assam | 90 |
| **Zimbabwe** | **103** |
| Orissa | 104 |
| Bihar | 105 |
| Rajasthan | 115 |
| **Sudan** | **121** |
| Uttar Pradesh | 123 |
| Madhya Pradesh | 138 |
| **Benin** | **157** |
| **India** | **95** |

Source: Registrar General of India; *World Health Report 2001*.

Generic health conditions tend to be reflected in overall life expectancy and infant mortality rates and many use these measures in studying the health conditions of society. Infant and child mortality ratios are considered to be indicative of the well being of the entire society. Not only are they considered to be representative of the effectiveness of preventive care, but also of attention paid to maternal and child health, as well as health care and health status of the population as a whole. However, with the changing nature of the types of ailments afflicting the population, the effectiveness of such indicators in representing the health status of the entire population is limited. Policies based purely on conclusions drawn from these indicators will not be able to attend to all the problems affecting the population.

We do not limit ourselves to the use of mortality or life expectancy rates. We use other measures as well. Take for instance DALYs - Disability Adjusted Life Years. DALYs are a measure of the time lost by a society due to different ailments. DALYs indicate the extent of time lost due to ailments, and as a result also the economic loss to society. DALYs are a good comparative measure across countries, and can prove useful in prioritizing health expenditures. However some information is not reflected in DALYs. That is better captured by *prevalence rates*. We also use 15-day prevalence rates of various ailments; prevalence is simply the number reporting ailments as a share of total population. This measure better reveals the ailment patterns. It can also help us in designing a policy that can better service requirements – serious as well as non-serious.

However, there is much that is hidden in these aggregated quantitative figures. Ailments may be acute (short-term) or chronic, communicable or non-communicable, life threatening or not, treatable or not, costly or cheap to treat, etc. Indeed, it is difficult to clearly categorize many diseases; they are too dependent upon particular and specific conditions. A purely statistical analysis of diseases is therefore fraught with the danger of missing out on the key insights. In the interest of lucidity and clarity, we focus on simply presenting the health status of Indians, and the patterns of ailments afflicting them.

This paper, therefore, seeks to present a perspective on the wide range of health issues facing India. It does so using information from many different sources. The key insights arising from such an analysis are:

- There is large heterogeneity in the requirement of health care.
- This care has to be made accessible at a low cost.
- Needs and requirements are changing rapidly with economic growth and shifts in demographic patterns.

Therefore, whatever system we come with, would also need to be one that smoothly changes its character with time. All of this, in the belief of the authors, can best be achieved through a strong reliance on private initiative – be it for profit or non-profit, and not by an over-dependence on public modes. The health policy for India should be one, therefore, that encourages the entry of all types of care providers, services, product suppliers, into the health care sector.

The rest of the paper proceeds as follows. The next section (Section 2) compares the health characteristics in India and the rest of the world. It finds that low incomes can explain much of the difference between India and the world; however, in many cases, India has performed more poorly than other non-developed countries.

Section 3 presents a brief State-wise analysis. It puts forth the argument that even the States that have performed much better than the rest of the country have important health care requirements, and need to be served by an efficient health care system. It goes on to underline the heterogeneity in the requirements of health care.

Section 4 studies the prevalence of ailments across different demographic segments. It finds that women and the old are two sections of the society that have significantly different requirements. Some public measures have been observed towards alleviating women's health conditions, however, little has been observed on the issue of better care for older population.

Section 5 underlines the heterogeneity of India, and suggests that a good policy would be one that does not seek to limit private initiative (whether for or not for profit) but promotes it. This is the only way to achieve coverage and quality for all at a low cost. Moreover, only a private system can rapidly adapt to changing requirements.

The concluding section (Section 6) lays out some characteristics of a public policy for India's health requirements. The appendix presents some information on India and its health patterns that is relevant but may not have been discussed in the text.

## 2. Illness in India and the World

While India has the second largest population in the world, it accounts for a larger percentage of the world's ailing in case of many ailments as compared to its share of the world's population. As per *The World Health Report-2001*, India shares 16 per cent of the world's population, but accounts for 20 per cent of the disability adjusted life year's (DALY's) lost in the world.

### *2.1 High Rates*

The following table (table 2) from the WHO shows a comparison of DALYs lost for India and the world.

**Table 2**

*Disability Adjusted Life Years (DALY's) Lost*

| *Disease/Condition* | *World* | *High income countries* | *Low and middle income countries* | *India* |
|---|---|---|---|---|
| Total Population | 5,884,576 | 907,828 | 4,976,748 | 982,223 |
| Total DALYs Lost | 1,382,564 | 108,305 | 1,274,259 | 268,953 |
| DALY Lost as a ratio of population | 0.235 | 0.119 | 0.256 | 0.274 |

Source: World Health Organization, 2001.

The number of days lost in India is much higher as a ratio of population than in the rest of the world. However, the difference is marginal when compared with low and middle-income countries. This is, of course, natural given poor living and work conditions as well as access to health care.

### *2.2 Second Stage Transition*

Given high poverty levels, it is not surprising that health conditions in India are poor in overall terms. However, rather than go into the poor overall conditions, we first discuss how India is different (or same) from other countries. To do this we first undertake an analysis of the distribution of DALY's lost.

**Table 3**

*Distribution of DALY's as per Major Categories of Ailments*

| Disease/Condition | *World (%)* | *High income countries (%)* | *Low and middle income countries (%)* | *India (%)* |
|---|---|---|---|---|
| I. Communicable diseases, maternal and perinatal conditions and nutritional deficiencies | 40.9 | 7.2 | 43.8 | 50.3 |
| II. Non-communicable conditions | 43.1 | 81.0 | 39.8 | 33.0 |
| III. Injuries | 16.0 | 11.8 | 16.4 | 16.7 |
| TOTAL | 100 | 100 | 100 | 100 |

Source: *World Health Report, 2001,* World Health Organization

According to epidemiological transition theories, as a country moves up the economic ladder, communicable diseases become relatively less important and non-communicable ones become more so. In the case of India, this distribution currently is highly biased towards communicable diseases – much more than an average low/ middle income country.

## *2.3 India Specific Patterns*

Later, we will discuss that this is not merely due to poor living or work conditions and access to health care. The age distribution also matters significantly in affecting this distribution. That is, the older age groups (who have a low share of India's population currently) tend to have a much higher prevalence of non-communicable ailments.

This is an important issue for India's health-economic policy. As the share of older age groups increase, and as rapid economic progress continues, the structure of ailment patterns will also change. However, this should not be taken to imply that economic factors are the only determinant. Further break-up of the first category shows that though India is similar to other low income countries in prevalence of infectious diseases, it has much higher DALY's lost due to maternal and perinatal conditions and nutritional deficiencies. Much has been written on the poor quality of health care provided and conditions during childbirth in India (IIPS, 1998-99a & 1998-99b), the figures below support these arguments.

**Table 4**

*DALY's due to category 1 Ailments as percentage of Total DALY's*

| *Disease/Condition* | *World (%)* | *High income countries (%)* | *Low and middle income countries (%)* | *India (%)* |
|---|---|---|---|---|
| I. Communicable diseases, maternal and perinatal conditions and nutritional deficiencies | 40.9 | 7.2 | 43.8 | **50.3** |
| A. Infectious and parasitic diseases | 23.4 | 2.8 | 25.2 | **25.1** |
| B. Respiratory infections | 6.2 | 1.4 | 6.6 | **9.5** |
| C. Maternal conditions | 2.3 | 0.4 | 2.5 | **2.9** |
| D. Perinatal conditions | 5.8 | 1.9 | 6.2 | **8.7** |
| E. Nutritional deficiencies | 3.2 | 0.9 | 3.4 | **4.0** |

Source: *World Health Report, 2001*, World Health Organization

In fact DALY's lost due to infections and parasitic diseases are similar to those in other countries. The relatively poor performance of India in category 1 ailments comes from the other sub-categories. According to *Bhandari and Dubey, 2001*, approximately 42.7 per cent of Indians do not receive their basic minimum calorific nutritional requirements (Refer table 5). The figures in all likelihood would be lower for women.

**Table 5**

*Proportion of Households with Calorie Deficiency: All India (%)*

| *Sector* | *Calorie Deficiency* |
|---|---|
| Rural | 48.7 |
| Urban | 25.4 |
| Total | 42.7 |

Source: Bhandari and Dubey, 2001

The top three categories of diseases that are causes of DALY's lost and deaths in India are presented in the table below.

**Table 6**

*Top Three Types of Ailments in India*

| | *DALY's lost* | *Deaths* |
|---|---|---|
| 1 | Infectious and parasitic ailments | Cardiovascular diseases |
| 2 | Unintentional injuries | Infectious and parasitic ailments |
| 3 | Cardiovascular diseases | Respiratory infections |

Source: *World Health Report, 2001,* World Health Organization

Evidence also suggests that the prevalence of infectious ailments may have reduced over time. India seems to be in the second phase of the epidemiological transition. The second stage is characterized by a reduction in infectious epidemics and the onset of non-communicable, degenerative diseases (such as diabetes), which have lifestyle related causes. In 1970, 17,268 cases of cholera were registered. In 1998 the number of cases had reduced to 7,151.[2] The trend is similar for ailments such as Malaria and Leprosy among others[3]. However, the absolute number of people suffering from such ailments continues to be large. In the following section, we will also show that prevalence rates for some degenerative ailments are quite high, not only among the aged but also among the working age population.

Table 6 suggests that not only infectious and contagious ailments but also degenerative ailments are showing up among the key health issues. This is indicative of India's entrance into the second stage of the epidemiological transition.

Also many ailments that afflict people in India today have long been eradicated from many other countries of the world. India's share in the burden of the world's ailing (in terms of the DALY's lost) is approximately 20 per cent, much higher than its share of the population. But for some ailments the shares are much higher.

**Table 7**

*India Largest Contribution to DALY's and Deaths in the World*

| | *DALY's lost* | *Deaths* |
|---|---|---|
| 1 | Leishmaniasis (66.8 %) | Leishmaniasis (70.8 %) |
| 2 | Dengue (63.2 %) | Dengue (63.2 %) |
| 3 | Leprosy (52.6 %) | Fires (47.7 %) |

Source: *World Health Report, 2001*. World Health Organization

India accounts for 66.8 per cent of the world's DALY's lost and 70.8 per cent of the deaths due to *leishmaniasis (kala-azar)*, found mostly in the states of Bihar, West Bengal and Uttar Pradesh.

Overall the situation in India differs highly between States. State level data on DALYs are not available, though the raw data is available to undertake estimates on the same. However we do have data on the prevalence of ailments[4].

## 3. Health Status of Indians: A State-wise Analysis

How do different states compare with each other? This question can be answered by taking a look at the average number of people who are ill in a 15-day period. The NSSO survey provides statistics for ailments afflicting the ill in India.[5] The fifty-second round of survey covered approximately 600,000 individuals residing in 120,942 rural and urban households in a representative manner. All spells of ailment suffered by each member of the household during the 15 days preceding the date of inquiry, whether or not the patient was hospitalized for treatment, were covered in the survey.

The table below shows State-wise data on prevalence of ailments. Unlike in the case of international data we find that there does not appear to be a direct relationship between aggregate health conditions (measured somewhat differently though) and how well the state is doing economically. We find that states with a larger share of the older population, states with hot and humid climate, tend to be the ones that have the highest prevalence rates.

## Table 8

*Prevalence of Ailments in India and the States*

| State | Persons ill in a 15 day span | Percentage population ill in a 15 day span | Per Capita State GDP (Rs.'000) |
|---|---|---|---|
| **Smaller States/UTs** | | | |
| Manipur | 10,478 | 0.7 | 11.5 |
| Mizoram | 7,344 | 1.6 | 15.5 |
| A & N Islands | 4,963 | 2.3 | . |
| Arunachal Pradesh | 14,431 | 2.7 | 15.9 |
| Meghalaya | 55,472 | 3.5 | 13.1 |
| Nagaland | 26,064 | 3.6 | 14.1 |
| Sikkim | 14,416 | 3.6 | 0.0 |
| Goa | 45,845 | 4.0 | 39.2 |
| Delhi | 418,013 | 4.2 | 36.6 |
| Daman & Diu | 3,890 | 4.3 | . |
| Lakshadweep | 4,682 | 5.5 | . |
| D & N Haveli | 8,944 | 5.7 | . |
| Pondicherry | 48,261 | 7.5 | 33.4 |
| Tripura | 358,444 | 11.5 | 12.3 |
| Chandigarh | 96,395 | 13.6 | 41.6 |
| **Larger States** | | | |
| Rajasthan | 1,151,114 | 2.9 | 12.0 |
| Bihar | 2,993,823 | 3.6 | 7.0 |
| Madhya Pradesh | 2,811,558 | 4.0 | 11.3 |
| Gujarat | 1,730,800 | 4.3 | 22.1 |
| Karnataka | 2,028,682 | 4.3 | 19.2 |
| Maharashtra | 3,955,976 | 5.0 | 26.7 |
| Jammu & Kashmir | 349,688 | 5.3 | . |
| Tamil Nadu | 3,099,601 | 5.4 | 20.7 |
| Haryana | 1,204,702 | 6.1 | 22.4 |
| Orissa | 1,860,213 | 6.2 | 10.7 |
| Andhra Pradesh | 4,530,187 | 6.3 | 16.7 |
| Uttar Pradesh | 8,911,460 | 6.3 | 10.8 |
| West Bengal | 4,247,918 | 6.5 | 16.6 |
| Punjab | 1,573,758 | 7.9 | 24.6 |
| Assam | 1,667,112 | 8.1 | 10.6 |
| Himachal | 449,301 | 8.8 | 16.9 |
| Kerala | 2,639,621 | 11.0 | 22.6 |
| **India** | **46,323,156** | **5.5** | |
| | **Standard Deviation** | 2.85 | |

Source: Authors' Calculation; NSSO 1995-96; CSO 1999-00; Census of India 2001

As per the NSSO survey, around 5.5 per cent of the Indian population is ill on any given span of 15 days. However, this is an average for India. The heterogeneity among the states is definitely obvious. Moreover, a close look at the figures reveals that a lot of the states that generally perform well socio-economically show very high numbers of ill people. Looking purely at the number of ill people as a share of population, States such as Chandigarh and Kerala would be termed as among the unhealthiest ones! That of course would be an incorrect conclusion to draw. To further understand this, let us first consider the association between life expectancy and ailments.

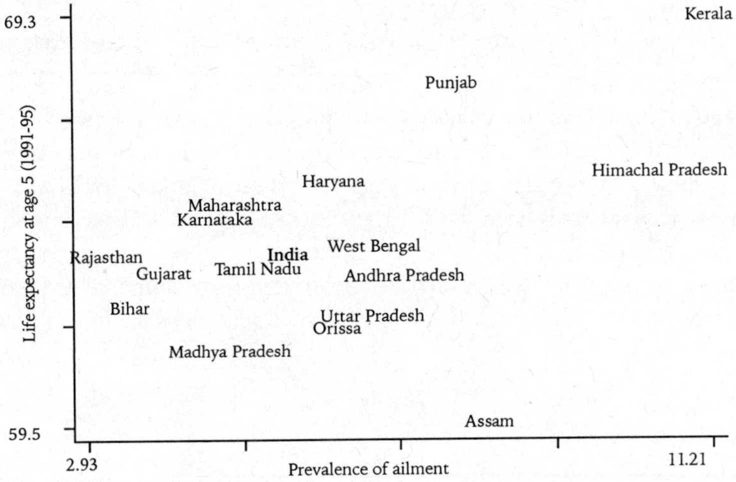


Source: Authors' Calculation. (NSSO Fifty-second Round; Sample Registration System)

We find a positive relationship between life expectancy and prevalence rates. The higher the life expectancy, the higher is the prevalence of ailments in the state. A policy based simply on the empirically established relationship between health status as represented by life expectancy or infant mortality rates and the socio-economy would not have accommodated the specific requirements of such states.

The difference is due to the parameters used to measure 'health'. In the initial case, we are measuring health from morbidity numbers, while in the latter case we are measuring it in terms of life expectancy. Health policy based only on vital indicators like mortality and life expectancy will ignore the needs of the better off states, who showed much higher prevalence of illness.

In other words, a policy based simply on prevalence of ailments would ignore the socio-economically worse off states, while a policy based on inferences from the vital indicators would ignore the problems affecting the better off states.

The above discussion reveals another fact; when studied with a geographical perspective, large differences are observed within the country. But what are the differences across different demographic groups?

## 4. Prevalence of Ailments across Demographic Segments

First, consider the overall prevalence rates of *all ailments* for the different demographic segments. The prevalence rates are, therefore, presented across sectors and according to sex. This is presented according to three age groups. Age less than or equal to 14 years categorized as Children, ages 15 to 59 categorized as working age adult population and 60 plus population comprising the group of elderly population. In the discussion that follow, some of the key aspects of the differences in ailment prevalence rates are presented.

**Table 9**

*Prevalence of Ailments as per Sector, Sex, Age*

| Prevalence of ailment | (%) |
|---|---|
| Rural Male Ailing 0-14 | 5.0 |
| Rural Female Ailing 0-14 | 4.5 |
| Urban Male Ailing 0-14 | 5.4 |
| Urban Female Ailing 0-14 | 5.0 |
| Rural Male Ailing 15-59 | 4.4 |
| Rural Female Ailing 15-59 | 5.5 |
| Urban Male Ailing 15-59 | 4.3 |
| Urban Female Ailing 15-59 | 5.4 |
| Rural Male Ailing 60+ | 19.2 |
| Rural Female Ailing 60+ | 17.9 |
| Urban Male Ailing 60+ | 15.8 |
| Urban Female Ailing 60+ | 17.6 |

Source: Authors' Calculation; NSSO 1995-96

On the whole, we find that:

1. Differences are not too large within an age group.
2. Differences are not too high across the rural-urban divide.
3. Differences are somewhat larger across sex.
4. The most significant differences are across age groups.

A more detailed break-up is essential to explain the numbers above. The types of ailments afflicting the various socio-economic groups are essential to come up with meaningful picture of the health status of Indians.

Now consider a more detailed break-up of the prevalence rates for India as a whole.

**Table 10**

*Prevalence of Ailments as per Categories of Ailments*

| Per 100 | Blood & Circulatory | Endocrine & Digestive | Genitourinary | Injury | Mouth, gums & teeth | Musculoskeletal | Nervous system disorders | Other Ailments | Parasitic | Respiratory | Total |
|---|---|---|---|---|---|---|---|---|---|---|---|
| 1 | 2 | 3 | 4 | 5 | 6 | 7 | 8 | 9 | 10 | 11 | 12 |
| Rural Male 0-14 | 0.02 | 0.48 | 0.02 | 0.10 | 0.03 | 0.01 | 0.18 | 0.85 | 2.96 | 0.35 | 5.0 |
| Rural Female 0-14 | 0.02 | 0.47 | 0.01 | 0.04 | 0.04 | 0.01 | 0.15 | 0.81 | 2.62 | 0.37 | 4.5 |
| Urban Male 0-14 | 0.03 | 0.39 | 0.02 | 0.18 | 0.05 | 0.02 | 0.18 | 0.89 | 3.03 | 0.60 | 5.4 |
| Urban Female 0-14 | 0.03 | 0.42 | 0.01 | 0.07 | 0.05 | 0.05 | 0.24 | 0.85 | 2.70 | 0.54 | 5.0 |
| Rural Male 15-59 | 0.15 | 0.42 | 0.06 | 0.16 | 0.04 | 0.15 | 0.18 | 1.06 | 1.91 | 0.30 | 4.4 |
| Rural Female 15-59 | 0.24 | 0.54 | 0.05 | 0.07 | 0.11 | 0.22 | 0.20 | 1.61 | 2.09 | 0.34 | 5.5 |
| Urban Male 15-59 | 0.21 | 0.47 | 0.06 | 0.19 | 0.07 | 0.09 | 0.21 | 1.04 | 1.61 | 0.31 | 4.3 |
| Urban Female 15-59 | 0.38 | 0.53 | 0.04 | 0.09 | 0.11 | 0.22 | 0.20 | 1.58 | 1.85 | 0.39 | 5.4 |
| Rural Male 60+ | 1.19 | 2.24 | 0.57 | 0.24 | 0.08 | 1.97 | 1.59 | 5.24 | 3.90 | 2.16 | 19.2 |
| Rural Female 60+ | 1.15 | 1.41 | 0.10 | 0.31 | 0.11 | 2.46 | 1.71 | 4.76 | 3.81 | 2.10 | 17.9 |
| Urban Male 60+ | 2.54 | 2.07 | 0.29 | 0.24 | 0.06 | 1.30 | 1.23 | 4.12 | 2.50 | 1.48 | 15.8 |
| Urban Female 60+ | 3.32 | 2.46 | 0.14 | 0.33 | 0.18 | 2.37 | 1.08 | 4.21 | 2.36 | 1.19 | 17.6 |

Source: Authors' Calculation; NSSO 1995-96

The above table shows the prevalence of ailments in the 15 days prior to the day of survey. What is most striking about the figures above (column 12) is the marked increase in prevalence between the younger age groups (<60 years) and the older age groups (>=60 years). On an average, 5 per cent of the children fall ill in any span of 15 days. The figures are not very different for the 15 - 59 age group. However, about 18 per cent of the elderly are suffering from some ailment or the other in any span of 15 days.

That the aged suffer more from health problems is well known, however, in the case of India bulk of health policy measures are oriented towards the younger age groups. Moreover, even where government health measures are universal in nature (such as free dispensaries) the conditions are such that the aged find it extremely difficult to access these services. These issues have been discussed further in Section 5.

### *4.1 Parasitic Ailments*

For a sub-tropical and poor country such as India, it is only expected that parasitic ailments form a large percentage of ailments. As expected, the figures above also reveal that across age, sex, and geography (rural and urban) parasitic ailments are a major component.

We have categorized parasitic ailments into three sub-sets:

- Ailments that have vaccines to prevent their prevalence (these include Tetanus, Diphtheria, Whooping Cough, Chicken Pox, Measles/German Measles, Mumps)
- Ailments that have no vaccines (these include Pulmonary Tuberculosis, Leprosy, Sexually Transmitted Diseases, Jaundice, Guinea Worm, Filaria (Elephantiasis)) and
- Short duration fevers, that are generally parasitic in nature.

The figures (table 11) show that amongst the three categories, fevers of short duration dominate. These cannot be further sub-categorized, as respondents themselves are not aware of their nature. Commonly, the bulk of the literature and discussion on health policy focuses on ailments such as TB, leprosy, jaundice etc. However, the common flu, or short duration viral fevers affect many more at a given period.

**Table 11**

*Prevalence of Parasitic Ailments*

(Per 10,000)

| *Prevalence* | *Age* | *Short duration fevers* | *Other parasitic ailments* | *Vaccination preventable* |
|---|---|---|---|---|
| Rural Male | 0-14 | 266.46 | 3.34 | 26.13 |
| Rural Female | 0-14 | 242.12 | 2.73 | 17.55 |
| Urban Male | 0-14 | 277.89 | 3.93 | 20.96 |
| Urban Female | 0-14 | 241.76 | 3.70 | 24.28 |
| Rural Male | 15-59 | 159.42 | 19.64 | 11.52 |
| Rural Female | 15-59 | 186.16 | 13.37 | 9.67 |
| Urban Male | 15-59 | 138.90 | 14.05 | 8.44 |
| Urban Female | 15-59 | 164.38 | 11.19 | 9.26 |
| Rural Male | 60+ | 296.17 | 43.65 | 50.46 |
| Rural Female | 60+ | 331.44 | 22.46 | 27.36 |
| Urban Male | 60+ | 191.23 | 38.77 | 20.44 |
| Urban Female | 60+ | 188.03 | 21.37 | 26.56 |

Source: Authors' Calculation; NSSO 1995-96

The fever of short duration is by far the most pervasive ailment in India. To the knowledge of the author, discussions on the ramifications of this fact have been more or less absent in the health policy debate. Three issues come to mind.

a) Can they be reduced? And how?

b) What is the impact on people's day-to-day lives?

c) What should be the public policy on short duration ailments

- Sanitation, garbage, mosquitoes
- Work conditions- forest/farms- protective clothing, creams etc.
- Proximity in living conditions
- Proper nutrition and rest during ailment period
- Loss of schooling of kids, loss of income, when parents fall ill,
- Public policy oriented towards better awareness

Prevalence figures (not reported here) suggest that seven per cent of those suffering from parasitic ailments could have prevented illness by means of adequate vaccines. However, five per cent of those suffering from parasitic ailments suffer from illnesses that do not have any vaccines. Increased awareness regarding these ailments can take us a long way in reducing their spread. The vast majority (88 per cent) being afflicted by parasitic illnesses, however, suffer from short duration fevers.

The situation of immunization in India appears to be poor. While the people who are currently over 60 years old do show to have a high prevalence of vaccination preventable ailments, children today seem to have a higher prevalence of such ailments as compared to the working age population. As mentioned before, a large part of the public policy discussions focuses on vaccinations. The above figures suggest that further improvements are required in the delivery of vaccination services.

Urban female children and rural male children suffer more from these ailments than their rural counterparts. Prevalence of parasitic ailments is also higher in the rural areas than in the urban areas. The elderly have a much higher difference between the rural and urban areas, however the difference among the children are lower. This might be due to more awareness over time and also due to targeted approach of the immunization drive in the rural areas.

### *4.2 Endocrine and Digestive System Ailments*

Many, if not most, of the digestive system ailments are caused by consumption of unhygienic food and unclean water. Water borne ailments are fairly wide spread in India even today. Clean and processed drinking water is available to a very small percentage of the population. In addition, water is also unavailable for purposes of cleaning and washing in adequate amounts. As a consequence sanitation conditions are poor. In a sub-tropical environment, the result of these conditions is the widespread prevalence of water-borne diseases.

Prevalence rates of endocrine and digestive system related problems are presented in the following table. Digestive system ailments include diarrhea and gastro-enteritis, dysentery, chronic amoebiosis, gastritis- hyper acidity, gastric/peptic/duodenal ulcers and piles. Endocrine problems include lifestyle related problems such as goitre and thyroid disorders, diabetes, Beri Beri, Ricket; as well as other malnutrition related ailments.

## Table 12

*Prevalence of Digestive and Endocrine Ailments per 10,000*

| *Group* | *Age* | *Digestive system (Per '0000)* | *Endocrine* | | |
|---|---|---|---|---|---|
| | | | *Nutrition (Per '0000)* | *Lifestyle (Per '0000)* | *Total (Per '0000)* |
| Rural Male | 0-14 | 45.82 | 1.65 | 0.15 | 1.81 |
| Rural Female | 0-14 | 45.55 | 1.03 | NA | 1.03 |
| Urban Male | 0-14 | 70.15 | 0.89 | 0.34 | 0.08 |
| Urban Female | 0-14 | 41.04 | 0.55 | 0.83 | 1.38 |
| Rural Male | 15-59 | 38.5 | 0.38 | 3.41 | 3.79 |
| Rural Female | 15-59 | 47.67 | 1.08 | 5.66 | 6.74 |
| Urban Male | 15-59 | 34.02 | 0.22 | 12.96 | 13.18 |
| Urban Female | 15-59 | 38.07 | 1.32 | 14.07 | 15.39 |
| Rural Male | 60+ | 166.43 | 7.04 | 50.82 | 57.87 |
| Rural Female | 60+ | 75.94 | NA | 65.07 | 65.07 |
| Urban Male | 60+ | 54.44 | NA | 152.44 | 152.44 |
| Urban Female | 60+ | 122.9 | NA | 123.55 | 123.55 |

Source: Authors' Calculation; NSSO 1995-96

Lifestyle related problems are more prevalent in the urban areas than in the rural areas. The prevalence rates in the urban areas are almost three times those in the rural areas for the adult population. On the other hand we find no such significant rural - urban differential in the case of either digestive or nutrition related ailments. Studying the same table we find that female children have marginally lower prevalence of nutrition related ailments but the condition is reversed among the 15-59 age group.

### *4.3 Respiratory Ailments*

Respiratory ailments include cough and acute bronchitis, also acute respiratory infection (including pneumonia). Lower respiratory ailments are the second largest cause of death in India. In 1999, lower respiratory ailments accounted for 10.4 per cent of the deaths. They were also the largest cause of DALYs (9.2 per cent) in India in 1999 (World Bank, 2001a). Of the three age groups being considered, the working age population has the lowest prevalence rate for respiratory ailments and the elderly have the highest, almost twice or thrice as much as the other age groups.

**Table 13**

*Prevalence of Respiratory Ailments*

| *Group* | *Age* | *Respiratory ailments (Per '0000)* |
|---|---|---|
| Rural Male | 0-14 | 35.1 |
| Rural Female | 0-14 | 37.2 |
| Urban Male | 0-14 | 60.3 |
| Urban Female | 0-14 | 53.9 |
| Rural Male | 15-59 | 30.3 |
| Rural Female | 15-59 | 34.5 |
| Urban Male | 15-59 | 31.3 |
| Urban Female | 15-59 | 39.4 |
| Rural Male | 60+ | 215.9 |
| Rural Female | 60+ | 210.3 |
| Urban Male | 60+ | 148.2 |
| Urban Female | 60+ | 119.2 |

Source: Author's Calculation, NSSO 1995-96

People in the rural areas suffer from respiratory ailments more than people in the urban areas . The higher prevalence of these ailments in the rural areas is difficult to explain. One contributory factor may be the widespread use of firewood and coal for cooking purposes within the residential area in rural households.

**Table 14**

*Sector wise prevalence of Respiratory Ailments (%)*

| *Prevalence* | *Respiratory* |
|---|---|
| Urban | 4.52 |
| Rural | 5.63 |

Source: Authors' Calculation; NSSO 1995-96

### *4.4 Ailment Pattern of Women vis-a-vis Men*

Differences in the nature of the tasks performed by the two sexes manifest themselves in different lifestyles for them while they may live in the same environment. A direct implication of this is differences in their ailment pattern.

Diseases relating to pregnancy and childbirth (including natural abortion) are included as a part of 'other' ailments. Prevalence of other ailments in the age group of 15-59 years is however not very much different for males and females. Women have only marginally higher prevalence rates of 'other' ailments, with a difference of only about 0.5 per cent. One may expect that women due to their specific reproductive role of child bearing may exhibit a higher prevalence of such ailments, thus accounting for the differences in the ailment pattern. However, this does not come across simply as we have clubbed such ailments with others where men have a higher prevalence.

It is in the case of blood & circulatory, musculoskeletal, and mouth related health problems that there is a stark difference between men and women. It is for such ailments that the argument of differences in the nature of work performed by the sexes may hold true. We now consider each of these in more detail:

- As per International Code of Diseases (ICD 9), joint pain and other disorders of the bones and joints are classified under musculoskeletal ailments. It is generally known that older women are more susceptible to bone loss and calcium deficiency. Our results support this claim (Refer table 10, column 7). Women more than men, especially elderly women, have a higher prevalence of musculoskeletal ailments. This is a characteristic observed in both the rural and the urban areas, for the working age and especially the elderly. Urban girl children also show a marginally higher prevalence of musculoskeletal ailments than their male counterparts.
- Blood and circulatory system related problems include anemia, heart failure, cerebral stroke, diseases of the heart and high or low blood pressure.

## Table 15

*Prevalence of Blood and Circulatory Ailments (per 10,000)*

| *Group* | *Age group* | *Blood diseases* | *Circulatory/heart diseases* |
|---|---|---|---|
| Rural Male | 0-14 | 0.06 | 2.25 |
| Rural Female | 0-14 | 1.05 | 1.18 |
| Urban Male | 0-14 | 0.00 | 0.01 |
| Urban Female | 0-14 | 0.63 | 2.73 |
| Rural Male | 15-59 | 0.20 | 14.62 |
| Rural Female | 15-59 | 3.43 | 20.39 |
| Urban Male | 15-59 | 0.40 | 20.35 |
| Urban Female | 15-59 | 3.09 | 35.21 |
| Rural Male | 60+ | 2.29 | 116.23 |
| Rural Female | 60+ | 6.06 | 108.79 |
| Urban Male | 60+ | 1.72 | 252.27 |
| Urban Female | 60+ | 10.50 | 321.18 |

Source: Authors' Calculation; NSSO 1995-96

A detailed view, presented in table 15 reveals that in the case of blood related ailments (anemia, general debility), men are far better off than women. The highest prevalence of anemia is among women in the working and elderly age groups. This is true across rural and urban areas. Much of this is probably due to greater low blood pressure prevalence among women.

- Women in India, more than the men are prone to diseases of the mouth, gums and teeth. This is true across sectors and for all age groups. However, it is difficult to explain this phenomenon.
- The most apparent difference between the sexes is for parasitic ailments, in case of which men are worse than women. (Refer table 10). The main type of parasitic ailments where males have a higher prevalence than females is in the case of vaccination non-preventable ailments (Refer table 11, 'other parasitic ailments'). For these parasitic ailments men more than women are ill across all age groups and across all sectors.

  Urban elderly males as well as male children from both the sectors are more prone to short duration fevers than females.

But in the working age groups and in the case of rural elderly, females have a higher prevalence of short duration fevers.

Childhood immunizable ailments are present to a higher extent in rural males than among rural females. While 17 out of every 10,000 rural female children suffer from immunizable ailments, 26 out of every 10,000 children suffer from them. This could be interpreted as female children in the rural areas receiving better care than male children. However, a more realistic interpretation can be made in conjunction with the sex-specific childhood mortality rates or sex ratios in the rural areas. A higher mortality rate among females indicates that female children suffering from these ailments do not receive as much care. In the urban areas on the other hand, more females than males suffer from immunization preventable ailments. This may be the direct outcome of better and more easily accessible health care facilities in the urban areas.

- Injuries due to accidents and violence: Injuries and accidents figure among the top 10 major causes of death in India. However, injuries are observed more in urban areas than in rural areas (Refer table 10). Children and adults in the working age group in urban areas travel by over-populated, badly maintained and congested roads and railways where there are more chances of facing an accident. Another possible cause of a higher prevalence of injuries in the urban areas may be the poor housing conditions.

### *4.5 Elderly*

The pattern of ailment for the elderly is different from the other age groups, first in terms of the overall higher prevalence rates and then in the nature of ailments that afflict them to a large extent. Prevalence of ailments among the elderly is almost three or four times the adult prevalence rates.

The most apparent difference from the other age groups is in the case of the single most prevalent ailment. For the elderly population, the set of other ailments shows the highest prevalence rate. For the urban elderly, this is followed by blood and circulatory ailments as the next set of most prevalent ailments. Elderly people in the rural areas however suffer most from parasitic ailments following other ailments.

Ailments are lesser among rural elderly females than among rural elderly males, however in the urban areas the situation is reversed. Blood and circulatory ailments are more prevalent in the urban areas than in the rural areas, especially in the case of urban women. Endocrine and digestive ailments are also more prevalent among the urban elderly than among the rural elderly. In case of all other ailments the rural elderly are worse off.

The urban elderly show the highest prevalence of heart problems. What is most apparent however is that women in the working age group are more adversely affected than men. In the working and elderly age groups, people in urban areas have a higher prevalence of circulatory ailments as compared to the rural areas.

*4.6 Higher and Lower Economic Classes*

Health care services are an important need not only for the lower income groups in India but also for people belonging to the higher income groups.

**Table 16**

*Prevalence of ailments Across Expenditure Groups, the top 10 and bottom 40 per cent*

| *Prevalence* | | *Lowest forty per cent* | *Top ten per cent* | *All* |
|---|---|---|---|---|
| | | Total | Total | Total |
| Rural Male Ailing | 0-14 | 4.1 | 7.5 | 5.0 |
| Rural Female Ailing | 0-14 | 3.6 | 5.8 | 4.5 |
| Urban Male Ailing | 0-14 | 4.9 | 7.1 | 5.4 |
| Urban Female Ailing | 0-14 | 4.0 | 6.6 | 5.0 |
| Rural Male Ailing | 15-59 | 3.6 | 7.1 | 4.4 |
| Rural Female Ailing | 15-59 | 4.2 | 9.1 | 5.5 |
| Urban Male Ailing | 15-59 | 3.4 | 6.4 | 4.3 |
| Urban Female Ailing | 15-59 | 4.8 | 6.2 | 5.4 |
| Rural Male Ailing | 60+ | 17.1 | 25.9 | 19.2 |
| Rural Female Ailing | 60+ | 16.2 | 20.9 | 17.9 |
| Urban Male Ailing | 60+ | 15.9 | 16.3 | 15.8 |
| Urban Female Ailing | 60+ | 16.6 | 18.8 | 17.6 |

Source: Authors' Calculation, NSSO 1995-96.

Across all age groups and sex, and in case of rural and urban sector, the economically better off have a much higher prevalence of ailments than the economically worse off. The lowest forty per cent, in terms of per capita monthly expenditure, is much lesser prone to illness than the top ten per cent of the population.

We believe that this is more an issue of self-perception. With greater awareness (which higher economic classes typically have) a better appreciation of 'good' health also emerges. And this is reflected in the greater reporting of ailments for the higher income groups.

In sum, we find that there are great differences across the country and between different demographic, social and economic segments. These differences require a health care system that is able to conform to the highly varying requirements of the population. These issues are discussed in the next section.

## 5. The Health Care System

The discussion in the previous section reveals the importance of accepting the high degree of heterogeneity across geography, sex, income, rural-urban boundaries, age, and so forth. This heterogeneity is also prevalent in the health care system in India. There are a wide variety of health care provision mechanisms available across urban and rural India. These range from conventional (allopathic) system, *ayurvedic, yunani,* homeopathy, naturopathy, *yoga*, bio-chemic medicine, local traditional providers, faith healers, and so forth. Over and above that, many illnesses are first treated through home remedies that have been passed down through the ages. And medical professionals are approached only after they have failed.

As per the Constitution, the responsibility of health care is to be shared by the Central, State and local governments. Effectively, though delivery of public health care is mainly conducted by the State government, health care delivery by the government is carried out by means of public institutions such as hospitals, primary health centres, sub-centres, government clinics, Auxiliary nurse-midwives (ANMs), etc. In addition to delivering curative health care, the public sector also implements a number of centrally sponsored programmes, relating to family welfare and disease control. The Centre and State governments as well as various other institutions provide primary health care, which is the first level of interaction between the population and health care services.

Primary health care is a three-tier system, consisting of sub-centres, Primary Health Centres (PHCs) and Community Health Centres (CHCs)[6].

- The Sub-center is the most peripheral contact point between the primary health care system and the community and has mainly promotional and educative functions relating to Maternal and Child Health, Family Welfare, Nutrition, Immunization, Diarrhea Control and Control of Communicable Diseases. A Sub-centre is manned by one Multi-purpose Worker (Male) and one Multi-purpose Worker (Female)/ANM. Sub-centres are also supposed to store basic drugs for minor ailments that are needed for taking care of essential health needs of women and children.
- PHCs are established and maintained by the State government under the Minimum Needs Programme (MNP). The PHC is the link between the village community and the medical officer. It acts as referral unit for six Sub-centres and has 30 beds. A PHC is manned by a medical officer and is supported by 14 paramedical and other staff. They undertake curative, preventive, promotion and family welfare services.
- CHCs are established and maintained by the state government under MNP. One CHC serves as a referral centre for four PHCs. Four medical specialists, i.e., surgeon, physician, gynaecologist and paediatrician supported by 21 paramedical and other staff, man each CHC. It has 30 indoor beds with X-ray and labour room laboratory facilities.

In addition to these health care services provided by the State government, the Department of Family Welfare supports personnel in rural family welfare centres, urban health posts, urban family welfare centres, district post partum-centres and sub-district post-partum centres. Broadly, most states have a similar structure, though administrative mechanisms may differ somewhat. More important, efficiency and coverage of public health services differ greatly across states.

This does not, of course, mean that the central government plays no role. The Department of Indian Systems of Medicine & Homoeopathy (ISM&H) also has its own dispensaries, hospitals and medical colleges. Central Government Health Services (CGHS) provides health care for Central Government employees. Railways, Defence and similar large Ministries/Departments have their own hospitals and dispensaries catering to their staff's health care needs. Public Sector Undertakings (PSUs) and large industries have their own medical infrastructure. Employees State Insurance (ESI) provides hospital and dispensary-based health care to employees.

Other government and non-private facilities include the municipal hospitals located in urban areas. In addition to all this, there are the voluntary organizations and the private sector that are providing health care. Many religious organizations also have their facilities in various parts of the country. The government also assists some of these.

**Table 17**

*Infrastructure and Personnel*

| | |
|---|---|
| **Health Care Infrastructure (Rural + Urban)** | |
| Sub centres | 137,000 |
| Dispensaries | 28,000 |
| PHCs | 23,000 |
| Urban Family Welfare Facilities | 3,500 |
| CHCs | 3,000 |
| Secondary and Tertiary hospitals | 12,000 |
| **Personnel in Public Sector in Rural Areas** | |
| Doctors | 29,000 |
| Nurse Midwives | 18,000 |
| Auxiliary Nurse Midwives (ANMs) | 134,000 |
| Male Multipurpose Workers | 73,000 |
| Pharmacists | 21,000 |
| Paramedical Staff | 60,000 |

Source: Ministry of Health and Family Welfare 2000, referred in *Raising the Sights*, World Bank (2001a).

Given India's demographic and geographical size, it is not surprising that there are many different types of organizations.

However that does not imply that this variety is effective. Many studies (Gupte *et al*, 2001; Das and Dasgupta, 2000) have critiqued public heath care provision and the lack of regulation of private providers. Figures such as maternal mortality figures also strongly reflect the poor quality and coverage of health care.

According to a World Bank study on the Health Sector[7], India's public sector is well below comparable ratios of manpower and hospital beds in other low-income countries. On adding the private sector figures to the public sector numbers in India they find that the number of physicians per 1000 population is about average for low-income countries though the ratio of nurses and midwives are much below average. This was also true in the case of the ratio of hospital beds per 1000. So while the infrastructure is vast in comparison to most countries in terms of absolute numbers the per capita availability of services is quite poor.

**Table 18**

*Health Infrastructure and Personnel*

| *Health infrastructure and Personnel* | *1st plan 1951-56* | *6th plan 1980-85* | *8th plan 1992-97* |
|---|---|---|---|
| Primary Health Centres | 725 | 11,000 | 21,854 |
| Sub-centres | NA | 83,000 | 132,730 |
| Total Beds | 125,000 | 514,989 | 596,203 |
| Medical Colleges | 42 | 106 | 148 |
| Annual admission in medical colleges | 3,500 | 8,000 | 11,389 |
| Dental colleges | 7 | 25 | 54 |
| Allopathic doctors | 65,000 | 297,228 | 410,800 |
| Nurses | 18,500 | 164,421 | 449,351 |
| ANM's | 12,780 | 85,630 | 203,451 |
| Health visitors | 578 | 13,612 | 22,144 |
| Health workers (males) | - | 80,000 | 124,680 |
| Health workers (females) | - | 80,000 | 63,871 |
| Village health guides | - | 372,190 | 410,904 |

Source: Ghai and Gupta (1999), as quoted in Gupte *et al* (2001)

According to Mukhopadhyay and Choudhury (1997, as quoted in Gupte *et al*), of the 21,802 PHCs operating in 1995, 416 were functioning with four doctors each, 777 with three, 4,062 with two, and 7,804 with one doctor. That is, 35 per cent of the PHCs functioned without a single doctor. The WHO recommends a doctor nurse ratio of 1:2. According to Gupte *et al*, until 1985 there were more doctors than nurses in India. However, this situation is changing as the table above shows.

The situation in the rural areas is worse than in the urban areas. Rural areas in India are characterized by shortages of manpower as well as equipment. As many have pointed out 80 per cent of the trained health manpower in all categories service 20 per cent of the urban population while only 20 per cent of manpower provide essential services to 80 per cent of the rural and poor urban population in the country. Such a distribution is indicative of the gross shortage in the rural areas.

The problem originates from the centralization of the health system. The state government bureaucracy holds financial and administrative powers. They are not delegated to district administrations, leave alone hospital administration. The personnel are also part of the state administrative system and have a similar perspective. The rules, procedures, orientation of care, etc. are decided at the state level and with a state-wide perspective; however as previous section shows, heterogeneity is endemic and the needs differ greatly even within the state.

Consequently, we find that public facilities are used by only a small part of the population. The utilization of these services is portrayed below, by means of NSSO data.

First consider ailments and treatment received. Of all those who were ailing in the 15 days prior to NSSOs survey, 91 per cent and 82 per cent in urban and rural areas respectively received some form of treatment. Receiving treatment here is defined as being treated using any system of formal medicine, be it conventional or non-conventional. However, faith healers and home remedies are not included.

**Table 19**

*Percentage Distribution of those not treated: Causes*

| *Reason for no treatment* | *Rural* | | *Urban* | |
|---|---|---|---|---|
| | *1986-87* | *1995-96* | *1986-87* | *1995-96* |
| No medical facility | 3 | 9 | 0 | 1 |
| Lack of faith | 2 | 4 | 2 | 5 |
| Long waiting | 0 | 1 | 1 | 1 |
| Financial problem | 15 | 24 | 10 | 21 |
| Ailment not serious | 75 | 52 | 81 | 60 |
| Others | 5 | 10 | 6 | 12 |
| All | 100 | 100 | 100 | 100 |

Source: *Morbidity and Treatment of Ailments*, NSSO 1998

The reason for no treatment reveals other aspects of health care provision across rural and urban areas. First, we find that the cause 'ailment not serious' is the most important cause. However, this share is falling over time. This only reveals that both rural and urban areas are increasingly paying more attention to their health requirements. However, financial constraints prevent some from visiting the health professional, and this share is increasing with time. Significantly, rural residents also report the lack of health facilities in their surroundings.

Of those who received some form of formal treatment we find the following:

**Table 20**

*Percentage Distribution of Non-hospitalized Treatments by Source*

| *Source of Treatment* | *Rural* | | *Urban* | |
|---|---|---|---|---|
| | *1986-87* | *1995-96* | *1986-87* | *1995-96* |
| Public Hospital | 18 | 11 | 23 | 15 |
| PHC/CHC | 5 | 6 | 1 | 1 |
| Public Dispensary | 3 | 2 | 2 | 2 |
| ESI doctor, etc. | 0 | 0 | 2 | 1 |
| All government sources | 26 | 19 | 28 | 20 |
| Private Hospitals | 15 | 12 | 16 | 16 |
| Nursing Home | 1 | 3 | 1 | 2 |
| Charitable Institution | 0 | 0 | 1 | 1 |
| Private Doctor | 53 | 55 | 52 | 55 |
| Others | 5 | 10 | 3 | 7 |
| All non-government sources | 74 | 81 | 72 | 80 |
| Total who received treatment | 100 | 100 | 100 | 100 |

Source: *Morbidity and Treatment of Ailments*, NSSO 1998

We find that four-fifths of ailing Indians who received some treatment did so from private providers. More importantly this share has increased over time. The above table reveals another interesting facet of health care provision. Government hospitals are becoming less and less important both in rural and urban areas. Instead we observe significant increase in nursing homes and private doctors. (Note that private doctors here refer to all, even those prescribing non-conventional medicine - homoeopathy, *ayurvedic, unani,* etc.) The largest increase is observed under the term 'Others'. This includes whatever is not covered under the preceding headers, private clinics or polyclinics is one such category.

The above also reveals that the share of broad sources of treatment is not very different across population residing in urban and rural areas. This can be seen in two ways. First, whatever be the failures of the public health care system; they are uniformly distributed across urban and rural areas. Second, the typically low-income rural areas have enough 'mass' to attract significant private sector response.

We have not discussed the distribution of care received while hospitalized. Though the difference between public and private facilities is not as high as in the case of treatment without hospitalization, it is in the same direction. (See appendix A3).

Both public (government) and private provisioning exists for almost all the different systems. However, public provisioning is weighed towards conventional medicine. And the non-conventional medicine is generally a private sector activity. Within the private sector we observe both consultation services, as well as institutional medicine through hospitals, clinics etc. There is some regulation, but as is the case in other sectors much of regulation is un-enforced. Regulatory activity in the health sector is currently very low and nowhere near the extent observed in developed countries.

As is the case for the prevalence of ailments, we also find that the extent of usage of health facilities is highly different across the country. The following table compares the treatment received from public sources across two points in time.

## Table 21

*Percentage of Ailments receiving Non-hospitalized Treatment from Government Sources*

| *States* | *Rural* | | *Urban* | |
|---|---|---|---|---|
| | *1986-87* | *1995-96* | *1986-87* | *1995-96* |
| Andhra Pradesh | 12 | 22 | 16 | 19 |
| Assam | 40 | 29 | 26 | 22 |
| Bihar | 14 | 13 | 17 | 33 |
| Gujarat | 28 | 25 | 18 | 22 |
| Haryana | 15 | 13 | 19 | 11 |
| Karnataka | 32 | 26 | 30 | 17 |
| Kerala | 32 | 28 | 33 | 28 |
| Madhya Pradesh | 24 | 23 | 28 | 19 |
| Maharashtra | 21 | 16 | 15 | 17 |
| Orissa | 37 | 38 | 43 | 34 |
| Punjab | 12 | 7 | 11 | 6 |
| Rajasthan | 46 | 36 | 52 | 41 |
| Tamil Nadu | 28 | 25 | 31 | 28 |
| Uttar Pradesh | * | 8 | 14 | 9 |
| West Bengal | 16 | 15 | 20 | 19 |
| **India** | **21** | **19** | **24** | **20** |

Source: *Morbidity and Treatment of Ailments*, NSSO 1998

We find that:

- Dependence on public sources is very low across the country.
- This rate differs greatly between parts of the country; it ranges from a low of 7 per cent in rural Punjab and 9 per cent in urban UP to 41 per cent in urban Rajasthan.
- In almost all the states the percentages of ailing using public facilities are falling, Andhra Pradesh is the lone exception.
- In some states such as Maharashtra, Gujarat, and Bihar, the usage by urbanites has improved. (Bihar improved significantly during the period).

In other words, the private sector health initiative is playing an extremely important role. It leads to some degree of health care where none would otherwise exist. Criticism that it is of low quality, not modern, etc. might be valid, but it should also be recognized that some health care is provided at very low cost to those for whom no other avenues are available.

We, therefore, arrive at three salient factors about India and its health sector:

1. ***Heterogeneity:*** Both needs and current private and public responses are highly heterogeneous. Uniformity in provision mechanisms would not succeed in India.
2. ***Low Cost:*** The only sustainable health care system would be a low cost one. Neither the beneficiaries nor the Central and State governments are capable of bearing high health costs in a sustainable manner.
3. ***Minimal Controls:*** A successful health system would be one that does not require high levels of regulatory or administrative capabilities. Quality regulation increases cost significantly.

Given these characteristics, health care policy has to ensure that private entities' entry into the health sector is maximized. The concluding section goes into some characteristics that a health care policy should have.

## 6. Conclusion

The above imply that Public Policy should be one that:

***does not discourage private sector involvement:*** Private sector includes the large informal sector, it includes the non-conventional systems of medicine, it includes formal private initiatives, etc. The private sector has the inherent flexibility to meet the requirements of a heterogeneous population and its heterogeneous requirements;

***does not prevent entry (conventional):*** Countries such as the USA have historically had many controls on the number of medical colleges, number of medical graduates, and so forth. The same is not advisable for India. Given the current conditions oversupply is not a problem for the fore-seeable future;

***does not prevent entry (non-conventional):*** Not much is known about the efficacy of different non-conventional systems of medicine. Many medical professionals discount their impact. At the same time many households have utilized their services for generations and continue to do so. A liberal and open-minded attitude would support their continuance;

***has minimal quality related regulations:*** Regulations lead to high costs, which one way or another pass down to the consumers. At the same time other means of ensuring the right incentives for quality provision should be encouraged. These include consumer's interest groups and consumer courts/arbitration mechanisms;

***does not depend on mandated public health insurance***: Health insurance is an extremely costly response to the problem of ensuring health care for all. It requires high levels of bureaucratic and administrative inputs that increase costs. Worse, it leads to incentives that create moral hazard like situations that further increase overall costs of health care. If a group of private individuals, however, would want to benefit from health insurance services, they should not be prevented from doing so, and therefore private health insurance should not be prevented;

***does not rest wholly upon the conventional judicial system* to enforce patients' or providers' rights**: The judicial system currently is not set up to handle matters of errors in health care. Moreover, it is time costly. If at all the conventional system is to handle such issues, an ongoing training mechanism would have to be built for the judiciary as well as legal professionals. Better alternatives are possible that do not depend upon the conventional justice mechanism (Refer to Box 1);

**does not give regulatory powers to providers or provider associations**: Experience in other countries suggests that incumbents tend to over-regulate in activities that limit entry, and under-regulate in areas that promote competition. Regulation has to be such that quality is not achieved at the cost of competition or entry. That would only lead to high costs.

The above points limit the areas that health policy should cover. Now we discuss what health policy should be about. For a country such as India, health policy should:

- Be dynamic and change over time with changing requirements;
- Increase accessibility through lower costs;
- Recognize that one size does not fit all;

- Encourage different types of provision models to function in parallel;
- Support natural market mechanisms to ensure high quality and low costs;
- Increase knowledge and information on health issues – only when consumers demand the best, will the private response provide the best;
- Support the formation of consumer interest groups and consumer courts/arbitration mechanisms in every town of India;
- Promote the study of efficacy of non-conventional systems of medicine.

**BOX 1**

*Reputation Vs. Regulation*

Health regulation in India is very poor. Perhaps that is one of the factors behind the prevalence of a large private sector in a wide range of medical care activities. And many believe that it is also one of the factors behind the poor quality of health care available to most Indians.

We, however, do not completely subscribe to such arguments. The fact remains that in India the central, state, or local governments do not have the necessary means to supply even basic health care to all its population. Even where the government has allocated adequate funds for a particular health care activity, we find that there is much to be desired. Government administrators are not specialized in health administration, and health administration is a highly specialized activity. It is, therefore, not surprising that even regulation is poor.

But should it be strengthened? The answer of course is yes, but only to a limited extent. We find that reputation of private agents achieves similar results as regulation, but at a much lower cost. In health care, as in other economic activities, quality is intimately associated with the incentives of the agents involved.

Two broad factors affect quality – the incentives, and the ability of health personnel. First, let us consider the incentives for quality health care. In almost all of economic activity, trust and reputation play an important role in smoothening the buying and

**Contd. ...**

selling of goods and services. In sectors such as finance, education, and of course, health, they become even more important.

In the case of Indian health sector as well, the reputation of the health care provider plays an important role. Long-term reputation creates similar incentives as efficient regulation. It is in the interest of the health care provider to treat their patient to the best of their ability. That is what ensures a good reputation and consequently higher expected income.

What are the characteristics of reputation? Some are mentioned below:

- It takes time to evolve and flow
- It flows through informal interactions of consumers and potential consumers and does not require high levels of education/human capital
- There are no explicit costs involved unlike in meeting with regulatory specifications
- It incorporates many different issues in one, though inexact measure
- The greater the competition, the greater is its importance, and therefore the larger are the incentives for quality care

The point being made is that reputation plays an important role and does so cheaply. Private sector initiative in the health sector will rest on reputation mechanisms and these should be strengthened. Consumer interest groups, Internet bulletin boards, and even informal arbitration mechanisms between providers and buyers of health services are some ways.

Now consider ability of providers. If the providers know of the importance of good reputation, then we will also observe a greater emphasis on quality education and skill enhancement. If effort is rewarded (which private efforts are better at) then better quality personnel will enter the sector.

Good regulation on the other hand requires extremely high levels of efficiency on the part of the regulatory bodies involved. Moreover, it needs to be backed by a large-scale monitoring and enforcement machinery, both of which are missing in India.

## Appendix – A1

*Distribution of Ailing by Source of Treatment (not as inpatient of hospital)*

| *States* | *Rural* | | | *Urban* | | |
|---|---|---|---|---|---|---|
| | *Percentage of ailments treated* | | | *Percentage of ailments treated* | | |
| | *Government sources* | *Other sources* | *All* | *Government sources* | *Other sources* | *All* |
| Andhra Pradesh | 22 | 53 | 75 | 19 | 68 | 87 |
| Assam | 29 | 27 | 57 | 22 | 41 | 62 |
| Bihar | 13 | 65 | 78 | 33 | 53 | 86 |
| Gujarat | 25 | 67 | 93 | 22 | 75 | 97 |
| Haryana | 13 | 84 | 97 | 11 | 87 | 98 |
| Karnataka | 26 | 51 | 77 | 17 | 74 | 91 |
| Kerala | 28 | 61 | 89 | 28 | 62 | 90 |
| Madhya Pradesh | 23 | 62 | 85 | 19 | 75 | 94 |
| Maharashtra | 16 | 73 | 89 | 17 | 77 | 94 |
| Orissa | 38 | 31 | 69 | 34 | 53 | 87 |
| Punjab | 7 | 92 | 99 | 6 | 91 | 87 |
| Rajasthan | 36 | 54 | 91 | 41 | 50 | 92 |
| Tamil Nadu | 25 | 54 | 79 | 28 | 65 | 93 |
| Uttar Pradesh | 8 | 83 | 91 | 9 | 85 | 94 |
| West Bengal | 15 | 65 | 80 | 19 | 72 | 91 |
| India | 19 | 64 | 83 | 20 | 72 | 92 |

Source: *Morbidity and Treatment of Ailments*, NSSO 1998

# Appendix – A2

*State-wise Registered Medical Practitioners*

| *States/UTs* | *Allopathic practitioners* | *ISM & H Doctors, Registered Practitioners IQ+NIQ* |
|---|---|---|
| Year | 2000 | 2000 |
| Andaman & Nicobar Islands | - | - |
| Andhra Pradesh | 41429 | 28371 |
| Arunachal Pradesh | - | - |
| Assam | 13293 | 714 |
| Bihar | 30720 | 160455 |
| Chandigarh | - | 297 |
| Dadra & Nagar Haveli | - | - |
| Daman & Diu | - | - |
| Delhi | 18567 | 10995 |
| Goa | 1569 | - |
| Gujarat | 29483 | 20750 |
| Haryana | 925 | 25850 |
| Himachal Pradesh | - | 8420 |
| Jammu & Kashmir | 5798 | 505 |
| Karnataka | 50077 | 18093 |
| Kerala | 23622 | 22574 |
| Lakshadweep | - | - |
| Madhya Pradesh | 16382 | 55097 |
| Maharashtra | 66477 | 78888 |
| Manipur | - | - |
| Meghalaya | - | 229 |
| Mizoram | - | - |
| Nagaland | - | 1998 |
| Orissa | 13057 | 8583 |
| Pondicherry | - | - |
| Punjab | 29170 | 33211 |
| Rajasthan | 18504 | 32327 |
| Sikkim | - | - |
| Tamil Nadu | 59305 | 35848 |
| Tripura | - | - |
| Uttar Pradesh | 38628 | 93259 |
| West Bengal | 46941 | 44660 |
| **India** | **503947** | **681124** |

Source: Rajya Sabha Unstarred Question No. 2991, dated 22.04.2002; Govt. of India (2002a).

## Appendix – A3

*Percentage of Hospitalized Treatments received from Public Provider*

| *States* | *Treated in government hospital* | |
|---|---|---|
| | *Rural* | *Urban* |
| Andhra Pradesh | 225 | 362 |
| Assam | 738 | 652 |
| Bihar | 247 | 346 |
| Gujarat | 321 | 369 |
| Haryana | 305 | 373 |
| Karnataka | 458 | 298 |
| Kerala | 401 | 384 |
| Madhya Pradesh | 533 | 560 |
| Maharashtra | 312 | 318 |
| Orissa | 906 | 810 |
| Punjab | 394 | 276 |
| Rajasthan | 649 | 731 |
| Tamil Nadu | 411 | 357 |
| Uttar Pradesh | 471 | 398 |
| West Bengal | 820 | 721 |
| India | 453 | 431 |

Source: *Morbidity and Treatment of Ailments*, NSSO 1998

## Notes

1 The authors would like to thank Bibek Debroy, Ajay Mahal, Amir Ullah Khan for their comments and critique. For any errors, authors are solely responsible and can be contacted at aartikhare@yahoo.com.

2 Government of India (2000b).

3 Government of India (2002c).

4 Prevalence of ailment is defined as (Numbers ailing/total population)*100.

5 A set of undiagnosed ailments is reported and we have included it among the set of other ailments.

6 Government of India (2001).

7 World Bank 2001a.

## References

Bhandari, Laveesh and Amaresh Dubey (2001): 'Calorie Deficiency, Poverty and the Public Distribution System- A Household Level Analysis', Rajiv Gandhi Institute for Contemporary Studies (RGICS), *Working Paper Series No. 24*.

Das, R.K. and P. Dasgupta (2000): 'Child Health and Immunization- A Macro Perspective', *Economic and Political Weekly*, February 19-26.

Government of India (1998a): *Morbidity and Treatment of Ailments*, National Sample Survey Organization (NSSO), November.

——— (1998b): SRS Analytical Studies Report No.1- 1998, Office of the Registrar General of India, New Delhi, India.

——— (2000a): Annual Report, 2000, Ministry of Health and Family Welfare, New Delhi. http://mohfw.nic.in/reports/index.htm.

——— (2000b): 'Health Information of India 1997 & 1998', Central Bureau of Health Intelligence, Directorate General of Health Services, Ministry of Health and Family Welfare, New Delhi.

——— (2001): Mid Term Appraisal of the Ninth Five Year Plan (1997-2000), Planning Commission, New Delhi. http://planningcommission.nic.in/mta-9702/ap9702cont.htm.

——— (2002a): Annual Report 2002-02, Ministry of Health and Family Welfare, New Delhi.

——— (2002b): *National Human Development Report 2001*, Planning Commission, India, New Delhi, March.

——— (2002c): *Economic Survey 2001-2002*, Ministry of Finance, Economic Division.

Gupte, M.D., V. Ramachandran and Mutatkar R.K. (2001): "Epidemiological Profile of India: Historical and Contemporary Perspectives", Journal of Biosciences, Vol. 26, No.4, November. http://www.ias.ac.in/jbiosci/nov2001/437.pdf.

Indira Gandhi Institute of Development Research (2002): *India Development Report 2002*, India, New Delhi.

International Institute for Population Sciences (1998-99a): "National Family Health Survey (NFHS-2)", India, Mumbai.

——— (1998-99b): "Reproductive and Child Health Project, Rapid Household Survey (Phase I & II)", India, Mumbai.

Narasipuram, M.M. (1994): "Hierarchical Modelling of Health Information Systems", Working Paper, Dept. of Information Systems, City University of Hong Kong, Kowloon, Hong Kong. http://www.is.cityu.edu.hk/Research/Publication/working_paper94.htm.

Pearson, M. (1999): India IHSD Country Briefing Paper, DFID Health Systems Resource Centre, London. http://www.healthsystemsrc.org/HBD/PDF/INDIA.PDF.

Shariff, Abusaleh (1999): *India Human Development Report- A Profile of Indian States in the 1990s*, National Council of Applied Economic Research, New Delhi.

United Nations Human Development Programme (2001): *Human Development Report 2001- Making New Technologies Work for Human Development*, New York, USA.

World Bank (2001a): "Raising the Sights: Better Health Systems for India's Poor", Report No. 22304, Washington (DC).

——— (2001b): *World Development Report 2000/2001- Attacking Poverty*, The World Bank, Washington D.C., USA.

World Health Organization (2001): "The World Health Report 2001, Mental Health: New Understanding, New Hope", World Health Organization, Geneva. http://www.who.int/whr/2001/main/en/annex/index.htm.

# 15

# Institutional Reforms in the Enforcement of Criminal Justice in India

ARNAB KUMAR HAZRA

## Introduction

There are three institutions that play a role in the enforcement of Criminal Justice system, in India — the Police, the Courts and the Prisons. Reforms in these institutions that foresee the enforcement of Criminal Justice, is a subject that is generally avoided. The reason for this is the pitiable condition that the administration of criminal justice in India is in at present. The quagmire of a nefarious institution called the Police, the overloaded Courts and the putrid Prisons is something most people wish to avoid.

However, not everyone can wish them away, especially the poor who invariably find themselves at the receiving end of the pitfalls of this system. This is essentially true of the undertrial prisoners languishing in jails throughout the country. This paper attempts to look at the problem essentially from the point of the under-privileged. Nevertheless, before drawing the correlation between the poor and the evils of the criminal justice system, it is imperative to provide a brief overview of the system.

Law enforcement and management of law and order, security, crime prevention and crime detection are essentially enforced and performed by the Police authorities. Three major laws, apart from the Police Act, 1861, govern the role and performance of police. These are The Indian Penal Code, 1860, The Indian Evidence Act, 1872 and The Code of Criminal Procedure 1973.

The Indian Penal Code (IPC) identifies the acts of omission and commission that constitute the offences and makes them punishable under this Act. It divides offences into several categories and embodies the substantial criminal law of the country. The Indian Evidence Act is a major law relating to evidence and applies to all judicial court or court martial. Criminal Procedure Code (CrPC) is the major procedural law relating to conduct of investigations, trial and appeal. It provides the mechanism for the punishment of offence against the substantial criminal law. The Code also formulates police duties.

Apart from these, to cater to various specific needs, several new laws have been enacted from time to time to meet the growing crime prevention needs. They are broadly categorized as (i) Special Law (vide Section 41 of IPC) which is applicable to a particular subject, and (ii) Local Law (vide Section 42 of IPC) which is applicable to a particular part of India. Collectively they are known as "Special and Local Laws" (SLL).

The Criminal Procedure Code divides all crimes into two categories — Cognizable Crimes and Non-cognizable Crimes. The Police deal with all cognizable crimes reported in the country. A police officer in a cognizable crime may arrest a person without a warrant. In such crimes, the police have a direct responsibility to take immediate action on receipt of a complaint or of credible information, visit the scene of the crime, investigate the facts, apprehend the offender and arraign him before a court of law having jurisdiction over the matter. Cognizable crimes are listed both under the IPC as well as under SLL.

Non-Cognizable crimes are those where the police cannot arrest a person without a warrant and so are generally left to be pursued by the affected parties themselves in the Courts. Police do not initiate investigation in non-cognizable crimes except with magisterial permission. This distinction, in practice, translates to the fact that the police normally do not investigate non-cognizable crimes unless specifically instructed by a magistrate to do so. The first schedule of the Criminal Procedure Code gives the classification of the offences of the IPC into cognizable and non-cognizable crimes.

It is now a well-established fact that the jail population of under trial prisoners is huge. These people, who are locked in a criminal case, are in jail simply because they have not been able to procure bail to come out of the jails. They have not been able to procure bail because they either have been unable to hire a lawyer to do the needful for them or have been unable to furnish the bail amount. This has happened simply because they are poor.

We next look at some Indicators on Crime and the Police in Table 1. From the Table, certain facts are evident like the total crimes in 2000 were around 51.6 lakhs which works out to more than 500 crimes per one lakh population and that there are only 13 lakh policemen in this country with only 41 policemen per 100 sq.kms. While this is certainly inadequate, the disturbing fact that emerge is that one out of every five IPC crimes remain completely uninvestigated by the police. More disturbing is the disposal rate by the Courts. It is paltry 18.3 per cent for IPC crimes and 45.7 per cent for SLL crimes. Thus a majority of the prisoners are undertrials, as the trial remains uncompleted in the courts. This has translated to a huge number of undertrials — more than 1.5 crores.

**Table 1**

*Various Indicators on Crime for the Year 2000*

| *Heads/Categories* | | *Figures for the Year 2000* |
|---|---|---|
| Crimes Committed (in Lakhs) | IPC | 17.7 |
| | SLL | 33.9 |
| | Total | 51.6 |
| Incidence of Crime per one lakh population | | 515.7 |
| Police Strength | Absolute No. (in lakhs) | 13 |
| | Per One lakh Population | 129 |
| Density of Police Personnel per 100 sq.kms. | | 41 |
| Workload per Investigation Officer | | 42.6 |
| Disposal Rate by Police | IPC Crimes | 79.1 |
| | SLL Crimes | 94.5 |
| Disposal Rate by Courts | IPC Crimes | 18.3 |
| | SLL Crimes | 45.7 |
| Persons Arrested | Under IPC Crimes | 26,75,923 |
| | Under SLL Crimes | 39,46,582 |
| Persons Undertrial | Under IPC Crimes | 105,32,307 |
| | Under SLL Crimes | 47,24,623 |
| | Total no. of undertrials | 152,56,930 |

Source: *Crime in India*, 2000, N.C.R.B., (M.H.A.), Government of India.

We next look at the cognizable crimes that have been registered between 1996 and 2000. From Table 2, we see that although the number of crimes under IPC has stabilized around 17 lakhs, the crimes under SLL have come down significantly. Nevertheless, crimes under SLL are around twice that of those committed under IPC.

**Table 2**

*Cognizable Crimes registered between 1996 and 2000*

| *Year* | *Cognizable Crimes registered in Lakhs* | | |
|---|---|---|---|
| | *Under IPC* | *Under SLL* | *Total* |
| 1996 | 17.1 | 45.9 | 63.0 |
| 1997 | 17.2 | 46.9 | 64.1 |
| 1998 | 17.8 | 44.0 | 61.8 |
| 1999 | 17.6 | 32.0 | 49.6 |
| 2000 | 17.7 | 34.0 | 51.7 |

Source: *Crime in India*, 2000, N.C.R.B., (M.H.A.), Government of India.

Note: In addition to the 51.7 lakh cognizable crimes in 2000, the other investigating agencies under the Central and State Governments registered another 70,646 cognizable crimes. Thus the total cognizable crimes in the country for the year 2000 was 52,38,396.

To further corroborate the fact that the poor are at the receiving end of the criminal justice system, we look at various crimes, both under IPC and SLL, that contribute towards maximum arrests, (Tables 3 and 4 respectively). Within Indian Penal Code crimes, 'other IPC crimes' or petty crimes constitute nearly 40 per cent of all arrests. The others categories where the number of poor in the total number of people arrested is significant are 'theft', 'riots' or 'hurt'.

As for SLL crimes, arrests for crimes outside the major 21 statutory laws account for almost 70 per cent of all arrests, here again the number of poor prisoners is significant. Even in arrests made under Acts like Gambling (the poor are naive and easy prey to activities like gambling) and Prohibition (essentially the people arrested under this category are the consumers of illicit locally made, liquor), the poor figure significantly.

## Table 3

*Crime Heads within IPC with maximum number of Arrests in the Year 2000*

| *IPC Crime Head (Over 1 Lakh People Arrested)* | *Number of Persons Arrested* | *Percentage to Total* |
|---|---|---|
| Cruelty by Husband or Relative | 1,05,547 | 3.94 |
| Theft | 1,66,867 | 6.24 |
| Riots | 4,30,593 | 16.09 |
| Hurt/Grievous Hurt | 4,55,332 | 17.02 |
| Other Indian Penal Code Crimes | 10,36,998 | 38.75 |
| Total No. of People arrested for IPC Crimes in 2000 | 26,75,923 | 100.00 |

Source: *Crime in India,* 2000, N.C.R.B., (M.H.A.), Government of India.

## Table 4

*Crime Heads within Special and Local Law with maximum number of Arrests in the Year 2000*

| *SLL Crime Head (Over 1 Lakh People Arrested)* | *Number of Persons Arrested* | *Percentage to Total* |
|---|---|---|
| Excise Act | 1,27,911 | 3.24 |
| Gambling Act | 3,01,866 | 7.65 |
| Prohibition Act | 5,36,379 | 13.59 |
| Other SLL Crimes | 27,54,205 | 69.79 |
| Total No. of People arrested for SLL Crimes in 2000 | 39,46,582 | 100.00 |

Source: *Crime in India,* 2000, N.C.R.B., (M.H.A.), Government of India.

Thus, the poorer section of society figure prominently in the arrests made, either under IPC or under SLL. The inability of this section of the society to secure release on bail was argued earlier. It is, therefore, no exaggeration to conclude that most of the undertrial prisoners in this country are people from a relatively poorer background. This perhaps compounds the duty of the State to enable these undertrials prisoners to lead a better life as the Preamble to our Constitution still boasts of India as a State with Socialist ideals.

On the other hand, contemporary jurisprudence exacts conviction and punishment for reparation of the accused and victim resulting in an equitable society, giving a chance to the convicted to re-merge with society. Unfortunately, these notions of the ideal society leave much to be desired as in the existing system there's a lot of reform still to be done. In dealing with the problem, three types of prisoners have to be considered.

1. Persons being tried for non-bailable offences, in respect of whom the courts have declined to pass an order for their release on bail.
2. Persons being tried for non-bailable offences, in respect of whom the courts have passed order for bail but who, because of the difficulty of finding appropriate surety or because of some other reasons, do not furnish the bail bond.
3. Persons, who are being tried for bailable offences but who, because of the difficulty of finding appropriate surety or some other reasons, do not furnish the bail bond.

Many of the persons who are lodged in the prisons are not dangerous or violent. Rather, they have family support and families to support. Perhaps they have become victims of circumstances. They would indeed leave the prisons in due course and live in society again. However, a long and overdue stay for these people, in the prison as an institution may create psychological harm and make them more prone to commit crime. The large number of undertrials lodged in the various jails of the country make this aspect really serious.

The sole basis of the detention of undertrials is to ensure their appearance at the trial. Consequently, thousands of them, arrested on suspicion of committing crimes (most cases are petty), languish in jails. Many remain in jail for a much longer period than the maximum punishment under the law for the crime committed. It was found that more than 85 per cent of the prisoners in Tihar Jail in Delhi were undertrials[1].

The reasons for overcrowding in jails are many. Inordinate delay in trials is the most important (as seen from Table 1), and results in many undertrials having to be detained in jail for unduly long periods — in many cases extending upto 10 years. The hardships that they face can surely be mitigated. There is a four pronged solution

(a) releasing the undertrials lodged in jail for sufficiently long periods of time, on bail and easing the procedure for procuring a bail; (b) expediting the process of trial. This entails reducing backlogs in Courts; (c) reducing the number of arrests on mere suspicion without any substantial evidence; and (d) improving the conditions of the jails and also building more prisons. However, there are also a lot more substantial issues involved and a wider look at these issues is imperative. This is attempted here.

We first look at the issue of Procedural Reforms, followed by discussions on Police Reforms, Judicial Delays and Prison Reforms. Finally a broad conclusion sums up the discussion. There are also five Appendices that follow. The first is on some of the Case Law pertaining to Undertrials. The Second is on the recommendations of the National Police Commission, the third on the Ribeiro Committee Report, the fourth on the Padmanabhaiah Committee Report and the fifth on the Mulla Committee Report.

## Procedural Reforms

Procedural Reforms can be sub-divided into two phases — Pre-Trial and during Trial.[2] The first remains within the domain of the Police, while the latter pertains to the Courts. However, we will be discussing aspects related to the first. This is because procedural reforms for the trial phase pertains to reforms in the Criminal Procedure Code and Criminal Law in general. This is a very vast topic and is beyond the scope of this paper. A Committee headed by Justice Malimath is presently looking into this aspect. We are however more interested in the institutional aspects that pertain to criminal justice system in India and therefore the focus of the paper is on the three institutions, namely, the Police, Courts and Prisons.

Let us first look at some of the Sections as provided for in our Constitution and the CrPC.

Constitution of India — Article 21: No one shall be deprived of his/her life or personal liberty except according to procedure established by law. This fundamental right incorporates, in its scope, the right to free legal aid to a person who is indigent or otherwise disabled from securing legal assistance. The Constitutional rights of the accused are also guaranteed under Article 22 of the Constitution, under which, anyone arrested under ordinary law has, a) the right to be informed as soon as possible on the grounds of arrest, b) the right to be defended by a lawyer of his choice, and c) the right to be produced before a Magistrate.

Code of Criminal Procedure, 1973 — Section 304 : Where, in a trial before the Court of Sessions, the accused is not represented by a pleader and where it appears to the Court that the accused has not sufficient means to engage a pleader, the Court shall assign a pleader for his/her Defence at the expense of the State.

Criminal Procedure Code, 1973 — Section 440 : (1) The amount of every bond executed under this chapter shall be fixed with due regard to the circumstances of the case and shall not be excessive. (2) The High Court or Court of Session may direct that the bail required by a police officer or Magistrate be reduced.

According to Section 57 of the CrPC, a person who has been arrested is supposed to be produced before a Magistrate within 24 hours of his/her arrest. This affords a possibility, for immediate release in case the arrest is not justified. The police is supposed to present charges in front of the Magistrate when the accused is placed before the Magistrate. However, it is well known that investigations cannot be completed within 24 hours in serious and complicated cases. The police then apply for remand either for police or for judicial custody.[3] Case diaries are required to be placed before the court when the accused is produced for remand. In case remand to police custody is not required, the accused is sent to judicial custody. The Supreme Court has further held that the police remand cannot be granted for more than 15 days under the existing law.[4] Under Section 167 of the Criminal Procedure Code, the accused is entitled to bail in case the investigation is not completed and the chargesheet not submitted within 90 days, in cases punishable with death, life imprisonment or imprisonment for 10 years. In the case of other offences, the period is 60 days. The police is supposed to release the person on bail in all bailable cases. If the bail is not granted, the arrested person would be entitled to a writ of Habeas Corpus directing his/her release.

At the pre-trial stage, every accused is presumed to be innocent until a competent Court finally disposes of the matter. He/she is entitled to all the rights enjoyed by other citizens and is thus entitled to his/her liberty under Article 21 of the Constitution. The Supreme

Court of India as also the High Courts have observed, "The normal rule is bail and not jail".[5] If the Courts are satisfied that the accused would appear for his/her trial and will not abscond or tamper with evidence, bail must invariably be granted. The Magistrate has no power to go into the merits of the case. Further, in view of the delay in disposing of bail application, it has been laid down that bail applications must be heard and disposed of the day they are filed.[6]

In many cases, police take an unreasonably long time to complete investigation. In such cases, where the accused has been in custody for a long time, the Courts have held that it is mandatory for the Magistrate to grant bail to the accused. In order to get the bail, a security deposit is mostly needed. Security deposits cannot be arbitrary and burdensome to the accused. When the Trial Courts impose higher burden of security deposits, the Apex Court unequivocally set them aside. In *Moti Ram vs. State of M.P.*[7] the Court expanded this concept to make it more responsive to the needy. The objective behind demanding security is to ensure that the person appears for his/her trial.

The Courts have repeatedly directed that the amounts fixed must be reasonable and a person can be released on his own bond, with or without surety. A Magistrate has no power to cancel bail, which has been granted in a bailable offence.[8] Lastly, the Magistrate must ensure that the police are not guilty of infringing any of the rights of the persons produced before him/her.

Like Article 22(1), Section 303 of the Criminal Procedure Code also provides every accused the right to be defended by a pleader of his/her choice. The right to consult a lawyer for the purposes of defence begins from the moment of arrest. If it is found that the accused was handicapped for want of legal aid, the Court may declare the trial as void, as the proceedings would amount to a negation of fair trial.[9] The fact that the accused could not afford a lawyer is no defence. Section 304 enjoins the State to provide legal aid to indigent persons.[10] The trial court is under an obligation to inform the accused that if he/she is unable to engage a lawyer on account of poverty, he/she is entitled to obtain free legal services at the cost of the state.[11] The Supreme Court, relating to undertrials, has laid down comprehensive guidelines in a series of judgments.[12]

The law enforcement authorities should ensure that any person who is accused of a bailable offence, and is arrested or detained without a warrant, should be released on bail as a matter of right. Further, if any person is ready to furnish the required amount for the bail, then he should not be refused bail under Section 436 of the Criminal Procedure Code. Otherwise, it should tantamount to illegal detention and any police officer causing such detention should be held guilty of wrongful confinement under Section 342 of the Indian Penal Code.

A trial continuing for an unreasonably long time is a violation of fair trial, especially if the accused is not released on bail.[13] Speedy trial is an essential ingredient of reasonable, fair and just procedure guaranteed by Article 21 and it is the constitutional obligation of the State to devise such a procedure as would ensure speedy trial for the accused.[14] The Courts have however not been consistent in quashing trials on the grounds of delay.

We, thus, find that the legal safeguards provided to the accused are quite vast and are adequate if followed properly. All that is required is to follow the law and the guidelines laid down by the courts especially the Supreme Court of India. Moreover, free and compulsory legal aid to the needy is a must and this is a Constitutional obligation too.

## Police Reforms

The police force in India is known for – inefficiency, high-handedness, brutalism, corruption, and being politicized. However, the police functions with a lot of constraints too. As a result, the issue of police reform assumes significance especially because the poor and the 'not-so-well-connected' people are invariably at the receiving end of the police action and inaction.

The birth of the police force in India can be traced back to 1860, when the British felt the need for a common pattern of police organization and properly trained and disciplined body of men exclusively devoted to the prevention and detection of crime. Consequently, the Indian Penal Code in 1860 and the Police Act in 1861 were enacted to give shape to the police force. The Police Commission of 1860 had observed that the organized police as proposed by them would be "politically more useful". The present culture of the police system appears to be a continuation of what was obtained under the British regime when the police functioned ruthlessly as an agent for sustaining the government in power.[15]

The subject of police reform is vast and covers many issues and concerns that is not just restricted to strengthening and improving the structural and administrative aspects of the police force, but also includes issues like changing the culture and ethos of policing. The police have an obligation to function within the Constitution, law and democratic aspirations of the people. With significant changes taking place in the country since the inception of the police as an organization and more so since independence, the complementary changes and reforms have been absent within the law-enforcement agency. Those who control and run the system have abused it beyond repair. There are problems concerning every aspect of the system, right from the stage of recording the First Information Report (FIR) to investigation of the case (which often involves search, arrests, detention and interrogation), prosecution, trial, conviction, imprisonment, parole, review, remission and rehabilitation, not to mention recidivism and relapse.

## Report of the National Police Commission, 1979-81

The first report after independence that looked into the issue of 'Police Reform' at large was that of the National Police Commission. Most of the recommendations have not been implemented although the report remains, in a way, the bible for police reforms in India.

The National Police Commission was formed in 1977 to look into the role of the police. The National Police Commission submitted its report in eight parts, between 1979 and 1981.[16] Each of the reports dealt with different aspects related to the police force and reforms pertaining to its image as well as functioning. A detailed summary of the recommendations of the National Police Commission on the various issues is in Appendix 2. Not all aspects discussed in the various Reports of the National Police Commission are of relevance to this discussion. We have focused on issues that are more general in nature (mostly related to the Indian Penal Code) and have or can have a bearing on the poorer segments of the society.[17]

The National Police Commission looked into issues like arrests, detention in police custody, interrogation of women and delay in investigation (which contributes to undue detention in custody of non-convicted persons). Besides highlighting the need to adhere to law, it made wide-ranging suggestions for amendment of the law and procedures to cut down delays at the investigation and trial stages and to obviate custodial violence and lock-up irregularities. The National Police Commission favoured a system of periodic visits to inspect and report on police lock-ups. It also laid down detailed guidelines for the organizational restructuring of the police force, including promotions, role, duties, functions, code of conduct, punitive measures and accountability of the police force.

The National Police Commission also acknowledged the extraneous pressures on the police. One needs to stop political interference in the process of investigation and also in the transfer of officers.

Too much distrust of the police is in-built in our system. The statements recorded by police officers during investigations of witnesses or the accused should be admissible in court. It should be left to the courts to rely on them or reject them. The National Police Commission recommended that the laws and procedures relating to arrest, search and seizure, recording of statements of the accused and witnesses by police officers, police remand, bail provisions, regulatory powers, and economic offences, specially section 161 and 162 of the Criminal Procedure Code should be amended keeping in view the changed role of the police and public interest.

The National Police Commission also recommended that Section 151 of the Criminal Procedure Code should be amended to facilitate remand to preventive police custody for a few days by a magistrate. This will help in a truthful record of First Information Reports (FIR) and avoid registration of false cases for investigation. The police may be empowered in law to compound offences even at the stage of investigation in certain situations when both parties to a dispute are themselves keen to settle the matter.

Public grievance and complaint cells, outside the police department, should inquire into complaints against police officers. The Commission recommended the creation of these cells to make the police more accountable and responsible.

Another reform that is long overdue is the separation of investigation from the police officers deployed in law and order duties. Successive police commissions including the National Police Commission have made this recommendation but owing to misplaced priorities and strong internal opposition from the police department, this recommendation has not been implemented.

Corruption adversely affects police performance. The Report went into this aspect in great details. Misuse of discretionary powers by a police officer is the main form of corruption in the police department. Obviously, the remedy lies in putting a check on these discretionary powers. This can be achieved in two ways — through procedural changes, and through tight supervision and inspections. The Police Rules provide for an elaborate system of inspections at all levels but unfortunately, the system is in disuse. The responsibility rests squarely with the senior officers who spend far too much time in their offices when they should be touring and inspecting their subordinate offices. Some procedural changes about arrests, searches and seizures should reduce the scope for the misuse of these powers. This is elaborated in the Report.

The legal wing of the police system needs to be strengthened by a Directorate of Prosecution as an integral part of the system. Co-ordination between the investigating wing and the legal wing would ensure thoroughness and fairness of investigation.

In the case of offences under the 'Social Legislations', the new concept of 'conditional cognizance' as recommended by the National Police Commission, giving all the essential powers of investigation to the police except the power of arrest, needs to be introduced in the Criminal Procedure Code.

The role, training and the status of the constable need up-gradation. To make the police more sensitive and responsive to public criticism, public grievances cells should supplement the efforts of vigilance cells within the department. Both training and equipment also need upgradation. Modernization of the police cannot be achieved without funds. The National Police Commission details the areas where upgradation of equipment and modernization is urgently required. It also calls for more financial powers to the Chiefs of the State Police.

The Police Act 1861 has become outmoded. It should be replaced by a new act to meet today's needs such as the new model Police Act, the National Police Commission had in its report.

## The Ribeiro Committee Report

In 1996, a civil writ petition was filed in the Supreme Court (Civil Writ Petition No. 316 of 1996) by two retired IPS officers, appealing for issue of orders to the Government to implement the recommendations of the National Police Commission. The petition is pending with the Supreme Court. In pursuance of the directions issued by the Court in the above case, the Central Government (Ministry of Home Affairs) set up in July 1998 a Committee on Police Reforms under the chairmanship of J.F. Ribeiro.

Besides visiting States and interacting with government officials, the Ribeiro Committee collected the views of different persons and organizations through a questionnaire. The Ribeiro Committee submitted its report in two parts. The highlights of the Ribeiro Committee report are given in Appendix 3.

The Ribeiro Committee finalized its report regarding the establishment of the State Security Commission; setting up of proper procedures to select the chiefs of police forces and providing a minimum secure tenure to them; and insulating the investigating wing of the police from its law and order functions. The Ribeiro Committee report is pending with the Supreme Court.

The Ribeiro Committee has more or less approved the recommendations of the National Police Commission except for minor changes. However, where it departs from the recommendations of the National Police Commission in a major way is *vis-à-vis* in the establishment of the State Security Commission as a statutory body. While the National Police Commission has recommended that the State Security Commission should be a statutory body, the Ribeiro Committee has recommended that it should be a *"non-statutory, advisory and recommendatory"* body.

## Padmanabhaiah Committee Report on Police Reforms

In January 2000, the Government of India announced the setting up of another Committee on Police Reform under the chairmanship of Mr. Padmanabhaiah. The terms of the reference assigned to the Committee were very wide, covering different aspects of police organization, structure, functioning and problems. The Committee completed its report in August 2000. The broad recommendations of the Padmanabhaiah Committee Report are given in Appendix 4.

The Padmanabhaiah Committee Report went into the issues of Police reforms in greater details than perhaps what the Ribeiro Committee did. Padmanabhaiah Committee Report tried to define the perspective roles of Centre and States in developing capabilities in the Police including funding. It also recommended a system of planned induction based on proper manpower planning and of career planning of individual group of officers.

The Padmanabhaiah Committee Report emphasized on a greater need to recruit more Sub-Inspectors instead of Constables. Incidentally, the National Police Commission recommended the opposite. The Padmanabhaiah Committee Report also recommends career planning at the level of Constables and says that it is very important. The Report laid special emphasis on the need for specialization in police.

The report also went into issues like political interference from outside and corruption within. The Padmanabhaiah Committee Report laid greater emphasis on forensic science and the role it can play in investigation of murder, sexual assault and terrorist cases, besides drug offences, vehicle crime and burglary. It recommended that the police manual must be amended to make it mandatory to collect samples and to obtain expert forensic opinion in all such serious crimes. This report is the first report that goes into issues like cyber crime and crimes related to terrorism.

The Padmanabhaiah Committee Report observes that the present classification of offences into cognizable and non-cognizable made almost 150 years ago is not very relevant today. It recommends that the Law Commission of India should review the entire classification and the powers of the police to investigate.

The Report also recommends a mandatory judicial inquiry into all cases of alleged rape of a woman or death of any person in police custody.

## Reports of the Law Commission of India

Several Reports of the Law Commission of India went into issues that fall within the ambit of Police Reforms or issues that the National Police Commission dealt with in its report. Specifically two reports are discussed here.

### *Report of the Law Commission of India — 78th Report*

The 78th Report of the Law Commission of India on "Congestion of Under Trial Prisoners in Jails", which was submitted in 1979, made the following recommendations with regard to release on bail.

- Release a person on bond without sureties, where such a release is permitted by court.
- Provide for release on bond without sureties in cases under Sections 395 (30) and 439 (1) (a) Criminal Procedure Code.
- Release on bond without sureties even in regard to non-bailable offences under Section 437 (1) Criminal Procedure Code.
- Create a new offence in the Indian Penal Code for punishing the failure of a person to appear and surrender to custody in conformity with a bond executed by him. However, there are two caveats. There should be due regard, before the bail is granted, for (i) the likely effect on public order and public peace by the release of such a person, and (ii) his conduct after release on bail on a previous occasion.

### *Report of the Law Commission of India — 142nd Report*

The 142nd Report of the Law Commission of India, submitted in 1994, was on "Custodial Crime". In the report, the Law Commission noted that the victims of Custodial Crimes and deaths usually belong to the weaker sections of society. "The poor, the downtrodden and the ignorant with little or no political and financial power are unable to protect their interests." (page 2).

Section 56 of the Criminal Procedure Code contains a mandatory provision requiring the police officer making arrest without warrant, to produce the arrested person before a Magistrate, without unnecessary delay. If the police wants to detain the person further, then an order from the Magistrate following the procedure, as prescribed under Section 167 of the Criminal Procedure Code, has to be obtained.

By Section 167 of the Criminal Procedure Code, the police are further required to make entry of his arrest in several documents under the Police Act and Police Manual, which includes information to the District Magistrate and the Sub-Divisional Magistrate about the date and time of the arrest. In order to avoid these regours of law, the police make informal arrest without making any entry into the records. Instances are not lacking where the police have arrested a person without warrant in connection with the investigation of an offence and the arrested person is subjected to torture to extract information from him for the purpose of further investigations or for recovery of weapons or goods and also for extracting confession in violation of the statutory law. The torture and injury caused on the body of the prisoner sometimes results into his death. The death in custody is not generally shown in records.

Consequently, even if the victim or the kith and kin launch a formal prosecution, no direct evidence is available to substantiate the charge of torture or causing hurt resulting into death. This is because in the police lock up, the sole witnesses are either policemen or co-prisoners who are highly reluctant to appear as prosecution. The Law Commission of India was of the opinion that "it is essential to make appropriate provisions in the Indian Penal Code, the Criminal Procedure Code, and the Indian Evidence Act to foreclose torture in custody by public servants and to protect the interest of the victims of custodial crimes" (page 51).

This difficulty was considered by the Supreme Court also in a series of cases and it observed that the situation required amendment of law relating to burden of proof in such cases. It is a matter of regret that in spite of the Law Commission's recommendations and the Supreme Court's observations in several cases, the requisite amendment in the law of Evidence has not been made.

## National Human Rights Commission – the Police

The National Human Rights Commission (NHRC) in all its Annual Reports, since the first one in 1993-94, expressed deep concern on the state of affairs afflicting the police in India. In particular, it made the following points in relation to a case in the Supreme Court[18], which was reiterated in the Annual Report of 1997-98.

- Separation of the Investigation Wing of the Police from executive crime detection duties so as to insulate the investigation wing from extraneous pulls and pressures.
- Constitution of the "Police Security and Integrity Committee" as a recommendatory and advisory authority to begin with who would recommend on (a) broad policy guidelines and directions for the performance of preventive tasks and service oriented functions by the police, and (b) illegal transfers, promotion orders, illegal or irregular orders in the performance duties, no premature transfers and by a competent authority only.
- District Police Complaints Authority to look into misuse of power and abuse of authority including wrongful arrests, detentions, custodial violence, etc.
- Institution of 'Lay Visitors' to Jails and Police lock-ups by respectable and independent members of the public without interfering in any manner.
- Improvement in the mode of appointment of prosecution personnel.

## Reforms in the Court System

The Courts are the second institution involved in the enforcement of Criminal Justice in India. Courts, in India, face widespread delays and a large backlog of pending cases. The deteriorating scenario of court arrears primarily reflects two things; growth in the number of cases instituted every year and failure to increase the infrastructure proportionately. An increased number of judges is an indicator of an upgradation in infrastructure. It was 278 in 1970 and increased to 587 in 1998 (although the working strength was only 466). During this period, when the number of judges doubled, total pending cases increased ten times. Again, in 1987, while there were only 10.5 judges per 1 million people in India, the corresponding figures were 50.9 in England, 57.7 in Australia, 75.2 in Canada, and 107 in USA. (Rao, 2001, pp.95).

The bulk of the literature that exists on Judicial Delays consists of reports by committees appointed by the Government, including the reports of the Law Commission of India.

The literature unanimously identifies inadequacy of Judge strength, delay in filling up of vacancies and unsatisfactory appointment of Judges as the main causes contributing towards for the accumulation of arrears in the courts. These reports, therefore, point out the infrastructure bottlenecks associated with dispute resolution as the main culprit. However, these reports have not tried to estimate the extent of infrastructure requirements. Also very little research, on the lower courts, have been attempted.

Most of the reports, on the other hand, expound in detail, various procedural aspects that the Courts as well as the cases are subjected to. In the process, the reports get caught in the quagmire of myriad procedural laws. This deters the policy-makers who do not have a legal background.

One of the first efforts to study the efficient functioning of the judicial system was undertaken by the *Civil Justice Committee* in 1924. This report is also known as the Rankin Committee Report as it was under the chairmanship of Justice Rankin. The report had a section titled 'Note on causes of delay in Civil Courts', and listed insufficient judge strength in some of the High Courts as the main cause for delay.[19] The *High Courts Arrears Committee* was set up under the Chairmanship of Justice S.R. Das in 1949. It recommended that inordinate delay in filling up of vacancies of the High Court bench should be avoided as much as possible and that there should be an immediate increase in the Judge strength of the High Courts where it was not commensurate with even the current volume of work.[20] Even the *Uttar Pradesh Judicial Reforms Committee* 1950, was of the unanimous opinion that the main cause of delay in the disposal of appeals in the Uttar Pradesh High Court was the shortage of Judges.[21]

The Law Commission of India was constituted in 1955 to undertake the task of reviewing the system of Judicial administration in all its aspects. The *14$^{th}$ Report of the Law Commission of India,* chided the bureaucratic obstacles posed by the Ministry of Home Affairs in increasing the Judge strength, which in its view led to the accumulation of arrears[22], and also mentioned the delay in filling up of vacancies as well as unsatisfactory appointments in the High Courts. It advocated a limited role to the State executive in the matter of appointment of Judges. This was later accepted. Even the *High Court*

*Arrears Committee* appointed in 1972 under Justice J.C. Shah expressed the same views[23]. It also recommended re-fixing of the permanent strength of High Court Judges making it commensurate with the rise in the volume of work and also the appointment of additional and *ad hoc* Judges for clearing the arrears. These observations were reiterated in the *79th Report* of the *Law Commission of India* on "Delay in High Courts and other Appellate Courts"[24] and also in the *Estimates Committee 31st Report* in 1986[25].

In 1979 the *80th Report* of the, *Law Commission of India,* on "The Method of Appointment of Judges" made detailed recommendations[26] regarding wrong and improper appointment procedure of Judges to the Supreme Court and the High Courts. The *Law Commission of India, 120th Report* was again on "Manpower Planning in Judiciary: A Blueprint", wherein it observed that judicial manpower planning was an area which has generally been ignored in India[27]. Among other things, it recommended for a re-thinking, whether expenditure on administration of justice can ever be called non-plan expenditure, as is the current practice.

In the *Law Commission of India, 121st Report* on "A New Forum for Judicial Appointments"[28] and also in the *Law Commission of India, 124th Report* on "High Court Arrears — A Fresh Look"[29], the earlier views on filing up vacancies expeditiously, augmenting the Judge Strength and appointment of *ad hoc* judges to tackle the problem of arrears were reiterated. Even the *Satish Chandra Committee"*[30], while dealing with the causes for accumulation of arrears, *inter alia,* identified inadequacy of Judge strength, delay in filling up of vacancies and unsatisfactory appointment of Judges as the main contributing causes. The *Malimath Committee Report*[31] also agreed with these views. It concluded that various reports 'in one voice' highlighted the same factors but 'nothing worthwhile appears to have been done, resulting in worsening of the problem of arrears'.

Therefore, the main highlight is the 'supply side' solutions to the problem. Nevertheless, there is also a need to tackle the problem from the 'demand side' by looking at the areas wherein litigation is maximum, and then looking for ways to curtail unnecessary litigation. Some of the Law Commission of India Reports deals quite extensively with the 'demand side' problems too, although the main recommendations remain improving the infrastructure. The *Satish*

*Chandra Committee Report* (1986) and the *Malimath Committee Report* (1990) are two such reports that deal extensively with these aspects.

## Prison Reforms

By our Constitution as well as the Indian Evidence Act, all undertrials are to be presumed to be innocent. This along with the right to be treated with dignity, are the two UN General Assembly adopted Undertrials Standards on Pre-Trial Detention, as enumerated in the UN Minimum Standard Rules for treatment of Prisoners.

Although we are primarily concerned with undertrials in Indian prisons, the question of Prison reforms has a much broader connotation. Prison reforms encompasses on one hand issues relating to diet, wages, buildings, sanitary conditions, and medical care, while on the other hand deals with issues like undertrials, segregation of women and children, issues of corruption, charter of relevance for prisoners and the need for more prisons. In this section, we will briefly discuss the various committees and their reports on the issue of undertrials in particular and recommendations on Prison reforms in general.

In the case of *Ramamurthy vs. State of Karnataka*[32], the Supreme Court discussed the complete case law on the subject of prisons. The Court concluded that there are nine major problems, which afflict the system and which needs immediate attention. These are, 1) Overcrowding, 2) Delay in Trial, 3) Torture and ill-treatment, 4) Neglect of health and hygiene, 5) Insubstantial food and inadequate clothing, 6) Prison vices, 7) Deficiency in communication, 8) Streamlining of Jail units, and 9) Management of Open Air Prisons.

At the end of 1991-92, there were 86 Central Jails, 252 District Jails, 11 Prisons for women, 718 Sub Jails, 21 Juvenile Jails, 46 Specialized Jails and 21 Open Jails in the country with a total jail population of 1,96,240 prisoners (including 5301 females). Out of this, 1,37,838 were undertrials i.e., over 70 per cent of prisoners were undertrials.

For the first time the terrible and inhuman conditions prevailing in the Indian Jails was brought to light by Lord Macaulay. On his suggestion, a Committee was appointed in 1836 to inquire into the affairs of Prison administration and Prison conditions. The report submitted in 1838 criticized the administration of prison, the "laxity of discipline, corruption and the system of employing the prisoners in extra manual-labour on public roads.[33] However, the report discussed issues related to prison administration only.

## The Prisons Act, 1894

There was no significant progress in the field of prison reforms and the concept of humane treatment of prisoners till 1894, when the Prisons Act was passed. It sought to streamline 'prison administration' and put it on a uniform footing throughout the country. It provided for separation of prisoners based on age, their civil or criminal status and on the basis of whether they were convicted or not. The Medical Officer was required to visit the prison daily and examine prisoners confined in cells for more than 24 hours. The Act also restricted employment of criminal prisoners sentenced to rigorous imprisonment to no more than nine hours on any day. The Medical Officer was made responsible for ensuring that the prisoners' health was not injured by the work in which they were employed. Nevertheless, the Act "was largely based on deterrent principles concerned more with prison management than with the treatment of prisoners and gave more consideration to prison offences and punishment than to their effect".[34] The Act still serves as the legal basis for the existing Prison system in India.

## Indian Jails Committee Report, 1919-20

Modern prison reform in the country can be said to emanate from the Indian Jails Committee of 1919-20. For the first time, this report identified reform and rehabilitation as the true objective of prison administration. The Committee recommended that the care of criminals should be entrusted to adequately trained staff, selected after careful scrutiny. The Committee made the important recommendation that separate jails should be earmarked for various categories of prisoners, prescribing a minimum area of 75 square yards per inmate within the jail walls. It took strong objection to the presence of children in jails meant for adults. It recommended the creation of special courts for hearing of cases of juvenile delinquents and their housing in remand homes. Many of the recommendations were not implemented on the ground that the subject of prisons was within the purview of the provincial governments.[35]

## Model Prisons Manual, 1960

An All-India Jail Management Committee was formed in 1957 and the report it submitted, became the Model Prisons Manual in 1960. This resulted in the setting up of the Central Bureau of Correctional Services, which was later re-designated as the National Institute of Social Defence. The report laid great stress on the reformative and correctional aspects as the major objective of incarceration of a person in jail, pursuant to his sentencing by a court, and also while awaiting trial.

Various state governments have also had a number of reports on Prison Reforms, as Prison is a state subject. However, most of these reports are in the local language and they were not available for the concerned central government agencies. So these have not been covered.

## All India Committee on Jail Reforms (1980-83)

All India Committee on Jail Reforms (1980-83) was headed by Justice A.N. Mulla, and is popularly known as the Mulla Committee Report. If the Report of the National Police Commission remains the guiding report for Police Reforms, then the Mulla Committee Report is the equivalent for Prison Reforms in India. A detailed summary of the recommendations made by the Mulla Committee Report is given in Appendix 5.

The Mulla Committee had noted that a majority of the persons lodged in prisons, especially the undertrials, consisted of people belonging to the underprivileged sections of society, and that the majority of the prison population was from rural and agricultural background[36]. First offenders involved in technical or minor violations of law accounted for a large number of them.

The Mulla Committee observed that a large number of offenders sent to prisons do not require any therapeutically correctional treatment. They are as normal as citizens outside prison walls and they need to be protected from the harmful effects of exposure to prison life. The Committee recommended that "protection of society as an objective of punishment has been universally accepted and this can be achieved through reformation and the rehabilitation of offenders." While taking due note of the need to keep out of circulation for a longer time, harmful, habitual, dangerous recidivist prisoners, the Committee came to the conclusion that a progressive prison system has to operate keeping in view the protection aspect as much as correctional and rehabilitation aspects.

The Mulla Committee examined all aspect of prison administration and made wide-ranging recommendations, which if implemented would go a long way to make prison administration efficient, humane and professional. The recommendations of the Mulla Committee touched upon legislative, operational, security aspects besides matters like classification of prisoners, living conditions in prisons, medical and psychiatric services, treatment programmes, vocational training for prison inmates, problems related to undertrials and other non-convicted prisoners, problems of women prisoners, etc. The report laid emphasis on the management of prisons to be entrusted to a cadre of professionals.

There is another category of prisoners *viz.* non-criminal mentally ill persons, who are held in various jails in India. In the normal course such persons should have been sent to Mental Hospitals, rather than to prisons. Recently an expert committee was set up by the Supreme Court of India, whose report has brought out that increasing number of poor people are seeking police assistance in throwing their kith and kin behind bars. The Mulla Committee found a close nexus between the police, magistracy, jail administration and relatives of the victims in this regard.[37]

## Law Commission of India

The 78$^{th}$ Report of the Law Commission of India on "Congestion of Under Trial Prisoners in Jails", made the following recommendations.

*Overcrowding*

Overcrowding leads to greater risk of disease, higher noise levels, surveillance difficulties besides physical discomfort. So the recommendation of the 78$^{th}$ Report of the Law Commission of India should be implemented within six months.[38]

*Alternatives to Prison Sentencing*

The Law Commission of India suggests among other remedial measures, the adoption of alternates to Prison sentencing or incarceration such as parole, premature release, probation, etc. The principle of suspended sentence has been successfully experimented in Japan and South Korea, particularly for first-time offenders in petty cases. The Report also suggests Probation to an experiment with suspended prosecution.

The Law Commission of India made the following recommendations in Chapter 9.[39]

- Suggestions of the Mulla Committee Report as contained in Chapter 20 of Vol. 1 relating to streamlining the remission system and premature release (parole).
- Producing under trial prisoners on remand dates without failure.
- Replacing the Indian Prison Act of 1894.
- A new Model All India Jail Manual.
- Mulla Committee Report on proper medical facilities.
- Complaint boxes in jails.
- Liberalization of communication facilities.
- Streamlining jail visits.
- Open-air prisons at least in the District Jails.

## National Human Rights Commission – Jails

The National Human Rights Commission (NHRC), in its first Annual report (1993-94), expressed its deep concern about the appalling conditions of overcrowding, lack of sanitation, poor medical facilities, inadequate diet, etc., in most of the jails of the country. These deficiencies are compounded by unconscionable delays in the disposal of cases for various reasons and mismanagement in the administration of jails, all of which needs to be remedied. It noted that the reasons for overcrowding are many. Inordinate delay in trials result in many undertrials having to be detained in jail for unduly long periods. This together with the routine new additions literally clogs the system.

### Other Reports

- Report of the National Expert Committee on Women Prisoners, 1987, led by Justice V.R. Krishna Iyer noted that the undertrials have a slightly elevated position but overcrowding does away with it. The report recommended that it is imperative to "identify the gaps in or drawbacks of the existing facilities and services and to evolve a more humane policy towards women offenders".
- Report of the Committee on Rationalization of Classification of Prisoners in Tihar Jail, 1997, led by the Justice Duggal reported that at the end of 1996, there were 9136 prisoners in Tihar Jail, out of which 7780 were undertrials, 1308 were convicts and 48 detainees. So more than 85 per cent of the inmates of Tihar Jail were undertrials. Moreover the stipulated capacity is only 2200.
- The Vohra Committee submitted its Report to the Government of India, Ministry of Home Affairs, in 1993. It was set up to take stock of all available information about the activities of crime syndicates/mafia organizations, which had developed links with and were being protected by Government functionaries and political personalities. (see page 4)

## Conclusion

It was seen that the legal safeguards provided to the accused were quite vast and adequate, if they were made use of. However, the illiterate poor are completely ignorant of the laws and they do not have the means to engage a lawyer either. The only way out, it was argued, is to have free and compulsory legal aid to the needy and this is a Constitutional requirement or obligation too. This must be provided for all prisons and the police must work out the arrangement so that this recourse is available to the accused. Proper and free legal aid will aid the poor in jails to secure bail. This would also reduce overcrowding in the jails and also reduce economic costs.

The criminal justice system in India is becoming progressively ineffective. Laws and procedures are so cumbersome that criminal cases keep accumulating and remain pending for years. The conviction rate has fallen so low that a resourceful criminal no longer fears punishment. Many cases are pending for over ten years. The Evidence Act and the Criminal Procedure Code need drastic amendments. The system must recognize the ground realities and not get caught in impractical laws and procedures. A balanced approach towards the rights of the accused and the needs of society should help in devising a system that will deliver justice in a reasonable time frame.

On the issue of Police Reforms, it was noted that Political interference at the stage of investigation has become a routine affair. Most reports of the various Police Commissions like that of the Punjab Police Commission (1961), Delhi Police Commission (1968), Public Police Relations Committee (1983), etc., all headed by eminent Judges, educationists, or outstanding civil servants have in one voice condemned political interference in the working of the police.

Separating the investigating wing from the regular police so that the police, who are subject to political pressures, do not handle the criminal administration of justice is one recommendation that was made by almost all the committees including the National Police Commission. The suggestion was to let the investigation be carried out by a group or body that is insulated from political influence. Yet this has remained unimplemented.

The requirement to produce the arrested person before a court within 24 hours is primarily a statutory requirement under the Constitution [Article 22 (2) and Section 57 of the Criminal Procedure Code], but this is not strictly observed.[40]

It is specifically laid down in the CrPC, that tasks related to investigation cannot be delegated to a constable. All the Police Manuals in the country repeat the same principle. This attitude towards constables is mainly responsible for the neglect of the most important rank in the police and as a result he has remained ill-trained, ill-equipped and is unwilling to take any initiative on his own.

And yet, this most important and visible rank in the police force, the person who interacts most with the general public, is distrusted and deliberately made ineffective. A constable responds to this distrust by his apathetic behaviour as he does not care and this is because he is not held accountable for the deterioration in law and order. The negative police image is created largely, owing to his callous unprofessional conduct. No improvement can take place without a reassessment within the police force of the constable's role.

Revamping of the law and order machinery to make it a citizen-friendly force requires both short-term and long-term measures. The short-term measures include insulating the police from external interference, specially political; the tightening of command and control systems; and ensuring that the leadership at all levels conducts itself in a professional manner and does not succumb to political pressures and, finally holding it accountable for the lapses of the force. Officers in sensitive posts should be assured of a fixed tenure. No officer should normally be transferred before the end of the tenure without valid reasons stated in writing.

The law and order cadre should be separated from the investigation branch. There should be separate cadres for the armed police, intelligence and traffic. The Police Act 1861, should be replaced by a new Act based on the model proposed by the National Police Commission. The criminal justice system should be strengthened by suitably amending the Criminal Procedure Code and the Indian Evidence Act. The old Police Manuals, some dating back to the nineteenth century, are in need of a major revision. The prosecution department should be brought within the police department.

The National Police Commission pointed out that 60 per cent of all arrests were either unnecessary or unjustified. This has resulted in overcrowding and accounts for 43.20 per cent of the expenditure of jails. Therefore, restraint by the police by following the five guidelines laid down by the Supreme Court in *Joginder Kumar vs. State of UP & others,*[41] regarding the procedure to be followed when a person is arrested, would go a long way in reducing overcrowding in jails.

One needs to minimize the scope of misuse or abuse of the power of 'arrests' without curtailing the powers of the police in effective protection and detection of crime and the maintenance of law and order. Changes in law are required to enable easier and quicker return of recovered property to the victims of crime at the stage of investigation and trial before the conclusion of trial.

The Courts found that the undertrials were not produced in courts on remand dates, which is a statutory obligation. On many occasions, they are either not produced or produced late, with the result that the hearing gets adjourned causing avoidable delay. This is due to the district police authority not making available police escorts on the ground of non-availability of manpower. In many districts, the sanctioned manpower is inadequate.

It was unequivocally stated that there is an urgent need to increase the infrastructure in the Courts. The literature unanimously identified inadequacy of Judge strength, delay in filling up of vacancies and unsatisfactory appointment of Judges as the main contributing causes for the accumulation of arrears in the courts. However, the infrastructure has failed to increase proportionately.

The problem of arrears in criminal cases is the maximum in the Lower Courts of the country. Total pendency in the Lower Courts has stabilized around 20 million or two crore cases. Around two-thirds of this figure is criminal cases. The Magisterial Courts alone has more than 90 per cent of all criminal cases and over 60 per cent of the total cases that are pending in the Lower Courts.

The problem of judicial delays is considered to be colossal in nature and perhaps beyond redemption. The situation has been allowed to develop primarily on account of the total apathy and lack of will on the part of all concerned. It is high time that urgent attention is paid to the resolution of the problems by taking appropriate remedial measures before the situation deteriorates any further.

Immediate remedial measures can essentially be in two directions. The first involves the improvement in the infrastructure requirements and the second involves reforms in the procedural aspects and law. If measures in these two directions can be implemented, the situation will improve drastically.

On the issue of Prison Reforms, broadly speaking there are 7 major problem areas, which afflict the system and need priority attention. These are, overcrowding, delay in trials, privacy and communication, hygiene, jail visits, review of sentences, and open jails.

There is no organized or systematic effort to bring about reforms in a sustained and institutionalized manner because of a variety of reasons like lack of formal policy, want of commitment by the government, budget inadequacies and the non-availability of the required number of professionals among jail administrators.

The failure of the NGOs to take full advantage of the available resources and facilities was another negative factor. Even though the Mulla Committee stressed the need for more Open Prisons, little has been done. Further, in many jails prisoners do not get the benefit of free legal aid. There is no standardization of the wages in the jails too. The legal profession has also not played its part fully in this regard. In short, the problems afflicting Prisons are many and are compounded by prolonged neglect.

Prison administration is a State subject and this is often cited as the main reason for the Centre not being able to implement the recommendations of the Mulla Committee. Similar reasons used to be given for not enacting an All-India Children's Act till the then Prime Minister put his full weight behind the Centre enacting legislation for the purpose. This shows that with political will, the Centre can take an active and direct interest in prison administration. If it becomes unavoidable, even the revolutionary step of making prison administration a Central subject should be seriously considered.

The Mulla Committee Report, in chapters 6 and 7, observed that no proper medical care was available in most prisons. Moreover, the extended exposure due to overcrowding makes the case of the prisoners really bad. One simple measure that the Prisons can undertake is to keep undertrials separately from the other convicts.

The State Secretariats do not have the requisite expertise in prison administration to assist the Government in taking appropriate policy decisions. To begin with, senior officer having experience of correctional administration and the requisite expertise should be posted in the Department of Prisons, both at the Centre and in the States. The Department of Prisons and Correctional Services, whose creation the Mulla Committee recommended, should invariably be headed by an officer from this Department.

The recommendations of the All India Committee on Jail Reforms (1980-83) headed by Justice A.N. Mulla, both in substance and in spirit, have not been implemented. This needs to be done immediately.

# APPENDIX 1

## Selected Case Law on Arrests, Undertrial Prisoners, Bail, Legal Aid and Jail Conditions

*Joginder Kumar vs. State of UP & others — 1994 (3) SCC 423*

The Supreme Court, in this case, laid down five guidelines regarding the procedure to be followed when a person is arrested.

1. the right of the arrested person to request that a friend, relative or other persons be informed of his arrest and the place where he is detained,
2. the duty of the police officer to inform the arrested person of this right,
3. an entry to be made in the police station diary as to who was informed of the arrest,
4. the duty of the Magistrate before whom the arrested person is produced, to satisfy himself that these requirements have been complied with, and
5. a police officer making an arrest should record in the case diary the reasons for making the arrest, implying thereby that every arrest by the police has to be justified.

*Sheela Barse (II) vs. Union of India — 1986 (3) SCC 632*

Right to a speedy trial is a fundamental right implicit in Article 21 of the Constitution.

*R.D. Upadhyay vs. State of A.P — 1996 (3) SCC 422*

This was a public interest petition filed under Article 32 asking the court to take cognizance of the fact that several undertrial prisoners were languishing in Tihar Jail for a very long period of time. The Court directed the authorities to file an affidavit giving a list of undertrial prisoners.

The court ordered the following:

1. For the murder cases pending, the Delhi HC should designate 10 Additional District Judges to take up the trials.
2. For cases related to attempted murder, undertrials in prison for longer than 2 years should be released on bail forthwith.

3. For those who were unable to provide surety, release on bail by furnishing personal bonds.
4. The Prisoners need not make applications for bail. The court is to consider their case *suo moto.*

*Hussainara Khatoon (IV) vs. Home Secretary — 1980 (1) SCC 98*

The Petition was on behalf of a large number of undertrial prisoners who could not afford lawyers to argue a case for bail on their behalf.

The Court directed that on the next remand dates, when the undertrial prisoners, charged with bailable offences, are produced before the Magistrates, the State Government should provide them a lawyer at its own cost for the purpose of making an application for bail, provided that no objection is raised to such lawyer on behalf of such undertrial prisoners.

*Mohammad Tariq vs. Union of India — 1990 Cri.L.J. 474*

The Court held that the amount fixed as surety bond was excessive and tends to defeat the very order of granting bail to the applicant. The rider (in this case the rider was that the applicant should not leave the city of Varanasi during the period of bail without prior permission of the Court) was also held to be unnecessarily severe.

*Mah Chand vs. State of Delhi — 1990 Cri.L.J. 682 (Del.)*

The accused petitioner was convicted for various offences under the Indian Penal Code. He was in custody with no legal recourse provided.

The Court held that it was a case of grave illegality as the petitioner, who was in custody all through the trial, was not provided with any counsel at the state expense and he had also not engaged any counsel of his own and violates Article 21 of the Constitution.

*Supreme Court Legal Aid Committee vs. Union of India — 1994 (6) SCC 731*

The petitioner represented a large number of undertrial prisoners arrested under the NDPS Act. The Act had extremely stringent provisions on the issue of bail. On the other hand, the constitution of special courts required under the Act was taking time. As a result a large number of persons were being detained without trial for a long time.

The Court held that such an unreasonable delay violated Article 21 and passed the following order:

(1) Where the prisoner is accused of an offence with a maximum imprisonment of 5 years; and has spent at least two and a half years in prison he should be released on bail.

(2) Where the offence also prescribed a maximum fine, the prisoner should be given bail if he deposits 50 per cent of the amount.

(3) Where the offence prescribes a minimum sentence of 10 years and minimum fine of Rs. 1 lakh, the prisoner should be given bail if he has been in jail for at least 5 years and deposited a fine of Rs. 1 lakh.

*Raj Deo Sharma vs. State of Bihar (1998) 7 SCC 507*

The Court held that in cases where there has been a long delay, if the accused has been in jail for a period not less than one half of the maximum period of punishment prescribed, the trial court shall release the accused on bail forthwith on conditions as it deems fit.

*Khatri (11) vs. State of Bihar — 1981 (1) SCC 627*

Prisoners were blinded due to police atrocities in Bihar jail. The petitioners were treated in Delhi and raised the plea that they should be allowed to stay in Delhi and further raised the issue of free legal aid. The petitioners raised the contention that since they were blinded by police officers who were government servants, it is a violation of Article 21 and they are entitled to compensation. The State contended that the role of police officers is not yet established and even if it is established and Article 21 is violated, the State is not liable to pay any compensation.

The Court, regarding the question of legal aid, held as follows:

(1) Right to free legal services is an essential ingredient of Article 21 of the Constitution.

(2) The State is under a Constitutional mandate to provide a lawyer to an accused person if the circumstances of the case

and needs of justice requires as long as the accused person does not object to such a lawyer.

(3) The State cannot avoid liability by pleading financial and administrative inability.

(4) The State is Constitutionally bound to provide free legal aid to poor or indigent accused who are incapable of engaging lawyers, not only at the stage of trial but also when they are first produced before the Magistrate or remanded from time to time.

(5) Magistrate's and Session's judges have a duty to inform the accused of his right to free legal aid at the cost of the State.

*Suk Das vs. U.T of Arunachal Pradesh — 1986 (2) SCC 401*

The appellant Government servant, tried and convicted to two years imprisonment for offences under Section 506 read with Section 34 of IPC was not represented at the trail by any lawyer by reason of his inability to afford legal representation. On appeal, the High Court held the trial could not be vitiated, since he made no application for legal aid. Therefore, the appeal went to the Apex Court.

Free legal assistance, i.e., at the cost of State, is a fundamental right of a person accused of an offence, which may involve jeopardy to the life or personal liberty. This fundamental right is implicit in the requirement of reasonable, fair and just procedure prescribed by Article 21. The exercise of this right is not conditional upon an application for the same by the accused and hence cannot be denied if the accused failed to apply for it. It would be a mockery of the legal aid programme if it were to be left to the poor, ignorant and illiterate accused to apply for free legal services. Every Magistrate or Sessions Judge, before whom an accused appears, is under an obligation to inform the accused that if he/she is unable to engage the services of a lawyer, on account of poverty or indigence, he/she is entitled to obtain free legal services at the cost of the state. The accused may however decide not to seek such service. Every state in India shall make provision for such free legal aid services. If the trial would result in a sentence of imprisonment and is of such nature that the circumstances of the case and the needs of social justice require that the accused be given free legal representation. Since the trial was vitiated, the conviction and sentence were directed to be set aside.

*Kadra Pahadiya vs. State of Bihar — 1983 (2) SCC 104*

A researcher and social scientists had addressed a letter dated November 28, 1980 to the Supreme Court pointing out that Kadra Pahadiya and three other young boys, aged between nine and eleven years and belonging a backward tribe, were put in a Bihar Jail about eight years back and were still languishing in the jail without trial and kept in leg irons and forced to do work outside the jail. Admitting this as a writ petition, the Court made certain directions.

The Court held that speedy trial is a fundamental right implicit in the guarantee to life and personal liberty enshrined in Article 21 of the Constitution and any accused who is denied of this right of speedy trial is entitled to approach this Court for the purpose of enforcing such right and this Court, in discharge of its Constitutional obligation, has the power to give necessary directions to the State governments and other appropriate authorities for securing this right to the accused.

*Rama Murthy vs. State of Karnataka — 1997 (2) SCC 642*

The petition was taken up by the Court on the basis of a letter written by one of the prisoners in the Central Jail, Bangalore regarding grievance about some jail matters.

The Court considered the matter as problems experienced in all jails and issued guidelines to be observed by the authorities. On the issue of overcrowding it stated that overcrowding has a detrimental effect on health and hygiene and must therefore be taken care of. Possibilities like release on bail/parole/remission should be considered. Alternative sentences like fine, etc. should be considered also. The Court referred to the 78th Report of the Law Commission of India and the Mulla Committee Reports on Jail Reforms (1983) and asked the Government to consider them and take an appropriate decision within six months.

# APPENDIX 2

## Some Selected Recommendations from the Report of the National Police Commission on Police Reforms

### The First Report

The Indian Police System and structure as presently organized, is based on the Police Act, 1861. The previous report before that of the National Police Commission was in 1902-03, by the Indian Police Commission. The Commission had concluded "the police force throughout the country is in a most unsatisfactory condition, that abuses are common everywhere, that this involves great injury to the people and discredit to the government, and that radical reforms are urgently required".[42] The National Police Commission remarks "what the Police commission said in 1903 appears to be more or less equally applicable to the conditions obtaining in the police force today". (Para 1.2, page 7)

*Constabulary*

The First Report of the National Police Commission confined itself to a detailed discussion on the Constabulary, who constitutes a large majority of the staff and form the foundation of the entire police structure. So any meaningful attempt at police reform has necessarily to start at their level since no restructuring of the system will be practicable or enduring unless the mass base of the system is redeemed healthy and efficient. The Report focused on aspects of the Constable's personality, status and role in the police.

The quintessence of efficient policing is the effective and amiable street presence of a well-trained and motivated Constable. However, the present position of the Constables is a far cry from this position. The First Report of the National Police Commission accordingly also went into issues of pay, housing, supply of essential commodities, removal of orderly systems, a machinery for redressal of grievances of the Constables, recruitment, training and career planning.

*Complaints Against the Police*

However, the most significant reforms and recommendations pertained to a detailed structure of modalities for inquiry into complaints against the police. Unfortunately, the follow up action and implementation of these recommendations is still in doubt.

According to the National Police Commission, any arrangement for inquiry into complaints against police should be acceptable both to police and public as fair and just. The Commission, therefore, suggested arrangements, which would include inquiries conducted by departmental authorities and those conducted by an independent authority outside the police. The Commission felt that a large number of complaints against police should be looked into and disposed of by the supervisory ranks in the police hierarchy. The Commission however recommended that a judicial inquiry should be made mandatory following complaints of alleged rape of a woman in police custody, death or grievous hurt caused while in police custody, and death of two or more persons resulting from police firing in the dispersal of unlawful assemblies, against the police. It will be also be mandatory on the part of the government to publish the report of the inquiry into these complaints, and the subsequent decisions taken thereon within two months of receipt of the report.

## The Second Report

### *Appointment of the Criminal Justice Commission*

According to the National Police Commission, the police cannot achieve complete success in their work unless all wings of the criminal justice system operate with simultaneous efficiency. It is therefore necessary to set up a body, which would comprehensively monitor the performance of all agencies and apply corrective measures from time to time. The existing Law Commission may be enlarged to function as a Criminal Justice Commission on a statutory basis. Such arrangements at the Centre should be supported by similar arrangements at the state level.

### *Police Role, Duties, Powers and Regulations*

The crux of police reforms, in this country, is to secure professional independence for the police to function truly and efficiently as an impartial agent of the law of the land, and at the same time to enable the government to oversee the police performance to ensure its conformity to law. A supervisory mechanism without the scope for illegal, irregular or mala fide interference with the police functions has to be devised. This is what the Second Report of the National Police Commission deals with.

The report went into several welfare measures to cover housing, education, medical care, recreational facilities, financial aid and special retirement benefits in distress situations arising from death or physical disability caused by service conditions, etc.

The National Police Commission remarked "there is an urgent need for a comprehensive reform in the procedural laws relating to investigation and trial in our system".[43] Further it commented that the "huddling together of a large number of undertrials with convicted prisoners and the mixing together of old and hardened criminals with the young first offenders tend to promote in the minds of all inmates feelings of criminalization instead of remorse and regret for their previous conduct and a desire to reform".[44] The rules that govern the present accusatorial system of criminal trials make various demands from and place various restrictions on the prosecution so that the defendant gets all the help he can do to defend himself. At the end of the trial the prosecution must prove their case beyond reasonable doubt, but the accused may, however, only raise a doubt and get its benefit to secure his acquittal. The severe limitations placed on the admissibility of evidence from the prosecution side and norms for determining the value of the admitted evidence make it difficult for the police as the investigating agency to carry forward all the material uncovered during the investigation to the final point of success in getting the offender convicted under the law.

The National Police Commission was of the view that the need for effective interaction between the police and the prosecuting agency at the stage of court trial for proper marshaling and presentation of all the evidence uncovered during investigation. The need for such interaction should also be suitably recognized in law instead of being left as a mere administrative arrangement.

There is considerable scope for exercise of discretion at various stages in the discharge of police functions, particularly in regard to preventive policing measures before a crime occurs, as distinct from investigation which starts after the occurrence of the crime (the responsibility of which is spelt out in the Police Act). The National Police Commission was of the view that the exercise of discretion in all such situations should be based on the assessment and judgment of the police functionaries concerned only. To prevent freakish or whimsical decision in such matters some broad guidelines should be laid down to cover all such conceivable situations. Police Manuals, which do not contain such guidelines at present, should be appropriately amplified. These guidelines should be set out in clear terms and also made known to the public.

The Second Report of the National Police Commission recommends the constitution of a statutory Commission in every state, which can be called the State Security Commission. This Commission can lay down broad policy guidelines for efficient functioning, evaluate the performance of the State Police, look into complaints of extraneous pressures in the form of illegal or irregular orders, look into discrepancies regarding promotions and transfers, and act as a forum of appeal. This can help considerably in making police performance politically neutral.

*Extraneous Political Pressures*

The Second Report also deals extensively with "Interference and misuse of police by illegal or improper orders or pressure from political executive or other extraneous sources". The Report noted that the influence is very strong.

The threat of transfer/suspension is the most potent weapon in the hands of the politician to bend the police down to his will. The National Police Commission recommended that the superintendence of the state government over the police should be limited to ensure that police performance is in strict accordance with law. In the performance of its tasks, the police should be subject to overall guidance from the government, which should lay down broad policies for adoption in different situations. There should, however, be no instructions in regard to actual operations in the field. In regard to investigation work, in any case, the police are beyond any intervention by the executive or politicians.

To help the state government discharge their superintending responsibility in an open manner under the framework of law, a State Security Commission should be set-up through law in each state. The State Security Commission should (a) lay down broad policy guidelines and directions for the performance of preventive tasks and service-oriented functions by the police; (b) evaluate the performance of the State Police every year and present a report to the State Legislature; (c) function as a forum of appeal to dispose of representations from officers regarding their being subjected to illegal orders and regarding their promotions; and (d) review the functioning of the police in the state.

The selection of Chief of Police should be from a panel of three Indian Police Service officers of that state cadre. A committee headed by the Chairman of the Union Public Service Commission should prepare the panel. The chief of police should also be assured of a fixed tenure of office. The tenure may be for four years or for a period extending up to retirement, whichever is earlier. The removal of the chief of police from his post before the expiry of the tenure should require approval of the State Security Commission.

Police officers should also be effectively protected against whimsical and mala fide transfer/suspension orders. There should be a provision in the Police Act, specifying the authorities competent to issue such order regarding different ranks. Any such orders passed by any authority other than those specified in the Act will be rendered null and void.

### *Gram Nyayalayas*

The National Police Commission also recommends the setting up of *Gram Nyayalayas*. The working of *Nyaya Panchayats,* though well conceived in principle, suffered in practice, mainly because of the lay members of the *Panchayats* being subjected to local influences and pressures, which defeated the purpose. The report also pointed out that a *Nyaya Panchayats* were solely made up of lay members who were unable to handle the judicial process. It was further recommended that *Nyaya Panchayats* would function far more efficiently if they were manned by trained persons with a certain minimum knowledge of law, rules and procedure.

## The Third Report

### *Weaker Sections of the Society*

The Third Report of the National Police Commission defines weaker sections of the society as those "who are subjected to social injustice and different forms of exploitation on account of poverty or ignorance besides age-old traditions, customs, beliefs and the interplay of vested interests that have grown around them."[45] The recommendations were as follows:

- The State Governments may set up Special Courts under section 15 A (2) (iii) of the Protection of Civil Rights Act, 1976, to bring down the large pendency of cases in Courts.
- The Ministry of Home Affairs may issue comprehensive guidelines for classifying crimes as 'atrocities' to ensure proper recording and analysis of all such offences over a period of time on a countrywide basis.
- Special cells may be set up in the Police Department in each state to, besides other thing, (i) monitor the progress of investigations of cases under the Protection of Civil Rights Act, 1976 or other atrocities against Scheduled Castes/ Scheduled Tribes registered in district police stations; (ii) make enquiries or investigations into complaints from Scheduled Castes/Scheduled Tribes or other weaker sections of the people that may be received directly in the cell; and (iii) discuss with the prosecuting staff the progress of cases pending. Trial to ensure satisfactory marshaling and presentation of evidence in Court.
- Importance should be given to causes for dissatisfaction of the weaker sections of society about lack of police response to their plight in certain situations and to the deficiencies in the scheme of allotment of land to the landless poor who include a large number of Scheduled Castes, cases related to Motor Vehicles Accidents, etc.
- Strengthening of the Village *Chowkidar*/Police.

*Corruption*

The Third Report of the National Police Commission looks at the crucial issue of Corruption in great details. The following recommendations were made.

- Insulate the Police system from political interference.
- Systems of surprise checks, inspections and effective supervision by honest and well-motivated officers, at different levels of command within the hierarchy itself.

- Posting of police officers be the exclusive responsibility of the Deputy Superintendent of Police (DSP) and likewise the Chief of Police for the DSPs.
- The provisions in the service rules for compulsory retirement after completion of 20 years of service should be restored to weed out Officers with corrupt reputation. A suitably constituted high-level committee in the police should assess evidence regarding this reputation. There can be one appeal against the recommendations of the committee and after the disposal of the appeal the matter will be closed.

*Arrests*

It is an accepted fact that the police makes far too many arrests that that are actually warranted. The low prosecution rate is, therefore, a natural corollary (although there are a host of other reasons too, which contribute to such a low rate). There is a clear case for reducing the number of arrests in police work. This will also reduce the scope for allied corruption. The Third Report of the National Police Commission made the following observations/ recommendations.

- Several policemen are under an erroneous impression that an arrest is mandatory under the law while investigating a cognizable offence.
- Section 2 (c) and 2 (1) Criminal Procedure Code should be amended to remove the emphasis on arrests in the definition of cognizable offences.
- Departmental instructions may insist that a police officer making an arrest should also record the reasons for making the arrest.
- The recommendations of the 78th Report of the Law Commission of India titled "Congestion of Under Trial Prisoners in Jails", on release of an arrested person on bail, should be implemented.

*Economic Offences and Modernization*

The report deals with Economic Offences like tax evasion, manipulation of stocks and shares, frauds in licenses and permits, black marketeering, hoarding, adulteration of drugs and food stuff, etc. in Chapter XXIII.

The Report also deals with the issue of modernization of law enforcement especially in transport, forensic science labs, scientific instruments, and wireless equipment, etc., in Chapter XXIV.

## The Fourth Report

### *Investigation*

In the first chapter of the Fourth Report of the National Police Commission matters related to 'Investigation' was discussed. The following recommendations were made.

- The cadre of investing officers must be increased.
- Provision of adequate transport, strengthening of forensic laboratory facilities and scientific aids to the detection of crime must be provided with the police force.
- Section 37 of the Criminal Procedure Code needs to be amended to facilitate the conduct of identification parades by the police themselves as an aid to investigation.
- Section 100 of the Criminal Procedure Code may be amended to facilitate the admission of search list as a piece of evidence without having to call upon search witness to depose in court, and further to facilitate public servants to function as search witness in certain situations.
- A new Section — 50 A — may be added to Chapter V of the Criminal Procedure Code requiring the police to give intimation about the arrest of a person to anyone who may be reasonably named by him/her for sending such intimation, to avoid agonizing suspense for the members of his family about his whereabouts.
- Surprise visits to the police stations by senior officers would help the immediate detection of persons held in unauthorized custody and subjected to ill treatment.
- A magistrate or Judge before whom an arrested person is produced by the police for remand to custody should be required by administrative rules of criminal practice to

specifically question the arrested person if he has any complaint of ill treatment by the police.

- To check third degree methods from being adopted, there should be a scheme for mandatory judicial inquiries into complaints of death or grievous hurt caused while in police custody.
- By sub-sections (3) and (4) of Section 167 of the Criminal Procedure Code, remand to police custody is exceptional and is actually dependent if the Investigating Officer pleads that the accused has already made a confession and his continued custody with the police is necessary. This is sometimes falsely made. These two sub-sections should be deleted and a new sub-section (3) may be added to facilitate remand to police custody in the interest of investigation whenever required.
- Section 2 of Criminal Procedure Code may be amended to facilitate the establishment of special police station to deal with particular cases or classes of cases.

*Court Trial*

The Fourth Report of the National Police Commission has been especially critical of the way Court Trials are held and its fall out. It noted that "protracted proceedings in courts followed by acquittal in heinous crimes tend to generate a feeling of confidence among hardened criminals that they can continue to commit crimes with impunity and ultimately get away with it all".[46] This can have a cascading effect on the poor who generally bear the brunt of lawlessness being the farthest from the corridors of power and protection.

The Fourth Report of the National Police Commission further mentions badly delayed trials arising from causes like non-appearance of witnesses, lack of preparedness of the prosecuting or defense counsel to get on with the day's work in court, frequent adjournments granted on the slightest pretexts, prolonged cross examinations without regard to its relevance or need, taking unduly long time for perusing records or otherwise getting prepared for the case at different stages of trial, etc. The National Police Commission accordingly raised the following broad points, which can lessen the present predicament affecting court trials to a significant extent.

- The Commission felt that several of these causes (listed above) could be eliminated "if the residing Magistrate/Judge adopts a positive approach to the daily proceedings in every case and adequately uses his powers under the Criminal Procedure Code and Section 165 of the Indian Evidence Act for expeditious disposal of the cases".[47]
- The National Police Commission suggests a whole time functionary at the rank of a Senior District and Sessions Judge who is qualified for appointment as High Court Judge may be attached to each High Court to inspect the District Courts periodically. A similar functionary of the rank of Additional Sessions Judge may be entrusted with the inspections at the district level.
- The Commission also suggests that Summary trial procedure should be made mandatory for offences specified in Section 260 of the Criminal Procedure Code. Accordingly, the words 'may, if he thinks fit' can be substituted by the word 'shall' in this Section.
- An adult who is proved to have organized a gang of juvenile criminals or otherwise abetted the commission of crime by a juvenile, should be held punishable under Chapter V of the Indian Penal Code which should provide for a more severe punishment than that stipulated for the main crime by the juvenile. A new Section may also provide for the mandatory award of a minimum punishment, except for special reasons to be recorded by the court.
- The National Police Commission also favours the institution of a Criminal Justice Commission at the Centre supported by a similar arrangement at the State level with special emphasis on the correctional services *vis-à-vis* the Protection of Offenders Act and the Children Act.
- Cooperation between the public prosecutors and the police at various levels aided by suitable additions to the Criminal procedure Code to specify this rule.

*Social Legislation*

The Fourth Report of the National Police Commission discusses in details the problem of social legislation. The normal role of the police as expected by the people is in the field of laws pertaining to the protection of life and security of property. The Indian Penal Code is the basic criminal law of the country for the police to perform this role. However, the police, as the premier law enforcement agency in the country, are frequently involved in the enforcement of a variety of laws aimed at social reforms. The National Police Commission categories social legislation into five groups, as follows.[48]

- The First Group covers laws regulating social institution like marriage, divorce, adoption, inheritance, etc. Here there is no role of the police that is envisaged in the enforcement of these laws.
- The Second Group pertains to laws dealing with social problem like prevalence of dowry, discrimination against women, begging, vagrancy, etc. The police should not have much role to play in the enforcement of these laws except in some cases like enforcing the law prohibiting begging which is solely from the point of view of maintaining public order at a specified place.
- The Third Group deals with laws aimed at prohibiting the deterioration of the health of the people. Offences under these laws which involve commercially organized activity (e.g. drug trafficking) or disturbance of public order, should be made fully cognizable by the police. Offences which do not have any such angle but involve individual behaviour and conduct without creating any public disorder may be made cognizable by the police only on a specific complaint from a person alleging annoyance or injury caused to him/her by such behaviour and conduct and not on any intelligence gathered by the police themselves.
- The Fourth Group of laws is aimed at prohibiting or regulating certain pastimes, which are likely to operate to the detriment of the earnings of the poor and their families. Laws that regulate gambling, horse racing, lotteries, etc., fall under this category. Police cognizance of offences, under these laws, should be limited to those that have a public aspect.
- The Fifth Group consists of laws that are meant for protecting and rehabilitating the handicapped and the weaker sections of

society and preventing their economic exploitation. Police should be fully involved in the enforcement of these laws. Protection of Civil Rights Act and the Suppression of Immoral traffic Act are examples of laws under these groups. Offences under these laws should be made cognizable and the general police should have full powers of enforcing them.

*Prohibition*

The Fourth Report of the National Police Commission comments that "the arrest of a large number of persons year after year and their passing through police custody for their involvement in prohibition offences alone would tend to 'criminalize' persons who are not perceived a criminal in the normal sense of the term by society at large". (Page 59) The prohibition law was conceived as a legislation primarily meant to benefit the ill informed and poorer sections of the community. Most of these in jail under this law are in prisons (and in large numbers) for their involvement in illicit liquor trade. However, most of them are the consumers of illicit liquor and thus belong to the poorer sections of the society. Illicit distillation of liquor is carried out in remote areas and safe hideouts, but is easily available. The profits from this business far outweigh the economic losses from punishment and provides for big business and consumption. This results only in consumers getting caught and languishing in jails. Consequently, the Fourth Report of the National Police Commission recommended the following.

- Cognizable offences under the prohibition law should be limited to manufacturer, transport and sale of liquor.
- Offences relating to possession of liquor and drinking of liquor or being found in a state of drunkenness should be made non-cognizable.

## The Fifth Report

*Recruitment and Training of Police Personnels*

The Fifth Report of the National Police Commission starts with a detailed discussion of Recruitment and Training of Police Personnels, especially for the Constables. Some of the important points raised and recommendations made are as follows:

- Limit recruitment at two levels only — Constables and Officers in Indian Police Service. The recruitment in the other levels should be eliminated in a phased manner.
- Recruitment of Constables only at the district level, to ensure adequate representation.
- A qualitative change in police perspective and approach is needed so as to result in a total change in the police culture. Much greater effort is required in training and education to develop greater professional competence, at the level of constables.
- This should be complemented with intelligent supervision, purposeful inspection, favourable environmental conditions, mutual trust and willingness to delegate.
- Training material and basic instructional literature should be easily made available.
- Better planning and training manpower is required.
- Attractive pay and other amenities are required.
- Recommendations of the 1973 Committee on Police Training should be implemented.
- Greater attention to the nature of the Constable's interaction with the public is needed.
- The Constable has to be made aware of the prospects of promotion.
- Constables like Sub-Inspectors should be attached to some social service organization.
- Periodical exposure is required by way of refresher courses to increase the sensitivity and understanding of psychology, management techniques and behavioral sciences.
- Special Courses at all levels for Constables, Sub-Inspectors and Inspectors.
- Deputy Superintendent of Police should go through the training imparted to the Indian Police Service Officers at the National Police Academy in Hyderabad.

### *District Police and the Executive Magistracy*

The next aspect (of relevance here) discussed in the Fifth Report of the National Police Commission pertains to the role of the District Police. The District Police and the Superintendent of Police are subjected to two kinds of control — a hierarchical control exercised by the officers in the police and an operational control exercised by the Chief Executive of the District or the District Magistrate (DM). The arrangement, contemplated in law, for the administration of the police in the district is set forth in paragraph 2 of Section 4 of the Police Act, 1861. The "general control and direction" of the District Magistrate mentioned in Section 4 governs the relationship between the police and the magistracy in most parts of the country. However, the words "general control and direction" have been left undefined in the law.

Police functions fall under two broad categories — investigative and preventive. The manner in which the investigative functions of the police are performed is described in details in the Criminal Procedure Code. On the other hand, the maintenance of public order is in a way part of the preventive function. Most actions of this type are justifiable in courts and should not be considered as left to unfettered executive discretion. However, the District Magistrate has come to acquire considerable authority to interfere with the internal management of the district police organization. Such control is not exercised only in the ares of drill, arms and discipline of the police force. The ground position of total subordination of the police to the executive magistracy is not contemplated under the law. This can only lead to distortion of police performance and dilution of police accountability to the law of the land. Consequently, the following recommendations were made:

- Any police rule or regulation which unnecessarily or without purpose subordinates the police to the District Magistrate should be removed or amended. The requirements of administrative and public interest should alone be kept in view.
- Suitable amendments to Section 4 of the Police Act, 1861, should be incorporated. All the provisions in the State Police Acts should also be suitably amended.

- The police should have a distinct identity, adequate competence and operational independence to play an effective role in the administration.
- The Superintendent of Police should be adequately armed under the law to deal with situation independently.

*Code of Behaviour for Police Personnels*

The report proposes a Code of Behaviour for Police personnels, which includes the non-occurrence of the following:

a) Neglect of duty, b) disobedience to orders without sufficient cause, c) discreditable conduct which is likely to bring discredit on the reputation of the police, d) misconduct towards a member of the police force without sufficient reasons, e) falsehood or prefabrication, f) corrupt or improper practice, g) abuse of authority, h) neglect of his health, i) improper dress and untidiness, j) reporting to duty in a state of drunkenness, k) be an accessory to a disciplinary offence, l) damage the unity of the police force especially on the grounds of religion, caste or community, and m) indulge in anti-national conduct.

*Police Public Relation*

According to the Fifth Report of the National Police Commission, police-public relations are in a very unsatisfactory state, essentially due to police partiality, corruption, brutality and failure to register cognizable offences.[49] Police do, in fact, harass even those who try to help them. The public, in general, does not think that the police are efficient. Again people who appear in courts as witnesses have to undergo considerable inconvenience and hardship and for this they blame the police more than the law courts because their appearance in a court of law is a consequence of their involvement in a police investigation. On the other hand, even though criminogenic factors are not under the control of police, the forces, which generate disorder, are confused with normal dissent and the police is blamed squarely for rise in crime and spread of disorder.

The Indian Police Commission of 1902-03 in Para 26 concluded, "what wonder is it that the people are said to dread the police, and to do all they can do to avoid any connection with a police investigation".[50] Hundred years on, the conclusion is still very much true. Policemen in general do not believe that very much is at fault and blame the system, which even according to some is beyond improvement. The recommendations to improve the police — public relations, were as follows:

- The major recommendations are in the directions of content of training in all orientation programmes and in the process of imparting the training wherein attitudinal changes can be bought about. The police service is a service dedicated to the protection of the common citizen and they should decide how best they could render the help sought and not how through subterfuge of law and regulation, evade their legitimate responsibility. They should also understand that dissent on the part of the citizen is not to be construed as a threat to law and order unless there is an apprehension of breach of peace.
- The police should place greater emphasis on service-oriented functions like rendering first aid to the injured, or helping in the distribution of food and clothing. Youth counselling should be made a regular feature.
- There should be the provision of a 'visitor's room' in the police stations.
- There should be high visibility in traffic policing and patrolling.
- The police should give up to a considerable extent the secrecy that surrounds their functioning.
- News of crime is of considerable interest to the people and therefore the press is interested in it. The police should establish a system of communication through which authentic facts relating to the crime and disorder can be quickly given to the press.

*Victim Compensation*

The police function in the context of a punishment-oriented judicial system. As a sub-system of the criminal justice system, the role of the police also becomes punitive and therefore negative. On paper, this is balanced by the right of every victim of a crime to claim damages in a civil court but it is common knowledge that very few can afford the excessively lengthy processes of civil courts, the end result of which are often uncertain and unsatisfactory. So there is little, even for the victim of a crime to motivate him/her to co-operate with the police except a wish to impose retribution. Although the National Police Commission recommends in its Fifth Report, to have a legislation of a Criminal Injuries Compensation Act, precious little on this subject was deliberated upon.

*Women Police*

Regarding the women police force, the Fifth Report of the National Police Commission makes the following recommendations:

- There should be a larger intake of women police especially in the ranks of Assistant Sub-Inspectors and Sub-Inspectors.
- The women police should be involved more in investigation related work especially relating to children and women.
- Delinquency among girls is a more serious problem than delinquency among boys. So women police can play a more useful role on both the spheres of investigation and prevention.
- Greater presence of women police in the police stations is required.
- Women police is essential for cities, urban police stations and in thickly populated areas.

## The Sixth Report

*Indian Police Service*

The first chapter of the Sixth Report of the National Police Commission deals with Indian Police Service. The National Police Commission calls for the equality in the pay scales and prospects of the Indian Police Service with the Indian Administrative Service. The Kothari Committee also recommended this. Most of the other recommendations of the National Police Commission for the Indian Police Service have more or less been implemented, except to an extent the issue of equality of pay.

*Police and Students*

The Sixth Report of the National Police Commission in view of the problems that the police face *vis-à-vis* the students and also regarding its image at large, devoted a chapter to this cause and had the following recommendations to make.

- The police should be kept out as far as possible from administrative problems in Universities and Colleges and their campuses. The primary responsibility for resolving and mitigating campus problems of indiscipline involving students shall be that of the academic authorities. Police intervention should be restricted to situations wherein the prevention of grave crime and other unlawful activities are needed, in the detection and investigation of a crime already committed and in cases where the authorities request for police intervention provided the police is satisfied that the situation is serious and is likely to result in a breach of law and order.
- The police should take actions as per law in off campus situations where violence can erupt or has erupted.
- Police interaction in non-conflict situations needs encouragement, as it will remove the impression among the students that the police are generally hostile to them.

*Urban Policing*

The National Police Commission with respect to urban policing envisaged a greater role for it in preventive and regulatory action. However, modernization along with greater manpower was urgently called for. The Report's other recommendations were for control room, single digit bureau, increasing use of computers especially for registration of motor vehicles and checking antecedents of persons with doubtful character, separate homicide squad, economic offences and forgery squad, auto thefts squad, etc., for all cities with over 5 lakh population. Although these measures have been implemented in most big cities, there are still cities with over 5 lakh population without these police facilities.

## The Seventh Report

*Organization and Structure of Police*

The National Police Commission made the following comments/ recommendations:

- The police stations need restructuring and a facelift. The buildings housing the police stations need improvement throughout the country. They need to be strengthened and made more effective.

- Should be free from political interference.
- Police stations in the rural areas are few and far between. They also have a very vast jurisdiction, which dilutes police presence and effectiveness. More police stations are required. The jurisdiction need to be delimited and made more compact and manageable.
- The criteria for creating police stations should be the number of crimes to be investigated, the area in which law and order has to be maintained and the population which they need to serve.
- The lock-ups are like dungeons with very poor sanitary conditions. These need improvement.
- Manpower commensurate with the volume of work should be available to the police stations and a committee should be constituted to work out suitable norms.
- An operative 'job content' needs to be developed for each rank.
- There should be a promotion scheme for every rank within the police structure. For example, a Constable should be able to become a Head Constable after 8 years of service provided he does not have unsatisfactory records and so on. However a bright Constable should be able to become an Assistant Sub-Inspector of Police through a competitive examination without necessarily having to become a Head Constable.
- Regarding the 'State Armed Police Battalions' and 'District Armed Reserve', the National Police Commission notes that these have not been accorded the importance they deserve.
- Transfer from armed police to civil police for Constables should be allowed after 3 years.

*Delegation of Financial Powers to Police Officers*

The Report of the National Police Commission calls for the delegation of financial powers to police officers, essentially more powers to the Chief of State Police, equivalent to the Director General, BSF or the Director General, CRPF. For example:

- Chief of State Police should be authorized to create temporary posts from the rank of Constables to Deputy Superintendent of Police for a period of two years.

- Chief of State Police should be authorized to make financial sanctions for the purchase and repair of motor vehicles, wireless equipment, etc., upto a certain amount.

*Ministerial Staff and other Administrative Work*

- The ministerial staff should be brought under the purview of the Police Act, 1861. They should be integrated with the rest of the policemen in respect of the terms and conditions of service, discipline, etc.
- In order to enhance the career prospects of the ministerial staff, they should be provided with openings in to regular police force.
- The Chiefs of State Police should take personal interest in making more effective use of computer both in operational matters and administrative matters.

*Home Guards*

Home Guards are a statutorily backed organizations that fills the gap between organized policing and individual self-policing in a society and consists of individuals who voluntarily organize themselves or who offer voluntarily their services. The National Police Commission noted the following:

- The Home Guards can employ a sizeable number of unemployed people if used more effectively.
- The Home Guards are used too infrequently and they should be utilized on many more occasions.
- If the regular use of Home Guards for patrolling proves to be more cost effective and commands greater public acceptability, then this could as well be made a regular feature and this will also promote the idea of self-policing.
- The Home Guards could be made to play a significant role in protecting the weaker sections of the society.
- Deficiencies in training staff, living accommodations, and apparatus must be removed wherever they exist.
- The daily allowance paid to the Home Guards should be realistic and not be unreasonably discriminatory.

*Performance Appraisal of the Police Personnel*

The National Police Commission makes the following recommendations in this issue.

- Use of annual confidential reports should be treated as a source of information for administrative purposes and for organisational development through improving the performance of the employee.
- The employee should be made aware of the quality of his performance, his shortfalls and failures, if any, so that he/she can correct himself/herself.
- The proximity between the officer reported upon and the reporting officer should increase.
- Monthly or quarterly counselling sessions should be carried out systematically.
- A superior inspecting officer should record their assessments.
- Annual performance appraisal report must contain an integrity column.
- A cell at the district and the state level be made responsible for follow up action both on the continuous appraisal as well as the annual appraisal.

*Disciplinary Action*

The Fifth Report of the National Police Commission detailed a 'Code of Conduct' for the Police. In breach of this code, certain disciplinary action was outlined in this report.

- Prompt and effective disciplinary action should be taken when departmental norms are broken.
- There should be a full proof grievance redressal machinery for the police personnel.
- Major punishments under the department involve (i) dismissal, (ii) removal, and (iii) reduction in rank. These should be awarded only after drawing up regular disciplinary proceedings.
- Minor punishments include (i) censure, (ii) withholding of increment, and (iii) withholding of promotion. These can be

awarded through a shorter procedure, in which, the delinquent officer should be confronted in writing with the facts of the case and the penalty proposed against him/her. He/she may then be asked to furnish his/her representation against the same within a specified period and the final order may be passed after taking the representation into consideration.

- Petty punishments may be awarded to the member of the constabulary in the orderly room and these may include (i) reprimand, (ii) confinement to quarter — guard for a period not exceeding 15 days, (iii) punishment drill, extra guard duty, fatigue or other punitive duty, not exceeding 15 days, with or without confinement and (iv) fine not exceeding one month's pay in a month.
- Against any of the major punishments awarded to a police official, there should be a provision of only one appeal to the authority just above the punishing authority, followed by one revision if necessary to an authority just above the appellate authority. There should be one appeal but no revision against minor punishments. There can be no appeal against petty punishments.
- Major punishments must be given after careful consideration and should not be resorted to in a routine manner.
- Suspension should not normally be ordered without getting the complaint looked into through a preliminary inquiry. Further suspension should not be resorted to unless facts and circumstances of the case indicate that the punishment will be a major one. Suspension should not be ordered for extraneous considerations.
- The charge must be furnished to the delinquent police official within a period of 15 days from the date of suspension, failing which, the incumbent would be entitled to automatic reinstatement.
- Time limits should be prescribed for completing various stages of disciplinary proceedings. In case, such time limits have to be exceeded, specific approval should be sought from the next higher authority.

## The Eighth Report

*Accountability of Police Personnel*

The responsibility should be squarely fixed on the officers of the level of Superintendent of Police and above to carefully watch the reputation of the SHOs and take appropriate measures whenever warranted. Any failure on their part, in this regard, should be seriously viewed. In those circumstances where the supervisory officer may either fail to assess the reputation of the SHO or fail to take appropriate action in a particular instance, the people have a right to petition to the State Security Commission. In the event of such complaints, the State Security Commission should gauge the reputation of the SHO concerned and take such actions as may be required.

Section 132 and Section 197 of the Criminal Procedure Code 1973 provide protection to various categories of public servants against any prosecution brought against them relating to performance of official duties. The protection available to the police officers under these sections should be withdrawn so that the private complainant is free to press his complaint against police official for a judicial pronouncement without there being a provision to obtain prior permission of the competent authority for such prosecution. However, the police officer against whom a complaint is brought in a court of law should be defended at the cost of the Government.

High Courts may impress upon subordinate courts that complaints against police officials should be disposed of on priority basis. The High Court may further draw the attention of the lower courts to the provisions of Section 202 Criminal Procedure Code, and advise them generally to ask for a report from the District Superintendent of Police on the complaint filed before them. It would be the responsibility, of the District Superintendent of Police to either make an inquiry himself or have it made by a sufficiently senior officer and submit a factual report to the court before the latter decides to proceed further with the case. On mere filing of a complaint, unless there is a *prima facie* case and justification for the same, transfer of the concerned official should not be ordered.

Functionaries in the department at each level should be held accountable only with respect to the functions and duties assigned to him and accountability should not extend to duties over which he has no direct control. Therefore, police functionaries from SHO to that of Chief of Police cannot be held accountable for each isolated incident in a particular region in their respective jurisdiction, however serious it may be, unless it is proved that the particular incident occurred because of act of omission or commission on the part of the police functionary or such incidents have been widespread and the official has failed to react adequately.

The sanction of fixing unreasonable or impossible targets, which cannot be achieved except through illegal or irregular means, should be effectively discouraged.

*Police Act*

- It is necessary to replace the existing outmoded Police Act of 1861. The recommendations made in the eight reports of the National Police Commission should be incorporated in the new legislation.
- The Central Government may enact the necessary legislation for the constitution of a Central Police Committee; define its role and such other details in terms of the following:
  a) Matters relating to police organization and police reforms of general nature;
  b) Matters relating to grants and loans to the State Police Forces for their modernization and development;
  c) Matters relating to budgetary allocations to the State Police Forces.

## APPENDIX 3

### Salient Features of the Ribeiro Committee's Recommendations on Police Reforms[51]

#### First Report (October 1998)

- A Security Commission should be set-up in each State consisting of the Minister in charge of Police as the Chairman, the Leader of the Opposition, the Chief Secretary of the State, a sitting or retired judge nominated by the Chief Justice of the

State's High Court and three other non-political citizens of proven merit and integrity as members. These three citizens should be chosen by a committee to be set-up by the Chairman of the National Human Rights Commission, which has taken much interest in the establishment of this proposed institution. The name of the Commission should be "The Police Performance and Accountability Commission." (PPAC)

- The four non-political members of this Commission excluding the Chief Secretary should hold office for three years after which persons of equal merit chosen in the same manner will replace them.
- The Security Commission will have advisory and recommendatory powers for the present. The State's Director General of Police will be its Secretary and Conveyer.
- The Security Commission will oversee the performance of the Police and ensure that it is accountable to the law of the land. Its functions will be as is spelt out by the National Police Commission in Para 15.48 of their report. In addition, Security Commission will ensure that no premature transfers of officers of the rank of Superintendent of Police and above are made without prior clearance from the Security Commission and that transfer are made only by the authority competent under the rules to do so.
- Besides the Security Commission, a District Police Complaints Authority will be set up in each Police District as a non-statutory body to examine complaints from the public of police excesses, arbitrary arrests and detention, false implications in criminal cases, custodial violence, etc. and to make appropriate recommendations to the Police Performance and Accountability Commission, as well as to the Government and to the State or National Human Rights Commission. The Principal District and Sessions Judge, the Collector of the district and the SSP would constitute this authority.
- In every State, a Police Establishment Board should be constituted with the Director General of Police (DGP) and his four senior-most officers, borne on the IPS cadre of the State but who are immediately junior to the DGP, as members to

monitor all transfers, promotions, rewards and punishments as well as other service-related issues. The Board should be given the legal authority to discharge its duties by amending the relevant Rules.

- Rules should be framed by the Government on transfers, tenures, promotions, rewards and punishments and the police authorities designated to administer these rules. Any departure from these norms and rules will be brought to the notice of the PPAC.
- The Director General of Police will be selected by the Chief Minister of the State from a panel of three names prepared by a Committee headed by the Chairman of the UPSC and consisting of the Union Home Secretary, the Director of Intelligence Bureau, the State's Chief Secretary and the State's incumbent DGP. This selection committee may consult the Chief Vigilance Commission before drawing up a panel. The DGP will have fixed tenure of three years. He can be removed within the period of tenure only on the recommendations of the PPAC and for specified reasons, made in writing to the Government.
- The investigation wing of the Police will be insulated from undue pressure if the DGP is selected in the manner prescribed above and given a tenure and also if the PPAC discharges its role of overseeing police performance and ensuring accountability. All investigating officers should be specially trained in scientific methods of investigation and not utilized for law and order duties except in small rural police stations where it may not be possible to strictly demarcate the two important police functions. The investigating officers should not be shifted to law and order or other duties for five years at least.

## Second Report (March 1999)

- The National Police Commission had recommended that there should be a State Security Commission at the Centre. There is no need for such an institution at the Central level. In case of CBI, the Supreme Court has already given directions. The intelligence Bureau is an intelligence organization and the BSF and the CRPF are paramilitary outfits that do not involve themselves with local politics and politicians.

- The Central Police Committee as recommended by the National Police Commission in its Seventh Report, should be constituted.
- The old Police Act of 1861 needs to be replaced by a new Police Act.
- The recommendations of the Law Commission about insulating the investigative functions of the police from its law and order work should be implemented urgently.
- The recommendations of the National Police Commission about recruitment, training and welfare of the constabulary should be implemented.
- The minimum educational qualifications for recruitment to the level of Constable should be Higher Secondary.
- The National Police Commission had recommended the reorganization of the hierarchy of the police, with an increase in the strength at middle levels of Assistant Sub-Inspectors/Sub-Inspectors/Inspector to be offset by reducing numbers at the lower levels of constabulary. This would improve promotion opportunities of lower ranks. We endorse the recommendations of the National Police Commission.
- Every State should establish an independent Police Recruitment Board and entrust to it the task of recruitment of all non-gazetted ranks.
- A qualitative change in the training being imparted in police training institutions is imperative to improve performance and behaviour of the police.

## APPENDIX 4

### Salient Features of the Padmanabhaiah Committee Report on Police Reforms[52]

- To define perspective roles of Centre and States in developing capabilities in the Police including funding.
- A system of planned induction based on proper manpower planning and of career planning of individual group of officers.

The Padmanabhaiah Committee on Police Reforms mentioned in Para 7.6, "we are yet to see a police department which has a well-thought-out and researched manpower plan for next five years and which knows what its growth rate should be".

- There should be a greater recruitment of Sub-Inspectors instead of Constables. This can be seen to be the opposite of the view taken by the National Police commission. Recruitment to constabulary should be restricted till a teeth-to-tail ratio of 1:4 is achieved as against present ratio, which ranges from 1:7 to 1:15 in different states.
- Ban the recruitment at the recruitment at the level of Inspectors and Deputy Superintendent of Police.
- Constables should be recruited young. Boys/girls, who have passed 10th Standard examination and are below 19 years in age, should be eligible to appear in a common competitive qualifying examination. The successful candidates should be put through a rigorous 2-year training programme and qualify for appointment as constables only after passing a final examination.
- The existing constabulary should be retrained to enable them to imbibe right attitudes to work. Those who do not successfully complete training should be compulsorily retired.
- A constable should be classified as a 'skilled worker' in view of the skills required and risks involved in the job.
- There should be a career plan in the police department. The Career plan should take into account: (a) promotional avenues and prospects, (b) the needs of specialization, (c) the training needs, and (d) posting policy.
- Career planning at the level of Constables is very important. Today only less than 25 per cent of Constables ever get any promotion. The remaining constables usually retire in the same rank in which they were recruited.
- The eligibility criteria for recruitment to the level of Sub-Inspectors should be 12th class pass and an upper age limit of 21 years. They should be recruited on the basis of a common written qualifying examination. The successful candidates

must pass a final examination after undergoing a 3-year training programme. Fifty per cent of vacancies of Sub-inspectors should be filled by direct recruitment and 50 per cent reserved for promotions.

- Promotions up to the level of Deputy Superintendents of Police should be based on undergoing certain mandatory training programmes and passing certain examinations.
- A constable would be eligible to appear for Assistant Superintendent of Police post in 3 years service and Superintendent of Police in 6 to 9 years of service and Inspector in 14 to 16 years of service. The average age of promotion to the post of Inspector therefore would be 35 to 40 years, which is young enough to hold SHO ship of a Police Station, but old enough to be mature and still energetic. In theory, an intelligent and lucky constable can hope to be a Deputy Superintendent of Police by 45 years and Additional Superintendent of Police by 52 to 55 years of age.
- Police Training Advisory Council should be set up at the Centre and in each state to advise the Home Ministers on police training matters.
- All promotions should be subject to completing the mandatory training programmes and passing of promotional examinations.
- There should not be more than one Director General post in the police department and that the Director General should have the right of writing the confidential reports of all officers at the level of Additional Director Generals and Special Director Generals.
- Special emphasis on the need for specialization in police. After a policeman, whether he is from the constabulary or from the officer ranks, spends the first eight years of service, his aptitude and potential for development in a particular area of specialization, like investigation, crime prevention, community policing, intelligence gathering, traffic, various branches of forensic work, fire arms, security, etc., should be assessed.
- The Indian Police should adopt the philosophy of community policing. The Government of India should support this by

bringing out a handbook on the subject, providing training inputs and funding pilot projects.

* Lack of a proper tenure policy for posting of officers at different levels and arbitrary transfers have been used by politicians to control and abuse the police for their own ends. To deal with this problem, following action is required:

  a) A body headed by the Chief Justice of the State High court as Chairman, State Chief Secretary and an eminent public person as members should be continued to recommend a panel of two names for appointment to the post of the Director General of Police.

  b) A police Establishment Board, consisting of DGP and three other members of the police force selected by him should be constituted to decide transfers of all officers of the rank of Deputy Superintendent of Police and above.

  c) The minimum tenure of all officers should be 2 years.

  d) Another Committee under the Chief Secretary, with Home Secretary and the DGP as members, should be constituted to hear representations from police officers of the rank of Superintendent of Police and above alleging violation of rules in the matter of postings and transfers.

- To deal with the problem of corruption in the police, which leads to the criminalization of the force, the committee has recommended a more serious enforcement of the code of conduct and simpler but more effective procedures for removing corrupt officers.

- Since police work cannot be organized on an 8-hour shift basis, police personnel should be given a weekly off and compulsorily required to go on earned leave every year. Holiday homes may be constructed for police personnel.

- Investigation should be separated from law and order work. In the first phase, this separation should take place at police station level in all urban areas. An Additional Superintendent of Police should be exclusively responsible for crime and investigation work.

- Sections 25 and 26 of the Indian Evidence Act should be deleted and confessions made to police officers of the rank of Superintendent of Police and above should be made admissible in evidence.
- Forensic science can play extremely dramatic role in investigation or murder, sexual assault and terrorist cases. It can play a very significant role in drug offences, vehicle crime and burglary. The police manual musts be amended to make it mandatory to collect samples and to obtain expert forensic opinion in all such serious crimes.
- The Government should create separate Department for Forensic Science and constitute an All India Forensic Science Service.
- Every police station should be equipped with 'investigation kits' and every sub-division should have a mobile forensic science laboratory.
- There has to be a two-phased programme for improving the upkeep of police stations. In the first phase, the minimum requirements should be provided. There should also be a conscious effort to locate new police stations, in residential and commercial areas, to make them easily accessible; incidentally such locations would act as a check on malpractice, third degree and violation of human rights, etc., at the station.
- The police leadership, through proper manpower and career planning, improved training, effective supervision and by inculcating a sense of values amongst the members of the force, can play an important role in encouraging specialization, promoting professionalism and increasing morale in the force.
- In each district, there should be a crime prevention cell manned by officers who have specialized in crime prevention work.
- To deal with cyber crime effectively, police capabilities in various areas need to be developed. Capabilities of some police institutions, like the National Police Academy in the field of training, CBI in investigation, Intelligence Bureau in cyber surveillance and the National Crime Records Bureau in cyber technology/forensics should be enhanced.

- The present classification of offences into cognizable and non-cognizable made 150 years ago is not very relevant today. The Law Commission of India should review the entire classification and the powers of the police to investigate.
- At present, investigative officer waste a lot of time in Court, where due to the prevailing backlog, their cases do not come up for hearing even though they might have been present in court for an entire day. As such, it is suggested courts should be advised to, as a rule, list cases police station-wise on each day. If this done, investigative officer will be attending court only on the days the cases of his police station are listed.
- The concept of VIP security has been grossly, blatantly and brazenly misused. The entire concept of personal security needs a careful review and dismantling.
- Certain offences having inter-state, national and inter-national repercussions should be declared "federal offences" to be investigated by the Special Crimes Division of the CBI, which should function under the administrative control of the Ministry of Home Affairs.
- Taking into account the wide ramifications of the terrorist crime, there have to be different norms regarding the burden of proof, degree of proof and the legal procedures in regard to trial of terrorist cases. There is a need for a special and a comprehensive law to fight terrorism.
- There should be a national counter terrorism coordinator to prepare a comprehensive counter-terrorism plan and budget.
- A statutory independent body of Police should be set up to carry out annual as well as thematic inspections of the police force and to report to the state government whether the police force is functioning efficiently and effectively.
- A non-statutory District Police Complaints Authority (DPCA) should be set up with the District Magistrate as the Chairman and a senior Additional Sessions Judge, the District Superintendent of Police and an eminent citizen nominated by the DM as members. Investigations into public complaints against the police should in the first instance be done by the

police department itself. Those who are not satisfied can approach the DPCA.

- There should be a mandatory judicial inquiry into all cases of alleged rape of a woman or death of any person in police custody.
- The Government of India should establish a permanent National Commission for Policing Standards to lay down norms and standards for all police forces on matters of common concern and to see that that the State Governments set up mechanisms to enforce such standards.
- The release of central grants for modernization or upgradation funds should be dependent upon compliance by state governments with certain basic issues, like each state having a manpower and career planning system, a transparent recruitment, promotion and transfer policy and meeting certain minimum standards for training.
- The Government of India should play a much more active role in
  1. All aspects of training like setting norms and standards for training for various levels of hierarchy, setting standards for training institutions and, in general, supporting and monitoring all training activities;
  2. Providing infrastructures and specialized support services, like communications and computers, forensic science, etc.
  3. Providing intelligence support,
  4. Maintaining crime records and data banks,
  5. Supplies of critical equipment, like night vision devices, BP jackets, BP cars and weaponry; and
  6. Funding of various innovative and pilot projects.
- The Police Act of 1861 should be replaced by a new Act.
- The State Government must give high priority to the allocation of resources to the police.

There should be a permanent National Commission for Police Standards (NCPS) to set standards and to see that State Governments set up mechanisms to enforce such standards.

# APPENDIX 5

## Salient Features of Report of the All-India Committee on Jail Reform or The Mulla Committee Report on Prison Reforms

- To define perspective roles of Centre and States in developing capabilities in the Police including funding.

*Legislation*

- The basic question is whether a prisoner continues to be a citizen or not.
- Need for a separate cell in the Ministry of Home Affairs, Government of India, to deal with jail reforms on an all India basis.
- Appointment of a high-powered commission to survey the criminal justice system in its entirety.
- In the case of young offenders, alternative punishments should be formulated.
- The subject of prisons and allied institutions should be included in the Concurrent List of the Constitution.
- A new uniform and comprehensive legislation should be enacted by Parliament for the entire country.
- State Governments and Union Territories should frame rules under the prison statute immediately.
- Revision of State and Union Territories' jail manuals should be given top priority.
- Operational manuals on various subjects of prison management should be prepared and made available to the staff for guidance.
- Civil prisoners should not be detained in jails for convicted and criminal offenders.
- A review on an all-India basis should be undertaken to find out whether the provisions of the Criminal Procedure Code in this regard have been implemented.
- Non-criminal lunatics should not be detained in prisons.

- Prisons are overcrowded with undertrials accounting for nearly 70-75 per cent of the prison population.
- Women and children should be kept in separate jails.

*Classification*

- The principles of classification included in the Report of the All-India Jail Manual Committee (1957-59) should be adopted on a national basis.
- The principles of keeping a prisoner as near his home as possible should be broadly kept in view at the time of classification of inmates.
- Panels of experts should be appointed by the Government of India on a regional basis to assist the States and Union Territories to prepare basic plans for setting up classified institutions.

*Buildings*

The State governments and Union Territories should immediately survey prison buildings with regard to minimum needs essential for the maintenance of standards of comfort and cleanliness in consonance with human dignity. The work plan prepared as a result of the survey should be completed within two years.

*Living Conditions*

a) Diet:

   i) Adequate checks should be provided to ensure that prison diets conform to the rules and the food is served in clean and hygienic conditions in covered places. The Medical officer should ensure these standards.

   ii) Adequate and nutritious diets should be given to nursing women and children.

b) Sanitation and hygiene:

   i) The ratio of latrines to prisoners should be 1:6.

   ii) Adequate number of separate urinals should be provided.

   iii) There should be provision of cubicles for bathing, with proper arrangements to ensure privacy.

iv) Medical officers must look after all aspects of prison sanitation and hygiene.

*Communication*

a) Letters:

i) On initial admission or transfer from another prison, a printed card should be sent to the family of the prisoner containing detailed information about him.

ii) Spouse/family members/close relative should be telegraphically informed of serious illness or injury, removal for medical care, or treatment of mental illness.

b) Interviews:

1. The scale of interviews for convicted and undertrial prisoners should be liberalized.

   i) Convicts should be granted six interviews a month.

   ii) There should be no restriction on the number of interviews sought by undertrial prisoners for legal assistance.

   iii) Interviews with family members and friends should, however, be restricted to two per week in the case of undertrials.

2. Properly designed tables and benches should be provided in the interview rooms. There should be no barriers between the prisoners and the interviewers. The duration of an interview should be at least one hour.

3. Family members, close relatives and close friends should be allowed to visit daily a prisoner, who is seriously ill and is in hospital.

*Medical and Psychiatric Services*

1. Every Central and district prison should have two or more medical officers.

2. A whole time lady medical officer should be appointed where there is a sufficiently large number of women prisoners.

3. Central and district prisons should have a qualified psychiatrist who should be assisted by a psychologist and a psychiatric social worker.

4. a) Non-criminal lunatics should not be kept in or sent to prisons.
   b) Criminal lunatics should be sent to the nearest prison having the services of a psychiatrist.
5. Sick women prisoners should be treated in a separate enclosure attached either to the hospital section or to the women section of the prison.

*Security and Discipline*

1. Fetters and handcuffs should not be imposed on undertrial prisoners except when they have a credible tendency to violence or escape.
2. Provisions regarding segregation and imposition of fetters as measures for ensuring security contained in the Prison Act, 1894 should be suitably revised.
3. The procedure for dealing with complaints against prisoners as well as genuine complaints and grievances of inmates should be rationalized.
4. Prisoner's panchayats should be involved in matters pertaining to inmates' self-management and self-improvement in day-to-day life.

*Treatment Programmes*

1. Inmate-prison personnel relationships should be based on mutual trust and confidence.
2. Treatment programmes should be individualized.
3. Educational programmes in prisons should be integrated with the educational system in the state/UT.
4. Inmates who have reached a certain stage of education should be allowed to continue their education either as regular students of schools/colleges or through correspondence courses.
5. Special attention should be paid to the development of suitable educational programmes for women prisoners.
6. Basic elements of recreational and cultural activities should be adopted.

*Works Programmes and Vocational Training*

1. Prison work programmes and vocational training should be integrated with national economic policies and development plans.
2. Vocational training programmes in self-employing trades and occupations should be organised in every Central and district prison.

*Undertrials and other Unconvicted Prisoners*

1. A review should be made of all police lock ups in each state and the living conditions in them should be improved.
2. A Board of Visitors should be appointed in each district to visit regularly all police lock ups.
3. Undertrial prisoners should be lodged in separate institutions away from convicted prisoners.
4. The feasibility of launching jail hostels on the lines of those sponsored and financed by Xenia Field Foundation (UK) should be examined under Indian conditions.
5. The rights of undertrial prisoners, including facilities for access to legal material, legal counsel and legal aid should be protected.
6. a) An effective mechanism should be evolved to review the cases of undertrial prisoners regularly, both at the district and state level.

   b) The Criminal Procedure Code should be suitably amended to provide that as soon as an undertrial prisoner competes the period of detention equal to half of the maximum sentence that can be awarded to him on conviction, he should be released immediately and unconditionally.
7. Broad guidelines should be laid down about the arrest of persons, specially those involved in minor violations of law.
8. Non-criminal lunatics, persons needing protective custody and children should not be sent to prison at all.
9. Persons detained under executive orders made under provisions of special legislations should be kept away from convicted and undertrial prisoners.

10. The Preventive sections of the Criminal Procedure Code, especially Section 109 of the Criminal Procedure Code, should be reviewed and suitably amended to restrict their use only in genuine cases.

*Women Prisoners*

1. Women should not be called to the police station for investigation. All police investigations, as far as possible, must be carried out in the presence of a relative of the accused or her lawyer and of a lady staff member.
2. Women in police custody should invariably be under the charge of women police officials.
3. Bail should be liberally granted to women undertrial prisoners.
4. Women prisoners should be lodged in separate institutions/ annexes meant exclusively for them.
5. Women personnel must staff all prisons/annexes for women only and women guards should be arranged to look after women in sub-jails.
6. Pregnant and nursing women prisoners should be prescribed special diet and exempted from unsuitable types of work.
7. Some self-contained units for groups of 8-10 women prisoners should be constructed to provide them a kind of family/group living.
8. Special consideration should be given to women prisoners in the matter of premature release.

*Open Institutions*

1. Open camp movement should be developed as a positive measure defined in the statute.
2. Open institutions in any state should be able to accommodate at least 20 per cent of the prisoners sentenced to one year and above.
3. All additional institutions for accommodating any future increase in the convict population should be open type.

*Leave*

1. There should be both i) leave and ii) special leave.
2. Procedures for grant of leave and special leave should be reviewed and liberalized.

*Organizational Structure*

1. The prison department in each state should be called the Department of Prisons and Correctional Services.
2. This department should invariably be headed and except where specialized services are required manned by persons belonging to the department.

*General*

The Government of India should set up a National Commission on Prisons and finalize a national policy on prisons.

## Notes

1. Report of the Committee on Rationalization of Classification of Prisoners in Tihar Jail, 1997.
2. Some also argue the need for reforms in post-trial procedures. But there are hardly many procedures in this phase except for adhering to certain norms within the confinements of the prison. As such this aspect is discussed within the gamut of prison reforms.
3. A heavy responsibility thus lies with the Court, which remands the accused to police custody as no person can be deprived of his life and personal liberty according to the procedures established by law within the ambit of Article 21 of the Constitution.
4. Many people arrested for specific offences pretend to be ill in an effort to hamper investigations. The police should request the Court that the period spent in hospital during the police remand be not counted.
5. State vs. Bal Chand — AIR 1977 SCC 2447.
6. Mahendra Pal Singh vs. State — 1990 SCC 18.
7. 1978 (4) SCC 47.
8. Sanjay Gandhi vs. Delhi Administration — 1978 Cri L.J. 952.
9. Janardan Reddy vs. State AIR 1951 SC 217.
10. Hussainara Khatoon (IV) vs. Home Secretary — 1980 (1) SCC 98.
11. Suk Das vs. U.T of Arunachal Pradesh — 1986 (2) SCC 401.
12. Supreme Court Legal Aid Committee vs. Union of India, 1994 (6) SCC 731; R.D. Upadhay vs. State of Andhra Pradesh 1996 (3) SCC 422; and Common Cause vs. Union of India 1996 (4) SCC 33.
13. Hussainara Khatoon (IV) vs. Home Secretary — 1980 (1) SCC 98.
14. Sheela Barse (II) vs. Union of India — 1986 (3) SCC 632.
15. First Report of the National Police Commission, page 7, Ministry of Home Affairs, Government of India.
16. The First Report was submitted in February 1979, the Second Report in August 1979, the Third Report in January 1980, the Fourth Report in June 1980, the Fifth Report in November 1980, the Sixth Report in March 1981, the Seventh Report in May 1981 and the Eighth and Concluding Report also in May 1981.
17. For example the Fourth Report of the National Police Commission also deals with issues like 'Industrial Disputes' and 'Agrarian Problems' and the role of the police in these areas. Again the Fifth Report discusses the detailed measures pertaining to Dacoity and the Arms Act 1959. The Sixth Report discusses the various administrative requirements and orientation to deal with situations of communal riots and urban policing. These themes have not been discussed, as they are more specific in nature.
18. Prakash Singh and Others vs. Union of India, Writ Petition No. 310 of 1996.
19. Government of India (1990), "Reports of the Arrears Committee", Supreme Court of India, New Delhi. pp. 50.
20. *Ibid*, pp. 50-51.
21. *Ibid*, pp. 51.
22. Law Commission of India (1958), "The Fourteenth Report on Reform of Judicial Administration", Ministry of Law, Government of India, Delhi.
23. Government of India (1972), "Report of the High Court Arrears Committee", Supreme Court of India, New Delhi.
24. Law Commission of India (1979), "The Seventy-Ninth Report on Delays and Arrears in High Courts and other Appellate Courts", Ministry of Law, Government of India, Delhi.
25. Government of India (1986), "The Thirty-First Report of the Estimates Committee to the Parliament", Ministry of Law, Government of India, Delhi.

26. Law Commission of India (1979), "The Eighth Report on The Method of Appointment of Judges", Ministry of Law, Government of India, Delhi.
27. Law Commission of India (1986), "The One Hundred and Twentieth Report on Manpower Planning in Judiciary: A Blueprint", Ministry of Law, Government of India, Delhi.
28. Law Commission of India (1987), "The One Hundred and Twenty-First Report on a New Forum for Judicial Appointments", Ministry of Law, Government of India, Delhi.
29. Law Commission of India (1988), "The One Hundred and Twenty-Fourth Report on High Court Arrears: A Fresh Look", Ministry of Law, Government of India, Delhi.
30. Government of India (1986), "Report of Justice Satish Chandra Committee", Supreme Court of India, New Delhi. This Report is also known as the Satish Chandra Committee Report.
31. Government of India (1990), "Report of the Arrears Committee", Supreme Court of India. New Delhi. This Report is also known as the Malimath Committee Report.
32. 1997 (2) SCC 642.
33. Report of the Indian Jail Committee, 1919-20, page 29-30.
34. Ananthachari, T. (1995), "Human Right Behind Prison Walls", in Behind Prison Walls : Police, Prisons and Human rights, Commonwealth Human Rights Initiative (35-47), page 36.
35. *Ibid*, page 36.
36. This has also been observed by the NHRC, see Annual Report, NHRC, 1998-99, page 19.
37. See Page 8, Mulla Committee Report.
38. As contained in Chapter 9.
39. (Para 22).
40. Annual Report of the National Human Rights Commission, 1999-2000, page 26.
41. 1994 (3) SCC 423. For details see Appendix 1.
42. Quoted in the First Report of the National Police Commission, page 7.
43. Para 18.29, Page 47, the Second Report of the National Police Commission.
44. *Ibid*, Para 18.31, page 47.
45. Third Report of the National Police Commission, Para 19.1, page 1.
46. Fourth Report of the National Police Commission, Para 34.24, page 48.
47. *Ibid*, Para 34.33, page 49.
48. *Ibid*, Para 32.12 to Para 32.17, pages 39-40.
49. Fifth Report of the National Police Commission, See Para 43.110 to Para 43.123, page 74-76.
50. *Ibid*, Page 74.
51. A Part of these comments were made by the Commonwealth Human Rights Initiative, India.
52. A part of these comments were made by the Commonwealth Human Rights Initiative, India.

## References


Ananthachari, T. (1995), *"Human Rights Behind Prison Walls"*, in Behind Prison Walls : Police, Prisons and Human Rights, Commonwealth Human Rights Initiative (35-47), page 36.

Government of India, (1972), *"High Court Arrears Committee"*, Supreme Court of India, New Delhi. [Also known as Justice Shah Committee Report]

——— (1979-81), *"Report of the National Police Commission"*, Ministry of Home Affairs, Government of India, New Delhi.

——— (1980-83), *"All India Committee on Jail Reforms Report"*, Ministry of Home Affairs, Government of India, New Delhi.

——— (1986), *"The Thirty-First Report of the Estimates Committee to the Parliament"*, Ministry of Law, Government of India, Delhi.

——— (1986), *"Report of Justice Satish Chandra Committee"*, Supreme Court of India, New Delhi. [Also known as the Satish Chandra Committee Report]

——— (1987), *"Report of the National Expert Committee on Women Prisoners"*, Ministry of Home Affairs, Government of India, New Delhi.

——— (1989-90 to 1999-2000), *"Annual Reports of the Ministry of Law, Justice and Company Affairs"*, Ministry of Law, Government of India, Delhi.

——— (1990), *"Report of the Arrears Committee"*, Supreme Court of India, New Delhi. [Also known as the Malimath Committee Report]

——— (1997), *"Report of the Committee on Rationalization of Classification of Prisoners in Tihar Jail"*, Government of India, New Delhi.

——— (2001), *"Crime in India, 2000"*, National Crime Records Bureau, Ministry of Home Affairs, Government of India, New Delhi.

Law Commission of India, (1958), *"The Fourteenth Report on Reform of Judicial Administration"*, Ministry of Law, Government of India, Delhi.

——— (1964), *"The Twenty-Seventh Report on Code of Civil Procedure, 1908"*, Ministry of Law, Government of India, Delhi.

——— (1973), *"The Fifty-Fourth Report on Code of Civil Procedure, 1908"*, Ministry of Law, Government of India, Delhi.

——— (1978), *"The Seventy-Seventh Report on Delays and Arrears in Trial Courts"*, Ministry of Law, Government of India, Delhi.

——— (1979), *"The Seventy-Eighth Report on Congestion of Under Trial Prisoners in Jails"*, Ministry of Law, Government of India, Delhi.

——— (1979), *"The Seventy-Ninth Report on Delays and Arrears in High Courts and other Appellate Courts"*, Ministry of Law, Government of India, Delhi.

——— (1984), *"The Ninety-Ninth Report on Oral and Written Arguments in the Higher Courts"*, Ministry of Law, Government of India, Delhi.

——— (1987), *"The One Hundred and Twentieth Report Manpower Planning in Judiciary: A Blue Print"*, Ministry of Law, Government of India, Delhi.

——— (1987), *"The One Hundred and Twenty-First Report on a New Forum for Judicial Appointments"*, Ministry of Law, Government of India, Delhi.

——— (1988), *"The One Hundred and Twenty-Fourth Report on High Court Arrears: A Fresh Look"*, Ministry of Law, Government of India, Delhi.

——— (1994), *"The One Hundred and Forty-Second Report on Custodial Crime"*, Ministry of Law, Government of India, Delhi.

——— (1996), *"The One Hundred and Fifty-Forth Report on The Criminal Procedure Code 1973"*, Ministry of Law, Government of India, Delhi.

National Human Rights Commission, Annual Reports, 1993-94 to 1999-2000.

Rajkumar C., (1988), *"Project Report on Standards of Prison Care"*, National Human Rights Commission, New Delhi.

# 16

## An Economic Freedom Index for India, 2004

BIBEK DEBROY • SHUBHASHIS GANGOPADHYAY • LAVEESH BHANDARI

### INTRODUCTION

This paper deals with the measurement of economic freedom in different States of India. The term 'economic freedom' has many connotations. The Index of Economic Freedom (Heritage Foundation, 2002) defines it as "the absence of government coercion or constraint on the production, distribution, or consumption of goods and services beyond the extent necessary for citizens to protect and maintain liberty itself". This definition however presumes that the mere absence of artificial constraints or those imposed by the government is sufficient for economic freedom. This paper takes a broader view; it considers economic freedom as "the unfettered ability of an individual to make economic choices".

Why should economic freedom have such a broad purview? For one, in developing countries such as India, family, community, and social constraints are also responsible for constraining an individual's options. Artificial constraints work to nullify human rights and the ability to choose, and therefore, freedom. Elements of social, civil and political freedom therefore also find a place in our view of economic freedom.

The concepts of economic, political and social freedom are integrated to form the concept of "human freedom". According to Milton Friedman political freedom is "the mode of representation in the political structure, the right to vote, the definition of democracy as the society in which the public servants - the people who determine public policy – are chosen by the votes of the citizens" while social/civil freedom is "the freedom to speak, the freedom to assemble, the freedom to express your views", that is, "human rights". To those we would also add the ability of an individual to take decisions unhindered by external forces, be they imposed by the government or society or even the inherent conditions that a person lives in.

Take for instance extreme poverty, or poor health, or lack of education/illiteracy. These may or may not be a result of government intervention, however they do hinder the ability of a person to make choices. In our view therefore, a poor person, or an unhealthy one, or someone whose awareness levels are low, should not be considered to be economically free. These are the essentials. Similarly, those who are not aware of the different choices that are available to them, however well off they may be, can also not be considered free. This of course should not take away from the important role that governments can play in ensuring adequate property rights, an environment where the law rules, and one that is safe and just.

This paper brings together about 50 different measures that in our view reflect different aspects of economic freedom for an individual and for an entrepreneur. Each of these measures reflects some aspect of economic freedom. The measures when aggregated reveal the levels of economic freedom in the largest 20 States of India.

Other studies have tried to objectively measure economic freedom. The Liberales Institute regularly publishes the *Economic Freedom of the World* (EFW, 2003). The index measures the consistency of a nation's policies and institutions with economic freedom. According to EFW, economic freedom mainly consists of personal choice, voluntary exchange, freedom to compete, protection of person and property and availability of legal and monetary arrangements that not only protect property right of owners, but also ensure an even-handed enforcement of contracts. EFW recognizes that economic freedom is furthered when the government does not interfere with personal choice, voluntary exchange, freedom to enter and compete in labor and product markets and the entry into occupations and business activities.

In order to measure the performance of different countries objectively, the EFW index is constructed for 5 major areas, namely, size of the government; legal structure and security of property rights; sound (legal and readily exchanged) money; freedom to trade with foreigners; and regulation of credit, labor and business. Together, these

5 major areas make use of 37 variables to measure economic freedom. They capture the extent to which the countries rely on government budget and political decision-making rather than personal choice and markets, the level of confidence among individuals and businesses that contracts will be enforced and that they will get to enjoy the outcome of their effort at economic activity, the ease with which economic agents can access and use alternative and more credible currencies and get access to credit and save their earnings; the ease (extent of red-tape and convertibility) and extent of international trade, and the extent of regulation in labor, business and credit markets.

In the case of sub-national economic freedom for India however, the laws are similar across different States. Freedom of entry into and exit from different activities is also similar across different States. By merely studying the existence of such freedoms one is not likely to obtain any differences between different sub-national units. However, the applications of such laws may vary, and the inherent conditions that allow such laws to translate into freedom may also vary. For instance, everyone in India has the freedom to purchase a refrigerator, however large parts of India do not have access to electricity. Effectively therefore, freedom is curtailed.

The EFW index value for a country for a particular indicator is calculated as follows. The value of the indicator for the country is subtracted from the highest value of the indicator and divided by the range (that is, its maximum value minus its minimum value). Many other ratings calculate index values in this way. However, there are some which use other criteria, or in which, the index was taken from other sources such as the *Global Competitiveness Report, International Country Risk Guide*, etc. Alternative basis of generating the index mainly involves assigning a subjective index value.

This paper attempts to minimize subjectivity by not using any qualitative measures. Instead it creates an index value for each measure on the lines above and then takes the geometric mean of the different measures to arrive at the composite economic freedom index at the sub-national level.

Byars *et al.* (1999) index economic freedom at the sub-national level for the United States. The study involved the creation of indices of economic freedom for the fifty U.S. States and ranked the same on the basis of measured economic freedom. They use the following definition of economic freedom: "The right of individuals to pursue their own interests through voluntary exchange under a rule of law". Using data from the mid- to late- 1990s, the study accumulates data on economic freedom. The study assembled State level data on a wide variety of economic activities. These were then categorized into five different sectors, fiscal, regulatory, judicial, government size, and welfare. From these five sectors, a number of indexes of economic freedom were created. Finally, one single index was derived using Principal Component Analysis.

Their index is based on more than 100 different individual measures of economic freedom, spanning government spending, regulation, welfare, school choice, taxation, and the judicial system. The index is somewhat subjective, since in some places, the authors used own judgment of relevance and importance of variables. However, the final aggregation makes use of Principal Component Analysis (PCA) and that eliminates subjectivity in aggregation.

This paper does not utilize PCA. Instead it relies on calculating the non-weighted geometric mean of each of the measures. This is similar to giving equal weights.

## This Study

As mentioned before, the indicators used in generating the index render the Economic Freedom Index for India broader and more inclusive. This economic index attempts to knit in aspects of social/civil freedom, absence of which constrains economic freedom. India boasts of being the largest democracy and elements of political freedom can be taken for granted. Government is chosen by vote and every citizen of India has a right to vote and elect the government. However, conditions vary in different States. Caste and gender biases, constraints in access to information and education, and quality of education being provided are some illustrations of the various dimensions of freedom that are captured by this index.

The index reflects conditions in developing countries where freedom does not translate into ability to make a choice. Freedom to exercise choice may show up as a positive indicator in a freedom index, but a lack of options to choose from renders such freedom redundant. Information and knowledge may be easily accessed, but the ability to process the information in a meaningful and useful manner may be missing. Existence of corruption, along with political and social freedom, makes economic freedom hollow. The Economic Freedom Index seeks to capture such fine aspects of freedom, which are integral aspects of the lack of economic freedom in most developing countries.

This paper therefore includes measures that reflect the ability of economic agents to make a choice. Ability to make a choice may be restricted by a general absence of a range of choice or artificially created due to absence of options. Social pressures have the capacity for limiting the options available to some people. Options are also considerably altered when there is an absence of physical mobility or if there is inadequate access to information. This is not enough. Information has to be meaningfully utilized in order to take rational, beneficial decisions. Further, economic agents should also be able to carry out the decisions that they judge as beneficial. Inefficiencies of the government or its interference in labor, product and credit markets may inhibit such decision-making capacities of economic agents. Realizing maximum returns from economic activities is curbed when there are artificial limits to trade, constraints in mobility of factors of production (labor and capital), free entry and exit of economic agents and also the impact of taxes. Protection of personal property rights and enforcement of contracts is also of importance in ensuring attainment of economic freedom.

Therefore, an economic freedom index that is appropriate for India should include measures that capture a range of factors and conditions. For an individual the following broadly classify the types of measures that should be included.

- Ability to make a choice
- Social and family biases
- Lack of available choices
- Lack of information
- Lack of physical mobility
- Lack of ability to process information
- Difficulty in taking most preferred actions
- Efficiency of governance

India has among the highest shares of those who are self-employed. Including its farmers, slightly less than half of all those employed can be considered to be entrepreneurs. Some aspects of the commercial side of an agent's economic freedom are captured by another set of factors.

- Limits on trade
- Constraints on realizing full returns from effort
- Limits on control over own business
- Issues in buying and selling of land/assets
- Availability and cost of capital

This paper is organized as follows. The paper is divided into 4 parts. This (first) section has presented a brief introduction of economic freedom and discussed other freedom rankings and motivated what follows. The second section presents the data and methodology used to arrive at the economic freedom index. It explains the variables included in the index and how they represent economic freedom. The third section presents the results of the composite economic freedom index. Finally, the last section presents a discussion on the situation of freedom in each of the larger 20 States.

## DATA & METHODOLOGY

The study deals with assessing the economic and business environment in different States. The term 'freedom' is wide and includes the freedom available to the agents for making a choice, ease in actualizing a consumption, employment, income earning, lifestyle, production, or commercial decision, given the inherent abilities and skill base, access to means of improving quality of human capital, safety of life and property, ability to retain one's share of fair profits, and access to efficient mechanisms that enforce contracts. It also encompasses the ease with which factors of production can be transferred, the ability of economic agents to take rational economic decisions and the extent to which they are able to carry out such decisions as assessed by the constraints of infrastructure and raw materials. The key economic agents that are considered are therefore workers, entrepreneurs and of course, consumers.

### Data

Data used for representing the level of economic freedom is defined in this section. Data have been taken from various government and private sources and a detailed list is presented in the appendix. Each of the different measures can broadly be categorized on the following lines:

- Ability to make a choice
- Social and family biases
- Lack of available choices
- Lack of information
- Lack of physical mobility
- Lack of ability to process information
- Difficulty in taking most preferred actions
- Efficiency of governance
- Limits on trade
- Constraints on realizing full returns from effort
- Limits on control over own business
- Issues in buying and selling of land/assets
- Availability and cost of capital

The economic freedom index however is not calculated for each of those categories, but only in the aggregate. In that sense, ease of exposition is the only objective of this categorization.

*Ability to Make Choice*

An economic problem, as the definition goes, is a problem of choice. The level of freedom that an individual enjoys is directly indicated by his or her ability to make a choice. Extreme income constraints therefore serve to limit the extent to which an individual can enter the ranks of those who make choices. The share of the population above the poverty line is included as an indicator to capture this aspect of economic freedom. However, mere basic economic ability will not translate into an ability to make a choice if basic lifestyle and health-associated amenities are absent. Inaccessibility or unavailability of basic amenities such as drinking water, sewage facilities and electricity, therefore, limit economic freedom. To capture the status of such amenities, we consider the percentage of all households that live in permanent (*pucca*) houses, have access to tap water, have electricity and a sewage system. A person may not be able to exercise his choice if he is not physically capable of accessing healthcare services or facilities. Health of an individual is highly dependent on health of the general public and the environment in which he survives. While life expectancy is a general indicator of the health of people, the morbidity rate is a more specific indicator of the quality of health.

1. Percentage of population above the poverty line: This is the percentage of total population above the absolute poverty line. Those lying below poverty line would be barely surviving and can be least associated with making a choice. Higher percentage therefore indicates better levels of economic freedom.
2. Percentage households living in permanent (*pucca*) houses: This is the percentage of total households that reside in permanent houses. Here, the permanent houses are considered to be the houses having walls and roofs made of permanent materials.
3. Percentage households having access to tap water: This is the percentage of households having tap water facilities. Higher percentage indicates better levels of economic freedom.
4. Percentage households having electricity: This is the percentage of households that have electricity. Higher percentage indicates better levels of economic freedom.
5. Percentage households having latrines within the house: This is the percentage of households that have latrines (water closets) available to them within the premises of the house. Higher percentage reflects better levels of economic freedom.
6. Percentage ailing in the last 15 days: The percentage of population in the age group of 15 to 59 years age group that has been ailing in the last 15 days has been considered here to assess the morbidity status of the work force. The value has been subtracted from 100 in order to ensure that a higher value of the indicator signifies greater choice making abilities and therefore, higher levels of freedom.
7. Life expectancy at birth: This is the number of years a person would be expected to live from the day he or she was born. This is considered for males and females separately and a higher life expectancy indicates better economic freedom.

*Social Constraints*

Social stigmas and taboos are effective at restricting the freedom of an individual. The fear of ostracism from the social circle works as an efficient tool for ensuring conformity with social norms and traditions. Often this leads to certain sections of the population becoming the 'privileged', thereby enjoying more freedom, while others become the 'underprivileged', whose freedom is limited, either because options are not available to them or because they do not have the ability to choose. Such social constraints have historically been a part of India in the form of the caste system. Difference in the spending capability of the population that belongs to the lower castes and the upper castes is considered as an objective measure of the prevalence of such socio-economic constraints to freedom. Further, even the means for building their human capital may be constrained by way of social norms and moves that ensure continuation of their status as the underprivileged. The educational attainment of children and youth belonging to the lower caste are also included to capture this.

8. Ratio of average Per Capita Monthly Expenditure of lower caste households to average Per Capita Monthly Expenditure of upper caste households: This is the ratio of average per capita monthly expenditure of lower castes to that of the upper castes. Ratio less than one would reflect that the lower caste is economically worse off than the upper caste and vice versa. A ratio close to one would suggest an egalitarian society and thus for the purpose of this study, a higher ratio would imply higher economic freedom.

9. Percentage persons 21 to 25 years old among the lower castes who have completed graduation & above: This is the share of lower caste adults in the 21 to 25 years age group who have completed graduation to the total lower caste population. A higher ratio would indicate better off lower caste individuals.

10. Percentage persons 16 to 19 years old among the lower castes who have completed high school: This is the share of lower caste population in the 16 to 19 years age group who have completed high school to the total lower caste population in that age.

*Family and Household Constraints*

Families and households are the basic units of society and it is within the institution of the household that an individual is introduced to the ways and customs of society. Households may seek to conform to the value system of the society of which they are a part in order to prevent ostracism. It becomes practical for a household to choose those options that the majority in the society considers to be good and avoid those that are considered bad. In many societies, the birth of a male child is welcomed more than that of a female child. Such attitudes also get reflected in the child sex ratio. The sex ratio in the 0 to 6 years age group is considered in the index. Females that grow up in such an environment find themselves severely inhibited as many restrictions are imposed upon them. Gender based differences may prevent females from learning skills that have economic value. Differences in literacy rates of males and females may reflect such attitudes and practices. Females are an essential part of the work force and limitation on their freedom has implications for the overall economic freedom; the overall sex ratio is also considered. Economic freedom of an individual is also restrained when an individual is unable to take risks, especially due to the burden of supporting others at a young age. Many if not most marriages occur during adolescence. Mean age at marriage is considered in order to capture this aspect of individual freedom.

11. Sex Ratio: This is defined as total number of females per thousand males. Lower ratio would indicate some kind of gender bias towards males and a ratio closer to one would reflect an unbiased society and thus higher economic freedom index.
12. 0 to 6 years sex ratio: This is the number of females in the age group 0 to 6 years per thousand males in that age cohort. A higher number indicates less male bias.
13. Ratio of female to male literacy rate: Literacy rate is defined as number of literates per number of persons above 7 years of age. This variable is the ratio of female literacy to the male literacy rate. A ratio close to 1 would suggest that females and males have similar access to education.
14. Mean age at marriage: A low age at marriage would reflect greater responsibilities at a young age and would hamper the

independent choice making ability of a person; a higher mean age therefore suggests higher economic freedom. Mean age at marriage is considered separately for males and females.

*Lack of Available Choices*

Economic freedom is reflected in the ability of a person to follow a profession of his/her choice. Inability of educated and skilled labor to find jobs that are suitable to their qualification and interests is indicative of lack of alternatives and options. This is a direct constraint on freedom. While this is one aspect of freedom, wages received and the economic independence gained thereby, widens freedom. High economic growth, with its manifestations in the form of high wages, jobs, returns to investment etc., allows us to objectively assess the existence or lack of such freedom. Disguised unemployment, especially in the agrarian sector, camouflages the inherent lack of options that is faced by a large section of the rural population. Such a situation is also prevalent in many other small scale and cottage industries where family labor continues to perform economic work without being remunerated.

15. Share of people employed: This is the share of people employed in an economic activity for a major part of the year. A lower percentage would mean lesser number of people employed and could indicate lack of career opportunities/choices and therefore lower level of economic freedom.
16. Work participation rate: This is the ratio of total workers (main + marginal) to total population. Unlike in the above case, this also includes those who are employed only partially.
17. Percentage of unpaid family workers: Unpaid family workers include persons who worked without regular money wages, for a relative who was a member of the same household. Those workers could be employed in other areas and would help in increasing the earnings of the household. The lower this variable, the better it is, because it makes members of the family available in the market. In order to achieve high levels of economic freedom, we have taken the inverse of this variable.

18. Economic growth rate: A lower economic growth rate would reflect lack of growth in job opportunities. Therefore, higher the rate, the better it is in terms of available choices.
19. Yearly average of daily wages for harvesting: This is the yearly average of daily wages for harvesting. Harvesting is a temporary employment that requires a minimal skill base. In that sense, this wage is the most comparable across the heterogeneous Indian States. Higher wages would therefore mean greater economic freedom. This variable is considered for both males and females.

*Lack of Information*

Access to timely information regarding various options that are available is a key determinant of whether an individual can exercise personal choice. There may be available optimal choices, but lack of information about their availability and feasibility may lead to inefficient or sub-optimal choices. Newspapers, telephones, and televisions, all serve as mediums of information. Inaccessibility of information, the most important input in any decision making process, therefore represents low levels of freedom. Ownership and access to information mediums therefore contribute to the freedom of choice.

20. Number of newspapers sold per household: A low value would reflect lack of awareness or flow/circulation of information. Conversely, a high value will imply easy access to information, signifying enhanced economic freedom.
21. Percentage households with telephones: Telephones are considered as one of sources of communication between individuals/households. A low value of this variable would mean lack of flow of information and vice versa.
22. Percentage households with mobiles: This is the share of all households owning mobile phones. This signifies a higher flexibility in accessing information than merely land lines.
23. Percentage of households with television: Similarly, televisions can cater to all sections of the population, including the illiterate section. This is the share of all households with

television sets to total households. A low value would again reflect lack of information flows.

*Physical Mobility*

While the condition of complete information amongst economic agents is essential for efficient functioning of the market mechanism, an additional requirement is that of mobility. This is directly influenced by the nature and extent of transportation infrastructure. A good transportation network not only enhances the environment for economic growth, but it also adds to the amount of freedom that is enjoyed by individuals, whether workers, entrepreneurs or consumers. Freedom to set up an industry or to access a better job in a location away from the place of residence is adversely constrained by unavailability of well-connected roads, and transportation options, especially public transport options that are the only option that may be available to the remote rural areas of India. Roads are essential for labor to seek work in new places, for raw material to reach the production unit and for the final product to reach the market place.

Moreover, mobility of entrepreneurs has a direct influence on the level of trade within a region. Ownership of private vehicles grants a certain freedom of movement that is different from traveling by the public transport system. There are lower constraints, lesser effort and wasted time to enable the exercise of choice. This translates into an extension of the trading activity and a wider 'catchment' for accessing inputs and markets.

24. Percentage of habitations connected by roads: This is the share of all habitations connected by roads to total habitations in the state. Connectivity by roads would directly influence the flow of individuals across borders and thus would result in greater physical mobility. Therefore, greater the number the better it is.
25. Number of buses registered per person: This is the number of registered buses within the State, per person. Buses occupy a vital component in the area of public transportation and thus a greater number of buses would result in better mobility for individuals and vice versa.
26. Percentage of households with 4 wheelers: This is the ratio of households having 4 wheelers to the total number of

households. 4 wheelers include a car, jeep or a van. Higher number of 4 wheelers ensures greater mobility for the household members and therefore, would signify higher levels of economic freedom.

27. Percentage of households with 2 wheelers: This is the ratio of households having 2 wheelers to the total number of households. 2 wheelers include a scooter, motorcycle or a moped. Higher number of 2 wheelers will ensure greater mobility for masses and therefore higher levels of economic freedom.

*Lack of Ability to Process Information*

Knowledge and information have to be adequately processed in order to get a realistic perception of the situations and opportunities that are available and to derive meaningful conclusions from the information that is available. Relying on spurious information or using wrong reasoning in evaluating a piece of information may lead to wrong decisions. Academic education provides the basic knowledge and reasoning skills that may help in processing myriad information. It may provide an individual with a better ability to sift out relevant information from all that he/she may encounter and also at reaching rational conclusions. Elementary and secondary education is extremely essential to gain the fundamentals of mathematics, science and language. The index therefore utilizes data on the extent to which children of school going age stay in/away from school. Besides the spread of education, its quality is extremely important in determining the extent to which the academic system may succeed in helping people become more effective in life. The attention that a student receives from a teacher is empirically known to influence the performance of a child in school.

28. Percentage children of 5 to 18 years currently studying: This is the percentage of children in the age group 5 to 18 years who are currently enrolled. A higher value indicates higher levels of economic freedom.

29. Teacher Pupil Ratio: This is the ratio of number of teachers available to the total number of students. Schools are where children are most likely to learn to process information in an organized and logical manner and teachers are a key element

in honing the ability of students to process information. Ratios are included separately for primary, middle and high school level of education.

*Safety, Law and Justice*

The level of safety that he/she lives in directly influences the freedom of an individual. A threat of physical harm or a threat to life is the most commonly understood violation of freedom of an individual. Lack of safety is the most effective deterrent of individual action and will. More violent the nature of the crimes that are being committed, the lower the feeling of safety and therefore, lower the level of freedom enjoyed by inhabitants of a region. However, violent crimes are not the only violations of law that adversely affect the level of economic freedom enjoyed by an individual. Persons arrested, as a share of total cases being investigated under Prevention of Corruption and related acts, is included along with recovery rate of stolen property, in order to capture these considerations. Ready settlement of disputes, especially those related to property and business are essential components in efficient functioning of free market forces. Enforcement of contracts and protection of personal property are equally important. Completion rate of cases and cases pending trial are included in the economic freedom index. The boost which protection of life, personal property and contracts can give to the sense of economic freedom of an economic agent is unparalleled by other determinants of economic freedom.

30. Percentage of violent crimes to total crimes: This is calculated as the total number of violent crimes divided by total number of crimes that are committed. The more violent the nature of the crimes that are being committed, the lower the feeling of safety and lower the freedom to take action. Therefore, a lower percentage of violent crimes would enhance the freedom to take preferred actions. This value has been subtracted from 100 in order to ensure that high values of the ratio would signify better levels of economic freedom.

31. Ratio of total value of property recovered to property stolen: One of the key ingredients of economic freedom is protection of property. This is the ratio of total value of property recovered to the total value of property stolen. Higher value

of this variable would mean higher efficiency of law enforcing agencies and thus would signify greater freedom.

32. Pendency rate: Pendency rate is the number of cases pending in the courts to the total number of newly registered cases and pending cases with the court. A higher pendency rate would reflect feeble governance and therefore, for better levels of economic freedom, the pendency rate should be low. Pendency rate is subtracted from 100 to ensure high values of the ratio, implying enhanced economic freedom.
33. Percentage cases where trials were completed: This is the ratio of total number of cases whose trial has been completed to the total number of cases. A higher value of the variable would have a positive influence on economic freedom.

*Efficiency of Governance*

Justice and safety levels can be positively altered to a large extent if the infrastructure meant to redress grievances is timely and efficient. Administering adequate punishment to those that have violated the law is an effective means of increasing the extent of freedom experienced by the public. This not only builds the faith of people in the law enforcement machinery, but also enhances compliance with the law by introducing a threat of punishment and an incentive for abiding by the law. Further, the trying of erring government and law enforcement officials, in case of violations by them, serves as an essential component of the economic freedom of an ordinary person, as it translates into the true spirit of democracy. The worst form of violation of law is when the guardians of laws themselves become its violators and the ability of the legal system to be even-handed is most limited in such a situation. Such unlawful acts allow other unlawful acts to take place and add to the transaction costs faced by an economic agent, directly attacking his/her economic freedom.

34. Persons arrested as a share of total cases being investigated, under Prevention of Corruption and related acts: This variable is an important measure of efficiency of government. A higher value would indicate greater efficiency of the government and would signify better levels of economic freedom.

35. Inverse of total cases for investigation under Prevention of Corruption act and related sections of IPC as a share of total government employees: This is total number of government employees divided by the number of cases of corruption under prevention of corruption act. In India where corruption is endemic across all states and all parts and levels of government, a higher number of instigations reflect the seriousness with which corruption is treated. It also reflects the efficient functioning of the system. A higher value of this indicator is preferable for economic freedom.
36. Cases pending investigation as a share of total cases registered: This is the total number of cases pending investigation registered under Prevention of Corruption and related acts as a share of total cases registered under the same acts in the previous year. A higher value of this indicator would negatively influence economic freedom.

*Limits on Trade*

Any form of government intervention, whether direct or indirect, except in case of violation of law, has the potential of becoming a danger to economic freedom as it interferes with market forces. This is especially true of governmental intervention or regulation in the form of requirement of licenses for setting up industries and businesses. Other forms of labor and product market interventions also hinder the freedom of an entrepreneur to set up an industry in an area that he may assess as lucrative. While on the one hand, high fees to be paid to government for setting up an industry in the formal sector may have negative connotations for the level of economic freedom in a country, on the other hand, a high number of markets in the country would translate into a wider realization of economic freedom. *Haats* and *Mandis* are important permanent or temporary markets that are accused by those hiring in rural and remote areas.

37. Market fees on all commodities as percentage of estimated value: Higher market fees will tend to decrease the liberty with which a person is able to sell his product in the market. The variable is calculated as the ratio of market fees on all commodities to the estimated value of the commodities. Inverse of this variable is taken into consideration for a higher level of the economic freedom index.

38. Minimum license fee for traders: Traders are required to pay a minimum amount of fees for obtaining a license from the government to indulge in market activities. Therefore, the higher the license fees, the move restricted traders get in trading in the market. Similarly, inverse of the variable is taken for higher levels of economic freedom.
39. Number of *haats* and or *mandis* as a ratio of population: This is the ratio of number of *haats* and *mandis* to the total population. Lower number of *haats/mandis* would mean lesser opportunities for the traders to sell their product and buyers to purchase their requirements.
40. Number of regulated markets as a ratio of population: Regulated markets tend to lower the transaction costs by reducing fraudulent activities, etc. that incur in trade activities. Therefore, a larger number of regulated markets would reflect greater economic freedom.

*Constraints on Realizing Full Returns from Effort*

Any economic agent gets involved in an economic activity only because he/she stands to benefit from it. There is little incentive for a rational individual to set up a business or perform a task without any self-interest. High levels of appropriations therefore work as a disincentive to economic activity. Taxes, whether direct or indirect, have a direct affect on the preferences of entrepreneurs and customers. They impose constrains on the ability of economic agents from realizing full returns from their effort and therefore result in limiting economic freedom.

41. State Taxes on income to GDP: This is the ratio of different types of State level taxes on income collected by the State to the State's Gross Domestic Product. The lower the State taxes on income, the higher the economic freedom.
42. Taxes on commodities and services to GDP: This is the ratio of taxes collected on commodities and services i.e. the sales tax, service excise, etc. to the State's Gross Domestic Product. Lower taxes on commodities would reflect a higher freedom index.

*Limits on Control Over Own Business*

An entrepreneur needs to take many decisions that cannot cater to the sentiments of all the workers and management that his firm employs. Decisions such as retrenchments etc. at the time of a slump are an essential part of maximizing profits. Constraints on exiting seriously hamper an entrepreneur's freedom. Labor laws for many decades have unduly favored the 'rights' of workers in the country. The number of strikes and industrial disputes that take place in the economy portray the amount of economic freedom in terms of the control that an entrepreneur has over his own business. Other areas where an entrepreneur may lack control over his own business is in terms of unavailability of adequate infrastructure and raw material. Such limitations severely constrain the entrepreneur's ability to enforce decisions that may be beneficial to his business.

43. Strikes as a share of factories: This is ratio of number of occurrence of strikes to the total number of factories. Higher number of strikes would curb the control of the entrepreneur over his business and adversely affect efficiency. Inverse of the variable is indicative of better levels of economic freedom.
44. Man-days lost: This is the ratio of man-days lost due to disputes resulting in stoppages to the total number of workers. A large number of man days lost would severely impact production and efficiency levels. Lower the man-days lost, the better it would reflect economic freedom. Therefore, inverse of the variable is taken for consideration.
45. Power shortage as a share of total demand: This is the ratio of power shortage to the total power demand. Higher power storage will tend to slow down the production process and constrain expansion and emergence of new businesses. Again, the inverse is taken to portray higher level of economic freedom.

*Issues in Buying and Selling of Land/Assets*

High transactions costs are well known deterrents of trade and economic activity. They also contribute to 'black' market transactions. Higher the costs, in terms of duties and taxes, the more constraints they impose on carrying out trade and economic activity and therefore, serve as restraints on economic freedom of agents. Stamp duty rates and taxes on property and capital transactions are used as indicators of constrains on this aspect of economic freedom.

46. Ratio of taxes on property and capital transactions to State GDP: This is the ratio of taxes on property and capital transactions to State GDP. High transaction costs and taxes tend to restrict trade activities. Therefore, the inverse of the variable is considered to get higher economic freedom index.
47. Stamp duty rate: Higher duties impose higher constraints on trade and economic activities and curb the economic freedom of agents. Inverse of this variable is taken to ensure higher values of the economic freedom index.
48. Percentage of census houses being used for residential cum commercial uses: This is the number of census houses used for residential cum commercial purposes as a ratio of all census houses. Lack of cheap commercial locations leads to double uses of residential property and are representative of constraints in economic freedom. Inverse of this ratio is taken, so that a higher value of the indicator represents higher economic freedom.

*Availability of Capital*

Cheap and abundant supply of capital is essential for the blossoming of new ventures and also for the expansion of existing businesses. The larger the amount of bank credit extended to businesses at lower interest rates, the more likely that new industries will be set up in the economy. The ratio of bank credit to SDP is used to represent availability of sound credit and the credit to deposit ratio is used to represent 'net' credit available to entrepreneurs in the State.

49. Bank Credit to SDP: This is the ratio of amount of bank credit to SDP. Smooth flow of bank credit ensures availability of capital to invest in new industries and thus a higher value of this variable would reflect better levels of economic freedom.
50. Bank credit to deposit ratio: This is ratio of bank credit issued by a commercial bank to amount deposited in the bank. Therefore, higher ratios would reflect larger amount of credit

and thus be indicative of high economic freedom in terms of availability of sound credit at a cheap rate.

Each measure in itself may not perfectly capture the full extent of economic freedom. It may not also individually capture some components of economic freedom. However, when taken together, these 50 odd measures reflect to a very large extent the amount of freedom enjoyed by an average individual in the State.

These 50 odd measures are then aggregated to arrive at the comprehensive index of economic freedom for the different States. This is discussed next.

## Methodology

The Economic Freedom Index has been calculated for 20 States of India. Ideally, all 35 States and union territories should have been included. However, data unavailability prevented this. As a result, only those States and union territories are included for which data were available for most of the variables that are used to construct the index. No imputations were made.

Further, many variables that would have found a suitable place in this index could not be included as data were not available for many States. Eventually, 53 variables covering diverse aspects of economic freedom from different areas were utilized to arrive at the composite freedom index. There were a few variables wherein data were not available for some of the 20 States. However, since the indicator was essential for the credibility of the index, such indicators were retained.

There are many different ways for constructing a composite index. One way to do this is to assign subjective weights to different variables. However, in order to ensure objectivity, this ranking refrains from such an exercise. No subjective weights have been used and as a result, each variable is considered to be equally important.

The following steps were followed in constructing the economic index:

- Identifying the appropriate variables: The variables in the freedom index were chosen such that a comprehensive view of economic freedom could be obtained while working within constraints of data availability. Variables not only represent aspects of economic freedom, but also stress on social and political freedom, without, which any economic freedom is meaningless.

- Normalizing the variables: The size and composition of States is not uniform. Indian States vary in their geographical area, topography, social and economic milieu. Depending on the variable and what it aspires to measure, each variable has been appropriately 'normalized'.
- Comparability of data: Since data are collected at the State level, care has to be taken to ensure that the data are defined in the same way for different States and also that they are for the same time point. Further, since the ranking exercise implies that higher values reflect better performance, appropriate ratios have been developed. Often, this implied taking an inverse of a particular indicator or subtracting a percentage from 100.
- Creating an index for each variable: While the composite index gives an overall view of freedom, it may be that while a State performs extremely well in certain indicators, its performance may not be as satisfactory in others. An index of each variable or indicator is also constructed so that a ranking of the States is available for a detailed understanding of the situation Details of the construction of individual indices are presented later.
- Calculating a composite/overall index: This final step required all 50 indices to be put together to come up with a composite indicator of relative economic freedom for 20 States.

The last two steps in constructing the economic freedom index are now explained in detail.

*Creating an index for each variable:* An index is obtained for each of the 50 ratios as mentioned earlier. The following formula was used to obtain each of the 50 indices:

$$I_{ij} = \frac{S_{ij} - \text{Min}(S_{1j}, S_{2j}, \ldots S_{20j})}{\text{Max}(S_{1j}, S_{2j}, \ldots, S_{20j}) - \text{Min}(S_{1j}, S_{2j}, \ldots, S_{20j})}$$

$S_{ij}$ represents the value of ratio $j$ for state $i$. The index is constructed for 20 States of India and therefore i ranges from 1 to 20. There are 50 ratios for which the indices have been constructed, j=1,2,...,50. $I_{ij}$ is the index value that is derived for state *i* over ratio *j*. The index value lies between 0 to 1 for each ratio. The state corresponding to index value 0 can be interpreted as having the lowest level of economic freedom and the state with index value of 1 can be said to have the highest level of economic freedom relative to other states.

*Calculating a composite/overall index*: Once all the indices for the 50 ratios were obtained, a composite index was obtained using all these indices. A geometric mean of all the indices helped to arrive at the multiplicative index. The formula used to calculate the multiplicative index is as follows:

$$M_i = Product\ (I_{i1}\ I_{i2}\ \ldots\ I_{in})^{1/n}$$

Where $M_i$ is the multiplicative index value for the $i^{th}$ state over the n indices of freedom. In most cases 50 indicators are included, that is, *n* is 50. There are a few indicators where n is lesser than 50. This however does not have an adverse impact on the index, as it includes only those states for which data are available. The multiplicative index or the geometric mean is designed for averaging ratio or proportion data and is therefore ideal for forming the composite freedom index.

**Final Indices & Ranks**

| *Rank* | *State* | *Economic Freedom Index* | *Rank* | *State* | *Economic Freedom Index* |
|---|---|---|---|---|---|
| 1 | Tamil Nadu | 0.44 | 11 | Jammu & Kashmir | 0.27 |
| 2 | Maharashtra | 0.44 | 12 | Haryana | 0.26 |
| 3 | Gujarat | 0.40 | 13 | West Bengal | 0.22 |
| 4 | Punjab | 0.39 | 14 | Uttar Pradesh | 0.21 |
| 5 | Andhra Pradesh | 0.36 | 15 | Madhya Pradesh | 0.19 |
| 6 | Karnataka | 0.35 | 16 | Orissa | 0.18 |
| 7 | Kerala | 0.35 | 17 | Assam | 0.17 |
| 8 | Uttaranchal | 0.29 | 18 | Jharkhand | 0.16 |
| 9 | Himachal Pradesh | 0.29 | 19 | Chhattisgarh | 0.14 |
| 10 | Rajasthan | 0.27 | 20 | Bihar | 0.11 |

## ECONOMIC FREEDOM INDEX

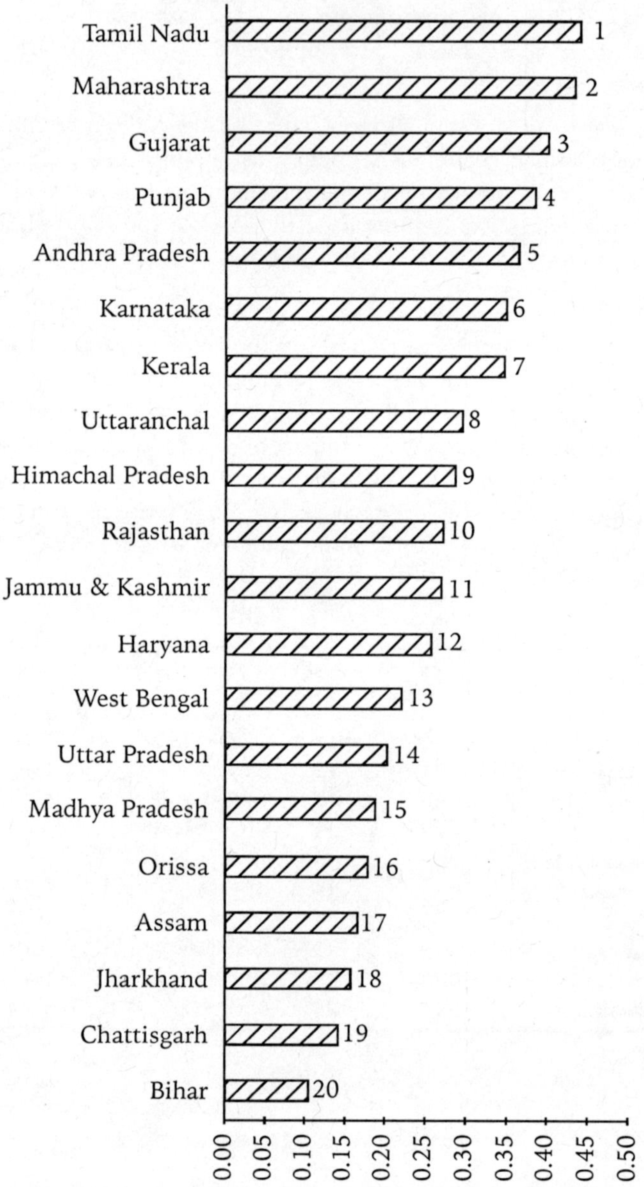

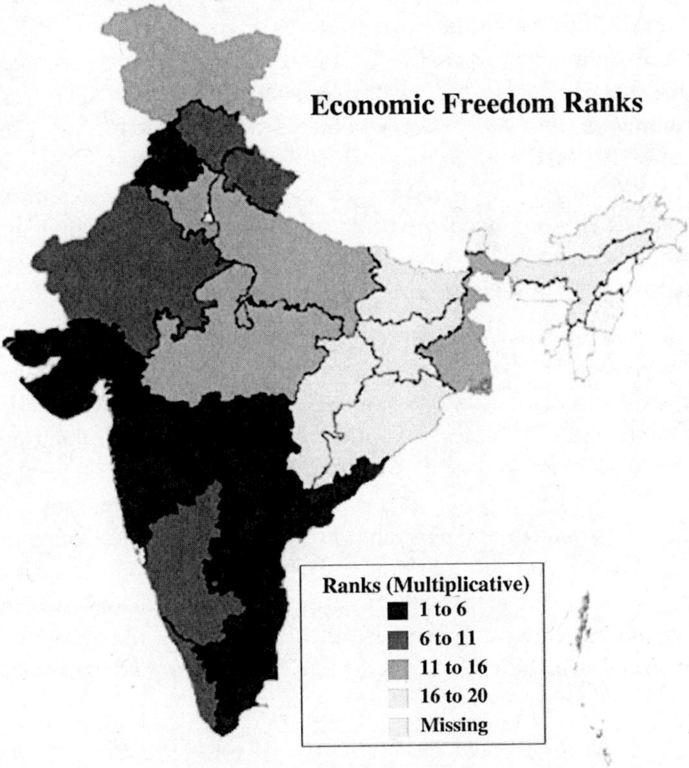


## SUMMARY OF STATES

The States within India show high levels of heterogeneity in their socio-economic conditions and governance. This also translates into highly varying levels of economic freedom. In a country such as India, where elements of political freedom are widely prevalent, there may not be undue legal and constitutional constraints to individual choice. However, there are many tacit constraints that are constantly at work. Family, community, and social constraints are the cause of some such tacit constraints. For instance, women and persons belonging to lower castes are often subjected to biases not suffered by the less disadvantaged.

Some broad insights can be obtained by studying the final rankings of the individual States and their performance in the individual measures. States such as Tamil Nadu, Punjab, Kerala, Uttaranchal and Himachal Pradesh tend to perform better in their overall socio-economic performance. However, States such as Maharashtra, Gujarat, Andhra Pradesh and Karnataka, as well as Jammu & Kashmir and West Bengal have a moderate performance in terms of ability of a person to choose, given the basic socio-economic constraints such as those related to poverty, health, education and gender and caste bias. Most other States fare poorly in these indicators.

In making any choice in order to arrive at an optimal decision, it is very essential that key information and knowledge is available and accessible and that it is processed in the right manner. Constraints in the availability and access of options and the decision making process severely hampers economic freedom. States, where an atmosphere of free flow of information is relatively better, include Tamil Nadu, Gujarat, Karnataka and Haryana. Punjab and Jammu & Kashmir fare extremely well on these grounds. Jharkhand and Bihar are worst off, with a poor performance in almost all indicators related to information flow and utilization. Other States that have a poor performance include Uttar Pradesh, Chhattisgarh and Orissa.

## Comparative Performance of Selected States

| | Low to Moderate | Moderate to High |
|---|---|---|
| Socio Economic | Maharashtra, Gujarat<br>Andhra Pradesh<br>Jammu & Kashmir<br>West Bengal | Tamil Nadu<br>Punjab<br>Kerala<br>Uttaranchal,<br>Himachal Pradesh |
| Information and mobility, trade | Jharkhand<br>Bihar<br>Uttar Pradesh<br>Chhattisgarh<br>Orissa. | Tamil Nadu<br>Gujarat<br>Karnataka<br>Haryana<br>Punjab |
| Governance, safety, law and justice | Bihar,<br>Uttar Pradesh<br>Haryana,<br>Chhattisgarh<br>Orissa<br>Assam | Karnataka<br>Gujarat<br>Punjab<br>Andhra Pradesh<br>Maharashtra |

In a free country, the government has a very important role to play. A key function of the government is to ensure the safety of citizens. Further, it has to safeguard ownership rights and enforcement of contracts. A country has to have a legal machinery in order that ensures that justice is served and that too evenhandedly. Such a legal machinery is helpful only when it is free of corruption and delivers justice in time. In India and in many other countries, the role of the government extends beyond that of safeguarding life and property. It intervenes in trade and indirectly affects business and economic decisions. Economic freedom requires that the market economy work in a free market environment characterized by laissez-faire. Therefore, while some aspects of governance are essential for economic freedom, other aspects become a hindrance to it.

In governance related indicators of freedom, Karnataka emerges as one of the best States. Other States showing a good to moderate performance are Gujarat, Punjab, Andhra Pradesh, Uttar Pradesh, Haryana and Madhya Pradesh. While Maharashtra is among the top States in this respect, it loses out in safety, law and justice. Similarly, Tamil Nadu loses out in the extent of limits to trade that exist in the State. Himachal Pradesh, Jammu & Kashmir and West Bengal are among the least well performing States in this category. Jharkhand and Bihar would also find a place among them, though they are better than others in some regards. Jharkhand performs well in terms of fewer limits to trade and low constraints in realizing full returns from effort. Bihar also has relatively fewer limits to trade. Chhattisgarh, Orissa, Uttar Pradesh and Assam have a moderate performance in terms of governance.

Most States that rank high in the overall economic freedom index also have excellent market conditions. Maharashtra performs exceptionally well in terms of product and factor market conditions, with a moderate performance only in the extent of limits in control over own business by entrepreneurs. Next is Tamil Nadu, where capital is easily available and buying and selling of land/assets is simpler than in most other States. Gujarat, Punjab, Karnataka and Haryana have moderate to good market conditions. Jharkhand is least well off. Other States with moderate to poor market conditions include Kerala, Uttaranchal, Himachal Pradesh, Jammu & Kashmir, and Uttar Pradesh. States slightly worse than these are West Bengal, Orissa, Assam, Chhattisgarh and Bihar.

The following figure (figure 1) plots the per capita SDP of the States against the final freedom index. We observe a clear positive correlation between the two series. Most States that are economically well off are also the ones that enjoy a higher degree of freedom.

**Figure 1**

*Per capita SDP and Economic Freedom*

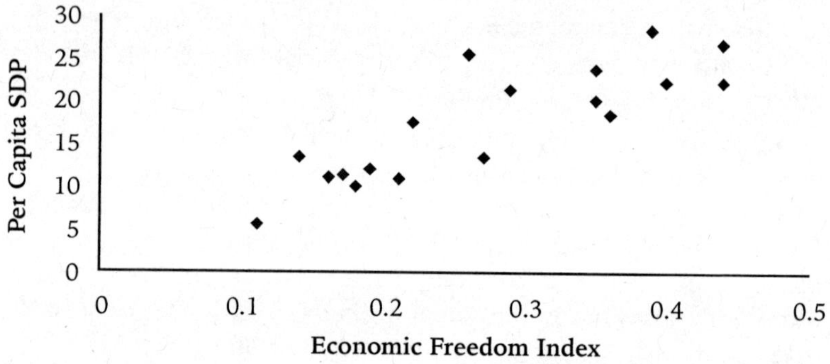


Figure 2 plots the economic freedom index against the per cent of population out-migrating from a State. Barring States that have a very low ranking, greater levels of economic freedom are associated with low out-migration. However for States that have a very low ranking - out-migration continues to be very low. This is likely because with extremely poor freedom of choice, even the ability to migrate and escape from poor conditions is affected adversely. This goes to show that after a certain satisfactory level of economic freedom is attained, there is an inverse relationship between economic freedom and out-migration.

Barring Uttar Pradesh, Bihar and Jharkhand, all other States have topped at least one of the 50 indicators of economic freedom. Andhra Pradesh, Karnataka and Maharashtra are the States that are never at the bottom in any indicator of economic freedom. Each State has some room for improvement. There is much that most States can learn from others.

## Figure 2

*Out-migration and Economic Freedom*

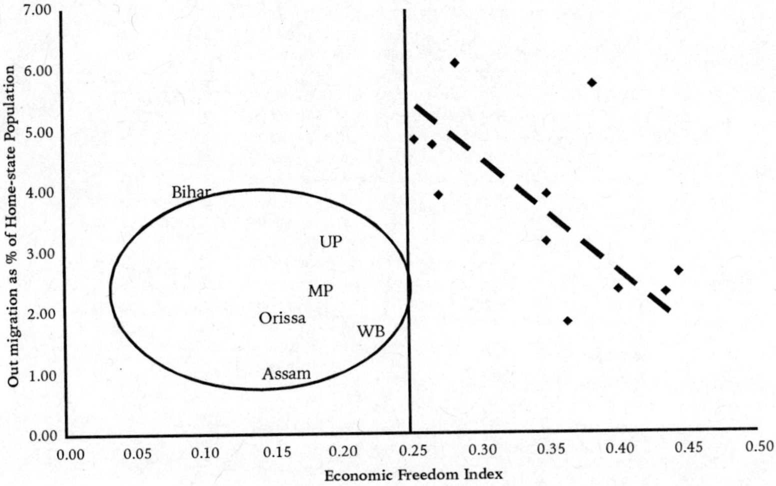


The following pages present a discussion on each State. There are three pages assigned to each State. The first page is utilized for presenting the performance of the State in each of the 50 indices that have been used in forming the composite index. The next two pages present the geographical location of the State and a summary view of the performance of the State is presented using a few statistics. This is followed by a discussion of the State's performance based on the overview statistics and its performance in each of the 50 indices.

All in all, we do not find any patterns that would fit the final rankings except one – the States that are economically the most free also tend to be those that have high per capita incomes. Which way the causality lies however is not clear – Does economic freedom lead to a greater economic progress? Or is it that stronger economies generate higher levels of economic freedom? These are empirical questions that we leave for the future to answer.

# ANDHRA PRADESH (5)

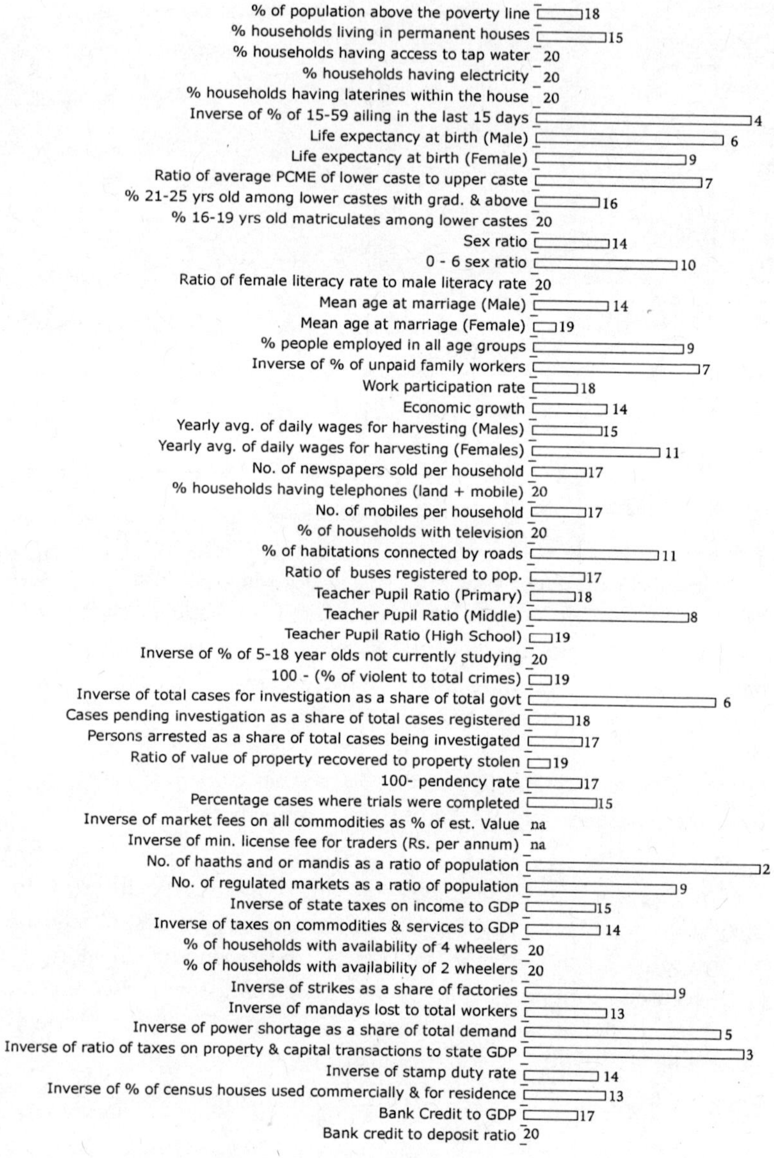

## ANDHRA PRADESH

| *Variables** | *Values* |
|---|---|
| Population Density (Persons/sq km) | 275 |
| PC SDP (Rs '000) | 18 |
| Share of Manufacturing SDP (%) | 14 |
| Share of Agriculture SDP (%) | 26 |
| Share of Services SDP (%) | 5 |
| % pop. above poverty line (%) | 84 |
| Literacy Rate (%) | 61 |
| % habitations connected with pucca roads (%) | 90 |
| % households with 2 & 4 wheelers (%) | 11 |
| Whether passed right to information act | No |

* For sources and units refer appendix.

Andhra Pradesh belongs in the top quartile in the composite economic freedom index. While Andhra is considered to be one of the fastest growing States, poverty continues to be a problem. Agriculture continues to be a large contributor to the State's domestic product. Literacy rate is low; approximately 29 per cent of the population is illiterate. However, approximately 90 per cent of the habitations are connected with roads.

Unlike most other States, Andhra has a sex ratio less unfavourable towards females. This is true not only in case of the child sex, ratio but also for the entire population. Work participation rate is high relative to other States. Andhra's legal machinery appears to be functioning much better than other States. Violent crimes are a lower share of all crimes. Further, more of the cases that are registered are being investigated, more suspects are caught, larger share of stolen property is recovered and many more of the cases that are tried in court are completed. Such a situation renders a feeling of safety, and therefore of freedom, to the common man and boosts business and other economic activity. Other actions that directly boost business and competition are low market fees on commodities and low license fees for traders. There are also many more regulated markets catering to the population than in other States. Favourable indirect taxation, supportive labour force, low stamp duty rates and availability of cheap capital, all add up to making Andhra an encouraging environment for setting up of business and industry.

Andhra Pradesh performs moderately in most social indicators of freedom, except when we consider caste-based differences. Only a small share of the low caste youth in the age group of 21 to 25 years are graduates or above. The share in most other States is higher. Other areas where Andhra performs worse than other States are primary level pupil to teacher ratio, transportation (buses as well as 4 wheelers), and the number of unregulated markets. Agricultural wages are lower than in other States, for males as well as females. It should also be mentioned that while many trials are being completed in courts there is still a large backlog of cases that are pending. Over the past few years, Andhra Pradesh has been exhibiting high growth rates. A significant contribution to this may be its admirable performance in economic freedom. There is however, still scope for improvement that could considerably enhance Andhra's performance.

# ASSAM (17)

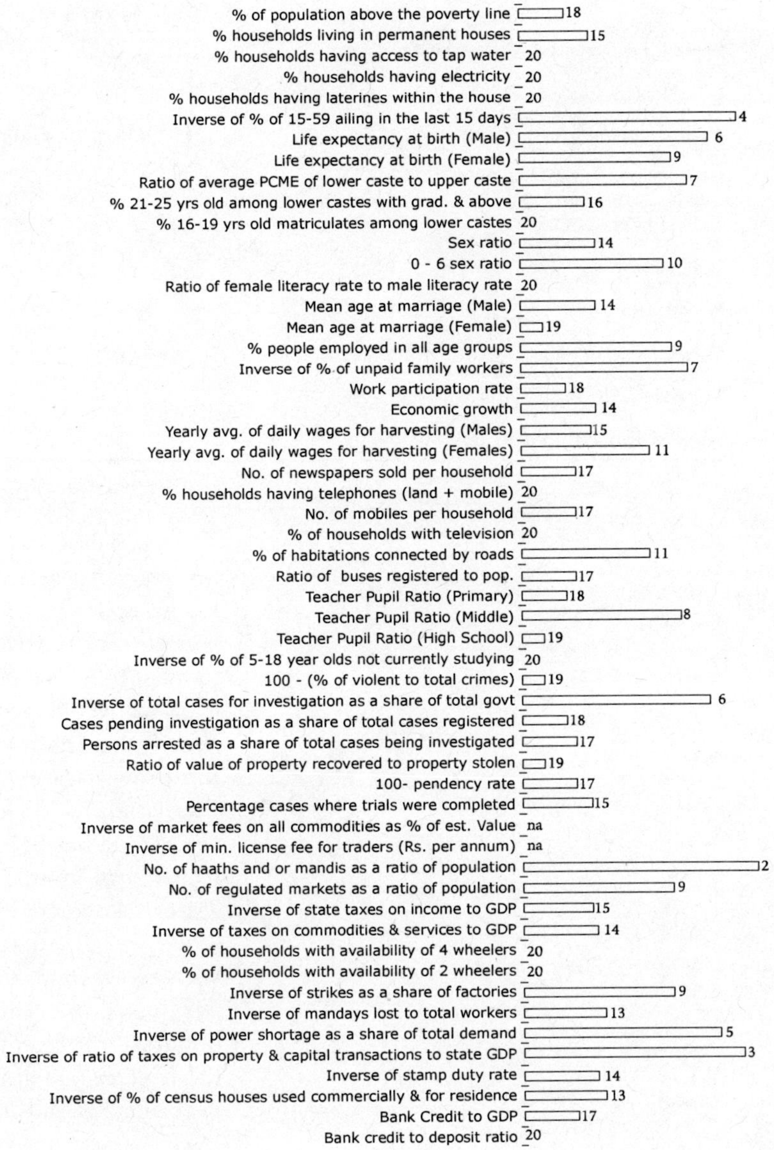

% of population above the poverty line 18
% households living in permanent houses 15
% households having access to tap water 20
% households having electricity 20
% households having laterines within the house 20
Inverse of % of 15-59 ailing in the last 15 days 4
Life expectancy at birth (Male) 6
Life expectancy at birth (Female) 9
Ratio of average PCME of lower caste to upper caste 7
% 21-25 yrs old among lower castes with grad. & above 16
% 16-19 yrs old matriculates among lower castes 20
Sex ratio 14
0 - 6 sex ratio 10
Ratio of female literacy rate to male literacy rate 20
Mean age at marriage (Male) 14
Mean age at marriage (Female) 19
% people employed in all age groups 9
Inverse of % of unpaid family workers 7
Work participation rate 18
Economic growth 14
Yearly avg. of daily wages for harvesting (Males) 15
Yearly avg. of daily wages for harvesting (Females) 11
No. of newspapers sold per household 17
% households having telephones (land + mobile) 20
No. of mobiles per household 17
% of households with television 20
% of habitations connected by roads 11
Ratio of buses registered to pop. 17
Teacher Pupil Ratio (Primary) 18
Teacher Pupil Ratio (Middle) 8
Teacher Pupil Ratio (High School) 19
Inverse of % of 5-18 year olds not currently studying 20
100 - (% of violent to total crimes) 19
Inverse of total cases for investigation as a share of total govt 6
Cases pending investigation as a share of total cases registered 18
Persons arrested as a share of total cases being investigated 17
Ratio of value of property recovered to property stolen 19
100- pendency rate 17
Percentage cases where trials were completed 15
Inverse of market fees on all commodities as % of est. Value na
Inverse of min. license fee for traders (Rs. per annum) na
No. of haaths and or mandis as a ratio of population 2
No. of regulated markets as a ratio of population 9
Inverse of state taxes on income to GDP 15
Inverse of taxes on commodities & services to GDP 14
% of households with availability of 4 wheelers 20
% of households with availability of 2 wheelers 20
Inverse of strikes as a share of factories 9
Inverse of mandays lost to total workers 13
Inverse of power shortage as a share of total demand 5
Inverse of ratio of taxes on property & capital transactions to state GDP 3
Inverse of stamp duty rate 14
Inverse of % of census houses used commercially & for residence 13
Bank Credit to GDP 17
Bank credit to deposit ratio 20

## ASSAM

| *Variables** | *Values* |
|---|---|
| Population Density (Persons/sq km) | 340 |
| PC SDP (Rs '000) | 11 |
| Share of Manufacturing SDP (%) | 12 |
| Share of Agriculture SDP (%) | 32 |
| Share of Services SDP (%) | 5 |
| % pop. above poverty line (%) | 64 |
| Literacy Rate (%) | 64 |
| % habitations connected with pucca roads (%) | 60 |
| % households with 2 & 4 wheelers (%) | 7 |
| Whether passed right to information act | No |

* For sources and units refer appendix

Assam is one of the key northeastern states of India. Its performance relative to most other States is dismal. Population density is high and the growth rate of population over the last decade has been higher than in other states. Poverty is widespread here with more than 35 per cent of the population below the poverty line and per capita SDP much lower than most other states. Agriculture is the largest contributor to SDP, while the service sector makes the smallest contribution.

Given that the State has such high levels of poverty it would seem realistic to expect that the level of economic freedom is low in the State, and this comes across from the overall economic freedom index where Assam ranks very low. However, there are indicators of economic freedom wherein Assam performs much better than most other States. In social indicators such as caste and gender based differences in the population, Assam's performance is exceptional. Female wages are not very different from those of males and male mean age at marriage is higher than most other States. There are fewer students per teacher in middle and high school relative to other States. Further, business environment is better than in other States in terms of direct taxes and market and license fee collections.

While Assam provides a freer environment for persons from a low caste and for females, it ranks extremely low in most other indicators of economic freedom. Appropriate infrastructure for basic amenities such as housing, water and electricity is not available with a large share of the households in Assam as compared to most other states. Health is poor, employment is low and so is economic growth. Adequate access to information is also missing. The situation of crime and redressal is very dismal. The state has high share of violent crimes, very low arrests as a ratio of crimes and very large number of pending cases in relation to total number of court cases. While collection from direct taxes is low, those from indirect taxes are high and taxes from property and capital transactions are also high.

Assam appears to be an extreme State — it either performs exceedingly well or its performance is very poor. Though indicators where it performs well are fewer and those where it performs poorly dominate, thereby leading to an overall low rank in the Economic Freedom Index.

# BIHAR (20)

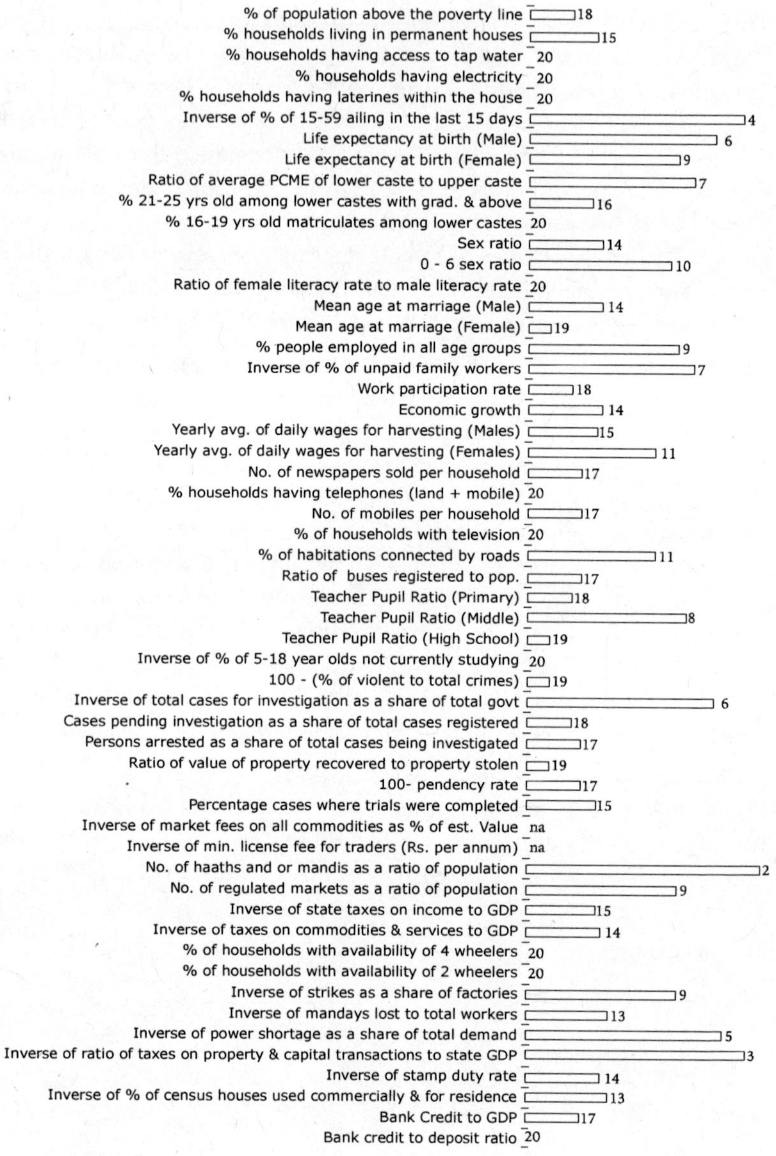
% of population above the poverty line 18
% households living in permanent houses 15
% households having access to tap water 20
% households having electricity 20
% households having laterines within the house 20
Inverse of % of 15-59 ailing in the last 15 days 4
Life expectancy at birth (Male) 6
Life expectancy at birth (Female) 9
Ratio of average PCME of lower caste to upper caste 7
% 21-25 yrs old among lower castes with grad. & above 16
% 16-19 yrs old matriculates among lower castes 20
Sex ratio 14
0 - 6 sex ratio 10
Ratio of female literacy rate to male literacy rate 20
Mean age at marriage (Male) 14
Mean age at marriage (Female) 19
% people employed in all age groups 9
Inverse of % of unpaid family workers 7
Work participation rate 18
Economic growth 14
Yearly avg. of daily wages for harvesting (Males) 15
Yearly avg. of daily wages for harvesting (Females) 11
No. of newspapers sold per household 17
% households having telephones (land + mobile) 20
No. of mobiles per household 17
% of households with television 20
% of habitations connected by roads 11
Ratio of buses registered to pop. 17
Teacher Pupil Ratio (Primary) 18
Teacher Pupil Ratio (Middle) 8
Teacher Pupil Ratio (High School) 19
Inverse of % of 5-18 year olds not currently studying 20
100 - (% of violent to total crimes) 19
Inverse of total cases for investigation as a share of total govt 6
Cases pending investigation as a share of total cases registered 18
Persons arrested as a share of total cases being investigated 17
Ratio of value of property recovered to property stolen 19
100- pendency rate 17
Percentage cases where trials were completed 15
Inverse of market fees on all commodities as % of est. Value na
Inverse of min. license fee for traders (Rs. per annum) na
No. of haaths and or mandis as a ratio of population 2
No. of regulated markets as a ratio of population 9
Inverse of state taxes on income to GDP 15
Inverse of taxes on commodities & services to GDP 14
% of households with availability of 4 wheelers 20
% of households with availability of 2 wheelers 20
Inverse of strikes as a share of factories 9
Inverse of mandays lost to total workers 13
Inverse of power shortage as a share of total demand 5
Inverse of ratio of taxes on property & capital transactions to state GDP 3
Inverse of stamp duty rate 14
Inverse of % of census houses used commercially & for residence 13
Bank Credit to GDP 17
Bank credit to deposit ratio 20

## BIHAR

| *Variables** | *Values* |
|---|---|
| Population Density (Persons/sq km) | 880 |
| PC SDP (Rs '000) | 6 |
| Share of Manufacturing SDP (%) | 5 |
| Share of Agriculture SDP (%) | 35 |
| Share of Services SDP (%) | 4 |
| % pop. above poverty line (%) | 59 |
| Literacy Rate (%) | 48 |
| % habitations connected with pucca roads (%) | 60 |
| % households with 2 & 4 wheelers (%) | 5 |
| Whether passed right to information act | No |

* For sources and units refer appendix

The economic freedom index for the new State of Bihar is presented, as the old State of Bihar was split into the 2 parts of Bihar and Jharkhand. The northern part of old Bihar now constitutes the new State of Bihar. Population density is very high, accompanied with low per capita SDP and high levels of poverty. A large part of the state's domestic product is accounted for by agriculture while share of manufacturing sector is very small. Bihar's literacy rate is lowest among the 20 States that are considered in the ranking.

In the overall economic freedom ranking, Bihar figures at the bottom. Its performance in most indicators is dismal. Surprisingly, however, it exhibits the low morbidity rate in the working age group. Apart from this, its performance is better than most other States only for number of mandis and haats as a ratio of population, power supply as ratio of total demand for power and for taxes on property and capital transactions.

Bihar performance is appalling in majority of the freedom indicators. Bihar has the lowest share of population that has access to tapped drinking water, electricity and sewage facilities within the premises. Its position relative to other States, in case of the number of children of school going age that are not currently studying and in the share of low caste persons in age group of 16-19 years who have completed high school, is lowest as well. Inaccessibility to information adds to the ignorance of the large section of the population who are also illiterate. Given that a large portion of the population is poor, it is not surprising that Bihar has the lowest share of households that own a telephone or a television. Also those households that own a 4 wheeler or even a 2 wheeler are few. Access to information and mobility of consumers are both, therefore severely limited in the State. Business environment is also not very favourable. Taxes on income are high. Indirect taxes such as those on commodities and services are also high. Further, there is a lack of adequate amount of credit. Credit to deposit ratio is the lowest in Bihar than in any other State. The law and order situation is far from satisfactory. Stolen property is rarely recovered. Investigation of cases and trails in court are not timely or efficiently carried out.

The level of economic freedom is lowest in Bihar. The situation is unfavourable for all economic agents, be it an entrepreneur, a worker or a consumer.

# CHHATTISGARH (19)

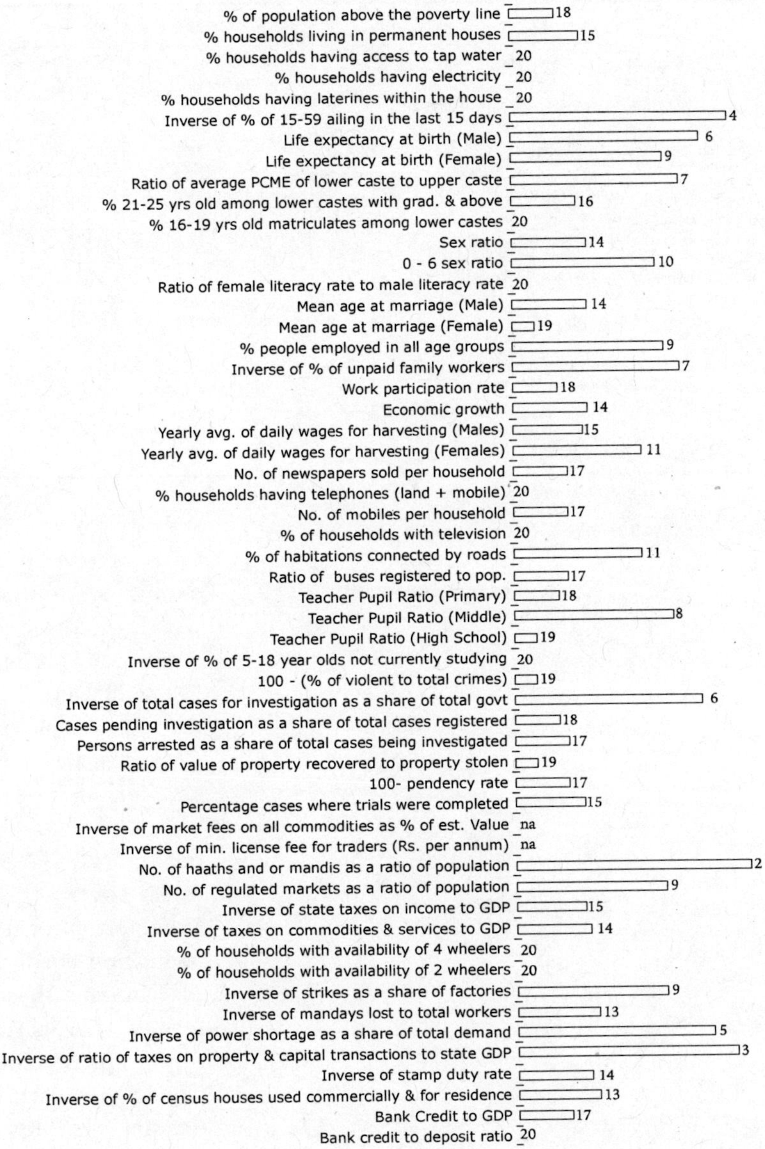

## CHHATTISGARH

| *Variables** | *Values* |
|---|---|
| Population Density (Persons/sq km) | 154 |
| PC SDP (Rs '000) | 13 |
| Share of Manufacturing SDP (%) | — |
| Share of Agriculture SDP (%) | — |
| Share of Services SDP (%) | — |
| % pop. above poverty line (%) | 59 |
| Literacy Rate (%) | 65 |
| % habitations connected with pucca roads (%) | 16 |
| % households with 2 & 4 wheelers (%) | 12 |
| Whether passed right to information act | No |

* For sources and units refer appendix

Chhattisgarh is a new State that was formed when state of Madhya Pradesh was split into two parts. Chhattisgarh is smaller than its sister State. It boasts of large forest cover and a large portion of its population is tribal that inhabit these forests. Given its topography, no wonder population density is low. However, approximately 41 per cent of the population is in poverty and a very small percentage of Chhattisgarh is approachable by roads.

Morbidity levels are low in Chhattisgarh than in most other states. In addition, females in Chhattisgarh seem to have a higher level of freedom, as indicated by the relatively higher sex ratio in the children's, as well as, the overall age group. Employment is high as indicated by the employment rate for all ages as well as the work participation rate. There are a large number of mandis and haats catering to the people and the demand for power is met more appropriately here than in many other states. Safety and governance indicators also show a moderately good performance.

While morbidity is low in Chhattisgarh, life expectancy is also very low. Such a situation may suggest that large number of people who fall ill, succumb to the illness. Availability of basic amenities is poor in comparison to other states. A large share of the population does not have permanent houses to live in. Further, access to potable tapped water, electricity and sewage system, are luxuries for most of Chhattisgarh. Caste differences are prevalent and are reflected in the low education levels of persons belonging to lower caste and from lower expenditures made by this section of society. Employment rate is high, but it is accompanied with large share of the work force's involvement in unpaid family work. Agriculture wages are also lower than in other states. The quality of education is poor as reflected by high pupil teacher ratios. The condition of poor literacy may continue in Chhattisgarh since many children of school going age are abstaining from school. Considering that 44 per cent of old Madhya Pradesh's forests are in Chhattisgarh it is natural that a large portion of the economy would be driven by forest produce. Taxes from commodities and services are high and so also the taxes on property and capital transactions. Poor connectivity by roads is a constraint on transportation, in addition, not many households own 4 wheelers.

In the over all, freedom index is second last. Poor condition of physical and human capital may be essential ingredients of Chhattisgarh's dismal performance. But if safety and governance performance is sustained, the State is likely to move up.

# GUJARAT (3)

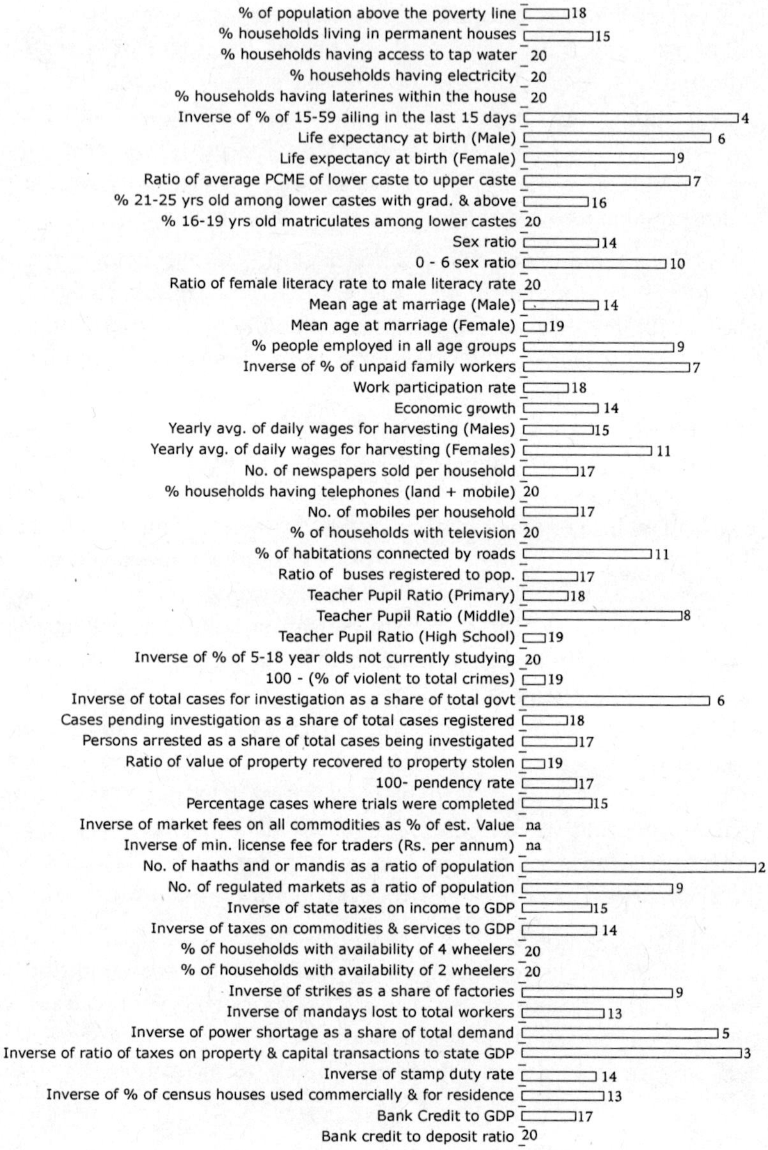
% of population above the poverty line 18
% households living in permanent houses 15
% households having access to tap water 20
% households having electricity 20
% households having laterines within the house 20
Inverse of % of 15-59 ailing in the last 15 days 4
Life expectancy at birth (Male) 6
Life expectancy at birth (Female) 9
Ratio of average PCME of lower caste to upper caste 7
% 21-25 yrs old among lower castes with grad. & above 16
% 16-19 yrs old matriculates among lower castes 20
Sex ratio 14
0 - 6 sex ratio 10
Ratio of female literacy rate to male literacy rate 20
Mean age at marriage (Male) 14
Mean age at marriage (Female) 19
% people employed in all age groups 9
Inverse of % of unpaid family workers 7
Work participation rate 18
Economic growth 14
Yearly avg. of daily wages for harvesting (Males) 15
Yearly avg. of daily wages for harvesting (Females) 11
No. of newspapers sold per household 17
% households having telephones (land + mobile) 20
No. of mobiles per household 17
% of households with television 20
% of habitations connected by roads 11
Ratio of buses registered to pop. 17
Teacher Pupil Ratio (Primary) 18
Teacher Pupil Ratio (Middle) 8
Teacher Pupil Ratio (High School) 19
Inverse of % of 5-18 year olds not currently studying 20
100 - (% of violent to total crimes) 19
Inverse of total cases for investigation as a share of total govt 6
Cases pending investigation as a share of total cases registered 18
Persons arrested as a share of total cases being investigated 17
Ratio of value of property recovered to property stolen 19
100- pendency rate 17
Percentage cases where trials were completed 15
Inverse of market fees on all commodities as % of est. Value na
Inverse of min. license fee for traders (Rs. per annum) na
No. of haaths and or mandis as a ratio of population 2
No. of regulated markets as a ratio of population 9
Inverse of state taxes on income to GDP 15
Inverse of taxes on commodities & services to GDP 14
% of households with availability of 4 wheelers 20
% of households with availability of 2 wheelers 20
Inverse of strikes as a share of factories 9
Inverse of mandays lost to total workers 13
Inverse of power shortage as a share of total demand 5
Inverse of ratio of taxes on property & capital transactions to state GDP 3
Inverse of stamp duty rate 14
Inverse of % of census houses used commercially & for residence 13
Bank Credit to GDP 17
Bank credit to deposit ratio 20

## GUJARAT

| *Variables** | *Values* |
|---|---|
| Population Density (Persons/sq km) | 258 |
| PC SDP (Rs '000) | 22 |
| Share of Manufacturing SDP (%) | 34 |
| Share of Agriculture SDP (%) | 12 |
| Share of Services SDP (%) | 6 |
| % pop. above poverty line (%) | 86 |
| Literacy Rate (%) | 66 |
| % habitations connected with pucca roads (%) | 85 |
| % households with 2 & 4 wheelers (%) | 25 |
| Whether passed right to information act | No |

* For sources and units refer appendix

Gujarat ranks very high among the 20 States ranked according to the economic freedom index. Situated in the west-most part of India, it performs well in almost all indicators of development. Gujarat has moderately low population density, only 14 per cent of the population is below the poverty line, which is much lower than most other States and per capita SDP is comparable to other economically well off States. The share of manufacturing sector's contribution to SDP is highest in Gujarat as compared to any of the other 20 States. While the agricultural sector contributes significantly to economy, the share is much larger in most other States.

Gujarat performs exceptionally well in terms of access to civic amenities by the general public. It has relatively high percentage of households that live in permanent houses that have access to tap water, electricity and sewage system. Larger share of youth in the lower caste are graduates or above and mean age at marriage of females is higher than in other states. Economic growth rate is relatively high and is accompanied with an employment rate that is higher than most other states as well. Ownership of assets that are a means of information and transportation are also relatively high. A large share of cases that are registered are investigated, the number of arrests as a ratio of the number of cases being investigated is high, and relatively low share of cases are pending in courts. The environment for trade is favourable with relatively low market fees on all commodities and low minimum license fees for traders.

In social indicators of freedom, Gujarat's performance is especially poor. Sex ratio, especially child sex ratio is among the lowest of that observed in the 20 States. The section of the population that belongs to the lower caste is worse off in relation to those belonging to the upper caste in terms of the average per capita monthly expenditure in the two sections. Males have a low mean age at marriage implying early restrictions on individual freedom due to added responsibility and lower ability to take risks. Labour available for the manufacturing sector is unsupportive with higher strikes than in other States. Power is not available in adequate amounts acting as a hurdle to efficiency in the industrial sector. Further obstructions come in the form of high taxes on property and capital transactions, which also leads to a higher number of residential houses being used for commercial purposes.

# HARYANA (12)

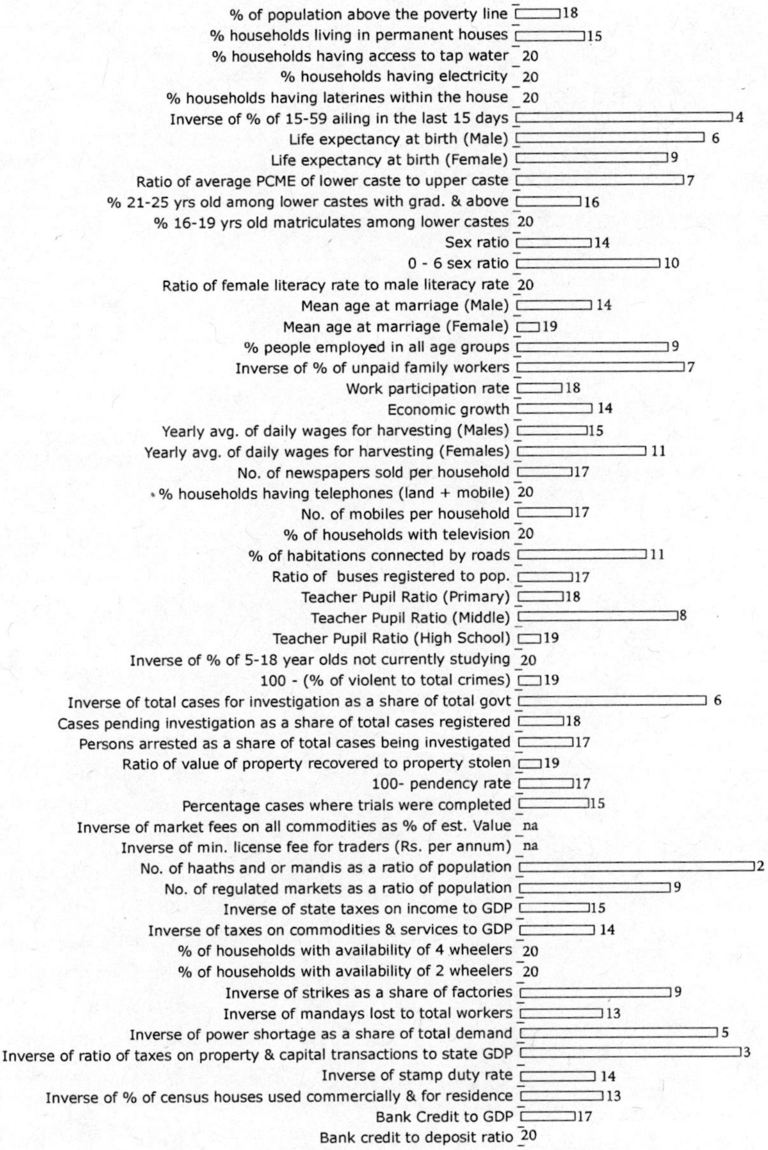
% of population above the poverty line 18
% households living in permanent houses 15
% households having access to tap water 20
% households having electricity 20
% households having laterines within the house 20
Inverse of % of 15-59 ailing in the last 15 days 4
Life expectancy at birth (Male) 6
Life expectancy at birth (Female) 9
Ratio of average PCME of lower caste to upper caste 7
% 21-25 yrs old among lower castes with grad. & above 16
% 16-19 yrs old matriculates among lower castes 20
Sex ratio 14
0 - 6 sex ratio 10
Ratio of female literacy rate to male literacy rate 20
Mean age at marriage (Male) 14
Mean age at marriage (Female) 19
% people employed in all age groups 9
Inverse of % of unpaid family workers 7
Work participation rate 18
Economic growth 14
Yearly avg. of daily wages for harvesting (Males) 15
Yearly avg. of daily wages for harvesting (Females) 11
No. of newspapers sold per household 17
% households having telephones (land + mobile) 20
No. of mobiles per household 17
% of households with television 20
% of habitations connected by roads 11
Ratio of buses registered to pop. 17
Teacher Pupil Ratio (Primary) 18
Teacher Pupil Ratio (Middle) 8
Teacher Pupil Ratio (High School) 19
Inverse of % of 5-18 year olds not currently studying 20
100 - (% of violent to total crimes) 19
Inverse of total cases for investigation as a share of total govt 6
Cases pending investigation as a share of total cases registered 18
Persons arrested as a share of total cases being investigated 17
Ratio of value of property recovered to property stolen 19
100- pendency rate 17
Percentage cases where trials were completed 15
Inverse of market fees on all commodities as % of est. Value na
Inverse of min. license fee for traders (Rs. per annum) na
No. of haaths and or mandis as a ratio of population 2
No. of regulated markets as a ratio of population 9
Inverse of state taxes on income to GDP 15
Inverse of taxes on commodities & services to GDP 14
% of households with availability of 4 wheelers 20
% of households with availability of 2 wheelers 20
Inverse of strikes as a share of factories 9
Inverse of mandays lost to total workers 13
Inverse of power shortage as a share of total demand 5
Inverse of ratio of taxes on property & capital transactions to state GDP 3
Inverse of stamp duty rate 14
Inverse of % of census houses used commercially & for residence 13
Bank Credit to GDP 17
Bank credit to deposit ratio 20

## HARYANA

| *Variables** | *Values* |
|---|---|
| Population Density (Persons/sq km) | 477 |
| PC SDP (Rs '000) | 26 |
| Share of Manufacturing SDP (%) | 21 |
| Share of Agriculture SDP (%) | 31 |
| Share of Services SDP (%) | 3 |
| % pop. above poverty line (%) | 91 |
| Literacy Rate (%) | 69 |
| % habitations connected with pucca roads (%) | 99 |
| % households with 2 & 4 wheelers (%) | 23 |
| Whether passed right to information act | No |

* For sources and units refer appendix

Haryana ranks in the bottom half of the economic freedom index. It exhibits one of the highest levels of per capita SDP accompanied with a low share of the population in poverty. A large share of the SDP is accounted for by the agricultural sector and the manufacturing sector is also performing well. There is much room for improvement in literacy. Haryana is, however, well connected with roads.

Not only is the head count ratio in Haryana low, but a high share of the population also lives in permanent or pucca houses. This may be due to high work participation rates and the fact that the share of unpaid family labour in total labour force is low. That is, more workers get compensated for their economic activities. While Haryana may be an agrarian State, there is not much disguised unemployment. There are a high number of regulated markets. Taxes on commodities and services are low. There are relatively lower power shortages and taxes on property and capital transactions are low. With large share of the households owning assets such as televisions, 2 and 4 wheelers, the situation of mobility and access to information also seems relatively better.

While Haryana performs well in many indicators of economic freedom, it fares very badly in others. Civic amenities in terms of sewage facilities are poor. Morbidity levels in the working age population are high. Caste and gender based differences are striking, leading to a social environment highly unfavouarble for large sections of the population. This hampers the level of freedom experienced by the 'underprivileged' sections. Sex ratio is the lowest in this state. Even the sex ratio in the 0-6 age group is very low. The education status of the children and youth in the lower caste in Haryana is poor. Only small shares of the youth and children in the state are graduates or have completed class 10. Agricultural wages are lower than in other states. Corruption levels appear to be high with a high share of cases investigated under the prevention of corruption act and other related acts against government employees. Income tax collections are high in comparison to SDP and stamp duties are high as well. A large number of houses are being used for commercial purposes and the number of unregulated *mandis* and *haats* is relatively low. The business and trade sector could receive a boost if taxes and duty collections are lowered to levels similar in other States and credit is made more easily available.

Though, Haryana is considered to figure among the economically well off States, when assessed in terms of economic freedom, there is a lot of scope for improvement. Slight improvements in social indicators of freedom and in the factors related to the business environment could considerably improve the relative position of Haryana.

# HIMACHAL PRADESH (9)

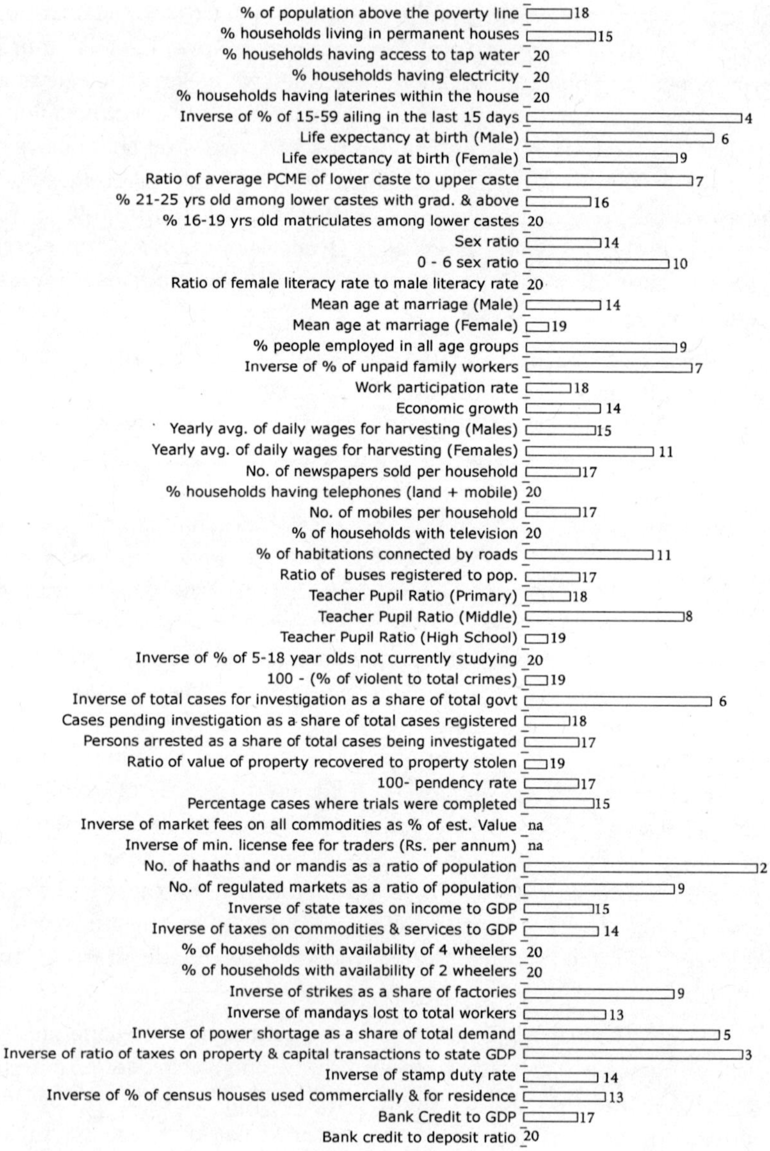

## HIMACHAL PRADESH

| *Variables** | *Values* |
|---|---|
| Population Density (Persons/sq km) | 109 |
| PC SDP (Rs '000) | 21 |
| Share of Manufacturing SDP (%) | 12 |
| Share of Agriculture SDP (%) | 22 |
| Share of Services SDP (%) | 4 |
| % pop. above poverty line (%) | 92 |
| Literacy Rate (%) | 76 |
| % habitations connected with pucca roads (%) | 35 |
| % households with 2 & 4 wheelers (%) | 10 |
| Whether passed right to information act | No |

* For sources and units refer appendix

Situated in the north, just below Jammu and Kashmir, Himachal Pradesh is one of the most picturesque States in India. Population density is very low, large population of the population is literate and only around 8 per cent of the population is in poverty. Among the three sectors, manufacturing, services, and agriculture, the latter is the largest contributor to the economy.

Low level of poverty is accompanied with a large share of the population having access to tapped drinking water and electricity.

Caste differences are not as prevalent as in other States. Lower caste households spend as much per person as those from the upper caste. Further, a large share of lower caste youth in the age group 21-25 years have completed graduation and many more lower caste children in Himachal have completed class X than in all other States. Moreover, most children of school going age are actually going to school and literacy among females, as a share of male literacy is amongst the highest.

Economic growth is higher than in other States and employment rate is also high. However, the share of unpaid family labour in the work force is high simultaneously. Agricultural wages are higher than in other States. Access to information is more by means of television and telephones than by means of newspapers. Road connectivity is poor though there are a high number of buses to cater to the population. Teacher pupil ratio is high in primary schools though in middle school there are a much higher number of students per teacher. The number of cases under prevention of corruption act as a ratio of total government employees is lower than in other States. Further, of all the cases that are registered, not many are being investigated. Business and trade environment is more or less moderate though the State could do with more *haats* and *mandis*. Taxes on property and capital transactions are high. However, not many houses are used for both residential and commercial purposes. Power is available in enough quantity to meet demand though capital is not as easily available.

Himachal could improve in its legal infrastructure and many changes are required to make the environment more conducive to business and trade.

# JAMMU & KASHMIR (11)

| | |
|---|---|
| % of population above the poverty line | 18 |
| % households living in permanent houses | 15 |
| % households having access to tap water | 20 |
| % households having electricity | 20 |
| % households having laterines within the house | 20 |
| Inverse of % of 15-59 ailing in the last 15 days | 4 |
| Life expectancy at birth (Male) | 6 |
| Life expectancy at birth (Female) | 9 |
| Ratio of average PCME of lower caste to upper caste | 7 |
| % 21-25 yrs old among lower castes with grad. & above | 16 |
| % 16-19 yrs old matriculates among lower castes | 20 |
| Sex ratio | 14 |
| 0 - 6 sex ratio | 10 |
| Ratio of female literacy rate to male literacy rate | 20 |
| Mean age at marriage (Male) | 14 |
| Mean age at marriage (Female) | 19 |
| % people employed in all age groups | 9 |
| Inverse of % of unpaid family workers | 7 |
| Work participation rate | 18 |
| Economic growth | 14 |
| Yearly avg. of daily wages for harvesting (Males) | 15 |
| Yearly avg. of daily wages for harvesting (Females) | 11 |
| No. of newspapers sold per household | 17 |
| % households having telephones (land + mobile) | 20 |
| No. of mobiles per household | 17 |
| % of households with television | 20 |
| % of habitations connected by roads | 11 |
| Ratio of buses registered to pop. | 17 |
| Teacher Pupil Ratio (Primary) | 18 |
| Teacher Pupil Ratio (Middle) | 8 |
| Teacher Pupil Ratio (High School) | 19 |
| Inverse of % of 5-18 year olds not currently studying | 20 |
| 100 - (% of violent to total crimes) | 19 |
| Inverse of total cases for investigation as a share of total govt | 6 |
| Cases pending investigation as a share of total cases registered | 18 |
| Persons arrested as a share of total cases being investigated | 17 |
| Ratio of value of property recovered to property stolen | 19 |
| 100- pendency rate | 17 |
| Percentage cases where trials were completed | 15 |
| Inverse of market fees on all commodities as % of est. Value | na |
| Inverse of min. license fee for traders (Rs. per annum) | na |
| No. of haaths and or mandis as a ratio of population | 2 |
| No. of regulated markets as a ratio of population | 9 |
| Inverse of state taxes on income to GDP | 15 |
| Inverse of taxes on commodities & services to GDP | 14 |
| % of households with availability of 4 wheelers | 20 |
| % of households with availability of 2 wheelers | 20 |
| Inverse of strikes as a share of factories | 9 |
| Inverse of mandays lost to total workers | 13 |
| Inverse of power shortage as a share of total demand | 5 |
| Inverse of ratio of taxes on property & capital transactions to state GDP | 3 |
| Inverse of stamp duty rate | 14 |
| Inverse of % of census houses used commercially & for residence | 13 |
| Bank Credit to GDP | 17 |
| Bank credit to deposit ratio | 20 |

## JAMMU & KASHMIR

| *Variables** | *Values* |
|---|---|
| Population Density (Persons/sq km) | 99 |
| PC SDP (Rs '000) | — |
| Share of Manufacturing SDP (%) | — |
| Share of Agriculture SDP (%) | — |
| Share of Services SDP (%) | — |
| % pop. above poverty line (%) | 97 |
| Literacy Rate (%) | 55 |
| % habitations connected with pucca roads (%) | 68 |
| % households with 2 & 4 wheelers (%) | 11 |
| Whether passed right to information act | No |

* For sources and units refer appendix

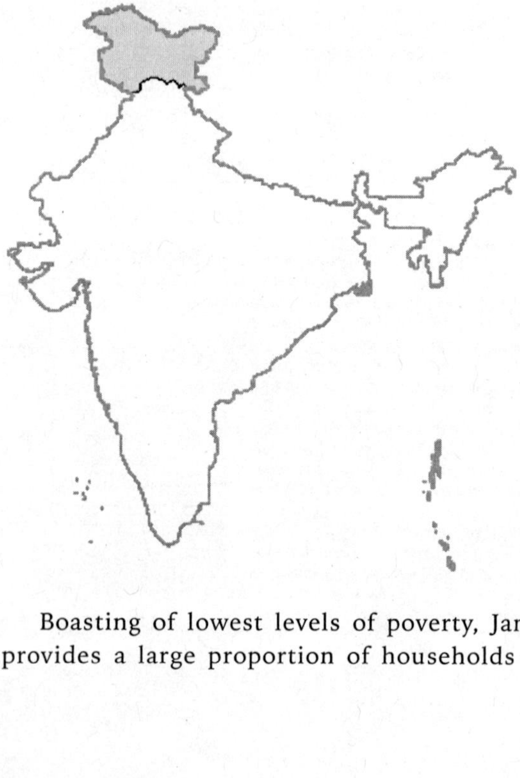

Jammu and Kashmir, constitutes the northern most State of India. Given the mountainous terrain, it is no wonder that the population density is the lowest in Jammu & Kashmir than in any other State. Moreover, the lowest share of the population in poverty is in this State. Literacy is of concern as almost 45 per cent of population is illiterate.

Boasting of lowest levels of poverty, Jammu & Kashmir also provides a large proportion of households with electricity. The situation of tapped water and permanent houses is moderate. Caste differences do not manifest into differences in spending capability. Agricultural wages for males are highest in J&K than in any of the 20 States. Though literacy is low the quality of education that is provided to the students is worth mentioning- at all levels of education, primary, middle or secondary, the number of students per teacher is low.

Gender differences are high in Jammu & Kashmir. Sex ratio is very low and the situation of literacy for females is much worse than it is for males. Employment situation is poor. Tourism was a large source of income for many in the State, but the constant violence has seriously affected the industry. Until very recently mobile phones were not allowed in the State, as a result the State ranks lowest in terms of number of households having mobile phones. Even newspapers are not a large source of information since very small shares of households buy newspapers. Of all kinds of crime that take place in Jammu & Kashmir, the majority are of a violent nature. Further not all cases that are registered are investigated and not many arrests are made in those cases that are investigated. Ready redressal is not available in courts with a large backlog leading to a large share of pending cases. Environment is not very conducive to trade and business. There are few *mandis* and *haats*. Indirect taxes are high, and transactions costs are high with high tax collections from property and capital transactions. Though commercial bank credit is available in large amounts, the credit deposit ratio is low.

It doesn't take an expert to identify the true problem faced by the State's economy. Threat to life and property is the biggest deterrent to economic growth in the State.

# JHARKHAND (18)

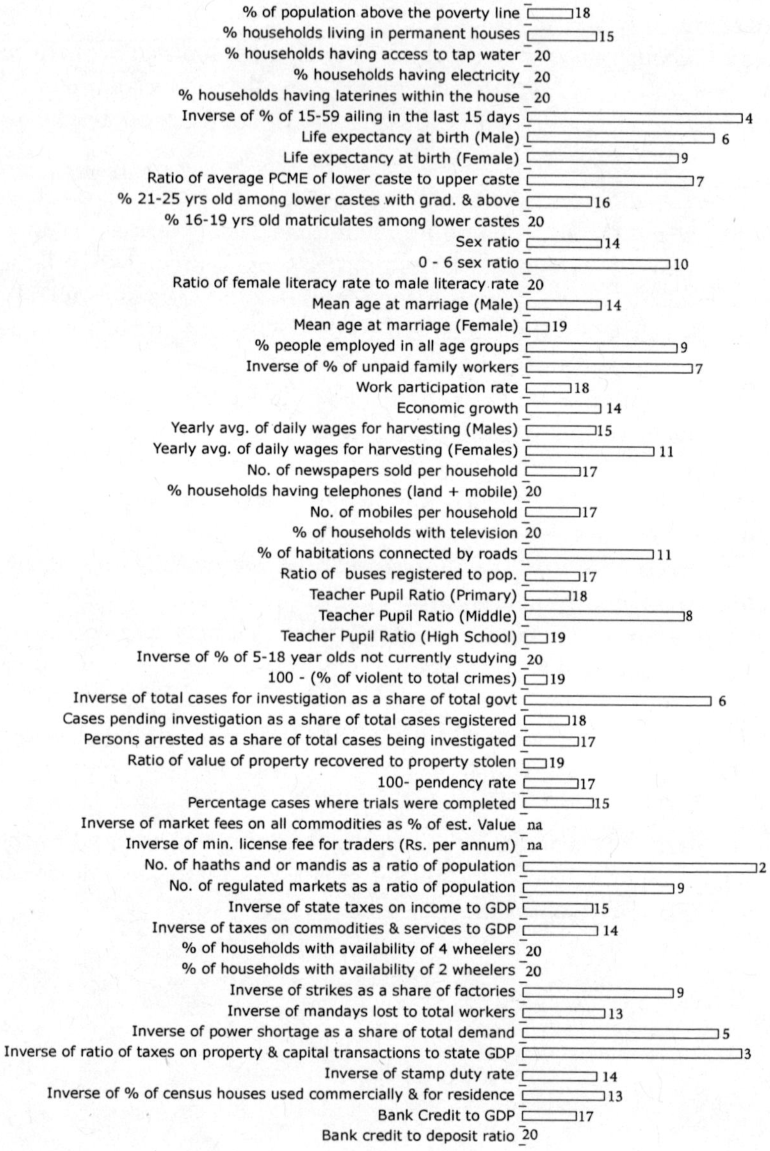

## JHARKHAND

| *Variables** | *Values* |
|---|---|
| Population Density (Persons/sq km) | 338 |
| PC SDP (Rs '000) | 11 |
| Share of Manufacturing SDP (%) | — |
| Share of Agriculture SDP (%) | — |
| Share of Services SDP (%) | — |
| % pop. above poverty line (%) | 56 |
| Literacy Rate (%) | 54 |
| % habitations connected with pucca roads (%) | 44 |
| % households with 2 & 4 wheelers (%) | 11 |
| Whether passed right to information act | 327 |

* For sources and units refer appendix

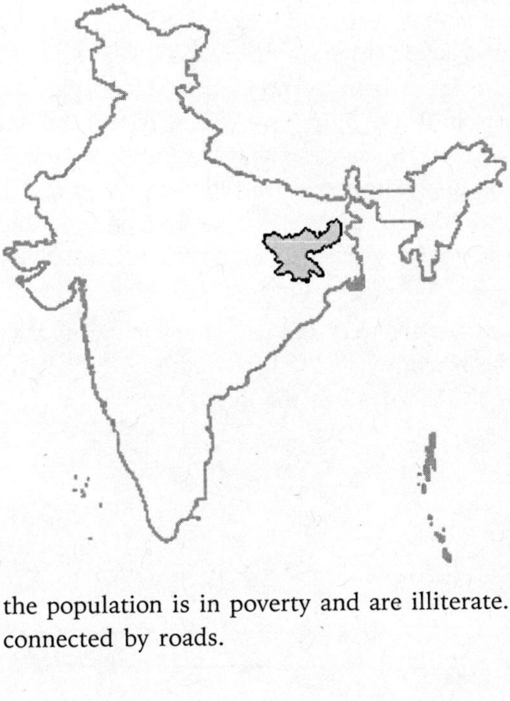

Jharkhand was recently formed when the old State of Bihar spilt into two parts. Geographically, it is only a little smaller than its sister State and is located south of the new state of Bihar. In the overall economic freedom index, it ranks very low, however, it performs better than Bihar. Population density is high. A large portion of the population is in poverty and are illiterate. It is also not very well connected by roads.

Its performance relative to other States is dismal in most indicators of freedom. However, its performance is relatively better in a few indicators. Just like Bihar, the working age population in Jharkhand exhibits low levels of morbidity. Child sex ratio is not as biased towards boys as in rest of the 20 States. In middle school, the number of children per teacher is low. Markets are abundant with a large number of *mandis* and *haats* catering to the demands of the people.

A large portion of the population is deprived of civic amenities. Caste differences are significant with large difference between expenditure per person in low caste households *vis-à-vis* that in upper caste households. Further lesser children belonging to the low caste have completed education till class 10. Gender differences are highlighted by the difference in male and female literacy rates. Females are worse off than males. People marry at an early age, reducing the risk taking ability and an early burden of family responsibility. While socio-economic conditions are poor, access to information is also not very good. Jharkhand ranks very low in ownership of telephones, mobiles or landlines; televisions; and not many households buy newspapers either. In primary and high schools, teacher to pupil ratios are lower than in most other states. The law and order situation is grim in Jharkhand where violent crimes account for a large share of total crimes. Many cases that have been registered are awaiting investigation and not many arrests have been made in those that are investigated. Stolen property is rarely recovered and many cases are pending in courts. Access to sound credit is relatively difficult.

The interest of consumers, labourers and entrepreneurs needs a lot of attention. However the recently gained autonomy from Bihar may lead to an improvement in Jharkhand in the near future.

# KARNATAKA (6)

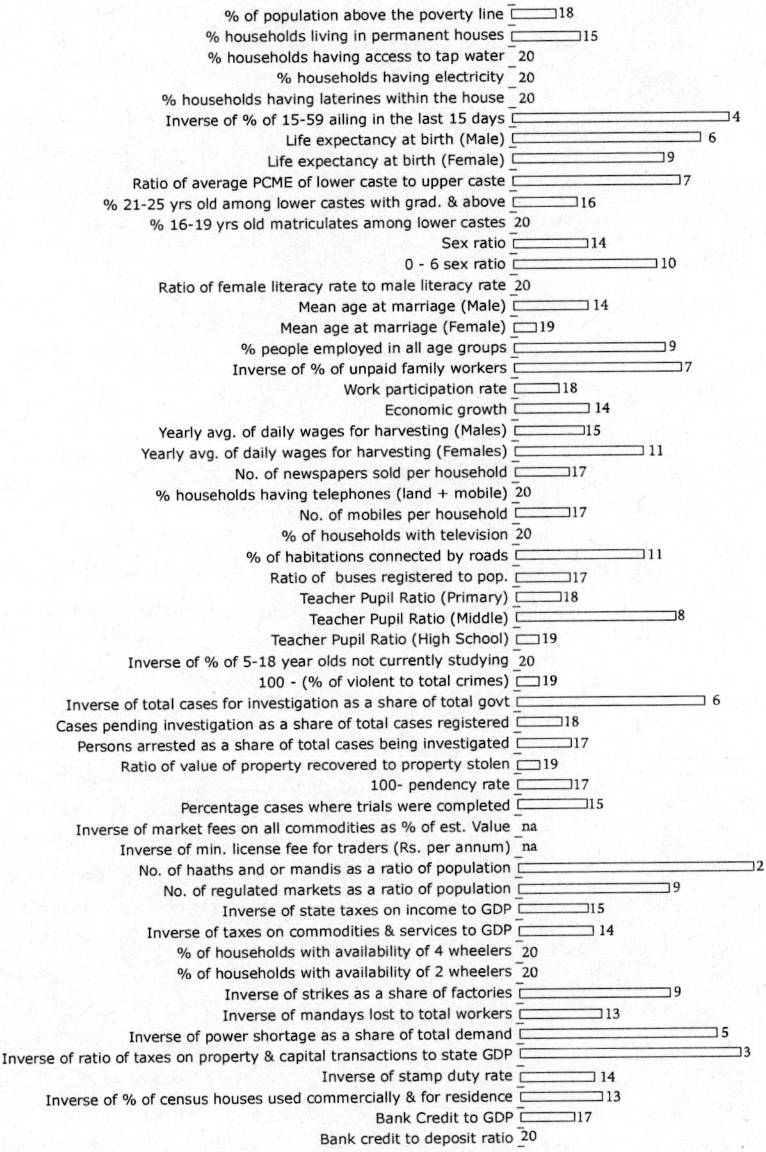
% of population above the poverty line 18
% households living in permanent houses 15
% households having access to tap water 20
% households having electricity 20
% households having laterines within the house 20
Inverse of % of 15-59 ailing in the last 15 days 4
Life expectancy at birth (Male) 6
Life expectancy at birth (Female) 9
Ratio of average PCME of lower caste to upper caste 7
% 21-25 yrs old among lower castes with grad. & above 16
% 16-19 yrs old matriculates among lower castes 20
Sex ratio 14
0 - 6 sex ratio 10
Ratio of female literacy rate to male literacy rate 20
Mean age at marriage (Male) 14
Mean age at marriage (Female) 19
% people employed in all age groups 9
Inverse of % of unpaid family workers 7
Work participation rate 18
Economic growth 14
Yearly avg. of daily wages for harvesting (Males) 15
Yearly avg. of daily wages for harvesting (Females) 11
No. of newspapers sold per household 17
% households having telephones (land + mobile) 20
No. of mobiles per household 17
% of households with television 20
% of habitations connected by roads 11
Ratio of buses registered to pop. 17
Teacher Pupil Ratio (Primary) 18
Teacher Pupil Ratio (Middle) 8
Teacher Pupil Ratio (High School) 19
Inverse of % of 5-18 year olds not currently studying 20
100 - (% of violent to total crimes) 19
Inverse of total cases for investigation as a share of total govt 6
Cases pending investigation as a share of total cases registered 18
Persons arrested as a share of total cases being investigated 17
Ratio of value of property recovered to property stolen 19
100- pendency rate 17
Percentage cases where trials were completed 15
Inverse of market fees on all commodities as % of est. Value na
Inverse of min. license fee for traders (Rs. per annum) na
No. of haaths and or mandis as a ratio of population 2
No. of regulated markets as a ratio of population 9
Inverse of state taxes on income to GDP 15
Inverse of taxes on commodities & services to GDP 14
% of households with availability of 4 wheelers 20
% of households with availability of 2 wheelers 20
Inverse of strikes as a share of factories 9
Inverse of mandays lost to total workers 13
Inverse of power shortage as a share of total demand 5
Inverse of ratio of taxes on property & capital transactions to state GDP 3
Inverse of stamp duty rate 14
Inverse of % of census houses used commercially & for residence 13
Bank Credit to GDP 17
Bank credit to deposit ratio 20

## KARNATAKA

| *Variables** | *Values* |
|---|---|
| Population Density (Persons/sq km) | 275 |
| PC SDP (Rs '000) | 20 |
| Share of Manufacturing SDP (%) | 16 |
| Share of Agriculture SDP (%) | 25 |
| Share of Services SDP (%) | 6 |
| % pop. above poverty line (%) | 80 |
| Literacy Rate (%) | 67 |
| % habitations connected with pucca roads (%) | 80 |
| % households with 2 & 4 wheelers (%) | 18 |
| Whether passed right to information act | Yes |

* For sources and units refer appendix

Karnataka is situated in south-west India, with Maharashtra to its north and surrounded by Kerala, Tamil Nadu, Andhra Pradesh and Madhya Pradesh. Population density is moderately high in comparison to other States and approximately 30 per cent of the population is in poverty. Agriculture is a large contributor to its economy, though manufacturing sector is also a significant contributor. Relative to other States, the service sector in Karnataka is much more active, although its contribution relative to other sectors is not very large.

Karnataka performs moderately well in many of the indicators of economic freedom. The availability of civic amenities is average and its performance in socio-economic indicators of freedom is not extraordinary either. Employment rate is high though unpaid family labour is high as well. The economy is growing at a rate higher than most other States. Communication and transportation infrastructure is also better than in most other States. Large share of the households have telephones and there are a good number of buses to cater to the needs of the population. Law and order machinery is functioning efficiently, most of the cases that are registered are actually investigated and most cases that are tried in court get completed within the year. Traders have to pay lower license fee, there are many regulated markets and the market fee on all commodities is also low. Direct and indirect tax collections are also low as a ratio of SDP. Credit is availability from banks is better than in most other States.

However there are some obstacles that industry may face. Stamp duty is higher than other States and many residential houses are used for commercial purposes as well, indicating lack of commercial space. Agricultural labour in Karnataka receives lower wages than similar labour in other States. This is true for male and female workers. Male life expectancy at birth is low though morbidity levels are moderate. Teachers in primary and high schools have to handle a large number of students, which may have a negative impact on the quality of education that is being provided. Newspapers are also not as widely read in Karnataka as in other States.

Karnataka is essentially an agrarian state, however recently it has made great strides in emerging sectors such as IT. The services sector can be expected to increase its contribution to the economy in future.

# KERALA (7)

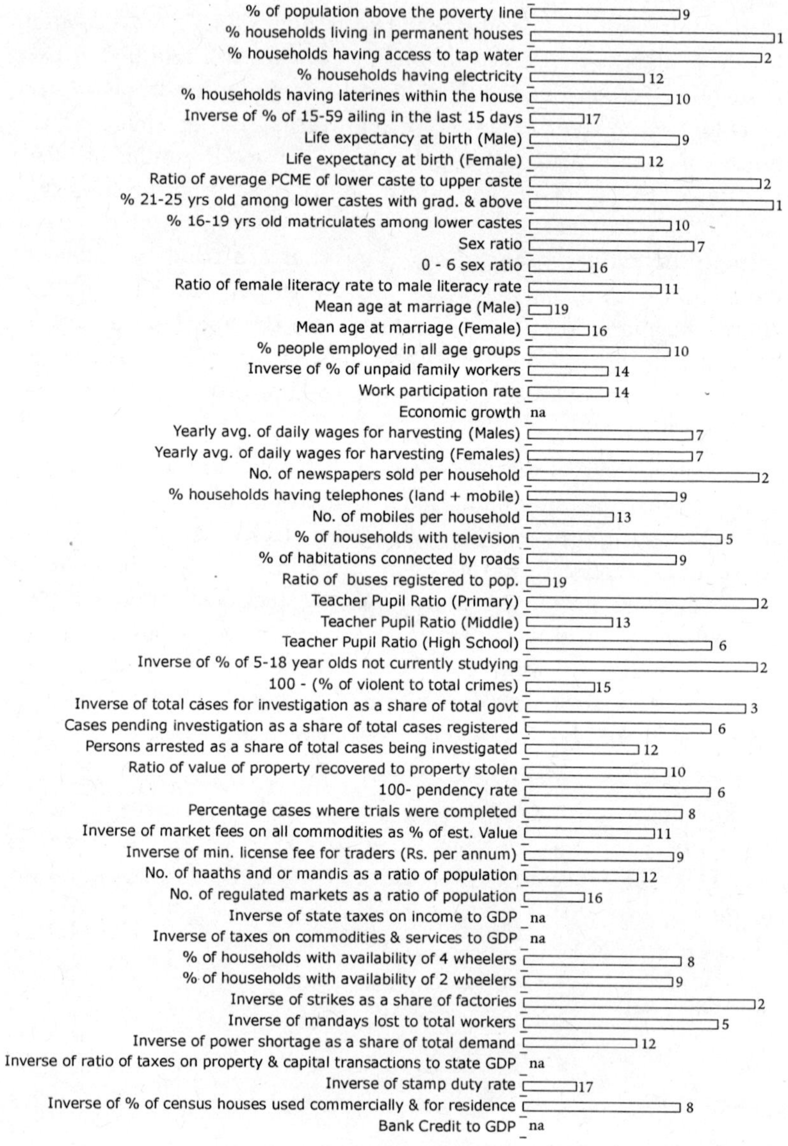
% of population above the poverty line 9
% households living in permanent houses 1
% households having access to tap water 2
% households having electricity 12
% households having laterines within the house 10
Inverse of % of 15-59 ailing in the last 15 days 17
Life expectancy at birth (Male) 9
Life expectancy at birth (Female) 12
Ratio of average PCME of lower caste to upper caste 2
% 21-25 yrs old among lower castes with grad. & above 1
% 16-19 yrs old matriculates among lower castes 10
Sex ratio 7
0 - 6 sex ratio 16
Ratio of female literacy rate to male literacy rate 11
Mean age at marriage (Male) 19
Mean age at marriage (Female) 16
% people employed in all age groups 10
Inverse of % of unpaid family workers 14
Work participation rate 14
Economic growth na
Yearly avg. of daily wages for harvesting (Males) 7
Yearly avg. of daily wages for harvesting (Females) 7
No. of newspapers sold per household 2
% households having telephones (land + mobile) 9
No. of mobiles per household 13
% of households with television 5
% of habitations connected by roads 9
Ratio of buses registered to pop. 19
Teacher Pupil Ratio (Primary) 2
Teacher Pupil Ratio (Middle) 13
Teacher Pupil Ratio (High School) 6
Inverse of % of 5-18 year olds not currently studying 2
100 - (% of violent to total crimes) 15
Inverse of total cases for investigation as a share of total govt 3
Cases pending investigation as a share of total cases registered 6
Persons arrested as a share of total cases being investigated 12
Ratio of value of property recovered to property stolen 10
100- pendency rate 6
Percentage cases where trials were completed 8
Inverse of market fees on all commodities as % of est. Value 11
Inverse of min. license fee for traders (Rs. per annum) 9
No. of haaths and or mandis as a ratio of population 12
No. of regulated markets as a ratio of population 16
Inverse of state taxes on income to GDP na
Inverse of taxes on commodities & services to GDP na
% of households with availability of 4 wheelers 8
% of households with availability of 2 wheelers 9
Inverse of strikes as a share of factories 2
Inverse of mandays lost to total workers 5
Inverse of power shortage as a share of total demand 12
Inverse of ratio of taxes on property & capital transactions to state GDP na
Inverse of stamp duty rate 17
Inverse of % of census houses used commercially & for residence 8
Bank Credit to GDP na

## KERALA

| *Variables** | *Values* |
|---|---|
| Population Density (Persons/sq km) | 819 |
| PC SDP (Rs '000) | 24 |
| Share of Manufacturing SDP (%) | 10 |
| Share of Agriculture SDP (%) | 18 |
| Share of Services SDP (%) | 5 |
| % pop. above poverty line (%) | 87 |
| Literacy Rate (%) | 91 |
| % habitations connected with pucca roads (%) | 56 |
| % households with 2 & 4 wheelers (%) | 14 |
| Whether passed right to information act | No |

* For sources and units refer appendix

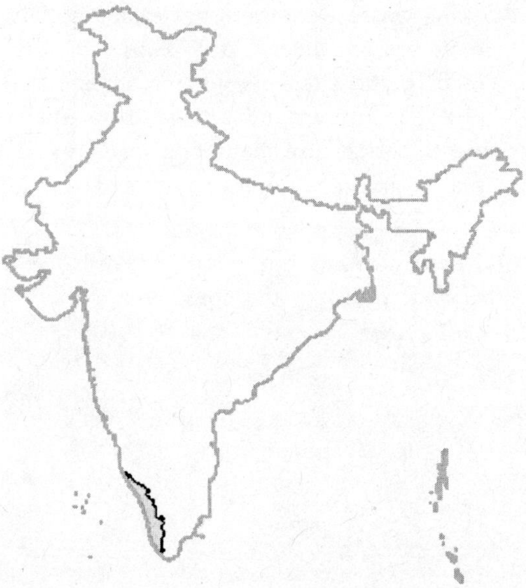

Kerala is well known for its attainment in the social sector. However, its excellent performance in the social sector has not translated into a freer economic environment. Population density is very high in Kerala and approximately 13 per cent of the population is below the poverty line. Literacy rate is highest in Kerala though it can no longer boast of 100 per cent literacy. 45 per cent of habitations are not yet connected with roads and personal transport is not available with a large share of the population.

Kerala tops the list in life expectancy at birth and age at marriage for males and females. However morbidity rates among working age population is high. Female agricultural wages are highest in Kerala and the share of workforce working as unpaid family labour is also the least in Kerala. Caste differences are not very marked as shown by education attainment of lower caste. People have good access to information as indicated by its exceptional performance in newspaper sales and ownership of telephones. It has the highest ratio of markets to population and collections from indirect taxes as a share of GDP are lowest in Kerala. Children of school going age do attend school in large numbers and high school teacher pupil ratio is also noteworthy. Education is widespread and its quality is also good. Violent crimes are not a large component of all crimes that are committed in the State. Socio-economic indicators of freedom are exceptional in the State.

On the other extreme, work participation rates are the lowest in Kerala and morbidity in the working age population is the highest. While a large share of the population lives in permanent houses, few have access to tapped drinking water. Redress is not easily available. Many cases that are registered are not investigated. Those cases that are investigated do not lead to the suspects getting arrested and property stolen is unlikely to be recovered. Industry can be warned of the nature of labour problems; strikes are many and result in large loss of mandays. Power situation in the State is also not as favourable as in other States.

Kerala has the social environment but needs to improve its economic environment to favour industry and commerce.

# MADHYA PRADESH (15)

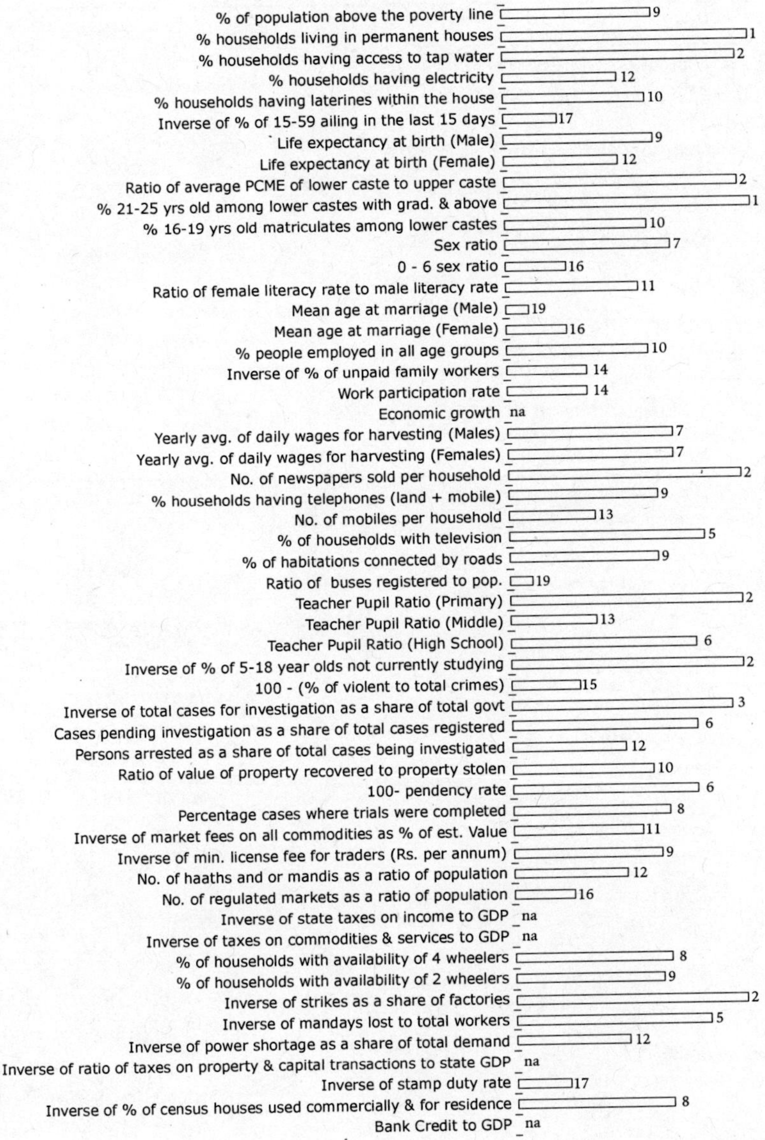

## MADHYA PRADESH

| *Variables** | *Values* |
|---|---|
| Population Density (Persons/sq km) | 196 |
| PC SDP (Rs '000) | 12 |
| Share of Manufacturing SDP (%) | 18 |
| Share of Agriculture SDP (%) | 25 |
| Share of Services SDP (%) | 4 |
| % pop. above poverty line (%) | 64 |
| Literacy Rate (%) | 64 |
| % habitations connected with pucca roads (%) | 15 |
| % households with 2 & 4 wheelers (%) | 14 |
| Whether passed right to information act | No |

* For sources and units refer appendix

Placed in the centre of India, Madhya Pradesh is geographically a very large State even after a part was chopped off to constitute the new State of Chhattisgarh. In the overall economic freedom index, it performs much better than Chhattisgarh. Though population density is not very high, there is wide spread poverty. Almost 37 per cent of the population survives in poverty and per capita Gross State Domestic Product is low. The share of manufacturing sector in the economy is high when compared with the share of the sector in the economies of other states. Road connectivity is the worst in this state.

Madhya Pradesh's performance is notable in very few indicators of economic freedom. Employment of all age groups is high though this is accompanied with very large number of people working as unpaid family workers. Violent crimes constitute a small share of all crimes committed and generally cases in courts are not pending. Investigations, arrests and recovery of stolen property are average. Income tax collections are a small share of State Domestic Product and stamp duty is not very high.

Socio-economic indicators of freedom portray a bleak picture of Madhya Pradesh. Large sections of the population do not live in permanent houses. The health environment is also poor as exhibited by low life expectancy at birth, for males as well as females. Caste differences are prominent. Spending per person is much lower among the lower caste than that among the upper caste indicating inequalities in economic well-being. Lower caste children in age group 16-19 years are not even educated till class 10. Also as compared to other states, greater number of youth from lower caste are not graduates. Moreover, of all children in age group of 5-18 years, only a small share attends school. Literacy levels among females are much worse than males and sex ratio is also biased towards males. Mean age at marriage of males and females is low, implying an early burden of family responsibility. Wages in the agricultural sector are lower than in other states. The legal machinery performs moderately though cases that are tried in court may not be completed quickly. Infrastructure for industry is also average though availability of power may be worse than in other states.

Poverty, gender gap and economic conditions of the most under privileged are the primary causes of Madhya Pradesh's relatively poorer performance.

# MAHARASHTRA (2)

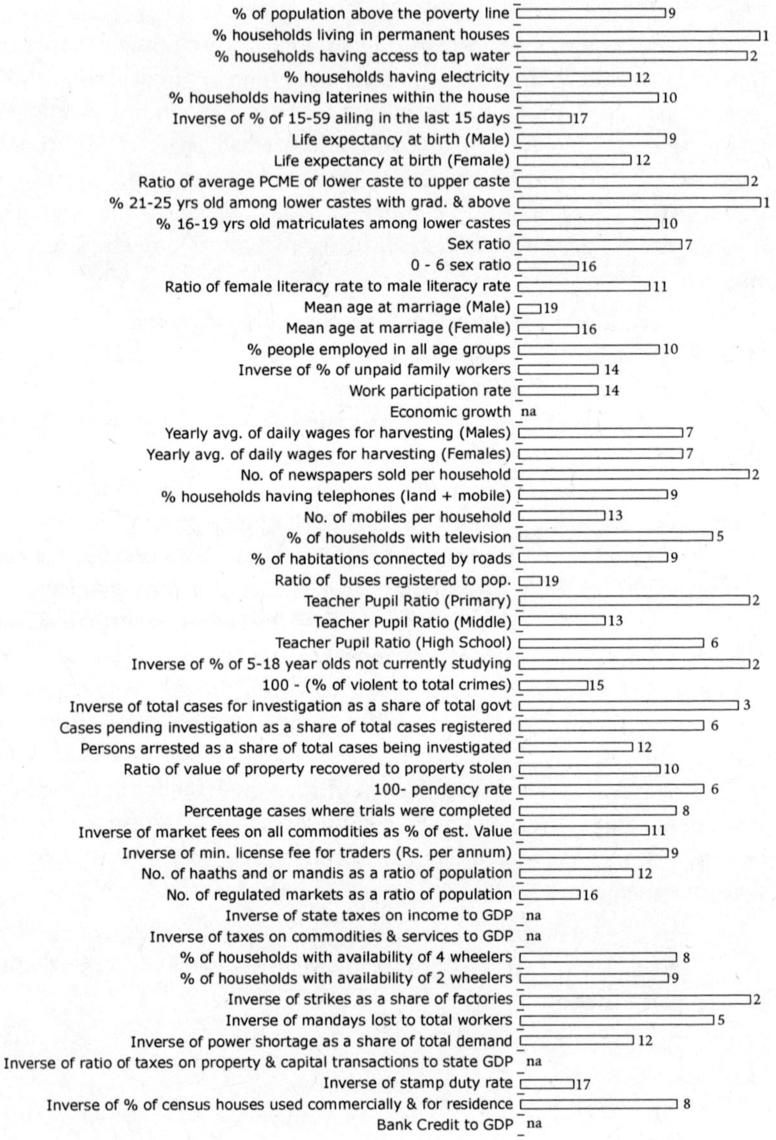

## MAHARASHTRA

| *Variables** | *Values* |
|---|---|
| Population Density (Persons/sq km) | 315 |
| PC SDP (Rs '000) | 27 |
| Share of Manufacturing SDP (%) | 26 |
| Share of Agriculture SDP (%) | 11 |
| Share of Services SDP (%) | 13 |
| % pop. above poverty line (%) | 75 |
| Literacy Rate (%) | 77 |
| % habitations connected with pucca roads (%) | 95 |
| % households with 2 & 4 wheelers (%) | 17 |
| Whether passed right to information act | Yes |

* For sources and units refer appendix

Maharashtra is India's most commercially and industrially active state. Population density is high and approximately 25 per cent of the population is in poverty. This is accompanied with high per capita SDP relative to other states. This may imply prevalence of inequalities. Share of services sector in the economy is highest in Maharashtra as compared to other states, though the manufacturing sector is the largest contributor to SDP. Literacy rate is high in comparison to other states.

A relatively larger number of households have access to tapped water and to sewage systems. Life expectancy at birth for males and females is high, signifying an overall healthy environment. Caste differences are not manifest in indicators of educational attainment. Also female literacy rate is comparable with that of males. Access to information is easy. Newspaper sales are high; many households have landlines, own mobile phones, and televisions. Mass media is a good way of increasing awareness in Maharashtra. Road connectivity is high and many more households in this state own 4 wheelers than other states. Labour is supportive of industry as the number of strikes are lower and not many mandays are lost. Taxes on property and capital transactions are lowest in Maharastra. This may also explain why few residential houses are used for commercial purposes. There are a large number of regulated and unregulated markets to cater to the needs of the population. Direct and indirect taxes as a ratio of SDP are small, implying an environment in which economic agents get to retain a large share of their profits or wages. Credit to SDP ratio is highest in Maharashtra and so also is the credit to deposit ratio. Labour and capital market conditions are therefore favourable for business and industry.

One important bottleneck may be power whose supply does not meet demand. The law and order situation is average though in most cases, stolen property is not recovered. Employment rate is low in all ages and agricultural wages for women are low. Child sex ratio and caste differences exhibited by large differences in spending capability of the lower and upper caste may be a cause of concern.

The atmosphere in Maharashtra is one of economic freedom, however, whether all regions and sections of the state live in it is an import and question that needs to be raised.

# ORISSA (16)

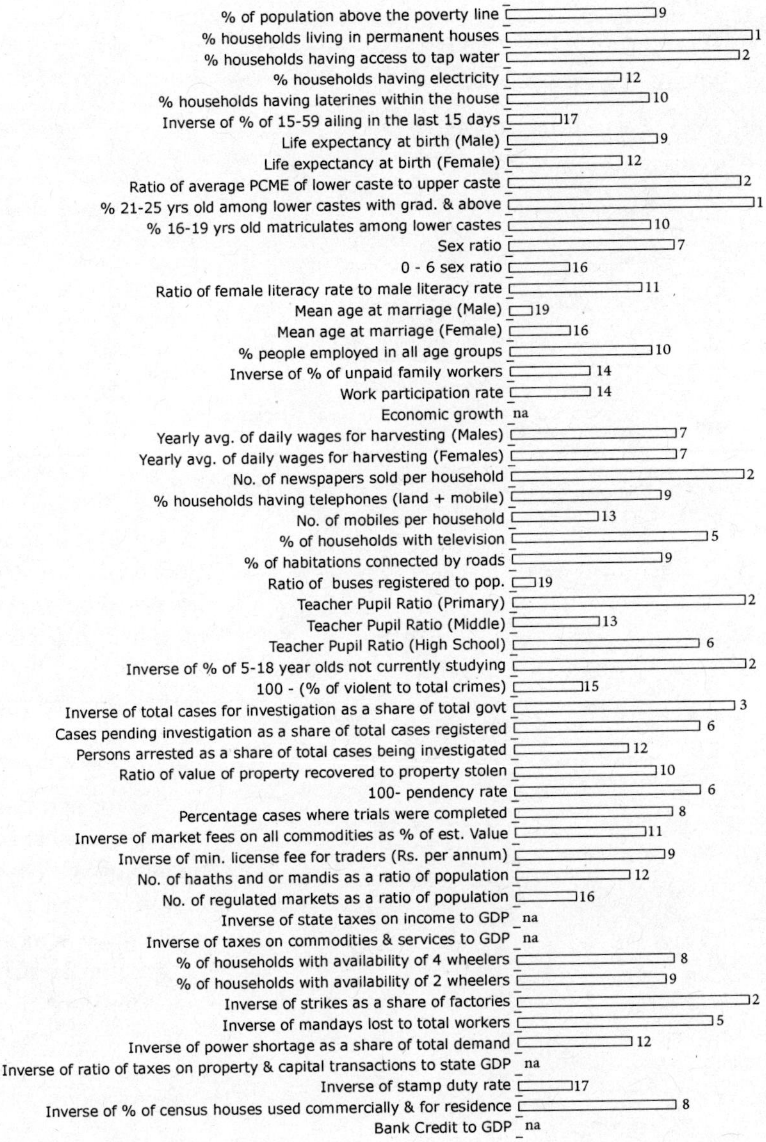
% of population above the poverty line 9
% households living in permanent houses 1
% households having access to tap water 2
% households having electricity 12
% households having laterines within the house 10
Inverse of % of 15-59 ailing in the last 15 days 17
Life expectancy at birth (Male) 9
Life expectancy at birth (Female) 12
Ratio of average PCME of lower caste to upper caste 2
% 21-25 yrs old among lower castes with grad. & above 1
% 16-19 yrs old matriculates among lower castes 10
Sex ratio 7
0 - 6 sex ratio 16
Ratio of female literacy rate to male literacy rate 11
Mean age at marriage (Male) 19
Mean age at marriage (Female) 16
% people employed in all age groups 10
Inverse of % of unpaid family workers 14
Work participation rate 14
Economic growth na
Yearly avg. of daily wages for harvesting (Males) 7
Yearly avg. of daily wages for harvesting (Females) 7
No. of newspapers sold per household 2
% households having telephones (land + mobile) 9
No. of mobiles per household 13
% of households with television 5
% of habitations connected by roads 9
Ratio of buses registered to pop. 19
Teacher Pupil Ratio (Primary) 2
Teacher Pupil Ratio (Middle) 13
Teacher Pupil Ratio (High School) 6
Inverse of % of 5-18 year olds not currently studying 2
100 - (% of violent to total crimes) 15
Inverse of total cases for investigation as a share of total govt 3
Cases pending investigation as a share of total cases registered 6
Persons arrested as a share of total cases being investigated 12
Ratio of value of property recovered to property stolen 10
100- pendency rate 6
Percentage cases where trials were completed 8
Inverse of market fees on all commodities as % of est. Value 11
Inverse of min. license fee for traders (Rs. per annum) 9
No. of haaths and or mandis as a ratio of population 12
No. of regulated markets as a ratio of population 16
Inverse of state taxes on income to GDP na
Inverse of taxes on commodities & services to GDP na
% of households with availability of 4 wheelers 8
% of households with availability of 2 wheelers 9
Inverse of strikes as a share of factories 2
Inverse of mandays lost to total workers 5
Inverse of power shortage as a share of total demand 12
Inverse of ratio of taxes on property & capital transactions to state GDP na
Inverse of stamp duty rate 17
Inverse of % of census houses used commercially & for residence 8
Bank Credit to GDP na

## ORISSA

| *Variables** | *Values* |
|---|---|
| Population Density (Persons/sq km) | 236 |
| PC SDP (Rs '000) | 10 |
| Share of Manufacturing SDP (%) | 8 |
| Share of Agriculture SDP (%) | 28 |
| Share of Services SDP (%) | 4 |
| % pop above poverty line (%) | 53 |
| Literacy Rate (%) | 64 |
| % habitations connected with pucca roads(%) | 41 |
| % households with 2 & 4 wheelers (%) | 9 |
| Whether passed right to information act | No |

* For sources and units refer appendix

Orissa is among the economically least well off states of India. Agriculture is the chief contributor to the state's GDP. The state has a low literacy rate and has the least number of people above poverty line. The per capita State domestic product is also low. The state also suffers from poor connectivity with pucca roads.

Though Orissa is ranked low in most categories, it has done well in some. The state can boast of a better sex ratio than most other states. Moreover, teacher pupil ratio in primary schools is better than many states. Furthermore, legal machinery appears to be efficient as percentage of cases where trials have been completed is high.

Orissa's performance is poorer than most other states in majority of the indicators of economic freedom. The state has a poor civic amenity provision such as tap water supply, sewage systems etc. Furthermore, many households still long for regular supply of electricity. Health situation in the state is poorer than in other states. Life expectancy at birth is low for both males and females. Morbidity rates are high in the working age population. Living conditions seem to be adverse in relation to other states. Social indicators of freedom appear biased against the underprivileged sections. Education level of persons belonging to the lower caste is worse in Orissa than in other states, as only a small share of the youth in the age 20-24 years are graduates or above. The share of lower caste children who have completed class X is also smaller here than in other states. Female literates form a small share of female population while male literates constitute a larger share of male population. The ratio of female to male literacy rate is lower in Assam than in many other states. Moreover, the state has a low overall literacy rate and a large number of children in school going age still stay away from schools. Teacher pupil ratio at the middle and high schools is lower than in many other states. Access to information by the masses is also low, since telephones/mobiles and television sets are not owned by a large share of the households. The state has a low percentage of households owning 2 or 4 wheelers, which implies constraints in mobility of factors of production. Other constraints to commerce and industry appear in the form of higher occurrence of strikes, lesser regulated markets that cater to the population, high stamp duty rates and moderate performance in availability of credit and power.

Orissa's performance is from mediocre to poor in most indicators of economic freedom. There is room for improvement in all aspects of freedom.

# PUNJAB (4)

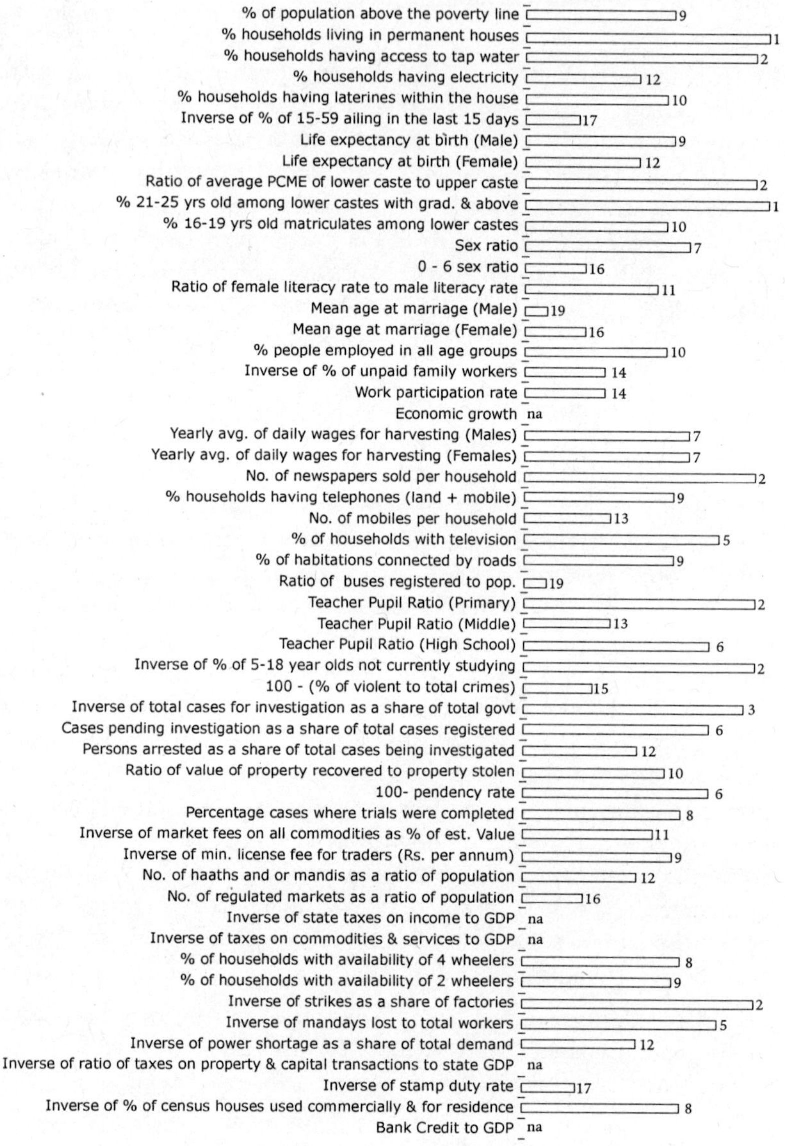
% of population above the poverty line 9
% households living in permanent houses 1
% households having access to tap water 2
% households having electricity 12
% households having laterines within the house 10
Inverse of % of 15-59 ailing in the last 15 days 17
Life expectancy at birth (Male) 9
Life expectancy at birth (Female) 12
Ratio of average PCME of lower caste to upper caste 2
% 21-25 yrs old among lower castes with grad. & above 1
% 16-19 yrs old matriculates among lower castes 10
Sex ratio 7
0 - 6 sex ratio 16
Ratio of female literacy rate to male literacy rate 11
Mean age at marriage (Male) 19
Mean age at marriage (Female) 16
% people employed in all age groups 10
Inverse of % of unpaid family workers 14
Work participation rate 14
Economic growth na
Yearly avg. of daily wages for harvesting (Males) 7
Yearly avg. of daily wages for harvesting (Females) 7
No. of newspapers sold per household 2
% households having telephones (land + mobile) 9
No. of mobiles per household 13
% of households with television 5
% of habitations connected by roads 9
Ratio of buses registered to pop. 19
Teacher Pupil Ratio (Primary) 2
Teacher Pupil Ratio (Middle) 13
Teacher Pupil Ratio (High School) 6
Inverse of % of 5-18 year olds not currently studying 2
100 - (% of violent to total crimes) 15
Inverse of total cases for investigation as a share of total govt 3
Cases pending investigation as a share of total cases registered 6
Persons arrested as a share of total cases being investigated 12
Ratio of value of property recovered to property stolen 10
100- pendency rate 6
Percentage cases where trials were completed 8
Inverse of market fees on all commodities as % of est. Value 11
Inverse of min. license fee for traders (Rs. per annum) 9
No. of haaths and or mandis as a ratio of population 12
No. of regulated markets as a ratio of population 16
Inverse of state taxes on income to GDP na
Inverse of taxes on commodities & services to GDP na
% of households with availability of 4 wheelers 8
% of households with availability of 2 wheelers 9
Inverse of strikes as a share of factories 2
Inverse of mandays lost to total workers 5
Inverse of power shortage as a share of total demand 12
Inverse of ratio of taxes on property & capital transactions to state GDP na
Inverse of stamp duty rate 17
Inverse of % of census houses used commercially & for residence 8
Bank Credit to GDP na

## PUNJAB

| *Variables** | *Values* |
|---|---|
| Population Density (Persons/sq km) | 482 |
| PC SDP (Rs '000) | 28 |
| Share of Manufacturing SDP (%) | 14 |
| Share of Agriculture SDP (%) | 38 |
| Share of Services SDP (%) | 4 |
| % pop. above poverty line (%) | 94 |
| Literacy Rate (%) | 70 |
| % habitations connected with pucca roads (%) | 92 |
| % households with 2 & 4 wheelers (%) | 37 |
| Whether passed right to information act | No |

* For sources and units refer appendix

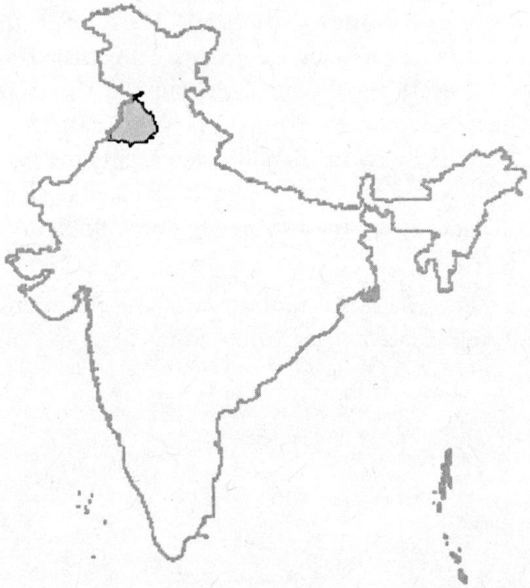

Punjab is ranked high in the composite economic freedom index. Famous, typically for agriculture, manufacturing does make its presence felt in the state's GDP. Punjab is generally considered to be one of the most economically prosperous state as indicated by relatively high per capita SDP and a high percentage of population above the poverty line. It has the highest share of households with 2 or 4 wheelers in comparison to other states and the state has a excellent connectivity with pucca roads. It also has a fairly high literacy rate.

Economic prosperity in the state is well illustrated by the large share of households living in permanent houses. The state has an excellent supply of electricity to the households as indicated by the high share of households that have electricity. In addition to favourable living conditions in terms of civic amenities, the state also boasts of high life expectancy at birth. The overall high literacy rate is well supported by high female to male literacy rate. Female age at marriage is higher than in other states as well. The state has excellent facilities for communication. It has the highest share of households with mobile phones and televisions. The situation of justice and governance is better than many states. Completion of trials and recovery of stolen property is more likely in Punjab than in other states. The state also has the highest number of regulated markets. Moreover, stamp duty rates are lower than that in most other states.

Indicators of freedom which pull down Punjab in the freedom ranking mainly include social indicators of freedom. Sex ratio in the state is more inclined towards males in all age groups. Punjab also has a large ailing population in the 15 to 59 years age group. Furthermore, Punjab has a large number of corruption charges against its government employees. Another area in which Punjab lags is the bank credit to deposit ratio. There are a higher share of houses used for residence and commercial purposes than in many states implying a dearth of commercial space.

Improving its performance in social indicators of freedom could immensely benefit the level of freedom experienced by large sections of its population.

# RAJASTHAN (10)

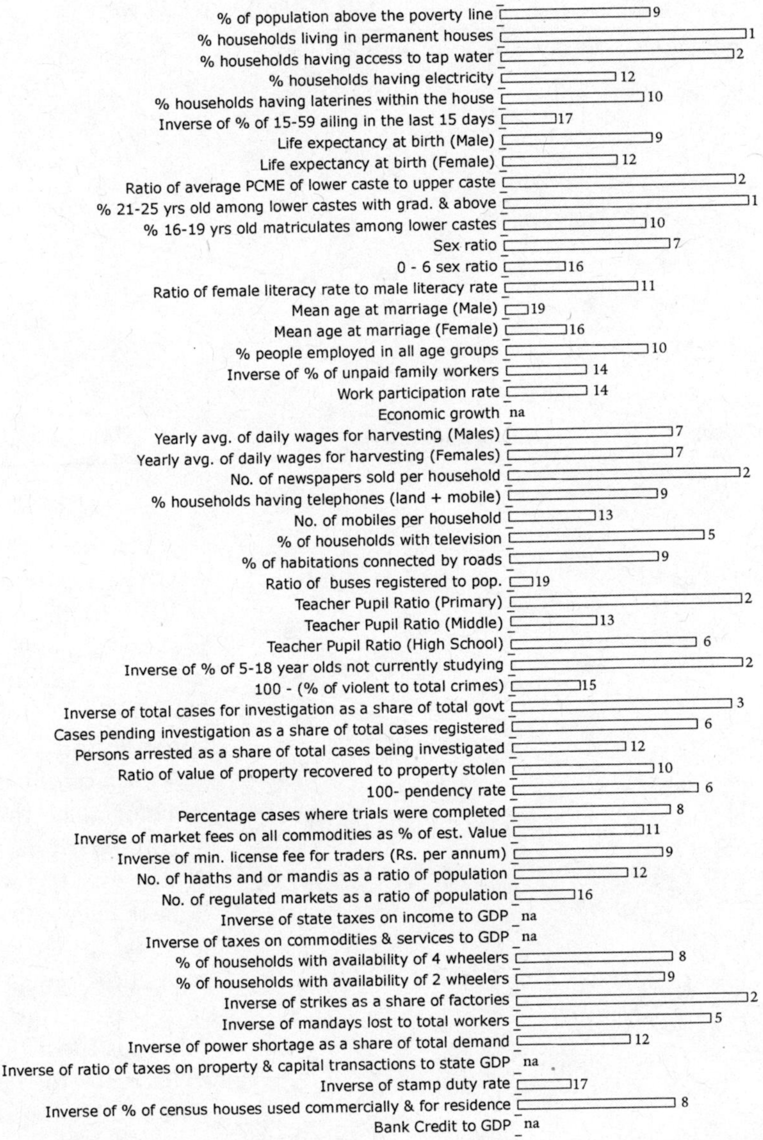

## RAJASTHAN

| *Variables** | *Values* |
|---|---|
| Population Density (Persons/sq km) | 165 |
| PC SDP (Rs '000) | 14 |
| Share of Manufacturing SDP (%) | 12 |
| Share of Agriculture SDP (%) | 26 |
| Share of Services SDP (%) | 4 |
| % pop. above poverty line (%) | 85 |
| Literacy Rate (%) | 61 |
| % habitations connected with pucca roads (%) | 42 |
| % households with 2 & 4 wheelers (%) | 16 |
| Whether passed right to information act | Yes |

* For sources and units refer appendix

Located in the northwest part of India, Rajasthan is identified as a desert region. However, the construction of Rajasthan canal has transformed the northwestern part of the state and Rajasthan is making fast progress even in the agriculture sector. Agriculture is the main contributor to the state's GDP. Population density is relatively low and a larger percentage of the population lies above the poverty line. In addition, a fair percentage of households own two and four wheelers. However, the state has a poor connectivity by pucca roads and literacy rate is amongst the lowest.

Rajasthan has a high percentage of populatio that is employed. Moreover, morbidity in the working age group is lowest here than in any other state. Wages are higher in Rajasthan than in most other states. Both males and females get relatively better pay here. Indicators of justice, such as recovery rate of stolen property and percentage of pending cases in court, show Rajasthan in good light. This is not all. Power supply meets demand more in this state than in other states.

While Rajasthan performs well in some areas, it does lag behind in many others. The state fails in providing electricity to a large share of the households. Life expectancy at birth is low in comparison to other states both in case of males and females. A large share of lower caste youth in Rajasthan are not even graduates. Child sex ratio is lower than in most other states. In addition, the ratio of female to male literacy rate is low. Another problem is that of early marriages. Age at marriage is lower than in other states for males as well as for females. In the field of education, a large share of the children of school going age do not attend school. Furthermore, a large share of the working population is accounted for by unpaid family workers. The law and order situation is also relatively worse than in other states. The violent crime rate is very high and lesser arrests are made. Rajasthan is also weighed down by corruption charges against government employees. There are limited number of *mandis/haath* and regulated markets where economic agents can trade. Business environment is blemished by loss of man-days much more than other states. Access to information in the state is not very easy; the share of households owning mobile phones or televisions is very low in comparison to other states.

In order to improve the situation of economic freedom in the state, Rajasthan will need to simultaneously improve in many different sectors. Indicators of social freedom are especially poor. Other areas are education, corruption, and product and labour market conditions.

# TAMIL NADU (1)

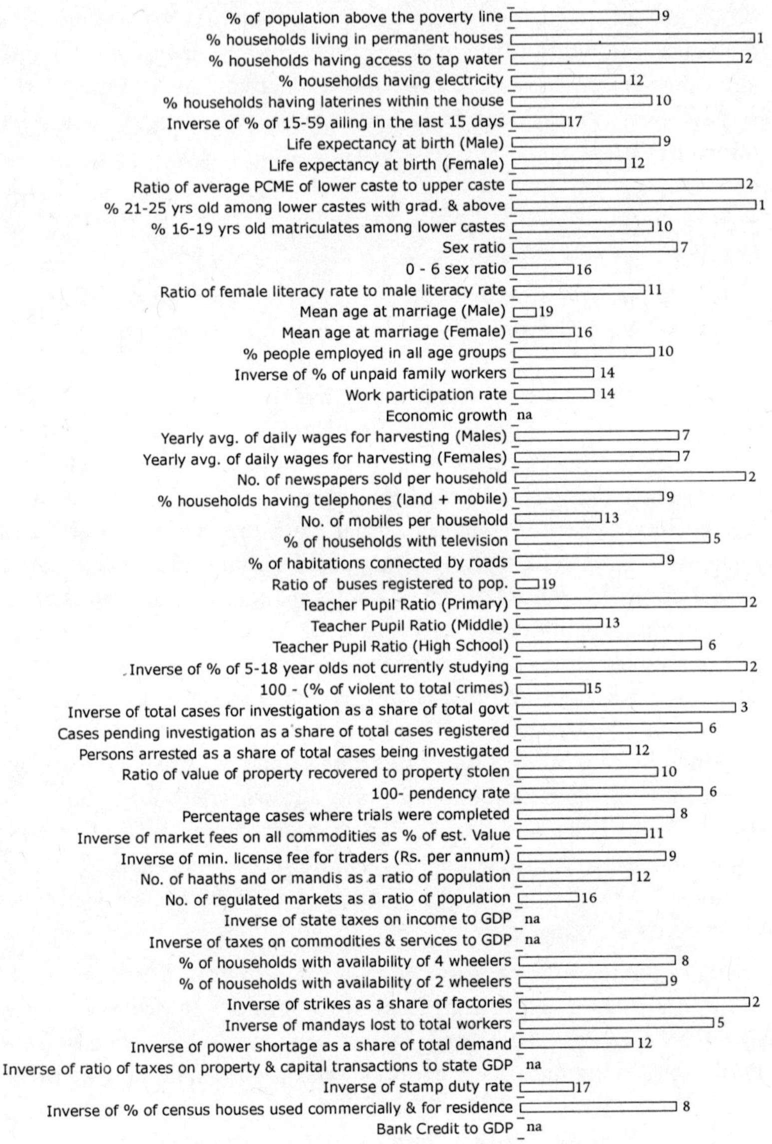
% of population above the poverty line 9
% households living in permanent houses 1
% households having access to tap water 2
% households having electricity 12
% households having laterines within the house 10
Inverse of % of 15-59 ailing in the last 15 days 17
Life expectancy at birth (Male) 9
Life expectancy at birth (Female) 12
Ratio of average PCME of lower caste to upper caste 2
% 21-25 yrs old among lower castes with grad. & above 1
% 16-19 yrs old matriculates among lower castes 10
Sex ratio 7
0 - 6 sex ratio 16
Ratio of female literacy rate to male literacy rate 11
Mean age at marriage (Male) 19
Mean age at marriage (Female) 16
% people employed in all age groups 10
Inverse of % of unpaid family workers 14
Work participation rate 14
Economic growth na
Yearly avg. of daily wages for harvesting (Males) 7
Yearly avg. of daily wages for harvesting (Females) 7
No. of newspapers sold per household 2
% households having telephones (land + mobile) 9
No. of mobiles per household 13
% of households with television 5
% of habitations connected by roads 9
Ratio of buses registered to pop. 19
Teacher Pupil Ratio (Primary) 2
Teacher Pupil Ratio (Middle) 13
Teacher Pupil Ratio (High School) 6
Inverse of % of 5-18 year olds not currently studying 2
100 - (% of violent to total crimes) 15
Inverse of total cases for investigation as a share of total govt 3
Cases pending investigation as a share of total cases registered 6
Persons arrested as a share of total cases being investigated 12
Ratio of value of property recovered to property stolen 10
100- pendency rate 6
Percentage cases where trials were completed 8
Inverse of market fees on all commodities as % of est. Value 11
Inverse of min. license fee for traders (Rs. per annum) 9
No. of haaths and or mandis as a ratio of population 12
No. of regulated markets as a ratio of population 16
Inverse of state taxes on income to GDP na
Inverse of taxes on commodities & services to GDP na
% of households with availability of 4 wheelers 8
% of households with availability of 2 wheelers 9
Inverse of strikes as a share of factories 2
Inverse of mandays lost to total workers 5
Inverse of power shortage as a share of total demand 12
Inverse of ratio of taxes on property & capital transactions to state GDP na
Inverse of stamp duty rate 17
Inverse of % of census houses used commercially & for residence 8
Bank Credit to GDP na

## TAMIL NADU

| *Variables** | *Values* |
|---|---|
| Population Density (Persons/sq km) | 478 |
| PC SDP (Rs '000) | 22 |
| Share of Manufacturing SDP (%) | 22 |
| Share of Agriculture SDP (%) | 14 |
| Share of Services SDP (%) | 7 |
| % pop. above poverty line (%) | 79 |
| Literacy Rate (%) | 74 |
| % habitations connected with pucca roads (%) | 93 |
| % households with 2 & 4 wheelers (%) | 18 |
| Whether passed right to information act | Yes |

* For sources and units refer appendix

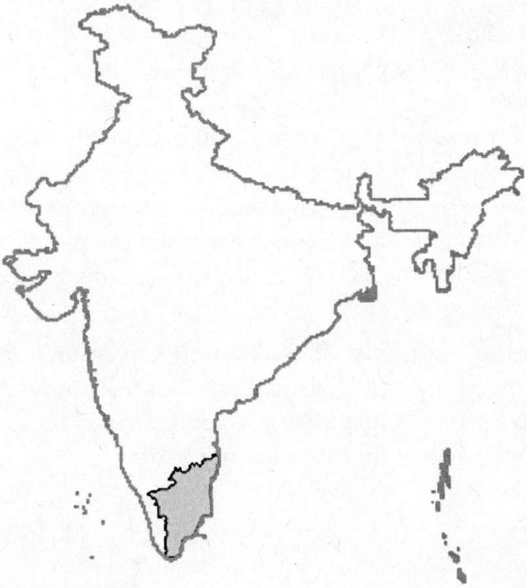

Tamil Nadu does exceptionally well in securing a high rank in the composite economic freedom ranking. Like in rest of the country, agriculture is the main source of livelihood for majority of the population. However, the chief contributor to the state's GDP is the manufacturing sector. Tamil Nadu has one of the highest literacy rates in India. Moreover, physical infrastructure is satisfactory, as indicated by very high connectivity by pucca roads.

Tamil Nadu excels in access to sanitation facilities and tap water by its citizens. Compared to other states, it has a relatively higher life expectancy at birth for both males and females. The lower caste people are also able to access education, not only at the school level but also higher studies. A large share of the children from lower caste in the age group of 16-19 years has completed class X. Similarly a large share of the youth belonging to the lower caste are graduates or above. The state has a sex ratio that is less unfavourable towards females. The ratio of female to male literacy rate is also amongst the highest. Mean age at marriage is not low for males as well as females. The work participation rate and economic growth rate is higher than in many states. It has the minimum ratio of violent crimes to the total crimes, fewer corruption charges against its government employees and the highest rate of trial completion amongst all states. Other categories in which it performs exceptionally well are the percentages of households with 2 wheelers, bank credit as a ratio of GDP and bank credit to deposit ratio.

While caste differences are not visible in terms of access to education, the difference is stark in terms of per capita monthly expenditure by households. The ratio of per capita monthly expenditure of lower caste households to upper caste households is the lowest in Tamil Nadu. Another area in which Tamil Nadu suffers is the teacher pupil ratio at the middle school level. Trade environment is severely hampered due to fewer number of *haats/ mandis* and regulated markets. Another significant deterring factor is the income tax collections, which are higher than in other states. Further, labour markets are characterized by strikes and loss of mandays.

In most indicators of economic freedom, the state performs moderately well, excelling in few, while also lagging in a few. The state manages the balance between economic, social and political freedom in a manner that is much better than most other states.

# UTTAR PRADESH (14)

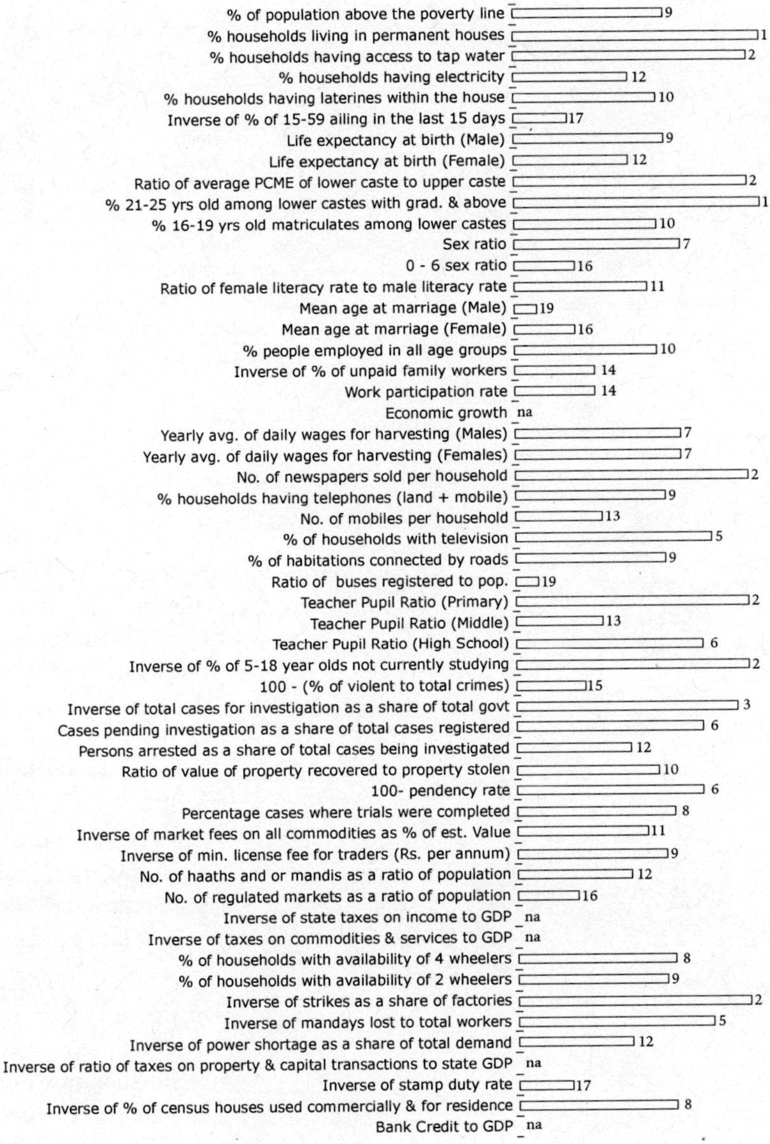

## UTTAR PRADESH

| *Variables** | *Values* |
|---|---|
| Population Density (Persons/sq km) | 689 |
| PC SDP (Rs '000) | 11 |
| Share of Manufacturing SDP (%) | 13 |
| Share of Agriculture SDP (%) | 32 |
| Share of Services SDP (%) | 3 |
| % pop. above poverty line (%) | 70 |
| Literacy Rate (%) | 57 |
| % habitations connected with pucca roads (%) | 44 |
| % households with 2 & 4 wheelers (%) | 13 |
| Whether passed right to information act | No |

* For sources and units refer appendix

Uttar Pradesh is the largest state in terms of population. Agriculture is the main contributor to the state's GDP. Poverty is widespread accompanied by low levels of literacy. It also has a fairly low connectivity with pucca roads.

UP's performance ranges from moderate to dismal in most indicators of economic freedom. However, there are some indicators where it manages to surface on the top. The share of households buying newspapers in UP is amongst the highest. It also has few corruption charges against its government employees. Labour market is relatively uninhibited by labour problems. This comes across from fewer strikes and lesser losses in mandays. The state can also boast of lower amount of tax imposed on property and capital transaction as compared to other states.

Basic living conditions of the masses are relatively worse than in most other states. A larger share of households is deprived of such basic amenities as lack of tapped water, electricity and sanitation facilities. In addition, many households do not have permanent houses to live in. Moreover even the health environment is not very good, since a high percentage of persons in the working age group suffer from ailments. Social indicators of freedom are especially unfavourable for females. Sex ratio is low for children as well as for all age groups. Also women are more deprived of education opportunities than men. The ratio of female to male literacy rate is lower in UP than in most other states. The state has an appalling education structure with very low teacher-pupil ratio in the middle and high schools. Furthermore, a major percentage of 5 to 18 year old children are out of schools. The law and order situation is also relatively worse than in other states. The violent crime rate is very high and fewer suspects are being caught. Other parameters that curb business are the lack of available regulated markets, *haats* and *mandis*. Apart from lack of markets, higher income taxes, taxes on commodities/services, and stamp duties further prevent smooth business activities. UP also ranks low in availability of bank credit as compared to other states. All these are also reflected in the relatively low economic growth rate exhibited by the state.

Uttar Pradesh requires change for the better in all aspects of freedom. Be it social, economic or political, there is much room for improvement in all spheres.

# UTTARANCHAL (8)

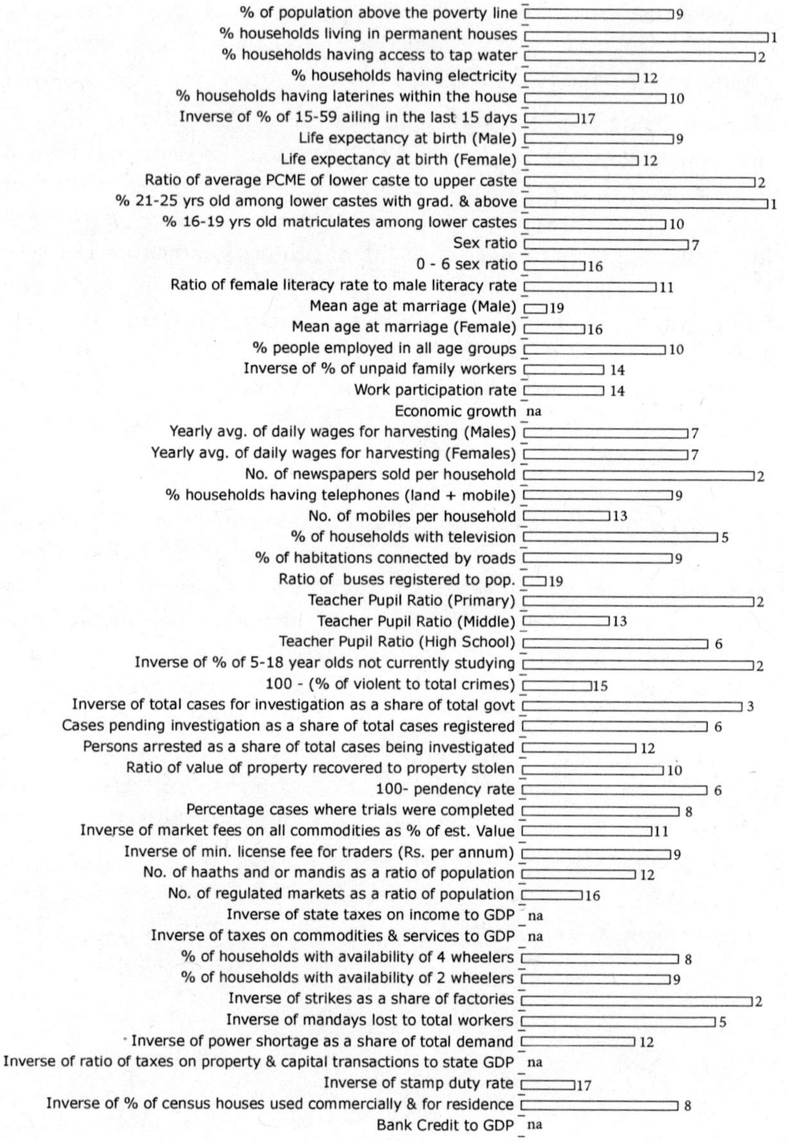

## UTTARANCHAL

| *Variables** | *Values* |
|---|---|
| Population Density (Persons/sq km) | 159 |
| PC SDP (Rs '000) | — |
| Share of Manufacturing SDP (%) | — |
| Share of Agriculture SDP (%) | — |
| Share of Services SDP (%) | — |
| % pop. above poverty line (%) | 83 |
| Literacy Rate (%) | 72 |
| % habitations connected with pucca roads (%) | 62 |
| % households with 2 & 4 wheelers (%) | 15 |
| Whether passed right to information act | No |

* For sources and units refer appendix

Uttaranchal parted from old Uttar Pradesh in 2002 and to become a state of India. Located in the north-west part of Uttar Pradesh, the state has a very low population density. Uttaranchal has a relatively high literacy rate. A relatively small share of the population lies below the poverty line, which is unlike its sister state of Uttar Pradesh. Approximately 1/4th of the state is not accessible by *pucca* roads; one reason for this may be the difficult mountainous topography of the state.

Uttaranchal has highest share of households living in permanent houses. Furthermore, a very high share of the households have access to tap water in this state than in any of the other 20 states. Caste differences are minimal in Uttaranchal. The share of lower caste youth that are graduates is the highest here. Furthermore, inequalities in terms of spending capability are also minimal. The ratio of lower to upper caste per capita monthly expenditure is very high in Uttaranchal. Information is widely accessed by means of newspapers and televisions. It has a very high teacher pupil ratio at primary schools and most children in the age group of 5 to 18 years study in schools. Unlike other states, industries in Uttaranchal are least inflicted by strikes and man-days loss. The share of government employees being tried under the prevention of corruption and other acts is very low in Uttaranchal as compared to other states.

Working age population in Uttaranchal is characterized by high morbidity rates. Work participation rate is low and a relatively large section of the work force is working as unpaid family workers. People marry early, whether males or females. In addition females also face a low child sex ratio. Though habitations in the state are fairly well connected by roads, it has a very poor bus transportation service in comparison to the 20 states. Another area, which has a negative impact on the state's performance in the economic freedom index, is the lack of bank credit. In fact, Uttaranchal sits at the bottom in the bank credit to deposit ratio. Uttaranchal has fewer regulated markets and stamp duty rates are higher than in many other states.

A fairly high literacy rate, easy flow of information and a more or less egalitarian socio-economic environment, all definitely have a positive impact on the economic freedom index.

# WEST BENGAL (13)

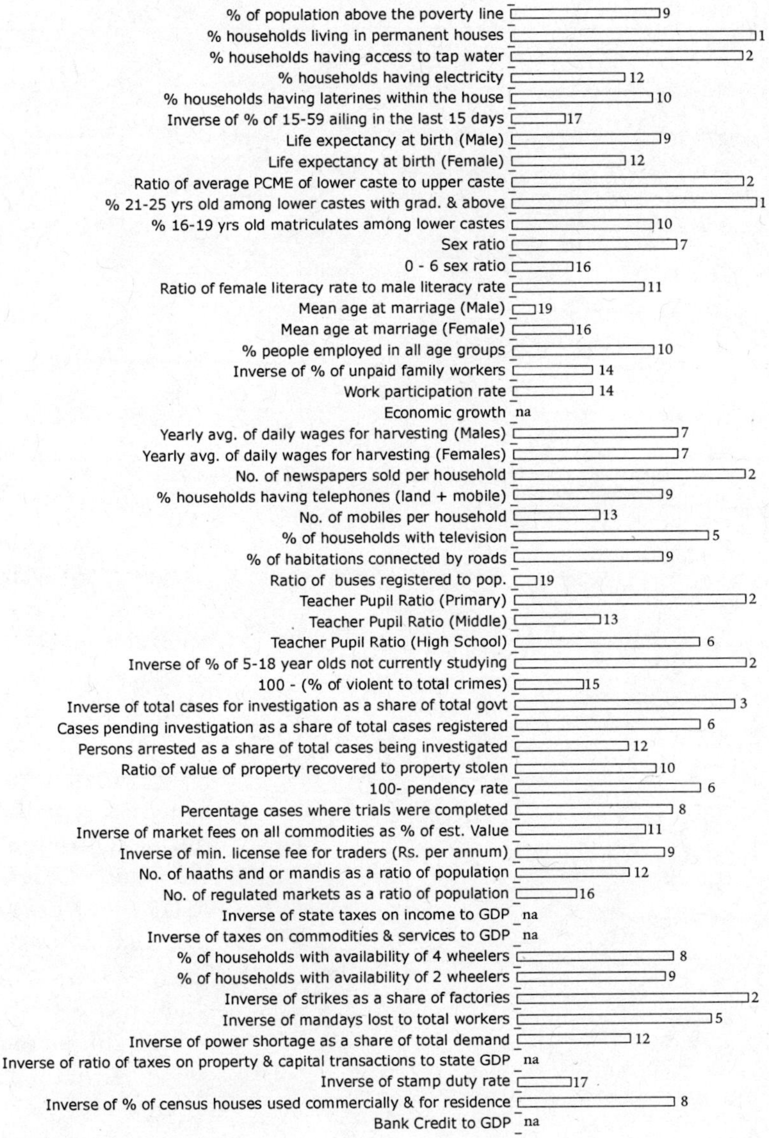

## WEST BENGAL

| *Variables** | *Values* |
|---|---|
| Population Density (Persons/sq km) | 904 |
| PC SDP (Rs '000) | 17 |
| Share of Manufacturing SDP (%) | 14 |
| Share of Agriculture SDP (%) | 23 |
| Share of Services SDP (%) | 11 |
| % pop. above poverty line (%) | 73 |
| Literacy Rate (%) | 69 |
| % habitations connected with pucca roads (%) | 49 |
| % households with 2 & 4 wheelers (%) | 7 |
| Whether passed right to information act | No |

* For sources and units refer appendix

West Bengal is not a big state in terms of area and also has the highest population density, with a sizable share of poor population. Agriculture is the major contributor to the state's GDP. Literacy rate is modest. Habitations in Bengal are fairly well connected with permanent roads. However, the percentage of households owning 2 and 4 wheelers is amongst the lowest in 20 states.

Bengal exhibits a high economic growth rate and has fewer unpaid family workers constituting the work force. Unlike other states, it has the least number of corruption changes against its government employees. Bengal is also very relaxed on trading practices with lower stamp duties and lower taxes on commodities and services. Ratio of income tax collections to SDP is lower than in other states. Teacher pupil ratio at the high schools is fairly high. Furthermore, sanitation facilities are fairly good. Life expectancy at birth, for males and females, is higher than in most other states. Caste differences have not manifested into differences in spending capacity and sex ratio is less unfavourable towards females.

Poverty in the state is reflected by means of small share of the households living in permanent houses, and also by lack of basic civic amenities such as tap water and electricity supply in the houses. Bengal has the minimum number of teenage matriculates among the lower caste. It also has a comparatively less percentage of 21 to 25 years old among lower caste with graduation. Though it exhibits a very high economic growth rate, Bengal has the highest share of unemployed people amongst the 20 states. Work participation rate is lowest here. The situation of justice and governance is poor in comparison to other states. There is a large backlog in cases and furthermore completion rate of trials is very low. The ratio of violent crimes to total crimes are also higher than in many other states and it has the least number of persons arrested as a share of total cases being investigated. Such weak law and order system acts as a deterrent to the safety of individuals and subsequently to the freedom of the common man and the economic activities. The industries in West Bengal are adversely affected by worker strikes and loss of man-days.

As a whole the state is amongst the worst in many areas and needs lot of improvement.

## Bibliography

Bhandari, Laveesh and Amaresh Dubey (2003), *Incidence of Poverty and Hunger in Indian Districts*, RGICS Working Paper, Rajiv Gandhi Institute for Contemporary Studies, New Delhi.

Byars, J., R. McCormick and B. Yandle, (1999) *Economic Freedom in America's 50 States*, Clemson University, Clemson, USA.

Debroy, B and Bhandari, Laveesh (2002), *How are the States Doing?*, Confederation of Indian Industry, New Delhi.

Debroy, B and Bhandari, Laveesh (edt.) (2003), *District-level Deprivation in the New Millennium*, RGICS, IDE (India) and Konark Publisher, New Delhi.

Liberales Institute, (2002) *Economic Freedom of the World: Annual Report*, The Fraser Institute, Vancouver, Canada.

National Commission on Population (NCP) (2001), *District Wise Social Economic Demographic Indicators*, Government of India, New Delhi.

## APPENDIX

### Table 1

| *Variables* | *Units* | *Sources* | *Year* |
|---|---|---|---|
| Population Density | Persons/sq km | Census of India | 2001 |
| PC SDP | Rs 000 | CSO | 2000-2001 |
| Share of Manufacturing SDP | % | CSO | 2000-2001 |
| Share of Agriculture SDP | % | CSO | 2000-2001 |
| Share of Services SDP | % | CSO | 2000-2001 |
| % pop. above poverty line | % | CSO | 1999-2000 |
| Literacy Rate | % | Census of India | 2001 |
| % habitations connected with pucca roads | % | Census of India | 2001 |
| % households with 2 & 4 wheelers | % | Census of India | 2001 |
| Accounts per thousand population | Number/ '000 | RBI | 2002 |

Note: Per capita SDP for Jharkhand and Chhattisgarh are estimates based on 7 year trend.